☆ ☆ ☆ ☆ ☆

THE National Directory of Corporate Training Programs

☆ ☆ ☆ ☆ ☆

by Ray Bard & Susan K. Elliott

COMPLETELY UPDATED SECOND EDITION
Previously titled *Breaking In*

A STONESONG PRESS BOOK

Doubleday

NEW YORK LONDON TORONTO SYDNEY AUCKLAND

Published by Doubleday, a division of
Bantam Doubleday Dell Publishing Group, Inc.,
666 Fifth Avenue, New York, New York 10103

Doubleday and the portrayal of an anchor with a dolphin
are trademarks of Doubleday, a division of
Bantam Doubleday Dell Publishing Group, Inc.

A Stonesong Press Book

Library of Congress Cataloging-in-Publication Data
Bard, Ray.
The National Directory of Corporate Training Programs / by Ray Bard and Susan K. Elliott. — 2nd ed.
p. cm.
"A Stonesong Press book."
Bibliography: p. 359.
Includes indexes.
1. Employees, Training of—United States—Directories.
2. Corporations—United States—Directories. I. Elliott, Susan,
1950– . II. Title.
HF5549.5.T7B29 1988
331.25'92'02573—dc19 88-298
CIP

ISBN 0-385-24203-4 (paperback)
ISBN 0-385-24202-6

PRINTED IN THE UNITED STATES OF AMERICA
OCTOBER 1988
SECOND EDITION

BG

Acknowledgments

This new edition was brought to press with the contributions of many people. Our editor at Doubleday, Alison Brown Cerier, continued to believe in the book and provided suggestions and guidance to make this new edition even better. Thanks go to the team who worked on this edition of the book: Teri Greene, for his mailing-list work; Margo McBride, for her assistance in getting out the corporate mailings; Frances Knight, for her reliable courier service; Sherry Sprague, for her able and timely word processing services; Linda Webster, for her fine research and indexing efforts; Sheree Bykofsky, for her assistance in shepherding the manuscript; and Dr. Howard Figler and Linda Johnson of the University of Texas at Austin Liberal Arts Placement Center, for their valuable research assistance and information. Many people in company training, personnel, and recruitment offices took time to complete our survey, respond to telephone questions, and be available for personal interviews. Their time and interest made the book possible, and we are most grateful.

Special thanks to those who granted interviews for the book: Jocko Burks, Manager of Recruiting and Staffing Services for Weyerhaeuser; Alyssa Carlson, College Recruitment Manager for Kay Jewelers; Pat Cataldo, Vice-President of Education Services at Digital Equipment Corporation; Dr. James Chastain, Director of the Center for Financial Services Education at Howard University; Dr. Howard Figler, Director of the University of Texas at Austin Liberal Arts Placement Center; William M. Fulton, Manager of Human Resources for Motorola in Phoenix; Baxter Graham, Vice-President of Human Resources at Chubb Insurance Companies; Dick Luongo, National Sales Manager of Sales Training and Development for R. J. Reynolds; Chris Mattern, Director of Organization and Development for R. J. Reynolds; Seth Moskowitz, Public Relations Representative for R. J. Reynolds; Dr. Glenn Payne, the Director of MBA Career Services in the Graduate School of Business at the University of Southern California; Sandy Shine, Sales Representative for John H. Harland Company; Charlotte Smoot, College Recruiter for Foley's Department Stores; and Steven Sanders, Partner in the firm of Hunt & Sanders.

Contents

Introduction

This new edition of *The National Directory of Corporate Training Programs* includes more training programs and more information about the companies and their programs. It will put you in touch with almost 1,500 valuable training programs nationwide. And it describes more than 450 programs in such areas as management, finance, computer science, engineering, accounting, electronics, and sales in a wide variety of companies.

Today, corporations understand that an investment in high salaries, sophisticated training, comprehensive benefits, and a wide-open career path will pay off by producing the top-of-the-line managers of tomorrow, and that is why they offer quality entry-level training and continuing professional development. Some companies have made significant investments in special facilities and instructional staffs. They offer state-of-the-art training through a wide range of learning methods and equipment. They know that training improves their bottom line and helps them attract the best talent in the job market. The type of training programs a company offers indicates how it uses human resources and treats employees. If a company has a comprehensive, well-planned training program, it values new employees and plans to develop and effectively use their expertise.

The growing corporate commitment to training and development is evidenced by the financial resources spent annually in this area. A 1986 study conducted by the Research Institute of America reported that more than $30 billion was spent in 1986 on formal employee training and about $180 billion on informal training, including on-the-job programs run by managers. *Training* magazine's 1987 annual survey showed that more than 38.8 million employees received training representing 1.2 billion person-hours. It also reported that in the first half of the 1980s there was a 38 percent increase in the number of people assigned to corporate training responsibilities full time.

Good training and orientation programs are as valuable to you as a future employee as they are to the employer. You will learn about the company and your role in it in an organized, efficient way. Often a program is a bridge from an academic environment to the world of work.

Unfortunately, most of the millions of aspiring young professionals who would jump to be considered for these programs either don't know they exist or are at a loss as to how to get enough information on the programs in operation. Corporations, if they recruit at all, often do so only at select campuses, and traditional job-hunting techniques have rarely taken these programs into consideration. *The National Directory of Corporate Training Programs* provides a reliable, well-documented, comprehensive source of information about the training programs.

Consider the following brief true examples of people who would have benefited from *The National Directory of Corporate Training Programs:* A computer sales rep with an associate's degree in computers grows more frustrated daily in a dead-end job, but he doesn't know how to find a position that will give him continued training and permit him to cross over to management. Meanwhile, a young man with two years of college inadvertently discovered corporate training programs while working as a sales rep for an employment agency. He landed a $23,000-a-year trainee position with a giant financial firm. A woman nearing thirty gave up on her bachelor's degree in sociology years ago and tried to find her way up in business. Despite five jobs in seven years, she's been unable to break out of the secretarial morass in which she's mired—or to earn more than $16,000 annually. Meanwhile, a college senior with a business degree and an unimpressive scholastic record learned through a relative about a training program offered by his company. The relative prepped her on how to apply and she won a place over several applicants with more impressive transcripts.

These capsules are about real people and situations. They illustrate not only what a corporate training program can mean to an individual but also how the inside track can be gained with the proper preparation.

Participation in a company training program is different from academic learning. Training programs prepare you for a specific job and focus on applied knowledge. Employers view training as an investment that is expected to yield results. The programs typically are more flexible and individualized than academic instruction. Some companies keep trainer-to-student ratio as low as one instructor for every six trainees. The learning is also more intensive. Often the training methods and materials used are specially designed to keep your interest while you learn.

An entry-level training program may last a few days or continue for several months or more as part of a long-term career development track. Some programs are structured and depend heavily on classroom instruction; others are more informal and rely primarily on experience gained on the job. A training program may include on-the-job experience; coaching by a supervisor; rotational assignments in different departments; outside self-study; consultation with an adviser or mentor; in-house classes; or university or college classes.

In-house classroom instruction may include lectures by company training staff, presentations by key company employees (sometimes even the president), audiovisual presentations, interactive video, computer-assisted programs, case studies, role play, small-group work, demonstrations, simulations, and practice sessions. Outside-the-classroom learning experiences may include self-directed learning with audio- and videotapes, computer-based learning programs, company-prepared manuals, other reading materials, and field trips.

In most entry-level programs you will learn company history, present operations, and plans for the future; company policies, products, and services; and information about the industry, the company's marketing approach, the competition, and the customer or client. The key skills and information specific to your new position will also be taught. General business skills (such as making presentations, conducting meetings, developing plans and budgets) that are used in supervisory, sales, and management jobs may be taught. It is unlikely that a program will include all these elements, but the more comprehensive programs include many of them.

Most companies agree that employees learn best on the job, but they differ widely in how they prepare employees to learn on the job.

Some companies provide a few hours of basic orientation to company background, policies, products, and services before quickly placing you in your first assignment. Your immediate supervisor is then responsible for orienting you to the department and your responsibilities. The companies that use on-the-job learning best encourage their supervisors to provide one-on-one coaching to new employees. In many cases a periodic evaluation of your progress (usually quarterly for the first year) is conducted by your supervisor, and a conference is held to discuss your performance and to set new learning goals.

Other companies provide longer instruction before starting you in a job. Often the initial training, which may last for several weeks, is conducted at the company's home office, but sometimes a few days of additional training at a regional or national training center are included. Many companies also provide classroom training at various intervals during the first few years and some even supplement your work experience later on. Many companies have developed supplemental self-study guides.

When you go to a training interview you should ask about the program itself, the work you will do, and the other people in the program. If possible, talk to someone who is in or has recently completed the program.

To illustrate what it's like to participate in a training program, we interviewed several recent graduates about their experiences. The interviews that appear in various places throughout the book are an excellent source of information about how the training programs operate. They include suggestions and strategies for making the most of these programs. They will also help you look at the programs from the perspectives of everyone involved, from university career-placement professionals to company recruiters and trainers, to corporate executives. The page location of each interview is listed on the Contents page.

Sandy Shine went through the sales associate training program at John H. Harland Company. Steven Saunders participated in the employee benefit training program at Aetna Life & Casualty and the commercial credit analyst training program at Mellon Bank. Alyssa Carlson completed the Kay Jeweler management training program.

Mr. Pat Cataldo, Vice-President of Educational Services at Digital Equipment Corporation, and Mr. Baxter Graham, Vice-President at Chubb Group of Insurance Companies, provide a broader, corporate perspective on the programs. Charlotte Smoot, college recruiter at Foley's Department Stores; Jocko Burks, Manager of Recruitment at Weyerhaeuser; and Dick Luongo, National Manager of Sales Training and Development, Seth Moskowitz, Public Relations Representative, and Chris Mattern, Director of Organization & Development for R. J. Reynolds Tobacco U.S.A. provide company perspectives on recruiting and training. Dr. Howard Figler, Director of the Liberal Arts Placement Center at the University of Texas at Austin; Dr. Glenn Payne, Director of MBA Career Services in the Graduate School of Business at the University of Southern California; and Dr. James Chastain, the Director of the Center for Financial Services Education and Professor of Insurance at Howard University offer an outside view and provide many good suggestions on how to approach the companies and the training programs.

The National Directory of Corporate Training Programs includes information about more than 450 training programs from 300 companies and lists an additional 1,000 programs. Company profiles include company background, training program description (length, type of training, location, time of year, methods of instruction, etc.), qualifications, how and where the company recruits, where you could be placed, salary and benefits, and the company's contact person. These profiles will help you narrow your choices when you schedule interviews or request information from companies.

Our research began with a questionnaire mailed to the companies included in the first edition. Telephone calls were used to solicit more information. Personal interviews helped supplement existing data and provide inside information. Many of the companies responded with complete information; others provided partial information. Some did not respond or did not have entry-level programs. In addition to our direct solicitation of company information, we used company recruitment information available at university placement centers and other sources.

This completely updated edition includes information about a corporation's position in *Fortune* magazine's annual financial ranking. If a corporation made the magazine's most admired list, that is also noted. In addition to the widely known Fortune 500, which annually ranks U.S. corporations according to sales, *Fortune* also annually ranks the 100 largest commercial banking companies by assets, the 100 largest diversified service companies by sales, the 50 largest retailing companies by sales, the 50 largest diversified financial companies by assets, the 50 largest life insurance companies by assets, the 50 largest utilities by assets, the 50 largest savings institutions by assets, and the 50 largest transportation companies by operating revenues. If a corporation was included in one of the industrial lists in the 1987 *Fortune* publication (1986 financial data), its ranking was included in the section called "The Company." *Fortune* compiles rankings of 300 companies in 33 industry groups. The 1987 list was created by asking 8,200 senior executives to rate the companies in their own industry on eight key measures of reputation. The survey was conducted late in 1986, and about half of those surveyed responded. If you are interested in this aspect of the company you are interviewing, obtain the current *Fortune* rankings. There is quite a bit of movement within the ranking each year; some companies join the list and others drop out.

Another addition to the 1988 edition of *The National Directory of Corporate Training Programs* is the inclusion of salary information from the College Placement Council. When we surveyed companies, we asked about the beginning salary for their entry-level positions. Some companies included salary information, others did not. When we did not have information from a company, salary information was included from the College Placement Council. The Council reports quarterly through its CPC Salary Survey, which collects beginning salary offers from 164 participating placement offices at 143 colleges and universities throughout the United States. The offers are base starting-salary offers and do not include fringe benefits or overtime. The comprehensive survey profiles salary information by curriculum, type of employer, technical or nontechnical degree, undergraduate or graduate degree, functional area, and sex. The information used in the book was reported from the July 1987 survey, which covered from September 1, 1986, through June 5, 1987. The salary information reported in the "Salary and Benefits" section of the company profiles includes starting-salary offers for bachelor's and master's degrees for nontechnical and technical majors from one of eighteen employer types. This information is provided only as a guide to what the beginning salary might be with a company. When you inquire about a position or interview with a company, that is the time to obtain more specific salary information. Salaries can vary significantly from industry to industry, from company to company, and with the geographic region and the condition of the economy.

Besides the valuable CPC Salary Survey, the College Placement Council also provides other helpful employment information such as the *CPC Annual,* a guide to career planning, the job search, graduate school, and work-related education. If you are on a college campus, the placement center probably has a copy of the latest survey and the *Annual.* If you want to obtain a copy, you can contact The College Placement Council at 62 Highland Avenue, Bethlehem, PA 18017 (215) 866-1421.

Undergraduates will find it helpful to use *The National Directory of Corporate Training Programs* throughout college to help them choose courses as their career choices take shape. Seniors can use it to map out postgraduation job-hunting strategies. It will help M.B.A.s locate the best salaries and opportunities in their field. Others with advanced degrees in less demand can use it to locate companies that recognize that intelligence and academic achievements can, with proper training, translate into top-notch business skills. Technologically and vocationally trained people can use it as a ladder to management and advanced skills positions. It is a tool, too, for minorities, women, and others concerned with affirmative action.

The National Directory of Corporate Training Programs is also a guide not only for recent graduates but also for the person wanting to break out of a dead-end job and find new career opportunities. Many companies are looking for employees with one to ten years of experience. These criteria are noted in the "Qualifications" section of the company profiles. If you have related work experience, you can usually complete the training program quicker and receive a full assignment sooner —which means more money.

Good luck with your job hunting. May *The National Directory of Corporate Training Programs* help you find the best job for you.

THE Programs

☆ ☆ ☆ ☆ ☆

ABBOTT LABORATORIES

MARKETING • SALES

THE COMPANY

Abbott has evolved from a U.S. prescription-pharmaceutical manufacturer into a broad-based health-care company serving a worldwide market. Founded in 1888 in Chicago by a neighborhood physician, Dr. Wallace Abbott, the company was originally known as the Abbott Alkaloidal Company. It changed to its present name, Abbott Laboratories, in 1914. Annual sales are more than $3 billion, as the firm continues to emphasize product diversification and acceleration of overseas expansion. Abbott markets products in approximately 130 countries around the world through its affiliates and distributors. Research focuses on new types of chemotherapeutic agents for cardiovascular disease, bacterial infections, and rheumatoid arthritis. Abbott sells professional pharmaceutical and nutritional products; hospital and laboratory products; and consumer, agricultural, and chemical products. Among its trade names are Sucaryl, Selsun and Selsun Blue, Murine, Similac, and Nembutal. About a fourth of the company's U.S. operations are located at the 480-acre headquarters site in Abbott Park, near Chicago. About 32,000 people work for Abbott worldwide. Listed among *Fortune*'s most admired corporations, Abbott is ranked number 96 in the Fortune 500 largest U.S. industrial corporations.

SALES TRAINING PROGRAM

Abbott's six-week sales training program will offer you strategically staggered classes during your first six months on the job. Training will cover products (taught to a great extent by the scientists who developed them), exposure to competitive products, and the Xerox Professional Selling Skills training course.

QUALIFICATIONS

Abbott looks for graduates with varied backgrounds who are self-starters and possess strong interpersonal skills. Science and chemistry knowledge are pluses.

RECRUITMENT AND PLACEMENT

Abbott recruits on college campuses around the country. After a recruiting interview you may be asked to visit the Chicago headquarters. Sales representatives work throughout the United States.

SALARY AND BENEFITS

The College Placement Council Salary Survey for September 1986–June 1987 indicates starting salaries for chemical, drug, and allied product companies to be $1,964 a month for those with a B.A. degree in nontechnical curricula and $2,457 with a B.A. degree in technical curricula. M.B.A. starting salaries were $2,886 for a nontechnical undergraduate degree and $2,794 for a technical undergraduate degree. Check with the company for more specific salary information. Benefits will include stock and profit-sharing plans.

CONTACT

Personnel Recruitment, Abbott Laboratories, Abbott Park, IL 60064.

ABRAHAM & STRAUS

BUYING · SALES

THE COMPANY

Abraham & Straus is a division of Federated Department Stores, Inc. Established in 1865 in Brooklyn, Abraham & Straus has 15 stores in New York, New Jersey, and Pennsylvania. The company combines a tradition of customer service and quality merchandise in a full-line department store with leadership in fashion merchandising. A&S has 17,000 employees.

MERCHANDISING TRAINING PROGRAM

After completing this training program, you will be prepared to work as a sales manager or assistant buyer. Your training will last ten to fifteen weeks, combining on-the-job experience and classroom seminars. During the training period you will work in two departments: home furnishings and apparel. The company also offers executive training programs for further career growth.

QUALIFICATIONS

A&S hires graduates in business, marketing, and the liberal arts. It is looking for individuals who are flexible, self-motivated, and creative. Experienced personnel with two to five years' work history are also encouraged to apply.

RECRUITMENT AND PLACEMENT

Department stores are located in New York, New Jersey, and Pennsylvania. The company hires about 350 trainees a year.

SALARY AND BENEFITS

Expect to start in the $18,000 to $20,000 range with a bachelor's degree. Benefits consist of medical, hospital, and life insurance, pension, profit-sharing, stock-purchase, deferred compensation, and incentive savings plans; relocation services; a liberal discount policy; and a career development program.

CONTACT

Walter J. Davis, Executive Recruitment Director, Abraham & Straus, 420 Fulton Street, Brooklyn, NY 11201.

ADDISON-WESLEY PUBLISHING COMPANY

SALES · MARKETING

THE COMPANY

Addison-Wesley is an independent worldwide publisher with divisions serving schools, colleges, and retail markets. The company publishes state-of-the-art training products for business and government; books and software for professional audiences; nonfiction trade books; and math, science, computer science, and engineering texts.

SALES/MARKETING TRAINING PROGRAM

The one-year training program prepares college graduates for the position of college textbook sales representative. It starts with two to three weeks of study about the books you will be selling to professors for course adoption and about your sales territory. General orientation covers company philosophy and policies. Basic sales techniques are taught through in-house classroom instruction, supervised on-the-job instruction, and feedback/coaching sessions. You will receive manuals for self-study. Your district sales manager accompanies you on campus sales calls during training. You will also attend regional and national sales meetings. The sales representative position is a stepping-stone to the positions of district sales manager, product manager, or acquisitions editor.

QUALIFICATIONS

The company is looking for highly motivated, articulate liberal arts graduates or those with backgrounds in the sciences, marketing, or data processing. A candidate should be able to work independently, enjoy challenges, and interact with a highly educated client base.

RECRUITMENT AND PLACEMENT

Addison-Wesley has regional offices in Reading, Massachusetts (the home office); Atlanta, Georgia; Rolling Meadows, Illinois; and Menlo Park, California.

SALARY AND BENEFITS

The College Placement Council Salary Survey for September 1986–June 1987 indicates starting salaries for merchandising (retail and wholesale) and service companies to be $1,594 a month for those with a B.A. degree in nontechnical curricula and $2,141 with a B.A. degree in technical curricula. M.B.A. starting salaries were $2,572 for a nontechnical undergraduate degree, and $2,735 for an M.B.A. with technical undergraduate degree. Check with the company for more specific salary information.

CONTACT

Manager of Human Resources, Addison-Wesley Publishing Co., Jacob Way, Reading, MA 01867, or Manager of Human Resources, 2725 Sand Hill Road, Menlo Park, CA 94025.

AETNA LIFE & CASUALTY COMPANY

ACCOUNTING • ADMINISTRATION • ANALYSIS/PROGRAMMING • ACTUARIAL SERVICES • AUDITING • BOND REPRESENTATIVE • BROKERAGE • CLAIM REPRESENTATIVE • ENGINEERING • PENSION ANALYSIS • RATING ANALYSIS • SALES • SERVICE REPRESENTATIVE

THE COMPANY

With assets of over $42 billion, Aetna is the largest diversified financial institution in the country, and the fourth largest life insurance company. It is also involved in satellite communications, real estate development, home construction, high technology, and investment management. Headquartered in Hartford, Connecticut, Aetna employs 40,000 workers in the United States and an additional 5,000 outside the country. It is listed among *Fortune*'s most admired corporations. There are many avenues at Aetna to lead you into the world of insurance, projected to be one of the leading financial industries of the twenty-first century.

ALL TRAINING PROGRAMS

Aetna believes in the value of on-the-job training but also makes available a wide array of classroom courses. Your supervisor will approve your courses. Each of the divisions offers insurance-related courses tailored to provide training for specific jobs, with computer-related courses through the Aetna Data Processing Education Program. You will be able to develop technical and supervisory skills and obtain information for making career decisions through courses offered by the company's Human Resources Department.

ACTUARIAL STUDENT PROGRAM

You will develop practical business ability through job assignments in the company's actuarial departments. You will be allowed substantial amounts of company time for study, as you prepare for your licensing exams. Aetna provides textbooks and other materials needed to prepare, with actuarial classes at the University of Connecticut paid for by Aetna. You will also receive salary increases after passing examinations, in addition to annual merit raises. A variety of work assignments will help you as you study. Actuaries at Aetna may expect to become officers of the company.

QUALIFICATIONS

You will need a mathematics degree, or an especially strong math background in another specialty such as chemistry, economics, or computer sciences. Aetna considers graduates who have passed one and preferably two of the actuarial exams.

PLACEMENT

You will begin in Hartford.

COMMERCIAL INSURANCE ENGINEER PROGRAM

You'll receive extensive training through a combination of on-the-job experience in a field office and formal classroom training in the home office. Your job is to provide accident-prevention services to business and industry. When a company applies for insurance coverage, an engineering representative surveys its facilities. Those findings assist the commercial insurance analyst in underwriting the risk and in determining the kind of insurance to provide. Once the insurance is in force, the engineer makes regular safety inspections and recommends protection techniques.

QUALIFICATIONS

Aetna looks for candidates with degrees in civil, chemical, environmental, mechanical, industrial, electrical, or fire protection engineering. A background in physics or chemistry will also be considered.

PLACEMENT

After being hired by a field office for the first segment of your training, you will go to headquarters, then transfer to another location within the territory of the field office where you were hired. You will travel regularly.

SALES MANAGEMENT PROGRAM

You will be immersed in an intensive twenty-four-month course of study and on-the-job experience. You will be expected to develop expertise in six critical areas: life insurance sales; time organization; recruiting; joint field work; study; and management assignments. In addition to following a prescribed course of study, you will spend a substantial amount of time selling during the first year. In the second year, focus shifts to management assignments. After successfully completing the program, you will be promoted to supervisor.

QUALIFICATIONS

A limited number of applicants are accepted, many with graduate degrees. You should have drive and a strong academic record.

PLACEMENT

You will begin at company headquarters in Connecticut.

ALL PROGRAMS

RECRUITMENT

Aetna is active on campuses across the country, often sending out tennis star Arthur Ashe (a member of its board of directors) to make speeches to students about careers.

SALARY AND BENEFITS

Salaries begin at $19,600 with a bachelor's degree, jumping to $37,000 with a business-related master's degree and nontechnical B.S. Benefits include life and business travel accident insurance, medical and dental expense coverage, long-term disability, an incentive savings and pension plan, profit sharing, flextime, relocation services, generous vacation and holiday policy.

CONTACT

Corporate Recruiting, 151 Farmington Avenue, Hartford, CT 06156.

ALCOA (ALUMINUM COMPANY OF AMERICA)

CHEMISTRY/METALLURGY · ENGINEERING · FINANCIAL SERVICES · HUMAN RESOURCES/INDUSTRIAL RELATIONS · INFORMATION SYSTEMS · RESEARCH AND DEVELOPMENT · SALES

THE COMPANY

Alcoa is the nation's and the world's largest producer of primary aluminum. Founded in 1888 by process inventor Charles Martin Hall, Alcoa produced the world's first economically viable aluminum, a metal that has been called "the metal of the twenty-first century." The company has annual sales of approximately $5 billion and employs more than 35,000 people domestically, and another 11,000 outside the country. Alcoa's principal operations include mining and processing bauxite and refining it into alumina, smelting metallic aluminum from alumina, processing aluminum and its alloys into mill products and finished products, and recycling aluminum products. Alcoa also produces a full line of alumina chemicals, licenses proprietary technology, and sells engineering and construction services. An offshoot of the company's interest in aluminum as a construction material is participation in real estate and land development through subsidiaries. Alcoa is also in the energy business, generating almost half the power used in its U.S. operations. Looking at its second century of growth, Alcoa plans to focus tightly on markets which support a special mix of high technology and large-volume production. Four such markets are aerospace, packaging, transportation, and electrical distribution. Company headquarters are in Pittsburgh, Pennsylvania. Listed among *Fortune*'s most admired corporations, it ranks number 79 in the Fortune 500 largest U.S. industrial corporations.

ALL TRAINING PROGRAMS

You will be trained on the job, with job rotation and special project assignments to develop your skills. An ongoing program of training and development covers personal skills and business-related areas.

QUALIFICATIONS

Alcoa hires graduates with degrees in transportation, business logistics, production/operations management, computer science, data processing, engineering, business administration, various technical and mathematical disciplines, personnel/labor relations, psychology, and organizational behavior. You may also need strong interpersonal skills in communication, conflict resolution and negotiation, personal integrity, sound logic, initiative, and be able to work well under pressure.

RECRUITMENT AND PLACEMENT

If you are still in college, make an appointment with an Alcoa recruiter and review a copy of *Alcoa Career News* in the placement office library. If you are no longer in college, send a résumé stating your area of interest to headquarters. Your first assignment could be in Pittsburgh or other Pennsylvania locations, Alabama, Arkansas, California, Indiana, Iowa, North Carolina, New York, Ohio, Tennessee, Texas, or Washington.

SALARY AND BENEFITS

The College Placement Council Salary Survey for September 1986–June 1987 indicates starting salaries for metal and metal product companies to be $1,782 a month for those with a B.A. degree in nontechnical curricula and $2,353 with a B.A. degree in technical curricula. M.B.A. starting salaries were $2,346 for a nontechnical undergraduate degree and $2,700 for a technical undergraduate degree. Check with the company for more specific salary information. Benefits include paid vacations, medical, vision and dental care, a contributory savings plan, and life and disability insurance, retirement, and vacation benefits that can be taken as cash or additional time off.

CONTACT

Director of Employment, Aluminum Company of America, Pittsburgh, PA 15219.

ALLIED BANCSHARES, INC.

AUDITING • BANK OPERATIONS • LENDING

THE COMPANY

Allied is a young organization. Begun in 1971 as a three-bank holding company with assets of $200 million, it now has more than 50 member banks, with combined assets of almost $10 billion, located in large and small Texas cities. Rather than going after big national accounts, Allied caters to the middle market. It is ranked number 53 in the Fortune 100 largest commercial banking companies.

ALL TRAINING PROGRAMS

You may select from three career directions with Allied—auditing, bank operations, or lending—without being channeled into a specific, pre-chosen area or generalized training. Allied's self-paced program eliminates months of classroom work under strict supervision. You'll begin working right away, side by side with senior professionals. You'll advance at your speed—the more responsibility you're ready to take on, the more Allied will be ready to give you. Your supervisor will provide formal performance reviews and informal feedback on a regular basis. By the time you've finished your training you'll have received a comprehensive exposure to your chosen area and a clear sense of your development within it.

QUALIFICATIONS

In addition to a degree and solid academic record, you should be self-motivated, energetic, hard-working, and competitive to catch the Allied recruiter's eye.

RECRUITMENT AND PLACEMENT

Allied recruits on college campuses and will send you to one of its major training centers in Houston or Dallas. In some cases, if you've chosen a member bank in another Texas city, it may be possible for you to begin working in that location immediately.

SALARY AND BENEFITS

The College Placement Council Salary Survey for September 1986–June 1987 indicates starting salaries for banking, finance, and insurance companies to be $1,889 a month for those with a B.A. degree in nontechnical curricula and $2,135 with a B.A. degree in technical curricula. M.B.A. starting salaries were $2,884 for a nontechnical undergraduate degree and $3,320 for a technical undergraduate degree. Check with the company for more specific salary information. Benefits include group life, health, and dental insurance, as well as profit sharing and stock savings plans.

CONTACT

Personnel, Allied Bancshares, P.O. Box 1515, Houston, TX 77251-1515.

ALLIED-SIGNAL, INC.

ADMINISTRATION • ENGINEERING • INFORMATION SYSTEMS AND PROCESSING • MARKETING • PRODUCTION • RESEARCH AND DEVELOPMENT • SALES

THE COMPANY

Allied-Signal (formerly the Allied Corporation), is a diversified firm that manufactures chemicals, fibers, plastics, aerospace systems, electronics, automotive and automation equipment, oil and gas, batteries, data processing equipment, motors, communications systems, and machine tools. It develops and applies technology for a broad range of markets. In 1983 Allied acquired Bendix in one of the most discussed mergers of the year. Headquarters for Allied-Signal are in Morristown, New Jersey. It employs 100,000 in the United States, and another 44,000 outside the country. Divisions and companies include: Union Texas Petroleum Division (gas and oil exploration), Semet-Solvay Division (ore refining), Agricultural Division (plant fertilizers), Specialty Chemical Division (primarily organic chemicals and plastics for various industries), Industrial Chemicals Division (primarily inorganic chemicals), Fibers Division (synthetic fibers), and Automotive Products Division (largest producer of auto seat-belt systems in the world). It ranks number 25 in the Fortune 500 largest U.S. industrial corporations.

ALL TRAINING PROGRAMS

You will receive on-the-job training under an experienced supervisor as you begin your career in one of Allied-Signal's divisions.

ENERGY PROGRAM

A new employee with the Union Texas Petroleum division is likely to be a geologist who will get hands-on training in geological mapping. When you become a full-fledged member of an exploration team, you will learn to analyze data and to assist in drilling operations under the tutelage of a senior geologist and team leader. Master's-level recruits will quickly find themselves accompanying teams in the field and studying seismograph printouts to discover promising resources.

In the Semet-Solvay Division, the technical trainee is assigned to one of the plants to be exposed to all facets of production, including manufacturing costs, marketing, labor relations, management, and quality assurance. After six months of this on-the-job training you will be assigned to the plant's maintenance or engineering functions.

The Specialty Chemicals Division lets you gain on-the-job training by assuming immediate responsibilities in process or maintenance engineering. In addition, this division has a special program for engineering development, offered to 20 technical graduates each year. These graduates have a six-month orientation in which each is assigned to a different plant for two- to three-month periods to work on special projects. The range of work is broad. If you are one of these technical trainees, you will be working closely with a technical adviser who will guide you and evaluate your progress.

CHEMICAL PROGRAM

The Industrial Chemicals Division has a comprehensive orientation and development program designed to prepare you for major management responsibilities. This one-year program familiarizes engineering trainees with all facets of chemical manufacturing. Your initial assignment will help you understand the complex process of chemical manufacturing. After six months you will be placed in an orientation program at divisional headquarters to learn about marketing, sales, advertising, and planning. Training for sales positions varies with the division assignment. For the Specialty Chemicals Division, you will spend six to eight months learning about products and marketing objectives.

FIBERS AND AUTOMOTIVE PRODUCTS PROGRAM

Engineers assigned to the Fibers and Automotive Products Division will be applying engineering principles immediately in maintenance and plant engineering or as a plant engineer. Your on-the-job training is supervised by a seasoned engineer. As part of your training you'll coordinate maintenance, assist with cost reduction programs, and update safety procedures. If you go to work in textiles, you might start as a product specialist; in this position you would learn to coordinate product evaluation, assess the potential impact of new processing technology, and support marketing by providing information on competitive products. If you begin as a sales or merchandising representative, you'll be based initially at one of the marketing centers for training. Your field training will cover making product presentations, taking and processing orders, and monitoring delivery.

ALL PROGRAMS

QUALIFICATIONS

The company is looking for men and women with strong academic preparation, the potential for achievement, and "the desire to build a rewarding career with a company that cares." Allied-Signal's various divisions are interested in engineering, chemistry, and physics majors at the bachelor, master, and doctoral levels. An M.B.A., primarily with a technical B.S., will also qualify you for employment with Allied-Signal.

RECRUITMENT AND PLACEMENT

The company recruits nationwide. You could begin work in California, Delaware, Florida, Illinois, Indiana, Kansas, Louisiana, Maryland, Michigan, New Jersey, New York, North Carolina, Ohio, Pennsylvania, South Carolina, Texas, or Virginia.

SALARY AND BENEFITS

A highly diversified company, Allied-Signal falls into several industry classifications, including aerospace, chemicals, and electronics equipment. The College Placement Council Salary Survey for September 1986–June 1987 indicates starting salaries for aerospace companies to be $1,943 a month for those with a B.A. degree in nontechnical curricula and $2,399 with a B.A. degree in technical curricula. M.B.A. starting salaries were $2,330 for a nontechnical undergraduate degree and $2,475 for a technical undergraduate degree. Chemical, drug, and allied products companies report average starting salaries of $1,964 a month for those with a B.A. degree in nontechnical curricula and $2,457 with a B.A. degree in technical curricula. M.B.A. starting salaries were $2,886 for a nontechnical undergraduate degree and $2,794 for a technical undergraduate degree. In the electronics field, average starting salaries are $1,861 a month for those with a B.A. degree in nontechnical curricula and $2,419 with a B.A. degree in technical curricula. M.B.A. starting salaries were $2,784 for a nontechnical undergraduate degree and $2,818 for a technical undergraduate degree. Check with the company for more specific salary information.

The benefits package includes medical, life, and dental insurance; a pension and stock-purchase plan; tuition reimbursement; relocation assistance; career counseling; and fitness programs.

CONTACT

Barbara B. Robbins, Manager, University Relations, Allied-Signal, Inc., P.O. Box 2245R, Morristown, NJ 07960.

ALLSTATE INSURANCE COMPANY

ACCOUNTING • CLAIMS • COMPUTER ANALYSIS AND PROGRAMMING • CONTRACTS • HUMAN RESOURCES • LAW • MANAGEMENT • SALES • UNDERWRITING

THE COMPANY

Allstate Insurance Company, a subsidiary of Sears, currently employs 46,000 people in offices throughout the United States. It sells and services auto, property, life, health, commercial, and worker's compensation insurance. Through affiliated corporations, it is involved in motor club, auto finance, savings and loans, and corporate and private mortgage insurance interests. A separate training division provides films, texts, and classroom instruction materials for company-wide use. Allstate's home office in Northbrook, Illinois, is one of the largest suburban office building complexes in the country. The company has assets of $14 billion and intends to remain nonunion. *Fortune* ranks Allstate number 38 in the 50 largest life insurance companies.

ALL TRAINING PROGRAMS

Training is designed to produce thoroughly knowledgeable employees for areas such as claims adjustment, settlement negotiations, contracts, and underwriting. Training usually consists of a combination of formal classes and on-the-job training. As a beginning claims adjuster, you will take classes that will teach you how to investigate liability, evaluate damages, negotiate statements, and interpret insurance contracts. Underwriters—those who evaluate insurance applications—attend underwriting courses and train on the job. The training program in sales consists of instruction in company procedures, rating, product knowledge, and sales skills. After this formal training, new agents are assigned to a field office where they work with district sales managers to develop practical skills.

QUALIFICATIONS

You should be in the top 25 percent of your class with a minimum G.P.A. of 3.0, related student work experience, and a record of achievement in extracurricular and leadership activities. The company is hiring primarily graduates with degrees in business, computer science, liberal arts, statistics, and physical science.

RECRUITMENT AND PLACEMENT

Applications are especially encouraged from students who have a technical degree and related work experience. The starting location is in Illinois.

SALARY AND BENEFITS

Salaries start at $19,500 with a bachelor's degree; $20,500 with an advanced social science/humanities degree; $20,500 for business-related master's and nontechnical B.S. ($22,000 to $28,000 with one to five years' experience); $24,000 with business-related master's and technical B.S. ($24,000 to $28,000 with one to five years' experience). Benefits include medical, life, and disability insurance, profit sharing, and a pension plan. A stock-purchase plan and flextime options are also offered.

CONTACT

Personnel Department, Allstate Insurance Company, Allstate Plaza, Northbrook, IL 60062.

AMAX, INC.

ACCOUNTING • AUDITING • ENGINEERING • FINANCIAL ANALYZING • MARKET RESEARCH ANALYZING • PRODUCTION • RESEARCH AND DEVELOPMENT • TECHNICAL SALES

THE COMPANY

In 1887, American Metal Company combined with Climax Molybdenum Company to form American Metal Climax, shortened to AMAX in 1974. AMAX mines more different kinds of metals, minerals, and other substances in huge quantities than any other company. AMAX is related to practically every other mining company through a web of interlocking financial arrangements. Through these partnerships, it has interests in all aspects of mining products. AMAX is the largest producer of molybdenum, a gray metal used as an alloy to toughen steel and iron. It is a major producer of coal, with 11 surface mines in Illinois, Indiana, Kentucky, and Wyoming, and the second largest tungsten producer. Employees are counted at over 11,000. Corporate headquarters are in Greenwich, Connecticut.

ALL TRAINING PROGRAMS

Most training is on the job but often is supplemented with technical courses and workshops. For those entering supervisory and management positions there are classes for the development of management skills.

QUALIFICATIONS

You should have an M.A. or M.B.A.; some undergraduate degrees are appropriate for positions in accounting, auditing, engineering, financial analyzing, market research analyzing, and mining engineering. Technical sales personnel need a bachelor's degree in metal or chemical engineering.

RECRUITMENT AND PLACEMENT

Recruiters visit two schools in the Northeast, six in the Midwest, three in the South, and six in the West. The most probable starting locations are in Louisiana, Colorado, or Connecticut. If you are a mining engineer, you will generally be located in Colorado, Illinois, Indiana, Missouri, or Wyoming.

SALARY AND BENEFITS

With a bachelor's degree, you can expect to start at about $24,000; and at $30,000 to $32,000 with a master's. Your benefits package will include medical, life, and dental insurance; a pension plan; relocation assistance; profit-sharing and stock-purchase plans; and a fitness program.

CONTACT

Eileen Jolly, Supervisor, Professional Employment, AMAX, Inc., AMAX Center, Greenwich, CT 06836.

AMERADA HESS

ACCOUNTING/FINANCE · ADMINISTRATION · EMPLOYEE RELATIONS · ENGINEERING · EXPLORATION/PRODUCTION · LAW · MARKETING · QUALITY CONTROL · REAL ESTATE · REFINING · SALES · TRANSPORTATION/SAFETY

THE COMPANY

Amerada Hess is a leader in the energy industry which explores millions of acres around the world and has thousands of producing oil and gas wells. Its refineries produce quality fuel oils, gasoline, and other petroleum products. Amerada Hess operates a fleet of tankers, including Very Large Crude Carriers (VLCCs), to move crude oil and refined products. Growing storage capacity, already the largest on the East Coast, is made up of strategically placed terminals distributing Amerada Hess products to all types of customers from Boston to Houston and beyond. Amerada Hess Corporation resulted from the 1969 merger of Amerada Petroleum Corporation and Hess Oil and Chemical Corporation. Corporate headquarters are in New York City. Amerada Hess ranks number 92 in the Fortune 500 largest U.S. industrial corporations.

ALL TRAINING PROGRAMS

Amerada Hess will train you on the job for most positions and offers formal training in some areas. You will be assigned a supervisor to oversee your progress and offer feedback. Your work unit will be relatively small.

QUALIFICATIONS

Amerada Hess hires from many degree disciplines at all levels. Specialties include: chemistry, chemical engineering, business administration, environmental science, marketing, economics, accounting, liberal arts, law, industrial relations, behavioral science, finance, computer science, safety engineering, mechanical engineering, marine transportation, civil engineering, petroleum, geology, physics, mathematics, land management, and geophysics. Work experience in the field is also considered a plus.

RECRUITMENT AND PLACEMENT

Recruiters visit campuses around the country. You are also invited to submit a résumé to headquarters. Your first job site could be in Texas, North Dakota, Mississippi, New York, California, Louisiana, Colorado, New Jersey, Oklahoma, Alaska, the Virgin Islands, or Canada.

SALARY AND BENEFITS

The College Placement Council Salary Survey for September 1986–June 1987 indicates starting salaries for petroleum and allied product companies to be $1,972 a month for those with a B.A. degree in nontechnical curricula and $2,497 with a B.A. degree in technical curricula. M.B.A. starting salaries were $2,629 for a nontechnical undergraduate degree and $2,970 for a technical undergraduate degree. Check with the company for more specific salary information. Benefits include medical, accident, and sickness insurance, savings and stock bonus plan, paid vacations and holidays, educational assistance, and retirement plan.

CONTACT

Corporate Recruiting Office, Amerada Hess Corporation, 1185 Avenue of the Americas, New York, NY 10036.

AMERICAN APPRAISAL ASSOCIATES, INC.

FINANCE APPRAISAL • ENGINEERING APPRAISAL • REAL ESTATE APPRAISAL

THE COMPANY

All types of businesses turn to this company to find out, "What's it worth?" American Appraisal Associates, Inc., was established in 1896 and is the leading international valuation consulting organization specializing in tangible and intangible assets; closely held securities; insurance services; and merger, acquisition, and divestment services. The company has 800 employees.

APPRAISAL TRAINING PROGRAM

You will be trained to evaluate one of three types of property. In the engineering program, you will inspect, quantity-survey, and value buildings; analyze and value machinery and equipment in a wide variety of manufacturing and process industries. For financial appraisals, you will value closely held businesses, privately held and publicly traded equity securities, and many types of intangible assets. To be a real estate appraiser, you will learn to render fair market value opinions and provide feasibility and highest-and-best-use studies of investment and industrial real estate. You will learn by doing as well as through formal classes. The company encourages its appraisers to attend short courses, seminars, workshops, and conferences to learn new methods and to keep in touch with other professionals in the field.

QUALIFICATIONS

You might have a degree in any engineering discipline; finance or accounting; or real estate. AAA looks for graduates with computer familiarity and excellent oral and written communication skills. You need a minimum G.P.A. of 3.0 and a record of extracurricular achievement.

RECRUITMENT AND PLACEMENT

The company recruits on campuses around the country. You will begin in a major city in California, Georgia, Illinois, Minnesota, New Jersey, New York, Oregon, Texas, Washington, or Wisconsin.

SALARY AND BENEFITS

American pays $21,000 to $24,000 for entry-level employees with bachelor's degrees; and $24,000 to $27,000 for those with a master's. Benefits will consist of life insurance, medical, hospital, dental, and incentive savings plans, as well as a deferred compensation program and tuition reimbursement.

CONTACT

Yvonne Gigstead, Manager, Employment Services, 525 East Michigan Street, Milwaukee, WI 53202.

AMERICAN CYANAMID COMPANY

INFORMATION SYSTEMS • MARKETING AND SALES • RESEARCH AND DEVELOPMENT

THE COMPANY

American Cyanamid is a large diversified company that sells agricultural products, specialty chemicals, medical products, consumer products, construction and building materials, cosmetics, health-care products, pharmaceuticals, and plastics. It has a large research and development organization. American Cyanamid was founded in 1907 and employs 25,000 workers in the United States; 38,000 worldwide. Annual sales top $3.8 billion, contributing to its status as one of *Fortune*'s most admired corporations. It ranks number 94 in the Fortune 500 largest U.S. industrial corporations.

ALL TRAINING PROGRAMS

American Cyanamid trains you to work and think independently. It also prepares you for future advancement within the company. Technical employees will have mostly on-the-job training supplemented with seminars. Sales trainees go through a formal training program.

QUALIFICATIONS

You need a bachelor's degree in engineering, chemistry, or computer science, or an M.B.A. You should have a minimum G.P.A. of 3.0. Applications are encouraged from candidates with three or more years' experience.

RECRUITMENT AND PLACEMENT

American Cyanamid recruits on about 50 college campuses each year, hiring up to 125 trainees. Starting locations include Connecticut, New Jersey, and New York. Sales positions can be anywhere in the United States. After a few years, you can be eligible for an overseas assignment.

SALARY AND BENEFITS

The College Placement Council Salary Survey for September 1986–June 1987 indicates starting salaries for chemical, drug, and allied products companies to be $1,964 a month for those with a B.A. degree in nontechnical curricula and $2,457 with a B.A. degree in technical curricula. M.B.A. starting salaries were $2,886 for a nontechnical undergraduate degree and $2,794 for a technical undergraduate degree. Check with the company for more specific salary information. Salaries are supplemented with a benefits package that includes medical, hospital, dental, and life insurance, pension, and profit-sharing plans; a career development program; and 100 percent tuition reimbursement.

CONTACT

Leo J. Medicus, Manager, College Relations and Professional Placement, American Cyanamid Company, One Cyanamid Plaza, Wayne, NJ 07470.

AMERICAN HOECHST CORPORATION

COMPUTER SCIENCE • DISTRIBUTION • ENGINEERING • MARKETING/SALES • PRODUCTION • RESEARCH AND DEVELOPMENT

THE COMPANY

American Hoechst makes more than 2,500 products, touching many diverse industrial and consumer markets. As the largest subsidiary of the Hoechst Group (487 companies that operate in 140 countries), American Hoechst is also the fastest-growing branch of the company. American Hoechst is a leader in the research, development, and manufacture of fibers, film, waxes, pharmaceuticals, chemicals, petrochemicals, resins, and graphic arts equipment. The company sees itself as blending chemistry, medicine, engineering, physics, and biology to improve the quality of life, preserve the environment, and help to shape the future of mankind. It has about 9,000 employees and headquarters in Somerville, New Jersey. Ranked number 210 in the Fortune 500 largest U.S. industrial corporations.

ALL TRAINING PROGRAMS

You will be given a combination of on-the-job and formal training when you join American Hoechst. The company also offers occasional courses in management, time management, and communications skills. You will be encouraged to continue training in your field to maintain and expand your expertise.

QUALIFICATIONS

Hoechst is looking for candidates with B.S., M.S., or Ph.D. degrees in a scientific or technical discipline such as biochemistry, computer science, engineering (ceramic, chemical, electrical, electronics, industrial, mechanical, software, and textile engineering), biology, chemistry, information systems, microbiology, pharmacology, polymer science, statistics, toxicology, and textile chemistry.

You should demonstrate that you are goal-oriented and a high-energy person to impress a Hoechst recruiter.

RECRUITMENT AND PLACEMENT

The company recruits nationwide. Hoechst locations include Spartanburg, South Carolina; Somerville, New Jersey; Branchburg, New Jersey; La Jolla, California; and Coventry, Rhode Island, to name a few. Your specialty will determine your placement.

SALARY AND BENEFITS

The College Placement Council Salary Survey for September 1986–June 1987 indicates starting salaries for chemical, drug, and allied product companies to be $1,964 a month for those with a B.A. degree in nontechnical curricula and $2,457 with a B.A. degree in technical curricula. M.B.A. starting salaries were $2,886 for a nontechnical undergraduate degree and $2,794 for a technical undergraduate degree. Check with the company for more specific salary information. Hoechst offers a complete benefits package, including life, dental, medical, accident, life, and disability insurance, tuition reimbursement, retirement and 401K plans, and paid holidays and vacations.

CONTACT

Employment Section, Corporate Headquarters, American Hoechst Corporation, Route 202–206 North, Somerville, NJ 08876; Fibers and Film Group, P.O. Box 5887, Spartanburg, SC 29301; Health Care and Agri-Vet Group, Route 202–206 North, P.O. Box 2500, Somerville, NJ 08876; or Specialty Products Group, 3070 Route 22, P.O. Box 3700, Branchburg, NJ 08876.

AMERICAN HOSPITAL SUPPLY CORPORATION

ACCOUNTING • CREDIT • ENGINEERING • FINANCE • LOGISTICS • MANAGEMENT • MANUFACTURING • PURCHASING • SALES

THE COMPANY

American Hospital Supply is the U.S. leader in manufacturing, marketing, and distribution of health-care products and services to hospitals, laboratories, and medical specialists. With more than 35,000 employees, it produces annual sales of more than $3 billion. American manufactures 27,000 of the 145,000 products it sells to 122,000 worldwide customers. Health-care expenditures worldwide have nearly tripled during the 1980s, and American, continuing its traditional pioneering efforts, has introduced a number of new technological innovations for the growing market. They include laser and other microsurgical techniques for low-trauma surgery; noninvasive diagnostic equipment such as cardiac monitoring computers; blood oxygenators and other life-support devices; therapeutic nutritional products such as instant foods for patients with chronic liver disease; advanced cardiac drugs; new polymers for contact lenses; and artificial skin for burn victims. The company was acquired by Baxter Travenol in 1985 for $3.7 billion.

ALL TRAINING PROGRAMS

You will be given immediate responsibility, learning as you work with supervision. You will not be locked into the area in which you start. Training may also include formal classes and self-study manuals.

ENGINEERING AND MANUFACTURING PROGRAM

Because American's divisions offer diverse technical and managerial opportunities within four engineering categories—process engineering, industrial engineering, research and development, or production supervision—you are encouraged to seek assignments in various manufacturing areas and in other functional areas. You will be conducting basic research that results in practical applications.

QUALIFICATIONS

Exceptional opportunities are available if you have a B.S. or M.S. in chemical, biomedical, mechanical, electronics, plastics, or industrial and civil engineering. Polymer chemists, materials scientists, and business graduates are also needed.

PLACEMENT

Manufacturing facilities are located in major cities throughout the country; opportunities exist for interim assignments in Puerto Rico.

FINANCE AND ACCOUNTING PROGRAM

You could begin as a staff accountant or financial analyst, or you could enter the Credit Understudy Program. You are exposed to all key financial functions within an operating unit. You learn on the job by maintaining general ledger accounts, preparing financial statements and tax data, and analyzing financial reports. Or you may develop financial forecasts or undertake special projects requested by senior management.

QUALIFICATIONS

You should have a bachelor's or master's degree in finance, accounting, or business.

PLACEMENT

American has offices throughout the country.

SALES AND MARKETING PROGRAM

The training will vary depending on your division or marketing group, but you will be expected to acquire a great deal of product knowledge on your own by studying manuals, asking questions, and observing closely. Supplementing your studies will be formal training. This may be either an intense, three- or four-month program combining classwork with field exposure or periodic, week-long sessions supplementing your on-the-job experience. The chairman, president, and many division presidents began as sales reps. Outstanding performers typically advance to a first-line management position within two years.

QUALIFICATIONS

American's sales force comes from a variety of academic backgrounds. They share an enthusiasm for learning and a strong desire to achieve, and they are hardworking, aggressive problem solvers. You must be willing to relocate. With a B.S. or M.S. in business, you qualify for a marketing position.

PLACEMENT

You could work anywhere in the United States.

UNDERSTUDY PROGRAM

Most people who join American begin as a management, logistics, credit, or purchasing understudy. The program provides a flexible, individualized series of assignments that puts you to work on the immediate needs of the center—anything from packing special orders to analyzing inventory forecasts. Working under an experienced supervisor, you will gain broad exposure to many aspects of the operation. As a management understudy, your assignments might include customer and order service, credit and collections, inventory control, logistics, materials, handling, distribution, and facilities planning. If you begin as a logistics understudy, you will work on materials handling, transportation and facilities functions, and special projects in traffic and warehouse management, inventory control, and transportation rates and traffic. Credit understudies use their accounting background to work on credit and collections activities. A variety of inventory and purchasing and systems assignments are provided for the purchasing understudy. When you complete several months of understudy training, you will be placed in a specific assignment in a distribution center. Although you may begin in the Understudy Program, you are encouraged to move ahead within operations or to a sales or management function. Because distribution is one of American's key strengths, professionals in this area are highly visible and able to advance rapidly.

QUALIFICATIONS

Although a college degree is required, your area of study is secondary to your energy, enthusiasm, and leadership abilities.

PLACEMENT

You will work in one of the company's 98 distribution centers around the country.

ALL PROGRAMS

RECRUITMENT

American recruits nationwide.

SALARY AND BENEFITS

The College Placement Council Salary Survey for September 1986–June 1987 indicates starting salaries for chemicals, drugs, and allied products companies to be $1,964 a month for those with a B.A. degree in nontechnical curricula and $2,457 with a B.A. degree in technical curricula. M.B.A. starting salaries were $2,886 for a nontechnical undergraduate degree and $2,794 for a technical undergraduate degree. Check with the company for more specific salary information. In addition to salary, American offers comprehensive medical and dental health-care coverage, disability benefits, and life insurance, as well as retirement, investment, and stock purchase plans. It also provides a credit union, tuition and relocation assistance, an educational gift-matching program, liberal paid holidays and vacations, and its own personal health/fitness program.

CONTACT

Corporate Recruitment, American Hospital Supply Corporation, One American Plaza, Evanston, IL 60201.

AMERITECH 

ADMINISTRATION • ENGINEERING • MARKETING • PROGRAMMING • SUPERVISION

THE COMPANY

Ameritech is one of the seven regional companies formed by the breakup of the Bell System in 1984. The backbone of the company is made up of the five Ameritech Bell companies: Illinois Bell, Indiana Bell, Michigan Bell, Ohio Bell, and Wisconsin Bell. These five companies serve 11.4 million business and residence customer accounts. Between them, they employ 67,700 people. Each Ameritech Bell company has its own subsidiary responsible for marketing telecommunications equipment. Together, the five Bell companies own Ameritech Services, a central source of staff support and technical and market expertise. Along with the five Ameritech Bell companies and their subsidiaries, Ameritech's family includes six other communications subsidiaries: Ameritech Communications, Ameritech Mobile Communications, Ameritech Credit, Ameritech Development, Ameritech Publishing, and Applied Data Research. Ameritech is among the top 25 Fortune 500 service businesses, has more than $18 billion in assets, annual sales exceeding $500 million, 1.4 million shareholders, and an outstanding financial track record. Listed among *Fortune*'s most admired corporations, Ameritech ranks number 440 in the Fortune 500 largest U.S. industrial corporations.

ALL TRAINING PROGRAMS

Training is similar in all the companies, which offer a combination of formal classes, self-study courses, and on-the-job training. You will be thoroughly prepared for your new job under the guidance of experienced supervisors. Some programs last as long as two years while others are much shorter.

ADMINISTRATION PROGRAM

With a degree in accounting, you might begin as an auditor. You'd probably have an opportunity to work on a number of internal audits during your first few months. If you have a strong background in mathematics or computer science, you could start your career as a staff assistant in corporate planning. After a brief orientation, you might be assigned to design a planning model. Public relations, advertising, and journalism specialists also belong to this department and receive on-the-job training through assignments with broad-ranging applications.

QUALIFICATIONS

Ameritech hires graduates with many different degrees for this department, some with technical depth in such areas as mathematics, statistics, and operations research, as well as strong analytical capabilities. Others—including personnel administration, training, and public relations—require special training and effective organizational and interpersonal skills.

ENGINEERING TRAINING PROGRAM

You will typically work closely with an experienced engineer on a project that will familiarize you with the company's systems and procedures while you apply your skills right away. Your work could entail on-site inspection of existing facilities to see if modifications might increase current capacity or if a new system is needed. As a switching engineer you could be asked to analyze the calling traffic handled by a particular central office with expanding and changing requirements. You would work closely with a design engineer to evaluate, then implement your plan. Formal technical training will also be part of your initial education. Some of that training takes place at the Bell Communications Technical Education Center in Lisle, Illinois. You'll be on a steep learning curve at the outset. Intensive training modules are designed to prepare you for more complex projects.

QUALIFICATIONS

Ameritech is interested in outstanding engineering graduates, particularly those with electrical and industrial degrees, as well as mathematicians and computer scientists with an interest in technical applications.

MARKETING PROGRAM

You will be assigned to a marketing team as an account executive or technical support person and given supervised assignments to broaden your knowledge of the company's operations. You will also receive formal training that encompasses systems-selling skills and instruction in product and service applications.

QUALIFICATIONS

To be an account executive, you will need a strong sales background, demonstrated leadership and management skills, and the analytical abilities necessary for effective decision making. To be a technical support specialist, you should have a technical degree with strong systems analysis and design skills, and excellent interpersonal skills.

PROGRAMMING PROGRAM

If you're a recent graduate, you'll usually begin with a self-paced training program to become familiar with the company's design and development methodology. Successful completion of the initial training phase will lead to an assignment with a line programming unit where you will apply your skills in coding and debugging computer programs under the guidance of an experienced computer programmer. If you perform well, you'll probably advance to a basic programmer position with responsibilities for developing program logic from specifications provided by a project leader.

QUALIFICATIONS

Ameritech is looking for technical graduates with strong academic records in computer science or mathematics. The company is also seeking experienced programmers.

SUPERVISION TRAINING PROGRAM

Training for supervisory positions is largely done on the job, so you'll have a chance to make significant contributions from your initial assignment. Several Ameritech companies have very competitive, accelerated development programs for those who demonstrate the capacity to move rapidly into higher levels of management. Your initial assignment will probably involve supervising non-management employees, such as customer service representatives or operators. Your daily work will involve reviewing the accuracy and quality of your subordinates' work and providing them with feedback and coaching.

QUALIFICATIONS

You should have a track record of demonstrating your abilities to achieve goals through others, such as leadership in campus groups or community organizations or through prior work experience. Ameritech is looking for graduates with good academic records in a range of disciplines.

ALL PROGRAMS

RECRUITMENT AND PLACEMENT

Ameritech recruits on college campuses and also solicits résumés from experienced applicants. Interviews will cover previous work experience, academic performance in school, outside activities and organizations, career interests and preferences, and geographical flexibility. Résumés and credentials are shared among the Ameritech companies, and company representatives at times travel in teams so that you may be considered by more than one Ameritech organization. You will work in the Midwest.

SALARY AND BENEFITS

Generally, you can expect to start at about $19,000 to $20,000 with a bachelor's and at about $10,000 more with a graduate-level degree. Benefits include: a savings plan with company matching contributions, tuition reimbursement for career-related study, comprehensive health-care plans for employees and dependents, including dental and vision-care insurance, group life insurance, liberal vacations, paid holidays and personal days, and a company-paid pension plan.

CONTACT

Ameritech Services, Management Employment-B86, 1900 East Golf Road, Schaumburg, IL 60173; Illinois Bell, Management Employment-B86, 212 West Washington Street, Chicago, IL 60606; Indiana Bell, Management Employment-B86, 220 North Meridian Street, Indianapolis, IN 46204; Michigan Bell, Management Employment-B86, 444 Michigan, Detroit, MI 48226; Ohio Bell, Management Employment-B86, 45 Erieview Plaza, Cleveland, OH 44114; or Wisconsin Bell, Management Employment-B86, 722 North Broadway, Milwaukee, WI 53202.

AMOCO

ACCOUNTING · BUSINESS ADMINISTRATION · CHEMISTRY · COMPUTER SCIENCE · CHEMICAL ENGINEERING · CIVIL ENGINEERING · ELECTRICAL ENGINEERING · GEOSCIENCES · MATHEMATICS · MECHANICAL ENGINEERING · MINING ENGINEERING · PETROLEUM ENGINEERING · PHYSICS

THE COMPANY

Formerly Standard Oil Company (Indiana), Amoco adopted its new name in 1985 but continues to protect the trademark in 15 states. Thirteenth among U.S. industrial companies and sixth among U.S. petroleum companies, Amoco continues to expand its areas of operations, using its existing resources to enter new fields. These include synthetic fuels, insurance, real estate, synthetic fabrics, and high-technology areas. In addition to its extensive domestic operations, Amoco is active in more than 40 foreign countries. As a parent company, Amoco operates three principal subsidiaries: Amoco Production Company, Amoco Oil Company, and Amoco Chemicals Company. Amoco employs about 53,000 people worldwide. Its annual sales exceed $18 billion, and the company is listed among *Fortune*'s most admired corporations.

ALL TRAINING PROGRAMS

Your training will be primarily on the job, supplemented by regularly scheduled training programs early in your career and periodically thereafter.

This is especially true in highly technical occupations utilizing the most advanced theoretical and practical technology to maintain leadership in capital-intensive industries. For example, Amoco Production Company has established a succession of technical seminars which are conducted at the Tulsa training center and at various work locations. They are carefully designed to contribute to your technical development and career opportunities. Similar training is provided in other subsidiaries and departments. Other programs help develop business and supervisory skills required in daily activities as well as oral and written communication skills to enhance presentations made to management, or when contact with the public and the media is called for in your assignments.

QUALIFICATIONS

You should rank in the top 10 percent of your class and have a G.P.A. of 3.0 or better. At the parent company offices in Chicago, bachelor's and master's degrees in accounting, business administration, computer sciences, and mathematics are most needed. Subsidiaries look for the following degrees: bachelor's or master's degrees in business administration; computer sciences; chemical, civil, electrical, mechanical, mining, and petroleum engineering; geosciences; mathematics; and physics. Doctoral degrees are also recruited in petroleum engineering, geosciences, and physics.

RECRUITMENT AND PLACEMENT

Amoco recruits continuously, visiting many college campuses around the country. Despite decreases in its work force, Amoco has increased its percentage of women and minority group members at all levels. At the beginning of 1985, 18 percent of the domestic employees were minority members, and women accounted for more than 24 percent. Most starting locations are in Colorado, Illinois, Indiana, Louisiana, Oklahoma, and Texas.

SALARIES AND BENEFITS

The College Placement Council Salary Survey for September 1986–June 1987 indicates starting salaries for petroleum and allied products (including natural gas) companies to be $1,972 a month for those with a B.A. degree in nontechnical curricula and $2,497 with a B.A. degree in technical curricula. M.B.A. starting salaries were $2,629 for a nontechnical undergraduate degree and $2,970 for a technical undergraduate degree. Check with the company for more specific salary information. Benefits include holidays and vacations, tuition reimbursement up to 75 percent, a sickness and disability plan, occupational illness and injury plan, comprehensive medical, health maintenance organization, dental assistance plan, long-term disability, group life insurance, savings and stock ownership plans, and retirement plan.

CONTACT

Corporate Recruiter, Amoco Corporation, 200 East Randolph Drive, Chicago, IL 60601.

AMWAY CORPORATION

ADMINISTRATION • INFORMATION SYSTEMS • PRODUCTION • RESEARCH AND DEVELOPMENT

THE COMPANY

Amway sales conventions have been compared to religious revivals for their intensity and the rah-rah enthusiasm that they generate. The manufacturer is well known for its direct sales force that offers a variety of health and home products. Based in Michigan, Amway employs 3,000 people in the United States, 6,000 worldwide.

ALL TRAINING PROGRAMS

You will begin working in your field right away, receiving on-the-job training as you learn Amway's procedures and policies. The company will support your efforts to continue your education after hours.

QUALIFICATIONS

Amway hires bachelor's and master's degree holders in the following fields: chemical engineering, chemistry, computer science, electrical engineering, industrial engineering, manufacturing engineering, mechanical engineering, packaging engineering, pulp and paper technology, and safety engineering. The company also needs doctoral-level graduates in analytical chemistry and chemistry. You should have a G.P.A. of 3.0 or higher, and above-average oral and written skills. Amway recruiters like candidates with at least some related student work experience.

RECRUITMENT AND PLACEMENT

Amway hires about 10 trainees a year. You will begin in Michigan.

SALARY AND BENEFITS

Starting salaries for those with bachelor's degrees are in the mid- to high twenties. You can negotiate for more with an advanced degree. Benefits consist of life insurance, medical, hospital, dental, vision, pension, and profit-sharing plans; 50 percent tuition reimbursement; and recreation and fitness programs.

CONTACT

Dan McCarthy, Supervisor, Human Resources Administration, Amway Corporation, 7575 East Fulton Road, Ada, MI 49355.

ANSER

INFORMATION SYSTEMS • RESEARCH AND DEVELOPMENT

THE COMPANY

ANSER (Analytic Services, Inc.) is an independent, nonprofit research corporation providing program analysis, systems analysis, and operations research for the U.S. Air Force and other defense-related agencies of the government. More than half of the firm's researchers hold at least one advanced degree, and about 15 percent have doctorates. ANSER is headquartered in Arlington, Virginia, with small affiliate offices in Colorado Springs, Colorado, and Dayton, Ohio. This think tank participates in a variety of challenging assignments ranging from analysis of voice and data communications, radar, identification and surveillance systems to intelligence planning. ANSER also handles research for both military and nonmilitary space programs. Succeeding here will give you considerable status in the scientific community. ANSER's analysts are frequently asked to participate in national and international conferences and to add their expertise to scientific boards and review panels.

ALL TRAINING PROGRAMS

You will continue to learn throughout your career with ANSER. On-the-job training will expose you to a variety of assignments in which you will contribute from the beginning. You will participate in multidisciplinary teams managed by both junior and senior staff members, working closely with corporate heads and top managers of client firms. In-house classes and seminars will supplement the education you bring with you to the job and prepare you for management.

QUALIFICATIONS

You should have a degree in: aeronautical/aerospace, electrical/electronics, industrial, logistics, mechanical, or systems engineering; computer science; mathematics; operations research; policy analysis; statistics; econometrics; or physics. Your class rank should be in the top 10 percent with a G.P.A. of 3.0 or higher. Writing skills, computer familiarity, and related job experience will be definite assets.

RECRUITMENT AND PLACEMENT

You will begin in either Colorado or Virginia.

SALARY AND BENEFITS

Salaries begin at about $23,000 with a bachelor's, and rise to the high twenties with a master's. Doctorates command $35,000 to $39,000. Your benefits package will consist of life insurance, medical, hospital, dental, pension, and deferred compensation plans; relocation assistance; and flextime options.

CONTACT

Personnel Director, ANSER, Suite 800, 1215 Jefferson Davis Highway, Arlington, VA 22202; or Personnel Director, ANSER, Suite 200, 2200 East Bijou Street, Colorado Springs, CO 80909.

APPLE COMPUTER, INC.

ENGINEERING • FINANCE • MANAGEMENT INFORMATION SYSTEMS • MANUFACTURING ENGINEERING • MARKETING • OPERATIONS/ MANUFACTURING • SALES

THE COMPANY

One of the most innovative computer companies, Apple holds a leading position in the education market with its Apple II products. Its Macintosh line is making inroads into the business world and dominates desktop publishing. Apple has tried to create computers that are flexible, technologically advanced, and easy to use. One example of Apple's forward-looking approach is an agreement with the National Geographic Society and LucasFilm Ltd. to undertake a long-term project to explore the use of new technologies in education. If you want to take an idea and soar with it, this is the company for you. With headquarters in Cupertino, California, Apple employs about 4,700 people and another 500 temporary employees and claims to have the highest productivity in the personal computer industry. Apple's annual sales are almost $2 billion. It is among *Fortune*'s most admired corporations and ranks number 190 among the Fortune 500 largest U.S. industrial corporations.

ALL TRAINING PROGRAMS

Apple offers internal and external classes regularly to fine-tune business, management, or technical skills. Through its Apple University program, Apple provides classes, on-the-job training, and other educational opportunities. In the Santa Clara Valley, Apple participates in the Stanford Honors Co-op, which offers advanced engineering education, and the Stanford A.C.E. program, which broadcasts college-level technical and supervisory courses, as well as M.B.A. courses, directly to classrooms at Apple. If you are in operations, an 18-month internal site rotation plan will acquaint you with the different specializations within the manufacturing operation.

QUALIFICATIONS

For most positions, Apple prefers M.B.A. graduates with at least one year's work experience. Engineers should have B.S. degrees and be familiar with 68,000 language programming, assembly language programming, and other languages such as UNIX, C, Pascal, and 6502 Assembly. Apple hires candidates with degrees in computer science, electrical engineering, materials and logistics management, and finance. Knowlege of Apple computers is a plus.

RECRUITMENT AND PLACEMENT

If an Apple recruiter does not visit your campus, send the company a résumé and letter of interest. You will be sent to Cupertino if you are a market development specialist, market analyst, product manager/coordinator, marketing engineer, financial analyst, IC/gate array design engineer, system design/logic design engineer, software engineer, or micro support analyst. Sales support analysts and marketing support representatives will be assigned to sales offices in major metropolitan areas throughout the country. Manufacturing engineering employees and those in operations/manufacturing will be sent to Fremont, California.

SALARY AND BENEFITS

The College Placement Council Salary Survey for September 1986–June 1987 indicates starting salaries for computer and business machine companies to be $1,880 a month for those with a B.A. degree with a nontechnical major and $2,389 with a B.A. degree with a technical major. M.B.A. starting salaries were $2,633 for a nontechnical undergraduate degree and $2,781 for a technical undergraduate degree. Check with the company for more specific salary information. Apple conducts regular reviews of nearby high-tech firms to insure that its salaries are competitive. Your performance and salary will be reviewed every six months. Benefits include the basics plus a loan-to-own program that puts an Apple computer in the hands of every employee (yours to keep after one year with the company), and a discount of 70 percent on company products. In addition, you will be eligible for educational assistance, medical, dental, vision, and life insurance, profit sharing, stock purchase, and a restart program that permits a six-week sabbatical after five years' service.

CONTACT

Personnnel, Apple Computer, Inc., 2052 Mariani Avenue, Cupertino, CA 95014.

APPLIED TECHNOLOGY

AUTOMATIC TEST ENGINEERS • MICROWAVE ENGINEERING PROCESS SPECIALISTS • MICROWAVE ENGINEERING SPECIALISTS • RECEIVER ENGINEERS • SCIENTIFIC ENGINEERS • SCIENTIFIC PROGRAMMERS • SOFTWARE ENGINEERS

THE COMPANY

A division of Litton Industries, Applied Technology is a major designer and producer of advanced electronic defense systems. Applied Technology has delivered over 18,000 radar warning systems for domestic and foreign military aircraft. Other areas of expertise include military/space computers, test/training/evaluation systems, and real-time electronic warfare systems. Much of its work is in state-of-the art electronics and applied physics. Applied Technology is expanding, so if you want to do advanced work on defense systems, this could be the right company for you.

ALL TRAINING PROGRAMS

In your first year you will receive on-the-job training and supplementary in-house seminars.

QUALIFICATIONS

You should have a bachelor's or master's degree in computer or electrical engineering, computer science, information science, systems engineering, mathematics, or physics. Applied Technology also encourages applicants with related work experience.

RECRUITMENT AND PLACEMENT

Applied Technology recruits nationwide. All jobs are in Sunnyvale, California.

SALARY AND BENEFITS

The College Placement Council Salary Survey for September 1986–June 1987 indicates starting salaries for electrical and electronic machine and equipment companies to be $1,861 a month for those with a B.A. degree in nontechnical curricula and $2,419 with a B.A. degree in technical curricula. M.B.A. starting salaries were $2,784 for a nontechnical undergraduate degree and $2,818 for a technical undergraduate degree. Check with the company for more specific salary information. Benefits include a choice of three medical plans, a dental plan, a tuition refund program, an eye-care program, and flexible working hours.

CONTACT

Patricia J. Marshall, College Relations Administrator, Applied Technology, 645 Almanor Avenue, Sunnyvale, CA 94040.

ARMSTRONG WORLD INDUSTRIES, INC.

SALES/MARKETING

THE COMPANY

Armstrong manufactures and markets a wide range of interior furnishings, including flooring, carpets, furniture, and specialty products for the building, automotive, and textile industries. Home office and training facilities are located in Lancaster, one of the most productive agricultural counties in the United States and the heart of Pennsylvania Dutch country. With $2 billion in annual sales, Armstrong ranks number 187 in the Fortune 500 largest U.S. industrial corporations.

SALES/MARKETING TRAINING PROGRAM

The program, designed to acquaint marketing trainees with Armstrong products, people, and business philosophy as well as sales and marketing skills, can lead you in a number of directions —larger sales territory responsibilities, specialized market development, sales territory management, or marketing management at the company's headquarters. For more than fifty years Armstrong has been offering a formal orientation for new employees at the headquarters in Lancaster. The twice-yearly orientation includes tours, seminars, and talks with company officers. Even the president makes a presentation. After the orientation you begin the three-month marketing training program. Your program will include a thorough introduction to company staff, products, marketing and production techniques, and trips to the field to observe marketing and manufacturing situations, as well as informal group seminars with product managers. Using videotape playback, you will be able to critique your sales presentations and polish them before going to the field. By the time you have finished the program, you will have a good grasp of advertising, promotion, distribution, inventory control, credit, and sales and be ready for your first call on a customer.

QUALIFICATIONS

You will have an advantage in an Armstrong interview if you maintained better-than-average grades and participated in extracurricular activities. The company is looking for people with well-rounded backgrounds and a high interest in sales and marketing.

RECRUITMENT AND PLACEMENT

After completing the training program you will be assigned to one of the 22 district offices around the country. By then you will be ready to become the company's resident expert for your assigned territory.

SALARY AND BENEFITS

The College Placement Council Salary Survey for September 1986–June 1987 indicates starting salaries for building materials manufacturers and construction companies to be $1,782 a month for those with a B.A. degree in nontechnical curricula and $2,156 with a B.A. degree in technical curricula. M.B.A. starting salaries were $1,666 for a nontechnical undergraduate degree and $2,677 for a technical undergraduate degree. Check with the company for more specific salary information. Armstrong offers an extensive employee benefits package including family hospitalization and surgical insurance, long-term income protection, travel insurance, annual active military duty makeup pay, a retirement and investment program, and an employee stock purchase plan. If you go back to school, Armstrong will reimburse you for approved courses taken on your own time.

CONTACT

W. J. Van Pelt, General Manager, Salaried Personnel Services, Armstrong World Industries, Inc., P.O. Box 3001, Lancaster, PA 17604.

ARTHUR ANDERSEN & COMPANY

ACCOUNTING • AUDITING • MANAGEMENT INFORMATION CONSULTING • TAX CONSULTING

THE COMPANY

Established in 1913, Arthur Andersen is one of the Big Eight certified public accounting firms. It is operated as a single worldwide organization owned and managed by partners in many countries. Every office shares equal status, standards, and policies. The company is administered by a cooperative based in Geneva, Switzerland. Auditing services make up a majority of its practice. Special divisions handle every size and type of business, from small operations to industrial giants.

ALL TRAINING PROGRAMS

The company will train you to become a certified public accountant for services in auditing, tax consulting, or management information consulting. Arthur Andersen was first in the accounting industry to establish an internal training program. It considers itself a leader in developing and operating a dedicated training facility. For its staff's professional development it maintains the Center for Professional Education in St. Charles, Illinois, about 45 miles west of U.S. headquarters in Chicago. The facility is on a 55-acre wooded site and has living accommodations for over 750 people. The center's impressive resources include color television studios, video recording and playback decks, personal computers, and other equipment needed to support classroom learning activities. The classes are taught by experienced managers and partners who can relate theory to actual situations. Classes usually are small, providing an opportunity for open discussions and problem solving. The center offers orientation programs and over 400 continuing-education courses.

ACCOUNTING/AUDITING PROGRAM

To prepare you for your first client assignment, you will attend the Firmwide Audit Staff Training School (FASTS). This three-week program is conducted regularly to accommodate new employees joining the firm at various times during the year. During the first week of the program you will stay in your local office and receive an orientation to the firm. Then you go to the St. Charles training facility for two weeks of intensive training, during which you get to meet peers from around the world and learn to apply theory to practice. The FASTS program provides you with a complete picture of business audit situations. You will work with a major case study involving a complete audit with the guidance of a partner or manager. After the initial training you begin your on-the-job experience, but you are expected to spend two to three weeks a year in various firm-sponsored training courses.

MANAGEMENT INFORMATION CONSULTING PROGRAM

The formal orientation program usually lasts about three weeks, beginning at the local offices and ending at the St. Charles education center. The initial training includes an orientation to the firm's consulting practice and range of services. Next, during the on-the-job phase of the training, you will learn about computers and their use in solving business problems, the company's methodology for analyzing and solving problems, the major business functions (finance, marketing, human resource management, and materials management), the information sources and data collection techniques used to fulfill business requirements, and the firm's professional procedures and work program techniques. The first two to three years of your career are your most intensive learning time. During that time you are encouraged to participate in the firm's continuing-education offerings.

TAX CONSULTING PROGRAM

You will be assigned to a project almost immediately. The on-the-job training will develop your skills and talents through working with skilled managers. You will then attend a three-week comprehensive tax course conducted at the Center for Professional Education. Specialized courses will be offered throughout your career depending on demand and your personal interests.

ALL PROGRAMS

QUALIFICATIONS

The company is looking for business administration graduates with backgrounds in accounting, business, finance, or economics; computer science personnel for systems; industrial engineering graduates with introductory accounting; and law graduates with an undergraduate accounting base.

RECRUITMENT AND PLACEMENT

The company recruits nationwide. There are offices in principal U.S. cities and foreign employment for nationals in Australia, Canada, Europe, Japan, Mexico, Puerto Rico, Singapore, South America, and South Africa.

SALARY AND BENEFITS

The College Placement Council Salary Survey for September 1986–June 1987 indicates starting salaries for public accounting firms to be $1,834 a month for those with a B.A. degree in nontechnical curricula and $2,155 with a B.A. degree in technical curricula. M.B.A. starting salaries were $2,335 for a nontechnical undergraduate degree, and $2,436 for an M.B.A. with a technical undergraduate degree. Check with the company for more specific salary and benefits information.

CONTACT

Firm Director, Recruiting, Arthur Andersen & Company, 69 West Washington Street, Chicago, IL 60602.

ATLANTIC RICHFIELD COMPANY (ARCO)

ACCOUNTING • AUDITING • CHEMISTRY • ENGINEERING • GEOCHEMISTRY • GEOLOGY • GEOPHYSICS • LAND MANAGEMENT • MARKETING • METALLURGY • RESEARCH AND DEVELOPMENT • SALES • SYSTEMS AND PROGRAMMING

THE COMPANY

One of the world's leading energy companies, Atlantic Richfield has divisions that produce oil and natural gas, petrochemicals, coal, and solar energy. Determined to shape its future rather than merely respond to the pressures upon it, Atlantic Richfield has recently streamlined its operations, selling off marginal enterprises to strengthen the remainder. Divisions operate in two major groups. The Resources Group includes ARCO Exploration Company, ARCO Oil and Gas Company, ARCO Alaska, Inc., ARCO International Oil and Gas Company, ARCO Resources Administration, and ARCO Resources Technology. The Products Group includes ARCO Transportation Company, ARCO Petroleum Products Company, ARCO Chemical Company, and ARCO Solar, Inc. Atlantic Richfield plans to focus its efforts on profit and performance rather than size and growth in the next few years. Most of its energy sources are domestic, including the vast Prudhoe Bay oilfield in Alaska. A concerned employer and citizen, ARCO donates generously to social service organizations and the arts, and keeps a keen eye on the welfare of its employees and the people who live in communities where it has plants. ARCO also emphasizes commitment to environmental protection. Listed among *Fortune*'s most admired corporations, ARCO ranks twentieth in the Fortune 500 largest U.S. industrial corporations.

ALL TRAINING PROGRAMS

ARCO takes a number of approaches to training, depending on the position. You may be trained entirely on the job or receive more formal classes to supplement on-the-job learning. Orientation will include an overview of ARCO's operations and products.

ACCOUNTING DEVELOPMENT PROGRAM

The Accounting Development Program, lasting from nine to fifteen months, provides you with information on current developments in accounting, the oil industry, and ARCO's policies and procedures. You will receive three-month assignments in several different accounting units or operational units at the Dallas headquarters as well as in district offices. Classroom courses to supplement on-the-job projects are also offered.

QUALIFICATIONS

ARCO is looking for college graduates with majors in accounting and business administration. Courses in data processing, computer science, and economics are valuable. You also need good interpersonal and communication abilities.

PLACEMENT

Your first placement will be in the Dallas headquarters or perhaps in a district office in Denver, Houston, Anchorage, Bakersfield, Tulsa, Midland, Tyler, or Lafayette.

SALES AND MARKETING PROGRAMS

Training prepares new employees for their first position as sales representative, whether their customers are retail outlets or industrial or wholesale consumers. Virtually everything you'll need to know to make your sales career a success can be learned on this job. You will learn about company products, sales techniques, customer needs, marketing plans, and company policies and procedures. You will spend time in the office and on the road with an experienced salesperson.

QUALIFICATIONS

ARCO recruits college graduates with backgrounds in business, liberal arts, and social sciences, as well as in more technical fields. An engineering background is required only in certain highly technical areas. The most important abilities for sales personnel are interpersonal and communication skills. Frequent travel is required.

PLACEMENT

Sales personnel work nationwide.

SYSTEMS AND PROGRAMMING PROGRAM

You will enter a several-month training program to prepare you for an initial assignment as a computer programmer or systems analyst. Skills in problem solving are stressed, as are analytical techniques, programming languages and practices, project planning and control, and computer operations. Initial assignments involve writing computer programs for a project.

QUALIFICATIONS

ARCO recruits bachelor's or master's degree candidates with backgrounds in mathematics, statistics, business, computer programming, and data processing. You will also need strong communication and interpersonal abilities.

PLACEMENT

Most new college graduates are placed in Los Angeles, Dallas, Denver, Philadelphia, Chicago, or Anchorage.

ALL PROGRAMS

RECRUITMENT

ARCO recruits nationwide. The company is making a strong effort to recruit and promote female and minority employees.

SALARY AND BENEFITS

The College Placement Council Salary Survey for September 1986–June 1987 indicates starting salaries for petroleum and allied products (including natural gas) companies to be $1,972 a month for those with a B.A. degree in nontechnical curricula and $2,497 with a B.A. degree in technical curricula. M.B.A. starting salaries were $2,629 for a nontechnical undergraduate degree and $2,970 for a technical undergraduate degree. Check with the company for more specific salary information. Benefits include life, medical, dental, and accident insurance; retirement plans; an employee savings program; and educational assistance of up to 80 percent of tuition and fees for approved courses.

CONTACT

College Relations, Recruitment and Placement, Atlantic Richfield Company, 515 South Flower Street, Los Angeles, CA 90071.

AT&T BELL LABORATORIES

NATIONAL DEFENSE • RESEARCH/DEVELOPMENT/DESIGN • SYSTEMS DEVELOPMENT • SYSTEMS ENGINEERING

THE COMPANY

AT&T Bell Laboratories is the corporation's research and development branch. Seven of its scientists have received Nobel prizes, and the company has averaged nearly a patent a day since its founding in 1925. Its 19,000 employees work in systems engineering; research, development, and design; and national defense. Examples of its work in national defense include undersea surveillance and military communications, command, control, and intelligence systems. The development and design group seeks to convert new knowledge into useful devices, equipment, and systems. Company headquarters is in Murray Hill, New Jersey.

ALL TRAINING PROGRAMS

Working at AT&T Bell Laboratories will mean that you must keep pace with new developments. Much of the knowledge you acquire in school will be out of date within ten years. Part of your training will be in the In-Hours Continuing Education Program (INCEP). These formal classes at the graduate and undergraduate level include short intensive courses as well as semester-long courses. During working hours you will attend classes taught by professors from local universities and AT&T Bell Laboratories professional staff. You will study both present and emerging technologies. As a member of the technical staff with a bachelor's degree, you will be given the option of several routes to expanding your knowledge, including acquiring a master's degree.

QUALIFICATIONS

AT&T Bell Laboratories hires graduates with degrees in computer science, electrical and mechanical engineering, mathematics, operations research, chemistry, physics, and psychology.

RECRUITMENT AND PLACEMENT

You should be able to arrange an interview with an AT&T recruiter on campus. If not, send a résumé and copy of your transcript directly to the company.

SALARY AND BENEFITS

The College Placement Council Salary Survey for September 1986–June 1987 indicates starting salaries for research organizations to be $2,116 a month for those with a B.A. degree in nontechnical curricula and $2,266 with a B.A. degree in technical curricula. M.B.A. starting salaries were $2,512 for a nontechnical undergraduate degree and $2,822 for a technical undergraduate degree. Check with the company for more specific salary information. The company also provides comprehensive benefits such as a major medical and dental plan, accident and sickness disability benefits, group life insurance, vision plan, deferred vested pensions and savings plan, and service pensions.

CONTACT

Director of Technical Personnel and University Relations, Dept. 169/3000/86, AT&T Bell Laboratories, 101 J. F. Kennedy Parkway, Short Hills, NJ 07078.

AT&T INFORMATION SYSTEMS

ACCOUNTING • ENGINEERING • FINANCE • INFORMATION SYSTEMS • MANAGEMENT • MARKETING • SALES

THE COMPANY

AT&T Information Systems designs, manufactures, markets, installs, and maintains state-of-the-art products, services, and systems in the fast-paced field of information collection and management. Headquartered in Morristown, New Jersey, AT&T Information Systems has five divisions: a national service group and four product lines: General Business Systems, Computer Systems, Large Business Systems, and Consumer Products division (which includes AT&T Phone Centers). Services is the largest division, employing 40,000 of AT&T's 90,000-plus work force at 1,000 locations nationwide.

ALL TRAINING PROGRAMS

AT&T will cover your expenses if you want additional education in your field. At work, you can expect informal workshops to supplement on-the-job training. The company selects prominent authorities to conduct workshops for employees on a variety of topics, both professional and personal.

MANAGEMENT PROGRAM

In this two-year program you will begin with an introduction to the company's basic operations, followed by training in supervisory skills, a special project assignment, and study of administrative techniques. You will learn through on-the-job training, formal classes, and seminars. Your supervisor will evaluate you every six months and offer coaching. Your progress must meet pre-established performance standards after each segment of training or you may be eliminated from the program.

QUALIFICATIONS

AT&T hires graduates with degrees in accounting and finance; business administration; marketing; mathematics and statistics; liberal arts; computer science; management information systems; and computer, electrical, and systems engineering. You should have an excellent academic record. Work experience will give you an edge in salary negotiation.

RECRUITMENT AND PLACEMENT

AT&T recruits on university campuses throughout the country. If you are unable to arrange an interview, send a letter describing your interests and résumé to headquarters. Your first assignment could be in Denver, Indianapolis, Illinois, or New Jersey.

SALARY AND BENEFITS

The College Placement Council Salary Survey for September 1986–June 1987 indicates starting salaries for electrical and electronic machinery and equipment companies to be $1,861 a month for those with a B.A. degree in nontechnical curricula and $2,419 with a B.A. degree in technical curricula. M.B.A. starting salaries were $2,784 for a nontechnical undergraduate degree and $2,818 for a technical undergraduate degree. Check with the company for more specific salary information. Benefits range from standard medical and life insurance to savings, vision, and dental plans, service pensions, and deferred vested pensions.

CONTACT

AT&T Information Systems, College and University Relations, Room 2H17, 100 Southgate Parkway, Morristown, NJ 07960.

AVERY INTERNATIONAL

ADMINISTRATION • BUSINESS • ENGINEERING • SALES

THE COMPANY

In 1935, Avery became the first company to manufacture self-adhesive labels. Now this international company is the leading manufacturer of a wide variety of self-adhesive materials and products used by business people every day. Its six operating groups create items used for marketing, identifying, labeling, decorating, fastening, filing and indexing. Avery employs 9,500 people in more than 100 manufacturing facilities and sales offices in 25 countries. Avery International's sales in 1986 topped $1 billion. It ranks number 273 in the Fortune 500 largest U.S. industrial corporations. Its divisions produce office products with the Aigner brand name in Schaumburg, Illinois; plastic and vinyl products through 20th Century Plastics in Los Angeles; tags and labels through the Soabar Group in Philadelphia; and appliance decorations through Thermark in Schereville, Indiana. In addition, Avery International's Research Center in Pasadena employs highly skilled scientists, chemists, and research engineers to conduct advanced adhesive research and development, using state-of-the-art computerized analytical and laboratory systems. The Venture Development Center in Pomona, California, studies new product or process prototypes away from the conventional business atmosphere to develop new business opportunities for the company.

ALL TRAINING PROGRAMS

Avery's approach to entry-level training is to provide immediate hands-on experience. An experienced supervisor will act as a coach and introduce you to the company's policies and procedures as you learn your new job. Avery's offering of ongoing internal classes are also available to you.

QUALIFICATIONS

Avery hires business and engineering majors. You will favorably impress a recruiter if you can demonstrate above-average oral and written communications skills, computer familiarity, and at least some work experience.

RECRUITMENT AND PLACEMENT

Avery recruits around the country. You will start in California, Illinois, Ohio, or Pennsylvania. After you have been with the company for five years, you may be eligible for assignments in Europe.

SALARY AND BENEFITS

The College Placement Council Salary Survey for September 1986–June 1987 indicates starting salaries for glass, paper, packaging, and allied products companies to be $1,865 a month for those with a B.A. degree in nontechnical curricula and $2,401 with a B.A. degree in technical curricula. M.B.A. starting salaries were $2,945 for a nontechnical undergraduate degree and $2,775 for a technical undergraduate degree. Check with the company for more specific salary and benefits information.

CONTACT

Director of Human Resources Planning, Avery International, 150 North Orange Grove Boulevard, Pasadena, CA 91103.

The Inside Story from a Training Graduate
Alyssa Carlson, Kay Jewelers

Alyssa Carlson is the College Recruitment Manager for Kay Jewelers. She graduated from California State University at Northridge in May 1985 and completed Kay Jewelers' manager training program. She was promoted to Store Manager after one year, and was promoted again in February 1987 to her present position.

☆ ☆ ☆ ☆ ☆

Tell me about how you interviewed on campus and how you made the decision to go to work with Kay Jewelers.

I think I was a lot like most seniors graduating from college in that I didn't have a clear idea of what I wanted to do. My business major was broad enough for me to interview for a lot of positions. Kay Jewelers was the only retailer I seriously considered. I was looking for corporations that had name recognition, a good training program, promotion from within. But ultimately I wanted to work for a company that appealed to me. Kay Jewelers is the second largest jewelry retailer in the nation, and I had an interest in jewelry. That's why I looked at Kay. Although I successfully interviewed with many other corporations, I decided to accept the Manager Trainee position with Kay Jewelers because it offered unlimited advancement, tremendous responsibility as a store manager, and an incentive-based pay plan with great earning potential.

Describe the training program and your experiences as you went through the first several months.

The Career Development Program consists of intensive in-store sales training through the use of role play, skills reviews, seminars, and testing modules. The testing modules are based on information pertaining to product knowledge, sales skills, store administration/operation and personnel policies. Most of this information is learned through store manager and training manuals. Your progress through the Career Development Program is monitored by the Central Office Training Department. Because you are responsible for pacing your work with the manuals, you need a lot of self-discipline and motivation to be ready when the tests are due. Every set of three tests constitutes a significant stepping-stone toward attaining your goal of Store Manager. After you have completed six training modules and have consistently demonstrated your ability to sell each month, you may be promoted to Assistant Manager. Then it is your responsibility not only to make your personal sales targets but to motivate others to reach theirs as well. You also take responsibility for running the repair department. How well you run your repair department indicates to the company how well you'll run your store, so profits are important. As an Assistant Manager you receive a percentage of store sales each month and 10 percent of the pretax profit of your repair department. Your training and testing continue, and you really get down to the specifics of running a Kay store. When you've completed all the testing modules you take a comprehensive final. The training usually spans about fifteen months, after which you're eligible for promotion to Store Manager.

When I first interviewed with the company I thought the tests would be no problem. In college I was very accustomed to taking tests. However, I must admit I was very surprised to find out how comprehensive these tests are. I remember my first test had 186 questions! If the truth be known I did procrastinate at first because of a fear of the unknown. But after the third test, the tests seemed much easier and I was anxious to take the next.

What is the promotion ladder in the program?

Everyone starts as a Sales Manager Trainee. Through a series of Manager and District Manager conferences, skills reviews, and testing, you gain promotions. Usually tests are taken one per month, and passing every group of three tests constitutes a promotion. As you progress through the Career Development Program and become a more integral part of the store, your salary grows with you. Your first major promotion occurs once you complete your sixth training test. At that time you should be ready to assume the role of Assistant Manager. That's a big job, but one that will groom you for management. Your training and testing continue until completion of the program, which, as I've said, is usually in fifteen months, although very motivated individuals have completed it in less time. Once you are promoted to Store Manager, you then move on to stores with larger and larger volume. From there you move to levels of District Manager and then Regional Vice-President.

You could take two tests in some months?

In the beginning that is very hard to do. The most important aspect of the job is learning how to sell. We believe that the best way to perfect your sales skills is by doing. So rather than having you spend a lot of extra time in test preparation, we prefer you to spend the time on the sales floor working with your peers, your customers, and the merchandise. After you have completed the first few tests, they become a little easier. At that time you are able to advance at a faster rate so long as you can do so while still keeping up with sales.

What are some other key points about the program?

One of the most notable aspects of the training program and about Kay Jewelers is that Kay promotes 100 percent from within, without exception. Everyone goes through the same process. Our Regional Vice-Presidents started as Manager Trainees in the stores. The same holds true for our District Managers. Promotions are based on merit, not seniority. This enabled me, as an overachiever, to be promoted in less than fifteen months. I opened a brand-new store in the West Los Angeles–Beverly Hills market. There's a lot to be said for the company because they really reward your achievements—especially in compensation. The compensation program is an incentive-based pay plan, so that when you look at your paycheck you can say, "I earned this, no more, no less." And there's no ceiling on what you can earn. Manager Trainees usually make between $18,000 and $21,000 their first year. However, there are some people who have made a lot more. Since it is the company's goal to increase sales, they make it so every salesperson shares in commissions on everything they sell. When you complete the training program and are promoted to the level of Store Manager, you are running a business within a business, and you share directly in the profits of your store. So, corporate philosophy and goals are congruent with the goals of the people who work for Kay.

As you look back at the training program and your experience with it, what for you personally were some of the most valuable aspects?

Learning to sell. I feel there's nothing I couldn't sell. I've also become far more personable and able to deal with a large variety of people on all levels. Graduating from college, you have a lot of textbook theory. At Kay Jewelers you are really responsible for the profits of your store, so the company provides you with the training and tools you need to do it. As a Store Manager, I had to learn how to use those tools to make the proper business decisions. It is an opportunity to put textbook theory into practice. You learn how to run a business.

How did you come to the corporate headquarters and to your present job?

At Kay the incentive is to remain in the field but our College Recruitment Program was expanding rather rapidly, and we didn't have a person specifically in charge of handling college recruitment until I came to headquarters. I was recommended for the position by my District Manager and my Regional Vice-President, and I was flown from California to headquarters for an interview along with several other people. Fortunately, I got the position but I took it with a two year option of returning to the field. I feel it's a very field- and sales-related position because now I'm looking for people who are capable of selling and running a Kay store at a profit.

What would you tell graduating seniors or people that were interviewing on campuses this coming spring about comparing training programs?

I think the most important thing is to look for promotional opportunities and an excellent training program. What percentage of a company's management is promoted from within? What kind of feedback will you be getting as you go through the training program? Is the company up front with you as far as what to expect and anticipate? I would tell any graduating senior to prepare for hard work. What you put into it is what you'll get out of it. Companies are investing a lot more time and money in developing their own training programs. Kay Jewelers certainly has done that. So if you have a willingness to learn and you're genuinely eager to apply that, you want to be working for a company that will give you that opportunity and will reward you based on your own deeds, not based on seniority.

B

☆ ☆ ☆ ☆ ☆

BABCOCK & WILCOX

ACCOUNTING • BOILERS AND REFRACTORIES • FINANCE • NUCLEAR ENERGY • RESEARCH AND DEVELOPMENT • STAFF • TUBULAR PRODUCTS

THE COMPANY

Babcock & Wilcox is a major manufacturer of heavy specially engineered industrial equipment. It specializes in the manufacturing of fossil and nuclear power systems, steel tubing, and pollution control systems. The corporate work force is more than 32,000 worldwide, 30,000 in the United States. McDermott paid $633 million for Babcock & Wilcox in 1977 in what was at the time one of the largest corporate takeovers.

ALL TRAINING PROGRAMS

Babcock & Wilcox offers a variety of entry-level programs in the following divisions: Research and Development, Tubular Products, Boilers and Refractories, Nuclear Energy, Finance and Accounting, and Staff. Trainees learn the ins and outs of their chosen division as well as general corporate policy and state-of-the-art applied technology. Depending on the program, you'll participate in on-the-job or classroom instruction for up to three months.

QUALIFICATIONS

Opportunities exist for graduates and postgraduates with degrees in engineering, law, business, and liberal arts.

RECRUITMENT AND PLACEMENT

About 250 applicants are hired annually. Depending on your specialty, you could start in Georgia, Ohio, Pennsylvania, or Virginia.

SALARY AND BENEFITS

The College Placement Council Salary Survey for September 1986–June 1987 indicates starting salaries for electrical and electronic machines and equipment companies to be $1,861 a month for those with a B.A. degree in nontechnical curricula and $2,419 with a B.A. degree in technical curricula. M.B.A. starting salaries were $2,784 for a nontechnical undergraduate degree and $2,818 for a technical undergraduate degree. Check with the company for more specific salary information. Benefits include life insurance, medical and dental plans, relocation assistance, and an incentive savings plan.

CONTACT

Robert Jongbloed, Manager, College Relations, Babcock & Wilcox, P.O. Box 61038, New Orleans, LA 70161.

BANKAMERICA

RETAIL BANKING: BRANCH ADMINISTRATION • RETAIL BANKING: CREDIT AND LENDING • SYSTEMS ENGINEERING • WORLD BANKING: SALES • WORLD BANKING: TRADING

THE COMPANY

BankAmerica is one of the best-known names in the financial world. Founded by A. P. Giannini in San Francisco in 1904, it was the first bank to break the monopoly of Eastern banks. It has assets of more than $100 billion. In an effort to improve its profitability, BA brought back A. W. Clausen as C.E.O. in October 1986. As a global financial services institution, it provides products and services—ranging from home banking and loan syndications to export financing—to consumers, corporations, and governments in 53 countries. Listed among *Fortune*'s most admired corporations, it ranks number 2 in assets in the Fortune 100 of the largest commercial banking companies.

ALL TRAINING PROGRAMS

You will participate in a carefully structured program that combines formal and on-the-job instruction in banking theory and operations. Hiring is extremely selective and competitive. Candidates should possess a proven academic and leadership record, strong interpersonal skills, and some applicable work experience.

Retail Bank Division

California Commercial Banking and California Sales & Service are two primary strategic business units within the Retail Bank Division. California Commercial Banking serves small businesses and middle market companies ranging from start-up companies with strong growth potential and small businesses earning up to $10 million a year to mature companies earning up to $250 million in domestic or international sales. BankAmerica's California Sales & Service unit is recognized as a market share leader within the state in serving the financial needs of the consumer market and the highly desirable upscale market. Management training within this division can lead you in one of two directions: branch administration or credit and lending.

BRANCH ADMINISTRATION PROGRAM

The Branch Administration Officer Training Program prepares you for a career in management within the branch network. An intensive nine- to twelve-month program provides complete training in customer service, management, human resources, and administration. Classroom instruction and on-the-job training prepare you for placement as a manager in customer service.

QUALIFICATIONS

A bachelor of arts or science degree in business administration, industrial relations, economics, or psychology is preferred. You should possess strong management and human relations skills. A background in supervision and technology is desired.

PLACEMENT

Placement can be within one of four California geographic regions; mobility within your chosen region is required.

CREDIT AND LENDING PROGRAM

As a financial services account officer (credit and lending), you will be prepared for a career in consumer or upscale banking. An intensive nine- to twelve-month program provides comprehensive training in consumer lending, branch operations, and sales techniques. Classroom instruction and on-the-job training lead to placement as an account officer.

QUALIFICATIONS

A bachelor of arts or science degree in business, finance, or economics is preferred; course work in accounting and finance is desired. Candidates should possess strong analytical and financial skills, as well as excellent communication and interpersonal skills.

PLACEMENT

You may work within one of four California regions. Mobility within your region is required.

Systems Engineering Division

Technology is managed and delivered through the BankAmerica Systems Engineering (BASE) Division. BASE operates from its new Technology Center in Concord, California, and data centers in San Francisco, Los Angeles, New York, London, and Hong Kong. Because BASE serves a large corporation with complex information needs, it offers exposure to an exceptional diversity of technologies. The division provides a wide range of production and development services to the corporation—from the daily processing of checks to the design of telecommunication systems for data and voice transmission worldwide. Upon successful completion of the program, you will be placed in entry-level positions in applications, systems, telecommunications, data management, or operations. Placement will be based upon your abilities and preference.

SYSTEMS ENGINEERING PROGRAM

Trainees will be provided a comprehensive twelve-week program covering an overview of the financial services industry, systems development methodology, systems architecture, core programmer/analyst tools, systems production/turnover processing methodology, and current major projects under development.

QUALIFICATIONS

Candidates with undergraduate degrees (B.A./B.S.) will be considered. It is expected that prospective candidates will have a minimum 3.3 grade point average and will demonstrate strong analytical and problem-solving skills. In addition, excellent interpersonal skills, leadership potential, attention to detail, and the ability to handle pressure are essential.

World Banking Division

The World Banking Division is one of the premier providers of financial services to major multinational corporations, financial institutions, and governments around the world. These clients require immediate access to financial services in a number of countries or use a broad range of worldwide banking services. North America Division (NAD) is a division of the World Banking Division that specializes in global wholesale banking, providing financial products and services to corporations, governments, and financial institutions.

NORTH AMERICA DIVISION PROGRAM

The account officer is trained to assess quickly the financial, legal, and tax aspects of a situation and to address them with the appropriate bank products or service structured in a manner that is most profitable for both the client and BankAmerica.

QUALIFICATIONS

A strong M.B.A. and undergraduate academic record is required, with excellent communication skills and the ability to solve problems aggressively.

PLACEMENT

NAD serves wholesale banking clients in the United States and Canada with staffs located in major market centers such as Chicago, Houston, Los Angeles, New York, San Francisco, and Toronto.

BANK INVESTMENT SECURITIES DIVISION PROGRAM

The Capital Markets Group (CMG) is a major unit of the World Banking Division. CMG provides clients with an international securities trading and distribution network featuring U.S. Treasury and federal agency obligations, municipal securities, commercial paper, and mortgage-backed securities. Additionally, CMG offers clients access to foreign exchange, money trading, currency and interest rate swaps, and financial futures. The Bank Investment Securities Division (BISD) is part of the Capital Markets Group in the World Banking Division. Specialists in BISD are engaged in activities related to issuing, distributing, and selling securities. Such activities include underwriting, market making, sales, bond redemptions, and securities safekeeping.

BISD has developed an intensive three-month training program that provides a comprehensive overview of the securities industry. The program consists of a series of seminars, workshops, and projects presented by professionals from all areas of finance. The goal is to provide practical, up-to-date training that will lead to a professional career as either a trader or salesperson.

A trader is a speculator who "makes markets" in a security, attempting to profit from movements in interest rates. Additionally, a trader facilitates transactions with bank customers.

A salesperson is a generalist who is familiar with all BISD investment instruments but usually specializes in one or two. The salesperson initiates and negotiates the purchase or sale of securities with institutional or individual investors. A key part of the process is analysis of market conditions and their effect on the value of customer holdings.

QUALIFICATIONS

To qualify as a trader you need an M.B.A., preferably with a finance concentration. A risk-taking, entrepreneurial attitude is essential as is the ability to work well in a high-paced, pressured environment. To qualify as a salesperson you need an M.B.A., preferably with a finance concentration. You must be highly motivated and excel at working independently. Interpersonal skills and perseverance, which are essential to the development of customer relationships, are mandatory.

ALL PROGRAMS

RECRUITMENT

BankAmerica recruits nationwide at job fairs, on college campuses, and through direct computer access to the personnel department.

SALARY AND BENEFITS

The College Placement Council Salary Survey for September 1986–June 1987 indicates starting salaries for banking, finance, and insurance firms to be $1,889 a month for those with a B.A. degree in nontechnical curricula and $2,135 with a B.A. degree in technical curricula. M.B.A. starting salaries were $2,884 for a nontechnical undergraduate degree, and $3,320 for an M.B.A. with technical undergraduate degree. Check with the company for more specific salary information. Benefits include preferred interest rates, a fully paid retirement plan and life insurance, group medical and dental plans, a matching contribution plan, a stock purchase plan, education tuition assistance, and paid vacations and holidays.

CONTACT

Sherrie D. Gong, Vice-President & Manager-DD, BankAmerica, Corporate College Relations, #3616, P.O. Box 37000, San Francisco, CA 94137; or, via computer, call 1-612-941-5723, press Return, and enter the password TOUCH BASE.

BARBER-COLMAN COMPANY

INFORMATION SYSTEMS AND PROCESSING • MARKETING • PRODUCTION • RESEARCH AND DEVELOPMENT • SALES • TECHNICAL SERVICES

THE COMPANY

Barber-Colman manufactures environmental controls and systems, industrial instruments and machines, cutting tools, and building automation systems. With a network of over 400 sales and service offices, representatives, licensees, and distributors around the world, Barber-Colman employs about 4,500 people. One of the oldest and largest privately held corporations in the United States, Barber-Colman was founded in 1894. The company's innovative TiNite process coats cutting tools with titanium nitride, prolonging their productive life substantially.

ALL TRAINING PROGRAMS

Training prepares new employees to perform in research and development, marketing and sales, production, technical services, or information systems and processing. When you join the engineering staff you will be provided with a twelve- to eighteen-month formal on-the-job training program to familiarize you with company operations and develop needed skills. Periodic reviews and technical and managerial development courses will help advance your career.

QUALIFICATIONS

Barber-Colman looks for candidates with engineering and technological expertise and B.S. and M.S. degrees in electrical, electronic, mechanical, computer, HVAC, industrial, and manufacturing engineering; electrical engineering technology; mechanical engineering technology; and computer science. A minimum G.P.A. of 3.0 is preferred. More than one year of technical experience will give you an edge.

RECRUITMENT AND PLACEMENT

The company recruits primarily in the Midwest. You will begin working in Rockford, Illinois, in most positions. Salespeople may be placed anywhere in the country.

SALARY AND BENEFITS

The College Placement Council Salary Survey for September 1986–June 1987 indicates starting salaries for automotive and mechanical equipment companies to be $1,907 a month for those with a B.A. degree in nontechnical curricula and $2,333 with a B.A. degree in technical curricula. M.B.A. starting salaries were $2,697 for a nontechnical undergraduate degree and $2,986 for a technical undergraduate degree. Check with the company for more specific salary information. Benefits consist of life, health, and dental insurance, disability insurance, profit-sharing and retirement plans, and tuition reimbursement.

CONTACT

Mike Carroll, Professional Employment Representative (Corporate, Aircraft, Air Distribution, Precision Dynamics, Motors, and Specialty Machine Tools), 555 Colman Center Drive, P.O. Box 7040, Rockford, IL 61125; Pam Morin, Personnel Representative, Energy Management, 555 Colman Center Drive, P.O. Box 7040, Rockford, IL 61125; Hal Sherran, Personnel Administrator, Industrial Electronics and Components, 555 Colman Center Drive, P.O. Box 7040, Rockford, IL 61125; or Jim Peterson, Robicon Corporation, 555 Colman Center Drive, P.O. Box 7040, Rockford, IL 61125.

BAUSCH & LOMB

ADMINISTRATION • CHEMISTRY • ENGINEERING • FINANCE • INFORMATION SYSTEMS AND PROCESSING • MARKETING • OPTICS • PHYSICS • SALES • TECHNICAL SERVICES

THE COMPANY

Bausch & Lomb, a leader in the vision-care field, is an aggressive company with competitive pricing. Innovation is the key to the company's success. B&L president David E. Gill explains his management philosophy: "Like IBM, we don't have to be first to become first." Besides the unique soft contact lens that held 100 percent of its market in the early 1970s, Bausch & Lomb also manufactures cosmetics, personal products, glass, health-care products, pharmaceuticals, and health-care instruments. Founded in 1853, Bausch & Lomb employs 8,200 people worldwide.

Although competitors have edged into the market, B&L still outsells all its competitors. About 47 million Americans need vision correction, and one fourth of these wear soft contacts. Sales of soft contacts abroad and increased demand for sunglasses added to revenues in 1986.

The company plans to continue emphasizing health and eye-care products. The company's high-volume, low-cost formula, which has served well in the soft contact lens market, may be applied to other products such as the cosmetic tint lenses now growing in popularity. With $700 million in annual sales, B&L ranks number 384 in the Fortune 500 largest U.S. industrial corporations.

ALL TRAINING PROGRAMS

Bausch & Lomb's training program combines on-the-job experience and classroom instruction. You will be reimbursed for tuition and fees up to 100 percent for job-related studies.

QUALIFICATIONS

Each year B&L hires about 20 people with bachelor's degrees and five with master's degrees in technical fields. You should rank in the top quarter of your class. B&L also encourages applications from people with one or more years of related work experience in financial analysis, purchasing, sales, accounting, chemistry, computer programming, and employee relations, as well as engineers concentrating in chemical, computer, electrical, industrial, manufacturing, and mechanical engineering, physicists specializing in optics, and chemists specializing in organic and polymer chemistry. Business majors also have an opportunity to be placed in the company.

RECRUITMENT AND PLACEMENT

Trainees recruited nationwide are placed in California, Florida, Maryland, Massachusetts, Mississippi, New York, South Carolina, and Texas. Summer employment is available to engineering, computer science, and physical and biological science students.

SALARY AND BENEFITS

The College Placement Council Salary Survey for September 1986–June 1987 indicates starting salaries for chemicals, drugs, and allied products companies to be $1,964 a month for those with a B.A. degree in nontechnical curricula and $2,457 with a B.A. degree in technical curricula. M.B.A. starting salaries were $2,886 for a nontechnical undergraduate degree and $2,794 for a technical undergraduate degree. Check with the company for more specific salary and benefits information.

CONTACT

Corporate Director, Staffing, Bausch & Lomb, 42 East Avenue, P.O. Box 743, Rochester, NY 14603.

BAXTER TRAVENOL LABORATORIES, INC.

ADMINISTRATION • CHEMISTRY • ENGINEERING

THE COMPANY

Baxter Travenol makes medical care products, including intravenous solutions and dialysis equipment for people with failed kidneys. This is a progressive company that works hard to maintain a family feeling—a challenge with 19 manufacturing plants and over 30,000 employees in the United States alone. It is also a very financially healthy organization, with three straight decades of strong sales and earnings increases. Baxter Travenol closely watches labor costs, holding them down by avoiding unions and by placing its plants in small towns, where the company gets and holds a loyal, long-term work force. It also has a strong commitment to physical fitness; corporate headquarters in Deerfield, Illinois, are surrounded by a running track and include an entire wing used as a gymnasium. Listed among *Fortune*'s most admired corporations, Baxter Travenol has $5 billion plus in annual sales. It ranks number 63 in the Fortune 500 largest U.S. industrial corporations.

ALL TRAINING PROGRAMS

Computer scientists participate in a three-month formal training program; for others, it's mostly on-the-job training.

QUALIFICATIONS

Baxter Travenol is looking for people with expertise in computers, chemistry, and business. There are openings at all degree levels for graduates in chemistry and business, and in computer, electrical, manufacturing, mechanical, and polymer science engineering.

RECRUITMENT AND PLACEMENT

Baxter Travenol recruits aggressively year round. The company will pay employees a $350 to $500 fee to recommend someone who is then hired. Your starting location will be in Illinois, but the company has operations all over the United States and the world.

SALARY AND BENEFITS

The College Placement Council Salary Survey for September 1986–June 1987 indicates starting salaries for chemicals, drugs, and allied products companies to be $1,964 a month for those with a B.A. degree in nontechnical curricula and $2,457 with a B.A. degree in technical curricula. M.B.A. starting salaries were $2,886 for a nontechnical undergraduate degree and $2,794 for a technical undergraduate degree. Check with the company for more specific salary information. Your benefits will include profit-sharing and thrift plans, subsidized day care, a flextime policy, summertime hours (so the office can be closed Friday afternoons), and other more traditional benefits.

CONTACT

Corporate Recruitment and Staffing, Baxter Travenol Laboratories, Inc., One Baxter Parkway, Deerfield, IL 60015.

BECHTEL

ADMINISTRATION • CONSTRUCTION • ENGINEERING

THE COMPANY

Bechtel is the nation's largest engineering and construction company. It is based in San Francisco but spans the globe with its many construction sites. Most major engineering feats throughout the world have had the assistance of Bechtel. Privately held and managed by the Bechtel family since its beginning in 1898, Bechtel has an image as a lumbering giant, strangely silent but ever present. About half of its business has been in constructing power plants. Major oil companies have been turning to Bechtel to build entire cities to help produce oil. The growth of Bechtel has been closely associated with the growth of the United States Government. With the oil glut of the past few years and increasing foreign competition, Bechtel has recently been forced to bid on smaller and smaller projects. It expects to secure a significant share of emerging worldwide markets for petrochemical plants, pipelines, and related facilities and to maintain its leadership position in filling the world's industrial and resource development needs.

ALL TRAINING PROGRAMS

You will be exposed to the wide variety of Bechtel's operations during the training period, participating in formal courses as well as learning by doing under the guidance of skilled supervisors.

ADMINISTRATION PROGRAM

The program prepares trainees to provide administrative support to the field and other line functions. You will be offered a variety of work assignments and company-sponsored external and in-house development programs. You learn to handle construction accounts, program computers for building needs, or use your knowledge to comprehend plans and apply them to schedules. Work-related training may emphasize new techniques to improve your supervisory skills, negotiating talents, or technical writing proficiency. The company wants you to participate in educational training or professional registration and thus help accelerate your advancement. You are offered ongoing opportunities to discuss career growth and planning, since Bechtel wants people who want to grow with the company.

QUALIFICATIONS

Bechtel seeks administrative and computer science personnel as well as cost, planning, and scheduling engineers with B.S. or M.S. degrees. Some jobs may require international relocation.

PLACEMENT

You will work in the home office in San Francisco.

CONSTRUCTION TRAINING PROGRAM

As a field engineer in the construction program you are responsible for communication between the design group and the construction superintendents who build the projects. A civil engineer learns about earthwork planning and construction and structural steel erection. Mechanical engineers are responsible for scheduling, inspecting, and interpreting drawings in their area of responsibility. The electrical engineer is concerned with the inspection, scheduling, and interpreting of drawings in areas such as conduit runs. Your training will be on the job, as a team member with experienced supervision. Training is ongoing and will continue as you grow with Bechtel. Promotional opportunities are excellent, and outstanding employees are recognized and promoted rapidly.

QUALIFICATIONS

For field construction work, you should have a B.S. or M.S. in construction management or in any engineering discipline.

PLACEMENT

You will work in the field, with assignments possible anywhere in the world.

ENGINEERING TRAINING PROGRAM

For the first six to twelve months you will calculate, supervise work on drawings, prepare specifications, route cable, check voltage regulations, work with line sizing calculations, study pipe stress, design control boards, or prepare nuclear shielding and radiation analyses. Your on-the-job experiences, along with training and development programs, are as varied as the jobs available. Bechtel wants you to become immediately involved, to enjoy seeing engineering projects come to life, and to relish working with others. The new engineering employee is encouraged to contribute and to learn to work on a team. How far you may advance from there is determined by your own personal commitment. Top management consists primarily of engineers.

QUALIFICATIONS

Openings exist for recent graduates with a B.S. or M.S. in all fields of engineering: chemical, civil, electrical, piping, mechanical, and nuclear. Related design, drafting, and technical opportunities are available.

PLACEMENT

You will work in the field with assignments possible anywhere in the world.

ALL PROGRAMS

RECRUITMENT

Bechtel recruits nationwide.

SALARY AND BENEFITS

The College Placement Council Salary Survey for September 1986–June 1987 indicates starting salaries for building materials manufacturers and construction companies to be $1,782 a month for those with a B.A. degree in nontechnical curricula and $2,156 with a B.A. degree in technical curricula. M.B.A. starting salaries were $1,666 for a nontechnical undergraduate degree and $2,677 for a technical undergraduate degree. Check with the company for more specific salary information. Benefits include medical, life, accident, and disability income protection, short- and long-term disability insurance plans, retirement income benefits through savings and profit-sharing plans, a federal credit union, tuition reimbursement, paid time off and holidays.

CONTACT

Personnel Manager, College Relations, Bechtel Power Corp., 50 Beale Street, San Francisco, CA 94119; Bechtel Power Corporation, P.O. Box 1000, Ann Arbor, MI 48106; Bechtel Power Corporation, 15740 Shady Grove Road, Gaithersburg, MD 20877; Bechtel Power Corporation, P.O. Box 60860, Terminal Annex, Los Angeles, CA 90060; or Bechtel Canada Ltd., 250 Bloor Street East, Toronto, Ont. M4W 3K5, Canada.

BELK STORES SERVICES, INC.

MANAGEMENT

THE COMPANY

With annual sales over $2 billion, Belk has 350 department stores throughout the South that dominate 85 percent of the markets in which they are located. Belk is a confederation of privately held store groups rather than a single corporate entity. Belk Stores is the largest family- and management-owned group of stores in the nation. In 1888, William Henry Belk founded the first Belk store. He started a tradition of rewarding good employees with partnerships instead of store management positions. Belk moved to new office space in 1988 (the company's hundredth anniversary), the first corporate office relocation since 1949.

MANAGEMENT TRAINING PROGRAM

Company representatives consider their eighteen-month Management Training Program to be well planned and note that a high number of trainees tend to stay with the company. Positions emphasized in the program are: area sales manager, assistant buyer, department manager/buyer, and division manager/buyer. You will be assigned to first-line management for on-the-job experience and given assignments throughout the store to develop an understanding of the basic functions performed in a store. Your progress will be reviewed periodically, background readings will be assigned, and classroom instruction will be provided. Specialized training is given in the last six months of the program. Optional self-study guides are also provided.

QUALIFICATIONS

If you have a bachelor's degree and/or previous retailing experience Belk will be interested in you.

RECRUITMENT AND PLACEMENT

Belk Stores plans to hire 200-plus management trainees annually. The 75 personnel managers in 16 states are encouraged to maintain contact with colleges and universities within the region. Recruitment from the part-time pool is also encouraged.

SALARY AND BENEFITS

Your beginning salary will be in the $15,000 to $16,500 range. Contact the company for details on benefits.

CONTACT

Alton Wright, Manager, Human Resources Utilization, Belk Stores Division, Inc., P.O. Box 31788, Charlotte, NC 28231.

BELL COMMUNICATIONS RESEARCH

APPLIED RESEARCH • NETWORK PLANNING • TECHNOLOGY APPLICATIONS AND SOFTWARE • TECHNOLOGY SYSTEMS

THE COMPANY

Bell Communications Research (Bellcore) was created to provide research and technology for the Bell Operating Companies. These divested Bell Operating Companies—seven of the largest telecommunications carriers in the country—rely on Bellcore for information systems, systems engineering, network planning services, projections of the types of equipment needed for network growth, and research and exploratory work in science and technology. Bellcore is owned by Bell Atlantic Corporation, BellSouth Corporation, NYNEX Corporation, AMERITECH, Southwestern Bell Corporation, Pacific Telesis Group, and US WEST. Headquarters are in Livingston, New Jersey, with the company's more than 7,000 employees spread out over northern and central New Jersey.

ALL TRAINING PROGRAMS

You will receive on-the-job training that will be supplemented by a variety of highly technical managerial and personal development courses offered by Bellcore's own education groups. You may also receive rotational assignments to broaden your knowledge. Bellcore encourages employees to obtain higher degrees through a Graduate Study Program that may be either full time or part time.

QUALIFICATIONS

Bellcore hires graduates with solid academic records in operations research, chemistry, physics, psychology, computer science, mathematics, operations research, and computer, electrical, and human factors engineering.

RECRUITMENT AND PLACEMENT

Bellcore recruits at 75 colleges and universities across the country. For further information, or to apply, contact the company directly. Positions will be in northern and central New Jersey. Bellcore makes a special effort to hire women, minorities, veterans, and the handicapped.

SALARIES AND BENEFITS

The College Placement Council Salary Survey for September 1986–June 1987 indicates starting salaries for research organizations to be $2,116 a month for those with a B.A. degree in nontechnical curricula and $2,266 with a B.A. degree in technical curricula. M.B.A. starting salaries were $2,512 for a nontechnical undergraduate degree and $2,822 for a technical undergraduate degree. Check with the company for more specific salary information. Benefits cover the basics and include life, health, vision, dental, and disability insurance, tuition reimbursement, and savings, investment, and retirement plans.

CONTACT

Manager, Technical Employment, RRC/169/3840/86, Bell Communications Research, P.O. Box 1300, Piscataway, NJ 08854.

THE BOEING COMPANY
COMPUTER SERVICES

THE COMPANY

The Boeing Company is best known as the world's largest producer of commercial aircraft, but is also heavily involved in space exploration, defense, strategy, helicopter, and hydrofoil manufacture. Boeing produced the first stage of the Saturn rocket that got our American team to the moon, and it was a Boeing-built four-wheeled vehicle that the American team drove while on the moon. It is among *Fortune*'s most admired corporations, and ranked number 16 in the Fortune 500 of largest U.S. industrial corporations.

The program described here is in Boeing's Computer Services company, which provides data processing service to its own operating companies as well as to both industry and government. Boeing Computer Services has over 9,000 employees and equipment valued at more than a half billion dollars. It provides computing services to over 200 of the Fortune 500 companies, U.S. federal and state customers, and other clients in the United States, Canada, Europe, Japan, and Saudi Arabia. Sales offices are located in virtually every major city in the United States. To support its geographically dispersed centers, Boeing Computer Services owns and operates one of the largest privately owned communications networks in the world, employing land, microwave, and satellite communications.

COMPUTER TRAINING PROGRAMS

Boeing will familiarize you with your new job through a combination of classroom instruction (up to six weeks) and supervised on-the-job training.

QUALIFICATIONS

Boeing is looking for graduates with degrees in computer science and related areas.

RECRUITMENT AND PLACEMENT

Recruiting is done nationally. You would work at one of Boeing Computer Services' major data centers in Puget Sound, Washington; Wichita, Kansas; Philadelphia; Huntsville, Alabama; and Vienna, Virginia.

SALARY AND BENEFITS

Boeing's salary program and fringe benefits—such as vacation, sick leave, voluntary investment plan, and insurance—are among the best in the nation. The company offers invention incentives of $1,000 to $10,000, and, in some cases, a share of the profits. The College Placement Council Salary Survey for September 1986–June 1987 indicates starting salaries for aerospace companies to be $1,943 a month for those with a B.A. degree in nontechnical curricula and $2,399 with a B.A. degree in technical curricula. M.B.A. starting salaries were $2,330 for a nontechnical undergraduate degree and $2,475 for a technical undergraduate degree. Check with the company for more specific salary information.

CONTACT

Recruiting, Boeing Computer Services, East Pike Office Building, Suite 200, 453 South Webb Road, Wichita, KS 67207.

BOISE CASCADE CORPORATION

ADMINISTRATION • ENGINEERING • FINANCE AND ACCOUNTING • FORESTRY • MANUFACTURING • MARKETING AND SALES • STAFF SERVICES

THE COMPANY

Boise Cascade is a diverse company with career opportunities in a variety of businesses: paper, wood products, packaging, office products and building materials distribution, and related staff services. With about 27,000 employees, its annual sales put the company in the top 100 of the *Fortune* 500. Boise Cascade is also listed among *Fortune*'s most admired corporations. In recent years the company has increased its timber ownership and yield from its timberlands as well as its leadership in paper manufacturing, building materials distribution, and office products distribution. Headquartered in Boise, Idaho, the company is also in a joint venture operating paper- and wood-products-manufacturing facilities in Louisiana. If you join Boise, you will participate in a fast-growing, decentralized company.

ALL TRAINING PROGRAMS

In many of Boise Cascade's businesses you will enter special sales, production, and management training programs that offer on-the-job experience as well as formal classroom instruction. Later in your career you will be eligible for personal development programs for supervisory or management training.

QUALIFICATIONS

Boise Cascade hires those with graduate and undergraduate degrees in: chemical, mechanical, industrial, electrical, and civil engineering; computer science; sales, marketing, and business; M.B.A.s with significant work experience between undergraduate and graduate school; finance and accounting; communications, public relations, and advertising; and law.

RECRUITMENT AND PLACEMENT

Boise Cascade has locations in Alabama, Arizona, Arkansas, California, Colorado, Connecticut, Florida, Georgia, Hawaii, Idaho, Illinois, Indiana, Kansas, Louisiana, Minnesota, Montana, New York, North Carolina, Ohio, Oklahoma, Oregon, Pennsylvania, South Carolina, Texas, Utah, Washington, Wisconsin, and Ontario, Canada.

SALARY AND BENEFITS

The College Placement Council Salary Survey for September 1986–June 1987 indicates starting salaries for glass, paper, packaging, and allied products companies to be $1,865 a month for those with a B.A. degree in nontechnical curricula and $2,401 with a B.A. degree in technical curricula. M.B.A. starting salaries were $2,945 for a nontechnical undergraduate degree and $2,775 for a technical undergraduate degree. Check with the company for more specific salary and benefits information.

CONTACT

College Relations, Boise Cascade Corporation, One Jefferson Square, Boise, ID 83728.

BOOZ•ALLEN & HAMILTON, INC.

BUSINESS CONSULTING

THE COMPANY

When a business needs answers to complex problems or to project the results of a contemplated move, it may turn to Booz•Allen for consulting services. The company's clients are the largest and best-managed businesses in the world. Booz•Allen's clients include more than 400 of the Fortune 500, 80 of the 100 top U.S. banks, and 70 of the 100 largest companies in the world. Three fourths of its clients are repeat customers. Using a team approach, its consultants combine analytical skills, technological knowledge, industry expertise, and functional capabilities to solve the problems put before them. A private corporation wholly owned by its 160 partners, Booz•Allen has 1,200 consultants on staff. This is a company that welcomes a variety of styles in its employees and offers a fast-paced, challenging, and entrepreneurial environment.

BUSINESS CONSULTING TRAINING PROGRAM

You will be a full team member from the beginning. Following an intensive course in consulting fundamentals, you will be assigned to projects where you can put your training to work. You might work on a team conducting interviews of all the key players in a particular industry to advise a company that is making an acquisition in an area unfamiliar to it. During your first years with Booz•Allen you will focus on mastering consulting skills, refining analytical techniques, developing a broad business perspective, and establishing initial client relationships. You will participate in a series of specialized training programs, including seminars. An objective appraisal system will help you evaluate your progress. You may spend as much as 25 percent of your time working away from home.

QUALIFICATIONS

The company hires outstanding graduates of leading business schools, as well as young and seasoned professionals who have excelled in a wide range of industries. Trainees might have worked as assistant product managers, bank lending officers, staff planners, or product development engineers. Booz•Allen looks for individuals with intellectual ability, curiosity, analytical skills, imagination and creativity, judgment and maturity, business experience, strong interpersonal skills, personal integrity, and a high energy level.

RECRUITMENT AND PLACEMENT

Booz•Allen recruits nationwide but welcomes applications to headquarters. Offices are located in New York, Atlanta, Bethesda, Chicago, Cleveland, Dallas, Düsseldorf, Houston, Jidda, London, Los Angeles, Mexico City, Milan, Paris, Philadelphia, San Francisco, Singapore, Tokyo, and Wassenaar (The Netherlands).

SALARY AND BENEFITS

The College Placement Council Salary Survey for September 1986–June 1987 indicates starting salaries for research and/or consulting organizations to be $2,116 a month for those with a B.A. degree in nontechnical curricula and $2,266 with a B.A. degree in technical curricula. M.B.A. starting salaries were $2,512 for a nontechnical undergraduate degree and $2,822 for a technical undergraduate degree. Check with the company for more specific salary information. Salaries are supplemented with a comprehensive benefits package that includes life insurance, medical, hospital, dental, and pension plans, relocation assistance, and career development programs.

CONTACT

Director, University Relations, Booz•Allen & Hamilton, Inc., 101 Park Avenue, New York, NY 10178.

BOURNS, INC.

ACCOUNTING AND FINANCE • INFORMATION SYSTEMS AND PROCESSING • MARKETING • PRODUCTION • RESEARCH AND DEVELOPMENT • SALES

THE COMPANY

Bourns is a production company that manufactures resistive circuit components, transducers, and potentiometric instruments. It employs 6,000 people worldwide, about half that number in the United States.

ALL TRAINING PROGRAMS

Training provides new employees with orientation to Bourns's policies and procedures. You will spend twenty-four months in a program that combines on-the-job and classroom instruction. Part-time study for advanced degrees is encouraged with a tuition reimbursement plan.

QUALIFICATIONS

Bourns is looking for graduates with bachelor's degrees in accounting and for M.B.A.s. Graduates with one to two years' experience are also encouraged to apply. You should have an excellent academic record (in the top 15 percent of your class) and be familiar with computers.

RECRUITMENT AND PLACEMENT

Starting locations are in California, Iowa, and Utah.

SALARY AND BENEFITS

Starting salaries range from the low to mid-twenties with a bachelor's degree; mid-twenties with a business-related master's degree and nontechnical B.S.; and upper twenties to low thirties with a business-related master's degree and technical B.S. Benefits include life insurance, medical, hospital, dental, pension, and profit-sharing plans, a career development program, and relocation services.

CONTACT

Tom Dickson, Human Resources, Bourns, Inc. 1200 Columbia Avenue, Riverside, CA 92507.

BRISTOL-MYERS U.S. PHARMACEUTICAL AND NUTRITIONAL GROUP

ACCOUNTING AND FINANCE • ENGINEERING • MANAGEMENT INFORMATION SYSTEMS • MARKETING • MATERIALS MANAGEMENT • PERSONNEL • PRODUCTION SUPERVISION • QUALITY ASSURANCE

THE COMPANY

In 1986, Bristol-Myers Company consolidated the business units dedicated to pharmaceutical and nutritional products to form Bristol Myers USPNG. Administrative and marketing headquarters is located in Evansville, Indiana, and includes Mead Johnson, Bristol Laboratories, Bristol-Myers Animal Health Care, and Bristol-Myers Oncology. The company is a leader in the research, manufacture, and marketing of pharmaceutical and nutritional products for the consumer and pharmaceutical markets. Listed among *Fortune*'s most admired corporations, it ranks number 75 in the Fortune 500 largest U.S. industrial corporations. Working with this company, you could assist in the development of a new infant formula or an entirely new type of food source, assure its quality, or create its packaging.

ALL TRAINING PROGRAMS

Bristol-Myers will start your career with a combination of on-the-job and formal training, giving you as much responsibility as you can handle from the beginning.

QUALIFICATIONS

Bristol-Myers hires from numerous degree specialties, including advertising, biochemistry, biological sciences, business administration, chemistry, communications, computer science, dairy science, engineering (chemical, civil, electrical, industrial, mechanical, packaging, food), food science, home economics, industrial management, journalism, marketing, mathematics/statistics, medical technology, microbiology/bacteriology, nutritional sciences, personnel, pharmacy, and psychology. Ph.D. graduates are employed in all areas of research.

FINANCE TRAINING

You will either be placed directly into a finance function or into the Finance Orientation Program. In the latter, the two- to three-month program will be tailored to your background and interests. You will be rotated to various departments to assist and learn numerous tasks in one- to two-week stints. You will also work in other areas such as manufacturing, distribution, marketing, and administration. The program will include counseling and preparation of written reports.

QUALIFICATIONS

You should have a B.S. degree in business administration with a major in accounting.

PLACEMENT

You will work in Evansville, Indiana.

ALL PROGRAMS

RECRUITMENT

Bristol-Myers sends representatives to many U.S. campuses.

SALARY AND BENEFITS

The College Placement Council Salary Survey for September 1986–June 1987 indicates starting salaries for chemical, drug, and allied products companies to be $1,964 a month for those with a B.A. degree in nontechnical curricula and $2,457 with a B.A. degree in technical curricula. M.B.A. starting salaries were $2,886 for a nontechnical undergraduate degree and $2,794 for a technical undergraduate degree. Check with the company for more specific salary and benefits information.

CONTACT

Manager, College Relations, Bristol-Myers USPNG, Evansville, IN 47721.

BROOKLYN UNION GAS COMPANY

MANAGEMENT

THE COMPANY

Brooklyn Union Gas provides natural gas for a territory of about 187 square miles in the New York City boroughs of Brooklyn, Staten Island, and two thirds of Queens—a population of more than 4 million. The American Gas Association ranks the company as the fifth largest natural gas utility in the country. As an energy firm with a reputation for sound management, Brooklyn Union develops its own supplies and has diversified into energy-related unregulated businesses. Its four wholly owned subsidiaries are Gas Energy, Inc. (markets energy-related equipment); Methane Development Corporation (reclaims methane from landfills); Star Enterprises, Inc. (sells propane, primarily in the Northeast, through its subsidiary, Delaware Valley Propane Company); and Fuel Resources, Inc. (gas exploration, development, and production, mostly in Appalachia). Brooklyn Union Gas employs about 3,700 employees and maintains headquarters in Brooklyn, New York.

MANAGEMENT TRAINING PROGRAM

As a new employee you will enter a seven-week Management Orientation Program conducted by the company's human resources department. This program covers the company's organization, operations, and key field personnel. You will then be given your first job assignment. Your supervisor will give you regular feedback on your progress and offer career guidance. Additional classes on technical and managerial subjects will be available in house for your development.

QUALIFICATIONS

Brooklyn Union looks for outstanding candidates with degrees in computer science and various types of engineering: civil, chemical, electrical, industrial, and mechanical.

RECRUITMENT AND PLACEMENT

The company's recruiters visit campuses around the country. You will be invited to visit the company for a tour of the facilities if you favorably impress the recruiter who visits your campus. Expect to begin your career in Brooklyn.

SALARIES AND BENEFITS

The College Placement Council Salary Survey for September 1986–June 1987 indicates starting salaries for utilities to be $1,905 a month for those with a B.A. degree in nontechnical curricula and $2,355 with a B.A. degree in technical curricula. M.B.A. starting salaries were $2,403 for a nontechnical undergraduate degree and $2,667 for a technical undergraduate degree. Check with the company for more specific salary information. Benefits include the following: medical, disability, and group life insurance, tuition reimbursement, and retirement.

CONTACT

Management Recruitment Administrator, Brooklyn Union Gas Company, 817 Neptune Avenue, Brooklyn, NY 11224.

BROWN & ROOT, INC.

ACCOUNTING • COMPUTER SERVICES • CONSTRUCTION • ENGINEERING • MATERIALS MANAGEMENT • RESEARCH AND DEVELOPMENT

THE COMPANY

Brown & Root is one of the largest engineering construction companies in the United States, serving all kinds of manufacturing and processing industries. The company was founded in 1919 when Herman Brown, who was building roads in central Texas, formed a partnership with his brother-in-law, Dan Root. In 1936 the company moved into heavy construction when it built Marshall Ford Dam on the Colorado River. The Halliburton Company purchased Brown & Root in 1962. B&R has a professional staff of about 15,000 in the United States and another 10,000 abroad. You might be part of a team designing a hydroelectric generating station for Thailand or a copper-refining facility in New Mexico.

ALL TRAINING PROGRAMS

You will be prepared to work in one of four engineering groups (power, petroleum and chemical, marine, and central engineering), industry design departments (based on specific industry requirements), construction groups, projects management services, or contract maintenance. A comprehensive training program for all new employees lasts three months and is held at corporate headquarters in Houston.

QUALIFICATIONS

Brown & Root recruits college graduates with backgrounds in accounting, business, computer science, engineering (architectural, chemical, civil, electrical, mechanical, nuclear, or ocean), environmental sciences, and mathematics.

RECRUITMENT AND PLACEMENT

The company recruits on campuses primarily in the South. Starting locations are in Houston or within 75 miles of Houston. All initial training takes place in Houston.

SALARY AND BENEFITS

With a bachelor's degree, salaries start at $26,400, climbing to $28,000 with a master's. Benefits consist of medical, life, and disability insurance; retirement, stock-purchase, and savings programs; and a tuition reimbursement program.

CONTACT

Personnel Manager, Brown & Root, Inc., P.O. Box 3, Houston, TX 77001.

BROWNING-FERRIS INDUSTRIES, INC.

ACCOUNTING · COMPUTER SCIENCE · ENGINEERING · FINANCE · MARKETING

THE COMPANY

Browning-Ferris, founded as a small waste collection company in 1967, has grown into the largest publicly held waste service company in North America. BFI's primary business is collecting, processing, and disposing of waste as effectively and economically as possible. All operations are conducted in a way that is compatible with the protection of the environment and conservation of natural resources. The 18,000 employees serve residential, commercial, industrial, and governmental customers in approximately 225 locations throughout the world. The company's subsidiaries also provide municipal and commercial street and parking lot sweeping; collection, treatment, and disposal services for health-care customers; and portable rest-room services. They are also active in the waste-to-energy field. The key word for this company is "professional." BFI identifies the waste handling problem, determines the best solution, and provides the necessary equipment, technology, and personnel for dependable, economical service. Annual sales are over $1.3 billion, and the company ranks number 51 in the Fortune 100 of largest diversified service companies.

ALL TRAINING PROGRAMS

Employee training for the various positions generally consists of supervised on-the-job training. In most areas, you will work with an experienced person until you've developed the skills and knowledge to work on your own. Seminars and continuing-education programs are encouraged and promoted.

QUALIFICATIONS

BFI offers professional opportunities for college graduates in the fields of accounting/finance, engineering, computer science, and business planning/marketing.

RECRUITMENT AND PLACEMENT

You can find out more about the company's opportunities by contacting the corporate offices in Houston. In addition to U.S. assignments, you might be sent to Canada, the United Kingdom, Kuwait, Puerto Rico, Saudi Arabia, Spain, Venezuela, or Australia.

SALARY AND BENEFITS

The College Placement Council Salary Survey for September 1986–June 1987 indicates starting salaries for merchandising (retail and wholesale) and service companies to be $1,594 a month for those with a B.A. degree in nontechnical curricula and $2,141 with a B.A. degree in technical curricula. M.B.A. starting salaries were $2,572 for a nontechnical undergraduate degree, and $2,735 for an M.B.A with technical undergraduate degree. Check with the company for more specific salary information. Company benefits include medical hospitalization, dental, life, and long-term disability insurance plans; retirement benefits; employee stockownership; and liberal vacation and holiday plans.

CONTACT

Browning-Ferris Industries, Inc., 14701 St. Mary's Lane, Houston, TX 77079.

THE BUDD COMPANY

ENGINEERING • INFORMATION SYSTEMS AND PROCESSING • PRODUCTION • OPERATIONS • RESEARCH AND DEVELOPMENT • TECHNICAL PROFESSIONAL SERVICES

THE COMPANY

The Budd Company, a subsidiary of Thyssen AG of Duisburg, West Germany, produces automotive and industrial components, railway cars, and truck trailers. Founded in 1912, Budd employs 10,000 people in the United States and another 5,000 abroad.

ALL TRAINING PROGRAMS

Training prepares new employees for their jobs in a program that combines classroom instruction and on-the-job experience. You will spend approximately twelve months in training.

QUALIFICATIONS

Budd recruits college graduates with degrees in business (B.S. or M.B.A.), chemistry, computer science, electrical engineering, manufacturing engineering, mechanical engineering, polymer chemistry, and structural engineering. Budd is also interested in technical graduates with one to two years of related work experience. Applicants should rank in the top 30 percent of their class, with a minimum G.P.A. of 3.0. Familiarity with computers will be a plus.

RECRUITMENT AND PLACEMENT

Starting locations are in Michigan, Ohio, and Pennsylvania.

SALARY AND BENEFITS

With a bachelor's degree, your starting salary will be about $27,000. Check with the company for more specific salary information. Benefits include life insurance; medical, hospital, dental, vision, pension, and incentive savings plans; a career development program; tuition reimbursement; and relocation services.

CONTACT

Assistant Personnel Manager, The Budd Company, 3155 West Big Beaver Road, Troy, MI 48084.

LEO BURNETT COMPANY

ACCOUNT MANAGEMENT

THE COMPANY

When Leo Burnett started in Chicago in the middle of the Depression, the ad agency welcomed visitors with a bowl of apples at the reception desk. Now the only major advertising agency in Chicago and the tenth largest in the country, Leo Burnett still gives away more than 272,000 apples a year. The company strives to develop long-term relationships with a few clients. It has fewer than 30 clients (who represent some 200 brands), half of whom have been with the company for more than fifteen years. Some of its more notable creations include the Jolly Green Giant, the Marlboro Man, Tony the Tiger, Charlie the Tuna, the Lonely Maytag Repairman, Morris the Cat, and the Pillsbury Doughboy. In addition to its domestic operation, the company serves international clients through 40 offices in 34 countries. Founder Leo Burnett felt as strongly about keeping employees as he did about keeping clients. About 30 percent of its employees have been with the agency more than ten years. The company promotes camaraderie and company spirit with an annual anniversary day celebration, annual bonus day breakfast, company sports teams, first-class air travel for company employees, and the continuation of the traditions established by Leo Burnett.

ADVERTISING TRAINING PROGRAM

The agency's Account Executive Training Program, with a reputation as one of the best in the business, is demanding. After a brief orientation, you begin as a trainee in the client service or media department. If you have an advanced degree or extensive work experience, initial training takes place in client service for approximately twelve months. Working under an account executive, you learn the fundamentals of developing, producing, and airing advertising. If you begin with an undergraduate degree and no experience, initial training is in the media department, where you learn the art of developing successful, effective strategies for spending the clients' advertising dollars. Most trainees spend fifteen to eighteen months before being promoted to assistant account executive. Every 120 days during the training program your supervisor assesses your growth and outlines a program of continued learning. Once you have demonstrated outstanding performance, you are promoted to assistant account executive as soon as a position becomes available.

As an assistant account executive you are assigned to one client and given responsibility for the day-to-day activities of that brand. You are also given full responsibility for at least two major projects from initial development through client presentation. On-the-job training is supplemented throughout the year by two series of seminars featuring the agency's top management as well as outside experts. The Wednesday Seminar Program is attended by all trainees and covers a wide range of topics: new product research, print production, Nielsen analysis, market testing, sales promotion, TV programming, and copy strategy. Often a successful advertising campaign is used as a case study. The Advanced Seminar Program is attended by those trainees assigned to client service. Each trainee also participates in a series of 20 media training classes prepared by the media research department.

An important component of your program is your adviser. At the beginning of the training program, you are assigned a mentor who plays a key role in your development. Your adviser not only shows you the ropes but also provides advice, an objective opinion, or a sympathetic ear—all in the strictest confidence.

QUALIFICATIONS

The company looks for college graduates who are intelligent, creative problem solvers, with excellent interpersonal and communication skills. Additionally, a superior track record of leadership and a strong interest in advertising and marketing are required. Prior experience is not necessary. Both undergraduate and graduate degree trainees are recruited.

RECRUITMENT AND PLACEMENT

Recruitment is conducted from November to February on 20 campuses nationwide. Even though the company receives over 4,000 unsolicited résumés each year, it takes time to review qualifications and respond in writing. About 45–55 trainees are hired annually, with starting dates staggered throughout the year. The training takes place in the Chicago office, where you will become an account executive upon completion of the training program.

SALARY AND BENEFITS

Check with the company for specific salary information. The annual profit participation bonus is good (20 percent for the last eight years), and the company has made the maximum contribution (15 percent) to the employee profit-sharing fund for the last forty years. The employee benefits package also includes tuition reimbursement and accident, life, medical/dental, and disability insurance. In addition, the company will pay up to $3,000 to help an employee adopt a child.

CONTACT

Recruitment Coordinator, Leo Burnett USA, Prudential Plaza, Chicago, IL 60601.

The Inside Story from a Training Graduate
Steven Sanders, Aetna and Mellon Bank

Steven Sanders is a partner in the financial consulting firm of Hunt & Sanders in Philadelphia. After graduating from Howard University he entered the Aetna Life Insurance Employee Benefit Training Program. Later he worked for Mellon Bank and went through their Commercial Analyst Training Program.

☆ ☆ ☆ ☆ ☆

Let's start with your college days—where you went to school and your major.

I was one of the first to enter the Risk Management Insurance Program at Howard University. Through that program I was exposed to the insurance industry.

Tell me about your first job and its training program.

I went to work for Aetna after getting my B.A. in business management and insurance. I got a chance to work with them through a summer internship. During the summer after my junior year, I spent time in their home office learning about the different divisions and operations of the company. I then interned as an employee benefit representative in one of the branch offices for Aetna Life Insurance Company. I talked to one of the employee benefit representatives, and he thought that I would be a good candidate for the employee benefits school.

Did you find the summer internship valuable?

Yes, I was very fortunate to have a chance to see what the actual job title entailed before I went into the training program. At the end of the summer, after working as an employee benefit representative, I went through the interview process, which was lengthy and extensive. And going into my senior year at Howard, Aetna decided to make me an offer. I told them I would take a couple of months to think about it. But I pretty much had my mind made up. I did interview with some other companies, but I was sold on the Aetna program. Once I graduated from Howard, I went right into the employee benefit training program.

Give me some background about the program.

The classroom part lasted for about three and a half months, and it gave me a round robin of what was available in the employee benefit arena. It took me through the background of the company and the specifics about group insurance and group pensions. During the sales aspect of the training we made a sales presentation and were taped so we could critique and learn from our own presentations. It was quite extensive and there was a very nice corporate learning atmosphere.

How large was your class?

There were twenty-eight and that was considered a large group.

What was the next step in the program?

After the training program I was assigned to an employee benefit office in Pittsburgh. Usually you don't have any idea where you're going to be assigned until the last week or two of the training. I took on the job of selling Aetna's group health, group life, and group pension programs to employers anywhere from a two-person shop to as large as U. S. Steel or Gulf Oil.

For the first month I traveled about two or three days with each person in the territory and got a chance to see different sales skills and how everyone managed their territory. Then I began to cultivate my own territory by making contacts on my own.

How long were you with Aetna?

About three years.

And then you made a career move?

Yes, that's correct. Mellon has a very big presence in Pittsburgh, and through a lot of civic and community organizations I was involved in I met a number of Mellon employees and management staff. Not being totally satisfied with what I was doing at Aetna, I was looking to make a career change at about the three-year mark. I wanted something new and different in the financial service arena. I decided to chose banking, and in Pittsburgh, Mellon had some of the best training programs.

Did you go through one of Mellon's training programs?

Yes, the commercial credit analyst training program. The formal classroom training lasted for about three months. Then a person remains in training on the floor as a commercial credit analyst for another fifteen months.

Tell me about the floor training.

You began analyzing different companies within an industry group. During this second stage of the formal training you were actually given a company to analyze their financial statement. You would spread them on the computer, draw up your analysis, write up a credit quality memo, and present that to your section head. Sometimes that also called for a presentation to the credit review committee. You had at least three or four formal presentations to the entire committee.

What role did your supervisor play?

He would give you feedback on a regular basis, comment on how your case analysis work was being done, and how your presentations were being made.

What was the determining factor in deciding to leave Mellon?

There were a number of reasons. I always wanted to start and run my own business. At the age of twenty-six, I began to recognize the things I really valued and things I really wanted to do. I wasn't going to necessarily have all the opportunities to do it within the corporate structure. I always felt I could run my own show, you know, do things my own way. I never wanted my income to be restricted by an annual review. I really wanted it to be based on my own skills and what I did on a daily basis. And that's the way it is now: my income definitely is a result of the number of people I bring into the firm.

Did the Aetna and Mellon programs help you to be a better, independent, successful business person?

I wouldn't trade those experiences for anything. Even the unpleasant parts taught me valuable lessons that I use now. Both programs taught me a lot of the basics that a person doesn't always get from an undergraduate or maybe even a graduate degree. And they gave me a lot of real-life experiences to draw on. The biggest thing was that I was exposed to my weaknesses. And that was very uncomfortable, but those times were the most powerful learning experiences that I've ever had. And I took note of all of the weaknesses and consistently knocked down each one of them.

Anything you would tell someone about to enter the job market?

I would definitely encourage them to get into a good training program. It will expose you to some of your weaknesses as well as your strengths, and give you the opportunity to learn some things that you didn't learn in college. I think it gives you an excellent rounding-out experience. I would also tell someone to go in with your own agenda. The corporation may have a certain way for you to go, they may have things mapped out for you which may not fit your entire career plan or your personal views or values. You should have a feel for where you are and where it is you're trying to go, and how you want to get there. You're going to have to make sacrifices.

How is your firm doing?

Fine. I now have about 250 clients. I also write on financial topics for the second largest paper in Philadelphia. And I'm making a few bucks too.

C

☆ ☆ ☆ ☆ ☆

CALCOMP
SALES

THE COMPANY

At about the same time that satellites were first launched into space, CalComp launched its first product, an electronic plotter that produced drawings and charts from computer data. CalComp maintains its leadership in the field. Its products are used for such diverse purposes as creating special graphic effects for movies and designing a new structural support system for the Statue of Liberty. CalComp has more than 2,500 employees with affiliates, subsidiaries, and distributors in 45 countries. Its divisional headquarters are located in Anaheim, California; Scottsdale, Arizona; and Hudson, New Hampshire.

SALES TRAINING PROGRAM

You will attend formal classroom training at company expense at corporate headquarters in Anaheim, followed by on-the-job training at your initial field sales office assignment. Within six months you will receive your first territory.

QUALIFICATIONS

You will catch a CalComp recruiter's attention if you have a B.S./B.A. or a master's in business with heavy emphasis on sales and marketing. Some sales experience would be very helpful along with a background that required public contact. Excellent verbal and written communication skills are mandatory. Some knowledge of the computer industry, hardware and software, particularly computer graphics, is a big plus.

RECRUITMENT AND PLACEMENT

CalComp recruiters visit many college campuses around the country. Your initial assignment will be in either the Houston or Dallas office, but you must be willing to relocate anywhere in the United States at the end of the training program.

SALARY AND BENEFITS

When you are assigned to a territory you will be placed on a base salary plus commission compensation plan. The College Placement Council Salary Survey for September 1986–June 1987 indicates starting salaries for electrical and electronic machine and equipment companies to be $1,861 a month for those with a B.A. degree in nontechnical curricula and $2,419 with a B.A. degree in technical curricula. M.B.A. starting salaries were $2,784 for a nontechnical undergraduate degree and $2,818 for a technical undergraduate degree. Check with the company for more specific salary information. Benefits include medical and dental plans; group life, disability, and business travel insurance; vacations and paid holidays.

CONTACT

Industrial Relations, CalComp, 2411 West La Palma Avenue, P.O. Box 3250, Anaheim, CA 92803.

CALGON CORPORATION

SALES

THE COMPANY

Calgon manufactures and sells filtering chemicals and equipment for air and water, and various industrial cleaning chemicals. The company is probably best known for its cleaning products, although it is also involved in large-scale service and sales involving water conservation, management and pollution control, energy conservation, desalination, and product recovery. Calgon works with industrial plants and municipalities throughout the world. The company markets over 500 products and services and has subsidiaries in Canada, Mexico, Venezuela, and Belgium.

SALES TRAINING PROGRAM

Training helps you become highly effective at selling Calgon products to industrial plants and municipalities. The focus is on selling techniques. You start on the job, in the territory, with your district manager. For the first week the manager will provide you with intensive coaching and instruction. As you need assistance, the manager will be available to assist you to continue to develop your sales skills and increase your performance. You will also go to St. Louis periodically for classroom training.

QUALIFICATIONS

A degree is preferred, with any major. Sales experience and mechanical and electrical aptitude and/or experience will boost your chances considerably.

RECRUITMENT AND PLACEMENT

Calgon has openings throughout the year, all over the country. Usually it takes from one to four months to complete the recruitment process; then you will work a territory.

SALARY AND BENEFITS

Starting guarantee for direct sales is in the high teens, and commissions start in the third month. Your potential earnings for the first year are in the mid-twenties, according to the company. Calgon has an extensive benefits program that includes a car program, life and survivor income insurance, a company-paid pension plan with eligibility beginning at age fifty-five, a company-matched stock-purchase plan, a liberal vacation plan, an educational assistance program, and paid holidays.

CONTACT

Calgon Corporation, Commercial Division, P.O. Box 3347, 14516 East Bonnelli Street, City of Industry, CA 91744.

CAMPBELL SOUP COMPANY

ADVERTISING • AGRICULTURE • AGRICULTURAL RESEARCH • BASIC RESEARCH • COMPUTER SYSTEMS • CONSUMER RESEARCH • CONTAINER MANUFACTURING • CONTAINER RESEARCH • CONTROLLERSHIP • CORPORATE RELATIONS • ENGINEERING RESEARCH AND DEVELOPMENT • GENERAL ENGINEERING AND MAINTENANCE • HUMAN RESOURCES • INDUSTRIAL ENGINEERING • INTERNATIONAL • LAW • LOGISTICS • MANAGEMENT INFORMATION SYSTEMS • MARKETING • PRODUCT DEVELOPMENT • PRODUCTION SUPERVISION • PROCUREMENT • SALES • TECHNICAL ADMINISTRATION • TREASURER'S DEPARTMENT

THE COMPANY

Campbell Soup Company began in Camden, New Jersey, in 1869 when Abram Anderson and Joseph Campbell established a canning and preserving business. These pioneers gained a reputation for quality food products. Camden is still the location of the world headquarters of Campbell, and one of its largest production facilities. While Campbell has been best known since 1897 for its popular canned condensed soups with the familiar red and white label, it also manufactures the brands Swanson, Hungry Man, Prego, Pepperidge Farm, Mrs. Paul's, and Le Menu, along with Recipe pet foods. Today, Campbell's 44,000 employees operate more than 90 manufacturing plants in the United States and 12 foreign countries and generate more than $4 billion in annual sales. The company ranks number 87 in the Fortune 500 largest U.S. industrial corporations.

ALL TRAINING PROGRAMS

You will begin your training with a general orientation to company philosophy and policies. Supervised on-the-job instruction will be combined with both in-house classroom training and outside classes. You can expect to be rotated to different departments to help you understand the overall workings of the company. Regular feedback sessions will keep you on track and awards for excellence will be part of your training motivation. Self-study is also part of the Campbell training program.

QUALIFICATIONS

Campbell's hires from every degree area and is aggressively recruiting minorities and women. Principal educational areas include engineering, life/physical sciences, computer science, math/statistics, business, accounting, and liberal arts.

RECRUITMENT AND PLACEMENT

Campbell recruits on college and university campuses. You may also contact company headquarters for an interview. Entry-level positions exist throughout the eastern United States, the Midwest, the South and Southwest, and on the West Coast.

SALARY AND BENEFITS

The College Placement Council Salary Survey for September 1986–June 1987 indicates starting salaries for food and beverage processing companies to be $1,834 a month for those with a B.A. degree in nontechnical curricula and $2,301 with a B.A. degree in technical curricula. M.B.A. starting salaries were $3,043 for a nontechnical undergraduate degree and $3,098 for a technical undergraduate degree. Check with the company for more specific salary information. Benefits include life, health, dental, and disability insurances, day-care and fitness centers at general offices, pension and savings plans, and educational opportunities.

CONTACT

Manager-Employment, Campbell Soup Company, Campbell Place, Camden, NJ 08101.

CENTRAL BANCORPORATION

COMMERCIAL LENDING • RETAIL MANAGEMENT • TRUST BANKING

THE COMPANY

The Central Bancorporation is one of the largest bank holding companies in the state of Ohio. With assets well over $4.5 billion, Central Bancorporation affiliates are organized into five regional Ohio banks, two Kentucky banks, a Kentucky bank holding company, a mortgage company, a real estate holding company, and a reinsurance company.

ALL TRAINING PROGRAMS

After interviews to determine aptitude, the Management Associates Program prepares new employees for one of three tracks: commercial lending, retail management, or trust. Each of the three areas provides a training sequence for its associates. On-the-job training and seminar instruction give an overview of the major divisions of the bank. You will spend one to two years as an associate in the program, depending on your academic background, rate of development, and available opportunities.

QUALIFICATIONS

Your degree and course of study in college may or may not have a direct application to a career in banking. The company is interested in your record of achievement in your major, in your extracurricular activities, and in any previous work experience. The diverse roles and responsibilities in banking today demand that personnel contribute a diversity of talents, backgrounds, and skills.

RECRUITMENT AND PLACEMENT

Central Bancorporation recruits at colleges and universities throughout the tristate area of Ohio, Kentucky, and Indiana. Most often, candidates will be placed in Greater Cincinnati.

SALARY AND BENEFITS

Your starting salary will range from $19,000 to $24,000, depending upon your degree, previous work experience, and type of position. A comprehensive benefits package is offered to all full-time employees, including dental, vision, and medical coverage, a retirement plan, and tuition reimbursement program, among other benefits.

CONTACT

Coordinator of College Recruiting, The Central Bancorporation, Fifth and Main Streets, Cincinnati, OH 45202.

CENTRAL INTELLIGENCE AGENCY

ANALYSIS AND RESEARCH • FOREIGN SERVICE

THE COMPANY

"The Company" is also the intelligence community's nickname for the Central Intelligence Agency, America's largest official collector and analyzer of information abroad. The agency says its positions are for "venturesome people who wouldn't be content with an ordinary job."

The CIA was established after World War II to coordinate the numerous intelligence efforts of the United States Government and to collect, evaluate, and analyze foreign intelligence. Prior to the war, intelligence gathering was a function of several agencies, and among other shortcomings, their poor coordination allowed the Japanese to launch their assault on Pearl Harbor without the foreknowledge of the United States. President Harry Truman oversaw the creation of the CIA, which is prohibited in its charter from most domestic intelligence gathering. The agency is under the direct authority of the President and releases only very general information about its structure to the public for security reasons.

ALL TRAINING PROGRAMS

The agency does not make its training program content public. It does note, however, that applicants for foreign service work undergo eighteen to twenty-four months of extensive classroom and supervised field training before assignment to regular posts. Courses are taught both on site in the Washington, D.C., headquarters and at leading universities throughout the United States.

ANALYSIS AND RESEARCH PROGRAM

QUALIFICATIONS

Candidates need to have or be actively pursuing a graduate degree. The agency wants to see good research and writing skills. Specific academic areas of interest are economics, foreign area studies, earth sciences, engineering, operations research, physics, mathematics, and the social sciences. U.S. citizenship and a medical exam are required.

FOREIGN SERVICE PROGRAM

QUALIFICATIONS

Foreign service officers serve almost half of their careers abroad. You'll need strong academic achievement, plus maturity and good writing skills. U.S. citizenship and medical exam are required. The agency also wants good foreign-language skills or aptitudes and a strong interest in foreign affairs, as shown by academic study or meaningful, extended experience abroad. You should be people-oriented, attracted to a life abroad, and able to deal effectively with people at all levels of a foreign culture.

ALL PROGRAMS

RECRUITMENT AND PLACEMENT

Arrange an interview through your college placement office, or send your résumé plus any pertinent transcripts or writing samples directly to the agency. Research and analysis positions are located at the CIA headquarters in Langley, Virginia, near Washington, D.C. Foreign service positions are assigned all over the world, depending upon your cultural and language skills and your suitability for specific situations.

SALARY AND BENEFITS

Starting salaries for research and analysis positions range from $18,358 to about $37,000 (GS-7 to GS-13). Starting salaries for foreign service officers range from $18,358 to $27,172 (GS-7 to GS-11). Increases for each level must be passed by Congress. Benefits include life and health insurance, retirement and leave programs, opportunities for further academic study with tuition paid, and government-sponsored language training.

CONTACT

Central Intelligence Agency, Department A, Room 821, P.O. Box 1925, Washington, DC 20013.

CHAMPION INTERNATIONAL CORPORATION

ACCOUNTING • ADMINISTRATION • BUSINESS • COMPUTER SERVICES • ENGINEERING • FINANCE • MARKETING • INSURANCE • PRODUCTION • SALES

THE COMPANY

Champion produces paper for all types of products that we use daily, including shopping bags, 20 of America's top-circulation magazines, milk cartons, direct mail brochures, and lumber and plywood for home construction. With more than 6.5 million acres of U.S. timberland and subsidiaries in Canada and Brazil, Champion is one of America's largest landholders. It has sales of more than $4 billion. It employs 27,000 people at over 400 locations in the United States, Canada, and overseas. The company is among *Fortune*'s most admired corporations and is 86 in the Fortune 500 largest U.S. industrial corporations.

ALL TRAINING PROGRAMS

Champion emphasizes on-the-job training for all positions, hiring only for jobs that actually exist rather than creating a pool of trainees to move into future slots. Formal instruction supplements on-the-job training, along with involvement in staff decision-making sessions and personal career counseling.

QUALIFICATIONS

Champion is looking for college graduates with the following degrees: wood technology, forestry, industrial management, accounting, business, chemistry, quality control, and engineering (mechanical, industrial, electrical, and chemical).

RECRUITMENT AND PLACEMENT

Champion recruiters visit college campuses to interview promising candidates, but you may also send a letter of interest and résumé directly to headquarters for consideration. Major employment centers are in the Hamilton-Cincinnati, Ohio, area; Pasadena–East Texas area; Canton-Asheville, North Carolina; Missoula, Montana; and Courtland, Alabama.

SALARY AND BENEFITS

The College Placement Council Salary Survey for September 1986–June 1987 indicates starting salaries for glossy paper, packaging, and allied product companies to be $1,865 a month for those with a B.A. degree in nontechnical curricula and $2,401 with a B.A. degree in technical curricula. M.B.A. starting salaries were $2,945 for a nontechnical undergraduate degree and $2,775 for a technical undergraduate degree. Check with the company for more specific salary information. Champion salaries are supplemented by basic benefits plus stock-purchase plan, educational assistance, and a credit union.

CONTACT

Manager College Relations, Department 204, Champion International Corporation, One Champion Plaza, Stamford, CT 06921.

CHAMPION SPARK PLUG COMPANY

ENGINEERING

THE COMPANY

Champion has capitalized on its strengths and diversified into related and nonrelated industries to establish itself as a multinational company grossing more than $800 million a year. Begun in Boston in 1907, Champion is now the world's largest spark plug company with manufacturing facilities in four U.S. cities, as well as Canada, England, Ireland, Belgium, South Africa, New Zealand, Australia, Mexico, and Venezuela. Headquarters are in Toledo, Ohio. Subsidiaries include the Anderson Company, maker of ANCO-brand windshield wiper blades; the DeVilbiss Company, a world leader in coating application equipment; the DeVilbiss Health Care Division, developer and manufacturer of respiratory and cardiopulmonary therapy equipment; Baron Drawn Steel Corporation; and Morenci Engineered Rubber Products. Champion also uses the trade name Ceraform for a line of ceramic products intended to replace corrodible metallic components. It currently has about 12,500 employees and ranks number 332 in the Fortune 500 largest U.S. industrial corporations.

ENGINEERING TRAINING PROGRAM

Champion will orient you to your new duties with informal, on-the-job training. Expect to be rotated to assignments within your division to work alongside experienced personnel in related departments for a period of approximately three months.

QUALIFICATIONS

You should have a degree in one of the following disciplines: chemistry; or chemical, electrical, ceramic, or mechanical engineering. Champion will look for a strong G.P.A. and solid analytical ability.

RECRUITMENT AND PLACEMENT

You should send a résumé to Champion or one of its subsidiaries for further information about its current needs. Company locations are primarily in the Midwest, but factory sites also exist around the United States.

SALARY AND BENEFITS

The College Placement Council Salary Survey for September 1986–June 1987 indicates starting salaries for automotive and mechanical equipment companies to be $1,907 a month for those with a B.A. degree in nontechnical curricula and $2,333 with a B.A. degree in technical curricula. M.B.A. starting salaries were $2,697 for a nontechnical undergraduate degree and $2,986 for a technical undergraduate degree. Check with the company for more specific salary information. Champion offers attractive benefits that are competitive with others in industry.

CONTACT

Manager—Personnel Relations, Corporate Personnel Relations Department, Champion Spark Plug Company, P.O. Box 910, Toledo, OH 43661.

CHASE MANHATTAN BANK
MANAGEMENT

THE COMPANY

Chase, once the country's largest bank, is now third behind BankAmerica and Citibank. Chase Manhattan's roots go all the way back to 1799, when Aaron Burr and others created the Manhattan Company to supply New York City with pure water during a yellow fever epidemic. Through Burr's skillful maneuvering, the Manhattan was able to open banking operations on Wall Street a few months after it began as a water company. In 1955 the Bank of Manhattan (which the Manhattan Company was then called), the nation's fifteenth largest bank, merged with the Chase National Bank, then the world's largest and under the control of the Rockefellers. Even though the 1970s were a rough time for Chase (they lost ground to aggressive Citibank and BankAmerica and were plagued by a number of bad loans), it remains a powerful international banking force with its global network of financial institutions covering 130 countries with more than 300 branches, nearly 50 major subsidiaries, and 6,000 correspondent banks. Long known as the "banker's bank," Chase primarily serves other banks, big corporations, and governments. The bank is especially known for its international lending activities and its ratio of nonperforming assets remains above that of its peers. The expense of acquiring several banks from outside the New York area temporarily depressed earnings in 1987, although analysts expect these purchases to pay off in the future. The bank provides services on the West Coast through the Chase Manhattan National Bank of California, operating from Newport Beach with branches in La Jolla, Palo Alto, and Walnut Creek. It has assets in excess of $94 billion and appears in *Fortune*'s listing of most admired corporations.

EXECUTIVE MANAGEMENT TRAINING PROGRAM

Chase's Executive Management Program prepares trainees for management positions in commercial banking. After a one-week orientation you'll start the one- to three-month training program. The classroom part will cover topics such as banking, financial analysis, and corporate finance. On-the-job training in one department (wholesale, international, commercial, institutional, Wall Street, operations, credit audit, or treasury) will familiarize you with Chase's systems and procedures and prepare you to assume the responsibilities of your first assignment. The length of the program varies with your experience and the type of training you receive.

QUALIFICATIONS

The bank is looking for trainees with degrees in business, liberal arts, or social sciences. You must be interested in banking as a career and be willing to work hard and learn the business. If you have a few years in banking or other related financial experience, Chase may consider you for the program.

RECRUITMENT AND PLACEMENT

Chase typically selects 100 to 125 persons a year for its program. You may work in the New York City headquarters or in any of its 300 branches. A lucky few are chosen to train in the London and Hong Kong branches.

SALARY AND BENEFITS

The College Placement Council Salary Survey for September 1986–June 1987 indicates starting salaries for banking, finance, and insurance firms to be $1,889 a month for those with a B.A. degree in nontechnical curricula and $2,135 with a B.A. degree in technical curricula. M.B.A. starting salaries were $2,884 for a nontechnical undergraduate degree, and $3,320 for an M.B.A. with technical undergraduate degree. Check with the company for more specific salary information. Chase offers medical and dental plans and savings incentive plans as part of its benefits package. Money is available for relocation expenses, and Chase reimburses for work-related courses.

CONTACT

Vice-President and Manager of Professional Recruitment, Chase Manhattan Bank, One Chase Manhattan Plaza, New York, NY 10081.

CHEVRON/GULF

ACCOUNTING • COMPUTER SERVICES • ENGINEERING • EXPLORATION • FINANCE • INDUSTRIAL RELATIONS • MANUFACTURING • MARKETING • PRODUCTION • RESEARCH • SALES

THE COMPANY

With the merger in 1984 of Chevron and Gulf, two powerful companies combined their resources. The new company is one of the top three energy producers in the nation, employing workers in 90 countries. The company is involved in petroleum exploration and production efforts as well as the exploration and production of alternative mineral resources. It also develops agricultural chemicals and synthetic fibers. Listed among *Fortune*'s most admired corporations, it ranks number 10 in the Fortune 500 largest U.S. industrial corporations.

ALL TRAINING PROGRAMS

Chevron emphasizes on-the-job training for most positions, augmented by formal instruction. For careers in finance, industrial relations, marketing, and accounting, you will participate in a one- to two-year program composed of rotational assignments aimed at giving you a wide variety of experience. In-house programs and workshops will develop your supervisory and management, business, and communications skills.

QUALIFICATIONS

You should have a bachelor's degree in engineering (civil, electrical, mechanical, or petroleum), computer science, earth science, chemistry, or business administration. Most entry-level positions require little or no prior experience.

RECRUITMENT AND PLACEMENT

You will be able to meet with a Chevron recruiter on college campuses around the country. Chevron locations are found throughout the world.

SALARY AND BENEFITS

The College Placement Council Salary Survey for September 1986–June 1987 indicates starting salaries for petroleum and allied products (including natural gas) companies to be $1,972 a month for those with a B.A. degree in nontechnical curricula and $2,497 with a B.A. degree in technical curricula. M.B.A. starting salaries were $2,629 for a nontechnical undergraduate degree and $2,970 for a technical undergraduate degree. Check with the company for more specific salary information. Benefits include medical, dental, and life insurance; long-term disability insurance; a stock-purchase plan; tuition reimbursement; annuity plan; and liberal vacations.

CONTACT

Professional Employment Manager, Chevron, P.O. Box 3495, San Francisco, CA 94119.

CHICAGO AND NORTH WESTERN TRANSPORTATION COMPANY

ADMINISTRATION • FINANCE • INFORMATION SYSTEMS AND PROCESSING • PRODUCTION • TECHNICAL SERVICES

THE COMPANY

The Chicago and North Western Transportation Company is the ninth largest freight railroad, a principal link in the central transcontinental freight corridor and a major shipper of coal and grain. The railroad operates 7,500 miles in an 11-state Midwestern region, employing approximately 10,000 people. It ranks number 23 in the Fortune 50 largest U.S. transportation corporations.

ALL TRAINING PROGRAMS

Training prepares new employees for positions in production, technical services, information systems and processing, and administration and finance. The six-month program includes both classroom instruction and on-the-job training.

QUALIFICATIONS

The company is looking for college graduates from the fields of computer science, statistics, and the following engineering specilizations: civil, electrical, electronics, industrial, mechanical, and transportation. It is also interested in people with one to ten years of related experience.

RECRUITMENT AND PLACEMENT

Starting locations are in Illinois, Iowa, Michigan, Minnesota, Missouri, Nebraska, South Dakota, Wisconsin, and Wyoming.

SALARY AND BENEFITS

The College Placement Council Salary Survey for September 1986–June 1987 indicates starting salaries for public utilities (including transportation) to be $1,905 a month for those with a B.A. degree in nontechnical curricula and $2,355 with a B.A. degree in technical curricula. M.B.A. starting salaries were $2,403 for a nontechnical undergraduate degree and $2,667 for a technical undergraduate degree. Check with the company for more specific salary information.

CONTACT

Assistant Vice-President—Personnel Services, Chicago and North Western Transportation Company, One North Western Center, Chicago, IL 60606.

CHUBB GROUP OF INSURANCE COMPANIES

ACTUARIAL SERVICES AND OPERATIONS • CLAIMS • UNDERWRITING

THE COMPANY

Established as an insurer of sailing ships in 1882, Chubb wrote the first war-risk policies during the Spanish-American War. Today, besides insuring more common ventures, it continues to insure unique and unusual risks, such as the three dolphins in the movie *Day of the Dolphin* and the ten seagulls that were trained for the lead in *Jonathan Livingston Seagull.* Chubb's parent organization (The Chubb Corporation) ranks number 28 in the Fortune 50 largest diversified financial organizations in the United States. It has $7 billion plus in assets, and $3 billion plus in annual revenues. Chubb makes an effort to give back to society through a matching gifts program, community outreach efforts, and vigorous support of public broadcasting. Employees describe Chubb as a "very conservative" company. In setting up personal insurance policies, Chubb agents establish an agreed value concept with customers that in effect settles a claim for a total loss before it occurs. This applies especially to unusual items such as art and collectibles whose values might be difficult to determine. Chubb does no direct selling; all of its business comes through 3,000 independent agents and brokers, served by 6,800 people in 50 branch offices in the United States and Canada.

ALL TRAINING PROGRAMS

Chubb offers individualized training through specific courses and, occasionally, a progression of job assignments. Informal performance review is a continuing process. Formal evaluations of your progress occur at least once a year.

ACTUARIAL AND OPERATIONS PROGRAM

As an actuarial trainee, you learn to solve business problems, develop profit opportunities, and make recommendations to line managers. In operations, you learn to perform the processing functions of recording information for senior management decisions. Training in the actuarial department is a combination of on-the-job experience and professional education through the Casualty Actuarial Society. You will work on a variety of projects and come into contact with many people in the company. Operations trainees start by spending a short time in each of the five operations sections. You spend time within the major underwriting groups and will be assigned a problem-solving project. After about six to eight months you will be eligible to supervise six to eight people.

QUALIFICATIONS

An actuary should be business-oriented, with instinctive mathematical abilities and training supported by strong communication skills. There is no single educational background or particular degree needed to succeed in operations. You should be people-oriented, innovative, decisive, responsible, and accomplished in a variety of interests.

CLAIMS PROGRAM

You spend about one year learning to be a claims adjuster. Three months are spent in each major claims area: property, liability, and worker's compensation. The last three months are spent in a supervised claims adjusting position. In addition to training seminars, programmed instruction, and written texts, a major portion of your training is on the job.

QUALIFICATIONS

Chubb hires people from all academic backgrounds. You should be capable, have good interpersonal skills, and possess the ability to make decisions, delegate authority, and exercise good judgment.

UNDERWRITING PROGRAM

First you are assigned to a specific underwriting department where, under the guidance of your supervisor, you begin to assume underwriting duties. In addition to this on-the-job training, you attend classes once or twice a week to learn insurance techniques as well as Chubb's particular philosophy and approach. After about six months you participate in a two-week home office seminar. Opportunities also exist for candidates with an international orientation as international underwriters. Underwriting surveyors become well-rounded safety experts.

QUALIFICATIONS

Rather than requiring a particular undergraduate degree, Chubb looks for people with a record of personal and academic achievement. You should have a business orientation and a desire to succeed. Candidates should show good judgment and strong interpersonal skills.

ALL PROGRAMS

RECRUITMENT AND PLACEMENT

Chubb recruits nationwide, selecting nearly 200 new trainees a year. If you contact the company directly, submit a résumé. You could be placed in any of Chubb's offices throughout the country.

SALARY AND BENEFITS

The College Placement Council Salary Survey for September 1986–June 1987 indicates starting salaries for banking, finance, and insurance firms to be $1,889 a month for those with a B.A. degree in nontechnical curricula and $2,135 with a B.A. degree in technical curricula. M.B.A. starting salaries were $2,884 for a nontechnical undergraduate degree, and $3,320 for an M.B.A. with technical undergraduate degree. Check with the company for more specific salary information. Benefits include medical, life, and travel accident insurance; profit sharing; tuition assistance; and a pension plan.

CONTACT

National Recruiting Coordinator, Chubb Headquarters, 15 Mountain View Road, P.O. Box 1615, Warren, NJ 07061-1615.

CIBA-GEIGY CORPORATION

BIOLOGY • BUSINESS • COMPUTER SCIENCE • ENGINEERING • SALES

THE COMPANY

CIBA-GEIGY is involved in the research, manufacture, and marketing of pharmaceuticals, agricultural chemicals, dyestuffs, pigments, additives, epoxy resins, and specialty chemicals. It employs 13,000 in the United States and 70,000 worldwide. Established by a merger in 1970, it is a wholly owned subsidiary of CIBA-GEIGY Limited, a publicly owned company headquartered in Basel, Switzerland. The seventh largest specialty chemical company in the world, the company consistently outspends several of its larger competitors in research investment.

ALL TRAINING PROGRAMS

Training prepares new employees for a variety of positions in research and development, production, and technical sales. The training program for chemists is a combination of on-the-job and classroom instruction lasting six to twelve months. You may participate in degree programs developed with leading universities, as well as periodic seminars and workshops.

QUALIFICATIONS

The company is looking for graduates with bachelor's or master's degrees in biology, chemistry, computer science, business, and information science. It is especially interested in those who rank in the top 30 percent of their class and have a G.P.A. of 3.5.

RECRUITMENT AND PLACEMENT

CIBA-GEIGY welcomes résumés sent directly to the company. It hires from 45 to 90 applicants a year. You will begin work in New Jersey, New York, or North Carolina.

SALARY AND BENEFITS

The College Placement Council Salary Survey for September 1986–June 1987 indicates starting salaries for chemical, drug, and allied products companies to be $1,964 a month for those with a B.A. degree in nontechnical curricula and $2,457 with a B.A. degree in technical curricula. M.B.A. starting salaries were $2,886 for a nontechnical undergraduate degree and $2,794 for a technical undergraduate degree. Check with the company for more specific salary information. Benefits include life insurance, medical, hospital, dental, pension, and savings plans; a career development program; relocation assistance; and flextime options. Tuition reimbursement of up to 75 percent is an additional benefit.

CONTACT

Corporate: Susan Santura, Personnel Administrator, Ciba-Geigy Corp., 444 Saw Mill River Road, Ardsley, NY 10502; Agricultural Division and Dyes & Chemicals Division: Jeff Owens, Supervisor of Employment and EEO, Ciba-Geigy Corp., P.O. Box 18300, Greensboro, NC 27419; Plastics and Additives: Janet Krikorian, Manager, Professional Employment and Relocation, Ciba-Geigy Corp., 3 Skyline Drive, Hawthorne, NY 10532; or Pharmaceuticals: Suzanne Matteson, Director, Staffing, Ciba-Geigy Corp., 556 Morris Avenue, Summit, NJ 07901.

CIGNA CORPORATION

ACCOUNTING · ACTUARIAL SERVICES · ADMINISTRATION · DATA PROCESSING · HUMAN RESOURCES · MANAGEMENT · SALES · UNDERWRITING

THE COMPANY

Formed from the merger of INA Corporation and Connecticut General in 1982, CIGNA Corporation provides worldwide business insurance. The breakdown of traditional boundaries between the functions of financial institutions—banks, insurance companies, and brokerage companies—has significantly changed the way CIGNA does business. The company has assets exceeding $50 billion and can provide virtually any insurance or financial coverage for its clients on a worldwide basis. Annual revenues top $17 billion a year. Listed among *Fortune*'s most admired corporations, it ranks number 6 in the Fortune largest U.S. diversified financial corporations. CIGNA has over 47,000 employees in 160 countries on five continents.

Subsidiaries include Connecticut General Life Insurance, Insurance Company of North America, Life Insurance Company of North America, INA Life Insurance, CIGNA Worldwide, Inc., CIGNA Healthplan, Inc., and the Horace Mann companies. The company's Employee Benefits and Health Care Group (EB&HC) ranks among the top five U.S. providers of group life and health programs. The Group Insurance and Services Division provides medical and dental coverage and life insurance products to single- and multi-employer groups, unions, and associations ranging in size from a few individuals to Fortune 100 companies with as many as 300,000 employees.

EB&HC's Group Pension Division provides full investment and administrative support for pension, profit-sharing, and retirement savings plans. CIGNA occupies a unique position in the insurance industry as a major provider of both indemnity and health maintenance organization (HMO) plans. The development, acquisition, and operation of CIGNA's health-care delivery operation are managed through the Affiliated Businesses Group (ABG), another segment of the EB&HC Group.

CIGNA Healthplan, Inc., the nation's largest investor-owned operator of prepaid health plans, operates health maintenance organizations in a number of states, providing service to more than 750,00 people. Through the formation of CIGNA Dental Health, Inc., CIGNA became one of the first major commercial insurance organizations to enter the prepaid dental field. ABG's Intracorp operation is a worldwide leader in the rehabilitation of injured workers.

Another division of EB&HC, the Life Insurance Company of North America (LINA), is the world's largest underwriter of accidental death insurance. As one of only two organizations in the United States able to combine domestic and overseas capabilities, CIGNA's Property and Casualty Group (P&C) delivers global service in the management of commercial risks, both large and small. CIGNA's Investment Group is ranked as the nation's fourth largest operation in terms of total assets managed.

The company makes a commitment to the communities it serves through sponsorship of such events as the Sunset Sounds Concerts in Hartford, Connecticut. CIGNA works hard to create an environment that attracts, motivates, develops, and retains high-quality people.

ALL TRAINING PROGRAMS

A training program in one of CIGNA's many divisions could last from one to nine months. Many professional training programs, seminars, and management conferences are held at Eagle Lodge Conference Center, a multimillion-dollar complex in suburban Philadelphia. Similar programs are available in Hartford training facilities as well as in learning centers throughout the CIGNA field office network. Tuition aid and professional education programs enable you to pursue academic, career-related courses outside the company. CIGNA offers a full range of development courses and programs to enhance career growth.

QUALIFICATIONS

CIGNA carefully assesses and selects new employees. It seeks accountants, actuaries, associate analyst programmers, claims representatives, financial analysts, and engineers with bachelor's degrees. It seeks new M.B.A.s as financial, investment, marketing, and strategic planning analysts. It also employs marine insurance trainees, sales personnel, and underwriters. Liberal arts majors with a solid academic background are also welcome. Business experience will be a plus in many positions.

RECRUITMENT AND PLACEMENT

Each year CIGNA hires about 100 of 5,000 interviewed with bachelor's degrees and 20 of 1,000 with master's degrees. Starting locations are in Connecticut, New Jersey, and Pennsylvania. Offices are located across the country. The location of your first CIGNA position depends upon the functional area in which you start. If your first assignment is with EB&HC, you would begin working in the Hartford area. Corporate headquarters are in Philadelphia. The possibility of relocation after your initial assignment depends upon performance, available positions, and your career direction.

SALARY AND BENEFITS

The College Placement Council Salary Survey for September 1986–June 1987 indicates starting salaries for banking, finance, and insurance firms to be $1,889 a month for those with a B.A. degree in nontechnical curricula and $2,135 with a B.A. degree in technical curricula. M.B.A. starting salaries were $2,884 for a nontechnical undergraduate degree, and $3,320 for an M.B.A. with technical undergraduate degree. Check with the company for more specific salary information. Benefits are generous and include all types of insurance, disability income, pension, and 401K plans.

CONTACT

Manager of Corporate University Relations, CIGNA Corporation, N-87, Hartford, CT 06152; or Manager of Corporate University Relations, CIGNA Corporation, 1600 Arch Street, 11 Pennwalt, Philadelphia, PA 19103.

CINCINNATI MILACRON, INC.

PRODUCTION • RESEARCH AND DEVELOPMENT • SALES • TECHNICAL SERVICES

THE COMPANY

Begun in 1884 as Cincinnati Screw & Tap Company, Cincinnati Milacron has produced manufacturing machinery since its beginning. For many years its chief engineer was Sol Einstein, cousin of Albert Einstein. During the 1950s the company expanded into electronics, and in the 1960s it moved into plastics-processing machinery. In 1977, Milacron started selling its first industrial robots. It ranks among the top U.S. sellers of robots, with competition from such large corporations as IBM, General Electric, Bendix, General Motors, and Westinghouse Electric Corporation as well as European and Japanese companies. Milacron plans to design and sell flexible manufacturing systems (FMS) incorporating a variety of stand-alone machines and robots—for the factory of the future. Milacron's materials-handling robot, called the T3-363, shook up the competition in 1985 when it came out at half the price of previous models—$30,000. The company's annual sales total more than $800,000, making Cincinnati Milacron number 339 in the Fortune 500 largest U.S. industrial corporations.

ALL TRAINING PROGRAMS

Training prepares new employees for positions in production, research and development, sales, and technical services. The program combines on-the-job assignments and classroom instruction for the first nine months of employment. Working under an experienced supervisor, you will be introduced to departmental and company operations and provided with the background information required to perform your first assignment successfully.

QUALIFICATIONS

Cincinnati Milacron hires 14–18 graduates a year in computer science, electrical engineering, electronics engineering, manufacturing engineering, materials science, mechanical engineering, systems engineering, and business. Personnel with three to ten years' experience are also encouraged to apply.

PLACEMENT

Your first assignment will be in Massachusetts, Ohio, or South Carolina.

SALARY AND BENEFITS

With a bachelor's degree, your starting salary will be in the low to mid-twenties. The College Placement Council Salary Survey for September 1986–June 1987 indicates starting salaries for electrical and electronic machine and equipment companies to be $1,861 a month for those with a B.A. degree in nontechnical curricula and $2,419 with a B.A. degree in technical curricula. M.B.A. starting salaries were $2,784 for a nontechnical undergraduate degree and $2,818 for a technical undergraduate degree. Check with the company for more specific salary information. The benefits package consists of medical, hospital, dental, pension, stock-purchase, and profit-sharing plans, as well as tuition reimbursement.

CONTACT

Manager, Educational Relations, Cincinnati Milacron, Inc., 4701 Marburg Avenue, Cincinnati, OH 45209.

CITICORP

BANKING MANAGEMENT

THE COMPANY

Citicorp, the first bank holding company, was formed in 1968 by Citibank, originally called First National City Bank of New York. Citibank is a tiger in the banking world, an innovator and fierce competitor. The list of "firsts" and "mosts" for this corporation is impressive: first U.S. national bank to go into the foreign market; movers and shakers behind the first transatlantic telegraph cable; first commercial bank to offer personal loans to consumers; largest U.S. bank overseas; originator of the certificate of deposit. This is a bank that bankrolls governments and huge industrial projects. At the same time it dominates New York State banking. The Citibank Visa and MasterCard credit card operation, headquartered in North Dakota to avoid New York's tougher usury laws, has garnered a strong national share of U.S. credit card business. Citibank holds 4 percent of all the money on deposit with U.S. banks—one dollar of every 25. Citicorp is one of the top three dealers in United States Government securities, a market maker and distributor of a wide variety of debt instruments worldwide. In 1985 the company spent approximately $50 million on new systems and technology, and plans to spend more in years to come. With more than $196 billion in assets, its net income each year is more than $1 billion. Listed among *Fortune*'s most admired corporations, Citicorp is number 1 among the Fortune 100 largest commercial banking companies.

Citicorp's other businesses include Carte Blanche, Nationwide Financial Services, Citicorp Leasing (aircraft and heavy equipment), and numerous consumer finance companies in Europe, Asia, and Latin America. It acquired the financial quotation service Quotron in 1986.

The staff is made up of 45,800 employees in the United States and almost 40,000 overseas. Relatively few Americans work outside the United States. Citicorp has approximately 2,600 locations, including branch banks, and affiliate offices in 41 states and the District of Columbia, and 91 other countries throughout the world. The atmosphere is highly competitive and employees are encouraged to develop new jobs for themselves as they perceive unfilled needs in the organization.

MANAGEMENT TRAINING PROGRAM

Although some observers say the company leaves off the frills in its training, preferring to weed out the swimmers from the nonswimmers by performance, you will receive on-the-job training with periodic workshops. Training may include computer simulations, small-group case studies, and question-and-answer sessions with senior management. Skills training focuses on computer literacy, systems, interpersonal, and management issues. Training lasts twelve to twenty-four months, and up to 100 percent tuition and fee reimbursement is possible for job-related graduate study.

QUALIFICATIONS

This company wants people who are aggressive and smart, not just content to pull in a paycheck but also able to keep Citicorp on the leading edge of continual expansion through boldness and innovation. You will be pushed hard for performance, but this is the kind of company that rewards it.

Citibank looks for bachelor's or master's degrees in computer science, information systems, software engineering, B.S., M.B.A. with technical B.S., and liberal arts.

Citicorp looks for B.B.A. degrees, with preference for management or marketing, or M.B.A.s.

RECRUITMENT AND PLACEMENT

Citicorp has locations all over the United States. Citibank starts trainees in New York City but makes international assignments of U.S. citizens with one to five years' experience. Citicorp has a very active campus recruitment system, but a large number of applicants are hired from write-ins, walk-ins, or personal referrals. The company has a strong minorities hiring policy, and 49 percent of employees are female.

SALARY AND BENEFITS

Citicorp aims to make its salaries some of the highest in banking. Average annual starting salaries with a bachelor's degree are in the low twenties; with a master's degree, about $30,000. Benefits include free banking services, a retirement plan, and a company store that sells a variety of merchandise at discount (mail order available).

CONTACT

Recruiting Manager, Citicorp Investment Bank, Citicorp Center, 153 East 53rd Street—6th Floor, New York, NY 10043.

THE CLOROX COMPANY

BUYING • FINANCE/ACCOUNTING • MANAGEMENT • MANUFACTURING • MARKETING • MARKETING RESEARCH • RESEARCH AND DEVELOPMENT • TRAFFIC

THE COMPANY

Based in Oakland, California, The Clorox Company is a diversified manufacturer and marketer of a wide range of consumer products. In addition to liquid bleach (its only product until 1969), the company's retail consumer products business includes household products and specialty foods. Some of the company's nonfood brands are Clorox 2 dry bleach, Formula 409 all-purpose cleaner, Liquid-plumr drain opener, Kingsford charcoal briquets, and Duraflame fireplace logs. Specialty food products include Hidden Valley Ranch salad dressing mixes, Kitchen Bouquet gravy-seasoning sauce, and B in B mushrooms. The Clorox Company expects to expand through the introduction of new products developed internally and through acquisitions. It currently has more than 50 manufacturing, distribution, and administration facilities in the United States, Puerto Rico, Canada, and England. Listed among *Fortune*'s most admired corporations, Clorox ranks number 282 in the Fortune 500 largest U.S. industrial corporations.

ALL TRAINING PROGRAMS

You will receive on-the-job training combined with in-house training courses covering a wide range of technical and managerial subjects. Buyers will be part of a management development program. Production supervisors will be rotated through various assignments to prepare them for plant manager positions.

QUALIFICATIONS

Clorox is looking for graduates with backgrounds in mechanical, chemical, civil, industrial, and electrical engineering; chemistry, accounting and finance; marketing; biochemistry; computer science; microbiology; and business (both B.S. and M.B.A.).

RECRUITMENT AND PLACEMENT

The company recruits nationally. Starting positions are available in California, Florida, Georgia, Illinois, Kansas, Kentucky, Maryland, Missouri, Nevada, New Jersey, North Carolina, Ohio, Oregon, Pennsylvania, Texas, West Virginia, and Wisconsin.

SALARY AND BENEFITS

With a B.A., starting salaries are in the $23,000 to $27,000 range, and with a master's, a few thousand dollars more. Benefits include a comprehensive medical and dental plan, group life and disability insurance, a stock-purchase and profit-sharing plan, an educational assistance program, and pension plan.

CONTACT

College Relations Coordinator, The Clorox Company, P.O. Box 24305, Oakland, CA 94623.

COASTAL GROUP, INC.

ACCOUNTING • MANAGEMENT • MARKETING

THE COMPANY

Coastal Group, Inc., is a privately owned group of corporations providing physician staffing services to hospitals and communities since 1975. Coastal has twelve regional offices in the South with several more planned. Individual corporations within the umbrella include Coastal Emergency Services, Inc., Coastal Physician Services, Inc., Medstaff, Inc., Sunlife Ob/Gyn Services, Inc., Medbill, Inc., and Medcollect, Inc. These companies provide temporary physicians for hospitals, emergency rooms, or short-staffed practices, and handle billing and payment collection for physicians and hospitals. This is a growing firm with many opportunities for advancement.

ALL TRAINING PROGRAMS

Training for all positions is provided by senior-level management at corporate headquarters in Durham, North Carolina. You will be trained in one of three areas: regional operations management, new business development, or financial management.

QUALIFICATIONS

Coastal wants college graduates with strong academic records. Health-care experience is not a prerequisite. To go into financial management, you will need an accounting background. Degrees in business or marketing will qualify you for regional operations management or new business development positions. Extensive travel will be part of your job as regional operations manager or for new business development.

RECRUITMENT AND PLACEMENT

Coastal representatives conduct interviews regularly on college campuses. Regional offices are currently located in the cities of Asheville, Atlanta, Augusta, Charlotte, Columbia, Columbus, Dallas, Durham, Fort Lauderdale, Memphis, Richmond, and Washington.

SALARY AND BENEFITS

The College Placement Council Salary Survey for September 1986–June 1987 indicates starting salaries for merchandising (retail and wholesale) and service companies to be $1,594 a month for those with a B.A. degree in nontechnical curricula and $2,141 with a B.A. degree in technical curricula. M.B.A. starting salaries were $2,572 for a nontechnical undergraduate degree and $2,735 for an M.B.A. with technical undergraduate degree. Check with the company for more specific salary and benefits information.

CONTACT

Personnel, Coastal Group, Inc., P.O. Box 15697, Durham, NC 27704.

COCA-COLA—FOODS DIVISION

FINANCE • INFORMATION SYSTEMS • SALES/MARKETING

THE COMPANY

Coca-Cola is the leading soft drink business internationally, outselling its nearest competitor by more than three to one outside the United States. The company's second most valuable trademark is Minute Maid, part of the Foods Division lineup. The company actively pursues new product introductions such as Bacardi tropical fruit mixers, and markets through restaurant chains such as Wendy's. Its products include such familiar names as Five Alive, Hi-C, Snow Crop, Ronco pasta, Tab, Fresca, Maryland Club Coffee, and Belmont Springs bottled water. Coca-Cola is listed among *Fortune*'s most admired corporations and ranks number 38 in the Fortune 500 listing of largest U.S. industrial corporations.

SALES PROGRAM

If you are convinced that "Coke is it," your entry-level position on the sales career ladder is territory manager. You may begin in the refrigerated products department or the grocery products department. After you are assigned a geographic area, your supervised on-the-job training will include selling store managers on new items, gaining increased shelf space, obtaining local advertising, informing the store manager of company promotional programs, and providing information about the local market condition to Coca-Cola regional management. This practical field experience and supplemental classroom instruction will provide a base for you to move to district sales manager and on up the company ladder.

QUALIFICATIONS

You should have a strong academic record along with good communication skills and a desire to exceed in sales.

SYSTEMS DEVELOPMENT PROGRAMMER PROGRAM

In your initial assignment as a programmer within Coca-Cola's systems development area, you will have many opportunities to use your educational training to develop productive information solutions. You will be developing programs primarily on-line, working with an IBM 30XX mainframe, CICS, programming primarily in COBOL or fourth-generation languages, and using support tools which include ADR Datacom database. As part of the applications staff, you will receive widely varied on-the-job and classroom training, including instruction in Method I, a structured programming methodology.

QUALIFICATIONS

For information management you should have a bachelor's degree in business/computer information curriculum. Coca-Cola looks for candidates with strong academic records and effective oral and written communication skills.

ALL PROGRAMS

RECRUITMENT AND PLACEMENT

Coca-Cola recruits throughout the country and places entry-level employees in metropolitan areas around the United States.

SALARY AND BENEFITS

The College Placement Council Salary Survey for September 1986–June 1987 indicates starting salaries for food and beverage processing companies to be $1,834 a month for those with a B.A. degree in nontechnical curricula and $2,301 with a B.A. degree in technical curricula. M.B.A. starting salaries were $3,043 for a nontechnical undergraduate degree and $3,098 for a technical undergraduate degree. Check with the company for more specific salary information. The company offers a wide variety of benefits, including medical and dental insurance, a survivors protection plan, a savings plan, tuition reimbursement, relocation assistance, a retirement program, and a company car for salespeople.

CONTACT

Manager of Recruiting, The Coca-Cola Company, Foods Division, P.O. Box 2079, Houston, TX 77001.

COLGATE-PALMOLIVE COMPANY

ENGINEERING · FINANCE · MANAGEMENT INFORMATION SYSTEMS · MANUFACTURING · MARKETING · RESEARCH AND DEVELOPMENT · SALES

THE COMPANY

Colgate is the best-selling toothpaste in the world, available even to schoolchildren in Africa. In 1806, William Colgate opened a soap and candle factory in New York City. The company sold toothpaste in jars in 1877 and toothpaste in a tube in 1908. In 1864 soap manufacturer B. J. Johnson began his operation in Milwaukee, and he introduced Palmolive soap in 1898. After World War I these soap companies merged. Currently, Colgate-Palmolive manufactures detergents, dental preparations, soaps, cleaners, sporting goods, leisure clothing, hygienic products for the medical profession and consumer, and industrial products and goods. A forerunner among multinational corporations, Colgate-Palmolive established 16 foreign subsidiaries between 1914 and 1933. More than 60 percent of its sales in a typical year come from outside the United States. The company was one of the first to use mass marketing aggressively. Its international structure and emphasis on promotion from within offer excellent opportunities for advancement to foreign management positions. Colgate-Palmolive emphasizes both career-long employment and a challenging environment for its employees. The company's annual sales are more than $5 billion. Listed among *Fortune*'s most admired corporations, it ranks number 71 in the Fortune 500 largest U.S. industrial corporations.

ALL TRAINING PROGRAMS

Your first assignment will give you hands-on experience and immediate responsibility. Colgate-Palmolive believes in frequent job rotation to create well-rounded employees. In-house seminars and outside classes may augment your training. A select number of applicants will be accepted for the International Marketing Training Program.

CORPORATE MANAGEMENT INFORMATION SYSTEMS PROGRAM

You might begin your career as a programmer, then become a systems analyst. You will learn through in-house educational programs as well as outside courses in special areas. By following your projects through to completion you will learn how the entire process works, rather than specializing in limited areas. Formal career development sessions every six months help lay out possible career steps and developmental activities to help you achieve them. You may follow either a technical or applications-oriented path.

QUALIFICATIONS

The company prefers to hire M.B.A.s and master's-level computer science graduates.

PLACEMENT

You will work in the company's state-of-the-art data center in Piscataway, New Jersey.

MANUFACTURING PROGRAM

Your first assignment will be very much "the real thing." Within certain parameters, you're fully responsible. You must learn to present your conclusions in such a way that senior plant management is convinced of the rightness of your plans. You will likely start in industrial engineering, which teaches you to think in terms of systems and interactions. You will soon develop an understanding of the entire operation: what resources and facilities are available, what some of the particular challenges are, how a change in one place alters procedures in another. Your next assignment might be on the line as foreman, followed by a period in project engineering. You will have hands-on experience, a lot of interaction with people, variety, and a broad role to play.

QUALIFICATIONS

You will need a degree in chemical engineering or related fields. Self-motivation will be an important characteristic to have.

PLACEMENT

Colgate has domestic plants in Kansas City, Kansas; Jersey City, New Jersey; and Jeffersonville, Indiana.

SALES PROGRAM

You will begin as a unit manager under the supervision of an area manager who is responsible for your training. You will work in tandem with customers, making sure that Colgate's products are displayed advantageously and attractively. With wholesalers, your job will be to pass along information about upcoming promotions or new product introductions. You may have as many as 300 accounts, most of them retail—food stores, drugstores, discount stores, and small chains. The sales organization is highly team-oriented. Bonuses go to regions that perform well rather than to individuals. You will be given a sequence of assignments to give you broad exposure to different regions of the country and different types of customers. You will be prepared to supervise and motivate others as you advance.

QUALIFICATIONS

Your degree might be in marketing, economics, or any business-related subject, although Colgate will consider prior experience in selling and a high degree of self-motivation to be equally important.

PLACEMENT

You could work anywhere in the United States.

ALL PROGRAMS

RECRUITMENT

The company recruits nationwide. You may contact the company directly with a letter of interest and résumé.

SALARY AND BENEFITS

Colgate's salary levels are maintained by periodic surveys of competitors. The College Placement Council Salary Survey for September 1986–June 1987 indicates starting salaries for chemical, drug, and allied products companies to be $1,964 a month for those with a B.A. degree in nontechnical curricula and $2,457 with a B.A. degree in technical curricula. M.B.A. starting salaries were $2,886 for a nontechnical undergraduate degree and $2,794 for a technical undergraduate degree. Check with the company for more specific salary information. The company offers a comprehensive benefits package.

CONTACT

Manager, Recruitment and Development, Colgate-Palmolive Company, 300 Park Avenue, New York, NY 10022.

COMERICA, INC.

MANAGEMENT

THE COMPANY

Comerica is a $9.8 billion bank holding company. Comerica provides complete financial services to corporate, consumer, and trust clients through a branch network of 200 offices in Michigan. It also offers consumer and corporate lending services through offices in other cities across the United States. Established in 1849 as the Detroit Bank & Trust Company, it now employs approximately 6,000. It is ranked number 50 in the Fortune 100 largest commercial banking companies.

MANAGEMENT TRAINING PROGRAM

Comerica Bank offers management careers in its Consumer Financial Services Division. This program is designed to provide in-depth training in selling the company's products and services as well as managing all administrative functions within the branch. The six-month training program combines classroom and on-the-job training, and consists of four modules: consumer banking, administrative skills, sales/product information, and supervisory skills. Part of the program is self-study with manuals, audio and videotapes, and computer programs.

QUALIFICATIONS

You will need a bachelor's degree in any of the following: marketing, finance, accounting, economics, or business administration. Since banking is now a sales-driven industry, candidates with previous exposure to basic marketing and sales principles are preferred.

RECRUITMENT AND PLACEMENT

Comerica recruits at major Midwest colleges and universities in the spring and fall. Highest recruitment is usually in the spring. After training in Detroit, you will locate at one of the branches throughout the Detroit metropolitan area.

SALARY AND BENEFITS

Salary ranges from $19,000 to $23,000. The bank offers a flexible compensation program.

CONTACT

Sue Carender, Human Resources Officer, Comerica Incorporated, 211 West Fort Street, Detroit, MI 48275-1235.

COMPUGRAPHIC CORPORATION

COMPUTER DESIGN • SOFTWARE DEVELOPMENT

THE COMPANY

Compugraphic designs, develops, manufactures, markets, and services graphic communications hardware and software, interactive work stations, and phototypesetting equipment. With 14 manufacturing facilities, the company is putting technology to work to solve the most complex problems of computer-aided printing and publishing. Headquartered in Massachusetts, Compugraphic has 4,500 employees in the United States, Ireland, Canada, and Mexico.

COMPUTER DESIGN/SOFTWARE DEVELOPMENT TRAINING PROGRAM

The company is a strong advocate of dual career paths; it provides training that allows employees to progress in either managerial or technical areas. You will begin working immediately in small groups on technical design, software design and development, or hardware design and development. Your supervisor will orient you to company operations and help you develop new skills. In addition, the company offers a liberal tuition reimbursement program (up to $3,000 a year) and in-house technical and/or managerial training.

QUALIFICATIONS

Compugraphic recruits bachelor's- and master's-level graduates in the following areas: computer science, electrical engineering, mathematics, mechanical engineering, and physics.

RECRUITMENT AND PLACEMENT

The company has an extensive college recruitment program. The starting location is in Massachusetts.

SALARY AND BENEFITS

Starting salaries are in the mid-twenties with a bachelor's degree, the high twenties with a master's degree. The extensive benefits package includes medical, life, disability, dental, and travel accident insurance; profit sharing; a retirement program; and a tuition reimbursement program. The company also has a credit union.

CONTACT

College Relations Director, Compugraphic Corporation, 200 Ballardvale Street, Wilmington, MA 01887.

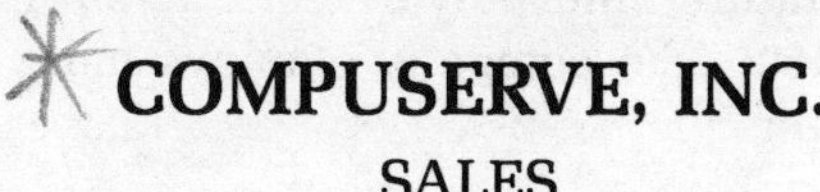

COMPUSERVE, INC.
SALES

THE COMPANY

CompuServe is one of the major information companies and computer networks in the United States. Electronic mail; business and financial databases; home shopping and banking; news, weather, and sports information; and on-line computer networking are some of its services for business, professional, and personal use. Established in 1970, it now has 30 sales offices in major cities and a research and development center in Tucson. The company has acquired 100,000 subscribers and expects to continue rapid subscription growth. Headquartered in Columbus, Ohio, it is a subsidiary of H & R Block. With about 800 employees, CompuServe hires more than 50 trainees a year.

SALES TRAINING PROGRAM

The sales program consists of six months of on-the-job training. Orientation to company practices and services, sales techniques, and support is provided by the immediate supervisor.

QUALIFICATIONS

Graduates with majors in business, information systems, and software engineering are sought.

RECRUITMENT AND PLACEMENT

Sales trainees are placed in the various sales offices in the 30 metropolitan areas in the United States.

SALARY AND BENEFITS

Starting salary for those with undergraduate degrees is about $20,000, and $21,000 with a master's. Job-related graduate study is reimbursed up to $1,500 a year. Your benefits package will include medical, hospital, dental, and profit-sharing plans; recreation programs; flextime; and a career development program.

CONTACT

Tamlyn E. Johnson, Vice-President, Human Resources, CompuServe, Inc., 5000 Arlington Centre Boulevard, Columbus, OH 43220.

COMPUTER ASSOCIATES INTERNATIONAL, INC.
SALES/MARKETING • SYSTEMS ANALYSIS • SOFTWARE ENGINEERING • TECHNICAL PUBLICATIONS • TECHNICAL SUPPORT

THE COMPANY

Computer Associates International was founded in 1976. Today it is one of the leading software suppliers in the world. It designs, develops, supports, and markets systems, applications, and database-management software products for IBM and IBM-compatible mainframe computers as well as for minicomputers and microcomputers. Its rapid market penetration is amazing—more than half of all IBM-based data centers use at least one Computer Associates product. Over 80 percent of the Fortune 500 companies are Computer Associates clients. The company has 50 offices in 19 countries around the world. Sales representatives and systems engineers enhance and install the firm's software products. Computer Associates is also creating user-friendly, on-line, interactive programming software for laymen. The company has its headquarters near New York City in Garden City, Long Island. Employees number about 1,100 in the United States and 1,600 worldwide.

ALL TRAINING PROGRAMS

You will begin learning on the job, with access to a complete training center maintained by Computer Associates. Seminars on a variety of topics will enhance your technical knowledge. There is also a company videotape library on Computer Associates products.

QUALIFICATIONS

The company is looking for graduates with specialization in computer programming, technical writing, and computer science.

RECRUITMENT AND PLACEMENT

Computer Associates lists jobs on campuses its recruiters do not visit. You may write to the company directly to apply. U.S. offices are located in Arizona, California, Colorado, Florida, Georgia, Illinois, Massachusetts, Michigan, Minnesota, Missouri, New Jersey, New York, Ohio, Texas, Virginia, Washington, and Washington, D.C. Foreign branches are scattered around the world.

SALARIES AND BENEFITS

The College Placement Council Salary Survey for September 1986–June 1987 indicates starting salaries for computer and business machine companies to be $1,880 a month for those with a B.A. degree in nontechnical curricula and $2,389 with a B.A. degree in technical curricula. M.B.A. starting salaries were $2,633 for a nontechnical undergraduate degree and $2,781 for a technical undergraduate degree. Check with the company for more specific salary information. Computer Associates reviews its benefits package regularly to be in step with industry standards.

CONTACT

Personnel Department, Computer Associates International, Inc., 711 Stewart Avenue, Garden City, NY 11530-4787.

CONE MILLS CORPORATION

COMPUTER SCIENCE • MANAGEMENT • PRODUCTION

THE COMPANY

Cone Mills manufactures, finishes, and sells textiles (including denim and corduroy), molded plastic furniture, and polyurethane foam. Established in 1895, the company employs more than 10,000 people.

ALL TRAINING PROGRAMS

Production managers participate in a nine-month on-the-job training program. Managers are placed in a six- to nine-month formal training program. Computer scientist managers receive a combination of on-the-job and formal training for six months.

QUALIFICATIONS

The company is recruiting college graduates (and technical graduates with three to ten years of related work experience) in the following fields: accounting, business, liberal arts, chemistry, computer science, materials science, mathematics, textile chemistry, and engineering (industrial, mechanical, chemical, civil, electrical, and transportation). The company prefers those who rank in the top 40 percent with a minimum G.P.A. of 3.0.

RECRUITMENT AND PLACEMENT

Cone Mills recruits in the East and Southeast. Starting locations are in Mississippi, New York, North Carolina, and South Carolina.

SALARY AND BENEFITS

Starting salary for those with a bachelor's degree ranges from $20,000 to $27,000. Benefits include tuition and fee reimbursement up to 75 percent; life insurance; medical, dental, vision, and hospitalization plans; relocation assistance; a fitness program; and profit-sharing and incentive savings plans.

CONTACT

N. Paige Stout, Manager, Manpower Recruitment, Cone Mills Corporation, 1201 Maple Street, Greensboro, NC 27405.

CONOCO, INC.

BUSINESS • ENGINEERING • PRODUCTION

THE COMPANY

Founded in 1875, Conoco is a major energy company that produces crude oil, natural gas, and a wide variety of petroleum-based products. It currently operates in about 25 countries on 5 continents and employs more than 20,000 people worldwide. Conoco holds leases on more than 16 million net acres in more than 15 countries. It is a wholly owned subsidiary of E. I. du Pont de Nemours & Co. (Inc.), the nation's largest chemical manufacturer. Conoco offers challenging career opportunities for college graduates who are innovative thinkers and problem solvers.

ALL TRAINING PROGRAMS

Conoco varies its approach to training depending on the type of work to be accomplished. You may be trained in a combination of on-the-job experience and formal classes, or through a series of rotational assignments.

BUSINESS TRAINING PROGRAM

The length of your training will vary from three to twelve months. You receive on-the-job training under an experienced supervisor. Formal training for new analysts emphasizes a variety of programming languages and techniques. Courses, lectures, and special seminars are available. A business graduate may be placed in the twelve-month Management Development Program.

QUALIFICATIONS

You should have a bachelor's or a master's degree in business, computer science, accounting, finance, economics, or employee or industrial relations. Engineering degrees are highly useful.

ENGINEERING TRAINING PROGRAM

Engineering training programs vary from department to department, and all have a built-in flexibility. On-the-job training and management development programs broaden your basic knowledge and foster leadership and administrative experience that can lead to management positions. You are trained by assignment, working with more experienced engineers on field trips and special projects. You will probably spend at least one year in training.

QUALIFICATIONS

You should have a bachelor's or a master's degree in any area of engineering, computer science, environmental or geological science, naval or marine science, petroleum science, or related areas. Some areas need master's or doctoral degrees.

PRODUCTION PROGRAM

You begin with eleven weeks of formal field training. You observe the drilling and completion of wells; study methods of producing and measuring oil, gas, and water; test various wells; and become familiar with computer systems used in oilfield operations. Two weeks of office orientation follow, during which you learn general office procedures, various accounting statements, and administrative systems.

QUALIFICATIONS

You need a degree in business administration, management, accounting, finance, statistics, general business, or industrial management.

ALL PROGRAMS

RECRUITMENT AND PLACEMENT

Conoco representatives, working through the college placement offices, call on approximately 50 colleges and universities, primarily in the Midwest, Southwest, and West. Your initial assignment will typically be in corporate headquarters in Houston; Ponca City, Oklahoma; or in one of Conoco's division offices.

SALARY AND BENEFITS

Starting salaries with a bachelor's degree are $22,000 to $30,000. A master's degree will increase the salary by a few thousand dollars. Conoco offers a competitive employee benefits package, including stockownership. The company matches your voluntary savings.

CONTACT

Gloria Sebor, Placement Counselor, Academic Services, Conoco, Inc., P.O. Box 1267, Ponca City, OK 74603.

CONTINENTAL ILLINOIS NATIONAL BANK

BANKING ASSOCIATE

THE COMPANY

A massive load of bad debts ($4.5 billion) brought the FDIC into Continental's boardroom in 1984, with the regulatory agency taking over two-thirds ownership of the bank. Observers quoted in business publications praise the bank's progress in coming back from the brink. The bank itself is candid with recruits about its problems. Continental says it is "determined to show how this bank with a very long and proud heritage faltered for a moment in history—then pulled itself back into the mainstream to resume its place among the world's pre-eminent financial institutions." The restructuring agreement for Continental solidly capitalized the bank, and many of its private sources of funding have returned. Despite its problems, opportunities exist to move up into positions vacated during troubled times. The bank has assets of more than $32 billion and it ranks number 14 in the Fortune 100 largest commercial banking corporations.

BANKING ASSOCIATES PROGRAM

Banking associates are trained to become bankers with a broad range of financial skills to provide insight and ingenuity in meeting the financial needs of a diverse customer base in global markets. Continental has a challenging eight-month Corporate Banking Training Program for the M.B.A. graduate, and a fourteen-month program for the non-M.B.A. graduate. You will receive a combination of line assignments, case studies, and financial analysis under strong supervision.

QUALIFICATIONS

You should have a degree in finance or accounting, U.S. citizenship, and such intangible attributes as the ability to make good decisions and handle multiple demands on your time. You'll have a lot of responsibility and should be comfortable with it.

RECRUITMENT AND PLACEMENT

Continental has overseas offices in 32 countries and domestic offices at 15 locations. You will train at corporate headquarters in Chicago.

SALARY AND BENEFITS

The College Placement Council Salary Survey for September 1986–June 1987 indicates starting salaries for banking, finance, and insurance firms to be $1,889 a month for those with a B.A. degree in nontechnical curricula and $2,135 with a B.A. degree in technical curricula. M.B.A. starting salaries were $2,884 for a nontechnical undergraduate degree, and $3,320 for an M.B.A. with technical undergraduate degree. Check with the company for more specific salary and benefits information.

CONTACT

Kevin Coleman, College Relations Manager, Continental Bank, 231 South La Salle Street, Chicago, IL 60697.

COOPERS & LYBRAND

ACCOUNTING

THE COMPANY

Founded in 1898, Coopers & Lybrand is an international firm of certified public accountants providing professional services in accounting and auditing, taxation, management consulting, advanced information technology planning, and actuarial benefits and compensation consulting.

The company employs 35,000 people in about 100 U.S. offices and 430 offices in 98 other countries. Its annual revenues exceed $1 billion. C&L was the first accounting firm to use computer specialists as technical resources on audit engagements. More than 500 other accounting firms use the microcomputer software developed by Coopers & Lybrand.

ACCOUNTING TRAINING PROGRAM

Training will allow you to function successfully as part of an audit team and will prepare you for the C.P.A. exam. Training combines on-the-job and classroom instruction. You will participate in courses in your office and at company regional education centers. Courses during your first year will include a two-part (eight-day) audit seminar, C.P.A. review program, and other courses in auditing specific to a variety of businesses and institutions. You will have access to more than 40 computer courses and more than 100 software programs developed by Coopers & Lybrand.

QUALIFICATIONS

The company is looking for graduates in business administration with accounting or finance backgrounds. It also is interested in graduates in law, taxation, data processing, actuarial science, mathematics, and computer science. The company wants people with an achievement orientation, communication skills, executive presence, intellectual abilities, good judgment, and leadership.

RECRUITMENT AND PLACEMENT

Coopers & Lybrand recruits nationwide. You could work in any of the company's 100 offices across the country.

SALARY AND BENEFITS

The College Placement Council Salary Survey for September 1986–June 1987 indicates starting salaries for public accounting firms to be $1,834 a month for those with a B.A. degree in nontechnical curricula and $2,155 with a B.A. degree in technical curricula. M.B.A. starting salaries were $2,335 for a nontechnical undergraduate degree, and $2,436 for an M.B.A. with technical undergraduate degree. Check with the company for more specific salary information. Benefits include insurance, medical, dental, savings, and pension plans. In addition, job exchange and rotation programs are available for assignments in offices overseas, at the national office, and with the federal government.

CONTACT

National Director of Recruiting, Coopers & Lybrand, 1251 Avenue of the Americas, New York, NY 10020.

CORDIS CORPORATION

ADMINISTRATION • DATA PROCESSING • ENGINEERING • FINANCE • MANUFACTURING • MARKETING • PRODUCT ASSURANCE • RESEARCH AND DEVELOPMENT • SALES

THE COMPANY

Cordis is one of the world's top manufacfurers of cardiac pacemakers and angiographic products. This company, established in 1957, is internationally recognized for its innovative approach to life-sustaining technology. The medical device industry is young, booming, and practically recessionproof. Cordis believes career satisfaction comes in as many shapes and sizes as the people who work there. Because it feels that creative participation demands an environment tailored to individual tempos, imaginations, and aspiration, Cordis has designed a Career Employment Program that gives you almost six months to define your own career path.

ALL TRAINING PROGRAMS

The programs provide an opportunity to sample the diverse challenges of the medical device industry. You'll make your way through the inner workings of the company in your choice of areas —from engineering, R&D, and manufacturing through marketing and sales to product assurance, data processing, administration, and finance. At Cordis, you set your own pace through a series of three seven-week working/training projects. You will then have on-the-job training for six months and a formal training program of six months in engineering, sales, or data processing.

QUALIFICATIONS

Although applications are encouraged from technical graduates with more than a year of related experience, you may also begin with a bachelor's or a master's degree in bioengineering, computer science, electronics engineering, engineering technology, industrial/management engineering, information science and systems, or mechanical and systems engineering.

PLACEMENT

The manufacturing facilities are in Miami. Sales representatives are needed nationwide.

SALARY AND BENEFITS

With a bachelor's degree, you will start out at $20,000; with a master's, $25,000. Experience could add $2,500 to $5,000 to your salary. Your benefits package will include life insurance, medical, hospital, dental, vision, and pension plans, savings and fitness programs, relocation assistance, and tuition reimbursement.

CONTACT

Dori Levenson, Senior Recruiting Representative, Cordis Corporation, P.O. Box 025700, Miami, FL 33152.

The Inside Story from a Training Graduate
Sandy Shine, John H. Harland

Sandy Shine is a sales representative with John H. Harland Company. Harland specializes in supplying checks and other printed products for banks and financial institutions and has representation in all 50 states. After she received her degree in journalism from the University of Wisconsin in 1985, Sandy went through Harland's training program.

☆ ☆ ☆ ☆ ☆

Tell me about your interview with Harland.

I had my first interview with them in November of my senior year. They contacted me about interviewing with them. At the time I really didn't know much about the company. I declined and the recruiter said oh, just spend a few minutes. So I interviewed with him, and it lasted a good half an hour. He gave me an overview of the company and what the sales associate position entailed. After the interview, I was invited to participate in the second step of the process, which was an assessment center held at corporate headquarters in Atlanta. I got my invitation in November and went in February.

How long were you in Atlanta?

The assessment process lasted two days. I was there with about forty or fifty other people from all over the nation. I guess they must have held about eight to ten assessment centers throughout the country, each with forty or fifty people.

What happened during those two days?

It was a great way to see exactly what the company was like and have them find out exactly what you were like. I don't think a person can be happy in a job unless you find a good match between you and the company. During the two days you give a presentation on what you've done in the past and what your plans are. We were also divided into discussion groups led by assessors. We were given a product and asked to give a presentation.

When did you get your offer from Harland?

Sometime in March they offered me a position and that's when I accepted.

What was it about Harland that was attractive to you?

During the initial interview I asked a lot of questions. After the interview I knew that I was very interested in the company. I guess the deciding factor was the training program. Also, there was something that was very compatible with my personality. They were a good solid company that really seemed to care about you and take an interest in what you want to get out of your job. It seemed like more than just a place where you go and do your work and go home. Even though it was a large company, it was evident there was a lot of support available to new employees. And it seemed like a close group, from the top managers down to the sales associates. There was a real sense of the staff wanting to know who you were. It was genuine, very genuine.

After you graduated you entered the training program?

Yes, I graduated at the end of May and a few weeks later I was in New Jersey working for Harland.

Tell me about the Sales Associate Training Program.

I started at our local imprinting plant for two weeks, seeing how the product is made, working in customer service, working in our billing department, just getting a feel for what we put out as a final product. I was assigned a trainer who was a sales representative. During those two weeks he was there to answer any question I had. He was always showing me what I was supposed to be doing, where I was supposed to be going. After I worked in the plant I went to the field with my sales representative and just did a couple of sales calls with him, like a shadow sitting back and taking it all in. I then went to Atlanta for two weeks and went back for a one-week follow-up course six months later. In Atlanta I learned the ins and outs of selling, and a lot more about the product. I went through the Xerox Professional Selling Skills Training Course there.

How many people were in your class?

I'd say about fifteen. They make it small because there's a lot of interaction.

What happened after the two weeks in Atlanta?

I came back to New Jersey and worked with my trainer for a while longer and he carved out a mini-territory for me. He let me work on some of his accounts under his supervision. So I started planning my sales day and going to work. Our job is very service-oriented, so we do a lot of service calls at the same time as sales calls. We sell to financial institutions. We call on advanced-level people—people who actually are going to be responsible for the use of our product. So service calls are important.

I worked my mini-territory and built it up. I set goals for it. During this time I worked under the supervision of my trainer. Next he gave me some prospects to call on. Then I began cold calling. This whole training period lasted nine months or so. I think on the average it lasts about a year. After you've proven yourself in the mini-territory, you're then promoted to a representative.

That means you have your own territory?

Right. It's got a base of existing accounts, it's also got a great potential because you're given a number of prospects to work on at the same time.

The training program profile for Harland indicated that twelve to eighteen months is usually the time needed to complete the course.

That is the case for certain territories. I know up here there's a lot of business so there are probably more opportunities. And the company is growing rapidly. I also think Harland is recruiting a very high-quality person right out of college now. And they're finding that they can move them along because they have a natural knack for selling. That is leading to a shorter training period, because they don't need as much work and sales grooming.

As you look back on your training, what part was the most valuable for you?

Probably knowing that I had somebody right there to lean on. My local sales representative–trainer was very helpful. Also my sales manager. He knew exactly what was going on all the time. He always wanted to know if he could help. The other sales representatives were willing to help also. I wasn't thrown cold turkey into a territory and told, "Go for it." There was a lot of one-on-one support.

D

☆ ☆ ☆ ☆ ☆

DAN RIVER, INC.

ENGINEERING • MANAGEMENT • MANUFACTURING

THE COMPANY

Dan River is a chemical and textile production company. It makes home furnishings; yarn; piece-dyed, woven, and knit apparel fabrics; chemicals; and dyes. It employs about 7,000 people and is based in Danville, Virginia.

ALL TRAINING PROGRAMS

Management trainees undergo a formal training period that lasts nine months. Engineers and other technical employees receive on-the-job instruction.

QUALIFICATIONS

For technical positions with the company, you should have a degree in chemical engineering, chemistry, mathematics, mechanical engineering, textile chemistry, or textile engineering. On the more general side, the company also may want you if you have a degree in business or liberal arts.

RECRUITMENT AND PLACEMENT

Starting locations are in South Carolina and Virginia.

SALARY AND BENEFITS

Your starting salary with a bachelor's degree will be $19,000. With a master's degree your starting salary will be in the mid-twenties. The company will reimburse up to half of your tuition and fees for job-related graduate study. You will also be eligible for medical and hospital plans, plus relocation assistance.

CONTACT

Mr. E. E. Carroll, Director of Employee Relations, Dan River, Inc., P.O. Box 261, Danville, VA 24541.

DATA GENERAL CORPORATION

ACCOUNTING • ADMINISTRATION • ENGINEERING • FINANCE • INFORMATION SYSTEMS AND PROCESSING • MANAGEMENT • MARKETING • SALES

THE COMPANY

Data General was founded in 1968 by two computer designers, a programmer, a salesman, and an attorney. With assets of over $1.2 billion, it now employs more than 17,000 people in the United States and another 4,000 abroad. It supplies small and medium-sized general-purpose computer systems and services to markets that demand products with increased productivity, decreased costs, and improved quality. Its systems are used in manufacturing, finance, commerce, science, engineering, communications, education, medicine, and government. The company owns two small software development firms—Design Data, Inc., and W.S.A., Inc.—plus a minicomputer manufacturing company, Digital Computer Controls, Inc. It also is an owner of Nippon Data General in Japan. Over 113,000 Data General systems have been installed worldwide. Many schools have received donated computer systems.

The company designed the computer industry's first 16-bit minicomputer with four accumulators in the central processor, a leading technology at the time. Data General has lots of firsts in the field: it offered a 15-inch circuit board, now standard; it developed automatic error correction; it offered a 16-bit minicomputer on a chip; it developed a programming language for small computers; and it offers compatibility with other systems.

Products range from the $100 microprocessor to more than $500,000 for a multiuser information system. Scientific and industrial models can be programmed for medical electronics, communications control, industrial automation, transportation, energy management, and computer-aided design. Commercial and computational models are used in manufacturing, distribution, finance, health care, insurance, and engineering analysis. Small-business models offer software for processing accounts payable and receivable, inventory, payroll, general ledger, and business modeling. Data General's key communications product, Xodiac X25, allows computers all over the world to communicate. Data General also provides office-automating systems.

The company has many channels of sales and distribution. Original-equipment manufacturers combine Data General's central processors, terminals, and other hardware products with their equipment to develop products such as body scanners or electronic cash registers, and then they resell the entire package. Systems integrators buy complete systems and use their own software for their specific job needs, such as accounting, inventory control, and order entry. The company also installs systems, diagnoses problems, and assists in maintenance. Retail stores sell complete systems to individuals. With more than $1 billion in sales, it ranks number 255 in the Fortune 500 largest U.S. industrial corporations.

ALL TRAINING PROGRAMS

Sales and systems engineers go through a twelve-month training program. Manufacturing management training is twenty-four months. Both programs combine classroom instruction with closely supervised on-the-job experience. Ongoing training is both internal and external, covering manufacturing, field engineering, management development, and marketing. Internal training is available to all employees and ranges from general development courses to specific technical courses to keep current with state-of-the-art technologies.

The company sponsors executive development programs and executive M.B.A. programs at universities such as Columbia, Cornell, Dartmouth, Harvard, and Stanford. The company pays for tuition, fees, and books.

QUALIFICATIONS

The company seeks people with a B.S. or an M.B.A. with a technical B.S. and one or two years of work experience. A minimum G.P.A. of 3.2 to 4.0 is preferred, with a ranking in the top 20 percent of your class. Computer familiarity will obviously be a plus.

RECRUITMENT AND PLACEMENT

Recruiters visit campuses and prescreen individuals from all regions of the United States. The company has over 200 sales and service offices, which are located in every state in the country and in more than 30 other countries. Corporate headquarters is in Westboro, Massachusetts, and the European headquarters is in Paris. If you enter the manufacturing area, you will be located in Southboro, Massachusetts; Westbrook, Maine; Portsmouth, New Hampshire; Clayton or Apex, North Carolina; Austin, Texas; or overseas in Hong Kong, Manila, or Bangkok. Product development areas are located in Westboro; Research Triangle Park, North Carolina; Austin; and Sunnyvale, California. Field engineering facilities are located in Milford, Massachusetts; Colorado Springs, Colorado; Eschborn and Schwabach, West Germany; and Feltham, England.

SALARY AND BENEFITS

The College Placement Council Salary Survey for September 1986–June 1987 indicates starting salaries for computers and business machine companies to be $1,880 a month for those with a B.A. degree in nontechnical curricula and $2,389 with a B.A. degree in technical curricula. M.B.A. starting salaries were $2,033 for a nontechnical undergraduate degree and $2,781 for a technical undergraduate degree. Check with the company for more specific salary information. The company encourages employee ownership through stock purchases. It offers various awards programs to recognize outstanding achievement. Classes are offered at company facilities, taught by local university faculty, to enable employees to receive graduate degrees in computer science or electronic engineering. The company also offers scholarships for employees' children. You will be eligible for flextime options and relocation assistance.

CONTACT

Steven Hobbs, Corporate Employment Manager, Data General Corporation, 4400 Computer Drive, Westboro, MA 01580.

DATA-TRONICS CORP.
COMPUTER SERVICES

THE COMPANY

Data-Tronics is a subsidiary of Arkansas Best Corporation, a large holding company. Data-Tronics provides data processing services for Arkansas Best and a large number of other clients, primarily other members of the transportation industry.

COMPUTER TRAINING PROGRAM

During an introductory period for new systems analysts/programmers, you will become acquainted with hardware, software, and systems analysis techniques. Then you will work one on one with an experienced employee. You also will participate in classes and seminars with other systems analysts/programmers.

QUALIFICATIONS

To qualify for a systems analyst/programmer position with the company, you must have at least a B.S. degree with courses in computer science, and your G.P.A. must put you in the upper third of your class.

RECRUITMENT AND PLACEMENT

Opportunities exist in teleprocessing applications, minicomputer applications, batch applications, and systems support. All positions are at the headquarters of Arkansas Best and all of its subsidiaries, in Fort Smith, Arkansas. Travel requirements are low.

SALARY AND BENEFITS

The College Placement Council Salary Survey for September 1986–June 1987 indicates starting salaries for merchandising (retail and wholesale) and service companies to be $1,594 a month for those with a B.A. degree in nontechnical curricula and $2,141 with a B.A. degree in technical curricula. M.B.A. starting salaries were $2,572 for a nontechnical undergraduate degree, and $2,735 for an M.B.A. with technical undergraduate degree. Check with the company for more specific salary information. Its benefits package includes medical insurance; long-term disability insurance; dental, vision, and life insurance; a retirement plan; and an educational assistance plan if you wish to return to school for an advanced degree.

CONTACT

Walter Echols, Data-Tronics Corp., Arkansas Best Corporation, P.O. Box 48, Fort Smith, AR 72902.

DEAN WITTER REYNOLDS, INC.

ADMINISTRATION • INVESTMENT BANKING • PUBLIC FINANCE

THE COMPANY

Since its acquisition by Sears, Roebuck & Co. in 1981, Dean Witter has been a company on the move. Its staff increased by almost 50 percent in the three years after the purchase, and the infusion of capital was used to open new branch offices as well. Along with Allstate Insurance and Coldwell Banker, Dean Witter is a world leader in the financial services industry. The new capital has allowed the firm to expand into a variety of consumer deposit operations, lending operations, and securities-related operations. Over half of its 20,000 employees sell securities. With 14 offices around the country, Dean Witter emphasizes its regional depth and service. The company is divided into three operating units: Capital Markets (made up of Investment Banking, Equity, Fixed-Income, and Realty divisions); Individual Financial Services (National Sales, Marketing, and Product divisions); and Consumer Banking (Sears Savings Bank, Sears Mortgage Securities Corp., Allstate Enterprises, Inc., Allstate Enterprises Mortgage Corp., Greenwood Trust Co., Discover Card Services, Inc., and the Hurley Bank of South Dakota). Headquarters are in New York.

CORPORATE FINANCE TRAINING PROGRAMS

You will begin as a generalist, working on a team with senior bankers. You will study all aspects of debt and equity financing, as well as sales and trading, in classes that supplement on-the-job experience. Lectures, accounting videotapes, and computer software classes will provide continuing education. After two years you may be selected to become an associate, and a few associates are selected to enter an executive M.B.A. program.

QUALIFICATIONS

You should have an M.B.A., a superior undergraduate record, excellent writing and communication skills, strong analytical ability, and a combination of initiative and teamwork. Exposure to accounting, finance, economics, and computer science is necessary.

RECRUITMENT AND PLACEMENT

The company recruits at Chicago, Colgate, Cornell, Dartmouth, Harvard, M.I.T., Northwestern, Stanford, and Wharton. After training you could work in New York or one of the regional corporate finance offices.

SALARY AND BENEFITS

Starting salaries for M.B.A.s begin at about $50,000. You will receive a semiannual bonus tied to performance. Dean Witter offers a comprehensive benefits program.

CONTACT

Marilyn McLeod, Manager of Recruiting, Investment Banking, Dean Witter Reynolds, Inc., Two World Trade Center, 15th floor, New York, NY 10048.

DEFENSE CONTRACT AUDIT AGENCY

AUDITING

THE COMPANY

The largest audit agency in the executive branch of the federal government, the Defense Contract Audit Agency (DCAA) is the Department of Defense's sole contract audit organization. A worldwide organization, DCAA performs all contract audits and provides accounting and financial advisory services on Department of Defense (DOD) contracts and subcontracts to procurement officials. This is the agency that checks the figures for accuracy, efficiency, and stability, sometimes blowing the whistle on fraudulent practices. The cost of operating the agency is returned to the government by a ratio of savings to cost as much as 44:1. Other government agencies may also hire DCAA. The agency's civilian director, appointed by the Secretary of Defense, manages an annual budget of about $160 million and oversees the audits of proposals topping $250 million. DCAA auditors study contractor price proposals, compliance with cost accounting standards, compliance with truth-in-negotiation guidelines (defective pricing), whether contractors performing government work are using economical and efficient methods and practices, and contractors' financial position. DCAA operates a modern training center in Memphis, Tennessee. Agency headquarters are in Alexandria, Virginia, with more than 4,500 employees working for DCAA worldwide.

AUDITOR TRAINING PROGRAM

You will attend formal technical classes at the Defense Contract Audit Institute in Memphis during your first six months with DCAA. You may take any of 22 courses, depending on your planned direction as an auditor. Meanwhile, you will be assigned a supervisor to guide you on the job at regional and field audit office locations, ensuring that you apply your degree training to real-life situations as smoothly as possible. Your experience as a DCAA auditor is creditable toward C.P.A. certification in most states and coaching is available at the agency to assist you in passing the examination.

QUALIFICATIONS

Your degree in accounting or twenty-four semester hours in accounting should show a high G.P.A.; particularly in cost accounting and auditing courses. DCAA wants candidates who demonstrate analytical ability in identifying and solving problems, ability to learn new concepts and procedures quickly, and strong interpersonal skills. You will have an edge if you have had courses in statistics and hands-on computer experience.

RECRUITMENT AND PLACEMENT

DCAA hires more than 500 auditors annually, most to enter their training program. You must first apply to the Office of Personnel Management (OPM) and be rated eligible according to the terms of Announcement No. 510 (Accountants and Auditors). There is no written examination, but you must provide a personal Qualifications Statement (SF-171), a college transcript (or OPM Form 1170-17), and a completed Occupational Supplement (Form B) to the OPM Staffing Service Center to receive a Notice of Results (rating). Fill this form out very carefully because the forms are computer scanned. After receiving this notice of rating, send the notice along with an SF-171 and college transcript to a regional office. In addition to DCAA's 6 regional offices, the agency has 420 field offices throughout the United States and overseas. Field audit offices are located at most defense contractor plants and in most major cities. You will be required to sign a rotation policy statement, agreeing to be moved to a different location every five to seven years. (This ensures that auditors do not work too long with contractors in a given area.) Overseas assignments may be obtained after three years' experience.

SALARY AND BENEFITS

If you enter DCAA with a bachelor's degree you will be hired at the GS-5 ($14,822 per year) or GS-7 ($18,350 per year) grade level, based on your academic qualifications. With an M.B.A. degree you could enter at GS-7 or GS-9 ($22,458 per year), based on work location and other factors. Benefits to expect will include health and life insurance, paid holidays, annual leave, retirement, travel expenses, and other allowances.

CONTACT

OPM Staffing Service Center (for a Results rating), Box 9800, Macon, GA 31298, then: Defense Contract Audit Agency, Boston Regional Office, Waltham Federal Center, 424 Trapelo Road, Waltham, MA 02154-6397; Defense Contract Audit Agency, Chicago Regional Office, 527 South LaSalle Street, Suite 652, Chicago, IL 60605-1096; Defense Contract Audit Agency, Philadelphia Regional Office, Federal Building, Room 4400, 600 Arch Street, Philadelphia, PA 19106-1604; Defense Contract Audit Agency, Atlanta Regional Office, 805 Walker Street, P.O. Box 1498, Marietta, GA 30060-2731; Defense Contract Audit Agency, San Francisco Regional Office, 450 Golden Gate Avenue, Box 36116, San Francisco, CA 94102-3563; or Defense Contract Audit Agency, Los Angeles Regional Office, 2500 Wilshire Boulevard, Suite 1270, Los Angeles, CA 90057-4366.

DELMARVA POWER AND LIGHT COMPANY

ENGINEERING AND OPERATIONS • MARKETING • PRODUCTION

THE COMPANY

Begun in 1909 as a small, independent utility in Delaware, the company expanded services in Delaware and incorporated subsidiaries in Maryland and Virginia to become the Delmarva Power and Light Company in 1950. Currently it provides electricity to more than 308,000 customers and natural gas service to 75,000 customers in the Wilmington, Delaware, area. To reduce dependency on oil, Delmarva is converting many of its oil-fired generating stations to burn domestic coal and is exploring options for the use of nuclear energy. Its Energy Management Program is designed to reduce customer costs. In addition, through Project Conserve, Delmarva conducts seminars and courses and offers low-cost computerized energy audits to promote energy efficiency efforts in both the residential and commercial/industrial sectors. Delmarva has more than 2,500 employees.

ALL TRAINING PROGRAMS

New employees learn about the electric utility industry through formal and on-the-job instruction as part of the Corporate Orientation Program. In addition, the Training and Development Department conducts over 10 different supervisory development and specialized training programs monthly. If you are new to supervision, you will attend a forty-hour program that reviews basic human relations and organizational skills needed for employee supervision. You can also participate in special informational programs, such as Basic Utility Economics, and enroll in job-related educational courses through the company's Educational Assistance Program.

QUALIFICATIONS

The company wants college graduates with backgrounds in civil engineering, computer science, construction engineering, electrical engineering, engineering technology, and mechanical engineering.

RECRUITMENT AND PLACEMENT

Starting jobs are in Delaware and Maryland. Job opportunities include power plant engineering, substation and transmission design, distribution engineering, substation construction and maintenance, distribution construction and maintenance, planning, and marketing. Summer positions for college students and co-op internship programs are available.

SALARY AND BENEFITS

The College Placement Council Salary Survey for September 1986–June 1987 indicates starting salaries for public utilities (including transportation) to be $1,905 a month for those with a B.A. degree in nontechnical curricula and $2,355 with a B.A. degree in technical curricula. M.B.A. starting salaries were $2,403 for a nontechnical undergraduate degree and $2,667 for a technical undergraduate degree. Check with the company for more specific salary information. Benefits include life insurance, medical, dental, and stock-purchase plans, and tuition reimbursement for employees who want to pursue a graduate degree.

CONTACT

Personnel Department, Delmarva Power and Light Company, 800 King Street, P.O. Box 231, Wilmington, DE 19899.

DEL MONTE

SALES MANAGEMENT

THE COMPANY

A division of RJR Nabisco, Del Monte is the largest fruit and vegetable canner in the United States. Although the company grows very little of the produce it cans, Del Monte does make its own cans, prints its own labels (2 billion-plus a year), and packs only for the Del Monte label. Del Monte canneries go at a frantic pace from June through November. In most products that it sells, Del Monte ranks number 1 or number 2 in sales. The company has more than 40,000 employees and headquarters in San Francisco.

SALES TRAINING PROGRAM

Your sales manager serves as your primary trainer-coach. Most of your training involves on-the-job development with limited classroom training. During your first two weeks on the job your manager will cover the basics, including company orientation, assignment of retail accounts and sales territory, assignment of company car and sales equipment, visiting stores with your manager, and building creative selling visuals. You'll also receive a sales training manual with individual units to complete during your first six months on the job, before attending a Central Training Workshop. This is an intensive, skill-building program that includes role-playing exercises, contests, self-paced instruction and testing, informal panel discussions, and knowledge-building sessions. Your progress will depend upon your ability to assimilate and use the new information and skills you've learned on the job. When you've successfully completed retail training, you will advance to direct selling and begin calling upon wholesalers and direct buying chains. After learning direct selling basics on the job, you will attend a direct selling seminar in San Francisco. Back on the job, you'll work closely with your sales manager to apply your skills and develop your potential through reading, projects, outside seminars, and additional training modules.

QUALIFICATIONS

Del Monte looks for candidates who are goal-oriented and possess strong interpersonal skills, energy, high standards, and intellectual capacity demonstrated by a solid grade point average.

RECRUITMENT AND PLACEMENT

You are encouraged to contact the company directly with a résumé and letter of interest. Del Monte sales offices are located in California, Colorado, Florida, Georgia, Illinois, Kansas, Maryland, Massachusetts, Michigan, Missouri, New York, Ohio, Oregon, Pennsylvania, Tennessee, Texas, Washington, and Wisconsin.

SALARY AND BENEFITS

The College Placement Council Salary Survey for September 1986–June 1987 indicates starting salaries for food and beverage processing companies to be $1,834 a month for those with a B.A. degree in nontechnical curricula and $2,301 with a B.A. degree in technical curricula. M.B.A. starting salaries were $3,043 for a nontechnical undergraduate degree and $3,098 for a technical undergraduate degree. Check with the company for more specific salary information. Del Monte offers a comprehensive benefits package averaging 30 percent of your base salary.

CONTACT

Del Monte, Sales Personnel—Room 1339, P.O. Box 3575, San Francisco, CA 94119.

DELOITTE HASKINS & SELLS

ACCOUNTING • MANAGEMENT CONSULTING

THE COMPANY

The accounting and law firm of Deloitte Haskins & Sells has specialized in professional tax practice since 1919. It has 26,000 tax specialists working in 430 offices in 70 countries, with about 8,000 employees in its 107 U.S. offices. The firm stresses comprehensive services to a varied clientele—from the largest multinational corporation to smaller, closely held companies. It also emphasizes personal tax and financial planning for corporate executives.

ACCOUNTING TRAINING PROGRAM

During your first year, client assignments and a variety of seminars will prepare you as a tax specialist. In states where audit experience is needed for the C.P.A. certificate, your assignments will be selected accordingly. In addition to in-house courses, you are also encouraged to participate in professional society seminars, postgraduate courses, and similar programs.

QUALIFICATIONS

The firm is looking for highly qualified students with academic backgrounds in accounting and tax law. You will also need to possess intellectual capacity and analytical ability, practical business sense, and sound judgment, and exceptional oral and written communication skills.

RECRUITMENT AND PLACEMENT

The company recruits nationwide. Offices are located in major cities across the country.

SALARY AND BENEFITS

The College Placement Council Salary Survey for September 1986–June 1987 indicates starting salaries for public accounting firms to be $1,834 a month for those with a B.A. degree in nontechnical curricula and $2,155 with a B.A. degree in technical curricula. M.B.A. starting salaries were $2,335 for a nontechnical undergraduate degree, and $2,436 for an M.B.A. with technical undergraduate degree. Check with the company for more specific salary and benefits information.

CONTACT

Gerald A. Sena, Director, Recruitment and College Relations, Deloitte Haskins & Sells, Dept. BI, 1114 Avenue of the Americas, New York, NY 10036.

DENNY'S INC.

ACCOUNTING • ARCHITECTURE • CONSTRUCTION • DATA PROCESSING • FINANCE • FOOD TECHNOLOGY • MANAGEMENT • MARKETING • QUALITY CONTROL

THE COMPANY

The next time you pull into Denny's at two in the morning for breakfast, consider the care and attention necessary to operate a restaurant providing full table service, a broad menu, moderate prices, convenient locations in 47 states, and twenty-four-hour availability. Behind this care is a company dedicated to quality products and friendly customer service in a clean and wholesome environment. Denny's was established in 1953. Since then it has had one of the most impressive growth records in the food service industry. It is a publicly held company, listed on both the New York and Pacific Coast stock exchanges, and has over 50,000 employees. Other divisions include Winchell's Donut House, El Pollo Loco (the newest, specializing in Mexican char-broiled chicken), Proficient Food Company, and Portion-Trol Foods. Because of its ongoing expansion, the company needs trainees to participate in all phases of its restaurant business. Corporate and division headquarters are located in Southern California. Denny's annual sales exceed $1 billion.

RESTAURANT MANAGEMENT TRAINING PROGRAM

The Manager-in-Training Program is designed to give prospective restaurant managers the background needed to succeed as leaders and achievers. Information is provided through training programs, seminars, workshops, organizational memberships, and periodicals. You begin with several weeks of on-the-job training, performing many of the tasks of all positions in your restaurant. Eventually you can become a manager or unit manager of a Denny's, Winchell's, or El Pollo Loco restaurant.

ALL PROGRAMS

QUALIFICATIONS

Almost all major disciplines are needed, from accounting to construction to food technology to real estate. Denny's is looking for people who can learn and perform quickly, have a sincere interest in working with people, and have a liberal arts degree or supervisory experience. All line vacancies are filled from within.

RECRUITMENT AND PLACEMENT

Write for more information or to get an application. As a restaurant manager, you could be placed anywhere in the country. Denny's, Inc., is headquartered in La Mirada, California; Proficient Food Company, a distributor, in Irvine, California. The processing division, Portion-Trol Foods, is located in Mansfield, Texas.

SALARY AND BENEFITS

Simply stated, Denny's philosophy regarding salary and benefits is "Be the best to attract the best." The College Placement Council Salary Survey for September 1986–June 1987 indicates starting salaries for merchandising (retail and wholesale) and service companies to be $1,594 a month for those with a B.A. degree in nontechnical curricula and $2,141 with a B.A. degree in technical curricula. M.B.A. starting salaries were $2,572 for a nontechnical undergraduate degree, and $2,735 for an M.B.A. with technical undergraduate degree. Check with the company for more specific salary information. Denny's has one of the best benefits programs in the food service industry and includes group life, health, major medical, and dental insurance, profit-sharing and retirement plans, and liberal paid vacations.

CONTACT

S. D. Phillips, Corporate College Relations, Denny's, Inc., 16700 Valley View Avenue, La Mirada, CA 90637.

DIGITAL EQUIPMENT CORPORATION

ENGINEERING • FINANCE • INFORMATION SYSTEMS • PERSONNEL • TECHNICAL WRITING

THE COMPANY

In 1957 three MIT engineers set out to change the world. They founded Digital to offer computers that were small and easy enough for almost anyone to use, and developed an entirely new technology for processing data. Their product, the minicomputer, would replace huge computer systems that once took up entire floors. Today Digital designs, manufactures, sells, and services the widest range of products in the interactive computer industry. The company employs over 111,500 people in North America, Europe, and the Far East. With sales over $9 billion, it is the second largest computer company. You will obviously work with state-of-the-art equipment, whatever your job at Digital. In the next few years Digital expects its employees to spawn the next generation of VLSI circuits, make artificial intelligence real, and develop faster, more responsive peripherals. You will be encouraged to set many of your own priorities and make your own decisions. Listed among *Fortune*'s most admired corporations, Digital ranks number 44 in the Fortune 500 of the largest U.S. industrial corporations.

ALL TRAINING PROGRAMS

Training and development at Digital are based on two concepts: the fastest way for you to learn is to encounter real-world situations as quickly as possible; and you need resources, support, and guidance to be successful in a new work environment. You'll be principally responsible for your own development with a supervisor there to guide and encourage you. You may attend structured workshops, seminars, and orientation sessions to supplement your on-the-job training, as your particular career requires. Digital offers a dual career path so that you may choose to excel in your own technical area, or move into management and administration.

QUALIFICATIONS

Digital wants candidates with a wide range of graduate and undergraduate degrees: engineering, computer science, finance and accounting, business administration, management, industrial technology, the physical sciences, economics, EDP, behavioral sciences, and related disciplines.

RECRUITMENT AND PLACEMENT

Check with your college placement office to find out when Digital representatives will visit, or send a letter of interest with a résumé directly to the company. Job locations exist in Arizona, Colorado, Connecticut, Georgia, Maine, Massachusetts, New Hampshire, New Mexico, South Carolina, and Vermont.

SALARY AND BENEFITS

Digital conducts salary surveys to ensure that theirs are competitive within the industry. The College Placement Council Salary Survey for September 1986–June 1987 indicates starting salaries for computer and business machine companies to be $1,880 a month for those with a B.A. degree in nontechnical curricula and $2,389 with a B.A. degree in technical curricula. M.B.A. starting salaries were $2,633 for a nontechnical undergraduate degree and $2,781 for a technical undergraduate degree. Check with the company for more specific salary information. Benefits include medical, dental and life insurance, disability income, retirement, vacations and holidays, stock purchase plan, and tuition reimbursement.

CONTACT

Digital Equipment Corporation, U.S. College Relations, 150 Coulter Drive (CF02-3K75), Concord, MA 01742.

R. R. DONNELLEY & SONS COMPANY

MANAGEMENT • SALES

THE COMPANY

R. R. Donnelley & Sons Company provides a broad range of printing and related services to publishers of magazines and books, as well as merchandisers, the telephone industry, financial institutions, and other firms requiring substantial printing. Donnelley sells printing to more than 3,000 customers and estimates that sales represent approximately 5 percent of total U.S. printing industry sales. Titles printed include the Sears, Roebuck and J. C. Penney catalogs and numerous popular magazines, such as *TV Guide, Life, Modern Maturity, Mademoiselle, The New Yorker,* and *Car and Driver.* Founded in 1864 and headquartered in Chicago, Donnelley has been publicly held since 1956. Sales, production, and operations facilities stretch from coast to coast, employing over 20,000. Sales in 1986 exceeded $2 billion. Listed among *Fortune*'s most admired corporations, Donnelley ranks number 164 in the Fortune 500 largest U.S. industrial corporations.

SALES AND MANAGEMENT TRAINING PROGRAMS

Sales and management training programs both last two years. Training includes on-the-job and classroom instructions. An orientation program familiarizes all new employees with company operations. The Manufacturing Management Trainee Program provides intensive individualized development for future management personnel.

QUALIFICATIONS

The company is recruiting business administration graduates with backgrounds in accounting, customer service, and management. It also is interested in graduates with degrees in electrical engineering, industrial engineering, mechanical engineering, computer science, and M.B.A.s.

RECRUITMENT AND PLACEMENT

Donnelley recruits nationwide. There are 24 manufacturing divisions, 50 other production facilities, and 35 sales offices where you could work.

SALARY AND BENEFITS

Check with the company for specific salary information. Benefits include a comprehensive major medical and prescription drug plan, long-term disability insurance, group life insurance, dental insurance, and a retirement plan.

CONTACT

Walter Hannan, Manager, Recruitment Planning, R. R. Donnelley & Sons Company, 2223 Martin Luther King Drive, Chicago, IL 60616.

DRESSER INDUSTRIES, INC.

ENGINEERING • FINANCE • MANAGEMENT

THE COMPANY

Dresser Industries, Inc., is a multinational corporation primarily involved in the energy and natural resource markets. Its sales and revenues are over $3.5 billion. Dresser's largest group is the Oilfield Products Group with five divisions: Magcobar—drilling fluids and instrumentation; Swaco—detection and control equipment; Dresser Minerals—mines and processing plants; Dresser Titan—pumping services; and the International Division—marketer of Dresser oilfield products and services outside the United States and Canada. Company headquarters are in Houston. Dresser ranks number 105 in the Fortune 500 largest U.S. industrial corporations.

ALL TRAINING PROGRAMS

Dresser is heavily committed to training for both employees and customers, and maintains a five-story Dresser Leadership Center in Dallas where employees go for management training. The leadership center is self-contained and provides computers for simulations, video and film equipment for presentations and role playing, a sauna and gymnasium. Swaco offers a cooperative program that allows college students to alternate working and studying each semester until graduation.

ENGINEERING TRAINING PROGRAM

Dresser offers several types of engineering programs to fit the needs of the division which you enter and your abilities. At Dresser Center, a facility that functions much like a university, you may attend mud school, DATA school, corrosion school, hydraulics and pressure courses, and even an advanced course in drilling engineering.

If you are selected for Magcobar's Special Projects Engineering Program, you will be trained for management. You begin with a field assignment to provide hands-on experience, a phase lasting eighteen months. You may be reassigned to two or three locations during that time. In phase two you join Magcobar's R&E operations in Houston for eighteen months of training, field service lab, and data services assignments. In phase three you spend two more years in Magcobar's R&E Houston operation as a technical service engineer. You will be expected to troubleshoot drilling mud problems worldwide, participate in the development of new technology and drilling mud products, and attend both internal and external advanced engineering, sales, and management training schools. Following phase three, you will be assigned to operations as a senior tech service engineer.

In the Associate Engineer Training Program, you begin with a week of orientation in Houston before beginning a ten-month program on all aspects of fracturing, acidizing, and cementing. Most of the training time is spent in the field working with experienced engineers.

QUALIFICATIONS

To be chosen for the Special Projects Engineering Program, you must have a high GPA, a degree in engineering, related oilfield experience, and achievements in extracurricular activities. A degree in engineering and academic achievement qualify you for the other programs.

RECRUITMENT AND PLACEMENT

Dresser recruiters visit college campuses, and the company also invites inquiries at headquarters about their hiring situation and operations. Positions exist throughout the world for Dresser employees, although the company will make an effort to place you near your home if possible and if that is your desire. In the United States, you might work in any of the major oilfield centers—Alaska, California, Louisiana, Nevada, Texas, or Wyoming.

SALARY AND BENEFITS

The College Placement Council Salary Survey for September 1986–June 1987 indicates starting salaries for petroleum and allied product companies to be $1,972 a month for those with a B.A. degree in nontechnical curricula and $2,497 with a B.A. degree in technical curricula. M.B.A. starting salaries were $2,629 for a nontechnical undergraduate degree and $2,970 for a technical undergraduate degree. Check with the company for more specific salary information. Benefits include group medical, dental, disability, and life insurance; an employee-owned credit union; retirement plan; educational assistance and special awards for suggestions, publications, patents, and public speaking.

CONTACT

Dresser Industries, Inc., Oilfield Products Group Employment Office, P.O. Box 6504, Houston, TX 77005.

DOW CHEMICAL

ACCOUNTING • ADMINISTRATION • CHEMISTRY • COMPUTER SCIENCE • ENGINEERING • FINANCE • GEOLOGY • MARKETING • OPERATIONS • RESEARCH AND DEVELOPMENT • SALES

THE COMPANY

Look through your kitchen or medicine chest and you will likely find at least one item from the diverse product line of Dow. The seventh largest chemical company in the world, second largest in the United States, Dow produces such familiar items as Saran Wrap and Cepacol mouthwash. Dow divisions also offer services such as mining, oilfield cementing, and enhanced oil recovery. Dow's 1986 sales were more than $11 billion. It employs more than 63,000 people who manufacture and market over 2,000 products. It maintains 103 manufacturing locations and 176 sales offices around the world. Despite its immense size, Dow retains a friendly, informal atmosphere. Through decentralization, Dow has created a number of smaller, more manageable organizations. Dow's worldwide operations are grouped into six geographic areas: United States, Canada, Latin America, Europe, Brazil, and the Pacific (Far East). Within each area are manufacturing divisions, sales offices, and research facilities. The company's 2,000-plus products are grouped into some 40 individual businesses directed by seven broad product departments. Dow emphasizes that "fences between departments are low, rules and policies seldom invoked, and requests for organizational charts are met with puzzled looks." The company encourages job changing between divisions, departments, and even functions. Headquarters are in Midland, Michigan. Dow is among *Fortune*'s most admired corporations and ranks number 27 in the Fortune 500 largest U.S. industrial corporations.

ALL TRAINING PROGRAMS

Recognizing that entry-level employees are emerging from sixteen or more years of an academic environment, Dow puts trainees to work right away. Two phrases you'll hear at Dow are "whole-job" concept and "on-the-job" training. Some areas of the company, such as sales, do provide formal training programs of three weeks or more, but most divisions will assign you to a team to orient you to Dow's procedures. Dow facilities in Midland, Michigan, and Freeport, Texas, recruit local university extension services to bring course work to the job site for additional technical training.

QUALIFICATIONS

For an accounting position, Dow wants candidates with a bachelor's degree in accounting or a closely related field. Although grades are important, other qualities are equally important. You should have good accounting knowledge coupled with a probing intellect, be an ambitious worker and self-starter. In distribution, Dow is looking for graduates with bachelor's degrees in transportation, logistics, economics, marketing, engineering, or a related discipline. You should demonstrate good human relation skills, an ability to make decisions independently and quickly, and a desire to build a career in the field. Successful computer candidates need not have a computer major or previous work experience if they show problem-solving skills and good judgment, can assume responsibility quickly and work with a minimum of day-to-day supervision. Computer-related courses are beneficial, but you might have a degree in engineering, accounting, chemistry, or industrial management. In general, Dow hires from a variety of degree specialties and is looking for employees who want to contribute to Dow's production and profitability.

RECRUITMENT AND PLACEMENT

Dow sends recruiters to campuses around the country, but you may contact a Dow regional office if you want to be placed in a particular area. Write to headquarters if you are willing to go anywhere in Dow's vast system. Dow actively recruits women and minority candidates.

SALARY AND BENEFITS

The College Placement Council Salary Survey for September 1986–June 1987 indicates starting salaries for chemical, drug and allied companies to be $1,964 a month for those with a B.A. degree in nontechnical curricula and $2,457 with a B.A. degree in technical curricula. M.B.A. starting salaries were $2,886 for a nontechnical undergraduate degree and $2,794 for a technical undergraduate degree. Check with the company for more specific salary information. Dow's benefits include life, medical, dental, and disability group insurance plans, a liberal retirement pension plan, relocation policy, tuition refunds, matching contributions to colleges and universities up to $2,000 a year, paid vacations and holidays, and a stock-purchase plan.

CONTACT

(Midland Dow Center, Any Dow Sales Office, Michigan division): Dow Chemical U.S.A., University Relations and Recruiting, Box 1713, Midland, MI 48640; (Texas Division): Dow Chemical U.S.A., Texas Division, Technical Placement/College Relations, A. P. Beutel Building, Freeport, TX 77541; (Dowell): Dow Chemical U.S.A., Dowell, Recruiting/College Relations, 400 West Belt South, Houston, TX 77042; (Louisiana Division): Dow Chemical U.S.A., Louisiana Division, Recruiting/College Relations, P.O. Box 150, Plaquemine, LA 70764; (Western Division): Dow Chemical U.S.A., Western Division, Recruiting/College Relations, 2800 Mitchell Drive, Walnut Creek, CA 94598; (Oyster Creek Division): Dow Chemical U.S.A., Oyster Creek Division, Recruiting/College Relations, P.O. Box BB, Freeport, TX 77541; (Eastern Division): Dow Chemical U.S.A., Eastern Division, Recruiting/College Relations; P.O. Box 36000, Strongsville, OH 44136; (Granville Research): Dow Chemical U.S.A., Granville Research, Recruiting/College Relations, Granville, OH 43023; (Houston Dow Center): Dow Chemical U.S.A., Houston Dow Center, Recruiting/College Relations, P.O. Box 3387, Houston, TX 77001; or (Consumer Products): The Dow Chemical Company, Health & Consumer Products Department, Recruiting/College Relations, Box 68511, Indianapolis, IN 46268.

E. I. DU PONT DE NEMOURS & COMPANY, INC.

ACCOUNTING • BUSINESS/FINANCIAL ANALYSIS • CHEMISTRY • MARKETING • SALES

THE COMPANY

The largest chemical company in the United States, Du Pont is a diversified international company backed by scientific and engineering capabilities, with operations in about 50 countries worldwide. Employees total approximately 140,000 and sales top $27 billion a year. Du Pont is involved in the development, production, and marketing of agricultural and industrial chemicals, biomedical products, including X-ray films, medical diagnostics, pharmaceuticals, coal, and minerals; electronic products, finishes, petroleum exploration and refining, polymer products, a broad range of engineering plastic resins; and textile fibers such as nylon, Orlon, and Dacron, for home furnishings and apparel. The company ranks ninth in the Fortune 500 largest U.S. industrial corporations. A pioneer in the area of employee benefits, Du Pont introduced a retirement plan in 1904 and paid vacations in 1934, among other innovations. The company provides country clubs near its Wilmington, Delaware, headquarters, encouraging employees to socialize during their off-hours. Du Pont workers tend to be loyal, but expect your rise to be slow and steady, not meteoric.

ALL TRAINING PROGRAMS

Du Pont offers formal training courses to all employees and will give you substantial responsibility early in your career. You will be given room to grow under experienced managers and are "not expected to know everything at once." Programmers and analysts will receive formal training. Courses available range from a review of effective oral and written communication skills to courses on financial management. Du Pont supports participation in industry and professional organizations.

QUALIFICATIONS

Demand at Du Pont is for business graduates with degrees in accounting, or M.B.A.s with undergraduate degrees in engineering. The company also hires engineers with a variety of specialties, biochemists, pharmacologists, and statisticians. Graduates with doctorates in these areas are also invited to apply.

RECRUITMENT AND PLACEMENT

Du Pont recruits nationwide. Plants are located in the mid-Atlantic, mid-South, Southeast, and Gulf Coast states. Sales offices are located in principal cities throughout the country. Most accounting employees work in Wilmington, except for those in auditing, which has locations at major plant sites.

SALARY AND BENEFITS

The College Placement Council Salary Survey for September 1986–June 1987 indicates starting salaries for chemicals, drugs, and allied products companies to be $1,964 a month for those with a B.A. degree in nontechnical curricula and $2,457 with a B.A. degree in technical curricula. M.B.A. starting salaries were $2,886 for a nontechnical undergraduate degree and $2,794 for a technical undergraduate degree. Check with the company for more specific salary information. The company has a published policy that it will provide benefits that are as good as or better than competitors'. The package includes relocation assistance, life, medical, hospital, and dental insurance, pension plans, and a stock-purchase program.

CONTACT

Professional Staffing, Employee Relations Department, E. I. Du Pont de Nemours and Company, 1007 Market Street, Wilmington, DE 19898.

E

☆ ☆ ☆ ☆ ☆

EASTMAN KODAK COMPANY

ENGINEERING · SALES AND MARKETING

THE COMPANY

Founder George Eastman began experimenting with photography in his mother's kitchen when he was twenty-four years old. His first box camera came out in 1888, and a year later he introduced transparent film in rolls. The rest is history. Professional and recreational photography was transformed by Eastman, who then went on to give away his great fortune while he was still alive.

Eastman was a major innovator in employee relations. He started the custom of sharing the company's success by making annual wage dividend payments to employees (some employees take home $2,000 to $3,000 extra each year this way). This Kodak benefits plan became a model far ahead of its time. Kodak inspires fierce loyalty in its people. Promotion is from within—it is virtually unheard of for outsiders to be brought into any power position. Kodak employees are encouraged to tinker on their own, which has led to millions of dollars' worth of new inventions. Kodak's suggestion plan, under which employees are rewarded with substantial cash for good ideas, has resulted in the company adopting 700,000 ideas submitted by employees and the reward of $20 million to those innovative employees.

Kodak today is involved in the research, design, development, manufacture, and sale of a wide range of photographic products as well as specialized optical, electronic, photographic, and mechanical equipment including copier/duplicator products, medical products, data storage and retrieval devices, synthetic textile fibers, plastics, fine and bulk chemicals, and vitamin concentrates. The company has annual sales in excess of $11 billion and ranks number 28 in the Fortune 500 largest U.S. industrial corporations. Eastman Kodak is listed among *Fortune*'s most admired corporations.

SALES AND MARKETING TRAINING PROGRAM

As a new sales representative you go through an extensive training program at Kodak's Marketing Education Center in Rochester, New York, for three to twelve months, depending on the products involved. During this period, at least two field trips allow you to observe sales representatives in action. Experienced sales representatives participate in ongoing training sessions at regional and national headquarters to become familiar with new products and to polish selling skills.

QUALIFICATIONS

Liberal arts or technical degrees are preferred. You'll also need strong interpersonal skills and the ability to function well both independently and on a team.

RECRUITMENT AND PLACEMENT

"Father Yellow," as Kodak is known internally, is everywhere; consequently, salespeople are assigned just about everywhere.

SALARY AND BENEFITS

Some divisions offer partial commission plans, while others offer a straight salary. Sales representatives receive use of cars, depending on geographic location, and financial support for necessary business expenses. The benefits are some of the best anywhere and include life insurance, comprehensive medical coverage, relocation assistance, fitness programs, profit sharing, and a pension plan. For every salary dollar Kodak spends, it spends another 51 cents in benefits.

ENGINEERING TRAINING PROGRAM

The Eastman Kodak Company provides individual, on-the-job training for all assignments. Your training commences when you report for work and continues during your career with the company. Your initial assignment will be working as a member of a small group with specific project assignments. This applied learning allows you to get your feet on the ground by working with experienced engineers. As you pursue your career, you may move into management positions or continue your development as a specialist.

QUALIFICATIONS

The Chemicals and Plastics Division of Kodak needs engineers: chemical, civil, electrical, electronics, industrial/management, applied mathematics, and mechanical. Opportunities exist for people with doctorates in analytical chemistry, chemical engineering, organic chemistry, and physical and polymer chemistry.

RECRUITMENT AND PLACEMENT

Your starting—and probably permanent—location will be Longview, Texas.

SALARY AND BENEFITS

The College Placement Council Salary Survey for September 1986–June 1987 indicates starting salaries for computers and business machine companies to be $1,880 a month for those with a B.A. degree in nontechnical curricula and $2,389 with a B.A. degree in technical curricula. M.B.A. starting salaries were $2,633 for a nontechnical undergraduate degree and $2,781 for a technical undergraduate degree. For companies in chemicals, drugs, and allied products, the CPC reports average salaries of $1,964 a month for those with a B.A. degree in nontechnical curricula and $2,457 with a B.A. degree in technical curricula. M.B.A. starting salaries were $2,886 for a nontechnical undergraduate degree and $2,794 for a technical undergraduate degree. Check with the company for more specific salary information. Kodak's benefits program is known as one of the best and includes life insurance, comprehensive medical coverage, relocation assistance, fitness programs, profit sharing, and a pension plan.

CONTACT

For sales and marketing: Personnel Resources, Eastman Kodak Company, 343 State Street, Rochester, NY 14650; for engineering: Nick Nabours, Senior Personnel Representative, P.O. Box 7444, Eastman Kodak Company, Kodak Boulevard, Longview, TX 75607.

EBASCO SERVICES, INC.

ACCOUNTING • BUSINESS

THE COMPANY

Since 1905, Ebasco has designed, engineered, or constructed power generators that use coal, gas, oil, nuclear power, or water. Ebasco Services also does consulting on all phases of electric utility administration. This New York company is a subsidiary of the Dallas-based ENSERCH Company. ENSERCH is a diversified energy company engaged in four major activities: providing gas utility service; exploring and developing oil and gas; providing petroleum production services and products; and providing specialized engineering, construction, and consulting services. The company has about 6,300 employees worldwide.

ALL TRAINING PROGRAMS

The unofficial training period usually lasts from eighteen to twenty-four months and includes on-the-job training and a series of lectures by in-house experts. The Entry-Level Employee Development Program shows how various engineering disciplines are integrated into Ebasco's services. The Corporate Training and Development Department offers over 50 courses, covering basic communication skills as well as high-level technical topics. Membership in professional, technical, and management organizations is encouraged, and reasonable expenses are reimbursed.

QUALIFICATIONS

A master's or a bachelor's degree is required in the fields of engineering, computer science, or business.

RECRUITMENT AND PLACEMENT

Ebasco recruits primarily from the following academic disciplines: chemical, civil, construction, electrical, environmental, industrial, mechanical, and nuclear engineering; and computer science. Placement for entry-level employees usually is in engineering, construction, quality assurance, and licensing.

Recruitment is nationwide and decentralized by region. Starting locations for any assignment usually are in offices in California, Georgia, New Jersey, New York, Texas, and Washington. Ebasco hires about 100 people annually.

SALARY AND BENEFITS

The starting salary with a bachelor's degree is in the mid-twenties. Those with a master's degree usually start a couple of thousand dollars higher. Tuition reimbursement and a complete employee benefits package are available. You will be eligible for stock-purchase and pension plans.

CONTACT

Employment Supervisor, College Relations, Ebasco Services, Inc., 79th Floor, 2 World Trade Center, New York, NY 10048.

EDISON BROTHERS SHOE STORES, INC.

BUYING • MANAGEMENT • MERCHANDISING

THE COMPANY

Edison Brothers is a major women's shoe retailer operating under the store names Bakers, Leeds, Size 5-7-9 Shops, Fashion Conspiracy, Joan Bari, Jeans West, Oak Tree, Burts, Chandlers, and The Wild Pair. The company employs about 17,000 people in its 2,400 shoe and apparel specialty stores throughout the United States, including Alaska, Hawaii, and Puerto Rico.

ALL TRAINING PROGRAMS

The program provides entry-level sales training that leads to management positions such as: assistant store manager, store manager, regional manager, merchandiser, and buyer. You learn the ins and outs of the shoe business with in-store work experience under the guidance of your store manager. Your on-the-job training is supplemented with classroom instruction.

QUALIFICATIONS

The company seeks applicants with bachelor's degrees in business or liberal arts and with an interest in a business career.

RECRUITMENT AND PLACEMENT

The company recruits nationwide. You will be placed in any of the 65 regional sales offices.

SALARY AND BENEFITS

Salaries are based on performance. The College Placement Council Salary Survey for September 1986–June 1987 indicates starting salaries for merchandising (retail and wholesale) and service companies to be $1,594 a month for those with a B.A. degree in nontechnical curricula and $2,141 with a B.A. degree in technical curricula. M.B.A. starting salaries were $2,572 for a nontechnical undergraduate degree, and $2,735 for an M.B.A. with technical undergraduate degree. Check with the company for more specific salary information. You will receive a comprehensive benefits package that includes a discount on merchandise.

CONTACT

Size 5-7-9 Shops, Kim Langmack, Training and Instruction Director, P.O. Box 14549, St. Louis, MO 63178; Fashion Conspiracy/Joan Bari, Jan Regazzi, Director, Sales Training and Inst., P.O. Box 14549, St. Louis, MO 63178; Jeans West/Oak Tree, Harold Johnson, Executive Vice-President and General Sales Manager, P.O. Box 14549, St. Louis, MO 63178; Bakers/Leeds, John Codespoti, Vice-President, General Sales Manager, P.O. Box 14020, St. Louis, MO 63178; Burts/Leased Departments, George Starmer, Vice-President, General Sales Manager, P.O. Box 14020, St. Louis, MO 63178; Chandlers, Murray Krinsky, Vice-President, General Sales Manager, P.O. Box 14020, St. Louis, MO 63178; or The Wild Pair, Les Cherry, President, P.O. Box 14020, St. Louis, MO 63178.

ELECTRONIC DATA SYSTEMS

ACCOUNTING • ENGINEERING SYSTEMS • FINANCE • MARKETING • NETWORK COMMUNICATIONS • OPERATIONS • SYSTEMS ENGINEERING • SYSTEMS PROGRAMMING

THE COMPANY

Through his vision, energy, and leadership, H. Ross Perot created EDS and built it into one of the largest data-processing service companies in the country. In 1962, Perot left IBM and struck out on his own. Lauded for his high standards, positive thinking, and aggressive sales methods, he built a company for which General Motors was willing to pay $2.5 billion twenty-two years later.

If you can feel comfortable in a work environment that stresses traditional dress codes and a drive to meet high quotas, this company offers an excellent opportunity to acquire and apply technical knowledge. If you are in a hurry to get to the top, there is no seniority system to get in the way. EDS promotes people based on performance, not seniority. So, if you're a high achiever, here's a company that will reward your hard work and productivity. EDS spends millions of dollars on internal training and development. The company employs more than 30,000 people with 1986 sales over $4 billion. EDS pioneered the facilities management concept of service, in which EDS assumes all information processing responsibilities of its customers. Systems analysis, systems design, programming, and computer operations are the thrust of EDS' business, not merely support. It is ranked number 8 in the Fortune 100 list of diversified service companies.

SYSTEMS ENGINEERING DEVELOPMENT TRAINING PROGRAM

In this three-phase program you will develop both business and technical skills during an eighteen-month period. Through Phase I, you will gain business exposure with on-the-job problem solving by working with customers. Phase II begins an intensive ten weeks of technical training in computer programming and systems analysis. Computer programming languages include COBOL, JCL, and ALC. In Phase III you will be assigned to an EDS account or a programming support team. Focus will be on programming, but you will be encouraged to explore alternate career paths.

ENGINEERING SYSTEMS DEVELOPMENT PROGRAM

You will work on the cutting edge in this program. The ESD Program is an exciting, rigorous, technical challenge involving high expertise and new technology. It encompasses a wide array of engineering and manufacturing computer processing applications, including CAE/CAD/CIM, robotics, and process control and simulation. Your training will prepare you to play a key role in designing, developing, and implementing sophisticated systems supporting GM clients.

ALL PROGRAMS

QUALIFICATIONS

You could be among the 100 or so trainees selected by EDS each year if you have maintained a B average or better and can describe yourself as a self-starter. Even though a degree in computer science, management information systems, or other technical areas is important, EDS also looks for people who possess energy and desire to become data-processing professionals.

RECRUITMENT AND PLACEMENT

EDS recruits nationwide for both entry-level and experienced professionals and accepts employment inquiries year round. The home office is in Dallas, but there are also offices in more than 100 other cities.

SALARY AND BENEFITS

The College Placement Council Salary Survey for September 1986–June 1987 indicates starting salaries for service companies to be $1,594 a month for those with a B.A. degree in nontechnical curricula and $2,141 with a B.A. degree in technical curricula. M.B.A. starting salaries were $2,572 for a nontechnical undergraduate degree and $2,735 for a technical undergraduate degree. Check with the company for more specific salary information. EDS offers comprehensive benefits, including medical coverage, stock-purchase plan, credit union, and a GM car-purchase program.

CONTACT

Electronic Data Systems Corporation, Corporate Recruiting, One Forest Plaza, 12200 Park Central Drive, Suite 200, Dept. O, Dallas, TX 75251.

EMERSON ELECTRIC COMPANY

ACCOUNTING • COMPUTER SCIENCE • ENGINEERING • FINANCE • OPERATIONS • PRODUCTION

THE COMPANY

"Farsighted" is one way to describe Emerson Electric. Established in 1890 when electricity was still a marvel, the company now applies its talents to a wide range of industrial, electrical, electromechanical, and electronic products. Emerson engineers design everything from armament systems and automatic test equipment systems to electronic warfare systems, and they conduct complex systems synthesis and analysis. With annual sales exceeding $5 billion, it ranks number 73 in the Fortune 500 largest U.S. industrial corporations and is listed among *Fortune*'s most admired corporations. The Emerson family includes 45 operating divisions with 148 manufacturing plants throughout the free world. Its products go to three markets—consumer, commercial and industrial, and government and defense. Corporate world headquarters are in St. Louis.

ALL TRAINING PROGRAMS

You will work one on one with a senior engineer who will introduce you to Emerson's policies and procedures. In-house seminars and product manuals will coordinate with your on-the-job training. The training period normally lasts three to nine months, depending on your area of employment.

QUALIFICATIONS

Emerson hires electrical, computer, electronics, and industrial engineers at all degree levels; engineering technologists; computer scientists; graduates with degrees in accounting, business, and related areas.

RECRUITMENT AND PLACEMENT

Emerson recruiters visit universities and colleges around the country. You may also send a résumé and transcript directly to the company. You will start in St. Louis.

SALARY AND BENEFITS

With a bachelor's degree, a typical starting salary would be in the $28,000 to $29,500 range; with a master's, $31,500 to $33,000. Salaries for doctorates are competitive. Your benefits package will include medical, dental, and life insurance, optional dependent life insurance, stock and savings plans, tuition reimbursement, and relocation assistance.

CONTACT

Manager, College Relations, Emerson Electric Co., 8100 West Florissant, Station 2218, St. Louis, MO 63136.

ERNST & WHINNEY

ACCOUNTING • MANAGEMENT

THE COMPANY

Ernst & Whinney is one of the world's leading public accounting, tax, and management consulting firms. Founded in 1903, the firm now has 12,600 people in the United States, and worldwide it has 28,000 people located in 400 offices in 75 countries. Ernst & Whinney provides services to a highly diversified group of over 14,000 organizations and many thousands of individuals. Clients range from high-technology and aerospace companies to sports teams and entertainment figures, from small enterprises just beginning to develop promising ideas to multinational corporations with extensive resources. As a result of a successful merger in Canada to form Thorne Ernst & Whinney, the firm is now the largest accounting firm in Canada.

ACCOUNTING/MANAGEMENT TRAINING PROGRAM

All Ernst & Whinney professionals are required to pursue 120 hours of continuing education every three years throughout their careers. The firm pays all costs associated with professional development, whether at the company's facilities or through approved outside resources. You will continue your formal education on the job and in the classroom. The firm offers seminars and workshops designed specifically for its accounting, tax, and consulting professionals. You will be expected to complete certain core courses. In addition, you can consider other courses that are directly applicable to a particular skill or industry. Individual career objectives and the future needs of the firm guide its ongoing development of new courses. Workshops offered include advanced microcomputer concepts, cost management for hospitals, advanced business analysis, consulting at E&W, structured systems analysis, and marketing yourself and company services. Some courses are self-study, using manuals, videotapes, and computer programs. Others are regional workshops, and many are held at the firm's national Education Center. Approximately 150 training programs are offered by the firm to meet the needs of its people. Instructors are experienced conference leaders who are experts in their subject matter. The fast-paced and highly interactive courses incorporate case studies and small group assignments to simulate actual work situations. E&W is a leader in professional development in range of curriculum, depth of course content, facilities, and commitment.

QUALIFICATIONS

Professionals are recruited from colleges and universities, business and industry. Candidates for accounting and auditing positions must have, at a minimum, an undergraduate degree and sufficient accounting and business credits to qualify for certification. Applicants for tax positions generally have advanced degrees in taxation or law. Those interested in management consulting opportunities should possess an advanced degree with some work experience in their specialty.

RECRUITMENT AND PLACEMENT

The firm recruits at approximately 450 campuses each year. Interested candidates should contact their campus placement office for the date and location of the next campus visit. Candidates may write directly to the E&W office location of their choice. A complete list of offices can be obtained through recruiting literature provided to placement offices or by requesting the company's recruiting brochure at the address below. You might work anywhere in the United States.

SALARY AND BENEFITS

The College Placement Council Salary Survey for September 1986–June 1987 indicates starting salaries for public accounting firms to be $1,834 a month for those with a B.A. degree in nontechnical curricula and $2,155 with a B.A. degree in technical curricula. M.B.A. starting salaries were $2,335 for a nontechnical undergraduate degree, and $2,436 for an M.B.A. with technical undergraduate degree. Check with the company for more specific salary information. Ernst and Whinney's benefits program is reviewed annually. On your visit to an E&W office, you will learn about the competitive holiday and vacation policies, comprehensive life, health, and accident insurance plans, and liberal pension plan.

CONTACT

James R. Peter, Partner, National Director of Recruiting, Ernst & Whinney, 2000 National City Center, Cleveland, OH 44114.

EXXON CORPORATION

BUSINESS • ENGINEERING • FINANCE • INFORMATION SYSTEMS

THE COMPANY

If you want to work for one of the biggest companies in America, look to Exxon. Besides oil and gas, this giant is also involved in shipping, real estate, coal and minerals, and petrochemicals. Listed among *Fortune*'s most admired corporations, Exxon ranks number 2 in the Fortune 500 largest U.S. industrial corporations. It has annual sales of more than $69 billion and net income in excess of $5 billion. The company is highly structured and bureaucratic but enforces an internal policy of high ethics and integrity. Exxon specifically prohibits employees from giving bribes to attract business, accepting gifts from customers, or creating off-the-record bank accounts. Each of the company's 210,000 employees is evaluated once a year and ranked against others in the same department. Job security prevails even during times of national hardship, such as the Depression and recent recessions. Most of Exxon's top people started as engineers. The company has 60,000 employees in the United States. Headquarters are in Houston.

ALL TRAINING PROGRAMS

You will train on the job under experienced supervisors and in formal classroom situations. Exxon's training programs are carefully individualized to develop your potential. A typical first assignment for an engineering graduate might be to analyze a problem such as why computer-developed cost estimates for various subsystems in a new major processing plant disagree with preliminary estimates and with vendor-supplied information. Your work will be significant from the beginning, giving you a chance to follow a project through to completion. Exxon also offers a formal management program. It is common for employees to switch between professional and managerial assignments during their careers.

QUALIFICATIONS

Exxon is in the market for people with strong academic backgrounds in business, computer technology, engineering, and the physical sciences. You should rank in the top 10 percent of your class with a minimum G.P.A. of 3.0. Familiarity with computers or programming will count in your favor. Strong leadership skills are a must.

RECRUITMENT AND PLACEMENT

Exxon sends recruiting personnel to colleges and universities around the country. While the company has operations throughout the United States, most people with degrees in business, engineering, or science will start in Houston, Baytown, Midland, or Corpus Christi, Texas; Florham Park or Linden, New Jersey; New Orleans or Baton Rouge, Louisiana; or Thousand Oaks or Benicia, California.

SALARY AND BENEFITS

Exxon says its salaries are some of the highest in the oil industry. Check with the company for specific salary information. Benefits are excellent and include all types of insurance, pension plan, disability income protection, medical and dental plans, a savings plan, relocation assistance, 100 percent tuition reimbursement, and liberal vacations.

CONTACT

Professional Employment, Exxon, P.O. Box 2180, Houston, TX 77252-2180.

A Recruiter's View of Training Programs
Jocko Burks, Weyerhaeuser

Jocko Burks is the manager of recruiting and staffing services for Weyerhaeuser at corporate headquarters in Tacoma, Washington. He has worked at Weyerhaeuser for twenty years, two years in his present job, and seven years in recruiting, staffing, and college relations.

☆ ☆ ☆ ☆ ☆

Let's start with the big picture. How do training and development fit into the overall corporate structure?

There are three major companies, or what we call companies, at Weyerhaeuser. Each is broken down into many different regions, by both geography and product. There are probably fifty or sixty separate units.

We have a central group called organizational development and training, which provides services to all those businesses and units. It tries to come up with courses that it thinks are attractive and to presell them. It also custom-develops courses—like one of our building products groups said, "We're going to hire this coming year X number of new salespersons, and we want you to develop eight one-week sessions to cover these subjects." The corporate group will put it together and then offer it to those sales people as they come on board. Training is paid for by the field unit. And the training department has to develop courses and programs that are going to sell, or they're not going to have any income.

How do you handle the initial orientation during that first week or two on the job?

In a remote unit, they do whatever they want to do. There's a lot of written material and video material they can use. In an area around corporate headquarters where there are probably one third of all Weyerhaeuser salaried employees in the country, we offer new employee orientation that involves one and a half days. Again, that's available for managers to send new employees to, but they have to pay for it. And it's offered on a regular basis, depending on the number of people signed up. It covers the company organization, company policy, ethics, and safety in a half-day sit-down session. And the next day is a full-day tour visiting several manufacturing facilities, forest operations to give people a background in the history of the company, and how it got to where it is and what the major divisions are.

Is that when the training begins to be tailored to the new employee, as in your example of the sales program?

Yes. Let's take someone in an engineering position. That person's supervisor would recommend him or her as a candidate for various programs that might last a week or two. Then the person would be on the job for a month or two months and then go to another program. We also have a lot of videos and textbooks that can be used by employees part time on the job and at home. Or they might go into a library to work six hours a day and spend two hours working with videos.

Is any of your training done with computers?

Yes, quite a bit. Plus we have a lot of computer programs here you just have to learn to do your job.

Have there been many changes in your programs?

At one time our engineering program was much longer and formal. Candidates were selected, hired, and trained for about eighteen months in a sequence of two or three different jobs. Then they were available for units to hire when they had openings. Well, it just didn't flow well. It worked, but the units didn't really know the people. Now we do a lot of interning. The potential candidates do a summer internship with a unit, and the unit pays for them to be there. If they like them, they are hired and brought on board. The units know exactly what they're getting so they're happier.

Tell me more about the internships.

The internships are mostly for college students between their junior and senior years. We'd like to do it with winter, fall, and spring.

And those would be co-op programs, then?

Yes, co-ops work nicely. The curriculum is designed around the student being here for six months.

How important is your summer intern program?

It's our primary selection device for hiring full-time entry-level staff. After that the individual and the supervisor really chart their own training course.

F

☆ ☆ ☆ ☆ ☆

FEDERAL BUREAU OF INVESTIGATION

COMPUTER SCIENCE • RESEARCH • SPECIAL AGENT

THE COMPANY

The FBI, under the aegis of the Department of Justice, investigates violations of U.S. laws, including kidnapping, extortion, and bank robbery. It also protects the national security by investigating subversive activities, spies, and saboteurs. In addition to its investigational responsibilities, its 21,000 employees correlate information and disseminate data to interested agencies of the federal government. Special Agents may help train state and local law enforcement officials and conduct background investigations for other United States Government agencies. No doubt it can prove to be exciting work; it will also require long hours of laborious, methodical investigation.

COMPUTER AND RESEARCH PROGRAMS

Nonagent personnel are given a formal orientation when they are first employed and receive ongoing on-the-job training.

QUALIFICATIONS

You can be hired for technical support positions with the FBI if you have a bachelor's degree in electrical or electronics engineering, computer science, or related fields. You must be a U.S. citizen and pass a background investigation.

PLACEMENT

You will work in the Washington, D.C., area.

SALARY AND BENEFITS

Depending upon qualifications and position, you may rank at GS-7 through GS-14, with salaries ranging from $18,358 to about $40,000. The FBI offers incentive awards; veterans' counseling and assistance; educational facilities; health, life, travel, and accident insurance; long-term disability insurance; accidental death and dismemberment insurance; and civil service retirement benefits.

SPECIAL AGENT TRAINING PROGRAM

To become a Special Agent you will go through an intensive sixteen-week training course at the FBI Academy in Quantico, Virginia, which covers investigative techniques, physical fitness, evidence, firearms, and crime-scene searches. Depending on your academic background, you will be placed in one of five entry programs—accounting, engineering/science, law, language, or diversified.

QUALIFICATIONS

You should be a U.S. citizen between the ages of twenty-three and thirty-five with a valid driver's license. The FBI requires a sound body as well as a sound mind. It is especially interested in applicants with degrees in electrical engineering or computer science. For the accounting program you will need a bachelor's degree in accounting and will have to be qualified to sit for the CPA exam. To enter the language program, you should have a bachelor's degree (in any discipline) and be fluent in a language for which the FBI has a need. For the law program, the FBI is looking for lawyers with degrees from accredited resident law schools. Applicants for the diversified program may have either a bachelor's degree and three years of full-time work experience, or an advanced degree and two years of full-time work experience.

PLACEMENT

You may be assigned to headquarters in Washington or to any of the 59 field divisions throughout the United States.

SALARY AND BENEFITS

Special Agents begin at the GS-10 level, $24,732, on the government pay scale, increasing to $32,568 including overtime compensation after completion of training. The FBI offers incentive awards; veterans' counseling and assistance; educational facilities; health, life, travel, and accident insurance; long-term disability insurance; accidental death and dismemberment insurance; and civil service retirement benefits.

ALL PROGRAMS

RECRUITMENT

The Bureau hires year round and is committed to affirmative action programs for minorities, women, veterans, and the handicapped.

CONTACT

Personnel Office, Federal Bureau of Investigation, 10th Street and Pennsylvania Avenue, N.W., Washington, DC 20535.

FERGUSON ENTERPRISES, INC.

ACCOUNTING • MANAGEMENT • PURCHASING • SALES

THE COMPANY

Ferguson is a wholesale distributor for a broad range of products for plumbing, heating, electrical areas, and waterworks. The operation began in 1953 with 14 employees and annual sales of almost $500,000. Today Ferguson Enterprises has more than 115 locations and generates sales in the neighborhood of $350 million annually. It has almost tripled sales and more than doubled locations during the eighties. This is a growing company, dedicated to superior customer service.

ALL TRAINING PROGRAMS

Ferguson offers an extensive on-the-job training program that prepares you for opportunities in accounting, management, purchasing, or sales. All new employees, including management trainees, begin their training in the warehouse. You can expect to work hard and get dirty. From there, you participate in an on-the-job management program.

QUALIFICATIONS

Ferguson is searching for people who are confident of their abilities and who recognize the commitment they must make to be successful. It wants people who have the self-confidence and determination to ask questions and to make decisions. If you're not afraid to make mistakes and learn from them, if you feel you can always grow and evolve, this may be the company for you. A degree is not essential.

RECRUITMENT AND PLACEMENT

For more information about recruiting dates, write to the home office in Newport News, Virginia. This company has most of its operations in the Southeast, Southwest, Midwest, and West.

SALARY AND BENEFITS

The company believes in high risk and high rewards. Each employee is expected to do more work than the typical person and is compensated accordingly. The College Placement Council Salary Survey for September 1986–June 1987 indicates starting salaries for merchandising (retail and wholesale) and service companies to be $1,594 a month for those with a B.A. degree in nontechnical curricula and $2,141 with a B.A. degree in technical curricula. M.B.A. starting salaries were $2,572 for a nontechnical undergraduate degree, and $2,735 for an M.B.A. with technical undergraduate degree. Check with the company for more specific salary information. There are generous bonus arrangements, opportunities for participation in limited partnerships, and stock-ownership by employees. A comprehensive group insurance program and an employee pension plan are also offered.

CONTACT

Steve Roznowski, Recruiting Director, Ferguson Enterprises, Inc., 618 Bland Boulevard, Newport News, VA 23602.

FIRESTONE TIRE & RUBBER COMPANY

ACCOUNTING/FINANCE • ENGINEERING • MANAGEMENT • SALES

THE COMPANY

Firestone is the nation's second largest tire company. It has 18 percent of the tire market in the United States, which accounts for 80 percent of its almost $4 billion in annual sales. Other divisions are in plastics, textiles, metals, synthetics, and chemicals. There are more than 100 manufacturing plants in 28 countries and a retail sales organization with more than 1,300 company-owned stores. Firestone is organized into four major divisions: North American Tire Group, the Diversified Products Group, the Chemicals and Raw Materials Group, and the International Company.

In 1900, Harvey S. Firestone founded the firm in Akron, Ohio. Although the company began strictly as a sales organization, he quickly got into the manufacture of the solid rubber tires needed for the new car market. The company has been closely associated with the Ford Motor Company since 1906, when Henry Ford ordered 2,000 sets of tires. Firestone has since diversified into other fields, but the tire and rubber business is still its mainstay. It remains a family-owned business and employs approximately 55,000 people around the world. Among *Fortune*'s most admired corporations, Firestone ranks number 102 in the Fortune 500 largest U.S. industrial corporations.

SALES MANAGEMENT TRAINING PROGRAM

You will learn the basic selling and management functions used in the replacement tire market to prepare you for an assignment as a store manager. The first module of training consists of orientation to the company, the products you will be selling, and your job responsibilities. In addition, you will be introduced to sales techniques. The development phase of your training at Firestone is on-the-job training in rotational assignments in several, if not all, of the following positions: retail sales manager, passenger tire sales manager, commercial salesperson, service manager, and assistant sales manager. You may have to do some dirty work, such as delivering merchandise, store cleaning and maintenance, receiving merchandise, and assisting in the service department during busy times. Expect to work long hours, to have sales quotas, and to be relocated as opportunities arise.

QUALIFICATIONS

No formal degrees are required, but you should be sales-oriented.

PLACEMENT

You could work anywhere in the country.

ACCOUNTING AND FINANCIAL MANAGEMENT PROGRAM

This three-year program will give you three or four assignments in corporate accounting, operational analysis and budgets, North American Tire

Group, treasury, tax, and portfolio. The program will give you broad-based experience in the company's operations and prepare you for promotion to an administrative or staff position in Akron or with one of the operating groups.

QUALIFICATIONS

You should have an M.B.A. in accounting or finance and be highly motivated.

PLACEMENT

You will be assigned to the Akron headquarters.

ALL PROGRAMS

RECRUITMENT

Firestone hires both from campus visits and by direct inquiries to the company.

SALARY AND BENEFITS

The College Placement Council Salary Survey for September 1986–June 1987 indicates starting salaries for automotive and mechanical equipment companies to be $1,907 a month for those with a B.A. degree in nontechnical curricula and $2,333 with a B.A. degree in technical curricula. M.B.A. starting salaries were $2,697 for a nontechnical undergraduate degree and $2,986 for a technical undergraduate degree. Check with the company for more specific salary information. Benefits include stock-purchase and savings plans, tuition reimbursement, insurance for medical, accident, hospital, disability, and life, as well as retirement and pension plans.

CONTACT

Employment Department, Firestone Tire & Rubber Company, 1200 Firestone Parkway, Akron, OH 44317.

FIRST INTERSTATE BANCORP

AUDITING • COMMERCIAL CREDIT • CORPORATE FINANCE • MANAGEMENT • MIDDLE MARKET LENDING • REAL ESTATE • SALES/CREDIT • SECURITIES SALES TRADING • SERVICE/OPERATIONS

THE COMPANY

This is a company on the move, all of it upward. First Interstate Bank currently maintains offices across more of the country than any other bank. The First Interstate system operates 23 wholly owned banks in 12 Western states and has licensing agreements in 6 additional states. It is the only commercial bank that offers a franchise option. *Fortune* ranks First Interstate number 9 among the top 10 bank holding companies in America by assets. Its region offers fertile territory with the country's fastest-growing population, number of new jobs, and personal income. The bank first spearheaded the formation of CIRRUS, a coast-to-coast ATM sharing network; twenty-four-hour banking, using ATMs; and an automated point-of-sale system. The bank was restructured in July 1985 to create a new division, First Interstate Bank, Ltd. As the system's merchant bank, Limited offers clients a full range of financial services, including round-the-clock world market and foreign exchange activities for institutional customers. First Interstate of California is the largest affiliate in the First Interstate organization, with more than $20 billion in asset strength. The entire system has assets of more than $55 billion. The bank has announced plans to streamline and restructure its branch offices to target specific needs of each market. It is among *Fortune*'s most admired corporations.

MANAGEMENT TRAINING PROGRAM

First Interstate expects to develop your leadership potential with an active, hands-on approach to learning the policies, procedures, and operations of each of the bank's divisions. You will acquire an overview of the bank's activities and philosophy, as well as practical experience and exposure to all functional areas in the Operating Services Group. You will be encouraged to network with senior management, who will share their expertise and visions for the future. After you are fully familiar with bank operations, you will be assigned to a management position with 10 to 15 employees.

QUALIFICATIONS

Successful OSG employees come from a diversity of backgrounds, including liberal arts, engineering and business, production and manufacturing, as well as those with extensive work experience in related environments.

PLACEMENT

You might work in any of the following states: Alaska, Arizona, California, Colorado, Hawaii, Idaho, Indiana, Iowa, Montana, Nevada, New Mexico, North Dakota, Oklahoma, Oregon, Utah, Washington, Wisconsin, or Wyoming.

REAL ESTATE LENDING PROGRAM

This one-year program begins in the summer. On-the-job training covers general banking, including operations, credit, marketing, and sales. In the specialized area of real estate, you will learn appraisals, as well as relevant engineering, credit analysis, and legal information.

QUALIFICATIONS

Interstate looks for candidates with B.A. and M.B.A. degrees who have completed at least two classes in accounting, in addition to having real estate experience or having successfully completed a real estate course.

PLACEMENT

The bank's primary market covers Alaska, Arizona, California, Colorado, Hawaii, Idaho, Indiana, Iowa, Montana, Nevada, New Mexico, North Dakota, Oklahoma, Oregon, Utah, Washington, Wisconsin, and Wyoming.

SERVICE/OPERATIONS TRAINING PROGRAM

This program is intended to expand your supervisory, interpersonal, and organizational skills. As a future officer in Retail Branch Operations, you must be prepared to assume responsibility for all aspects of branch operations and quality customer service. In this nine- to twelve-month program, your responsibilities will be varied, ranging from budget planning to employee evaluations, and implementing advanced techniques for customer relations.

QUALIFICATIONS

Candidates with bachelor's degrees are preferred, but you may also be hired with significant work experience in a related business area.

PLACEMENT

You could work anywhere in the bank's primary market: Alaska, Arizona, California, Colorado, Hawaii, Idaho, Indiana, Iowa, Montana, Nevada, New Mexico, North Dakota, Oklahoma, Oregon, Utah, Washington, Wisconsin, and Wyoming.

ALL PROGRAMS

RECRUITMENT AND PLACEMENT

For the real estate positions, First Interstate is the only bank recruiting on campuses exclusively. For all other trainee programs, campus recruiting is supplemented by hiring at regional offices. Securities traders will work in New York, Los Angeles, San Francisco, Chicago, London, or Tokyo.

SALARY AND BENEFITS

The College Placement Council Salary Survey for September 1986–June 1987 indicates starting salaries for banking, finance, and insurance companies to be $1,889 a month for those with a B.A. degree in nontechnical curricula and $2,135 with a B.A. degree in technical curricula. M.B.A. starting salaries were $2,884 for a nontechnical undergraduate degree and $3,320 for a technical undergraduate degree. Check with the company for more specific salary information. First Interstate benefits include: banking privileges, educational reimbursement programs, and comprehensive medical, dental, and life insurance plans.

CONTACT

First Interstate Bancorp, College Relations Representative, 707 Wilshire Boulevard, Los Angeles, CA 90017.

FIRST NATIONAL BANK OF CHICAGO

AUDITING • BANKING • MANAGEMENT

THE COMPANY

First Chicago has a mission—to become one of the top five financial institutions in the United States. This is a strategically driven, diversified, financial services organization whose assets total well over $39 billion and that now ranks as the eleventh largest bank in the nation. Listed among *Fortune*'s most admired corporations, First Chicago offers commercial lending and related financial services, training through the Asset and Liability Management Group, and local and national consumer services. First Chicago stresses cohesive strategic planning, development of preferred positions through relationships with its customers, high standards, teamwork, and development of its employees.

MANAGEMENT TRAINING PROGRAM

The key employee, the relationship manager, markets the full array of First Chicago's services and products, develops marketing plans and relationship objectives, and implements the plans. The training program for a relationship manager's position is divided into carefully planned phases. The first phase is a banking credit course of fourteen weeks. The next phase provides experience in using credit analysis skills on actual loan projects. Finally, one or two two-month rotational assignments give you a feel for the role of RM. This program lasts seven to ten months, depending on your background and progress. When you're through, you will take a first-level line position in the U.S. banking department, worldwide banking department, credit policy committee, or trade finance.

QUALIFICATIONS

This position is designed for someone with an M.B.A. First Chicago wants mature, energetic, and articulate people who are attracted to a fast-paced financial environment. You can impress the recruiter with an excellent academic record, well-developed leadership abilities, and superior interpersonal skills. A graduate degree should demonstrate a background in finance, accounting, and economics.

RECRUITMENT AND PLACEMENT

First Chicago sends recruiters to the best undergraduate and business schools. Although the company is based in Chicago, it has U.S. regional offices and 61 installations in 35 countries around the world.

SALARY AND BENEFITS

The College Placement Council Salary Survey for September 1986–June 1987 indicates starting salaries for banking, finance, and insurance firms to be $1,889 a month for those with a B.A. degree in nontechnical curricula and $2,135 with a B.A. degree in technical curricula. M.B.A. starting salaries were $2,884 for a nontechnical undergraduate degree, and $3,320 for an M.B.A. with technical undergraduate degree. Check with the company for more specific salary information. First Chicago's benefits include flexible vacation time and tuition reimbursement.

CONTACT

College Recruitment Manager, First Chicago Corp., One First National Plaza, Chicago, IL 60670.

FIRST WISCONSIN CORPORATION

ACCOUNTING • COMPUTER SCIENCE • MANAGEMENT

THE COMPANY

First Wisconsin is a full-service bank located in Milwaukee, Wisconsin. It provides commercial, leasing, real estate, international, and retail banking services. It employs over 5,000 people and has 14 branches and 18 affiliated banks in Wisconsin. It has assets of $7 billion-plus and ranks number 70 in the Fortune 100 largest banking companies.

ALL TRAINING PROGRAMS

Programmer trainees are trained formally for three months. Other programs combine on-the-job supervised and in-house classroom instruction with self-study and feedback/coaching sessions.

QUALIFICATIONS

First Wisconsin is looking for accountants, auditors, business programmers, and management trainees. If you have a degree in business data processing or business, you are especially encouraged to apply.

RECRUITMENT AND PLACEMENT

Recruiting is limited to the Midwest; placement is in Wisconsin.

SALARY AND BENEFITS

The College Placement Council Salary Survey for September 1986–June 1987 indicates starting salaries for banking, finance, and insurance firms to be $1,889 a month for those with a B.A. degree in nontechnical curricula and $2,135 with a B.A. degree in technical curricula. M.B.A. starting salaries were $2,884 for a nontechnical undergraduate degree, and $3,320 for an M.B.A. with technical undergraduate degree. Check with the company for more specific salary information. The company will reimburse all tuition and fees for job-related graduate study.

CONTACT

Deborah Choren, Personnel Officer, First Wisconsin Corporation, 777 East Wisconsin Avenue, Milwaukee, WI 53202.

FISCHER & PORTER COMPANY

ACCOUNTING • ADMINISTRATION • ENGINEERING • FINANCE • INFORMATION SYSTEMS/PROCESSING • MARKETING • RESEARCH AND DEVELOPMENT • SALES

THE COMPANY

Founded in 1937, Fischer & Porter manufactures analog and digital systems, electronic and pneumatic instruments, and specific process analyzers. Headquartered in Warminster, Pennsylvania, Fischer & Porter has a worldwide staff of about 4,500.

ALL TRAINING PROGRAMS

The training program provides information about company policies, operations, systems, and products to all new employees. Other classroom and on-the-job instruction is provided on an individual basis. Complete tuition reimbursement is available for job-related course study.

QUALIFICATIONS

To be considered for employment with Fischer & Porter, a bachelor's, master's, or doctoral degree in engineering is preferred. An equal number of computer science and business majors are also recruited. Your G.P.A. should be at least 3.0. If you are a technical graduate with one to ten years of related experience, you will be given extra consideration by Fischer & Porter recruiters.

RECRUITMENT AND PLACEMENT

The company hires about 30 trainees a year. Computer science and engineering majors with specialties in chemical, electrical, electronics, mechanical, and software engineering work in R&D positions. Computer science, engineering, and physics majors work in technical services positions. Marketing and sales positions are filled by engineering, computer science, and systems engineering majors. Administrative positions are generally filled by information systems majors. You will work at corporate headquarters in Pennsylvania. International assignments are available to U.S. citizens with one to five years' experience.

SALARY AND BENEFITS

With a bachelor's degree, you will receive between $23,000 and $24,000 as a new hire. If you have a master's, you can expect a starting salary of $25,000 to $28,000. With a doctorate, the starting salary range is between $28,000 and $35,000. Benefits are standard for the industry, including relocation assistance and a savings plan.

CONTACT

Caesar DiSoro, Manager, Employment and Hiring, Fischer & Porter Company, 125 East County Line Road, Warminster, PA 18974.

FLORIDA POWER & LIGHT COMPANY

ACCOUNTING · ENGINEERING · FINANCE

THE COMPANY

Florida Power & Light is one of the nation's largest investor-owned electric utilities. It has 2.6 million customers and assets totaling nearly $9 billion. FPL adds nearly 100,000 customers each year, and expects a 3 percent compound annual growth of new customers through 1994. The company has 11 generating plants, including 3 nuclear units. FPL is developing such alternative sources of fuel as coal, garbage, and sugarcane-refinery residue, and continues to lessen its dependency on oil. It is considered a leader in promoting energy efficiency among customers and has received numerous awards for using this policy to benefit its communities. The company serves more than 5.7 million Floridians in 700 communities, primarily along the east and southwest coasts. FPL has more than 13,500 employees.

ALL TRAINING PROGRAMS

On-the-job training is emphasized for technical and managerial positions. Some classroom training is also provided. You are encouraged to attend company seminars and training by outside groups.

QUALIFICATIONS

FPL looks for recent graduates as well as experienced professionals in the following fields: accounting, finance, business administration, computer science, engineering technology, and engineering—electrical, electronics, industrial, mechanical, nuclear, and chemical.

RECRUITMENT AND PLACEMENT

Recruitment and placement are in Florida.

SALARY AND BENEFITS

The College Placement Council Salary Survey for September 1986–June 1987 indicates starting salaries for public utilities to be $1,905 a month for those with a B.A. degree in nontechnical curricula and $2,355 with a B.A. degree in technical curricula. M.B.A. starting salaries were $2,403 for a nontechnical undergraduate degree and $2,667 for a technical undergraduate degree. Check with the company for more specific salary information. Benefits include medical, dental, and life insurance; retirement benefits; a stockownership plan; an investment program; and educational assistance.

CONTACT

T. Studer, Corporate Recruiting, Florida Power & Light Company, P.O. Box 029100, Miami, FL 33102.

FLUOR CORPORATION

ENGINEERING

THE COMPANY

Fluor started as a general contracting business seventy years ago in Santa Ana, California. Today the firm employs over 20,000 people throughout the world, specializing in serving the energy and natural resources industries. It is made up of five operating groups: Engineering and Construction (the largest), Drilling Services, Oil and Gas, Minerals and Metals, and Distribution. Listed among *Fortune*'s most admired corporations, Fluor ranks number 5 in the Fortune 100 largest diversified service companies. Its annual sales exceed $4 billion.

ENGINEERING TRAINING PROGRAM

New engineering employees participate on task forces where they receive on-the-job training. Some engineering departments also offer daily classes; others offer half-day classes with half-day on-the-job training. The human resource development departments conduct management development courses in supervision, management practices, negotiating techniques, performance measurement, and counseling. Additionally, the company has an education refund program for job-related graduate study.

QUALIFICATIONS

You should have a degree or background in management, engineering, construction, design, procurement, sales, geology, mining, drilling, or computer sciences.

RECRUITMENT AND PLACEMENT

Fluor has offices scattered throughout the United States and in many areas of the world. The two largest engineering divisions are in Irvine, California, and Greenville, South Carolina.

SALARY AND BENEFITS

The College Placement Council Salary Survey for September 1986–June 1987 indicates starting salaries for building materials manufacturers and construction companies to be $1,782 a month for those with a B.A. degree in nontechnical curricula and $2,156 with a B.A. degree in technical curricula. M.B.A. starting salaries were $1,666 for a nontechnical undergraduate degree and $2,677 for a technical undergraduate degree. Check with the company for more specific salary information. Benefits include health, life, and travel insurance, flexibility in the use of time off with pay, long-term disability, a profit-sharing trust fund, and a savings investment plan.

CONTACT

General Manager, Human Resources, Fluor Corporation, 3333 Michelson Drive, Irvine, CA 92730.

FMC CORPORATION

ACCOUNTING/FINANCE • APPLICATIONS ENGINEERING • APPLICATIONS PROGRAMMING/ANALYSIS • DESIGN ENGINEERING • MANUFACTURING ENGINEERING • PROCESS ENGINEERING • PRODUCTION SUPERVISION • RESEARCH AND DEVELOPMENT • SALES • SYSTEMS PROGRAMMING/ANALYSIS

THE COMPANY

As one of the world's leading producers of machinery and chemicals for industry, agriculture, and government, FMC addresses the markets for industrial chemicals, petroleum equipment and services, defense systems, performance chemicals, and specialized machinery. Founded as the Bean Spray Pump Company in 1884, the company went through numerous name changes before settling on its current less restrictive name. The company employs approximately 30,000 people worldwide with more than 95 production facilities and mines in 25 states and 15 other countries. Its products include fire engines, insecticides, earth-moving equipment, guided missile launching systems, and air pollution control equipment. Listed among *Fortune*'s most admired corporations, FMC has annual sales totaling more than $3 billion and is number 131 in the Fortune 500 largest U.S. industrial corporations.

ALL TRAINING PROGRAMS

FMC emphasizes on-the-job training for new employees. You will be supervised in your first assignments as you learn the company's policies and procedures. Through assignments of increasing complexity and frequent discussions with your supervisor, you'll begin to shape your career. FMC promotes from within whenever possible.

QUALIFICATIONS

FMC hires graduates from many disciplines, including engineering (agricultural, chemical, computer science, electrical/electronics, industrial, materials, mechanical, and technology); science (agricultural, life, and chemistry); and business (accounting/finance, business/marketing, and information systems). You are invited to discuss other areas or possibilities with the company.

RECRUITMENT AND PLACEMENT

FMC recruits around the country. Headquarters are in Chicago, and other major offices are in San Jose, California; Minneapolis; Philadelphia; Princeton, New Jersey; and Houston.

SALARY AND BENEFITS

The College Placement Council Salary Survey for September 1986–June 1987 indicates starting salaries for chemicals, drugs, and allied products companies to be $1,964 a month for those with a B.A. degree in nontechnical curricula and $2,457 with a B.A. degree in technical curricula. M.B.A. starting salaries were $2,886 for a nontechnical undergraduate degree and $2,794 for a technical undergraduate degree. Check with the company for more specific salary information. FMC offers comprehensive medical and dental coverage, short-term disability protection, life insurance, a retirement plan, an employee thrift and stock-purchase plan, and tuition reimbursement.

CONTACT

Manager, College Relations, FMC Corporation, 200 East Randolph Drive, Chicago, IL 60601.

FOLEY'S DEPARTMENT STORES

ACCOUNTING AND FINANCE · ADMINISTRATIVE AND TECHNICAL SUPPORT MANAGEMENT · ART · BUYING · HUMAN RESOURCES · INFORMATION SYSTEMS · MERCHANDISE MANAGEMENT · RESEARCH · STORE MANAGEMENT · WRITING

THE COMPANY

Foley's is the largest full-line department store operation between Atlanta and Los Angeles. It serves six major Texas markets—Dallas, Houston, Austin, San Antonio, Bryan/College Station, and Corpus Christi—as well as Oklahoma, New Mexico, and Arizona. As a result of the 1987 merger by the parent company, Federated Department Stores, of Foley's and Sanger Harris, Foley's expanded to 38 stores. It is a $1 billion-plus retailer, with sales that make it the sixth largest department store in the country. Foley's makes a commitment to giving back to the communities it serves through support for the arts, United Way charities, and local events. A Purdue University survey named Foley's Retail Management Training Program number one in the nation.

MANAGEMENT TRAINING PROGRAMS

You will be introduced to Foley's philosophies and policies in a ten-week training course. Classroom instruction is combined with on-the-job training. You will attend class for fifteen full days during the ten-week period. The sessions are designed for participation rather than straight lecture. Instructors are members of upper and middle management who can relate firsthand experiences and realities of the job. As part of the on-the-job training, you and your manager have shared responsibility for your training. You are responsible for demonstrating a desire to enhance your knowledge and skills by asking questions and actively seeking information. Your manager has the responsibility to answer your questions, expose you to the many functions which go on in the department, and challenge you to initiate new ideas. As part of Foley's ongoing training, seminars are conducted regularly on managerial techniques, new supervisory models, situational leadership, merchandising tools, negotiation skills, time management, and more.

QUALIFICATIONS

College degrees are preferred but not required. Personality, alertness, and a good attitude will catch the attention of recruiters. Retail experience will help.

RECRUITMENT AND PLACEMENT

Foley's hires between 50 and 100 trainees per year. It recruits in the Southwest. There are two or three programs per year, with all training in Houston. You will work in one of the stores in a major metropolitan area.

SALARIES AND BENEFITS

The College Placement Council Salary Survey for September 1986–June 1987 indicates starting salaries for merchandising (retail and wholesale) and service companies to be $1,594 a month for those with a B.A. degree in nontechnical curricula and $2,141 with a B.A. degree in technical curricula. M.B.A. starting salaries were $2,572 for a nontechnical undergraduate degree, and $2,735 for an M.B.A. with technical undergraduate degree. Check with the company for more specific salary information. Your benefits will include major medical and dental insurance as well as a substantial employee discount on purchases.

CONTACT

Foley's, c/o Manager Executive Recruiting, P.O. Box 1971, Houston, TX 77251.

FORD MOTOR COMPANY

EMPLOYEE RELATIONS • ENGINEERING • FINANCE • MANUFACTURING • MARKETING • PRODUCT PLANNING • SALES • SYSTEMS

THE COMPANY

Ford sells more than 5 million vehicles annually, has approximately 380,000 employees, and spans an array of transportation, electronics, aerospace, and materials technologies. In 1986 it was the most profitable automobile company in the world with earnings of $3.3 billion on sales of $62.7 billion. The company provides financial and land development services as well. Job functions at Ford often cross divisional, organizational, and even international lines. Listed among *Fortune*'s most admired corporations, Ford ranks number 3 in the Fortune 500 largest U.S. industrial corporations.

ALL TRAINING PROGRAMS

You will be given challenging assignments as well as formal classes to introduce you to Ford's operations and your job responsibilities.

EMPLOYEE RELATIONS PROGRAM

During your first two years, you may have up to four assignments, possibly in several company locations, to develop your understanding of problems and solutions in employee relations. Your first assignment could be to a Ford plant where you can gain experience in salaried personnel, training, personnel services, and hourly personnel and labor relations. You may, at this point, participate in resolving plant labor relations issues in accord with collective bargaining agreements. Some new professionals begin with staff assignments such as personnel planning, salary administration, benefits planning and administration, or special employee communications projects. Employee relations professionals are involved with more than a dozen unions, more than 300 plant and office locations, and national as well as international personnel issues.

QUALIFICATIONS

You will need a graduate degree in industrial relations, labor relations, human resource management, or business administration, and will have to rank in the top third of your class.

ENGINEERING PROGRAM

There are many engineering groups—engine, transmission and axle, chassis, climate control, body, electrical and electronics, and materials engineering. The initial phases of your career give you on-the-job experience in several of these engineering groups and exposure to virtually all of them. During this time you will be expected to define general career interests and to prepare yourself for advancement. You may specialize, but Ford prefers to develop well-rounded engineers. You may learn many perspectives—design, component engineering, overall vehicle engineering, manufacturing engineering, perhaps even plant engineering. Your advancement could be upward in engineering, across to manufacturing, over to product planning, or to general management.

QUALIFICATIONS

You should have a degree in mechanical, electrical, automotive, chemical, or electronics engineering; physics, engineering mechanics, or computer science. Ford prefers graduates who rank in the top third of their class.

FINANCE PROGRAM

You will gain experience quickly through a variety of assignments. You may start with the corporate staff, with a division, or at a plant. Your early assignments may include: budgeting and cost control; manufacturing and capital investment analysis; market and price analysis; product analysis; profit planning and forecasting; treasury (everything from funding analysis and actions to portfolio investments); and accounting and auditing. Ford works hard to make certain that senior management knows how you are progressing and that you receive both line and staff assignments. Finance people are excellent candidates for senior management positions worldwide.

QUALIFICATIONS

Ford will consider you if you rank in the top third of your class and have a graduate degree in finance, accounting, economics, engineering/business, business administration, industrial management, or management science.

MANUFACTURING PROGRAM

Ford sees a great competitive advantage in moving manufacturing and product engineering groups closer together. Some Ford facilities no longer distinguish between manufacturing and product engineers. Your on-the-job training will prepare you to be part of teams that do both. Other Ford operations, such as body and assembly, will provide you with product and manufacturing engineering experience during your first two years on the job. You might spend time in component engineering, move to a line automation project, or work in both stamping and assembly plants during your first two years. After you have a broad base of experience, you will be ready to move between manufacturing and engineering and upward in both.

QUALIFICATIONS

You may have any of the following degrees: mechanical, electrical, chemical, metallurgical, industrial, manufacturing, environmental, automotive, or ceramic engineering; business administration, industrial management, computer science/systems engineering. The company prefers graduates who rank in the top third of their class.

MARKETING AND SALES PROGRAM

Initially, you will receive on-the-job training in a district sales office. Early assignments might include forecasting sales in specific market segments, analyzing dealer operating and financial statements, planning sales development strategies, and managing customer relations. On-the-job experience will be supplemented by self-study programs and structured training. If you begin with the Ford or Lincoln-Mercury divisions, you will participate, generally within six months of your start, in the fifteen-week field manager training program. This program includes intensive training in dealer operations, credit and zone management. You will also work for several weeks in a dealership. The Field Manager Training Program, which includes structured training at the Ford Marketing Institute, is recognized as among the best in the industry. Ford Parts and Service Division provides similar training through a career development program that includes customer relations, sales and service strategies, and all facets of dealer parts and service operations.

QUALIFICATIONS

You should have a graduate degree in marketing, business administration, economics, finance, management, or automotive technology, and be in the top third of your class.

PRODUCT PLANNING PROGRAM

You will probably begin as an analyst, learning on the job from senior professionals on one or more project teams. You will quickly become involved in both the advanced planning and the implementation stages of various product programs. During your early assignments you may undertake market analyses, cost/benefit studies, pricing determinations, sourcing analyses, and technology evaluations. As a product planner, you are in close touch with corporate management as well as with engineering, finance, marketing and sales, purchasing, and the other functions that turn product concepts into reality. Successful product planning professionals are considered candidates for management positions.

QUALIFICATIONS

You should have a graduate degree in business administration, finance, marketing, or industrial management, with an undergraduate degree in engineering or science. Ford prefers graduates who rank in the top third of their class.

SUPPLY PROGRAM

You will begin your career in the Ford College Graduate Program. You will be given assignments to develop your knowledge, then monitored and directed as necessary. Your assignments will be supplemented by Ford-sponsored supply education and general training courses. During this period you will be given challenging assignments to gain maximum exposure to a variety of commodities, components, manufacturing processes, and procurement strategies. You will be expected to develop your own commodity/component plans, which will be monitored by senior professionals. You will be encouraged from the beginning to seek as much responsibility as you can handle.

QUALIFICATIONS

Depending on the area of supply you go into, your degree might be in any of the following: business administration, materials and logistics management, marketing, finance, economics, management science, industrial engineering or management, statistics, transportation, business logistics, traffic management, or mathematics. Your G.P.A. should put you in the top third of your class.

SYSTEMS PROGRAM

You may join the Ford systems team as a programmer or analyst in several ways: as a trainee working to acquire specific skills, as a technical specialist making use of knowledge or skills learned in school or on previous jobs; or as a member of a development team tackling a specific problem. A sample of some areas in which you will have the opportunity to gain experience include: applications such as engineering information systems, manufacturing and supply management systems, office automation, finance, and personnel systems; and computer systems and communications such as: operating systems, database management, software development, local area networks, and telecommunications. Ford's annual systems budget is in the hundreds of millions.

QUALIFICATIONS

Your degree may be in quantitative methods, industrial administration, industrial engineering, statistics, combined technical and business administration, computer science, or management science. You should rank in the top third of your class.

ALL PROGRAMS

RECRUITMENT AND PLACEMENT

Ford recruits nationwide. The company generally does not recruit U.S. citizens for employment outside the country. You will likely spend at least part of your career in Dearborn, Michigan; but branch offices are located throughout the country.

SALARY AND BENEFITS

The College Placement Council Salary Survey for September 1986–June 1987 indicates starting salaries for automotive and mechanical equipment companies to be $1,907 a month for those with a B.A. degree in nontechnical curricula and $2,333 with a B.A. degree in technical curricula. M.B.A. starting salaries were $2,697 for a nontechnical undergraduate degree and $2,986 for a technical undergraduate degree. Check with the company for more specific salary information. Ford offers the following benefits: retirement and investment plans; profit sharing; medical care, dental- and vision-care plans; life and accident insurance; disability benefits; paid holidays and vacations; and car-purchase plans.

CONTACT

Your college placement office for dates of recruiter visits, or Department CR, Ford Motor Company, The American Road, Room 450, P.O. Box 1899, Dearborn, MI 48121-1899.

FOREIGN SERVICE, U.S.

ADMINISTRATOR · CONSULAR OFFICER · CULTURAL AFFAIRS OFFICER · ECONOMIC OFFICER · INFORMATION OFFICER · NURSE · PHYSICIAN · POLITICAL OFFICER

THE COMPANY

The Foreign Service of the United States is America's diplomatic, consular, commercial, and overseas cultural and information service. It assists the President and Secretary of State in planning, conducting, and implementing our foreign policy at home and abroad. Some 4,000 Foreign Service officers of the Department of State serve as administrative, consular, economic, and political officers in more than 230 U.S. embassies and consulates in over 140 nations, in Washington, D.C., and with other government agencies. Some 850 Foreign Service officers of the United States Information Agency serve abroad as public affairs, information, and cultural affairs officers; at headquarters in Washington; and elsewhere in government. The Foreign Commercial Service has some 165 officers. Some 3,500 Foreign Service specialists support diplomatic offices around the world. Personnel spend an average of 60 percent of their careers abroad, moving every two to four years. This imposed mobility presents challenges to family life and raising children not found in more settled careers. To potential recruits, the Service emphasizes the likely hardships, not the adventure and intrigue. But for those who are motivated and dedicated to public service, a Foreign Service career offers unique rewards and opportunities such as frequent travel, a stimulating work environment, and the enriching cultural and social experience of living abroad.

ALL TRAINING PROGRAMS

The purpose of training is to acquaint you fully with the four main career areas in the Foreign Service: administrative, consular, economic/commercial, and political. As a newly appointed career officer, you will receive as much as eight months of training. This will include language instruction, if needed. You will be rotated among several functional areas in your first years of service.

QUALIFICATIONS

You should have a liberal arts or social science degree, preferably with courses in history, government, economics, law, literature, and international relations. Recent candidates selected have ranged in age from the early twenties to the middle fifties, with a median age of thirty-one. Of those officers recently appointed, 54 percent had master's degrees, 11 percent had law degrees, and 6 percent had Ph.D.s. Many had some years of professional work experience as well. You should have a keen awareness of the significance of current events and trends, breadth of knowledge of domestic and international affairs, and a wide range of interests. "Acceptable skills" in at least one foreign language are a real plus. You and all dependents must meet medical fitness standards.

RECRUITMENT AND PLACEMENT

You could be assigned just about anywhere in the world.

SALARIES AND BENEFITS

New entry-level officers are appointed at Foreign Service classes 6, 5, or 4, depending on qualifications, experience, and salary record. Appointment at entry FS-5 normally requires a master's degree. Appointment at entry-level F-4 normally requires a master's degree and eighteen months of experience in a field closely related to the Foreign Service and in a position equivalent to at least the F-5 level. Specialists are appointed at classes FS-9 through FS-2. Appointments to top-ranking FS-1 are rare. Typical salaries range from $15,000 to $62,000. Benefits include cost-of-living allowance, hardship differentials, medical benefits, educational allowances for children, and a retirement program.

CONTACT

Foreign Service, Department of State, U.S.A., Washington, DC 20520.

FRITO-LAY, INC.

ENGINEERING • INFORMATION SYSTEMS • PRODUCTION • RESEARCH AND DEVELOPMENT • SALES • TECHNICAL SERVICES

THE COMPANY

Frito-Lay, headquartered in Plano, Texas, manufactures a full line of snack foods. Founded as two regional snack companies in the twenties and thirties, the two had merged only four years before joining Pepsi-Cola in 1965. Today, Frito-Lay is one of the largest contributors to the profits of the parent company. It employs about 27,000 people throughout the country.

ALL TRAINING PROGRAMS

The length of the training program will depend on your starting position. The training includes on-the-job experience complemented with classroom instruction. Complete tuition reimbursement is available for job-related courses.

QUALIFICATIONS

Most positions require either a bachelor's or a master's degree. The company prefers graduates who rank in the top 25 percent of their class, with a minimum G.P.A. of 3.0. Some research positions require a doctorate. If you are seeking a business position, an M.B.A. with up to three years of experience is preferred. Graduates with one or more years of related work experience have an advantage. Familiarity with a foreign language will count in your favor.

Engineering majors (chemical, civil, construction, electrical, technology, environmental, industrial/management, manufacturing, and mechanical) usually find positions at Frito-Lay in technical services. Some engineering majors (such as environmental, food science, industrial management, and manufacturing) may find a job in the production end of making snack foods. Computer engineering and computer science majors will be placed in information systems jobs. Other production jobs are available for chemistry majors and mathematics majors. Environmental engineering majors may also be placed in research positions. Operations research majors are in technical services jobs. M.B.A.s may be placed as assistant product managers, business analysts, business planners, consultants, distribution supervisors, employee relations associates, sales personnel, or systems analysts.

PLACEMENT

Starting locations for manufacturing and sales are throughout the United States. Other positions are headquartered near Dallas.

SALARIES AND BENEFITS

The College Placement Council Salary Survey for September 1986–June 1987 indicates starting salaries for food and beverage processing companies to be $1,834 a month for those with a B.A. degree in nontechnical curricula and $2,301 with a B.A. degree in technical curricula. M.B.A. starting salaries were $3,043 for a nontechnical undergraduate degree and $3,098 for a technical undergraduate degree. Check with the company for more specific salary information. Benefits include tuition reimbursement; major medical, life, and long-term disability insurance; savings and retirement plans; and relocation assistance.

CONTACT

David L. Koch, Associate Manager, College Relations, Frito-Lay, Inc., P.O. Box 660634, Dallas, TX 75266-0634.

FURR'S CAFETERIAS, INC.

FOOD MANAGEMENT

THE COMPANY

Furr's Cafeterias, a subsidiary of the K mart Corporation, has operated in the Southwest since 1947. The company has 130 cafeterias employing about 10,000 people in 11 states and is still expanding.

FOOD MANAGEMENT TRAINING PROGRAM

The cafeteria management program provides comprehensive on-the-job training in all phases of cafeteria operations and lasts six months. Your training will include quality food production, cost control methods, personnel policies, management styles, and corporate philosophies. In addition, corporate management development seminars are conducted quarterly for your continual training.

QUALIFICATIONS

If you have a business-related degree, prior management responsibilities, and a stable employment history, Furr's is looking for you. It wants people who are genuinely interested in a management career in the food service industry.

RECRUITMENT AND PLACEMENT

Career opportunities are available in various cities in Arizona, Arkansas, California, Colorado, Kansas, Missouri, Nebraska, Nevada, New Mexico, Oklahoma, and Texas.

SALARY AND BENEFITS

Including salary and bonus, managers can expect to receive between $25,000 and $85,000 a year, based on their cafeteria's performance. Your base starting salary will be about $16,000. Benefits include medical and life insurance, a pension plan, a savings plan, free meals while on duty, and a stock-option plan.

CONTACT

J. Wilson Tye, Manager of Recruitment, Furr's Cafeterias, Inc., P.O. Box 6747, Lubbock, TX 79413.

G

☆ ☆ ☆ ☆ ☆

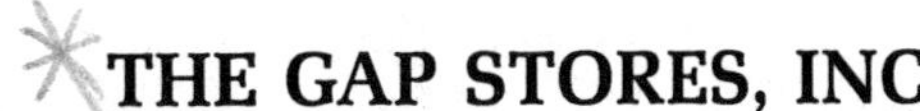

THE GAP STORES, INC.

ACCOUNTING · DISTRIBUTION · FINANCE · INFORMATION SYSTEMS · MANAGEMENT · MARKETING · MERCHANDISING

THE COMPANY

The Gap sells more jeans and tops than any other specialty retailer in the United States. Since 1969, when the first Gap store opened in San Francisco, the company has grown to more than 600 stores in 80 of the top 100 national markets. Its newest project is the development of "Super Gap" stores, which are three to five times larger than most Gap stores.

MANAGEMENT TRAINING PROGRAM

A four-month, on-the-job training program in any one of the Gap stores prepares you for your first position as assistant store manager. In addition, you will participate in seminars and training sessions in the field and at corporate headquarters in San Francisco.

QUALIFICATIONS

The Gap recruits college graduates with a variety of backgrounds. Retailing requires leadership and decision-making skills, an entrepreneurial approach, and supervisory abilities. If you possess these abilities and are interested in a rapidly growing retailing company, The Gap may be for you.

RECRUITMENT AND PLACEMENT

The Gap recruits nationwide. It has positions not only in store management but also in finance, management information systems, distribution, merchandising, and marketing. You will probably start in California if you are not in store management.

SALARY AND BENEFITS

The College Placement Council Salary Survey for September 1986–June 1987 indicates starting salaries for merchandising (retail and wholesale) and service companies to be $1,594 a month for those with a B.A. degree in nontechnical curricula and $2,141 with a B.A. degree in technical curricula. M.B.A. starting salaries were $2,572 for a nontechnical undergraduate degree, and $2,735 for an M.B.A. with technical undergraduate degree. Check with the company for more specific salary information. Benefits include medical, dental, and life insurance; an accidental death and dismemberment insurance package; supplemental life insurance; and long-term disability insurance. In addition, you can take advantage of a savings/retirement plan, tuition reimbursement, and a discount on merchandise.

CONTACT

Joan Witterholt, Recruiting and Placement Specialist, The Gap Stores, Inc., P.O. Box 60, 900 Cherry Avenue, San Bruno, CA 94066.

GE

ACCOUNTING • CHEMISTRY-METALLURGY • COMPUTER SCIENCE • ENGINEERING • MARKETING • RESEARCH TECHNOLOGY • SALES

THE COMPANY

Recent mergers and acquisitions (including RCA, Kidder, Peabody, and Employers Reinsurance) make GE one of the most diversified companies in the world. It is involved in 14 different businesses in technology, services, and core manufacturing. The technology businesses—aircraft engine, aerospace, plastics, medical systems, and factory automation—represent a significant thrust into the global market for advanced technology. The service businesses—financial, communications, and NBC—give GE a major position in the fastest-growing segment of the economy. The core manufacturing businesses—major appliances, lighting, power systems, construction equipment, transportation systems, and motor—are high-quality competitors in the world marketplace. In addition, GE has 5 important divisions that enhance its ability to compete successfully in domestic and foreign markets: consumer electronics, international, corporate trading, petroleum, and semiconductor. In 1986 GE accelerated the use of joint ventures and other alliances to open or expand world market opportunities. GE Factory Automation formed an alliance with FANUC LTD of Japan; GE Plastics and PPG Industries, Inc., created Azdel, Inc.; and GE Medical Systems increased its investment in a Japanese joint venture, Yokogawa Medical Systems. GE is working to increase its number of women and minorities in management positions each year. Minorities account for 11.4 percent of GE's employees, and women account for 27.6 percent. GE's annual sales exceed $35 billion a year. The company is listed among *Fortune*'s most admired corporations and ranks number 6 in the Fortune 500 largest U.S. industrial corporations.

ALL TRAINING PROGRAMS

Each year about half of GE entry-level candidates begin their careers in professional development programs. Most programs represent a broad range of GE businesses; some a small number of businesses with similar personnel requirements. A few businesses, such as GE Aircraft Engines, administer their own development programs. All GE programs combine rotating work assignments with required functional and business management courses. Some incorporate options to pursue graduate degrees at nearby universities.

CHEMICAL-METALLURGICAL MANAGEMENT PROGRAM

The Chem-Met Program prepares engineers for manufacturing management positions in GE's chemical, metallurgical, plastics, and materials businesses. The two-year program includes four manufacturing assignments in two locations. You will also participate in educational courses at your work location.

QUALIFICATIONS

You should have a B.S. or M.S. degree in chemical, metallurgical, or materials engineering.

CORPORATE RESEARCH PROGRAM

The Research Technology Program (RTP) involves a variety of projects over two years at the GE Research and Development Center. The Software Technology Program (STP) involves three years at the R & D Center while pursuing an M.S. in computer engineering or computer science at local universities.

QUALIFICATIONS

RTP candidates should have B.S. or M.S. degrees in chemistry, ceramics, metallurgy, physics, computer science, or engineering. STP candidates should have a B.S. degree in computer science or engineering.

EDISON ENGINEERING PROGRAM

The Edison Engineering Program will help you develop broad technical competence in product and process design engineering. In the two-year program you will receive rotational work assignments, take a course in applied engineering problem solving, and attend a one-week in-residence engineering leadership course.

QUALIFICATIONS

Most of the candidates accepted have B.S. or M.S. degrees in electrical, mechanical, or nuclear engineering.

FIELD ENGINEERING PROGRAM

This program seeks engineers who want hands-on experience and enjoy working with customers in the utility, industrial, transportation, marine, and mining industries. During the one-year program you will be given work assignments in field offices or product businesses with technical training at the Training and Development Center in Schenectady, New York.

QUALIFICATIONS

Most candidates have B.S. degrees in electrical or mechanical engineering.

FINANCIAL MANAGEMENT PROGRAM

In the Financial Management Program you will receive rotational work assignments as well as attend seminars in accounting, finance, and operational analysis. Depending on your background in accounting, the program should take two to two and a half years.

QUALIFICATIONS

You should have a degree in accounting, finance, business administration, economics, mathematics, or liberal arts.

INFORMATION SYSTEMS MANAGEMENT PROGRAM

This program will prepare you for professional and managerial positions in information technology. During the two-year program you will combine six-month rotational job assignments with graduate-level courses in information technology.

QUALIFICATIONS

You need an interest in business information systems and quantitative analysis, and a bachelor's or master's degree with a minimum of two computer science courses.

MANUFACTURING MANAGEMENT PROGRAM

The Manufacturing Management Program is for engineers who want to develop their skills in manufacturing automation and management. It is a two-year program with four assignments in two locations. You will attend a one-week in-residence program each year and follow a nine-month manufacturing leadership curriculum.

QUALIFICATIONS

Most of the candidates accepted have B.S. or M.S. degrees in electrical, mechanical, or industrial engineering.

TECHNICAL SALES PROGRAM

The Technical Sales Program will prepare you for sales or application and systems engineering for businesses serving the industrial, electric utility, construction, manufacturing automation, communications systems, and medical equipment markets. During the eighteen-month program you will be sent to work in field sales offices and product business locations. You will attend sales and marketing courses at GE's Management Development Institute in Crotonville, New York.

QUALIFICATIONS

You should have a B.S. degree in electrical, mechanical, or industrial engineering.

ALL PROGRAMS

QUALIFICATIONS

In addition to specific degree requirements, you should have a high G.P.A. (in the top quartile of your class), combined with work experience and activities indicating leadership potential.

RECRUITMENT AND PLACEMENT

GE recruits primarily through campus interviews conducted at 110 universities from September through February. You could work anywhere in the GE system. Plants and laboratories are located in over 200 locations in 34 states and Puerto Rico. The majority of U.S. facilities are in states east of the Mississippi River. Sales offices and service facilities are nationwide.

SALARY AND BENEFITS

The College Placement Council Salary Survey for September 1986–June 1987 indicates starting salaries for electrical and electronic machine and equipment companies to be $1,861 a month for those with a B.A. degree in nontechnical curricula and $2,419 with a B.A. degree in technical curricula. M.B.A. starting salaries were $2,784 for a nontechnical undergraduate degree and $2,818 for a technical undergraduate degree. The CPC Survey gives average starting salaries for automotive and mechanical equipment companies of $1,907 a month for those with a B.A. degree in nontechnical curricula and $2,333 with a B.A. degree in technical curricula. M.B.A. starting salaries were $2,697 for a nontechnical undergraduate degree and $2,986 for a technical undergraduate degree. Check with the company for more specific salary information. GE's benefits are comprehensive, including substantial life and medical insurance, a savings and security program with the company matching 50 percent of the employee's investment, pension plan, sick leave and vacations, discounts on some products, and tuition refunds.

CONTACT

GE Applicant Referral Center, Bldg. 36-1, Schenectady, NY 12345.

GEARHART INDUSTRIES, INC.

ENGINEERING

THE COMPANY

Gearhart is an oil- and gas-well service company that was begun in 1955. The company also provides international wire-line drilling.

ENGINEERING TRAINING PROGRAM

Field engineer trainees begin their careers with field instruction supplemented with formal training schools conducted by the company at its training center in Fort Worth. These sessions include management and sales training as well as technical instruction. After completing this initial training, engineers are sent to the field for further training under a qualified engineer. Then the new employee will be promoted to the position of field engineer and assigned a unit and crew with corresponding supervisory responsibilities.

QUALIFICATIONS

The company hires graduates in electrical engineering, computer science, and mechanical engineering.

RECRUITMENT AND PLACEMENT

The company has field offices throughout the United States and Canada.

SALARY AND BENEFITS

The College Placement Council Salary Survey for September 1986–June 1987 indicates starting salaries for petroleum and allied products (including natural gas) companies to be $1,972 a month for those with a B.A. degree in nontechnical curricula and $2,497 with a B.A. degree in technical curricula. M.B.A. starting salaries were $2,629 for a nontechnical undergraduate degree and $2,970 for a technical undergraduate degree. Check with the company for more specific salary information. Benefits consist of medical, dental, and disability insurance; a retirement program; bonus payments; and use of a company vehicle.

CONTACT

Gearhart Industries, Inc., Personnel Department, P.O. Box 1936, Fort Worth, TX 76101.

GENERAL DYNAMICS

ENGINEERING • HARDWARE/SOFTWARE PROGRAMMING • RESEARCH AND DEVELOPMENT

THE COMPANY

As a leading defense contractor, General Dynamics is active in five major markets: electronics, shipbuilding, aerospace, military land systems, and resources and building products. It is one of the country's 50 largest industrial companies and employs more than 100,000 people. Its 14 divisions and subsidiaries are spread across most of the United States and into 45 foreign countries. In 1986, General Dynamics' sales topped $9 billion with a backlog of almost three times that amount. Among the products that its various subsidiaries provide are: Tomahawk Cruise missiles, Cessna airplanes, Trident submarines, computer-output microfilm systems and equipment, and advanced missile systems. The company employs engineers of all types, ranging from electro-optical to composite and aerospace/aeronautical. Regional centers in California, Michigan, Connecticut, and Texas design, develop, and operate advanced computer-based information systems to support the engineering and business activities of the company's operating units. Headquarters are in St. Louis, Missouri. General Dynamics is listed among *Fortune*'s most admired corporations and ranks number 36 in the Fortune 500 largest U.S. industrial corporations.

ALL TRAINING PROGRAMS

As a student or recent graduate you will be encouraged to participate in one of General Dynamics' co-op or summer intern programs. You will work side by side with experienced engineers, many of whom are recognized as leaders in their field. In the co-op program you will alternate semesters of study with work. You will be exposed to a wide variety of technical and managerial development courses during your career with General Dynamics to ensure that your knowledge is current.

QUALIFICATIONS

General Dynamics looks for candidates with strong academic achievement and degrees in the following specialties: aerospace/aeronautical, civil/structural, electrical/electronics, industrial, manufacturing, marine, mechanical, metallurgical/materials, mining, naval architecture, nuclear systems, and welding engineering; engineering technology/science; computer science, mathematics, operations research; physics.

RECRUITMENT AND PLACEMENT

General Dynamics recruits extensively on campuses around the country. Placement could be almost anywhere in the United States.

SALARY AND BENEFITS

The College Placement Council Salary Survey for September 1986–June 1987 indicates starting salaries for aerospace companies to be $1,943 a month for those with a B.A. degree in nontechnical curricula and $2,399 with a B.A. degree in technical curricula. M.B.A. starting salaries were $2,330 for a nontechnical undergraduate degree and $2,475 for a technical undergraduate degree. Check with the company for more specific salary information. The company's benefits are comprehensive.

CONTACT

Corporate College Relations Administrator, General Dynamics Corporation, Pierre Laclede Center, St. Louis, MO 63105.

GENERAL FOODS CORPORATION
SALES/MARKETING

THE COMPANY

The world's largest diversified food company traces its roots to health food zealot Charles William Post, who developed the coffee substitute Postum in 1895, Grape-Nuts cereal in 1897, and Post Toasties (originally named Elijah's Manna) in 1904. What is now General Foods was formed in the 1920s when several food-processing firms—notably Maxwell House Coffee and Jell-O gelatin desserts—joined forces with the Post cereal business. Most of the original companies started before the turn of the century. One, the Walter Baker chocolate business, predates the American Revolution. The frozen foods industry had its start when General Foods bought the quick-freezing process from inventor Clarence Birdseye in 1929. General Foods acquired Kool-Aid soft-drink mixes in the 1950s, Burger Chef restaurants in the 1960s, and the Oscar Mayer meat products company in 1981. General Foods' products are among the best known and strongest in the country, with sales of almost $10 billion a year. The company puts more funds into research and development than any other company in the U.S. food industry and ranks among the top U.S. advertisers. General Foods became part of Philip Morris Companies, Inc., late in 1985.

SALES/MARKETING TRAINING PROGRAM

Initial training will prepare you to be a sales representative in 100 to 120 individual stores. Your supervisor will provide orientation in sales techniques in merchandising, advertising, shelving and distribution, and on-the-job training for your first position as sales representative. During the early months of your career you'll also attend the General Foods Professional Selling Skills Program conducted in your sales region. In addition, training workshops are conducted at district meetings. As you advance in your career, you'll receive training in account management, supervisory skills, and management development.

QUALIFICATIONS

General Foods is looking for sales management candidates who are self-reliant and goal- and achievement-oriented, and who have good judgment and creative problem-solving ability.

RECRUITMENT AND PLACEMENT

General Foods recruits on college campuses across the country. Openings exist throughout the United States.

SALARY AND BENEFITS

The College Placement Council Salary Survey for September 1986–June 1987 indicates starting salaries for food and beverage processing companies to be $1,834 a month for those with a B.A. degree in nontechnical curricula and $2,301 with a B.A. degree in technical curricula. M.B.A. starting salaries were $3,043 for a nontechnical undergraduate degree and $3,098 for a technical undergraduate degree. Check with the company for more specific salary and benefits information.

CONTACT

Sales Management Careers (S2-3), General Foods Corporation, 250 North Street, White Plains, NY 10625.

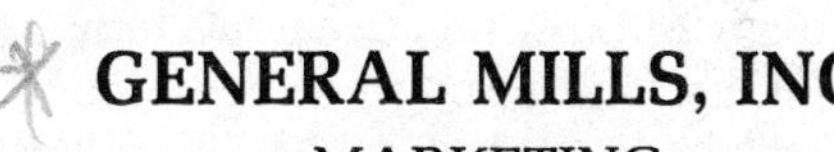

GENERAL MILLS, INC.
MARKETING

THE COMPANY

General Mills used to be all about food. Today the main emphasis is still on food, but the company announced a restructuring in mid-1986 to strengthen its profit picture that resulted in the divestiture or spin-off of about 30 percent of General Mills' assets. The newly streamlined company is divided into three divisions: consumer foods (Betty Crocker and Gorton's); restaurants (Red Lobster and The Olive Garden); and specialty retailing (Talbot's, Eddie Bauer, and Furniture Group America). The company believes in a decentralized management structure with decisions made at the lowest possible level. It is very protective of its employees—anyone who works for the company at least ten years cannot be fired without the personal permission of the president. Teamwork is the name of the game. General Mills does not have one-man or one-woman projects; you have to learn to fit in well in a team. The company promotes from within, so you'll be groomed for career advancement. Listed among *Fortune*'s most admired corporations, it ranks number 80 in the Fortune 500 largest U.S. industrial corporations.

MARKETING ASSISTANT TRAINING PROGRAM

In this intensive program you will work with a specific product during your first few months, assisted by a product manager, assistant product manager, and perhaps another marketing assistant. You will absorb a lot of information about your product, your profession, and your company. It's not uncommon for marketing assistants to become involved with multimillion-dollar budgets, promotional plans, and package design projects. Your success will lead to the next level, assistant product manager, then to product manager, and possibly beyond to other divisions or subsidiaries.

QUALIFICATIONS

You'll need an M.B.A., an ingenious mind, good analytical skills, and strong communication and interpersonal skills. You should be a self-starter who is comfortable making decisions.

RECRUITMENT AND PLACEMENT

Lots of people want to work for this company, and the recruitment process is not easy. General Mills recruits extensively on campus, and before someone is hired, he or she typically goes to headquarters in Minneapolis for two more days of interviewing (or to Florida for a position in the Restaurants Division, New York for the Fashion Division). Marketing assistants start in Minneapolis and will be assigned to one of the divisions making up the Consumer Foods area. But as a company spokesperson wryly notes, "Your initial product assignment at General Mills isn't a life sentence." Marketing people frequently move among products and divisions.

SALARY AND BENEFITS

The College Placement Council Salary Survey for September 1986–June 1987 indicates starting salaries for food and beverage processing companies to be $3,043 a month for those with an M.B.A. degree in nontechnical curricula and $3,098 with an M.B.A. degree in technical curricula. Check with the company for more specific salary information. Benefits include the basic hospitalization, life insurance, and investment plans; a pension plan; stockownership and educational assistance plans; scholarships to children of employees; and relocation reimbursement.

CONTACT

Director, Corporate Recruiting, General Mills, Inc., P.O. Box 1113, Minneapolis, MN 55440.

GENERAL MOTORS CORPORATION

ACCOUNTING • ADMINISTRATION • ENGINEERING • FINANCE • INFORMATION SYSTEMS AND PROCESSING • MARKETING • PRODUCTION • RESEARCH AND DEVELOPMENT • SALES • TECHNICAL SERVICES

THE COMPANY

Headquartered in Detroit, General Motors is a highly diversified manufacturing firm creating products for many different markets. Products range from automobiles, buses, and trucks to diesel and electric locomotives, construction equipment, and moon rovers. The company is also active in data processing, defense, electronics, information services, and telecommunications. Founded in 1908, GM has 560,000 employees in the United States, and another 150,000 outside the country. They work in 152 facilities operating in 26 states and 93 U.S. cities. Thirteen plants operate in Canada with assembly, manufacturing, distribution, sales, or warehousing operations in 37 other countries. GM is listed among *Fortune*'s most admired corporations and has annual sales of $100 billion-plus. It ranks number 1 in the Fortune 500 of the largest U.S. industrial corporations.

ALL TRAINING PROGRAMS

You will receive on-the-job training under the guidance of experienced supervisors. Depending on your position, you may be eligible for additional training through short courses, seminars, and workshops. GM encourages study for advanced degrees with tuition reimbursement and offers educational leaves of absence.

QUALIFICATIONS

You could be hired at GM with a bachelor's or master's degree in aerospace sciences, engineering (aerospace, ceramic, chemical, computer, electrical, electronics, management, mechanics, technology, industrial, manufacturing, mechanical, metallurgical, packaging, plastics, or software), chemistry, mathematics, or statistics. You should rank in the top half of your class and have a strong record of academic and extracurricular achievement.

RECRUITMENT AND PLACEMENT

GM recruits around the country and hires on a decentralized basis for each division, selecting almost 2,000 trainees a year. You could work in Alabama, Arizona, California, Connecticut, Delaware, Georgia, Illinois, Indiana, Kansas, Kentucky, Louisiana, Maryland, Massachusetts, Michigan, Mississippi, Missouri, New Jersey, New York, Ohio, Oklahoma, Pennsylvania, Tennessee, Texas, Virginia, or Wisconsin.

SALARY AND BENEFITS

With a bachelor's degree, you can expect to start at about $29,000; at $33,000 with a master's; and at $42,000 with a doctorate. Your benefits package will include medical, life, and dental coverage; pension and profit-sharing plans; flextime options; relocation assistance; and stock-purchase and savings plans.

CONTACT

Salaried Personnel at the division nearest you; or write General Motors Corporation, 3044 West Grand Boulevard, Detroit, MI 48202.

GENERAL TELEPHONE COMPANY OF FLORIDA, INC.

ACCOUNTING • COMPUTER SCIENCE • ENGINEERING • MANAGEMENT

THE COMPANY

General Telephone is a telecommunications utility in Florida that has been in business since 1901. It is the third largest operating company in the GTE Corporation of Stamford, Connecticut, and employs 11,200 in Florida. Its modern facilities include a new headquarters building in downtown Tampa equipped with an employee Health Fitness Center. General Telephone was the first company to use a fiber-optic system to relay the network transmission of a National Football League playoff game to television viewers. It operates throughout the state's west coast and serves more than 1.3 million customers in a 6-county area including the cities of Tampa, St. Petersburg, Clearwater, Sarasota, and Lakeland.

ALL TRAINING PROGRAMS

You will receive on-the-job training with orientation and rotational assignments to familiarize you with the scope of General Telephone's operations.

COMPUTER SCIENCE PROGRAM

Your training will be primarily on the job, building on your formal education. As a technical adviser you may assist other departments in the analysis and design of mainframe- and minicomputer-based mechanized systems. Other responsibilities may include assisting in the design, coding, testing, documenting, and maintenance of computer programs. You may be able to move into GTE Data Services, a subsidiary of GTE.

QUALIFICATIONS

You will need an undergraduate degree in computer technology, management information systems, or a related discipline. Knowledge of mainframe or minicomputers and COBOL, FORTRAN, BASIC, assembler, or PASCAL languages is desirable.

PLACEMENT

You will probably begin at headquarters in Tampa.

MANAGEMENT PROGRAM

You will begin an eighteen- to twenty-four-month training program with assignments in the customer service department as a first-line supervisor, the engineering and construction department, or business-related areas such as rates and tariffs, revenue development, or business relations. Orientation lasts several weeks. It highlights various departmental functions and offers supervisory training on company policies and labor relations. The second stage of orientation training involves classes tailored to the department of your initial assignment.

QUALIFICATIONS

You should have an undergraduate degree in engineering, computer science, or a business-related discipline. A graduate degree is desirable but not required.

PLACEMENT

You will probably be trained at headquarters in Tampa.

ALL TRAINING PROGRAMS

QUALIFICATIONS

General Telephone hires people with bachelor's and master's degrees in all areas of engineering (including electrical, systems, electronics, technology, and industrial/management), and math. Applications are also encouraged from graduates with a technical or nontechnical degree in business. You should rank in the top 50 percent of your class and have a minimum G.P.A. of 3.0. It hires U.S. citizens and holders of permanent residence visas as well as Canadian citizens.

RECRUITMENT

You may contact the company directly with a copy of your róoumé.

SALARY AND BENEFITS

The College Placement Council Salary Survey for September 1986–June 1987 indicates starting salaries for public utilities (including transportation) to be $1,905 a month for those with a B.A. degree in nontechnical curricula and $2,355 with a B.A. degree in technical curricula. M.B.A. starting salaries were $2,403 for a nontechnical undergraduate degree and $2,667 for a technical undergraduate degree. Check with the company for more specific salary information. Benefits will include medical, hospital, dental, pension, profit-sharing, stock-purchase, incentive savings plans; relocation services; tuition reimbursement; and a career development program.

CONTACT

Management Staffing, General Telephone Company of Florida, P.O. Box 110, MC77, Tampa, FL 33601.

GENERAL TELEPHONE COMPANY OF THE SOUTHWEST, INC.

ACCOUNTING · ADMINISTRATION · ENGINEERING · FINANCE · INFORMATION SYSTEMS · MARKETING · SALES · TECHNICAL SERVICES

THE COMPANY

General Telephone Company of the Southwest provides telecommunication services for businesses and residential customers in West Texas. The company is a subsidiary of GTE Corporation in Stamford, Connecticut, and employs 11,000 people in the United States.

ENGINEERING TRAINING PROGRAM

Engineers participate in a six- to twelve-month program that includes supervised on-the-job experience and classroom instruction.

QUALIFICATIONS

Applications are encouraged from graduates with engineering degrees in the following fields: computer science, civil engineering, electronics, electrical engineering, general engineering, engineering technology, industrial/management engineering, information science, mechanical engineering, mathematics, and business. The company prefers graduates who rank in the top quarter of their class and have some work experience.

RECRUITMENT AND PLACEMENT

You will work in West Texas.

SALARY AND BENEFITS

Bachelor's-level trainees start at salaries in the low twenties. The College Placement Council Salary Survey for September 1986–June 1987 indicates starting salaries for public utilities (including transportation) to be $1,905 a month for those with a B.A. degree in nontechnical curricula and $2,355 with a B.A. degree in technical curricula. M.B.A. starting salaries were $2,403 for a nontechnical undergraduate degree and $2,667 for a technical undergraduate degree. Check with the company for more specific salary information. Your benefits package will include tuition reimbursement up to 100 percent; a stock-purchase and pension plan; and medical, dental, and hospital insurance.

CONTACT

Michael Millegan, Personnel Administrator, General Telephone Company of the Southwest, Inc., P.O. Box 1001, San Angelo, TX 76902.

GRUMMAN DATA SYSTEMS CORPORATION

ENGINEERING • INFORMATION SYSTEMS AND PROCESSING • RESEARCH AND DEVELOPMENT • TECHNICAL SERVICES

THE COMPANY

Established in 1970 as a subsidiary of the Grumman Corporation, Grumman Data Systems provides comprehensive computer services to government, business, and industry as well as to the Grumman family of corporations. The company is involved in graphics and advanced robotics technology; mathematical modeling; scientific programming, including automated telemetry systems; business systems, including software transition; and the NASA space shuttle program. Its headquarters are on Long Island, New York. Grumman Data Systems employs about 2,500 people in the United States.

INFORMATION SYSTEMS TRAINING PROGRAM

You will participate in an orientation program followed by on-the-job and formal training in the equipment and languages you'll be using. Most of the training is devoted to real-time computer systems, with emphasis on assembly language, programming-structured software engineering techniques, and operating-system development and modifications.

QUALIFICATIONS

Grumman wants college graduates in electrical and manufacturing engineering, computer science, mathematics, and business. You will need a strong academic record, preferably with a minimum G.P.A. of 3.5 or higher.

RECRUITMENT AND PLACEMENT

Grumman recruits on college and university campuses during February and March and hires 30 to 35 trainees a year. Entry-level positions involve data processing; scientific programming; on-line business and financial systems; computer-output microfilming; and systems design, development, and implementation. You will work on Long Island.

SALARY AND BENEFITS

With a bachelor's degree you can expect to start at about $23,000 and at $26,500 with a master's. Your benefits package will consist of tuition reimbursement; hospital, medical, and dental insurance; life insurance; a pension plan; and an employee investment plan. The company sponsors a recreational program for all employees and pays all relocation expenses.

CONTACT

Administrator, College Relations, Grumman Data Systems Corporation, 1111 Stewart Avenue, Bethpage, NY 11714.

GTE CORPORATION

DATA PROCESSING • FINANCE • HUMAN RESOURCES • MARKETING

THE COMPANY

Because of the nearly unbounded potential in the decades ahead for each of its businesses—information, electronics, and communications—GTE considers itself almost a new company. With assets of more than $27 billion to underwrite its future, GTE should continue to be a leader in exploring new technologies. Annual revenues exceed $15 billion. Excitement at GTE is generated by new services and products brought about by digital, fiber optic, and packet switching technologies. One of the leading telephone systems in the nation, GTE serves over 12 million telephones. In addition, three GTE international telephone operating subsidiaries serve more than 2 million telephones in Canada and the Dominican Republic. The company manufactures sophisticated communications products and produces a broad range of lighting products and precision materials such as metal-cutting tools. More than 185,000 employees work for the Stamford, Connecticut-based company. *Fortune* lists GTE as the largest utility among its top 50 and reports that it is among America's most admired corporations.

ALL TRAINING PROGRAMS

You can enter GTE as a direct hire of a specific department, or you may be selected to join an associate training program. In the associate program you will be rotated through a series of three six-month assignments in different areas of the country, then interview for the permanent position you want. In either case, you will participate in hands-on training with real responsibility.

QUALIFICATIONS

GTE hires candidates with undergraduate degrees in accounting, finance, computer science, industrial relations, psychology, and graduate degrees in business, organizational development, labor relations, behavioral psychology, and related fields.

RECRUITMENT AND PLACEMENT

Interviews are held around the country by the company's numerous divisions, or you may contact headquarters directly to be considered for jobs throughout the system. You might work for GTE anywhere in the country.

SALARIES AND BENEFITS

GTE's salary structure is based on a job evaluation system used by over half of the Fortune 500 companies to ensure consistency across organizational lines. Check with the company for specific salary information. Benefits will average 40 percent of your salary, with comprehensive hospital, medical, and dental coverage; a savings and investment plan; stockownership plan; and a relocation package.

CONTACT

Associate Development Programs: Manager-Human Resources Associate Development Program; Manager-Marketing Associate Development Program; or Manager-Financial Associate Development Program: GTE Corporation, One Stamford Forum, Stamford, CT 06904; All positions: Manager-College Relations, GTE Corporation, One Stamford Forum, Stamford, CT 06904.

GULF STATES UTILITY COMPANY

ENGINEERING • PRODUCTION

THE COMPANY

Half a century ago, Gulf States Utility began as a company that traded in ice, water, and electricity. The ice and water divisions were sold, and the company focused solely on the generation of energy, including both electricity and natural gas. Today Gulf States ranks number 37 in the Fortune 50 largest utilities, with yearly revenues of $1.4 billion. In recent years the company has constructed two coal-fired plants to reduce its dependence on oil. It draws about a third of its electricity from the technically successful, albeit expensive, River Bend nuclear plant. Troubled financially since this plant went into operation in 1986, the company nonetheless offers employment opportunities for new hires. Gulf States is headquartered in Beaumont, Texas, and provides electricity and natural gas to over half a million customers in East Texas and South Central Louisiana. It has about 5,000 employees.

ENGINEERING AND PRODUCTION TRAINING PROGRAMS

A large part of your training program will consist of on-the-job experience. But there is much more: seminars, workshops, and special programs developed by the in-house training staff. Additional academic study is encouraged, and the company will reimburse you for the entire cost of obtaining an advanced degree. The program is designed to allow a participant to enter a large number of positions within the company after completion.

QUALIFICATIONS

You may have a degree in engineering (general, electrical, mechanical, civil, structural, industrial, chemical), environmental sciences, chemistry, physics, accounting (tax, fuels, general), economics, mathematics, or computer science.

RECRUITMENT AND PLACEMENT

College recruiters will interview all students who sign up. In addition to the Beaumont headquarters, Gulf States has divisional headquarters in Conroe and Port Arthur, Texas; and Baton Rouge and Lake Charles, Louisiana. There is no choice of placement.

SALARY AND BENEFITS

Gulf States offers starting salaries of $26,000 to $29,000, depending on your degree level. You can expect to receive benefits that include life, business travel, hospitalization, dental, medical, and surgical insurance; a retirement plan, paid holidays and vacations; a stockownership plan; and relocation assistance.

CONTACT

Director of Employment, Gulf States Utilities Company, P.O. Box 2951, Beaumont, TX 77704.

A Recruiter's View of Training Programs
Charlotte Smoot, Foley's

Charlotte Smoot, a college recruiter for Foley's Department Stores, has worked there since high school. She moved up into the executive ranks, left briefly, and has been back for three years.

☆ ☆ ☆ ☆ ☆

How many schools do you call on and how do you go about that?

We go to about 8 to 15 schools. We visit more in the spring because there are more graduates in the spring. A lot depends on budget as to how many I go to. Ideally, I'd like to go to every school in the spring that I go to in the fall so that I can look at students who are graduating in the semesters beyond, getting to know the students. We primarily go to schools that are in our market area: Texas, Oklahoma, Arizona, and New Mexico. We also do go to the Midwest—Illinois and Indiana.

How many candidates do you interview in both the spring and fall periods?

Just on campus, I would say anywhere from 500 to 600. Probably 50 positions are available to be filled during an average year. You can see that we hire about one out of ten applicants we interview. That number will change with the merger. In January of 1987 Federated merged the Foley's and Sanger Harris divisions, which has of course made us much stronger in our marketplace. Our training programs will be combined.

How many come into the training program from campus recruitment and how many from other means?

Probably about 75 to 80 percent are from campus recruiting. The rest would be either in-store promotes, hourly supervisors becoming executives, or walk-ins (those who mail in résumés).

So if someone living in Tallahassee, Florida, wanted to relocate to the Southwest and sent you a résumé, you would read and pay attention to it if he or she seemed to have the right qualifications, and you would follow up on it?

Certainly.

How many résumés have you gotten from people who mention reading about Foley's in the first edition of this book?

It's around ten a month. It's hard to generalize, but I would probably say that they have been more qualified than the average applicant.

How do you do noncampus recruitment?

I go through every résumé that I get and, if I like what I see, I invite that person for an interview.

What do you look for in résumés that you receive?

I'm going to look at a résumé differently if the person is someone on campus versus one that I get in the mail. People who send in résumés usually have more experience than a college student would. If I'm interviewing on campus I'm going to look at grades, I'm going to look at activities, what kind of leadership role they played, and so forth. And it goes without saying, I look at their degree plans. I'm open to looking at a lot of different degree plans, but I have my preferences as to what background will do better in retailing.

What degree plans seem to fit best for a retailing trainee?

Marketing, management, and some schools even have retailing degree plans, but those are usually in the business school. Those curriculums really relate to the type of business we're in.

What about liberal arts graduates?

Sure, we'll look at liberal arts, but I have to tell you that the bulk of the people who come into our program have business backgrounds.

So you're saying that 75 percent are probably people twenty-two to twenty-four years old, right off the campus, who come into your program, and the other 25 percent are often older.

Yes, the other 25 percent come to us from the stores and are already proven. They come to us with store recommendations, and they are looked at as being upwardly mobile in the company. I'm sure that they're strong performers. They already know what they're getting into. It's no surprise to them what a retail job is. I'm not really taking a risk on these people. I have to report back to the store backing them, saying this person does have potential, but with a student many times I'm taking a risk.

Any recommendations for students on how they can approach interviews?

I would recommend that before going into an interview they do their homework. If they don't have information available to them in the placement office, write the company for recruiting brochures or whatever is available. Know what's going on with that business. For example, in the case of Foley's, know that the company just merged with Sanger Harris. I see people who don't even realize that that happened. They're just not with it. I want to know that they've done their homework. They should know what the career path is. They should know what to expect in this company. They should know the size of the company, they know where we're located. They just need to do their homework.

How important is grade point average? Is there a cutoff point in terms of whom you will consider seriously?

I think in retail generally it's not important to have a 4.0 G.P.A. Some students will have a lower grade point because they had to work forty hours or more to support their education. Their G.P.A. might be 2.5. I've really got to jump in and challenge to find out why their grades are the way they are. If I come across a student who has a 2.5 and has not been involved in any campus activities, I probably will not be interested.

What about those so-called "people skills" that many companies say they want?

If you're in a management position where you have to count on people supporting you to make you successful, those people skills are critical. In an interview I'm not terribly structured. I let applicants talk to me about their strengths, about their leadership roles, how they got their peers motivated to do those tasks, and how they dealt with peers that they couldn't motivate. I try to learn how they would motivate and deal with a staff on a sales floor. It's hard to say how one discovers "people skills," because it's not a 1-2-3 process.

How long does a good interview usually take if you're interested in that person?

Oh, about thirty minutes.

How about the résumés that you get through the mail? What do you look for?

I look for a clear objective. They need to know what they want. Are they applying to everybody across the board, or are they specifically interested in what I have to offer? Of course I'll look for grades. I am not interested in a listing of all these courses they take. I am interested in, obviously, retail experience. I am interested in what their community involvement has been, their activities on campus. If they don't have those activities, maybe they're older applicants and they've been out of school for a while and that wouldn't apply, but I'm interested in any community or volunteer or specifics that they can parallel to retail. They might not be in the same industry now but perhaps they have qualities that will match up to what I want.

Walk me through your training program.

That first day may be information overload. We have our senior vice-president in charge of executive development talk to them about administrative development at Foley's. A member of senior management comes in and talks about Foley's and the mission of the organization.

That first day we also have people from the placement office talk about the role of placement in the trainee's career. Each store handles its own placement, but the executive personnel office works with them throughout their careers. So we talk about how to open those doors. Some of the other information we give is about hiring. As I say, it's kind of an information overload.

Then, over ten weeks, they come in for training one to two days a week and are exposed to a variety of material. They learn how to set up a store, how to analyze, how to do retail math, how to communicate with the buying office, supervisory techniques—a barrage of information. Then when they go back to their store they start applying what they're learning in the classroom so they have the on-the-job experience as well.

It sounds like the nice part is that they can start applying what they learn immediately.

Right. During that ten-week period we give them the tools they need to start to become a manager and then they are assigned to a manager so that they have a trainer, kind of like a mentor relationship. Between the tenth and twelfth weeks, we determine where they are. It's not a formal review, but just an update to let placement know. They may have come to us with a lot of retail background. Are they ready to be promoted already? Or do they need more time, and if so, how much time? We also want to know what their challenges are.

And their title during this ten- to twelve-week period is what?

Basic trainee.

They have one supervisor who serves as trainer and mentor. Is that the same person who makes the evaluation?

Yes.

After completing training, what title is the trainee given?

Sales manager or buyer.

At the next level, is there more training?

No. It is truly a comprehensive program. It helps them start out on the right foot. We give them the tools to go into the unknown and be productive. I don't see how you could do it any other way.

H

☆ ☆ ☆ ☆ ☆

HALLMARK CARDS, INC.

ACCOUNTING • DATA PROCESSING • ENGINEERING • FIELD MARKETING • FINANCE • GRAPHIC SERVICES • MATERIALS MANAGEMENT • PACKAGING • PRODUCTION • PRODUCT MANAGEMENT • WRITING

THE COMPANY

If you care enough to send the very best, 25 percent of the time you'll choose Hallmark, the world's leading creator and publisher of "social expression" products. The company has come a long way since eighteen-year-old Joyce C. Hall began selling postcards in 1910 to shopkeepers in Kansas City, Missouri; Hallmark is now the world's largest manufacturer of greeting cards. Its 19,000 employees include the largest force of artists (300 to 400) working under one roof. A Hallmark Christmas card—just one of 12.5 million products made by Hallmark each day in more than 20 major product lines—can take up to two years to complete. Some of the products include gift wrap, stationery, writing instruments, candles, puzzles, crystal and pewter gifts, decorative bath accessories, and greeting cards. Hallmark also owns the Trifari Jewelry Company; photo frame manufacturer Charles D. Burnes Co.; Binney & Smith, makers of Crayola crayons; and a diversified media and publishing company, SFN Companies. You will find that Hallmark makes a concerted effort to use its profits for social good. In addition to sponsoring the highly acclaimed Hallmark Hall of Fame television series, it has established a job training center in Kansas City's inner city area, and sets aside about 5 percent of its pretax profit, plus other resources, to benefit society. College scholarship programs and a national art competition are expressions of social commitment from Hallmark. Although the company is privately held, Hallmark employees participate in the company's successes through a profit-sharing plan from stock sold to a trust by family members.

ALL TRAINING PROGRAMS

Hallmark tailors its training to specific departments and individuals. As an engineer, you will spend three months gaining on-the-job experience. Data processors combine formal training and on-the-job experience for two months. Management trainees learn from seminars, classrooms, and work experience. Workshops are available. Based on their portfolios, new artists are assigned to various design departments, where an assigned supervisor helps them become oriented to the broad spectrum of Hallmark products. Artists are frequently sent on research trips to galleries and special exhibits to gather innovative ideas. Writers and editors work on a line development team consisting of an editor, a product line designer, and a planner. Even at entry level, you will be given a significant degree of immediate responsibility.

QUALIFICATIONS

Hallmark is interested in graduates with degrees in engineering, computer science, math/statistics, business planning/marketing, and accounting/finance, but the company is most interested in liberal arts graduates with artistic and literary backgrounds. Portfolios must show a strong grasp of fundamentals of drawing, design, and color as well as creativity and idea content.

RECRUITMENT AND PLACEMENT

Trade journal and newspaper ads, employment agencies, and college campuses are all fertile grounds for attracting prospective employees. Hallmark visits colleges, universities, and professional art schools seeking the finest talent among graduating seniors. Interviews are held at the schools, and students who qualify are asked to submit their portfolios to a review committee. Placement may be at one of the production centers in Missouri or Kansas, or at the distribution divisions and subsidiaries scattered around the country.

SALARY AND BENEFITS

With a bachelor's degree, you will start out at about $22,500; with a master's, $25,000. Benefits include vested profit sharing, retirement, savings, medical and life insurance, discounts on merchandise at company-owned retail stores, and disability plans. Tuition refunds, matching gifts to educational institutions, and two weeks of paid vacation are also features.

CONTACT

For professional positions: College Relations Manager, Hallmark Cards, Inc., 25th and McGee Trafficway, Kansas City, MO 64108; for creative services positions, contact your art department or placement office, or write to the Director of Creative Recruiting at the same address.

JOHN HANCOCK MUTUAL LIFE INSURANCE CO.

ACTUARIAL SCIENCE • PROGRAMMING • SALES

THE COMPANY

Celebrating its one hundred and twenty-fifth anniversary in 1987, John Hancock Mutual Life Insurance Company is a Boston-based financial services firm with offices throughout the United States, Puerto Rico, and the Virgin Islands. It is the nation's sixth largest life insurer, with assets under management of $40 billion. Once a traditional provider of life and health insurance products, Hancock has diversified and expanded its product line to include virtually all financial services—annuities, consumer banking, equipment leasing, investment banking, mutual funds, pension investment management, commercial/residential mortgages, securities brokerage, and others. The company has 17 subsidiaries doing business in many of these areas and presently derives a third of its total revenue from business outside traditional life insurance operations. The company sponsors major sporting events such as the Boston Marathon and John Hancock Sun Bowl. Hancock has about 6,500 employees in its Boston home office and 10,000 sales representatives throughout the United States. Most of the company's Boston employees work in the 60-story Hancock tower or one of three neighboring buildings named after the streets they are located on: Berkeley, Clarendon, and Stuart.

ALL TRAINING PROGRAMS

Hancock provides training for actuarial, programming, and sales positions. In the Actuarial Development Program you will have several assignments in major actuarial areas and prepare for your fellowship in the Society of Actuaries, which usually can be acquired within four to six years.

QUALIFICATIONS

John Hancock is seeking college graduates with degrees in accounting, business, finance, economics, and applied mathematics.

RECRUITMENT AND PLACEMENT

Except for sales positions, all trainees begin at the Hancock home office in Boston.

SALARY AND BENEFITS

The College Placement Council Salary Survey for September 1986–June 1987 indicates starting salaries for banking, finance, and insurance firms to be $1,889 a month for those with a B.A. degree in nontechnical curricula and $2,135 with a B.A. degree in technical curricula. M.B.A. starting salaries were $2,884 for a nontechnical undergraduate degree and $3,320 for an M.B.A. with technical undergraduate degree. Check with the company for more specific salary information. Hancock offers competitive benefits and generally promotes from within. You will have access to a job posting program, corporate education courses, a tuition assistance program, and a commuter services department.

CONTACT

Mary K. Milley, Coordinator of College Recruiting, John Hancock Mutual Life Insurance Company, John Hancock Place, Personnel Operations, P.O. Box 111, Boston, MA 02117.

JOHN H. HARLAND COMPANY

PRODUCTION/OPERATIONS MANAGEMENT · SALES/MARKETING

THE COMPANY

Headquartered in Atlanta, the John H. Harland Company has been in business since 1923. It specializes in printing personal checks, business checks, deposit tickets, internal forms, computer printing, and in other printed products and services for banks and other financial institutions. Harland is the second largest check printer in the country and has 44 production plants nationwide. The company has an outstanding financial record with over 35 consecutive years of increased sales, profits, and dividends. Over 5,000 employees contribute to the company's successful record, including 350 sales representatives in 50 states. Potential for upward mobility is excellent for new employees due to the growth in the company. Harland does all promoting to management from the sales force.

PRODUCTION/OPERATIONS MANAGEMENT TRAINING PROGRAM

You will work in a plant for twelve to eighteen months, as well as attending seminars in Atlanta at the Corporate Training Center, learning the check-printing process and developing management skills.

QUALIFICATIONS

You will need a college degree, record of academic excellence, leadership ability, hands-on work experience, and a willingness to relocate.

RECRUITMENT AND PLACEMENT

Harland recruits at over 50 colleges and universities across the country. It operates 42 imprinting plants with locations in California, Florida, Illinois, Louisiana, New Jersey, New York, Puerto Rico, and Texas.

SALARY AND BENEFITS

The College Placement Council Salary Survey for September 1986–June 1987 indicates starting salaries for glass, paper, packaging and allied products companies to be $1,865 a month for those with a B.A. degree in nontechnical curricula and $2,401 with a B.A. degree in technical curricula. M.B.A. starting salaries were $2,945 for a nontechnical undergraduate degree and $2,775 for a technical undergraduate degree. Check with the company for more specific salary information. The benefits include a company-funded profit-sharing plan, stock-purchase plan, scholarships, medical insurance, life insurance, and disability benefits.

SALES/MARKETING TRAINING PROGRAM

You will be hired as a sales associate and have a training period of twelve to eighteen months. During this time you will work in the field with sales representatives and managers, attend professional sales seminars in the Corporate Training Center in Atlanta, and spend time training in a check-printing plant. This training period focuses on becoming familiar with the company philosophy; learning product knowledge; developing selling skills; and learning about the financial industry. You will be provided with guidance, feedback, and performance evaluations throughout your training period and career. After training you will be assigned a permanent sales territory.

QUALIFICATIONS

Harland requires a four-year college degree, preferably in business, marketing, or communications. Other requirements include a professional image, academic excellence, campus activity leadership, a willingness to relocate, and a desire to work in outside sales.

RECRUITMENT AND PLACEMENT

Harland recruits nationwide at over 50 colleges and universities, resulting in the hiring of sales associates across the country. The hiring process consists of your initial on-campus interview with a corporate recruiter, from which sales associate candidates are selected to attend a two-day Assessment Center program at the corporate headquarters in Atlanta. At the Assessment Center, candidates will meet Harland management and staff and become fully informed about the company and the training program. You will also make individual presentations and participate in group activities and exercises which are evaluated by a team. Potential sales associates receive offers based upon their performance in the Assessment Center.

SALARY AND BENEFITS

The College Placement Council Salary Survey for September 1986–June 1987 indicates starting salaries for glass, paper, packaging and allied products companies to be $1,865 a month for those with a B.A. degree in nontechnical curricula and $2,401 with a B.A. degree in technical curricula. M.B.A. starting salaries were $2,945 for a nontechnical undergraduate degree and $2,775 for a technical undergraduate degree. Check with the company for more specific salary information. The benefits include a company-funded profit-sharing plan, stock-purchase plan, scholarships, medical insurance, life insurance, disability benefits, and full sales expense coverage.

CONTACT

Employment Manager, John H. Harland Company, P.O. Box 105250, Atlanta, GA 30348.

THE HARTFORD INSURANCE GROUP

ACCOUNTING • ACTUARIAL SCIENCE • FINANCIAL CONTROLS • INFORMATION MANAGEMENT • MARKETING • SALES • UNDERWRITING

THE COMPANY

Begun in 1810, Hartford is one of the nation's largest multiline insurance operations, offering diverse personal and commercial insurance coverage. The Hartford has been a subsidiary of ITT since 1970. The company's 19,000 employees are located in hundreds of offices throughout the United States and Canada, including regional offices in 30 states and the District of Columbia, as well as the corporate office in Connecticut. Additionally, the Hartford's international operations in Great Britain, Germany, Bermuda, and the Netherlands employ 4,000 people.

ALL TRAINING PROGRAMS

Training programs last from six to twelve months, depending on subject, and are conducted primarily at the regional level. Training combines on-the-job supervised and classroom instruction, feedback sessions, outside classes, and independent study using manuals and computer programs.

FINANCIAL CONTROLS PROGRAM

The junior insurance accountant position trains college graduates in accounting controls, collectioner, statutory, and GAAP accounting, consolidation, and management reports. On-the-job training is tailored to your assigned area.

QUALIFICATIONS

You should have an accounting degree, computer science classes and/or PC exposure. A G.P.A. of 3.0 is preferred, with a 2.8 minimum.

RECRUITMENT AND PLACEMENT

Recruitment is primarily on the East Coast with placement in Greater Hartford.

INFORMATION MANAGEMENT PROGRAM

You will be trained in Hartford's home office for an intensive eight weeks. The program begins with an introduction to the history of data processing, information management organization at Hartford, and internal data representation and number systems. Proficiency is tested through a series of increasingly difficult programming exercises. Retention of factual material is tested by weekly quizzes, and a mid-term examination in computer concepts, JCL, and COBOL.

QUALIFICATIONS

College graduates with a background in information management, computer science, or data processing are preferred.

RECRUITMENT AND PLACEMENT

Recruitment is nationwide. Placement is in the Hartford Financial Controls Division in Hartford.

SALES PROGRAM

You will be trained in a regional office with manuals, classroom activities, and on-the-job experience. Training will include product knowledge and sales technique. You will interact with related departments such as claims, underwriting, and administration.

QUALIFICATIONS

Candidates will have undergraduate degrees in business administration, marketing, economics, or other liberal arts-related fields. Sales experience is desirable.

RECRUITMENT AND PLACEMENT

Recruitment and placement are nationwide during the spring with emphasis on May and August graduates. In 1987, Hartford made more than 50 campus visits.

ALL PROGRAMS

SALARY AND BENEFITS

The College Placement Council Salary Survey for September 1986–June 1987 indicates starting salaries for banking, finance, and insurance firms to be $1,889 a month for those with a B.A. degree in nontechnical curricula and $2,135 with a B.A. degree in technical curricula. M.B.A. starting salaries were $2,884 for a nontechnical undergraduate degree, and $3,320 for an M.B.A. with technical undergraduate degree. Check with the company for more specific salary information. You will be eligible for insurance plans covering personal illness and catastrophe, including life, health/medical/dental, homeowner's, and auto. The company also offers an investment savings plan and ITT stock-purchase plans for qualified employees.

CONTACT

Director of Placement and College Relations—The Hartford Insurance Group, 690 Asylum Avenue, Hartford, CT 06115.

HEB FOODS/DRUGS

MANAGEMENT

THE COMPANY

HEB Foods/Drugs is one of the nation's twenty largest supermarket companies. In 1905, Florence Butt founded the company by opening a small grocery store in Kerrville, Texas. The company expanded store by store into almost 80 Central and South Texas cities. Today, more than 20,000 employees operate close to 150 stores throughout the HEB marketing area. In addition to its food retailing outlets, the company operates manufacturing and distribution facilities in San Antonio and Corpus Christi. The company's headquarters complex is located in San Antonio.

MANAGEMENT TRAINING PROGRAM

You will be assigned to the company's College Skilled Training (CST) Program. For forty-seven weeks you will learn the food retailing industry at HEB Foods/Drugs from the bottom up. You will be exposed to every facet of the business—from company philosophy to customer service to technical and management skills. After successfully completing the CST Program, you can expect to be assigned to a management position in one of the company's stores. As you grow with HEB, you may choose to continue on your career path in store operations or direct your career in another area of the company such as finance, corporate planning, human resources, marketing, or real estate.

QUALIFICATIONS

HEB describes its ideal candidates as well-rounded individuals with strong educational backgrounds and the motivation to succeed.

RECRUITMENT AND PLACEMENT

HEB recruiters visit college campuses in the spring and, to a limited extent, in the fall. But don't wait to be asked—résumés are reviewed and considered for openings. Training will be in one of four divisions in San Antonio, Austin, Corpus Christi, or South Texas.

SALARY AND BENEFITS

The College Placement Council Salary Survey for September 1986–June 1987 indicates starting salaries for merchandising and service companies to be $1,594 a month for those with a B.A. degree in nontechnical curricula and $2,141 with a B.A. degree in technical curricula. M.B.A. starting salaries were $2,572 for a nontechnical undergraduate degree and $2,735 for a technical undergraduate degree. Check with the company for more specific salary information. In addition to annual merit increases, HEB offers performance/incentive bonuses. Benefits include educational assistance, employee relocation, vacation, paid holidays, medical, dental, and life insurance, short- and long-term disability, investment and retirement plan, a credit union, and profit sharing.

CONTACT

HEB Foods/Drugs, Corporate Staffing Department, P.O. Box 9999, San Antonio, TX 78204-0999.

HEWLETT-PACKARD COMPANY

CHEMISTRY/CHEMICAL ENGINEERING • COMPUTER SCIENCE • ELECTRICAL ENGINEERING • FINANCE • INDUSTRIAL ENGINEERING • MANUFACTURING • MARKETING • MECHANICAL ENGINEERING • PERSONNEL • PHYSICS • RESEARCH AND DEVELOPMENT

THE COMPANY

Hewlett-Packard is a company that considers how it operates as important as what it produces. Its more than 7,000 advanced computation, information, and instrumentation products serve worldwide technical, professional, and business markets. With 84,000 employees worldwide, HP emphasizes management by objective. Individual creativity is encouraged in small business units of around 800 people in its profit-centered divisions. MBWA (management by wandering around) is an established concept at Hewlett-Packard, contributing to the informal atmosphere and open communication lines. Since Hewlett-Packard developed its first computer in 1966, computers, peripherals, and calculators have grown to make up more than half of the company's revenues. Listed among *Fortune*'s most admired corporations, Hewlett-Packard ranks number 51 in the Fortune 500 largest U.S. industrial corporations.

ENGINEERING TRAINING PROGRAMS

You may begin your Hewlett-Packard career with on-the-job training, supplemented by developmental programs on topics ranging from improving time management skills to giving effective presentations. Honors cooperative programs in engineering and science are offered by leading universities such as Stanford, the University of California at Berkeley, Massachusetts Institute of Technology, and National Technological University. These interactive classes are delivered to your work site from campus via television or videotaped instruction. In addition, more than 1,700 internal training courses are offered annually to employees worldwide.

QUALIFICATIONS

Hewlett-Packard looks for candidates with graduate and undergraduate degrees in business administration, computer science, engineering, and related fields.

PLACEMENT

HP has 55 divisions around the country that produce and manage their own products, more than 200 field sales offices, and 6 research and development centers. Headquarters are in Palo Alto, California.

MANAGEMENT DEVELOPMENT PROGRAM

The Management Development Program helps both new and experienced managers develop their skills in personnel supervision, problem solving, communications, and decision making. Your training program provides information about your assigned division, corporate objectives, and personnel policies. You will have the opportunity to improve your time-management skills and learn how to give effective presentations and lead effective meetings. In addition, you will receive training on how to interview and select new employees, conduct performance evaluations, make salary decisions, and carry out the company's commitment to affirmative action. There are over 20 internal management courses available, which may use videotapes, films, computer simulation, skill practice, and case studies.

QUALIFICATIONS

Hewlett-Packard looks for college graduates from the fields of engineering, computer science, business administration, and related fields. Joining the summer internship program often leads to a permanent position after graduation.

PLACEMENT

Main employment centers are in northern California and Colorado. Other manufacturing facilities are in Idaho, Massachusetts, New Jersey, Oregon, Pennsylvania, and Washington.

FIELD SALES REPRESENTATIVE PROGRAM

You will be prepared to be a customer representative, with responsibilities for site preparation and on-site installation of major HP systems and equipment, preventive maintenance, and repair service. You will participate in a five- to seven-month training program before you are assigned to accounts. During the first months of training in the sales office you become acquainted with the job responsibilities and intelligent on-line terminals. Next you will spend two to three months in the classroom, and then you will work with experienced customer representatives in the field for one to three months.

QUALIFICATIONS

Hewlett-Packard recruits college graduates from the fields of electronic engineering, physics, mathematics, biomedical engineering, and related disciplines. You need a high degree of technical, analytical, and problem-solving abilities. You must be capable of managing your time and priorities and be able to deal with a wide variety of people.

PLACEMENT

You could be assigned to any one of 80 nationwide sales offices.

ALL PROGRAMS

RECRUITMENT

Hewlett-Packard recruits heavily on college campuses, but it hires at least 20 percent of its new employees from other sources, so send your résumé. When you arrive for a campus interview, be sure to bring an unofficial copy of your academic transcript if it's available, as well as examples of work showing your ability to understand and solve problems.

SALARY AND BENEFITS

The College Placement Council Salary Survey for September 1986–June 1987 indicates starting salaries for computers and business machine companies to be $1,880 a month for those with a B.A. degree in nontechnical curricula and $2,389 with a B.A. degree in technical curricula. M.B.A. starting salaries were $2,633 for a nontechnical undergraduate degree and $2,781 for a technical undergraduate degree. Check with the company for more specific salary information. Hewlett-Packard's benefits package includes medical and dental insurance, a profit-sharing plan, and a stock-purchase plan. Employee surveys have led to benefits such as flexible time off (up to three weeks paid during an employee's first year). The company maintains recreation areas for employees and their families in the Santa Cruz Mountains in northern California, three sites in Colorado, a site in the Pocono Mountains of Pennsylvania, a beach villa in Malaysia, a lake resort in Scotland, and a ski chalet in the German Alps.

CONTACT

Manager, Corporate Staffing, Hewlett-Packard Company, 3000 Hanover Street, Palo Alto, CA 93403.

HOLIDAY CORPORATION

ACCOUNTING • DEVELOPMENT • FOOD AND BEVERAGES • FRONT OFFICE • GUEST SERVICES • HUMAN RESOURCES • LAW • MARKETING • REAL ESTATE • ROOMS • SALES • SITE SELECTION

THE COMPANY

Think of Holiday Inns as the friendly family chain? Well, they're also part of a $1.6 billion diversified international corporation, providing services and products in lodgings, casinos and gaming, and food service—all part of the world's largest hotel company. Holiday has more than 1,850 hotels in 50 states and 53 countries. Divisions include: Holiday Inn Hotels, the world's largest full-service mid-priced hotel chain; Holiday Inn Crowne Plaza Hotels, top-of-the-line properties; Harrah's, a leading hotel/casino company with five properties in the four major U.S. gaming markets; Embassy Suites, leader and fastest-growing all-suite hotel chain; Hampton Inn Hotels, an economy, limited-service chain; and the Residence Inn Hotels, apartment-like suites for extended-stay customers. You'll have lots of opportunities for assignments to interesting locations with this ever expanding company. Holiday uses system-wide job posting to inform employees of openings. Holiday ranks number 41 in the Fortune 100 largest diversified service companies.

MANAGEMENT TRAINING PROGRAMS

The Holiday Inns program is the prototype for all Holiday's training. In operations management development you will learn all phases of managing hotel operations. You will go through three phases of the program before being assigned to a hotel. The program begins with a short orientation in the company headquarters. Then you'll spend several weeks at Holiday Inn University. Upon graduation you will be assigned to a specific management support position in food and beverage, sales, or guest service, and you'll work ultimately with the general manager. The hotel manager who will provide on-site supervision will have been selected for exceptional leadership and operational skills, so you will receive an introduction to the Holiday Inns system from one of its best. Working at your own pace, you will probably complete the training within a year. After you finish the last phase of the program, you'll usually assume a management position.

QUALIFICATIONS

The formal education requirements aren't tough, but Holiday Inns puts a lot of emphasis on "real world" hotel experience. You need at least a high school diploma and two to three years' experience in food and beverage, sales, front-office work, or supervision. If you've graduated from a technical school or university in food service, business, or hotel administration, you have a real advantage.

RECRUITMENT AND PLACEMENT

Although Holiday likes to promote from within, it does recruit for the program. After the orientation in Memphis you'll move down the road and over the Tennessee state line to the training center in Olive Branch, Mississippi, a small town of about 2,000 people. After you graduate you'll work in one of the company's top hotels until you receive a permanent assignment.

SALARY AND BENEFITS

The College Placement Council Salary Survey for September 1986–June 1987 indicates starting salaries for merchandising (retail and wholesale) and service companies to be $1,594 a month for those with a B.A. degree in nontechnical curricula and $2,141 with a B.A. degree in technical curricula. M.B.A. starting salaries were $2,572 for a nontechnical undergraduate degree, and $2,735 for an M.B.A. with technical undergraduate degree. Check with the company for more specific salary information. Holiday provides life, medical, and dental insurance, savings and retirement plans as part of its benefits package. When traveling, you can also get discounts on lodging and related services in Holiday hotels.

CONTACT

Corporate Manager, College Relations, Holiday Corporation, 1023 Cherry Road, Memphis, TN 38117.

THE HOME INSURANCE COMPANY

CLAIMS • INSPECTION/SAFETY ENGINEERING • PREMIUM AUDITING • UNDERWRITING

THE COMPANY

Since its founding in 1853, The Home Insurance Company has helped people overcome crisis and catastrophe. The company came through the Chicago fire of 1871, the San Francisco earthquake of 1906, and Hurricane Camille in 1969, and it continues to provide property and casualty insurance for thousands of industries, homes, personal property, and individuals. The Home Insurance Company pioneered the concept of discount premiums for safe drivers. The company is a leader in volume of all property/casualty companies in the United States. It has a sales force of independent agents and brokers, with a work force of more than 6,000 employees. About four fifths of its accounts are commercial.

ALL TRAINING PROGRAMS

Entry-level professional and technical training prepares you for careers in four areas: claims, inspection/safety engineering, premium auditing, and underwriting. You are first assigned to one of the 95 branch offices or to the executive offices in New York City. Your first two or three months will acquaint you with the fundamentals of your job. The second phase of training consists of three to seven weeks of classroom work at one of the company's training centers. The final phase of the program is structured on-the-job training. Under guided supervision, you are assigned specific projects, tasks, and responsibilities to develop practical applications of knowledge and theory learned earlier in training. The company plans for you to be in a supervisory position within five years or less. You are encouraged to attend company-sponsored and outside training courses to increase your technical and management skills. The Tuition Prepayment Plan pays the full cost of tuition for job-related, approved graduate courses.

QUALIFICATIONS

The Home Insurance Company is looking for college graduates in business and liberal arts with an interest in claims, inspection/safety engineering, premium auditing, or underwriting. You will need a strong academic record and class ranking in the top 10 percent. The company wants graduates who have demonstrated achievement in extracurricular activities.

RECRUITMENT AND PLACEMENT

The company recruits nationwide, hiring about 30 trainees a year. You will be able to begin your career in the branch office of your choice. Branch offices are located in large and small cities throughout the United States and Canada.

SALARY AND BENEFITS

Expect to start at about $20,000 with a bachelor's degree; $22,000 with a master's. Your benefits will include life, medical, long-term disability, automobile, and personal property insurance; a stock-option plan; and retirement.

CONTACT

Cindy deLuise, Personnel Specialist, The Home Insurance Company, 59 Maiden Lane, New York, NY 10038.

HONEYWELL, INC.

ACCOUNTING • COMPUTER SCIENCE • ENGINEERING • MANAGEMENT • SALES

THE COMPANY

Honeywell places great emphasis on employee involvement in decision making at all levels. Honeywell, which celebrated its hundredth anniversary in 1985, is a multinational high-technology corporation with more than 94,000 employees, revenues of over $7 billion, and headquarters in Minneapolis. It is involved in computers, aerospace and defense, environmental and industrial process controls, electronic components, and international products. It is among *Fortune*'s most admired corporations and ranks number 52 in the Fortune 500 largest U.S. industrial corporations.

ALL TRAINING PROGRAMS

Honeywell's commitment to training is seen in its comprehensive videotape library with 100 ongoing technical courses for use by technical professionals. You will be able to study courses ranging from software management to various kinds of state-of-the-art technology in small groups using study guides. You may tailor your own development program at Honeywell.

ADVANCED ENGINEERING TRAINING PROGRAM

In this program, Honeywell provides internal training in areas such as database systems, new and competitive products, and various computer languages. You may study for a master's or doctoral degree at Arizona State University or Worcester (Massachusetts) Polytechnic University on company time at Honeywell expense. Corresponding to your course work, your six-month rotational work assignments will give you practical experience in areas such as business analysis and fault analysis/simulation.

QUALIFICATIONS

You must be a highly ranked graduate in electrical engineering or computer science, with leadership ability and motivation to pursue graduate work.

MANUFACTURING MANAGEMENT TRAINING PROGRAM

In the three-year Manufacturing Management Program, you will attend after-hours in-house courses in manufacturing, human relations, and financial aspects of manufacturing management. You may also pursue a master's degree at Arizona State

University or Worcester (Massachusetts) Polytechnic Institute at Honeywell's expense. Your six-month rotational work assignments will expose you to computer systems configuration/testing, production/materials control, factory planning and product assurance, process and equipment engineering.

QUALIFICATIONS

To qualify for this selective program, you must have a bachelor's degree in industrial, electrical, mechanical, or chemical engineering or a similar engineering science, high academic standing, and a strong interest in manufacturing.

ALL PROGRAMS

RECRUITMENT AND PLACEMENT

Honeywell representatives visit college campuses to recruit graduates in engineering and computer science; occasionally they seek candidates for sales and accounting positions. For information about other jobs, contact the company directly. Management and engineering trainees will be placed in either Boston or Phoenix. Honeywell also has divisions in California, Colorado, Florida, Illinois, Maryland, Minnesota, New York, Pennsylvania, Texas, Virginia, and Washington. It offers a limited number of technical summer intern positions, primarily for electrical engineering students.

SALARY AND BENEFITS

The College Placement Council Salary Survey for September 1986–June 1987 indicates starting salaries for computers and business machine companies to be $2,389 a month with a B.A. degree in technical curricula. Check with the company for more specific salary information. Honeywell salaries are supplemented by comprehensive group life, medical, and dental insurance, stock-option and retirement plans, tuition refunds, and liberal holiday and vacation schedules.

CONTACT

Ernie von Heimburg, Corporate Manager of University Relations, Honeywell, Inc., Honeywell Plaza, Minneapolis, MN 55408.

HOUSTON LIGHTING & POWER COMPANY

ACCOUNTING · ARCHITECTURE · CUSTOMER RELATIONS · ENGINEERING · INFORMATION SYSTEMS · LAW · PURCHASING

THE COMPANY

Houston Lighting & Power Company started in 1882 as a small utility company supplying electricity for Houston's streetlights. Today it's the fourth largest investor-owned electric utility in the United States, providing services to over 3 million people in Houston and 157 other Texas cities. Its 10,000 employees serve 21 percent of the state's population. The company has more than doubled its generating capacity during the last decade, and by 1990 expects to build an additional 6 units at 3 plants, and make other capital expenditures totaling $13 billion.

ALL TRAINING PROGRAMS

Most entry-level positions are in engineering, accounting, and customer relations, and training is provided by the personnel department. Some departments use a formal training program, some will start you with informal, on-the-job training. Several departments use rotational work assignments within the department. When you begin, you will attend a one-day company-wide orientation program. You will later be encouraged to attend company seminars, workshops developed by professional organizations, and job-related courses offered by nearby colleges and universities as well as to participate in professional and technical societies. If you demonstrate potential for management positions, you may be selected for the in-house Leadership Development Program and for selected off-premises management development programs designed to broaden your managerial skills and to prepare you for higher-level positions.

QUALIFICATIONS

HL&P is looking for electrical and mechanical engineers with bachelor's and master's degrees, and has more limited needs for chemical, civil, nuclear, and industrial engineers. It also is recruiting college graduates with degrees in accounting, architecture, marketing and management, computer science, math, and law.

RECRUITMENT AND PLACEMENT

Entry-level professionals may find themselves working on plant construction, electricity production and distribution, customer relations, fuel acquisition, purchasing, accounting and finance, or computer programming in the Houston area.

SALARY AND BENEFITS

The College Placement Council Salary Survey for September 1986–June 1987 indicates starting salaries for public utilities to be $1,905 a month for those with a B.A. degree in nontechnical curricula and $2,355 with a B.A. degree in technical curricula. M.B.A. starting salaries were $2,403 for a nontechnical undergraduate degree and $2,667 for a technical undergraduate degree. Check with the company for more specific salary information. You will enjoy the following benefits: medical and life insurance, retirement, savings and employee stock options, and an educational assistance program. In addition, you may purchase electric appliances at a discount through the company appliance store.

CONTACT

Director of Recruiting, Houston Lighting & Power Company, P.O. Box 1700, Houston, TX 77001.

I

☆ ☆ ☆ ☆ ☆

IBM CORPORATION

ADMINISTRATION · FINANCE · MANAGEMENT · MARKETING · SYSTEMS ENGINEERING

THE COMPANY

A leader in information processing, one of the world's fastest-growing and most competitive industries. IBM attracts high-caliber employees. Only "highly motivated" individuals need apply. The company designs, manufactures, markets, and services products for problem solving in business, science, government and education—creating a wide variety of jobs. IBM has employees in almost every U.S. city of any size. Never unionized, the company nonetheless virtually guarantees lifetime employment and blurs the distinction between blue collar and white collar. Headquarters are located in Armonk, New York. The company does business in over 125 countries, employing predominantly nationals of those countries.

ALL TRAINING PROGRAMS

IBM training methods vary, depending on where in the company one begins, but expect a combination of approaches: assignment to a branch office; classes at the lavish and modern education center in Armonk to learn about IBM policies, practices, and products; classroom and on-the-job training with (naturally) computer-aided instruction. Employee education and training receive high priority, with the company budgeting as much as $500 million a year.

MARKETING REPRESENTATIVE AND SYSTEMS ENGINEERING PROGRAMS

QUALIFICATIONS

Those who succeed in these areas of IBM thrive in a fast-paced environment and are able to adapt to constant development and change. Training and education are ongoing. Marketing representatives may have backgrounds in business, engineering, sciences, or liberal arts. Most important is the ability to understand and solve business and technical problems and to communicate solutions with precision and skill. Systems engineers usually have backgrounds in science, engineering, business, computer science, or mathematics. IBM wants people who can be creative technically but who also work well with people.

ADMINISTRATION PROGRAM

QUALIFICATIONS

Many IBM jobs that do not require college degrees—secretarial, data entry, clerical, and technical—may be steppingstones to other areas of the company such as programming, customer service, software development, marketing, personnel, purchasing, management, and finance. Secretaries need the flexibility to work under deadlines as well as good typing and other business skills. Administrative people should have good communication skills, an eye for detail, some knowledge of business mathematics, and possibly some experience with office and business practices. Data entry people should have good typing and related business skills. Computer operators must be attentive to detail and have strong observational skills.

FINANCE PROGRAM

QUALIFICATIONS

Recruits should have a well-rounded business and finance education. You will be placed on the management track with training that will cover financial planning, analysis, accounting, and information systems.

ALL PROGRAMS

RECRUITMENT AND PLACEMENT

The company recruits nationwide, with regularly scheduled visits to college campuses. Starting locations can be anywhere in the United States. IBM receives more than a million applications a year, so it can afford to be selective in hiring. The company still advocates regular transfers for employees, maintaining the insider's joke that IBM stands for "I've Been Moved."

SALARY AND BENEFITS

IBM offers high salaries, generous pension, health, and dental insurance plans for employees and their families, plus benefits such as exercise classes and physical examinations, adoption assistance (up to $1,500 a year), and inexpensive company-sponsored recreation facilities. In addition, IBM offers a Tuition Refund Program, which reimburses employees completely for courses taken off company time that are related to job responsibilities or career development. The Graduate Work Study Program reimburses employees for courses at the master's degree or doctorate level in such engineering and scientific disciplines as electrical, mechanical, industrial, and chemical engineering, chemistry, materials science, solid state physics, information science, and metallurgy. In this program, supported classes may be taken on company time. A third program, the Resident Study Program, sponsors full-time study on campus in areas relevant to the business with expenses and salary paid by IBM. Educational Leave of Absence allows employees to complete personal educational goals related to their IBM career. The company's own Systems Research Institute in New York City offers graduate-level study in information processing.

CONTACT

C. F. Cammack, IBM Corp., 400 Colony Square, Suite 1111, Atlanta, GA 30361, (404) 885-7000; S. J. Cook, IBM Corp., One Barker Avenue, White Plains, NY 10601, (914) 686-3300; I. C. Pfeiffer, IBM Corp., One IBM Plaza, Chicago, IL 60611, (312) 245-2000; or J. J. Halsey, IBM Corp., 3424 Wilshire Boulevard, Los Angeles, CA 90010, (213) 312-5400.

ILLINOIS BELL TELEPHONE COMPANY

ACCOUNTING · FINANCE · INFORMATION SYSTEMS · MARKETING · SALES

THE COMPANY

Illinois Bell provides telephone service and equipment to the residents and businesses of Illinois. A subsidiary of Ameritech, it has about 22,000 employees.

ALL TRAINING PROGRAMS

There are training programs for sales representatives and technical employees. As a sales rep, you will enter a six-month formal training program. Computer scientists and engineers receive an equally long training program that combines formal classroom training and on-the-job experience.

Illinois Bell provides a summer employment program for students who may be interested in working for the company after they graduate. You will be eligible for this program if you are majoring in computer science and have completed at least two years of college.

QUALIFICATIONS

The company is looking for graduates who rank in the top half of their class. If you have a degree (undergraduate or graduate) in computer programming; electrical, general, or industrial engineering; or marketing, Illinois Bell will certainly consider your application. Related work experience and accomplishments outside the classroom will weigh in your favor.

RECRUITMENT AND PLACEMENT

Illinois Bell is looking for computer scientists, engineers, mathematicians, and business graduates. All placements are in Illinois, with most of the openings in the Chicago area.

SALARY AND BENEFITS

Salary for holders of bachelor's degrees is in the $19,000 to $20,000 area; holders of master's degrees receive about $10,000 more, with consideration given for related experience. Benefits include medical, hospital, dental, and vision plans; life insurance; stock-purchase, savings, and pension programs; flextime options; tuition reimbursement; and assistance when you relocate.

CONTACT

Elizabeth Tarbell, Manager, Illinois Bell Telephone Company, 212 West Washington Street, Room 3-H, Chicago, IL 60606.

INLAND STEEL COMPANY

BUSINESS · COMPUTER SCIENCE · ENGINEERING · SALES

THE COMPANY

The fifth largest steel producer in the United States, Inland was one of the first companies in the country to adopt an eight-hour workday and in 1920 was the first steel company to have a pension plan. The company has more University of Chicago M.B.A.s than any other Chicago company (about 200), and 90 percent earned their degrees by going to night school while working at Inland. Most of its 24,500 employees work at the Indiana Harbor Works in East Chicago, Illinois, or inside the Loop in Chicago. Inland's annual sales exceed $3 billion, and it is listed among *Fortune*'s most admired corporations. The company ranks number 123 in the Fortune 500 largest U.S. industrial corporations

ALL TRAINING PROGRAMS

Inland emphasizes on-the-job training as well as formal classes for all entry-level employees.

QUALIFICATIONS

The company hires about 15 business majors, 15 social science/humanities majors, 75 engineering majors, and 15 computer science majors each year. You should have a record of extracurricular and leadership activities; strong communication skills; and above-average writing ability. Related work experience will be a plus. Liberal arts graduates are hired for sales.

RECRUITMENT AND PLACEMENT

Inland is one of the few steel companies to recruit on college campuses—about 80 a year. You will likely work in the Chicago area or northern Indiana.

SALARY AND BENEFITS

With a bachelor's degree, you will start at $20,400; with advanced social science/humanities degree, $21,600; with business-related master's degree and nontechnical B.S., $30,000 ($31,200 with one to five years' experience); with business-related master's degree and technical B.S., $31,200 ($33,600 with one to five years' experience). Your benefits package will include life insurance; coverage for medical, hospital, and dental; pension, profit-sharing, and stock-purchase plans; and relocation assistance.

CONTACT

Manager—Recruiting, Inland Steel Company, 30 West Monroe Street, Chicago, IL 60603.

INTEL CORPORATION

ACCOUNTING AND FINANCE · ADMINISTRATION · COMPUTER SCIENCE · ENGINEERING · SALES

THE COMPANY

In 1968, Intel was founded in Santa Clara, California, by Gordon Moore and Robert Noyce, both involved in the development of the integrated circuit and both with reputations in microelectronics. Intel is a leading high-tech company. IBM is Intel's largest stockholder and largest customer. Among Intel's "firsts" are the microprocessor, the erasable programmable read-only-memory (EPROM), the single-board computer, the microcomputer development systems, and the million-bit bubble memory. Intel is heaven for high achievers—it offers a tough, demanding work situation in which you are constantly being challenged to perform and to create. It has a very young staff and a very intense atmosphere. With annual sales of more than $1 billion, it intends to stay at the cutting edge of the computer revolution. Employees currently number 16,000 in the United States, 22,000 worldwide. Intel ranks number 256 in the Fortune 500 largest U.S. industrial corporations.

ALL TRAINING PROGRAMS

In addition to the special programs described below, Intel conducts about 32,000 hours of training per month for all its employees. It has its own in-house training center complete with a catalog of courses.

FIELD APPLICATION ENGINEER PROGRAM

Training prepares new employees for positions in design engineering, process engineering, research, software engineering, systems analysis, production, and product and test engineering. The Field Application Training Program prepares you to integrate fully customer software and hardware requirements. The program begins with twelve to fourteen weeks of on-the-job training with Intel's technical organizations in California, Oregon, or Arizona. It gives you an opportunity to learn the company philosophy, its products, and their applications. After the training on the West Coast you will be assigned to a sales office where you will work closely with experienced field application engineers. Under their guidance you will meet the district's customers and learn their specific application requirements.

QUALIFICATIONS

Intel is recruiting college graduates and experienced personnel from the following fields: chemical, computer, electrical, and mechanical engineering; computer science; solid-state physics; chemistry; and business administration. The company places a high premium on creativity and achievement.

PLACEMENT

Employment centers are located in the San Francisco area; Portland, Oregon; Phoenix; Austin, Texas; and Albuquerque.

FIELD SALES PROGRAM

The Field Sales Training Program lasts twelve to fourteen weeks and includes on-the-job training with Intel's technical and marketing organizations in California, Oregon, or Arizona. You will receive a complete orientation to the company's philosophy and objectives, detailed technical training, and hands-on lab experience with the microcomputer products. The program also provides comprehensive nontechnical training in order entry, customer service, contracts, law, and other key areas that will add to your effectiveness. After this formal training program, your on-the-job training continues in one of the company's sales offices.

QUALIFICATIONS

Intel is recruiting college graduates from engineering, computer science, business, and related fields. The company places a high premium on creativity and achievement.

PLACEMENT

Sales and field support offices are located worldwide.

ALL PROGRAMS

RECRUITMENT

Intel has an aggressive program of on-campus recruiting throughout the country.

SALARY AND BENEFITS

The College Placement Council Salary Survey for September 1986–June 1987 indicates starting salaries for computers and business machine companies to be $1,880 a month for those with a B.A. degree in nontechnical curricula and $2,389 with a B.A. degree in technical curricula. M.B.A. starting salaries were $2,633 for a nontechnical undergraduate degree and $2,781 for a technical undergraduate degree. Check with the company for more specific salary information. You will be eligible for stock-purchase and profit-sharing plans. Intel has a sabbatical program that provides eight weeks off with full pay after you've worked for the company for seven years. In addition, you may also apply for six months off with pay for public service, teaching, or educational opportunities.

CONTACT

Manager, Corporate College Relations, Intel Corporation, 365 Bowers Avenue, Santa Clara, CA 95051.

INTERNATIONAL PAPER COMPANY

ENGINEERING • FINANCE • MARKETING • RESEARCH AND DEVELOPMENT • SALES

THE COMPANY

International Paper is one of the world's largest forest products companies. It owns more than 7 million acres of U.S. timberland and 24 paper mills around the world, 93 packaging plants, and numerous lumber mills, plywood facilities, and other plants. With worldwide sales exceeding $2 billion, IP is the world's leading supplier of printing and writing papers. Other operations include oil and gas drilling, agriculture, and the development of mineral properties. The company employs more than 30,000 people worldwide. It also owns Davol, a maker of innovative medical and health products. International Paper encourages its employees to set goals through career planning seminars. Among *Fortune*'s most admired corporations, it ranks number 66 in the Fortune 500 largest U.S. industrial corporations.

ENGINEERING TRAINING PROGRAM

You will participate in the Manufacturing Technical Management Program (MTMP), a two-year rotational program that mixes on-the-job work assignments and classroom instruction. You will learn about the papermaking process and spend rotational periods in the major areas of the mill: paper machines, pulp mill, power plant, quality control, process computer, environmental, plant engineering, and maintenance planning.

QUALIFICATIONS

International Paper hires from the following degree programs: chemical, mechanical, electrical, and pulp and paper engineering, accounting, finance, marketing, computer sciences, and liberal arts.

FINANCE PROGRAM

International Paper's Financial Entry-Level Program (FELP) prepares you to deal with all aspects of the company's business. In this two-year rotational program you will combine on-the-job training with exposure to various departments within Finance, and courses on the forest products industry and IP's financial reporting system.

QUALIFICATIONS

International Paper hires from the following degree programs: chemical, mechanical, electrical, and pulp and paper engineering, accounting, finance, marketing, computer sciences, and liberal arts.

SALES AND MARKETING TRAINING PROGRAM

Your training will be balanced with both challenging assignments and classroom instruction. On the job and in the classroom, you will learn about the company's products, markets, and strategies, and how to apply this knowledge to customer needs. After you complete training, you may move into a specific territory as a sales representative or join the marketing staff in customer service.

QUALIFICATIONS

International Paper hires from the following degree programs: chemical, mechanical, electrical, and pulp and paper engineering, accounting, finance, marketing, computer sciences, and liberal arts.

ALL PROGRAMS

RECRUITMENT AND PLACEMENT

IP visits 130 campuses. Some schedules are by invitation, and résumés are prescreened. The company's Corporate Research Center is located at Sterling Forest, New York, providing corporate-level research direction and multidisciplinary research and development. Another research facility is located in Mobile, Alabama, and regional forest research centers are located in Bainbridge, Georgia; Natchez, Mississippi; Bangor, Maine; and Portland, Oregon. Additional facilities exist throughout the United States and in various foreign countries.

SALARY AND BENEFITS

The College Placement Council Salary Survey for September 1986–June 1987 indicates starting salaries for building materials manufacturers and construction companies to be $1,782 a month for those with a B.A. degree in nontechnical curricula and $2,156 with a B.A. degree in technical curricula. M.B.A. starting salaries were $1,666 for a nontechnical undergraduate degree and $2,677 for a technical undergraduate degree. Check with the company for more specific salary information. Benefits include medical and dental coverage, life and disability insurance, retirement, savings and investment plans, relocation assistance, tuition reimbursement, and liberal holiday and vacation time.

CONTACT

Manager—College Recruiting, International Paper Company, International Paper Plaza, 77 West 45th Street, New York, NY 10036.

ITT COURIER TERMINAL SYSTEMS, INC.

COMPUTER SCIENCE • ENGINEERING • MARKETING • PRODUCTION • RESEARCH AND DEVELOPMENT

THE COMPANY

A subsidiary of ITT Corporation in New York, New York, ITT Courier was founded in 1969 by a group of engineers formerly with General Electric Computer Products. In only a few years the company has grown into a leading manufacturer of computer terminals and controllers, employing 2,500 people. The company is also active in printers and modems.

ALL TRAINING PROGRAMS

ITT Courier has a unique training method that utilizes the company's in-house television studio. Training and demonstration tapes are produced for marketing, engineering, field engineering, and manufacturing personnel. The TV programs are interactive, and you will be able to study at your own pace. Many accredited college classes are offered on site, and employee development seminars are held regularly. Additionally, you are encouraged to continue your studies at universities in the area to upgrade your professional skills.

QUALIFICATIONS

ITT Courier is primarily looking for graduates with bachelor's or advanced degrees in electrical engineering. Applications from technical graduates with related work experience are also encouraged. The company prefers graduates who rank in the top quarter of their class.

RECRUITMENT AND PLACEMENT

Recruiting is done nationwide. You will work at company headquarters in Tempe, Arizona.

SALARY AND BENEFITS

You can expect to start at about $30,000 with a bachelor's degree, adding about $4,000 each for a graduate or doctorate degree. A liberal tuition reimbursement plan covers approved refresher courses and degree programs. In addition, you will be eligible for pension, stock-purchase, and savings plans; life insurance; relocation assistance; and medical, hospital, and dental plans.

CONTACT

Manager, Technical Staffing, ITT Courier Terminal Systems, Inc., P.O. Box 29039, Phoenix, AZ 85038.

ITT DEFENSE COMMUNICATIONS DIVISION

ENGINEERING • INFORMATION SYSTEMS AND PROCESSING • RESEARCH AND DEVELOPMENT

THE COMPANY

The International Telephone and Telegraph Defense Communications Division (ITTDCD) conducts research and manufactures sophisticated communications equipment such as digital telephone circuit switching, message switching, narrow-band digital voice processing, radio transmission, and satellite communications and navigation. ITTDCD has been a leader in the electronics industry since 1945. It continues to stress research and development. Almost half of the 1,900 employees are members of the technical staff; 40 percent have advanced degrees. A subsidiary of ITT Corporation in New York, New York, ITTDCD's headquarters are in Nutley, New Jersey.

ENGINEERING TRAINING PROGRAM

New engineers are placed directly in jobs in functional or project areas and receive supervised on-the-job training. Engineers can continue their education at one of the universities in the area or take continuing education courses offered on site by the New Jersey Institute of Technology.

QUALIFICATIONS

ITTDCD is primarily looking for graduates with bachelor's or advanced degrees in electrical engineering, computer science, and mechanical engineering. You should have a G.P.A. of 3.0 or higher.

RECRUITMENT AND PLACEMENT

ITTDCD recruits at many college campuses. You will work at sites in California, Florida, Nebraska, or New Jersey.

SALARY AND BENEFITS

The College Placement Council Salary Survey for September 1986–June 1987 indicates starting salaries for electrical and electronic machines and equipment companies to be $1,861 a month for those with a B.A. degree in nontechnical curricula and $2,419 with a B.A. degree in technical curricula. M.B.A. starting salaries were $2,784 for a nontechnical undergraduate degree and $2,818 for a technical undergraduate degree. Check with the company for more specific salary information. A relocation coordinator will help you find a suitable home in the area of your job assignment. All tuition for job-related graduate study will be reimbursed. You will be eligible for life insurance; pension and stock-purchase plans; and medical, hospital, and dental programs.

CONTACT

Manager, Employee Relations, ITT Defense Communications Division, 492 River Road, Nutley, NJ 07110.

J

☆ ☆ ☆ ☆ ☆

JERRICO, INC.
MANAGEMENT

THE COMPANY

Jerrico has three main divisions: Jerry's Restaurants, Long John Silver's Seafood Shoppes, and Florenz Restaurants. Jerry's Restaurants, the first of Jerrico's endeavors, has evolved from its original drive-in sandwich shops to full-service family restaurants. Long John Silver's, established in 1969, is now the nation's largest seafood chain. Florenz, Jerrico's latest innovation, is a full-service restaurant specializing in northern Italian cuisine.

MANAGEMENT TRAINING PROGRAM

Jerrico maintains comprehensive training and development programs for personnel at successive stages of managerial and operational development. The Management Training Program includes both classroom and in-field instruction. Structured on-site programs will begin your training. Each level has specific modules that must be completed. Some sections rely mainly on an instructional format, while others are learner-controlled, permitting progress at an individual pace. Initial on-the-job training focuses on development and practice of basic operational skills.

As you progress in your career, Jerrico offers a series of individual field courses for ongoing professional development. These courses cover specific areas of performance and provide opportunities for promotion into multi-unit supervision. The in-field programs are designed to guide you in advancement from assistant manager to district director.

All classroom instruction takes place at the Jerrico Center for Training and Development in Lexington, Kentucky. You will learn management concepts and gain practical experience in technical aspects of restaurant management. Advanced courses provide an introduction to the techniques and requirements of mid-level management.

QUALIFICATIONS

Jerrico is looking for individuals who will uphold standards of quality and guest service required in its restaurants. All management personnel must have a high school degree or the equivalent. Additional education or food service experience will be considered.

RECRUITMENT AND PLACEMENT

Recruitment generally takes place at the local level. Applications are available at individual restaurants or from the personnel office in Lexington, Kentucky.

SALARY AND BENEFITS

The College Placement Council Salary Survey for September 1986–June 1987 indicates starting salaries for merchandising (retail and wholesale) and service companies to be $1,594 a month for those with a B.A. degree in nontechnical curricula and

$2,141 with a B.A. degree in technical curricula. M.B.A. starting salaries were $2,572 for a nontechnical undergraduate degree, and $2,735 for an M.B.A. with technical undergraduate degree. Check with the company for more specific salary information. A full benefit package includes hospitalization and dental insurance, quarterly and annual bonuses, and stock options in the advanced management levels.

CONTACT

Vice-President of Personnel, Jerrico, Inc., P.O. Box 11988, Lexington, KY 40579.

JOHNSON & JOHNSON

FINANCE • MANAGEMENT • MANUFACTURING • MARKETING • SALES

THE COMPANY

Johnson & Johnson, the world's largest healthcare product manufacturer, was incorporated in 1887. Its founder, Robert Wood Johnson, developed sterile bandages in the 1890s and the Band-Aid in 1920. The company ranks at the top in sales of adhesive bandages, headache remedies (Tylenol and Medipren), contraceptives (Ortho creams and foams), disposable diapers, and shampoo (baby shampoo marketed successfully to adults). Consumer products account for about 45 percent of sales. Today the corporation is a highly decentralized family of 150 companies operating in 50 countries on 6 continents and employing more than 80,000 people worldwide. Johnson & Johnson ranks number 53 in the Fortune 500 largest industrial corporations and has annual sales of more than $7 billion. The Robert Wood Johnson Foundation, the country's second largest, grants an estimated $50 million annually to health and medical research. J & J is listed among *Fortune*'s most admired corporations.

ALL TRAINING PROGRAMS

On-the-job learning is the primary training method. Most training lasts six to twelve months and also includes classroom instruction. J & J provides degree programs developed jointly with nearby colleges and universities, as well as periodic workshops and seminars to enhance your professional growth.

FINANCIAL PROGRAM

On-the-job learning is the primary training method. Training lasts six to twelve months and includes classroom instruction. Financial management trainees often complete a planned rotation of assignments to expose them to all the interrelated financial areas, such as financial analysis, general accounting, cost accounting, marketing accounting, financial planning, and data processing.

QUALIFICATIONS

The company is looking for graduates with degrees in accounting, business, and international business. You will impress the recruiter favorably with demonstrated leadership ability, a class ranking in the top 20 percent, and a G.P.A. of 3.2 or higher.

PLACEMENT

Headquarters are in New Brunswick, New Jersey. You could also be assigned to other New Jersey locations, or to positions in California, Florida, Georgia, Illinois, Massachusetts, Pennsylvania, or Texas.

OPERATIONS MANAGEMENT PROGRAM

Operations management trainees supervise staff in manufacturing facilities early in their careers. The majority of trainees are needed in marketing management. Your on-the-job experience is designed to familiarize you with the products and markets of the company in your home country as well as effective sales and marketing management techniques. You may spend time in the company sales force to learn about its customers and markets.

QUALIFICATIONS

You will need a degree in engineering or business, along with a personal commitment to excellence demonstrated by your achievements in school and extracurricular activities. J & J prefers graduates who rank in the top 20 percent of their class with a G.P.A. of 3.2 or higher.

PLACEMENT

J & J facilities are located in California, Florida, Georgia, Illinois, Massachusetts, New Jersey, Pennsylvania, and Texas.

MARKETING PROGRAM

Marketing positions are found in consumer and professional areas. Training involves on-the-job and classroom learning as well as a brief stint in the company sales force to learn customers and markets. You will work with experienced personnel to learn planning production on objectives, pricing strategies, promotional programs, packaging changes, and advertising content and schedules for products. After training, you will be assigned to a team responsible for a particular product or group of products.

QUALIFICATIONS

J & J looks for marketing and business graduates who demonstrate leadership ability and have high personal integrity. You should rank in the top 20 percent of your class with a G.P.A. of 3.2 or higher.

PLACEMENT

You could be assigned to any of the following states: California, Florida, Georgia, Illinois, Massachusetts, New Jersey, Pennsylvania, or Texas.

SALES PROGRAM

In sales, you will enter an intensive program to learn about the company, its products, and effective sales techniques. In the pharmaceutical professional products area, you will be trained to present products to physicians, nurses, hospital administrators, and other health-care professionals. With consumer products, you will be dealing with many distribution channels, such as drugstores, supermarkets, discount stores, syndicates, and department stores. You will learn to advise retailers on promotion and placement of products to build their volume and profits. The last phase will be to accompany an experienced sales representative through a regional area to begin to apply your skills. Then you will be assigned your own territory.

QUALIFICATIONS

Previous selling experience will be a plus, as will a high academic standing in your class (top 20 percent preferred, with a G.P.A. of 3.2 or better). You should be organized and a self-starter.

PLACEMENT

J & J has sales offices all over the country.

INTERNATIONAL M.B.A. PROGRAM

If you are a foreign national who has pursued an M.B.A. in the United States, you may qualify for a two-year, highly competitive financial training program that helps develop local nationals for management positions worldwide. In this program you are assigned a sponsor to guide you throughout your training, which consists of rotational work in four major financial fields: financial accounting, data processing, operations accounting, and marketing accounting.

QUALIFICATIONS

You should have an excellent academic record to go with your M.B.A. as well as leadership ability.

PLACEMENT

The company has operations in 50 countries around the world.

ALL PROGRAMS

RECRUITMENT

The company recruits on a nationwide basis and has offices in all 50 states.

SALARY AND BENEFITS

Starting salary with a bachelor's degree is in the mid-twenties; a master's degree will earn you a few thousand dollars more. Check with the company for more specific salary information. You will receive life and accident insurance, medical and dental health-care coverage, disability benefits, tuition reimbursement, and retirement benefits. You also participate in the Live for Life Program, which provides facilities, guidance, and motivation to enhance your health.

CONTACT

Director of Personnel, Johnson & Johnson, One Johnson & Johnson Plaza, New Brunswick, NJ 08933; or you may write directly to any of the company's divisions if you have a preference.

JOHNSON CONTROLS, INC.

ENGINEERING · SALES

THE COMPANY

The Globe Battery Division of Johnson Controls manufactures automotive, industrial, and communications batteries. Its Systems and Services Division designs and manufactures heating, ventilating, and air conditioning systems; computerized building automation/energy management systems; and physical and fire security systems for commercial and industrial buildings. The Control Products Division makes and wholesales a wide range of controls and control systems. Established in 1885, Johnson Controls has more than $2.6 billion in annual sales. It ranks number 147 in the Fortune 500 largest U.S. industrial corporations.

ALL TRAINING PROGRAMS

Training prepares beginning engineers for positions in design and development, project engineering, and technical sales. The program provides on-the-job supervision supplemented with classroom instruction.

QUALIFICATIONS

You should be in the upper third of your class with a B.A. or a master's in engineering, computer science, materials science, or business.

RECRUITMENT AND PLACEMENT

The company recruits nationwide for sales engineers. Midwest recruiting for Globe Battery and Systems and Services sends employees to Milwaukee positions primarily. The Systems Engineering and Construction Division recruits in the Southwest and Northeast for positions in Dallas and Philadelphia. In the Control Products Division, you could work anywhere in the United States.

SALARY AND BENEFITS

For those with a bachelor's degree, starting salaries in the Systems and Services Division are in the $21,000 to $27,000 range; with a master's degree, from $23,000 to $31,000. Ask for specifics from the other divisions. There is a full benefits program.

CONTACT

Professional and Technical Recruitment, Systems and Services Division, Johnson Controls, Inc., 507 East Michigan Street, P.O. Box 423, Milwaukee, WI 53201; Battery Division, Professional and Technical Recruitment, Johnson Controls, Inc., 5757 North Green Bay Avenue, P.O. Box 591, Milwaukee, WI 53201; Control Products Division, Professional and Technical Recruitment, Johnson Controls, Inc., 1250 East Diehl Road, Naperville, IL 60540; or Systems Engineering and Construction Division, Professional and Technical Development, Johnson Controls, Inc., 1201 West Crosby Road, Carrollton, TX 75006.

From the Training Manager's Perspective
William M. Fulton, Motorola

William M. Fulton, manager of human resources and training at the Motorola semiconductor plant in Phoenix, Arizona, has been with the company for twenty-three years.

☆ ☆ ☆ ☆ ☆

What does your job involve?

I do recruiting, but not full time. I fill in occasionally and go out on campus but my primary function is the planning and delivery of training in a segment of the semiconductor division here at Motorola.

How is your program structured for engineers?

We have a rotation program. We go out once a year, typically for the spring graduates, recruiting normally 20 graduates. Usually we hire electrical engineers, but that may vary. We may go get some chemical engineers, or some industrial engineers, or some materials science engineers—basically engineering people.

Those people are then brought on the payroll in a department which is administered by the personnel department. It takes care of all the salaries, fringes, payroll taxes, and expenses, that sort of thing. The operations do not pay that budget. The cost gets allocated back to the operations, obviously, but they're not in control of the budget. As long as we control the budget we control the destiny of the rotational engineers in terms of getting them assigned to permanent jobs until they've been in the program for a year.

We put them through four three-month rotations. For the first one, we try to match what the trainees said they think they want to do with openings that we have when they arrive. For example, if we hire an engineer to start on July 1 and he said he wanted to be a device engineer, we would try to start his rotation somewhere in the device engineering department.

We decided all our incoming people should know how the quality organization operates and what some of its problems are. So there is a three-month rotation in the quality organization.

Then the last two—and understand that this is not necessarily in chronological order, except for the first one—are basically elective. We let them decide what area they would like to participate in for three months. One stipulation is that they cannot be where they have been before. We want these people to have as broad, in-depth knowledge of operations as they can get within a one-year period. Then at the end of the one-year period they are assigned to a regular full-time job.

We try as much as we can to get the rotational engineer to negotiate with hiring managers and work out their own bargain, but we in the personnel department do try to guide them in the right direction.

Has the program changed in its structure in the last few years?

We have always basically had this approach. We have changed by adding more structure. At one time the college fresh-outs would arrive and in fact we would put them in an office with a telephone and a list of telephone numbers and say, "Call these numbers until you find yourself a position." That's obviously not the best way to infuse new blood into an organization. We have found that the rotation plan that has evolved seems to work the best, from both the new hire's personal standpoint and the company's.

Is the program limited to on-the-job training or does it include classwork?

There are some classes, in total cycle time management and statistical process control. Typically, the instructional materials are given in a lecture type of environment and the application is done within their rotations.

So the trainee gets a chance to put the information to work right away?

Exactly.

What should a trainee do to be most successful in your program?

Complete the rotational projects successfully (there are some who do that better than others), and absorb as much knowledge of the business operation as possible in each rotation. Once a month part of the rotational group gives presentations to selected managers. They discuss their rotation and what's been good about it, what they've learned. We think that it's mandatory to success in the organization to be able to get up in front of people and tell them what you've been doing and what the outcome has been.

Do you keep track of the trainees after they leave the program?

Once they've been given their regular full-time assignment, we do keep track of them, but we've only started doing this in the last eighteen months or so. However, I can point to some of our very senior executives who were graduates of that program twenty years ago.

Do you monitor trainees' progress or give them additional support once they leave the program?

We in personnel don't formally monitor these employees, with one major exception. Should we go through a downturn in business and need to reduce the work force, the rotational engineers are protected while they're in the rotational program and for one year thereafter.

K

☆ ☆ ☆ ☆ ☆

KAISER ALUMINUM & CHEMICAL CORPORATION

ACCOUNTING • ADMINISTRATION • ENGINEERING • FINANCE • INFORMATION SYSTEMS • MARKETING • PRODUCTION • RESEARCH AND DEVELOPMENT • SALES • TECHNICAL SERVICES

THE COMPANY

Henry J. Kaiser started in the construction business in 1913 when he acquired a road-building company. Together with five other large firms, Kaiser helped build the Hoover, Bonneville, and Grand Coulee dams. When World War II started, the same six companies went into shipbuilding. In 1946, Kaiser purchased several aluminum processing plants from the federal government, and today 75 percent of the company's business is in aluminum production. It also has branched out into the production of agricultural and industrial chemicals and real estate in Southern California and Hawaii. A company with a long history of community involvement, Kaiser has built 19 hospitals and has been a principal backer of the Oakland Renaissance Program to restore the city's downtown area. Kaiser has about 11,500 U.S. employees, and another 2,000 outside the country. Listed among *Fortune*'s most admired corporations, Kaiser has more than $2 billion in annual sales and ranks number 165 in the Fortune 500 largest U.S. industrial corporations.

ENGINEERING TRAINING PROGRAM

Training prepares new employees for a variety of production responsibilities, including production management. The program consists of on-the-job and classroom instruction. It lasts eighteen months for industrial engineers and fifteen to eighteen months for maintenance engineers.

QUALIFICATIONS

Kaiser is looking for college graduates with bachelor's and master's degrees in the following fields: business, accounting, computer science, industrial relations, and engineering (ceramic, chemical, electrical, industrial, mechanical, and metallurgical). A year or more of technical experience is helpful.

RECRUITMENT AND PLACEMENT

Starting positions are available in California, Louisiana, Ohio, Pennsylvania, Washington, and West Virginia.

SALARY AND BENEFITS

Starting salaries range from the low to high twenties, depending on your degree level. The College Placement Council Salary Survey for September 1986–June 1987 indicates starting salaries for metals and metal products companies to be $1,782 a month for those with a B.A. degree in nontechnical curricula and $2,353 with a B.A. degree in technical curricula. M.B.A. starting salaries were $2,346 for a nontechnical undergraduate degree and $2,700 for a technical undergraduate degree.

Check with the company for more specific salary and benefits information.

CONTACT

Director, Human Resources Planning, Kaiser Aluminum & Chemical Corporation, 300 Lakeside Drive, Oakland, CA 94643.

KAY JEWELERS, INC.

MANAGEMENT

THE COMPANY

Kay Jewelers currently operates more than 450 stores in 34 states, making it the world's second largest jewelry retailer. The firm chooses to sell jewelry only, with no giftware or other merchandise in its inventory. Its stores are generally located in corner, high-traffic locations within major shopping malls. Kay's merchandise buyers strive to appeal to a broad-based clientele. Approximately half of the company's sales are in diamonds. In 1986, Kay acquired J. B. Robinson Jewelers, a 94-store chain in the Midwest. It also operates Black, Starr & Frost, Ltd. stores in upscale markets, and Marcus & Co. leased in major department stores. In addition to planning more acquisitions, Kay continues to add 20 to 30 new stores each year, opening up new opportunities for store managers to join the company. Fairfax Distributing Co. is the marketing and distributing arm of Kay Jewelers, with diamond-buying offices in Antwerp, the Netherlands, and in Israel. Corporate headquarters are in Alexandria, Virginia, just outside Washington, D.C. In 1987 there were record sales of 368 million dollars and record profits which are steadily increasing at a 23 percent annual rate.

MANAGEMENT TRAINEE PROGRAM

Most of your training occurs on the job and consists of a structured program of intensified sales training, role play, skills reviews, manager and district manager conferences, and several testing modules. These modules are comprised of information pertaining to product knowledge, sales skills, store administration, and personnel policy. You are taught how to analyze and interpret operational and inventory information to improve management decision-making and enhance store profits. On-the-job training is supplemented with seminars and professional speakers in all districts.

By the end of nine months, you will have completed six training modules and will be eligible for promotion to assistant manager. As an assistant manager you receive a percentage of store sales and 10 percent of repair department profits! Promotion to store manager is possible within fifteen to twenty-four months, based on performance and availability.

As a store manager you will continue your training. Kay's Store Management Career Development Program is designed to increase a manager's ability to deal successfully with operational and interpersonal dimensions of store management. Seminars delivered include Interviewing Skills, Time and Stress Management, Administration and Profitability, and Management Style and Employee Motivation. Kay Jewelers is continually enhancing its Career Development Program on all levels to ensure that Kay store personnel are given the opportunity to develop their professional sales skills and lead with the confidence of a winner.

QUALIFICATIONS

Kay is looking for college graduates with an interest in sales and retail management. Prior experience is not required, but you should be a confident, independent person projecting poise and enthusiasm. Listening and communication skills are also considered important. You must be willing to relocate as the job demands.

RECRUITMENT AND PLACEMENT

Kay recruits on college campuses across the country. Stores are located in Alabama, Arizona, California, Colorado, Connecticut, Florida, Georgia, Illinois, Indiana, Iowa, Kansas, Kentucky, Louisiana, Maryland, Massachusetts, Michigan, Mississippi, Missouri, Nevada, New Hampshire, New Jersey, New York, North Carolina, Ohio, Oklahoma, Pennsylvania, Rhode Island, South Carolina, Tennessee, Texas, Virginia, Washington, D.C., and West Virginia.

SALARY AND BENEFITS

Usually manager trainees make between $18,000 and $21,000 their first year. Store managers' compensation averages above $40,000, although many earn much more. The rates vary by region, but you will receive base salary, commission, and performance-based incentives. Kay also offers a comprehensive benefits package including free medical and life insurance, a dental plan, a pretax savings plan, sick days, holidays, vacation, and an employee stock-purchase plan. Contact the company for further details on benefits.

CONTACT

Eric Mayer, Divisional Vice-President, Personnel, Kay Jewelers, Inc., 320 King Street, Alexandria, VA 22314.

KEARFOTT DIVISION, SINGER COMPANY

AEROSPACE · ENGINEERING · INFORMATION SYSTEMS · RESEARCH AND DEVELOPMENT

THE COMPANY

Kearfott manufactures navigation and communications systems for airplanes, missiles, and spacecraft. The company employs about 5,500 people in the United States, and more than 2,000 outside the country.

ALL TRAINING PROGRAMS

Six months of supervised on-the-job experience and classroom instruction get you started. Seminars and conferences will be provided to build your technical expertise. You will be encouraged to continue your professional development with 100 percent reimbursement of approved graduate study.

QUALIFICATIONS

Kearfott is looking for people with degrees in computer science, engineering (computer, electrical, manufacturing, mechanical, software, and systems), engineering technology, and business. Three or more years of related work experience is a plus. The company prefers candidates in the top 25 percent of their class but will interview those with G.P.A.s as low as 2.8. You must be familiar with computer systems and software, and be able to program. Doctoral candidates in physics are also in demand.

RECRUITMENT AND PLACEMENT

You will start your new job in New Jersey.

SALARY AND BENEFITS

With a bachelor's degree, you can expect to start at about $28,000; at $30,500 with a master's; and at $38,500 or more with a doctorate. Benefits include medical, hospital, dental, and vision plans; life insurance; relocation assistance; and pension and stock-purchase programs.

CONTACT

Carol Batte, Employment Supervisor, Kearfott Division, Singer Company, 1150 McBride Avenue, Little Falls, NJ 07424.

KELLOGG COMPANY

ACCOUNTING · ADMINISTRATION · CHEMISTRY · COMPUTER SCIENCE · ENGINEERING · FINANCE · FOOD SCIENCE · HUMAN RESOURCES · RESEARCH AND DEVELOPMENT

THE COMPANY

William Keith Kellogg was the business manager of the Battle Creek Sanitarium in Michigan, where his brother Dr. John Harvey Kellogg was chief surgeon and superintendent. Since patients and staff observed a strict vegetarian diet, the Kellogg brothers experimented with various foods in the sanitarium kitchen to try to add variety to the regimen. During one of those experiments in 1894, they accidentally produced individual wheat flakes. W. K. Kellogg began the Battle Creek Toasted Corn Flake Company in 1906. Today Kellogg ranks first in breakfast cereals and owns several subsidiaries that make other types of food—Mrs. Smith's frozen pies, Eggo frozen waffles, LeGout canned dinners, nondairy toppings and creamers, and Salada teas. This is a highly competitive field with only a few top players battling it out for dominance. Kellogg's annual sales exceed $3 billion, and it ranks number 120 in the Fortune 500 largest U.S. industrial corporations.

ALL TRAINING PROGRAMS

Training prepares new employees for careers in food research, nutrition, engineering, plant operations, accounting and finance, data processing, employee relations, marketing research, and sales positions. On-the-job training lasts from six to twelve months, depending on the requirements of the position. Sales training is personalized and is conducted on an individual basis. There are opportunities to work with experienced Kellogg personnel to learn sales methods and company products. For the first several months, progress is reviewed and coaching provided to the trainee. In many positions you will be offered in-house management development seminars.

QUALIFICATIONS

The company is looking for college graduates and experienced personnel in the following fields: accounting, business administration, chemistry, computer science, food science, biological sciences, food technology, marketing and marketing research, nutrition, and engineering—agricultural, electrical, electronics, and industrial.

RECRUITMENT AND PLACEMENT

The company recruits nationwide. Starting locations are in California, Michigan, Nebraska, Pennsylvania, and Tennessee.

SALARY AND BENEFITS

Salaries are in the low to mid-twenties with a bachelor's degree; mid-twenties with a master's; and low thirties with a doctorate. You will participate in a benefits package that consists of medical and dental, life and disability insurance plans, savings and investment plans, a pension plan, a performance bonus plan, tuition reimbursement, and a credit union.

CONTACT

College Recruitment, Senior Employment Representative, Kellogg Company, One Kellogg Square, P.O. Box 3599, Battle Creek, MI 49016-3599.

KENNECOTT CORPORATION

ENGINEERING • PRODUCTION •
RESEARCH AND DEVELOPMENT •
TECHNICAL SERVICES

THE COMPANY

After Meyer Guggenheim made $15 million by buying into two lead and silver mines in Colorado, he gathered his seven sons around the table to show them how to become multimillionaires. He gave them each a stick, telling them to break it. Then he passed around a bundle of sticks, tied together, and told them to break it. When none of them could, he pointed out that together they, too, were invincible. "Stay together, my sons, and the world will be yours." The sons stuck together and soon controlled 80 percent of the silver, copper, and lead market. The Kennecott name still is synonymous with copper. But today less than half of Kennecott's sales come from this shiny metal. Additional revenues come from the mining of gold, silver, and molybdenum. The company owns the largest copper reserves in the United States, the largest open-pit mine in the world, and over 80 processing plants.

ENGINEERING MANAGEMENT TRAINING PROGRAM

If you want to use your engineering background to move into management, you can go through Kennecott's formal, six-month College Hire Management Development Program. You train at your choice of locations—Ely, Nevada; Hayden, Arizona; Hurley, New Mexico; or Salt Lake City or Tintic, Utah.

QUALIFICATIONS

Kennecott needs people with bachelor's degrees in business, chemistry, civil engineering, engineering, and mechanical engineering. It also needs people with metallurgy, mineralogy, geology, and mineral economics backgrounds.

RECRUITMENT AND PLACEMENT

The headquarters are in New York City; 40 percent of the metal-processing plants are scattered across the United States. Major locations for placement are in Arizona, Nevada, New Mexico, and Utah, while remaining plants are in Latin America, Europe, Canada, Australia, and New Zealand.

SALARY AND BENEFITS

The College Placement Council Salary Survey for September 1986–June 1987 indicates starting salaries for metals and metal products companies to be $1,782 a month for those with a B.A. degree in nontechnical curricula and $2,353 with a B.A. degree in technical curricula. M.B.A. starting salaries were $2,346 for a nontechnical undergraduate degree and $2,700 for a technical undergraduate degree. Check with the company for more specific salary information. You will receive benefits that include medical, hospital, and dental insurance, a pension plan, and life insurance.

CONTACT

Larry King, Director of Compensation and Personnel, Kennecott Corp., P.O. Box 11248, Salt Lake City, UT 84133.

KIDDER, PEABODY & CO., INC.

EQUITY SALES AND TRADING • FIXED-INCOME SALES AND TRADING • INVESTMENT BANKING • MUNICIPAL SECURITIES • RESEARCH • RETAIL SALES

THE COMPANY

In 1985, Kidder, Peabody marked its one hundred and twentieth anniversary as a private investment banking firm. Since its inception, Kidder, Peabody has grown from a small Boston-based brokerage firm to a leading international investment banking house with approximately 70 offices and over 6,000 employees worldwide. A full range of investment banking services are offered in corporate finance, municipal securities, international finance, fixed-income sales and trading, financial futures, market making, research, and sales. The investment banking business has grown at unprecedented rates in recent years, which has increased the amount of capital required to compete effectively in all investment banking markets. In response to these competitive pressures, Kidder, Peabody chose to end its long-standing position as a private firm when it agreed to sell a majority interest (80 percent) to General Electric Company for approximately $600 million. The introduction of General Electric as Kidder, Peabody's corporate partner provides the firm with an effective capital base and capital-raising ability unparalleled on Wall Street. Equally important, certain Kidder, Peabody employees will retain a 20 percent equity ownership position in the firm, which will provide them with the continued opportunity to participate directly in the firm's future successes.

ALL TRAINING PROGRAMS

You will be trained through a variety of approaches: job rotation, formal classes and on the job. You will be given responsibility from the beginning.

EQUITY SALES AND TRADING, RESEARCH, MUNICIPAL SECURITIES PROGRAMS

Training for these departments is conducted on the job to give you an accelerated understanding of job functions and results.

FIXED-INCOME SALES AND TRADING PROGRAM

The Fixed-Income Sales and Trading Training Program for both B.A.s and M.B.A.s consists of two main components. First is a rotation through the three chief areas of fixed-income trading. Second is classroom instruction, including talks by a number of key Kidder, Peabody professionals. You will spend approximately eight weeks in the program, which is conducted in the New York office. Upon completion of the training program you may be sent to Dallas, Atlanta, San Francisco, Los Angeles, Boston, Philadelphia, or Chicago.

INVESTMENT BANKING PROGRAM

If you are a B.A. candidate, Kidder, Peabody offers a two-year corporate finance associate internship designed to introduce recent college graduates to investment banking before returning to business school. The program is currently comprised of approximately 50 associate interns who are divided between generalists, covering a broad range of clients, and specialists working in varied industry and technical groups. Following four weeks of formal training, you will receive on-the-job instruction.

M.B.A. candidates enter the investment banking department as associates. Following a two-week training program, you will be assigned to account teams consisting of a senior broker, an assistant vice-president, and an associate. Once assigned to a specific account team, associates remain members of that team, servicing all the financing, merger and acquisition, and advisory needs of each of their clients. This focused approach to client relationships offers incoming associates substantial client contact, up-front responsibility, and constant exposure to senior bankers.

RETAIL SALES PROGRAM

Individual branch offices hire retail and account executives. Upon passing the Series 7 examination and within six months of hiring, you will have spent one week in a regional training program and four weeks in sales training in the New York office.

ALL PROGRAMS

QUALIFICATIONS

The company is looking for individuals who demonstrate a strong desire to achieve individual excellence while maintaining an established appreciation for the importance of teamwork. Additional characteristics Kidder, Peabody looks for are creativity, well-developed communication and interpersonal skills, a sense of humor, and a high energy level. Intelligence and creativity are required to grasp the various financial, accounting, and legal considerations involved in transactions and to develop sound business judgment. Communication and interpersonal skills are necessary to work effectively with clients and other members of the firm. A sense of humor and a high energy level are crucial in meeting the varied, sometimes unpredictable needs of a diverse client base.

RECRUITMENT AND PLACEMENT

Each department hires independently. The company recruits nationwide. You could be placed in any of Kidder, Peabody's 70 offices in major U.S. cities.

SALARY AND BENEFITS

The College Placement Council Salary Survey for September 1986–June 1987 indicates starting salaries for banking, finance, and insurance firms to be $1,889 a month for those with a B.A. degree in nontechnical curricula and $2,135 with a B.A. degree in technical curricula. M.B.A. starting salaries were $2,884 for a nontechnical undergraduate degree, and $3,320 for an M.B.A. with technical undergraduate degree. Check with the company for more specific salary information. The company offers a full package of benefits.

CONTACT

Kidder, Peabody & Co., Inc., 10 Hanover Square, New York, NY 10005; Equity Research, Mr. George H. Boyd III, Managing Director; Equity Trading, Mr. Anthony C. Woodruff, Managing Director; Fixed-Income Sales, Trading, and Research, Ms. Glorianne Pheloung, Recruiting Coordinator; Institutional Equity Sales, Mr. Theodore J. Johnson, Managing Director; Investment Banking, Ms. Sharon Henning, Recruiting Coordinator; Municipal Securities, Ms. Lynne R. Davidson, Vice-President; Retail Sales, contact manager of individual branch.

KIMBERLY-CLARK CORPORATION

ACCOUNTING · ENGINEERING · FINANCE · LOGISTICS · RESEARCH

THE COMPANY

Kleenex is perhaps the most famous of Kimberly-Clark's product line, but the company also produces and markets a wide range of products for health care, personal care, and other uses in the home, business, and industry. K-C groups its products and services into three categories. The first includes disposable diapers, household towels, feminine pads, and surgical gowns. The second includes newsprint; groundwood; correspondence, cover, and text printing papers; base papers for abrasives, labels and tapes; film and foils; and specialty envelopes. The final category illustrates the company's diversity and includes aircraft maintenance, finishing, and refurbishing; commercial airline service; machinery design, fabrication, and installation; and truck transportation services. The company employs approximately 16,000 people in the United States and 40,000 worldwide. Among *Fortune*'s most admired corporations, it ranks number 90 in the Fortune 500 largest U.S. industrial corporations.

RESEARCH TRAINING PROGRAM

You will begin with a multiassignment program in which you work and learn as a team member with project leaders, scientists, and technicians in one of K-C's five major research areas: consumer products; health care, nonwoven and industrial products; newsprint pulp and forest products; technical paper and specialty products; and corporate science and technology. For growth and job satisfaction, K-C offers innovation time to all research employees: 10 percent of your time may be spent working on individual ideas, plans, and projects.

QUALIFICATIONS

You should have a B.S. or advanced degree in a discipline such as chemistry (physical, colloid, surface, polymer, organic), biotechnology, chemical engineering, paper sciences and technology, engineering science, textile chemistry, materials science (polymers, fibers), biochemistry, mathematics, mechanical engineering, or physics.

GENERAL TRAINING PROGRAMS

Your training will last for several months in engineering, logistics management, or finance, combining classroom instruction and supervised on-the-job experience. The length of training will depend on your ability, experience, and progress.

QUALIFICATIONS

In addition to engineering, chemistry, and physics graduates, K-C hires entry-level employees with degrees in business or with technical or nontechnical B.S. You may have a bachelor's, master's, or doctoral degree. Skills in human relations are especially valuable for logistics management candidates.

ALL PROGRAMS

RECRUITMENT AND PLACEMENT

Competition will be stiff, so make your letter of inquiry and application shine. K-C hires only about 10 percent of all applicants each year: 100 with bachelor's degrees, 30 with master's degrees, and 15 at the doctoral level. Your starting location could be in any of the following states: Alabama, Arizona, Arkansas, California, Connecticut, Georgia, Massachusetts, Michigan, Minnesota, Mississippi, New Jersey, New York, North Carolina, Ohio, Pennsylvania, South Carolina, Tennessee, Texas, Utah, or Wisconsin.

SALARY AND BENEFITS

The College Placement Council Salary Survey for September 1986–June 1987 indicates starting salaries for glass, paper, packaging, and allied product companies to be $1,865 a month for those with a B.A. degree in nontechnical curricula and $2,401 with a B.A. degree in technical curricula. M.B.A. starting salaries were $2,945 for a nontechnical undergraduate degree and $2,775 for a technical undergraduate degree. Check with the company for more specific salary information. K-C offers comprehensive benefits including health, life, dental, disability, and business travel insurance, educational funds for employee and family members, educational leave, holidays, and vacations.

CONTACT

Corporate Recruiter, Kimberly-Clark Corporation, 401 North Lake Street, Neenah, WI 54956.

K MART CORPORATION

RETAIL MANAGEMENT

THE COMPANY

Described as one-stop shopping centers, K mart stores emphasize quality merchandise at discount prices. With more than 2,100 stores, the company boasts that more than 80 percent of all consumers in America shop at K mart, and half the American population visits one of its stores at least once a month. It has twice as many stores as its nearest competitor, with stores falling into three size categories, ranging from 40,000 to 80,000 square feet. Each store stocks clothing for the entire family, home improvement products, electronics, cookware, home furnishings, sporting goods, automotive accessories, toys, jewelry, camera supplies, records, books, and health and beauty aids. Central buying offices are located at K mart International Headquarters in Troy, Michigan, a Detroit suburb. K mart subsidiaries include Builder's Square, a chain of warehouse home centers; Pay Less Drug Stores Northwest, Inc., with more than 200 stores; and Waldenbooks, with over 1,000 bookstores. The S. S. Kresge Company, founded in 1899, developed the discount store concept, opening the first K mart store in 1962.

K mart is now one of the largest mass merchandisers in the world, with more than 340,000 employees, mostly in the United States. It ranks number 2 in the Fortune 50 largest retailing companies and has annual sales of more than $24 billion. K mart appears among *Fortune*'s most admired corporations. All the top executives started in the training program, showing that you'll have opportunities to climb the corporate ladder as well.

MANAGEMENT TRAINING PROGRAM

You will spend one to two years in the Management Training Program, specializing in general merchandising, apparel, or automotive and sporting goods. The program begins with an intensive sixteen-week orientation, introducing you to all phases of K mart operations, including basic store procedures, processing center training, personnel training, an overview of sporting goods and automotive departments, general merchandising, office training, and apparel merchandising overview. You will also be learning cash register operations. In the final four weeks of orientation you will supervise four departments within the store and complete a review of what you have learned. You will work in a store for firsthand experience. In Phase II you will be promoted to assistant manager and possibly transferred to another store in your region where you will put your training into action. Your next step is to become merchandise manager, with total responsibility for all merchandise in your store, approving all orders and maintaining the optimum level of inventory in each department. At this position you are eligible for a yearly bonus based on the store's profitability. Store manager position comes next, making you responsible for the total operation and profitability of the store.

QUALIFICATIONS

You might have a degree in liberal arts, business, or other area, but more important is your willingness to work hard, the ability to get along with people and take the initiative. You should be willing to relocate frequently.

RECRUITMENT AND PLACEMENT

K mart recruits year round. You will work in the region in which you are hired and trained.

SALARY AND BENEFITS

The College Placement Council Salary Survey for September 1986–June 1987 indicates starting salaries for merchandising (retail and wholesale) and service companies to be $1,594 a month for those with a B.A. degree in nontechnical curricula and $2,141 with a B.A. degree in technical curricula. M.B.A. starting salaries were $2,572 for a nontechnical undergraduate degree, and $2,735 for an M.B.A. with technical undergraduate degree. Check with the company for more specific salary information. Your benefits will include a comprehensive medical plan, pension, sickness and accident disability coverage, paid vacation, and employee savings plan.

CONTACT

The Regional Personnel and Training Manager at the office nearest you: K mart Western Regional Office, 1184 North Citrus Avenue, BIN-K, Covina, CA 91722; K mart Southwestern Regional Office, 703 South Industrial Boulevard, Euless, TX 76040; K mart Midwestern Regional Office, 2300 B. W. Higgins Road, Hoffman Estates, IL 60195; K mart Central Regional Office, 41425 Joy Road, P.O. Box 8310C, Plymouth, MI 48170; K mart Southern Regional Office, 2901 Clairmont Road, N.E., Atlanta, GA 30029; or K mart Eastern Regional Office, 645 Highway 18, East Brunswick, NJ 08816.

THE KROGER CO.

ACCOUNTING • ADVERTISING • CORPORATE PLANNING • DATA PROCESSING • DISTRIBUTION MANAGEMENT • ENGINEERING • FINANCE • FOOD TECHNOLOGY • HUMAN RESOURCES • LABOR RELATIONS • MANAGEMENT • MANAGEMENT INFORMATION SYSTEMS • MERCHANDISING • OPERATIONS MANAGEMENT • PLANT MANAGEMENT • PROCUREMENT • PRODUCT MANAGEMENT • PUBLIC AFFAIRS • QUALITY CONTROL • REAL ESTATE • RESEARCH AND DEVELOPMENT • RISK MANAGEMENT • TRANSPORTATION

THE COMPANY

Kroger is the largest domestic food retailer in the United States, with over 1,300 food stores and over 700 convenience stores. Founded by twenty-three-year-old Bernard H. Kroger in 1883, the chain has shaped the structure of grocery retailing as it exists today. Among Kroger's firsts were the introduction of meat markets in grocery stores (and a pitched battle forcing butchers to follow ethical business procedures); in-store bakeries; a laser-based scanning system installed in a Cincinnati store in 1972; and fresh seafood departments. In addition, Kroger is the world's largest retail florist and largest importer of cheese, and operates the largest privately owned trucking company. It manufactures more than 4,000 food and nonfood products in 27 manufacturing plants. New Kroger stores are over 47,000 square feet and have up to 200 employees. The chain has a total of more than 150,000 workers. The industry's most complete research and development facility, the Kroger Technical Center, employs over 80 scientists and support technicians to study new manufacturing processes. Restructuring in 1986 maintained the company's profitability by closing 100 unprofitable food stores and divesting 870 drugstores.

Kroger is listed among *Fortune*'s most admired corporations and has annual sales of more than $18 billion. It ranks number 4 in the Fortune 50 largest retailing companies.

ALL TRAINING PROGRAMS

The Kroger Education Center in Cincinnati offers courses in operations methods and management skills to over 1,000 employees a year. Much of your training will be on the job, as you are taught all aspects of grocery retailing while working in a store environment. The company offers over 300 different jobs.

QUALIFICATIONS

College degrees are valuable, but you should also demonstrate the ability to work hard and get along well with people.

RECRUITMENT AND PLACEMENT

Kroger recruits year round. The company has stores all over the country.

SALARY AND BENEFITS

The College Placement Council Salary Survey for September 1986–June 1987 indicates starting salaries for merchandising (retail and wholesale) and service companies to be $1,594 a month for those with a B.A. degree in nontechnical curricula and $2,141 with a B.A. degree in technical curricula. M.B.A. starting salaries were $2,572 for a nontechnical undergraduate degree and $2,735 for an M.B.A. with technical undergraduate degree. Check with the company for more specific salary information. Your benefits package will contain group life and accident insurance; basic medical, major medical, orthodontia, dental, and vision care; a savings plan; stock-purchase plan; retirement plan; credit union; educational assistance program; and paid vacations and holidays.

CONTACT

Manager of Human Resources, Corporate Headquarters, Retail/Manufacturing Divisions, The Kroger Co. Executive Offices, 1014 Vine Street, Cincinnati, OH 45201.

KRAFT, INC.

FINANCE · SYSTEMS SERVICES

THE COMPANY

Kraft, Inc., is a leading producer, marketor, and distributor of processed food products. Kraft products are known to consumers, retail grocers, and food service and industrial customers in more than 130 companies. In 1980 Kraft merged with Dart Industries to form Dart & Kraft, Inc., a multinational consumer and commercial products company ranked number 37 in the Fortune 500 and included in *Fortune*'s most admired companies. Today, Kraft continues to operate independently as the largest business unit of the corporation. Kraft employs over 40,000 persons worldwide and is headquartered in Glenview, Illinois, a Chicago suburb.

FINANCE TRAINING PROGRAM

Training is a continuing process at Kraft, with all professionals kept up to date on developments in their specialties and in the business as a whole. You will train on the job with rotation of assignments to give you the broadest understanding of Kraft's operation.

QUALIFICATIONS

In financial analysis and control, Kraft considers a wide range of candidates, including M.B.A. graduates and undergraduates with business or accounting degrees. The company also wants those with broad interests who can communicate well, function easily as part of a team, and take on leadership roles.

SYSTEMS SERVICES TRAINING PROGRAM

You will probably enter this department as a systems engineer. Training begins with an orientation to both Kraft and the department. After orientation, which normally lasts three weeks, you'll be assigned to a project team composed of from three to ten professionals. Your group might be responsible for the program development for a product pricing system or a new cost accounting system. You and your team, under the direction of a project manager, will analyze all requirements, design the system, complete the programming, execute the testing, and take on systems implementation. You'll have a specific measurable portion of the project and the resources and guidance needed to achieve your goals. You will be given a broad charter in working at Kraft, not slotted into a narrow specialty. The projects you receive could last from two days to two years.

QUALIFICATIONS

In systems services, Kraft hires graduates from a wide range of disciplines, interests, and backgrounds. Recruiters look for M.B.A.s in computer science, graduates with business knowledge, and those who combine a business degree with an understanding of technology. Previous experience is desirable; excellent interpersonal skills are essential.

ALL PROGRAMS

RECRUITMENT AND PLACEMENT

Recruiters regularly visit college campuses throughout the United States. Kraft operates nearly 50 processing plants from coast to coast. Seven are multiproduct plants located in Buena Park, California; Pocatello, Idaho; Springfield, Missouri; Garland, Texas; Decatur, Georgia; Champaign, Illinois; and Allentown, Pennsylvania. Approximately 14,000 Kraft employees work outside the United States. Finance staff work in budgeting, financial planning, and other administrative positions. Systems staff work throughout the manufacturing process.

SALARY AND BENEFITS

The College Placement Council Salary Survey for September 1986–June 1987 indicates starting salaries for food and beverage processing companies to be $1,834 a month for those with a B.A. degree in nontechnical curricula and $2,301 with a B.A. degree in technical curricula. M.B.A. starting salaries were $3,043 for a nontechnical undergraduate degree and $3,098 for a technical undergraduate degree. Check with the company for more specific salary information. Kraft offers the following benefits: a comprehensive medical benefit plan, long-term disability, tuition reimbursement, paid vacations and holidays.

CONTACT

For financial positions: Manager of Placement, Kraft Retail Food Group, Kraft, Inc., Kraft Court, Glenview, IL 60025; and for systems services: Manager of Corporate Staffing, Kraft, Inc., Kraft Court, 2 West, Glenview, IL 60025.

L

☆ ☆ ☆ ☆ ☆

LAND O' LAKES, INC.

ACCOUNTING · AG MANUFACTURING/DISTRIBUTION · AG RESEARCH/TECHNICAL SERVICES · AGRICULTURAL SALES/MERCHANDISING · AGRICULTURAL SERVICES · DAIRY MANUFACTURING/PRODUCTION · FINANCE · FOOD RESEARCH/DEVELOPMENT · FOOD SALES · INFORMATION SYSTEMS · MARKETING · MARKETING SERVICES

THE COMPANY

Don't make the mistake of thinking this company is old-fashioned. It may have started out just selling butter, but now Land O' Lakes is a cooperative of more than 350,000 farmers whose commitment has transformed it from a single-line dairy operation in 1921 to today's multiline company. Organized in the 1920s to give farmers in the upper Midwest economic clout, it now represents itself as a bastion for farmers to ward off control by government and by large private corporations. Sales are over $2 billion annually. It has two types of owners: individual farmers who sell their milk, turkeys, and cattle directly to Land O' Lakes, and farmer-owned local cooperatives that buy farm supply products from Land O' Lakes and market soybeans and dairy products through the organization. The company stresses that its career opportunities encourage individual creativity, permit you to specialize in your area of interest, and provide the learning advantages of seeing your project through from conception to completion. It ranks number 167 in the Fortune 500 largest U.S. industrial corporations.

ALL TRAINING PROGRAMS

In-house training seminars for all employees develop management skill in three areas: technical skills of the job specialty; managerial skills of planning, organizing, directing; and interpersonal skills to include courses in coaching, counseling, and motivating.

AG MANUFACTURING AND DISTRIBUTION PROGRAM

You may begin as an order service specialist and learn the operation of a manufacturing or distribution facility as your responsibility grows. The rotation of assignment used for some individuals provides them with a two- to three-week orientation to each position in the plant. After about six months the trainee will be assigned to a permanent position in the facility.

QUALIFICATIONS

Successful candidates usually possess degrees in ag business, business administration, or ag mechanization. Positions in manufacturing and distribution frequently require knowledge of specific products systems or commodities, and related experience is often mandatory. Leadership skills which are oriented to serving customers as well as to motivating employees are highly desirable, as is strong mechanical aptitude.

FOOD RESEARCH AND DEVELOPMENT PROGRAM

You will have the option of going into one of six research areas where you will be trained one on one. Special projects will give you in-depth knowledge of all phases of your department. You might go into: development of new competitive products; development of line extension products; cost reduction of products and processes without detracting from quality; product and process improvements; technical support for Land O' Lakes production facilities by helping plant management solve problems; or exploratory research related to major raw materials of interest to the company.

QUALIFICATIONS

Depending on the area of expertise, you will need a B.S., M.S., or Ph.D. degree in food science and technology, dairy science, meat science, microbiology, biochemistry, organic chemistry, or food process engineering and chemical engineering.

MARKETING SERVICES PROGRAM

Working with marketing research, you will initially learn techniques of test study and analysis, reporting analysis, and research methodologies. You will learn to present your data effectively in a critical and understandable way. Your first work assignments as a product specialist will be conducting tolerance testing for recipes to assure good results in different cooking situations, such as changes in cooking temperatures or levels of ingredients. As a product specialist, you will also handle food styling for photography, develop recipes for cookbooks, brochures, magazine ads, newspapers, and television publicity, and put on training sessions for the Land O' Lakes sales force and brokers.

QUALIFICATIONS

Land O' Lakes wants M.B.A. graduates with an emphasis in marketing or marketing research. You should be quantitatively oriented and capable of seeing the broader marketing picture. Product specialists must have an undergraduate degree in foods and nutrition, consumer food science, dietetics or institutional management.

ALL PROGRAMS

RECRUITMENT AND PLACEMENT

Land O' Lakes recruits mainly in the Midwest, concentrating on hiring for positions in Minnesota, Iowa, Wisconsin, Nebraska, and the Dakotas, although job opportunities also exist in major metropolitan areas in the Midwest, South, and East.

SALARY AND BENEFITS

The College Placement Council Salary Survey for September 1986–June 1987 indicates starting salaries for food and beverage processing companies to be $1,834 a month for those with a B.A. degree in nontechnical curricula and $2,301 with a B.A. degree in technical curricula. M.B.A. starting salaries were $3,043 for a nontechnical undergraduate degree and $3,098 for a technical undergraduate degree. Check with the company for more specific salary information. To all its professional employees, Land O' Lakes offers a full range of personal benefits, including comprehensive life, medical, dental, short- and long-term disability, and accidental death insurance. It also provides vacations, holidays, short-term illness leaves, savings plans, pension program, and tuition assistance.

CONTACT

College Relations Representative, Land O' Lakes, Inc., Corporate Headquarters, P.O. Box 116, Minneapolis, MN 55440; or College Relations Representative, Land O' Lakes, Inc., Agricultural Services Division, P.O. Box 1395, Minneapolis, MN 55440.

LA QUINTA MOTOR INNS
HOTEL MANAGEMENT

THE COMPANY

La Quinta Motor Inns began in San Antonio in 1968, the same year HemisFair was hosted in that city. Today, in 26 states, there are 130 of the company's motor inns, each known for its Spanish architectural style and its comfortable, affordable accommodations primarily geared to business travelers. Regional offices are in San Antonio, Dallas, Houston, New Orleans, Atlanta, Phoenix, Denver, and Chicago. La Quinta means "country house" in Spanish. Couples selected for La Quinta's husband/wife management teams have the potential of operating a business generating over $1 million in annual revenues.

HOTEL MANAGEMENT TRAINING PROGRAM

You and your spouse will attend six-day-a-week training consisting of classroom instruction with company orientation and explanation of job skills. You will study procedures, learn La Quinta's operating systems, complete assignments, and pass tests. The program continues with on-the-job training with top-rated managers and staff at selected La Quinta inns, or at the San Antonio training property. Managers in training receive instructions and perform the tasks of the front desk sales representatives, the night auditor, the housekeeper, the room attendant, the laundry worker, and the maintenance person—employees whose work you will ultimately supervise. Throughout this period, property managers and staff provide feedback and coaching for continued development. Upon successful completion of this portion of training, you will be assigned to vacation relief; after approximately three to six months of relief assignments, you will be given a permanent property assignment.

QUALIFICATIONS

La Quinta will be interested in you if you're a dependable, hardworking couple with management, sales, and customer relations experience, have no live-in dependents, and are willing to relocate.

RECRUITMENT AND PLACEMENT

Send a résumé to the company headquarters for consideration. La Quinta hotels are located primarily in the South and Southwest.

SALARY AND BENEFITS

The College Placement Council Salary Survey for September 1986–June 1987 indicates starting salaries for merchandising (retail and wholesale) and service companies to be $1,594 a month for those with a B.A. degree in nontechnical curricula and $2,141 with a B.A. degree in technical curricula. M.B.A. starting salaries were $2,572 for a nontechnical undergraduate degree and $2,735 for an M.B.A. with technical undergraduate degree. Check with the company for more specific salary information. La Quinta offers a base salary plus quarterly bonuses (upon permanent assignment). Benefits include a monthly car allowance, company-paid medical and life insurance, retirement plan, paid vacation, stock-purchase plan, and free on-property furnished apartment with utilities paid (after permanent assignment).

CONTACT

Motor Inn Management Recruiting, La Quinta Motor Inns, P.O. Box 790064, San Antonio, TX 78279-0064.

LAVENTHOL & HORWATH
ACCOUNTING AND AUDITING

THE COMPANY

Laventhol & Horwath is an international firm of certified public accountants. Its services include professional accounting, auditing, tax, and management consulting services to clients in industrial, commercial, hospitality, real estate, and health-care fields. Established in 1915, Laventhol & Horwath now has offices in major cities throughout the United States and associates in more than 60 other nations. A special national tax division in Washington, D.C., has a reputation for being innovative and sophisticated. You will be exposed to a variety of clients and business types in this growing firm.

ACCOUNTING TRAINING PROGRAM

The company requires a minimum of forty hours of continuing education each year. During your first year you'll participate in the following company-designed courses: one-day orientation to company policies and procedures: an intensive six-day national seminar to prepare you for your initial job responsibilities; and one-day courses in taxes, accounting and auditing, the code of professional ethics, and basic computer operations. The company will also provide a comprehensive self-study C.P.A. review course. These courses are supplemented by on-the-job training and self-study materials. Regular performance reviews will let you know your progress.

QUALIFICATIONS

In addition to an accounting or business degree, you will need excellent interpersonal skills and good business understanding. Be prepared to demonstrate that you are a self-starter.

RECRUITMENT AND PLACEMENT

The company recruits and places new employees nationwide.

SALARY AND BENEFITS

Salaries are competitive, beginning in the low twenties. The College Placement Council Salary Survey for September 1986–June 1987 indicates starting salaries for public accounting firms to be $1,834 a month for those with a B.A. degree in nontechnical curricula and $2,155 with a B.A. degree in technical curricula. M.B.A. starting salaries were $2,335 for a nontechnical undergraduate degree, and $2,436 for an M.B.A. with technical undergraduate degree. Check with the company for more specific salary information. Benefits include profit sharing; life, medical, and travel accident insurance; and tuition reimbursement.

CONTACT

National Director of Human Resources, Laventhol & Horwath Executive Offices, 1845 Walnut Street, Philadelphia, PA 19103.

LAWRENCE LIVERMORE NATIONAL LABORATORY

CHEMISTRY • COMPUTER SCIENCE • ENGINEERING • MATERIALS SCIENCE • PHYSICS

THE COMPANY

Lawrence Livermore National Laboratory, established in 1952, is operated by the University of California under a contract with the U.S. Department of Energy. It specializes in basic and applied nuclear research for industrial applications, environmental effects, magnetic fusion, weaponry, and natural resource development. The laboratory's work depends heavily on the use of state-of-the-art computer technology. Its CRAY supercomputers and CDC 7600s make it one of the world's largest high-speed computing facilities. Research projects involve nonnuclear energy research such as oil shale retorting and underground coal gasification, aluminum-air batteries to power electric vehicles, and the safe disposal of hazardous and radioactive wastes. LLNL employs about 8,000 people in the Livermore Valley of California, forty-five miles southeast of San Francisco.

ALL TRAINING PROGRAMS

On-the-job training is provided for twelve months for some positions. Postdoctoral appointments of six to twelve months are available in engineering and applied sciences. You will be encouraged to maintain your expertise through advanced study with complete tuition reimbursement, and at professional seminars and conferences. In addition, Livermore has cooperated in developing degree programs with nearby universities to benefit its employees.

QUALIFICATIONS

The company is looking for applicants with bachelor's, master's, and doctor's degrees (as well as those with one to ten years of related experience) in the following areas: computer science, chemistry, bioengineering, geology, hydrology, information science, materials science, mathematics, mining and mineral engineering, physics, polymer chemistry, statistics, health physics, and the following engineering specializations—electronics, mechanical, ceramic, chemical, electrical, environmental, geological, nuclear, and structural. Applicants should have a minimum G.P.A. of 3.0. A class ranking in the top 10 percent is preferred. You must be familiar with computer systems and software.

RECRUITMENT AND PLACEMENT

The company recruits nationwide. Starting location is in California.

SALARY AND BENEFITS

With a bachelor's degree, you will start in the $29,000 to $33,500 range; at $32,000 to $35,000 with a master's; and at $41,400–45,600 with a doctorate. Your benefits package will include life, medical, hospital, and dental insurance; a fitness program; relocation assistance; flextime options; three weeks vacation; a tax-deferred annuity program; savings plans; and career counseling.

CONTACT

Kathy Hanks, Recruitment Administrator, Lawrence Livermore National Laboratory, P.O. Box 5510, Livermore, CA 94550.

LEEDS & NORTHRUP (L&N)

ENGINEERING • INFORMATION SYSTEMS • MARKETING • RESEARCH AND DEVELOPMENT • SALES • TECHNICAL SERVICES

THE COMPANY

Leeds & Northrup supplies process control instrumentation to over 36,000 customers, including 80 percent of the companies on the Fortune 500 list. Growth averages 20 percent a year. Leeds & Northrup is a division of General Signal Corporation, a leading manufacturer of a broad spectrum of specialty control systems. The company headquarters are in North Wales, Pennsylvania (suburban Philadelphia), with field sales and service personnel at 45 locations throughout the United States. The company is concerned with the advancement of industrial production, environmental management, and scientific research. One of its recent accomplishments was development of the first domestic optical electrical highway in 1982.

ALL TRAINING PROGRAMS

New trainees get several months of on-the-job training in a field office to become familiar with the general nature of the business. Then those interested in sales engineering attend a formal training program at headquarters to orient them to products, markets, and selling techniques. Professional development at L&N includes day-to-day professional on-the-job consultation with supervisors, advisers, and other specialists; inhouse training programs; tuition refund for job-related courses at local universities; participation in activities of professional associations; and interaction with customer engineers. Company commitment to state-of-the-art instrumentation and systems demands not only that L&N employees use their engineering knowledge but also that they constantly update it. You will have long-term opportunities for continual career development in research, product development and design, systems engineering, software development and application programming, and field sales or systems support engineering.

QUALIFICATIONS

A college degree in electrical engineering, mechanical engineering, chemical engineering, mathematics, computer science, metallurgical engineering, or physics is required. In addition, there are occasional openings for financial personnel, systems analysts, programmers, industrial relations personnel, and other specialists. You must have a G.P.A. of 2.5 or higher and be familiar with computer systems, software, and programming.

RECRUITMENT AND PLACEMENT

L&N recruits nationwide. You may work in the home office or in one of the 45 field offices.

SALARY AND BENEFITS

The College Placement Council Salary Survey for September 1986–June 1987 indicates starting salaries for electrical and electronic machines and equipment companies to be $1,861 a month for those with a B.A. degree in nontechnical curricula and $2,419 with a B.A. degree in technical curricula. M.B.A. starting salaries were $2,784 for a nontechnical undergraduate degree and $2,818 for a technical undergraduate degree. Check with the company for more specific salary information. Your benefits package will include tuition reimbursement; pension and stock-purchase plans; and medical, hospital, and dental insurance.

CONTACT

Manager of Professional Employment, Leeds & Northrup, Sumncytown Pike, North Wales, PA 19454.

KENNETH LEVENTHAL & COMPANY

ACCOUNTING • AUDITING • MANAGEMENT CONSULTING • TAX SERVICES

THE COMPANY

KLCO is the country's largest C.P.A. firm with its founder still active in day-to-day operations. Founded in 1949, the company's growth was initially tied to the dramatic real estate expansion in California. Today, KLCO has offices in major cities nationwide and is regarded as the foremost real estate accounting firm in the nation. KLCO provides the full spectrum of accounting, taxation, auditing, and management consulting services—all with the goal of solving business problems.

ALL TRAINING PROGRAMS

KLCO recognizes the importance of continuing education for its professional staff. Each staff member is required to participate in a minimum of 120 hours of formal training over a three-year period. The firm pays the cost of approved conferences and seminars and will reimburse you for 75 percent of the cost of tuition and books for approved college and university courses. When you join KLCO, you will attend an extensive two-week orientation program designed to bridge the gap between your college experience and the business world. You will learn about the audit function, real estate accounting, individual and partnership taxation, and the business aspects of the real estate industry; you will also obtain a comprehensive introduction to the firm. During your first year as a staff accountant, you will work on a variety of auditing assignments, as well as tax and special projects that bring you into close contact with the firm's tax and management consulting experts. You will also participate in an intensive two-person assignment or as one of several individuals to audit a large, publicly held client. The firm offers top-notch continuing education throughout your career—at least forty hours of training a year. Each year, staff below the managerial level attends a one-week seminar away from the office. Partners and managers attend an annual three-day seminar. Shorter, specialized training programs put on by local offices supplement these seminars.

QUALIFICATIONS

KLCO is looking for the college graduate with a questioning mind, adeptness at problem solving, flexibility, an eagerness to respond to challenges, and a readiness to tackle many diverse business situations. You may find a slot in this firm even though you graduated from college without a traditional accounting background. KLCO takes an interdisciplinary approach and wants its management services staff to have skills ranging from business management and real estate finance to computer and behavioral sciences.

RECRUITMENT AND PLACEMENT

The company recruits nationally. Generally, you select the KLCO office location of your choice.

SALARY AND BENEFITS

The College Placement Council Salary Survey for September 1986–June 1987 indicates starting salaries for public accounting firms to be $1,834 a month for those with a B.A. degree in nontechnical curricula and $2,155 with a B.A. degree in technical curricula. M.B.A. starting salaries were $2,335 for a nontechnical undergraduate degree, and $2,436 for an M.B.A. with technical undergraduate degree. Check with the company for more specific salary information. You are compensated for overtime either by cash payment or by accruing time off. All seniors and managers participate in annual bonus programs. Benefits include major medical, life, and long-term disability insurance, a pension plan, and membership in a health club.

CONTACT

The personnel director in any KLCO office; or Douglas M. Hecox, National Director of Personnel, 2049 Century Park East, Suite 1700, Los Angeles, CA 90067.

LEVER BROTHERS COMPANY

SALES MANAGEMENT

THE COMPANY

Lever manufactures high-quality household, personal-care, and food products sold through virtually every grocery and drugstore across the United States. This multibillion-dollar American corporation is currently revitalizing itself through an expanded program of research and development; accelerated new product introductions, record capital spending for new facilities and equipment; and streamlined, decentralized management. Founded in 1895 in New York City by English soapmaker William Hesketh Lever, the company is now a part of Unilever, the world's largest producer of packaged consumer goods, and the world's number one advertiser. Unilever is comprised of more than 500 companies in some 75 countries. The parent company is larger than Procter & Gamble and General Foods combined. A few of Lever's familiar products are Dove, Signal, Aim, Mrs. Butterworth's syrup, and Imperial margarine. Listed among *Fortune*'s most admired corporations, Lever has annual sales of more than $2.4 billion and ranks number 155 in the Fortune 500 largest U.S. industrial corporations.

SALES MANAGEMENT TRAINING PROGRAM

You will be part of an individualized, field-oriented training program that is designed to continually develop your abilities. The program initially consists of one week of classroom training and thirteen weeks of field training in your assigned territory. After six months of service you will attend an advanced sales seminar designed to sharpen your selling skills and prepare you for increased responsibility. Your manager will provide supervision throughout your sales career through field contacts and performance appraisals.

QUALIFICATIONS

Your degree area is not as important as your ability to be self-motivated, organized, and productive. Proven selling experience would be a definite plus.

RECRUITMENT AND PLACEMENT

Lever recruits nationally. Your sales territory might be anywhere in the United States.

SALARY AND BENEFITS

The College Placement Council Salary Survey for September 1986–June 1987 indicates starting salaries for chemicals, drugs, and allied products companies to be $1,964 a month for those with a B.A. degree in nontechnical curricula and $2,457 with a B.A. degree in technical curricula. M.B.A. starting salaries were $2,886 for a nontechnical undergraduate degree and $2,794 for a technical undergraduate degree. Check with the company for more specific salary and benefits information.

CONTACT

Corporate Recruiting, Lever Brothers Company, 390 Park Avenue, New York, NY 10022.

LIBERTY MUTUAL INSURANCE GROUP

AUDITING · AUTOMOTIVE ENGINEERING · CHEMISTRY · CLAIMS · DATA PROCESSING · ERGONOMY · FINANCIAL FIELD SERVICES · SALES · UNDERWRITING

THE COMPANY

Liberty Mutual, based in Boston, is one of the largest multiline insurance companies in the world. It employs 20,000 people and has more than 190 offices in the United States, Canada, the United Kingdom, and Bermuda. Liberty provides all types of insurance, including property, casualty, and life insurance, and workers' compensation. It insures several million individuals and more than 100,000 businesses. Liberty goes beyond merely insuring against loss; it tries to prevent and repair losses. It operates the only private rehabilitation facility in the United States devoted wholly to work-related injuries; a skid control school that travels the country showing police and driver trainers how to teach safe driving; and an 86-acre research center to develop new ways to safeguard people at home, on the highway, and at work.

ALL TRAINING PROGRAMS

The training program varies with the position. Claims adjusters begin their training with a general orientation, followed by six to seven weeks of classroom and on-the-job training. After some experience on the job, advanced training in technical areas will prepare you for advancement. Loss prevention representatives receive an initial two weeks of basic training followed by on-the-job training and advanced seminars. Underwriters receive on-the-job training, study programs, and seminars.

QUALIFICATIONS

The company has a wide assortment of entry-level positions. In general, an undergraduate degree in the relevant area, math, or in business administration is preferred; a liberal arts degree with prior business experience is also acceptable. Loss prevention representatives need an engineering, industrial management, or physical sciences degree. Auditors must have a degree in accounting. Programmers must have a degree in a business-related subject, although work experience in data processing may serve as a suitable alternative. Prior business experience or demonstrable ability that shows you have the necessary educational background may also be enough.

RECRUITMENT AND PLACEMENT

The company recruits nationally. You may be placed anywhere in the United States.

SALARY AND BENEFITS

With a bachelor's degree, you will start in the high teens. The College Placement Council Salary Survey for September 1986–June 1987 indicates starting salaries for banking, finance, and insurance firms to be $1,889 a month for those with a B.A. degree in nontechnical curricula and $2,135 with a B.A. degree in technical curricula. M.B.A. starting salaries were $2,884 for a nontechnical undergraduate degree and $3,320 for an M.B.A. with technical undergraduate degree. Check with the company for more specific salary information. Benefits include medical coverage, life insurance, disability income protection, accidental death and dismemberment insurance, a savings and investment fund, paid vacations and holidays, and pension and retirement benefits.

CONTACT

Dennis Nicholls, Personnel Development Department, Liberty Mutual Insurance Group, 175 Berkeley Street, Boston, MA 02117.

THE LIBRARY OF CONGRESS

LIBRARY SCIENCE

THE COMPANY

The Library of Congress is the largest library in the world. It employs approximately 5,000 people and serves as the national library of the United States. It is organized into four major departments: the Congressional Research Service; Processing Services; the Copyright Office; and Research Services. These departments serve the Congress, the nation's libraries, and the learning community in general.

ALL TRAINING PROGRAMS

The Library of Congress Intern Program considers outstanding library science graduate students who are nominated by their dean. Current Library employees may nominate themselves for the program. This internship introduces participants to a broad range of Library activities through a twenty-week program of seminars, rotational work assignments, and tours. The Library offers more than 50 in-house training programs for employees, covering topics from basic automation, effective communications, and research techniques to a complete supervisory/management development series.

QUALIFICATIONS

Applicants with backgrounds and degrees, especially graduate degrees, in library science, economics, foreign affairs, government, science policy, and language specialties will find a variety of entry-level career opportunities as librarians, research assistants, analysts, and subject area specialists with the Library.

RECRUITMENT AND PLACEMENT

The Library recruits nationally. Interested applicants are encouraged to contact the Library directly. You will work in Washington, D.C.

SALARY AND BENEFITS

The Library's salary levels follow the federal government's General Schedule (GS). Generally, completion of a graduate degree qualifies an applicant for analyst/specialist positions at the GS-7 ($18,358) and GS-9 level. Current graduate students who have not yet completed an advanced degree but have completed at least one year of graduate study would qualify as research assistant or technician at the GS-5 and GS-7 level. Benefits include medical and life insurance, annual and sick leave, and a competitive retirement plan. An additional benefit available to Library employees, and not to the general public, is book-borrowing privileges.

CONTACT

The Library of Congress, Recruitment and Placement Office, Room LM-107, 101 Independence Avenue, S.E., Washington, DC 20540.

LINK FLIGHT SIMULATION DIVISION—SINGER COMPANY

ENGINEERING • INFORMATION SYSTEMS • RESEARCH AND DEVELOPMENT • TECHNICAL SERVICES

THE COMPANY

Link is the world's leading manufacturer of flight training simulators for commercial airlines and military aircraft flight training. Established in 1929 by Edwin A. Link, inventor of the synthetic flight trainer, the company was acquired by the Singer Company in 1968. Recently Link has experienced dramatic growth, with sales more than doubling since 1979. It has three major domestic facilities and one in Lancing, England. Binghamton, New York, the largest domestic facility, is corporate headquarters and location of the design and production of total simulator systems for both military and commercial airlines. The Houston operation maintains and updates spacecraft simulation equipment for NASA and fighter aircraft simulators. The plant in Sunnyvale, California, is developing the next generation of real-time computer graphics for out-the-window scene simulation and radar display simulation. If you are interested in a career at the forefront of the developing computer and simulation technologies, Link offers exciting opportunities.

ENGINEERING TRAINING PROGRAM

The New Engineering Training Program provides a smooth transition from college into the work environment. You will enter a four- to six-week formal training program that includes an orientation to the company, an introduction to flight simulation, the basics of aircraft performance and theory of flight, and an overview of all systems engineering departments and their tasks. Then you will be given an in-depth introduction to your own department. Ongoing training in technical and management skills is provided to improve your performance and advancement potential.

QUALIFICATIONS

Link wants people with college degrees in aeronautical, computer, electrical, electronics, industrial, and mechanical engineering; mathematics; computer science; physics; and M.B.A.s with technical bachelor's degrees. You are required to pass a physical examination and be eligible for security clearance, which is required for most technical areas.

RECRUITMENT AND PLACEMENT

Link recruits in Eastern, Southern, and Western states and places new employees in Sunnyvale, California; Binghamton, New York; or Houston.

SALARY AND BENEFITS

If you have a bachelor's degree, your starting salary is in the $26,000 to $29,000 range. The comprehensive benefits program includes medical coverage, dental insurance, disability coverage, life insurance, travel accident insurance, a retirement program, stock-purchase plan, and a credit union. In addition, value engineering awards, writing incentive awards, software development awards, and a patent award program are offered.

CONTACT

Employee Administrator, College Recruiter, Link Flight Simulation Division, The Singer Company, Corporate Drive, Binghamton, NY 13902.

THOMAS J. LIPTON, INC.

SALES

THE COMPANY

In 1871, Sir Thomas Lipton's idea was novel: he would package, market, and sell his tea with a brand name. Established in Glasgow, Scotland, Lipton's has grown into the largest seller of teas and soup mixes in the United States, and the largest profit contributor to the highly diverse multinational Unilever family of 500 companies. Lipton purchased Lawry's, a respected manufacturer of high-quality seasonings, in 1979, and uses both companies' sales forces to jointly market their products. The company's annual sales top $1.3 billion and continue to grow. Company headquarters are in Englewood Cliffs, New Jersey. Lipton ranks number 250 in the Fortune 500 largest U.S. industrial corporations.

SALES TRAINING PROGRAM

Your four-week orientation begins with personalized instruction from a district sales trainer. You will work both in the sales office and in the field, learning about the company, its products, the grocery trade, selling, in-store merchandising, your territory, and all the details of your job. After orientation, you will join a sales management team under the guidance of a unit sales manager. After about six months you will be sent to the Professional Sales Institute at Lipton's headquarters for a week of advanced sales training. This course increases your knowledge of the company and its products to make you a more effective salesperson. In addition, you may attend a Career Development Institute to strengthen any weaknesses you may have. Sales managers retain responsibility for your ongoing training, which will be supplemented by seminars, bulletins, and sales meetings. Management training will also be available to you later in your career.

QUALIFICATIONS

Lipton hires graduates with degrees in management, marketing, and liberal arts. Highly motivated and organized candidates with records of extracurricular achievement will be most likely to impress Lipton recruiters.

RECRUITMENT AND PLACEMENT

Lipton sends recruiters to campuses across the country. If an interview is not possible in your area, send a cover letter and résumé directly to company headquarters. Lipton's sales territories cover the entire United States.

SALARY AND BENEFITS

The College Placement Council Salary Survey for September 1986–June 1987 indicates starting salaries for food and beverage processing companies to be $1,865 a month for those with a B.A. degree in nontechnical curricula and $2,401 with a B.A. degree in technical curricula. Check with the company for more specific salary information. You can expect to receive a company car and an expense account for travel, in addition to your salary. Incentive bonuses based on the sales performance of your assigned district during the year can increase your base salary by as much as 25 percent. Benefits include life, health, dental, and disability insurance, a tuition refund program, and pension and savings plans.

CONTACT

Personnel Division—Sales Division, Thomas J. Lipton, Inc., 800 Sylvan Avenue, Englewood Cliffs, NJ 07632.

LITTON INDUSTRIES, INC.

ACCOUNTING · ENGINEERING · MANAGEMENT · PRODUCTION · RESEARCH AND DEVELOPMENT

THE COMPANY

Founded in 1953, Litton currently has more than 80 different businesses under its corporate umbrella. The company is known for buying successful businesses and letting them operate without a lot of interference. To consumers, Litton is probably best known for its microwave ovens. The company also makes Monroe office calculators, Sweda electronic cash registers with an optical scanner, steel office furniture, machines that make automobile brake parts, printed circuit boards for computers, and warehouses manned by robots. The company also publishes medical magazines and produces navigation and guidance systems for airplanes, helicopters, and missiles used by the U.S. Air Force. Listed among *Fortune*'s most admired corporations, it has annual revenues of about $4.5 billion. Litton ranks number 83 in the Fortune 500 largest U.S. industrial corporations.

ALL TRAINING PROGRAMS

Training prepares new employees for positions in manufacturing and management as well as research and development. Whether your position is technical or managerial, you'll benefit from on-the-job training supplemented with classroom instruction. You are encouraged to attend outside seminars and trade shows and to join job-related associations.

QUALIFICATIONS

Litton hires graduates in accounting and finance, liberal arts, and engineering.

RECRUITMENT AND PLACEMENT

Recruitment and placement are nationwide.

SALARY AND BENEFITS

With a bachelor's degree, you will start in the low to mid-twenties. The College Placement Council Salary Survey for September 1986–June 1987 indicates starting salaries for electrical and electronic machines and equipment companies to be $1,861 a month for those with a B.A. degree in nontechnical curricula and $2,419 with a B.A. degree in technical curricula. M.B.A. starting salaries were $2,784 for a nontechnical undergraduate degree and $2,818 for a technical undergraduate degree. Check with the company for more specific salary information. Benefits include medical, dental, and life insurance, tuition reimbursement, a stock-purchase plan, and a pension plan.

CONTACT

Director of Personnel, Litton Industries, Inc., 360 North Crescent Drive, Beverly Hills, CA 90210.

LOCKHEED MISSILES AND SPACE COMPANY

ADMINISTRATION • ACCOUNTING • CHEMISTRY • COMPUTER SCIENCE • DATA PROCESSING • ENGINEERING • FINANCE • PRODUCTION • RESEARCH AND DEVELOPMENT

THE COMPANY

Lockheed Missiles and Space Company, a subsidiary of Lockheed Corporation, has designed the U.S. Navy's Polaris, Poseidon, and Trident submarine-launched missile systems as well as a wide variety of NASA and U.S. Air Force spacecraft and space systems. Begun as an aircraft company in 1916 by brothers Allan and Malcolm Loughhead (who later changed the spelling of their name), the company developed in 1926 the Vega plane, which Amelia Earhart later flew solo across the Atlantic. In 1938, Lockheed entered the weapons industry, producing the Hudson bomber for the British, and has been involved in military contracts—both U.S. and foreign—ever since. In addition, Lockheed scientists and engineers are working at the frontiers of microelectronics and energy, especially ocean thermal energy conversion and solar power. The company is at the leading edge in database technology, on-line computer systems, and scientific computing. Lockheed went through a period of great turmoil in the 1970s—a financial debacle in the early 1970s, and the 1975 disclosure of massive bribery to win overseas contracts. But it has completely recovered its credibility. Corporate sales exceed $6 billion a year, with employment of over 26,000 worldwide (the majority in the United States).

ALL TRAINING PROGRAMS

For many jobs your beginning training is on the job. Engineering trainees go through a six-month training program that offers classroom instruction and supervised on-the-job training. You can also participate in a variety of other training and career advancement programs offered by the company: tuition reimbursement plans, on-site university extension courses, management development workshops, and seminars and courses offered at some of the nation's finest colleges and universities in the San Francisco Bay area.

QUALIFICATIONS

The company is recruiting college graduates with backgrounds in astronomy, earth science, materials science, metallurgy, meteorology, ocean sciences, optical sciences, and physics. You can also pursue careers in computer systems, manufacturing, and administration. You should be familiar with computers and have a G.P.A. of at least 2.8.

RECRUITMENT AND PLACEMENT

The company recruits nationwide. You will start in Alabama, California, or Texas.

SALARY AND BENEFITS

Starting salaries are about $29,000 with a bachelor's degree, $32,500 with a master's, and about $42,500 with a doctorate. Benefits include life, health, and dental insurance, tuition assistance, a savings plan, and a retirement program.

CONTACT

Gil Chavez, College Relations Coordinator, Lockheed Missiles and Space Company, 1184 North Mathilda Avenue, Sunnyvale, CA 94086.

LONE STAR GAS COMPANY

COMPUTER SCIENCE • ENGINEERING • MARKETING • PRODUCTION • SALES

THE COMPANY

Lone Star Gas is in the business of natural gas transmission and distribution and the sale of natural gas appliances. It employs 4,500 people and is a division of Enserch Corporation of Dallas, Texas.

ENGINEERING PROGRAM

You will receive six months of on-the-job training with orientation from experienced supervisors to Lone Star's policies and procedures.

QUALIFICATIONS

You must have a bachelor's or a master's degree in any of the following engineering specialties: chemical, civil, electrical, general, industrial, mechanical, or petroleum. Applicants with two to five years' experience are also encouraged to apply.

COMPUTER SCIENCE/PROGRAMMING PROGRAM

You will be given six months of training that combines formal classroom instruction and on-the-job experience.

QUALIFICATIONS

You will need a bachelor's or master's degree in computer science. A business background is also desirable. Applicants with two to five years' experience are also encouraged to apply.

ALL PROGRAMS

RECRUITMENT AND PLACEMENT

The company recruits in Texas where the job will be.

SALARY AND BENEFITS

The College Placement Council Salary Survey for September 1986–June 1987 indicates starting salaries for public utilities to be $1,905 a month for those with a B.A. degree in nontechnical curricula and $2,355 with a B.A. degree in technical curricula. M.B.A. starting salaries were $2,403 for a nontechnical undergraduate degree and $2,667 for a technical undergraduate degree. Check with the company for more specific salary information. Benefits include pension and stock-purchase plans; medical and hospitalization coverage; dental and vision plans; and tuition reimbursement of 75 percent for job-related study.

CONTACT

Placement Manager, Lone Star Gas Company, Enserch Corporation, 301 South Harwood Street, Dallas, TX 75201.

LUBY'S CAFETERIAS
MANAGEMENT

THE COMPANY

If you would like to combine culinary skills with budgeting and management, this public cafeteria corporation may be your cup of tea. Luby's is a growing San Antonio, Texas, company that owns and operates 108 cafeterias in the Southwest. Begun in 1947 by Robert W. Luby and Charles R. Johnson, the company now employs 6,500 full-time employees.

MANAGEMENT TRAINING PROGRAM

Four times a year a 15- to 20-member class enters a three-month "introductory education period" at the training school in San Antonio to learn cafeteria management. You will move through every department in the Luby system—preparing salads, clearing tables, and operating the cash register. The training program, characterized by hands-on experience and personal instruction, is augmented by the company's video program. It includes a large library of training tapes designed and produced especially for cafeteria training and continuing education. Luby's also uses "training partners," experienced employees who work alongside the new trainees to teach them the Luby way. Upon completion of this fundamental training you will be assigned to one of the cafeterias as assistant manager. Then you begin a traditional five to seven years of training leading to the position of manager. During this time you will undergo formal periodic testing and performance reviews as you master the day-to-day intricacies of purchasing, managing, and operating a cafeteria.

QUALIFICATIONS

A college degree is preferred, but you don't need food experience to get into the program. You must be at least twenty-two years old and willing to relocate.

RECRUITMENT AND PLACEMENT

Luby's recruits in the Southwest. After training, you will be placed in one of the cafeterias in Arizona, New Mexico, Oklahoma, or Texas.

SALARY AND BENEFITS

You can expect a starting salary in the high teens, plus relocation expenses. By the time you are qualified as an assistant manager, part of your compensation will be based on a percentage of your cafeteria's profits. As you move up the management ladder the potential for a six-figure income is excellent. Luby's offers participation in life, health, and disability group insurance programs, as well as profit-sharing and retirement plans.

CONTACT

Rick Philpoot or Dave Simpson, Luby's Cafeterias, P.O. Box 33069, San Antonio, TX 78265.

From the Training Manager's Perspective

Dick Luongo, Seth Moskowitz, and Chris Mattern, R. J. Reynolds Tobacco U.S.A.

Dick Luongo, national manager of sales training and development, and Seth Moskowitz, public relations representative, explain the sales training at R. J. Reynolds Tobacco U.S.A., a part of RJR Nabisco.

☆ ☆ ☆ ☆ ☆

How is your entry-level sales training program structured?

LUONGO: STEP, the Sales Training Entry Program, is a comprehensive thirteen-week program combining on-the-job and classroom training. It has over five hundred pages of printed material and eight videotapes, each anywhere from fifteen to thirty-five minutes in length. But the key to the program is the on-the-job training. The training takes place in the individual's actual assignment area, and while there is classroom training, the majority of training is on the job in the assignment the individual will have.

MOSKOWITZ: We've got over 150 sales training offices around the country. Anywhere from 100 to 300 enter the program each year.

LUONGO: The program is very structured but it's also flexible to allow individuals to progress at their own pace. As an example, during the first week a member of management might be with an individual the entire week. The first two days would be classroom followed by three days' on-the-job training. The second week would also be very structured and the trainer would be with that individual three or four days and allow the individual to go out on his or her own for a couple of days that second week.

Have there been any changes in the program in the last few years?

LUONGO: Yes, we're constantly changing and updating the program. A major change we made at the beginning of this year was adding video to the program. Prior to 1987 we had a series of slides and sound tracks. We've upgraded that to all video.

Do you do any videotaping or role playing with trainees?

LUONGO: We don't have any taping in this phase of the program, but we have another program on professional selling—a comprehensive, three-day classroom program—that does include videotaping and role playing.

MOSKOWITZ: Within the training videotapes there is some role playing.

LUONGO: Yes, there are a number of examples of role playing within the eight videos I mentioned that demonstrate to the individual how to do something and how to perform. But there is no actual interaction of the individual in participating in role plays.

How should trainees expect the program to advance their careers or help them in the transition from an academic environment to the workplace?

LUONGO: We believe very strongly that the proper training up front will pay dividends in the long run for both the company and the individual. We expect our people to do a lot, we expect a lot of them, and obviously to do that we must provide them with the proper tools. What they can expect to get out of it is satisfaction in their job and the opportunity for advancement.

What should trainees do to be successful in the program?

LUONGO: First of all, they need to work hard. They need to be a self-motivated type of individual who is eager to work, because training and learning never stop. They must be willing to try new procedures and approaches to see what works best for them. I think most important, they need to enjoy what they're doing.
MOSKOWITZ: Although the program is very comprehensive and highly structured, it still leaves a great deal of room for each individual to play up his or her own talents, abilities, and skills.
LUONGO: The key to the program is its flexibility. I mentioned earlier that it's a thirteen-week program. Well, that's the average length. The training can last anywhere from eleven weeks to sixteen weeks, depending on individual progress.

Are regular performance reviews part of the training schedule?

LUONGO: Yes, we monitor trainees very closely during the initial training period. Our managers learn performance management, which is designed to set specific objectives and provide timely feedback. So our managers are trained on how to train, and we provide a very challenging, motivating atmosphere.

As far as keeping track of the trainees goes, a member of management is with that individual over 50 percent of the time during the initial training. After that, we work with them, counseling each on an ongoing basis, depending upon their needs. That continues throughout every individual's career with us.
MOSKOWITZ: There is another important aspect of the program. All sales reps who have been with the company for between one and two years are brought to our home office in Winston-Salem, North Carolina, for a sales orientation program. We usually have, what, about 250 people?
LUONGO: Usually about 200. They're brought in for four days and the objective is to show them the support that they have back here in the home office.
MOSKOWITZ: They get a close look at our sales departments and various aspects of it, such as merchandising, our manufacturing plants and R & D facilities. They get a good overview and a lot of detailed information. They get a much better appreciation of what the company is, what it's doing, and also a better appreciation when they're back out in the field of the very strong support that we provide from the home office.

What are some of the other training programs you offer?

LUONGO: When salespeople are promoted to an entry-level management position, they go

through exactly the same type of program to learn how to be a successful manager. When they're promoted to the next level of management, we have another program for that particular level.
MOSKOWITZ: I think that the efforts we take in training contribute to our very stable sales force. Especially once an individual reaches management, there are fairly clear career progression paths. I'm not going to say that the steps are easy, but it's easy to succeed if you're willing to work hard. We provide as much background and foundation as we possibly can. We want people to succeed because, when they succeed, we succeed.

Chris Mattern, director of organizational development for R. J. Reynolds Tobacco USA, describes the company's marketing program:

How is the marketing entry-level program structured?

MATTERN: The marketing training program is set up for folks who are entry-level brand management people. It is a three-month program similar to a college-level classroom in its intensity. The new people come into the company and are here for three months to give them some familiarity with what we do, and then they come right into this training program. It is a highly structured classroom situation that includes eight modules covering marketing development, promotion, media, research and development, sales, law, advertising agency, and brand.

Have you made any changes in your approach in the last few years?

MATTERN: We only started this formal program in 1983. Before that we had on-the-job training. The new marketing person was sent to each of the departments I mentioned, to work with people in those areas, but training was somewhat erratic depending on what was going on in that department during the time the person was there. The program is now more formal and sequential.

How should trainees expect the program to enhance their careers?

MATTERN: It provides them with a comprehensive overview of what goes on in each department in a very short time period, so it helps them become effective much more quickly. We have begun to make this program available to others outside the marketing department as well.

So a trainee might be in class side by side with an upper-level employee?

MATTERN: Yes, in a few cases.

How many trainees enter the program each year?

MATTERN: About 12.

What should the trainee do to be most successful in the program?

MATTERN: Work hard, listen, study. It is very, very intense and there are assignments every night for most of the modules. You really have to get into it. If you don't apply yourself, you won't get anything out of it, but that's true for any kind of training.

Is there a predictable failure rate in the program?

MATTERN: There is no failure. Someone who is not doing well in a particular area will get individual help. It's not a pass-fail situation. In addition to the formal marketing program, there are two-day and four-day workshops in specific skills such as making oral presentations, conducting productive meetings, stress management, supervisory skills, time management, and general management techniques.

Do you keep track of the trainees after they leave the program or provide additional support?

MATTERN: We have a formal evaluation process each year. We've set up a training matrix which is taking a look at each job we have in the company and determining what the training needs are for those jobs. And then we schedule people into the programs. So we've got a very formal process going on. The marketing program is just one piece of everything we have.

Would the marketing graduate work in Winston-Salem after completing training?

MATTERN: Yes, although there are occasionally opportunities for people to move into one of the other divisions of RJR Nabisco. That's the exception rather than the rule.

This marketing training program was not put together by the training staff. Over 220 people in these various departments put this program together, and the training staff provided the methodology. I think it is rather amazing to have the input of so many people.

Has the more formal approach measurably improved the efficiency of your new marketing employees?

MATTERN: I think so in terms of their quickness of learning what all these other departments do and what they have to do in their job to deal with these departments. I would say yes, definitely.

M

☆ ☆ ☆ ☆ ☆

MAAS BROTHERS
MANAGEMENT

THE COMPANY

Maas Brothers is a full-line department store on the west coast of Florida and southern Georgia. The company's 20 stores maintain the dominant position for fashion retailing in its market. In early 1987, Maas Brothers merged with Jordan Marsh, another division of Allied-Campeau Corporation. Jordan Marsh's 17 stores on the east coast of Florida will be headquartered in the Maas Brothers corporate offices in Tampa.

MANAGEMENT TRAINING PROGRAM

The Executive Development Program is structured to teach policies, procedures, and the merchandising and leadership skills necessary to manage a group of departments within a retail store. Training lasts from four to five months and combines classroom instruction, observation, and on-the-job experience. In class, you'll learn department store policies and procedures, advanced selling skills, and management techniques. You'll spend three days on a whirlwind tour of all major departments in the company, including control, operations, credit, collections, visual merchandising, advertising, data processing, customer service, and distribution services. Your on-the-job assignment lasts from two to four months in a unit store with an experienced area sales manager. You'll spend two weeks of this time with a buyer learning the function of a retail buyer.

QUALIFICATIONS

All college degrees are acceptable. However, most trainees have a marketing or management background. You will receive favorable attention if you have work or school experiences that demonstrate your leadership skills and if you exhibit energy, competitiveness, flexibility, and strong communication skills.

RECRUITMENT AND PLACEMENT

Maas Brothers recruits on Florida campuses. Aproximately 100 trainees are hired annually. Training takes place in Tampa and Miami. Placement after completion of training may be in any of the Florida or Georgia locations.

SALARY AND BENEFITS

Starting salary is in the $18,500 to $20,000 range. Benefits include group medical, salary disability, group life, accidental life, and in-hospital cash income insurance. Generally, the premiums are shared by the company and the employee. Profit sharing and retirement benefits, including an employee stock-option plan, are also available. All employees enjoy discounts on purchases. Paid holidays and a generous vacation plan are based on length of service.

CONTACT

Judy B. Tibma, Director of Executive Personnel, Maas Brothers, P.O. Box 311, Tampa, FL 33601.

R. H. MACY AND COMPANY, INC.

ART • FINANCE • GRAPHICS • HUMAN RESOURCES • MANAGEMENT • MERCHANDISING • VISUAL MERCHANDISING

THE COMPANY

This department store chain continues to expand throughout the country, operating under four divisions: Macy's New York, Bamberger's, Macy's California, and Macy's Atlanta. New stores have recently opened in Texas, Maryland, California, Georgia, and Louisiana. Merchandising focuses on upper to moderate-priced lines with a diversity of products: men's, women's, and children's ready-to-wear apparel and accessories, housewares, electronics, home furnishings, and furniture. Macy's New York division operates stores in New York, Connecticut, Texas, and Florida, and has expanded by nearly 25 percent in recent years. The company employs 50,000 people nationwide and maintains headquarters in New York City. Growth is projected for the next few years, causing a need for skilled executives to guide the expansion. Macy's began employee training more than sixty years ago and has been described as "the Harvard of retailing" by *The Wall Street Journal.* The majority of its top executives began their retailing careers in Macy's training programs.

MERCHANDISING, SALES TRAINING PROGRAMS

To ensure a broad understanding of Macy's operations, all employees begin their training with retailing fundamentals. In classroom and on-the-job training you will learn about Macy's managerial and merchandising philosophies and methods. If you are to work in merchandising, you will begin a series of job rotations, moving from store-line to buying-line positions. Your first assignments will be as sales manager and assistant buyer, then group manager (managing a merchandise category within a store), and ultimately buyer. Sales support executives also train in the classroom and on the job before being given their first assignments.

QUALIFICATIONS

Macy's hires graduates with degrees in liberal arts, accounting, finance, business, human resources, marketing, and merchandising. You should be strong in analytical and interpersonal skills to handle the demands of making far-reaching decisions and dealing with people at all levels. Macy's also values flexibility in employees.

RECRUITMENT AND PLACEMENT

Contact the company directly to apply for training classes offered several times during the year. You will be tested extensively to determine your abilities, interests, and motivation before Macy's accepts you. You will be placed by the division that hires you.

SALARY AND BENEFITS

The College Placement Council Salary Survey for September 1986–June 1987 indicates starting salaries for merchandising companies to be $1,594 a month for those with a B.A. degree in nontechnical curricula and $2,141 with a B.A. degree in technical curricula. M.B.A. starting salaries were $2,572 for a nontechnical undergraduate degree and $2,735 for a technical undergraduate degree. Check with the company for more specific salary information. Macy's benefits vary slightly from division to division, but generally include health and life insurance, pension plan, long-term disability insurance and salary continuance. Macy's recognizes that retailers often work long hours, necessitating a liberal vacation policy. Generous merchandise discounts apply in all stores.

CONTACT

Executive Development, Macy's New York, 17th Floor, 151 West 34th Street, New York, NY 10001;

Executive Development, Bamberger's, 131 Market Street, Newark, NJ 07101; Executive Development, Macy's California, Stockton at O'Farrell Street, San Francisco, CA 94108; or Executive Development, Macy's Atlanta, 180 Peachtree Street, N.W., Atlanta, GA 30303.

MARRIOTT CORPORATION

ACCOUNTING • BEVERAGE MANAGEMENT • CATERING • CONVENTION SERVICES • ENGINEERING • FOOD PRODUCTION • FRONT OFFICE • GIFT SHOPS • HOUSEKEEPING • RESTAURANTS • SALES/MARKETING

THE COMPANY

Since J. Willard Marriott opened his small root beer stand in Washington, D.C., in 1927, the Marriott Corporation has been an innovator. One of the first to provide meals for airline travelers, Marriott's contract food service is the world's leading independent in-flight caterer, with 87 flight kitchens serving more than 150 carriers around the world. Its 1986 merger with Saga Corporation brought Marriott's work force to nearly 200,000 employees and made it the largest contract food service company in North America. Half of the company's earnings come from its extensive hotel chain, with additional revenues from its fast food restaurants (including Roy Rogers and Big Boy's), and gift shops in airports and theme parks and on cruise ships. Taking its hospitality into new areas, Marriott is developing life care communities (elegant retirement living) in San Ramon, California; Haverford, Pennsylvania; and Fort Belvoir, Virginia, with other sites under investigation around the country. Nineteenth among the Fortune 50 largest retailing companies, Marriott has more than doubled its size in recent years. Annual sales exceed $5 billion. Headquarters are in Washington, D.C.

MANAGEMENT TRAINING

In Marriott's Hotels and Resorts Management Program, called "ID" for individual development, you will set your own pace. In-depth training will focus on a particular area such as food production, housekeeping, or front desk. Your training will last from nine to twenty-four weeks, shorter than most other hotel programs. You will receive full salary and travel expenses during training. After selecting the area you wish to pursue, you will be assigned to an adviser. A weeklong Introduction to Management course will cover such skills as motivation, coaching and counseling, and problem solving in a team. You may attend Food School at Marriott headquarters, studying techniques of food procurement and preparation, equipment operations, and restaurant kitchen specifications and procedures. Upon completion, you'll be assigned to a hotel as a manager or assistant manager.

QUALIFICATIONS

For housekeeping management, you should have a four-year degree and excellent organizational and motivational skills. Front office candidates need particularly strong personal qualities of enthusiasm, caring, efficiency, and resourcefulness. In addition, a four-year degree, previous desk experience, and a knowledge of computer systems are helpful. Gift shop managers will need a merchandising/retailing degree and some supervisory experience. Human resources managers must meet higher entry-level requirements: four to eight years' work experience and possibly an advanced degree. Accounting candidates need a four-year degree in accounting or substantial accounting experience. For sales and marketing, a four-year degree and direct sales experience. An outstanding candidate with intern credentials might be hired upon college graduation. Experience in food service will be needed for banquet chefs and restaurant managers. A catering service manager should have strong interpersonal skills and good organizational abilities.

RECRUITMENT AND PLACEMENT

Marriott recruits at campuses nationwide. You could work anywhere in the United States.

SALARY AND BENEFITS

Entry-level salaries are in the mid- to upper teens. Your benefits package will include medical, dental, and life insurance, profit-sharing and stock-purchase plans, gift shop, cruise, and hotel discounts, paid vacations and holidays, and tuition reimbursement.

CONTACT

Marriott Hotels and Resorts, Hotel Human Resources, 1 Marriott Drive, Washington, DC 20058.

MARSHALL FIELD AND COMPANY

FINANCE • FOOD SERVICES • HUMAN RESOURCES • INFORMATION SYSTEMS • LOSS PREVENTION • MANAGEMENT • OPERATIONS

THE COMPANY

In the early 1860s, Marshall Field and Potter Palmer joined forces to open "a six-story dry goods palace" in Chicago. Burned out during the Great Fire of 1871, Field persevered and rebuilt. Widely acknowledged as the pioneer of the retail business, Marshall Field was the first to introduce an exchange-and-full-credit policy; to open a buying office abroad; to offer a personal shopping service; to open a tearoom for customers; and to establish a value-oriented downstairs store. Today, the chain is a division of BATUS, a member of the British-based B.A.T. Industries. In 1986, Marshall Field opened five new stores in Wisconsin and added a San Antonio store, expanding its Texas presence. It employs about 15,000 people in 30 stores located in Illinois, New York, Texas, and Wisconsin.

MANAGEMENT TRAINING PROGRAM

In this twelve-week program you will be taught by senior executives in a classroom setting and by rotational job assignments. The first few weeks are spent introducing you to the company's overall organization. Seminars during this period focus on topics such as operations, customer service, loss prevention, human resources, finance, merchandise reports, and many more. Another part of the program is devoted to sales, with the majority of time spent on the selling floors to develop effective selling skills. Several more weeks are spent in the Central Buying Office. Buyers will familiarize you with buying responsibilities. Buying seminars will continue one day each week. In the weeks that follow, you'll be assigned to individual stores to work with a department manager. You will be evaluated every four to eight weeks during the training program. After training, you may select new areas to pursue as you learn more about the company's operations.

QUALIFICATIONS

Marshall Field's hires top graduates from a variety of fields—from marketing to human resources, communications to finance, visual arts to security to operations. You should be in the top 10 percent of your class with a minimum G.P.A. of 3.0. Related student work experience would be a plus.

SALES SUPPORT TRAINING PROGRAM

Individuals hired for finance, food services, human resources, information systems, loss prevention, and operations will enter a rotational assignment program. Your training begins in the buying offices and stores, experience that will be necessary wherever your career may take you in Marshall Field's. Seminars will be available in specific subjects to help you develop your knowledge of retailing.

QUALIFICATIONS

Your degree might be in business, social science, or the humanities, but you should have a strong academic record, ranking in the top 10 percent of your class. Above-average communication skills and related work experience are important.

ALL PROGRAMS

RECRUITMENT AND PLACEMENT

Marshall Field recruits around the country. You will be trained in Chicago.

SALARY AND BENEFITS

With a bachelor's degree, you can expect to start in the high teens or low twenties. The College Placement Council Salary Survey for September 1986–June 1987 indicates starting salaries for merchandising (retail and wholesale) and service companies to be $1,594 a month for those with a B.A. degree in nontechnical curricula and $2,141 with a B.A. degree in technical curricula. M.B.A. starting salaries were $2,572 for a nontechnical undergraduate degree, and $2,735 for an M.B.A. with technical undergraduate degree. Check with the company for more specific salary information. Your benefits package will consist of life insurance, medical, hospital, dental, pension, and savings plans.

CONTACT

College Relations Manager, Marshall Field's, 111 North State Street, Chicago, IL 60690.

THE MAY DEPARTMENT STORES COMPANY

RETAIL MANAGEMENT

THE COMPANY

Challenging. Dynamic. Fast-paced. Diverse. Rewarding. This is how May Department Stores' employees describe their retailing careers. And these adjectives could also be used to describe May Department Stores. It is the third largest department store retailer in the nation, with 146 stores coast to coast. It also operates 62 Venture quality discount stores, primarily in the Midwest, and nearly 1,900 Payless ShoeSource stores in 40 states—the largest self-service specialty shoe retailer. Through subsidiaries, the May Company is one of the largest developers and operators of shopping centers in the United States. The company expects to continue an aggressive expansion through 1989, adding 17 department stores, 19 Venture stores, and 1,100 Volume Shoe Stores. It has nearly 80,000 employees in 43 states and in 12 offices overseas. Annual revenues exceed $10 billion, making May number 10 in the Fortune 50 largest retailing companies. Corporate headquarters are in St. Louis.

RETAIL MANAGEMENT TRAINING PROGRAM

The Executive Training Program provides a foundation of technical retail knowledge and supervisory skills through a combination of on-the-job and classroom learning experience. It will prepare you to be a department store manager, then assistant buyer, then buyer, and finally an upper-level manager in a variety of areas. Your first several months will be spent in the Executive Training Program learning selling skills, merchandise presentation, merchandising math, advertising preparation, shortage control, statistical analysis, and supervisory skills. Your first assignment as a department manager will put all these skills to immediate use.

QUALIFICATIONS

Retailing is intense and competitive. The company is looking for exceptional college graduates with both liberal arts and business backgrounds.

RECRUITMENT AND PLACEMENT

The company recruits throughout the United States, hiring about 350 trainees a year. You will go to work in the May store where you are hired. You could work in California, Colorado, Connecticut, District of Columbia, Florida, Kansas, Missouri, Ohio, Oregon, or Pennsylvania.

SALARY AND BENEFITS

With a bachelor's degree, you can expect to start at about $22,500. You will also receive a number of attractive benefits: merchandise discounts, relocation assistance, comprehensive medical and hospitalization insurance, life insurance, disability coverage, travel accident insurance, a retirement plan, and a profit-sharing and savings plan.

CONTACT

Director, Executive Recruiting, The May Department Stores Company, 611 Olive Street, St. Louis, MO 63101.

OSCAR MAYER FOODS CORPORATION

ACCOUNTING · ENGINEERING MANAGEMENT · FINANCE · INFORMATION SYSTEMS MANAGEMENT · PRODUCTION MANAGEMENT · QUALITY ASSURANCE · SALES/MARKETING

THE COMPANY

In 1883, Oscar Mayer, a German immigrant, established a small sausage shop on Chicago's North Side with his two brothers. From making sausages the company expanded to manufacturing processed meats of all kinds, pickles and sauerkraut from C. F. Claussen & Sons, and turkey from Louis Rich, Inc., by buying those two companies. Oscar Mayer developed machines to package products automatically in Saran plastic tubes and in vacuum-sealed packages. In 1981, Oscar Mayer merged with General Foods Corporation, making it one of the largest food processors in the United States. The company considers quality control so important that 10 percent of its employees work in this area.

ALL PROGRAMS

You will receive close supervision during your training as you learn Oscar Mayer's policies and procedures through on-the-job experience and formal classes.

ACCOUNTING, FINANCE, AND INFORMATION SYSTEMS PROGRAM

You'll work under senior staff members while gaining experience in programming, testing, and documentation of selected phases in computer systems now being developed. You'll work as part of a management team while learning financial planning, cost analysis, business analysis, accounting, asset management, and strategic planning.

QUALIFICATIONS

You need a bachelor's degree in information systems or computer science.

PLACEMENT

Starting locations are in California, Illinois, Iowa, Missouri, Pennsylvania, Tennessee, Texas, and Wisconsin.

ENGINEERING MANAGEMENT DEVELOPMENT PROGRAM

The six-month Engineering Management Development Program includes a variety of basic engineering assignments with primary emphasis on the application of broad knowledge of engineering and management principles. Your learning opportunities may range from designing buildings or machines to supervising personnel within a plant engineering environment. The program's focus is on preparing you to manage people and projects in the engineering and maintenance functions to reduce cost and increase output.

QUALIFICATIONS

The company wants applicants with a bachelor's or a master's degree with majors in any of the following areas: mechanical, electrical, civil, chemical, agricultural, or general engineering.

PLACEMENT

Starting locations are in California, Illinois, Iowa, Missouri, Pennsylvania, Tennessee, Texas, and Wisconsin.

PRE-MANAGEMENT TRAINING PROGRAM

The Pre-Management Training Program is a structured six-month program that provides a thorough orientation to the full scope of the company's operations as well as actual management experience. The program prepares you for positions in marketing and sales, management information systems, production management, accounting/financial management, quality assurance, materials management, and industrial engineering. You will be placed in each department of the company to learn about its operations. You will participate in special projects in communications, time management, decision making, quality assurance, and sales and will spend six weeks managing a production department and supervising plant employees. In addition, you will travel to other Oscar Mayer plants and sales centers and will be encouraged to participate in seminars and courses conducted by the American Meat Institute, the American Management Associations, and the Management Institute at the University of Wisconsin. This program has been successfully preparing people for management positions for more than thirty years. In fact, the current president of Oscar Mayer went through the program.

QUALIFICATIONS

Those interested in the Pre-Management Training Program should have an M.B.A. or a master's degree in finance, marketing, operations, materials management, or food science. Applicants are evaluated on the basis of intelligence, communication skills, judgment, motivation, and management potential. You must be willing to relocate.

PLACEMENT

Starting locations are in California, Illinois, Iowa, Missouri, Pennsylvania, Tennessee, Texas, and Wisconsin.

PRODUCTION MANAGEMENT DEVELOPMENT PROGRAM

The program prepares trainees for a management position in production. Before you move into a supervisory role in production, you will receive several months of training that cover all aspects of the department. By working on the job, you learn about the people, machines, and supplies, and how to produce a product efficiently and economically. You coordinate your operations with other departments, such as industrial engineering, quality assurance, inventory control, personnel, and maintenance.

QUALIFICATIONS

You will need a bachelor's or a master's degree with a major in industrial management, agriculture, food science, business, sociology, or education.

PLACEMENT

Starting locations are in California, Illinois, Iowa, Missouri, Pennsylvania, Tennessee, Texas, and Wisconsin.

SALES/MARKETING TRAINING PROGRAM

Before being assigned to a territory, you participate in a program that combines travel with an experienced sales representative and classroom instruction in key areas. The classroom part of the program sharpens selling skills, develops product knowledge, provides an opportunity to make practical applications of marketing principles, and teaches effective management of administrative functions. When traveling with the sales representative, you learn to make calls on individual grocers, corporate chains, food-service distributors, and major institutions. You will be able to observe the rep working in areas such as advertising, promotional programs, collections, and new account selling. When you finish the program you will be ready to start in your assigned territory selling Oscar Mayer products.

QUALIFICATIONS

Oscar Mayer is looking for people with a bachelor's degree or a master's degree in business, preferably with an emphasis on marketing.

PLACEMENT

Starting locations are in California, Illinois, Iowa, Missouri, Pennsylvania, Tennessee, Texas, and Wisconsin.

ALL PROGRAMS

RECRUITMENT

Oscar Mayer recruits nationwide. The company is striving for a 10 percent increase in its hiring of women and minority employees.

SALARY AND BENEFITS

The College Placement Council Salary Survey for September 1986–June 1987 indicates starting salaries for food and beverage processing companies to be $1,834 a month for those with a B.A. degree in nontechnical curricula and $2,301 with a B.A. degree in technical curricula. M.B.A. starting salaries were $3,043 for a nontechnical undergraduate degree and $3,098 for a technical undergraduate degree. Check with the company for more specific salary information. Benefits include medical, dental, and life insurance; a stockownership plan; a voluntary investment program; profit sharing; and tuition reimbursement up to 80 percent.

CONTACT

Martha L. Winston, Corporate Recruiting Manager, Oscar Mayer Foods Corporation, 910 Mayer Avenue, Madison, WI 53704.

McDONNELL DOUGLAS CORPORATION

COMPUTER SCIENCE • ENGINEERING

THE COMPANY

McDonnell Douglas is a leader in the aerospace industry. The company produces commercial and military transport aircraft and researches, develops, and designs spacecraft, missiles, photo-optic systems, and data-processing systems. In 1967 McDonnell and Douglas were merged to form McDonnell Douglas Corporation. Douglas's line of DCs (Douglas Commercial) is famous in more ways than one. The DC-3 became the mainstay of many emerging airline giants, including TWA. The DC-4 became the first presidential plane. The DC-10s became notorious from several well-publicized crashes and near crashes. McDonnell was the first to make jet-propelled planes to operate from the decks of aircraft carriers. McDonnell specialized in fighter and other defense-related planes. The McDonnell Douglas companies are: Douglas Aircraft Company, McDonnell Aircraft Company, McDonnell Douglas Astronautics Co.—St. Louis, McDonnell Douglas Astronautics Co.—West, McDonnell Douglas Helicopter Company, McDonnell Douglas Electronics Company, and McDonnell Douglas Aerospace Information Services. Its work force is approaching 100,000 worldwide. Sales in 1985 of $11.48 billion placed it first in the total value of defense contract awards, ninth in value of exports, and thirty-fourth in sales among U.S. industrial corporations. In 1986 sales exceeded $12 billion. Listed among *Fortune*'s most admired corporations, McDonnell Douglas ranks number 23 in the Fortune 500 largest U.S. industrial corporations.

ALL TRAINING PROGRAMS

You will receive a combination of formal and on-the-job training as you begin your career with McDonnell Douglas. Engineers spend six months in training, computer scientists two months.

QUALIFICATIONS

Generally, holders of both bachelor's and master's degrees are employed as new hires. Doctoral-level opportunities also exist. You should be familiar with computers and have above-average communication skills, both oral and written. You should rank in the top half of your class.

RECRUITMENT AND PLACEMENT

The company recruits nationwide. You may work in Long Beach or Cypress, California, or in St. Louis.

Douglas Aircraft Company recruits engineers: aeronautical, civil, computer, electrical, industrial, and mechanical.

McDonnell Aircraft Company recruits engineers: aeronautical, civil, computer, electrical, industrial, and mechanical, and computer science majors.

McDonnell Douglas Astronautics Co.—St. Louis needs engineers: aeronautical, civil, computer, electrical, industrial, mechanical, and computer science majors.

McDonnell Douglas Astronautics Co.—West hires engineers in aeronautics, civil, electrical, and industrial specialties, and computer science majors.

McDonnell Douglas Helicopter Company hires engineers: aerospace, computer, electrical, and mechanical.

McDonnell Douglas Electronics Company needs electrical engineers and computer science majors.

McDonnell Douglas Aerospace Information Services hires computer specialists.

SALARY AND BENEFITS

With a bachelor's degree, your salary could range from $19,000 to $31,000; and with a master's, from $23,000 to $34,000. Benefits include tuition reimbursement, medical plans, relocation assistance, life insurance, a Salaried Savings Plan, and company-sponsored recreation programs.

CONTACT

David R. Estes, Manager, College Relations, McDonnell Douglas Corp., P.O. Box 516, St. Louis, MO 63166 (for McDonnell Douglas Aircraft Co. and McDonnell Douglas Astronautics Co.—St. Louis); Sally Ghan, Professional Employment, Douglas Aircraft Company, 3855 Lakewood Blvd., Long Beach, CA 90846; Barry Waller, Professional Employment, McDonnell Douglas Astronautics Co.—West, 5301 Bolsa Ave., Huntington Beach, CA 92647; Marti Vargas-Tous, College Relations, McDonnell Douglas Helicopter Company, 4645 South Ash, Tempe, AZ 85282; Darry Dugger, Professional Employment, McDonnell Douglas Electronics Company, P.O. Box 426, St. Charles, MO 63102; Tom Drury, Section Manager, Employment, McDonnell Douglas Aerospace Information Systems, P.O. Box 516, St. Louis, MO 63166.

McGRAW-HILL, INC.

CIRCULATION • FINANCE • MANUFACTURING • PUBLISHING • SALES

THE COMPANY

James H. McGraw, Sr., and John Hill founded the company in 1909. McGraw-Hill is primarily known as a publisher of technical magazines and textbooks. It puts out over 60 magazines, such as *Business Week, Chemical Engineering, Aviation Week, Space Technology, Electronics,* and *Medical World News.* The company ranks as the largest publisher of trade magazines, newsletters, and textbooks. The corporation has distribution centers in Highstown, New Jersey; Manchester, Missouri; and Novato, California. It also owns 4 television stations. Listed among *Fortune*'s most admired corporations, McGraw-Hill has annual sales of $1.5 billion and ranks number 217 in the Fortune 500 largest U.S. industrial corporations.

FINANCIAL PROGRAM

TRAINING PROGRAM

In the Corporate Financial Training Program you will be rotated from job to job among various divisions to acquaint you with McGraw-Hill's operations. Financial seminars are held regularly to maintain technical proficiency.

QUALIFICATIONS

You will need a bachelor's or master's degree in business administration or should be a C.P.A.

PUBLISHING PROGRAM

TRAINING PROGRAM

You will learn on the job, working with experienced supervisors who will guide you as you develop your skills in the publishing world. You can go into advertising sales, sales promotion and research, circulation, or manufacturing and distribution. There is a good chance for advancement in all areas.

QUALIFICATIONS

Editorial positions require a degree in a technical discipline and the ability to write, as well as resourcefulness and a willingness to accept responsibility. Other publishing positions require a college degree.

ALL PROGRAMS

RECRUITMENT AND PLACEMENT

McGraw-Hill recruits nationally. You may work in the New York City headquarters, in a division or district office, or in one of the company's 18 overseas offices.

SALARY AND BENEFITS

Check with the company for specific salary information. Your benefits package will include medical, life, disability, and accident insurance, retirement plans, a credit union, a book and magazine discount, and a tuition reimbursement plan.

CONTACT

Personnel Department, McGraw-Hill, Inc., 1221 Avenue of the Americas, New York, NY 10020.

MEAD CORPORATION

ACCOUNTING · ADMINISTRATION · COMPUTER SCIENCE · ENGINEERING · FINANCE · MARKETING · PRODUCTION · RESEARCH AND DEVELOPMENT · SALES · TECHNICAL

THE COMPANY

Mead Corporation manufactures paper, paperboard, corrugated containers, packaging, systems, precision castings, school and office supplies, and rubber products. Established in 1846, Mead is a packaging pioneer for the food and beverage industries. In addition, it has 1.4 million acres of U.S. timberland and three paper manufacturing plants—at Chillicothe, Ohio; Kingsport, Tennessee; and Escanaba, Michigan. One of its newest ventures is data processing. The company has developed LEXIS, a computer database for lawyers, and NEXIS, a computer database accessing newspapers and magazines. It has about 17,000 employees worldwide. Mead's annual sales exceed $3 billion, making it number 125 in the Fortune 500 largest U.S. industrial corporations.

ALL TRAINING PROGRAMS

Training prepares new employees for research and development positions, technical areas, production management assignments, and sales positions. The formal training lasts four to six months and is supplemented with on-the-job training and outside seminars.

QUALIFICATIONS

Mead Corporation is looking for college graduates in all engineering areas, computer science, and business. A minimum G.P.A. of 2.7 is required. One or two years of related work experience will give you an edge.

RECRUITMENT AND PLACEMENT

The company recruits nationwide. You could start in Alabama, Georgia, Michigan, Ohio, Tennessee, or Virginia.

SALARY AND BENEFITS

The College Placement Council Salary Survey for September 1986–June 1987 indicates starting salaries for glass, paper, packaging, and allied products companies to be $1,865 a month for those with a B.A. degree in nontechnical curricula and $2,401 with a B.A. degree in technical curricula. M.B.A. starting salaries were $2,945 for a nontechnical undergraduate degree and $2,775 for a technical undergraduate degree. Check with the company for more specific salary information. The comprehensive benefits package includes major medical insurance, a health- and dental-care plan, a stock-purchase and -ownership plan, educational reimbursement, long-term disability insurance, and life insurance.

CONTACT

Patricia Barnard, Manager, College Recruiting, Mead Corporation, Courthouse Plaza, N.E., Dayton, OH 45463.

MEASUREX CORPORATION

COMPUTER SCIENCE · ENGINEERING · MANUFACTURING · MARKETING · RESEARCH AND DEVELOPMENT · SALES

THE COMPANY

Measurex is a growing electronics company that produces digital-based process control systems for a variety of industries. It employs over 1,300 people in this country and another 1,200 overseas. Established in 1968, Measurex is located in Silicon Valley.

ALL TRAINING PROGRAMS

Computer scientists follow a six-month formal training program. Other new employees take part in a one-month program.

QUALIFICATIONS

You should have a bachelor's degree in engineering, computer science, information science, physics, or paper technology.

RECRUITMENT AND PLACEMENT

Measurex hires about 35 trainees a year. All starting positions are in the Cupertino, California, headquarters.

SALARY AND BENEFITS

With a bachelor's degree, you could expect to start in the $26,000 to $31,000 range; and at $32,000 to $36,000 with a master's. The comprehensive benefits package includes major medical insurance, a health- and dental-care plan, a stock-purchase and -ownership plan, educational reimbursement, long-term disability insurance, and life insurance.

CONTACT

W. H. Guengerich, Employee Relations Manager, Measurex, One Results Way, Cupertino, CA 95014.

MELLON BANK CORPORATION

AUDITING · CAPITAL MARKETS · COMMUNITY BANKING · CORPORATE BANKING · CORPORATE CONSULTING · CREDIT POLICY · FINANCE · FINANCIAL INSTITUTIONS · HUMAN RESOURCES · INFORMATION MANAGEMENT AND RESEARCH · INTERNATIONAL BANKING · LEASING · MARKETING AND COMMUNICATIONS · NATIONAL BANKING · OPERATING SERVICES · PORTFOLIO AND FUNDS MANAGEMENT · REAL ESTATE · TECHNOLOGY PRODUCTS · TRUST AND INVESTMENT

THE COMPANY

Recent mergers have increased Mellon's assets to more than $34 billion and its employees to more than 12,000. These mergers (with Girard Company of Philadelphia; CCB Bancorp, based in State College, Pennsylvania; and Mortgage and Trust, Inc., of Houston, Texas) offer many new opportunities and work locations to trainees joining the company. Mellon is recognized as a leader in shaping computer systems for the banking industry. The departments of Mellon's banking subsidiaries are organized into three broad areas: Market, Product, and Support. Market departments—Community Banking, International Banking, Corporate Banking, and Financial Institutions—deal directly with Mellon customers, individual and corporate alike. Product departments are concerned with specialties such as Capital Markets, Finance, Leasing, Real Estate, Technology Products, and Trust and Investment. Support departments—Auditing, Corporate Consulting, Credit Policy, Finance, Information Management and Research, Marketing and Communications, and Operating

Services—are involved with every area. Many departments expect to double in size in the next few years. Mellon is ranked number 12 in the Fortune 100 largest commercial banking companies.

AUDITING PROGRAM

Actual on-the-job assignments begin your first two weeks and are combined with classroom training over six months. In addition, EDP auditing recruits will receive six weeks of technical training prior to assignment.

QUALIFICATIONS

The department selects recruits with undergraduate degrees (B.A., B.S.) in accounting or business systems. Applicants with other majors who have received credits in accounting are also considered.

CAPITAL MARKETS PROGRAM

On-the-job training provides money market and investment banking experience and is supplemented by classes and seminars. Early on, you will become familiar with sophisticated techniques such as interest rate arbitrage. You will also gain experience in identifying yield spreads, interpreting Federal Reserve activity, funding domestic and overseas affiliates, and marketing interest and currency swaps. For traders, feedback is virtually instantaneous. Capital Markets has doubled its staff over the past five years and will continue to expand.

QUALIFICATIONS

The company recruits primarily M.B.A. and B.A. candidates with concentrations in finance, economics, and mathematics.

COMMUNITY BANKING PROGRAM

After a short orientation in Community Banking, candidates continue learning on the job, serving actual clients and assuming bona fide responsibilities. Community office management requires a fifteen- to twenty-four-month training period that takes place primarily on the job, supplemented by classroom work. After training, individuals are assigned titles and managerial positions.

QUALIFICATIONS

Mellon wants candidates from both graduate and undergraduate programs with a broad range of business, accounting, and financial skills. In addition, you should thrive on the challenge of responsibility, have an outstanding ability to communicate, a high energy level, a capacity to solve problems creatively, and a desire to be part of an effective performance team.

CORPORATE BANKING PROGRAM

Corporate Banking's training program involves both classroom and on-the-job instruction. Initially, recruits take part in Mellon's Credit Training Program, which is recognized industry-wide and is taught by senior Mellon officers and nationally known university professors. Here, recruits develop skills in credit analysis, become familiar with banking regulations, and gain a broad-based knowledge of the financial services industry. After three months of formal training, recruits become credit analysts and are assigned a portfolio of 100–200 companies. The next assignment is in Cash Management, followed by a line position in the Capital Markets Department.

QUALIFICATIONS

Mellon selects M.B.A.s with backgrounds in finance, economics, and accounting. A limited number of outstanding undergraduates will also be considered. More than academic credentials alone, the bank seeks graduates who want responsibility quickly, have excellent analytical and interpersonal skills, and who can readily adapt to an evolving industry and the changing needs of customers.

CORPORATE CONSULTING PROGRAM

Corporate Consulting substitutes on-the-job training for a more formal program. New members will have an immediate opportunity to contribute while assigned to work teams in one of the department's six divisions. There, your assignments will include market research, product development, strategic planning, and operations design.

QUALIFICATIONS

Mellon selects academically distinguished M.B.A. graduates, generally with degrees in engineering, mathematics, marketing, and economics. Mellon also prefers a year or more of full-time work experience. Although a technical background is helpful, general analytical and problem-solving skills are more essential than any specific area of expertise. In addition, Mellon looks for those with outstanding communication and interpersonal abilities.

CREDIT POLICY PROGRAM

Recently restructured, this program provides all the basic credit skills needed to do a thorough credit analysis, training recruits from the major lending departments of the bank as well as from Credit Policy. Now twelve weeks long for recruits from graduate programs and seventeen weeks for undergraduates, much of the program's classroom instruction is provided by highly respected instructors from outside Mellon Bank. After completing this program you will be assigned for six to nine months to a credit management section, where you will learn to evaluate actual corporate credit situations.

QUALIFICATIONS

The department looks for people with strong academic backgrounds in finance or accounting, preferably at the master's level.

FINANCE PROGRAM

The Finance Department does not have a formal training program. Rather, experience is gained through a series of on-the-job assignments designed to foster broad corporate perspective. Early assignments will develop your skills in financial analysis, presentation techniques, and working as part of a team.

QUALIFICATIONS

Mellon wants academically distinguished M.B.A. graduates with backgrounds in accounting and finance. Work experience in public accounting or financial planning and analysis is particularly useful. The department needs people with an aptitude for creative quantitative analysis and highly developed planning skills. Close involvement with the bank's management and professional staff also requires the ability to make oral presentations and prepare effective written communications.

FINANCIAL INSTITUTIONS PROGRAM

A combination of classroom and on-the-job training offers Financial Institutions professionals the solid background they need to manage effectively the changing requirements of a diverse customer base. As a Financial Institutions associate, you'll participate in Mellon Bank's Credit Training Program to develop expertise in credit analysis and a thorough understanding of the financial services industry. After sixteen weeks of credit training, you will inherit a portfolio of 100–200 companies and perform all credit analysis in support of their lenders to financial institutions. After training, you may be assigned to a cash management area to gain expertise in the bank's noncredit areas. Other associates have spent a period of time on the bank's trading floor or the department's own Product Development section. The Financial Institutions Department plans to double in size in the next few years.

QUALIFICATIONS

Mellon selects M.B.A.s with backgrounds in finance, economics, and accounting. A limited number of outstanding applicants from undergraduate programs will also be considered. The ablity to work effectively in teams as well as excellent communication and analytical skills are all important qualities for success in the department.

HUMAN RESOURCES PROGRAM

Not all skills for successful personnel management in a changing bank are acquired in university classrooms. Therefore the department assigns new recruits to rotational projects and planning assignments. Recruits are also exposed to in-house classes and workshops and can obtain additional instruction at local colleges and universities.

QUALIFICATIONS

Mellon selects only top candidates with graduate and undergraduate degrees in industrial relations, business administration, and human resources management, among others. Requiring from people the ability to deal with both the human and technical aspects of personnel management, Human Resources seeks applicants with a balance of analytical, communication, and interpersonal skills.

INFORMATION MANAGEMENT AND RESEARCH PROGRAM

For B.A. and B.S. recruits, a formal training program provides a complete overview of how the department functions. The length and content of this training are tailored to the individual, with skills such as programming taught to those who need them. Activities during training include both course work and on-the-job experience. Recruits from graduate programs attend a shorter version of the training program, with skills taught as needed. In addition, further personal and academic development is encouraged through continuing education. Regularly scheduled training sessions, bank-administered programs, and continued university course work are offered to the entire staff. The department continues to expand at a rapid rate—about 10 percent a year.

QUALIFICATIONS

Mellon wants both graduate and undergraduate candidates with a range of computer science, business, mathematics, and engineering backgrounds. Advanced programming training is not a prerequisite. You should be a person who seeks responsibility, possesses keen analytical skills, and enjoys working in a team environment.

INTERNATIONAL BANKING PROGRAM

International Banking's comprehensive Management Development Training Program will be tailored to your background and needs. It will provide classroom training and credit analysis assignments, and may include special work in such areas as international economics, money desk, planning and development, and international cash management. During your credit analysis assignment you will be given a credit portfolio of 75 to 100 banks and corporations. Initially, you will be exposed to global industries, and then you'll concentrate on international credit. The skills you develop, combined with country risk evaluation, will help you anticipate and understand the changing complexities of international banking. Upon completion of the Management Development Training Program, a series of assignments will deepen your knowledge of international finance, your analytical skills, and your familiarity with the many products and services Mellon Bank offers its international customers.

QUALIFICATIONS

The rapidly expanding International Banking Department hires M.B.A., B.A., B.S., and international graduates with backgrounds in banking, finance, political science, languages, and economics. Applicants should have both analytical and interpersonal skills—the ability to motivate others and to supervise banking activities. Depending on your area of responsibility, travel may be frequent and extensive. Assignments in other countries may also require a capacity for working and living among people whose social and business customs may be quite different from your own.

LEASING PROGRAM

Depending on your assignment, Leasing offers both formal and on-the-job training. The formal training program is designed to provide knowledge in pricing, documentation, accounting, and the legal aspects of leasing. In addition, exposure to credit analysis techniques is provided through the Mellon Bank Credit Policy Training Program. Assignments offering on-the-job training develop similar skills in multiyear forecasting and planning. Leasing doubled its staff in the past three years and will double again in the next few years.

QUALIFICATIONS

Leasing selects highly qualified recruits, with both graduate and undergraduate degrees, who have backgrounds in finance, economics, or accounting. Prior leasing experience, while helpful, is not required. For a combination of detail-oriented work and close involvement with customers,

Leasing seeks people with analytical, planning, communication, and leadership abilities.

MARKETING AND COMMUNICATIONS PROGRAM

New recruits are assigned directly to a division for on-the-job training. Further personal and academic development is encouraged. Opportunities to attend in-bank as well as outside courses, seminars, and trade meetings are offered to the entire professional staff of the department.

QUALIFICATIONS

One of banking's few marketing departments to recruit from universities, the Marketing and Communications Department hires a few select graduates each year. Generally, the department hires M.B.A.s with degrees in marketing. However, those with other commercial, design, and business backgrounds are also considered. The ability to assess and solve problems quickly and innovatively is more important than familiarity with any specific academic function. Analytical and communication skills, creativity, and the ability to work well under pressure are the characteristics of successful members of this project-oriented department. Good interpersonal skills are equally important.

NATIONAL BANKING PROGRAM

Recently, the National Banking Department restructured and shortened its training program for lenders. The program's classroom instruction is provided by senior Mellon relationship officers and nationally known university professors. Your training continues with on-the-job assignments. Future members of Regional Lending Groups will be assigned to Credit Policy, evaluating corporate credit situations, monitoring a portfolio of 75 to 100 companies, and providing valuable support to relationship officers in the field. This will be followed by an assignment in cash management to gain familiarity with noncredit services. Future members of the Financial Institutions and Corporate Services Groups will, after completing classroom training, be assigned directly to their area of specialty.

QUALIFICATIONS

One of the fastest-growing areas of Mellon Bank, the National Banking Department plans to double its staff in the next few years. Mellon selects M.B.A.s with backgrounds in finance, economics, and accounting. A limited number of outstanding applicants from undergraduate programs will also be considered.

OPERATING SERVICES PROGRAM

You will begin with an assignment to a particular position within one of the four department groups. This initial assignment will be either a line or staff position, working along with skilled professionals while gaining experience that only hands-on responsibility can provide. In addition, during your first twelve months, you will participate in a Management Development Program that is tailored to meet the group's specific needs.

QUALIFICATIONS

Mellon selects recruits from both graduate and undergraduate programs, with backgrounds as varied as finance, economics, business administration, industrial engineering, production management, and information management. Some knowledge of computer science is helpful. People who combine technical, interpersonal, and analytical skills are needed throughout Operating Services.

PORTFOLIO AND FUNDS MANAGEMENT PROGRAM

Mellon's on-the-job training provides direct marketing experience, supplemented by classes and seminars. This department supervises the bank's investment portfolio and is responsible for funding the corporation through short-term debt and certificates of deposit. Early on, you will become familiar with such sophisticated techniques as interest rate arbitrage. You will also gain experience in identifying yield spreads, interpreting Federal Reserve activity, and researching market opportunities. Having doubled its size over the past five years, Portfolio and Funds Management continues to expand.

QUALIFICATIONS

Mellon is recruiting M.B.A. and B.A. candidates with a wide variety of educational backgrounds. However, degrees in economics and mathematics are particularly useful. You should also have an aptitude for quantitative analysis and an ability to make decisions. Steady nerves, quick thinking, and a high energy level characterize the successful members of Portfolio and Funds Management.

REAL ESTATE PROGRAM

The Real Estate Department Training Program seeks to foster good judgment, management ability, and technical expertise—skills not easily or speedily learned. The department's fifteen- to eighteen-month Management Development Program helps new recruits acquire and develop them. A combination of course work and practical experience in the field, the program provides recruits with the ability to analyze the three essential aspects of real estate banking: the developer, the project, and credit needs.

QUALIFICATIONS

Mellon wants recruits with graduate degrees in finance, economics, and real estate. Backgrounds in engineering and architecture are also useful. Consider the Real Estate Department if you have highly developed analytical skills and outstanding interpersonal skills. Requiring total involvement with developers and their projects, the department seeks mature, determined, well-rounded professionals who are willing to spend up to one third of their time traveling to serve customer needs.

TECHNOLOGY PRODUCTS PROGRAM

Training programs vary, owing to the wide variety of unique products and markets served by the four product/market divisions in the Technology Products Department.

Associates in Datacenter and Network Services begin their careers as either production or customer service representatives, serving approximately 300 correspondent banks in 20 states. Production representatives train customer bank personnel in the technical aspect of applications and delivery systems, such as automated teller, home banking, and point-of-sale systems that allow consumers to use debit cards to make purchases. Customer service representatives work with associates in servicing the ongoing needs of Datacenter and Network Services customers. Initially, associates participate in a one-week overview of the Datacenter and Network Services Division. They then have classroom instruction and on-the-job training experiences. These programs last three to four months and include in-depth experiences with one or more of the operating systems sold to customer banks.

Individuals joining Global Cash Management may begin their careers in a marketing representative or product management position. On-the-job training is supplemented by Mellon's highly respected "Cash Management University." Here the individual develops a thorough understanding of the bank's cash management products and services and their applications for corporate customers.

Product management trainees complement their formal training by attending product development sessions, customer presentations, and strategic planning sessions with experienced product managers. Associates are assigned responsibility for a specific product area and will work in teams to service domestic and international corporate customers' financial needs.

QUALIFICATIONS

Mellon will consider you for the Technology Products Department if you have a graduate or undergraduate degree in data processing, marketing, economics, accounting, or finance.

TRUST AND INVESTMENT TRAINING PROGRAM

Your training and orientation depend upon the division for which you are hired. In all cases, you will gain a broad overview of how that division operates and relates to other divisions. You will participate in planning your own development program.

QUALIFICATIONS

Reorganization in this department is keeping recruiting needs at a minimum. Generally, however, the department selects recruits from both graduate and undergraduate programs with accounting, economics, and finance backgrounds. These recruits must possess outstanding academic records and exhibit excellent judgment, analytical skills, and communication ability.

ALL PROGRAMS

PLACEMENT

You may work in Pittsburgh or at new locations throughout Pennsylvania or in Houston.

RECRUITMENT

Mellon seeks its potential trainees on college campuses.

SALARY AND BENEFITS

The College Placement Council Salary Survey for September 1986–June 1987 indicates starting salaries for banking, finance, and insurance firms to be $1,889 a month for those with a B.A. degree in nontechnical curricula and $2,135 with a B.A. degree in technical curricula. M.B.A. starting salaries were $2,884 for a nontechnical undergraduate degree and $3,320 for an M.B.A. with technical undergraduate degree. Check with the company for more specific salary information. Mellon was the first bank to offer a flexible benefits program, in which you select the benefits that are most useful to you. It is effective the second year you are with the company. Benefits include health insurance, dental assistance, life insurance, long-term disability insurance, vacation, holidays and personal days, cash awards, profit-sharing and thrift plans, retirement, bank services, tuition refund, and scholarships for employees' children.

CONTACT

Your college placement office, or Manager of College Relations and Recruiting, Mellon Bank, Mellon Square, Pittsburgh, PA 15230.

MERCK & COMPANY, INC.

ACCOUNTING • ENGINEERING • INFORMATION SYSTEMS • MANAGEMENT • PHARMACY • RESEARCH • SALES

THE COMPANY

Although most of Merck's products are not household names, its contributions to the health of the world are significant. Merck makes 75 percent of all childhood vaccines, including those for mumps, measles, and rubella. It is a worldwide corporation engaged in the discovery, development, manufacture, and marketing of products to maintain or restore health in two broad spheres: human, animal, and other agricultural health products, and environmental health products and systems. You could work in any of seven divisions, including Merck, Sharp & Dohme, which produces, packages, and markets Merck pharmaceutical and biological human health products in the United States. Another possibility, the Calgon Corporation, supplies water and wastewater treatment chemicals, services, and systems for industrial and municipal use (see separate entry). A third subsidiary, the Baltimore Aircoil Company, manufactures process cooling systems, cooling towers, industrial fluid coolers, pumps, and other equipment to conserve water and prevent thermal pollution. Together, Merck's divisions account for more than $4 billion in annual sales, placing the company at number 91 in the Fortune 500 of largest industrial corporations. It is also listed among *Fortune*'s most admired corporations. Merck is an international enterprise, manufacturing products in 27 countries and marketing them worldwide. The corporation and most of its divisions are headquartered in Rahway, New Jersey. Merck employs over 32,000 people worldwide, 16,000 in the United States, in more than 12,000 different jobs.

ALL TRAINING PROGRAMS

You will receive on-the-job training, supplemented by courses in management and career development. Managers can develop analytical and "people skills" in seminars, leadership training and performance workshops. You will be able to take courses in such diverse subjects as finance, marketing, business, reading, writing, and secretarial skills.

PROFESSIONAL REPRESENTATIVE PROGRAM

The Field Development and Training Department structures its sales training program so that, even with a minimal science background or little experience in the health science fields, you can receive a solid educatonal foundation in these areas. You will spend ten to twelve weeks in the initial training phase, including programs at the Merck, Sharp & Dohme home office at West Point, Pennsylvania, as well as your local regional office. The instruction course and audiovisual tools will be taught by experienced training personnel, including physicians with long and varied experience in the pharmaceutical industry.

QUALIFICATIONS

You should have a college degree or equivalent, the ability to communicate effectively, and an interest in the medical and health fields. The company looks for those with degrees in science fields, such as pharmacy, premed, chemistry, or biology, and also considers those with liberal arts degrees or majors in other fields with few or even no science courses. M.B.A.s must start in sales to advance into management.

PLACEMENT

Regional offices are located in Needham Heights, Massachusetts; Oak Brook, Illinois; Arlington, Texas; Overland Park, Kansas; Commerce, California; Teterboro, New Jersey; King of Prussia, Pennsylvania; Atlanta; Denver; and Columbus.

ALL PROGRAMS

RECRUITMENT AND PLACEMENT

Merck recruits at over 75 colleges each year. The company has 6 research and development centers and 23 production plants.

SALARIES AND BENEFITS

The College Placement Council Salary Survey for September 1986–June 1987 indicates starting salaries for chemicals, drugs, and allied products companies to be $1,964 a month for those with a B.A. degree in nontechnical curricula and $2,457 with a B.A. degree in technical curricula. M.B.A. starting salaries were $2,886 for a nontechnical undergraduate degree and $2,794 for a technical undergraduate degree. Check with the company for more specific salary and benefits information.

CONTACT

Director, Corporate Personnel Relations, Merck & Company, Inc., P.O. Box 2000, Rahway, NJ 07065.

MERRILL LYNCH, PIERCE, FENNER & SMITH, INC.

FINANCIAL CONSULTING

THE COMPANY

The largest brokerage firm in the world, Merrill Lynch is involved in more than stocks these days. The company has renamed its 10,110 account executives "financial consultants" and wants them to broaden out from traditional sales of stocks, bonds, and the occasional mutual fund or cash management account into insurance, estate planning, and real estate. The company estimates that by 1991 about 70 percent of the FCs will be licensed for real estate sales. (Only 10 percent currently have real estate licenses.) The rechristened FCs should be able to enter into every one of their clients' financial decisions "from the time they begin earning income to the day they retire," according to *Institutional Investor.* A new headquarters building opened on Fifth Avenue in 1986 with 275 brokers, making it Merrill Lynch's largest office. Changes have also been made in the training program, making an excellent program even better. A new training center in Plainsboro, New Jersey, will be broadcasting live training classes to branch offices throughout the year over the company's internal television network. The company has more than $53 billion in assets, with more than $9 billion in annual revenues. Listed among *Fortune*'s most admired corporations, Merrill Lynch ranks fifth in the Fortune 50 largest U.S. diversified financial corporations.

FINANCIAL CONSULTANT TRAINING PROGRAM

The nine-month Operations Management Program acquaints the trainee with the variety of functions involved in processing transactions and maintaining customer accounts. Training can take place in New York or at various operating centers throughout the country. Extensive classroom instruction focuses on the individual aspects of operations. Training assignments give participants the opportunity to apply what they have learned in the classroom. Trainees work closely with the operations staff to enhance their technical and managerial skills. You will then be sent to Plainsboro for in-depth training in two areas that you choose in consultation with your branch manager —financial planning and insurance, for example. You will participate with other brokers in seminars and training classes on a regular basis via the television network.

QUALIFICATIONS

Merrill Lynch is looking for highly motivated individuals with college degrees who are eager to stand on their own, make decisions that count, and lead others.

RECRUITMENT AND PLACEMENT

Merrill Lynch recruits nationwide. The company's training program prepares you, usually within a year, to manage your own staff within one of the several hundred branch offices or operations centers. Few other corporations offer this level of managerial responsibility so soon.

SALARY AND BENEFITS

Merrill Lynch offers first-rate salaries based on performance. The College Placement Council Salary Survey for September 1986–June 1987 indicates starting salaries for banking, finance, and insurance firms to be $1,889 a month for those with a B.A. degree in nontechnical curricula and $2,135 with a B.A. degree in technical curricula. M.B.A. starting salaries were $2,884 for a nontechnical undergraduate degree and $3,320 for an M.B.A. with technical undergraduate degree. Check with the company for more specific salary information. A wide variety of benefits include comprehensive insurance coverage, a pension plan, a stock-purchase plan, and a credit union.

CONTACT

Director of Personnel, Merrill Lynch, Pierce, Fenner & Smith, Inc., 717 Fifth Avenue, New York, NY 10022.

METROPOLITAN LIFE INSURANCE COMPANY

ACTUARY

THE COMPANY

Metropolitan Life provides life and health insurance plans and annuities through personal and group insurance to 47 million people in the United States and Canada—about one of every five persons. Metropolitan is the largest insurance company in New York and the second largest in the United States. The company has over $81 billion in assets and employs more members of the Society of Actuaries than any other insurance company. It was founded in 1863 to provide insurance to Yankee soldiers fighting in the Civil War but did not prosper until it turned to industrial insurance in 1879. It now employs over 42,000 people in more than 950 offices. Listed among *Fortune*'s most admired corporations, Metropolitan ranks second in the Fortune 50 largest life insurance companies.

ACTUARIAL TRAINING PROGRAM

A goal of your training will be to prepare you to be a fellow of the Society of Actuaries by giving you practical work experience. Emphasis will be placed on business and management development leading to executive positions. You will be given access to senior management during the intensive six-week orientation program. This is followed by new job assignments every eighteen months and liberal study-time arrangements (up to seventeen days per examination), both of which continue until fellowship.

QUALIFICATIONS

You will need a strong mathematical aptitude and background, and an excellent academic record. The recruiter will also be looking for interpersonal and communication skills, leadership qualities, business acumen, and management potential. Actuarial exam credit is preferable but not required, although passing at least one exam is necessary for summer employment.

RECRUITMENT AND PLACEMENT

Metropolitan recruits candidates nationwide. The company is headquartered in New York City and also has limited openings in Hauppauge, New York; Aurora, Illinois; and San Francisco.

SALARY AND BENEFITS

Basic starting salary for 1986 was $27,300 for those with 0–2 exams. Higher starting rates are provided for additional exam credit. The benefits package includes a savings and investment plan and a tuition aid program.

CONTACT

Lewis Borgenicht, F.S.A., Metropolitan Life Insurance Company, Area 21-V, One Madison Avenue, New York, NY 10010-3690.

MICHIGAN BELL TELEPHONE COMPANY

INFORMATION SYSTEMS AND PROCESSING · MARKETING · SALES · TECHNICAL SERVICES

THE COMPANY

Michigan Bell, a subsidiary of Ameritech in Chicago, is a telecommunications utility company. It employs 19,000 people.

ALL TRAINING PROGRAMS

New employees learn basic company information and procedures for positions in technical services, marketing and sales, and information systems and processing. Sales trainees participate in a formal training program that lasts twelve months. Other positions have a combination of on-the-job training and classroom instruction that lasts twelve months.

QUALIFICATIONS

The company is recruiting college graduates (and technical graduates with one to ten years of related experience) in computer engineering, computer science, electrical engineering, electronics engineering, information science, mechanical enigneering, software engineering, systems engineering, economics, and business (M.B.A. with technical B.S.). The company requires that you rank in the top 50 percent of your class and prefers a minimum G.P.A. of 3.0.

RECRUITMENT AND PLACEMENT

You will work in Michigan.

SALARY AND BENEFITS

Generally, you can expect to start at about $19,000 to $20,000 with a bachelor's degree, and at about $10,000 more with a graduate-level degree. Benefits include tuition and fee reimbursement up to 75 percent; programs for medical, hospital, and dental insurance; and pension and stock-purchase plans.

CONTACT

Bob Nikolas, Assistant Director of Management Employment, Michigan Telephone Co., 444 Michigan Avenue, Detroit, MI 48226.

MILLER & RHOADS
RETAILING MANAGEMENT

THE COMPANY

Miller & Rhoads is a full-line retail department store with 16 stores in Virginia and one in Raleigh, North Carolina. It sells fashion-oriented merchandise and offers full customer services.

RETAILING MANAGEMENT TRAINING PROGRAM

The Executive Management Training Program is carefully structured to prepare you for entry-level management positions. Classroom curriculum is coordinated with on-the-job assignments in different company positions from sales associate to department sales manager. All pertinent aspects of department store operations are included. You will be expected to demonstrate competency in each phase of the program. After successfully completing the program, you will be placed within the executive merchandising or store line organization. The program begins in the summer, but there may also be an early spring class. Training includes assigned readings and feedback sessions.

QUALIFICATIONS

Miller & Rhoads is looking for four-year college graduates, preferably with business, retail, or fashion degrees. You need leadership experience in college, strong self-motivation, entrepreneurial talents, good written and verbal communication skills, and a good analytical ability. Retail experience is helpful.

RECRUITMENT AND PLACEMENT

The company recruits in Washington, D.C., Virginia, North and South Carolina, and Tennessee. All training takes place in Richmond; placement can be anywhere in the company system.

SALARY AND BENEFITS

The College Placement Council Salary Survey for September 1986–June 1987 indicates starting salaries for merchandising (retail and wholesale) and service companies to be $1,594 a month for those with a B.A. degree in nontechnical curricula and $2,141 with a B.A. degree in technical curricula. M.B.A. starting salaries were $2,572 for a nontechnical undergraduate degree, and $2,735 for an M.B.A. with technical undergraduate degree. Specific salary and benefits will be discussed at time of interview.

CONTACT

Russ Consaul, Executive Recruiter, Miller & Rhoads, 517 East Broad Street, Richmond, VA 23219.

MILLIKEN & COMPANY
ENGINEERING • MANUFACTURING MANAGEMENT • SALES

THE COMPANY

Milliken & Company manufactures a broad range of textiles for clothing, industrial applications, and home furnishings, as well as specialty chemicals. The company employs computer-aided manufacturing, using the latest machinery and process controls. Established in 1865, it employs about 18,000 people in the United States. It has 56 manufacturing plants at 45 locations in the Carolinas and Georgia.

ALL TRAINING PROGRAMS

Training prepares entry-level personnel for manufacturing management, plant engineering, process engineering, industrial engineering, and sales positions. The program combines on-the-job and classroom training and lasts from eight to ten months.

QUALIFICATIONS

You'll need a college degreee in chemical engineering, chemistry, computer engineering or computer science, electrical engineering, electronics engineering, engineering technology, industrial management engineering, manufacturing engineering, mechanical engineering, technology or economics, textile chemistry, textile engineering, business, or liberal arts. A minimum G.P.A. of 3.0 and a ranking in the top third of your class are preferred.

RECRUITMENT AND PLACEMENT

Starting positions in manufacturing are located in Georgia and in North and South Carolina. Sales positions are available in New York City and branches. Milliken hires about 250 to 350 trainees a year.

SALARY AND BENEFITS

Starting salaries for bachelor's degree employees are in the mid-twenties. Benefits include relocation assistance, pension and deferred savings plans, comprehensive medical and hospitalization plans, life insurance, and career counseling.

CONTACT

Paul Loadholdt, Director, College Relations, Milliken & Company, P.O. Box 1926, Spartanburg, SC 29304; for sales, contact: Personnel Director, Milliken & Company, 1045 Avenue of the Americas, New York, NY 10018.

MOBIL CORPORATION

COMPUTER SCIENCE • ENGINEERING • EXPLORATION • MARKETING • RESEARCH

THE COMPANY

Mobil Corporation is the second largest U.S. petroleum company, with revenues of approximately $44 billion in 1986. Mobil companies do business in more than 100 countries and employ approximately 164,000 people. The company dates back to 1866 but took its present form in 1976 as the publicly held holding company for Mobil Oil Corporation and the newly acquired Marcor, Inc., the parent company of Montgomery Ward & Co., Inc., and Container Corporation of America. The company actively supports cultural, civic, art, and educational organizations. Listed among *Fortune*'s most admired corporations, Mobil ranks number 5 in the Fortune 500 largest U.S. industrial corporations. Mobil Chemical and its affiliates are major producers and marketers of petrochemicals worldwide, focusing on plastic resins. Mobil aggressively pursues new product development and efficient production techniques.

ALL TRAINING PROGRAMS

You will receive training throughout your career with Mobil, beginning with courses in basic management skills and specific content workshops. You will most likely receive rotational assignments to familiarize you with various aspects of company operations. As you advance, you will be eligible for the Home Study Program, offering over 200 courses in 15 categories to fit your individual training needs and interests. Outside speakers and consultants cover technical and personal skills development with courses on topics such as refinery operations, effective writing, and computer programming. An educational assistance program permits you to continue your education outside the company.

ENGINEERING PROGRAM

Rotational assignments during the first three years of your career with Mobil may include both land and marine field activities.

QUALIFICATIONS

You should have a degree in mechanical or electrical engineering. Specific educational requirements vary with the demands of each position.

PLACEMENT

Expect to be based in Dallas with rotational field assignments during your first three years.

EXPLORATION PROGRAM

As a geologist, you will expand your skills with on-the-job training, learning about well log analysis, economics, and computer applications. You will also take part in geological and geophysical exploration seminars. Rotational assignments will be given to broaden your knowledge. As a geophysicist, you will work on an exploration team to gather, process, and analyze geophysical data. Land agents also begin work as part of a team for on-the-job training.

QUALIFICATIONS

To be a Mobil geologist, you will need a master's degree in geology or a bachelor's degree in geological engineering. In addition, geophysicists should have a varied technical background generally emphasizing mathematics or physics with some exposure to geology and engineering. Land agents need a bachelor's or master's in business administration or a degree in law.

PLACEMENT

You could be sent to Denver, Houston, Dallas, or New Orleans (except for land agents, who do not go to Dallas).

MARKETING PROGRAM

You will be expected to complete a six-month Resale Marketing Representative Training Program. The course covers all aspects of financial management, selling techniques and product knowledge, hiring, and promotion of gasoline, motor oil, and lubricants. The company operates a state-of-the-art Marketing Training Center in Fairfax, Virginia.

QUALIFICATIONS

In addition to a bachelor's degree, you will need to demonstrate that you are well organized and a self-starter.

PLACEMENT

Your territory could be anywhere in the United States. Expect to be relocated.

ALL PROGRAMS

RECRUITMENT

Mobil recruiters visit colleges and universities throughout the country. Make an appointment through your college placement center or write directly to the company for additional information about hiring possibilities.

SALARY AND BENEFITS

The College Placement Council Salary Survey for September 1986–June 1987 indicates starting salaries for petroleum and allied products (including natural gas) companies to be $1,972 a month for those with a B.A. degree in nontechnical curricula and $2,497 with a B.A. degree in technical curricula. M.B.A. starting salaries were $2,629 for a nontechnical undergraduate degree and $2,970 for a technical undergraduate degree. Check with the company for more specific salary information. Mobil salaries are supplemented by benefits such as comprehensive medical and dental plans, liberal vacations, and plans for disability income, savings, employee stockownership, life insurance, pension, and continuing education.

CONTACT

Manager, Campus Relations and Recruitment, Mobil Oil Corporation, 150 East 42nd Street, New York, NY 10017.

MONOLITHIC MEMORIES

ENGINEERING

THE COMPANY

Monolithic Memories produces integrated computer circuits and other electronic equipment. Located in the Silicon Valley, in Santa Clara, California, the company has 3,000 employees, almost half of whom are overseas.

ENGINEERING TRAINING PROGRAM

The training program is designed to help you apply your technical or business education to entry-level positions. Supervised on-the-job instruction is supplemented by job rotation and self-study. The yearlong graduate training program gives new technical hires four three-month assignments—one each in design, products, processing, and testing.

QUALIFICATIONS

You need a G.P.A. of at least 3.0, and you should be in the top half of your class. Monolithic Memories is interested in people with a bachelor's degree in one of the engineering fields (chemical, electrical, mechanical, polymer, or metallurgical engineering), computer science, materials science, and business.

RECRUITMENT AND PLACEMENT

Training and initial assignments are all at headquarters in Santa Clara. After one year you can be eligible for an overseas assignment.

SALARY AND BENEFITS

Starting technical salaries are in the $27,000 to $35,000 range and are competitive with those of other electronics companies. Benefits are also competitive and include insurance and a tuition refund program.

CONTACT

Tom A. Bianda, Supervisor Professional Staffing, Monolithic Memories, 2151 Mission College Boulevard, Santa Clara, CA 95054.

MONSANTO COMPANY

CHEMISTRY · COMPUTER SCIENCE · ENGINEERING · MANAGEMENT · SCIENCE

THE COMPANY

The nation's fourth largest chemical company, Monsanto got its start in 1901 manufacturing saccharin. Today the company makes more than a thousand products including chemicals, agricultural products, man-made fibers, plastics, resins, and specialized electronics and process control systems. Monsanto has annual sales over $6 billion and approximately 38,000 U.S. employees, 53,200 worldwide. The company places great emphasis on environmental and employee safety and assigns more than 1,000 managers, scientists, and technicians worldwide to work full time to ensure worker, product, and environmental safety. Headquarters are located in St. Louis. Listed among *Fortune*'s most admired corporations, it ranks number 55 in the Fortune 500 largest U.S. industrial corporations.

ALL TRAINING PROGRAMS

Monsanto favors on-the-job training, during which you can apply your skills, try innovations, produce results, and have the opportunity to learn from mistakes. You will be closely monitored by a supervisor who shares the responsibility for your development. In annual performance reviews, the two of you will discuss your career interests, plans to improve, and preparation for future assignments.

QUALIFICATIONS

Roughly 40 percent of the trainees hired by Monsanto are from engineering disciplines, 40 percent are from scientific disciplines (such as chemistry, computer science, toxicology, industrial hygiene, biochemistry, and botany), and 20 percent are from nontechnical fields (such as business administration, accounting, journalism, law, and personnel). You may have either a bachelor's or advanced degree, depending on your specialty.

RECRUITMENT AND PLACEMENT

In a typical year Monsanto hires more than 500 new management and professional employees. Monsanto offices are located throughout the country—in metropolitan areas like Boston, New York, Philadelphia, San Francisco, and Chicago, and in smaller towns like Soda Springs, Idaho; Pensacola, Florida; Muscatine, Iowa; and Decatur, Alabama. In the United States there are 61 manufacturing locations, 13 laboratory technical centers, and 100 sales, merchandising, and warehousing locations.

SALARY AND BENEFITS

The College Placement Council Salary Survey for September 1986–June 1987 indicates starting salaries for chemical, drug, and allied product companies to be $1,964 a month for those with a B.A. degree in nontechnical curricula and $2,457 with a B.A. degree in technical curricula. M.B.A. starting salaries were $2,886 for a nontechnical undergraduate degree and $2,794 for a technical undergraduate degree. Check with the company for more specific salary information. Benefits include medical and dental insurance, disability income, life insurance, retirement plans, savings and investment plans, paid holidays and vacations, housing and transfer allowances, leaves of absence, tuition reimbursement, membership in professional organizations, and a matching college gift program.

CONTACT

University Relations and Professional Employment Department-F4EE, Monsanto Company, 800 North Lindbergh Boulevard, St. Louis, MO 63167.

MONTGOMERY WARD AND COMPANY

COMPUTER SCIENCE • FINANCE • MARKETING • PRODUCTION • RETAIL BUYING • SALES • STORE MANAGEMENT

THE COMPANY

Montgomery Ward has celebrated over a hundred years in the mail-order catalog business. Its catalog is found in one of seven U.S. homes and is used by over 25 million customers. Catalog sales represent over $1 billion of annual business. Forty-three credit service centers handle 7 million active charge accounts. The parent company is Mobil Corporation. Wards has its headquarters in Chicago and has 1,600 catalog stores and 350 conventional Wards stores. It is diversifying into innovative Jefferson Stores, outlets that combine the promotional pricing and self-service of a discount store with the wide selection, attractive display, and product service of mass merchandising. Jefferson subsidiary headquarters are in Miami, with facilities throughout the East and Southeast. Wards also owns subsidiaries in insurance, financial marketing, and chemical products. It has about 60,000 employees in the United States. Annual sales top $4 billion. Wards is ranked number 22 in the Fortune 50 largest retailing companies.

ALL TRAINING PROGRAMS

Montgomery Ward uses both formal and on-the-job training programs to prepare employees for their careers in retailing. You will learn the functions of all departments with which you will have contact by working on the line. Regular performance reviews will help you assess your progress.

STORE MANAGEMENT PROGRAM

As a store management trainee, you start with a six-week program in a store in your area or nearby. The training focuses on store activities essential to sales profits and on customer and employee relations. Training is intensive and broad so you will understand all areas of the retail business. You will use self-instruction materials to learn about the company, methods of business, and the merchandise. You will be introduced to effective selling techniques and support systems, including computerized recordkeeping and inventory control methods. Most of your time will be spent in planned rotation assignments throughout the store. In the on-the-job phase, you will work directly with store staff managers, who will encourage you to show initiative in seeking out the information you feel you need. You will be assigned a sponsor, who is responsible for your training and counseling and for guiding you through temporary assignments in each area of the store. Your assignments will be operating cash registers, selling merchandise to customers, creating and monitoring promotional displays, and scouting competitive stores in your area. You will handle merchandise from the receiving dock to the sales floor, learn the operation of the catalog department, and help complete the payroll schedule. At intervals you will review your performance and career development with your sponsor. Finally, you will complete a special project related to management duties, such as conducting a training class for new store personnel. Your sponsor will constantly evaluate your progress. Ongoing training and development programs are provided for employees at all levels of the organization. It takes about seven years to be promoted through several positions to store manager.

QUALIFICATIONS

Your degree might be in retailing, although the area of study is less important than personal qualities such as being able to take the initiative, being goal-oriented, and working well with people. In addition, you should want responsibility and like rewards, have the capacity to develop and execute plans, and be able to establish and work within a budget. Montgomery Ward prefers that you rank in the top tenth of your class with a G.P.A. of 3.4 or higher.

PLACEMENT

You could work anywhere in the country.

ASSISTANT BUYER PROGRAM

The Assistant Buyer Training Program prepares you to handle buying assignments by exposing you to every facet of retail store management, from customer service to shipping and receiving. Merchandising assignments will include product presentations and firsthand sales experience in the retail store. As an assistant buyer, you will be working with a buyer making up orders, preparing information for entry into automated systems, and working with catalog and retail copywriters, display managers, and package designers. You will begin to establish vendor relationships and plan promotions. Reaching the position of associate buyer takes about two years, and full buyer takes five years. In the buying capacity, you will study the sources of supply for the highest quality, develop supplier relations, arrange financing, and supervise production. If a product is not found on the market, it must be produced to specifications. You must guide product testing, advertising, packaging, display, and promotion cycles. Buyers must assure a continuous supply of parts and service for merchandise at locations close to Wards selling and distribution facilities.

QUALIFICATIONS

In addition to having a college degree, you should rank in the top 10 percent of your class with a G.P.A. of 3.4 or higher. You will need a high energy level and be able to work well with people, as well as take the initiative.

PLACEMENT

Corporate buying offices are in Illinois and New York, but you could be assigned to a retail store anywhere in the country.

FINANCE PROGRAM

Wards offers financial careers in four different areas: controllership, auditing, treasury, and tax. As a finance trainee, you spend the first few years in one area before moving to another. Training begins in the retail store, where you learn every aspect of store management, from merchandise to personnel. At the same time, you are working on store accounting problems and internal audits. After six months to a year you will have full responsibility for coordinating accounting functions with a field accounting office.

QUALIFICATIONS

You will need a degree in accounting, finance, or business, with a solid academic record. Wards prefers graduates who rank in the top 10 percent of their class and maintain a G.P.A. of 3.4 or better.

PLACEMENT

You might work at corporate headquarters in Chicago or at corporate buying offices in Illinois or New York. District offices are in Baltimore; Chicago; Detroit; Tampa; Kansas City, Missouri; Dallas; San Antonio; Oakland; Los Angeles; and Denver.

ALL PROGRAMS

RECRUITMENT

Wards recruiters visit some campuses. However, they hire only when there is a need. You may submit a résumé, which will be retained until a position becomes available.

SALARY AND BENEFITS

Whatever your degree, you can expect to start at about $15,000 to $18,000. Your benefits package will consist of life, health, and disability insurance, illness and relocation benefits; and merchandise discounts. You will also be eligible for a pension plan, savings, profit-sharing and stock-purchase plans.

CONTACT

Executive Staffing Department, Montgomery Ward and Company, One Montgomery Ward Plaza, Location Two South, Chicago, IL 60671.

MOORE

ACCOUNTING · INDUSTRIAL ENGINEERING · INFORMATION SYSTEMS · SALES

THE COMPANY

Moore is a leader in the design, manufacture, sale, and distribution of business forms and systems for electronic and manual data processing. Established in 1882, Moore now has annual sales over $1.4 billion. A wholly owned subsidiary of Moore Corporation Limited of Toronto, Canada, the firm has an extensive network of facilities throughout the United States, with national headquarters in the Chicago suburb of Glenview. The multimillion-dollar Moore Research Center in Grand Island, New York, is one of the most advanced of its kind and has been responsible for major innovations such as the Compurite ink jet printing system. The company's divisions include: Moore Business Centers, a retail operation that markets microcomputers and computer supplies to small-system users; the Moore Business Products Catalog, which offers computer supplies by mail; the Data Management Services Division; Moore Business Information Centers; and the Response Graphics Division, which uses proprietary computerized presses to personalize and produce direct mail and gaming products. Moore has over 2,000 sales representatives.

SALES TRAINING PROGRAM

Training enables new sales representatives to create, design, and sell business forms. You will undergo extensive sales and product training at the company's Education Center in Northbrook, Illinois. The program is conducted in five phases by a skilled office staff. Your training will begin with a comprehensive self-study program on the basics and progresses to more advanced selling techniques and product applications. A course on dimensional management training will be part of the program.

QUALIFICATIONS

Positions are open for college graduates who are self-motivated, accept responsibility, and have initiative, enthusiasm, and drive.

RECRUITMENT AND PLACEMENT

Hiring is done through the local district sales offices. You should send a résumé to the district manager of the local Moore office, listed in the Yellow Pages under "Business Forms and Systems."

SALARY AND BENEFITS

Salaries are based on performance. The College Placement Council Salary Survey for September 1986–June 1987 indicates starting salaries for merchandising (retail and wholesale) and service companies to be $1,594 a month for those with a B.A. degree in nontechnical curricula and $2,141 with a B.A. degree in technical curricula. M.B.A. starting salaries were $2,572 for a nontechnical undergraduate degree and $2,735 for an M.B.A. with technical undergraduate degree. Check with the company for more specific salary information. Your benefits will include hospitalization and major medical insurance, a dental program, tuition reimbursement, life insurance, a stock-purchase plan, retirement program, and an employees' credit union.

CONTACT

Manager, Human Resources, Moore, P.O. Box 1116, Glenview, IL 60025.

MORSE INDUSTRIAL CORPORATION

CUSTOMER SERVICE · SALES/ MARKETING

THE COMPANY

Morse Industrial Corporation is a subsidiary of Emerson Electric Company, a diversified manufacturing company founded in 1890. Emerson Electric, headquartered in St. Louis, Missouri, is a multibillion-dollar corporation ranking in the top third of the Fortune 500. Emerson has had over twenty-five consecutive years of increased net earning and sales during a period that included seven economic recessions. Morse Industrial produces mounted ball/roller bearings, chain drives, gear reducers, overrunning clutches, and couplings for industrial applications. It is headquartered in Ithaca, New York, fifty miles southwest of Syracuse in the beautiful Finger Lakes district and has 5,000 employees worldwide. Manufacturing facilities are located in Ithaca; Aurora, Illinois; Denver, Colorado; and Osaka, Japan. Service and product distributors are in Florence, Kentucky; Dallas, Texas; Los Angeles, California; and Toronto, Ontario, Canada.

ALL TRAINING PROGRAMS

You will receive five months' formal training in Ithaca, consisting of two weeks of orientation and core training and product lines training for each Morse product line. You will be instructed in and observe the following areas: manufacturing—all phases of product manufacturing and quality control; sales service—handling customer requests, pricing products, and preparing orders for data processing; sales engineering—culmination of training for each product line by applying knowledge gained to actual customer design and pricing projects; design school—detailed training in product applications, product engineering, and competition; Service Center training—handling customer design applications and order follow-up at one of the Morse Service Centers; and associated training—assisting in supervising Morse-sponsored distributor training schools and marketing projects.

If you become a sales representative, you will then spend nine months in on-the-job field training. You will call on company officials, purchasing agents, and engineers to help resolve power transmission requirements. You will assist distributors in a mutual sales effort. In effect, you will manage your own business territory by opening new accounts, developing existing accounts, and building a stronger customer-supplier relationship.

If you become a customer service representative, you will spend six weeks training at a Morse

Service Center after completing your training in Ithaca. At the Service Center, you will solve technical and policy questions, order follow-up and gather information essential to successful sales efforts.

QUALIFICATIONS

Candidates must have a bachelor's degree in mechanical engineering, industrial engineering, business administration, or marketing.

RECRUITMENT AND PLACEMENT

After training in Ithaca, you will be assigned to one of the company's sales districts and could work anywhere in the country.

SALARY AND BENEFITS

The College Placement Council Salary Survey for September 1986–June 1987 indicates starting salaries for automotive and mechanical equipment companies to be $1,907 a month for those with a B.A. degree in nontechnical curricula and $2,333 with a B.A. degree in technical curricula. M.B.A. starting salaries were $2,697 for a nontechnical undergraduate degree and $2,986 for a technical undergraduate degree. Check with the company for more specific salary information.

CONTACT

Scott A. Anderson, Director of Training, 620 South Aurora Street, Ithaca, NY 14850.

MOTOROLA, INC.

COMPUTER/PROGRAMMER ANALYSIS • ENGINEERING • FINANCE • PROCESS ASSEMBLY • QUALITY ASSURANCE • SALES

THE COMPANY

Since the early 1960s, Motorola has been a major force in the electronics industry. Its Semiconductor Products Sector is a leader in state-of-the-art technology, manufacturing microprocessors for automotive applications, smoke detectors, electronic watches, digital voltmeters, and other consumer products. The Communications Sector specializes in the development, manufacture, and marketing of advanced two-way communications technology. This division has annual sales of over $2 billion, a major part of the company's total $5.8 billion in sales. Additional divisions include the Government Electronics Group (making electronic hardware and systems for government agencies), the Automotive and Industrial Electronics Group, and the Information Systems Group (Codex and Four-Phase). Motorola has about 90,000 employees worldwide. Listed among *Fortune*'s most admired corporations, it ranks number 60 in the Fortune 500 largest U.S. industrial corporations.

ENGINEERING TRAINING PROGRAM

Engineers undergo a combination of on-the-job and formal training. The Semiconductor Group offers a special Engineering Rotational Program that will expose you to a variety of job experiences. You will have your choice of four three-month assignments in research and development, design, processing, production, quality control, and marketing. At the same time you'll work at obtaining your master's degree at the rate of six hours in the fall and the spring. If you already have a master's, you will be encouraged to pursue other postgraduate work. An important part of the program is regular counseling and performance ratings. The Government Electronics Group offers a twenty-four-week Engineering Training Program twice yearly. In the first twelve weeks you will participate in a series of technical lectures and design projects; the second twelve-week segment focuses on a hands-on model project. After completion of the program you will be assigned to the Communications, Aerospace, Tactical Electronics, or Radar Laboratories.

QUALIFICATIONS

You should have a bachelor's, master's, or doctoral degree in any of the following engineering specialties: ceramic, chemical, electrical, electronics, industrial, or mechanical. You might also have a degree in chemistry, computer science, finance, mathematics, or physics.

RECRUITMENT AND PLACEMENT

Your starting location will be in Alabama, Arizona, Florida, Illinois, Massachusetts, or Texas. Motorola hires as many as 1,000 trainees a year.

SALARY AND BENEFITS

Salaries start in the high twenties with a bachelor's degree, jumping about $2,000 with a master's and another $4,000 with a doctoral degree. Benefits include life and health insurance, tuition assistance, and a retirement plan.

CONTACT

Government Electronics Group, Engineering Training Program: University Relations/Staffing, Motorola, Inc., Box 1417, Scottsdale, AZ 85252; Communications Sector: Staffing, Motorola, Inc., 8000 West Sunrise Boulevard, Plantation, FL 33322; Staffing, Motorola, Inc., 1301 East Algonquin Road, Schaumburg, IL 60196; Staffing, Motorola, Inc., 5555 North Beach Road, Fort Worth, TX 76113; Semiconductor Products Sector: Staffing, Motorola, Inc., P.O. Box 20903, Phoenix, AZ; Staffing, Motorola, Inc., P.O. Box 6000, Austin, TX 78762; Automotive and Industrial Electronics Group: Staffing, Motorola, Inc., 1299 Algonquin Road, Schaumburg, IL 60196; or Information Systems Group: Staffing, Codex Corporation, 20 Cabot Boulevard, Mansfield, MA 02048; or Staffing Manager, Four-Phase Systems, 10700 North DeAnza Boulevard, Cupertino, CA 95014.

MOUNTAIN BELL TELEPHONE COMPANY

ACCOUNTING · ADMINISTRATION · COMPUTER SCIENCE · ENGINEERING · FINANCE · TECHNICAL SERVICES

THE COMPANY

Mountain Bell provides telephone, information, and other communications services in the Mountain States. It is a subsidiary of U.S. West, Inc., headquartered in Denver. Mountain Bell has about 34,000 employees.

ALL TRAINING PROGRAMS

Both on-the-job and classroom training are offered to new employees. Tuition reimbursement for job-related courses is also available if you choose to pursue an advanced degree.

QUALIFICATIONS

If you have been trained as an engineer or in management-related programs, you might consider Mountain Bell as an employer. The company prefers applicants with mostly bachelor's and some master's degrees. A minimum G.P.A. of 3.0 is preferred. Mountain Bell hires U.S. citizens and permanent-residence visa holders. Some domestic assignments are open to foreign nationals. Either a business-related B.S. or an M.B.A. with a technical or nontechnical B.S. is required for some administrative/finance positions. Experienced technical graduates with one to ten years of related work experience are encouraged to apply.

RECRUITMENT AND PLACEMENT

Mountain Bell seeks communications systems representatives for communications analysis and implementation. Civil, computer, construction, electrical, and electronics (telecommunications) engineers find placement with Mountain Bell. You may be recruited if you majored in information services, engineering (civil, electrical, electronics, industrial/management, software, or general), computer science, engineering science, information science, mathematics, physics, technology and economics, or business.

Placement for graduates in engineering (civil, electrical, electronics, general, or industrial/management), engineering technology, information systems, and mathematics is in technical services. If you majored in computer science, engineering (electrical, electronics, or industrial/management), information science, information systems, mathematics, physics, or software engineering, you may be assigned to an information systems job. You may be assigned to an administrative position if you majored in engineering (electrical, electronics, industrial/management, or general), engineering science, engineering technology, mathematics, business, or technology and economics. You will start in Colorado. Mountain Bell hires about 150 trainees a year.

SALARY AND BENEFITS

With a bachelor's, you will start in the $23,000 to $26,000 range; and at $26,000 to $28,000 with a master's. Your benefits package will include health plans, life insurance, pension and stock-purchase plans.

CONTACT

Placement Manager, Mountain Bell Telephone Company, 1005 17th Street, Room S-40, Denver, CO 80202.

Advice from a University Career-Placement Center
Dr. James Chastain, Howard University

Dr. James Chastain is the Director of the Center for Financial Services Education and Professor of Insurance at Howard University in Washington, D.C.

☆ ☆ ☆ ☆ ☆

Tell me about the program at Howard.

The job of the Center for Financial Services Education is to bridge the gap between the campus and the companies. There are twenty-two hundred students in the School of Business, and I work with about two hundred and fifty of them who have indicated a special interest in financial service careers—through insurance companies, banks, or brokerage houses. We interview the students and build a file on each one from their freshman year and then we help them get internships. We had about a hundred internships with companies last year, in which the students went out and worked for the summer. And, when the students are ready to graduate, we publish a résumé collection of students who are looking for jobs, and we mail that to about two hundred banks and insurance companies, then coordinate the interviewing for these students on campus.

How would you describe financial training programs in general?

I would describe them more in terms of great diversity, because some companies have quite extensive programs and others depend largely on hiring people who are already trained. For example, most of the major insurance brokerage houses have very modest educational programs. They depend more on hiring people who have some background. Whereas some companies, like Aetna or Allstate or State Farm, have some of the best career path programs, and they work out a ten- or fifteen-year development program for their people.

Can you profile a good program that offers a mix between in-house classroom instruction and on-the-job learning with supervision?

Yes. For example, one type of job is an employee benefits representative for a company. Employee benefits has been a rapidly growing area in the last few years. And most insurance companies feel that new employees need about six months of intensive training to get ready to be representatives of this kind. So they will probably hire them and bring them into an office for a month or two, and then put them into an intensive five- to nine-month training program. And then put them out in the field and follow through with specialized training after that. Many companies have programs like that.

What's the value of these entry-level training programs?

Well, students get a chance to learn more rapidly in the first year or two if they're involved in an official training program. And this should make them more valuable. Then the company almost has to recognize this increased value of an individual or the person will leave.

So greater compensation comes faster for those going through the training programs.

I think it has to. I just talked to a student recently who had been hired by a bank fast-track management training program. Banks have done a good job of bringing college graduates into a loan officer training program which might run six to nine months. This particular student had gone through the company's training program and then within a matter of six months after he finished the training program he switched to a bank that didn't have such a program. And I'm sure they paid him handsomely to get somebody with his training.

What trends have you seen in entry-level training programs and recruitment in general?

There are a lot of trends. Hiring women is clearly one. Ten or fifteen years ago the percentage of women who were students in schools of business was about 10 or 15 percent. And now it's at least 50 percent. And not only that but the number of good women students is disproportionate. Even though about 55 percent of our students are women, perhaps 75 percent of our best students are women. And that's not only at Howard, that's at other schools also. And so it's very common to hire women now for whatever kind of job is available.

I would say that the insurance companies, particularly the property and liability companies, are subject to violent cycles. One of the distressing things is that many of these companies have treated employment as the deferrable expense. So when they are in a down part of the cycle, when they're losing money, they'll cut their training programs and cut their hiring. And then when they get back in the up part of the cycle, they've got a lot of catch-up to do. And so everybody will want to hire and they'll want to generate some instant underwriters, and it's very hard to do.

Have you seen much change in the way the companies are recruiting and looking for minority candidates for their entry-level programs or fast-track programs?

Yes, there are some companies that aren't particularly interested, but there are many companies that are intensely interested and go all out to hire minority students. One field where this is particularly true is actuarial science. There are ten thousand actuaries in the country, and there are probably less than fifty black fellows or associates in the Society of Actuaries. The companies are working very hard to try to increase this number.

Do you have any tips that might help people research and compare programs?

I guess they would just have to learn as much as they could, find out how long a program is and as much as they can about what they'll be doing. One thing the student should look for is that some companies have special fast-track management development programs. Many companies now feel like they want to get a small group of students out of college and attempt to move them ahead as rapidly as they can. And this will frequently involve more concentrated classroom activity and then job rotation over a period of three or four years. Companies may only put five percent of their college hires in these programs, but those are the training programs students are on the lookout for. The really good students begin to hear companies talking about that kind of fast-track program, so they begin to ask other companies about their programs. So I would say they get pretty sophisticated in a hurry about looking at the kind of management training programs a company has, comparing fast-track programs with regular programs.

As far as comparing regular programs goes, I'd guess the main thing would be to study them very carefully. I think that any professor would want to emphasize the values of the programs as opposed to money, but there is great competition among the students as to who can go out at the best salary. And this is unfortunate because there are many other things to take into consideration. One of them is geography. Our students who go to New York at $26,000 may not be nearly as well off as somebody who goes to Indianapolis or Dallas at $23,000. You never hear somebody say, "Well, I had an offer at $23,000, but I have a better training program."

So the strong advice I hear is to take a three- and five-year perspective and see what kind of training program a company has to get your salary up to $40,000 or $50,000 rather than that $23,000 or $26,000.

Yes, I'd say that it's kind of a general sign of maturity as to how a person sees the future. If you put a sucker in front of a baby and say, "Would you rather have this sucker now or five suckers tomorrow?" he'd probably take the sucker today. So it's a sign of maturity if a person can visualize the value in the future as opposed to the present value, and some students have that more than others.

N

☆ ☆ ☆ ☆ ☆

NASA—LYNDON B. JOHNSON SPACE CENTER

ADMINISTRATION • ENGINEERING • RESEARCH AND DEVELOPMENT

THE COMPANY

NASA's Lyndon B. Johnson Space Center is responsible for the development and operation of the Space Shuttle, which is designed to minimize the cost of using space for commercial, scientific, and defense needs. This center, an arm of the federal government, is also responsible for the design, development, and testing of space flight payloads and associated systems for manned flights; for planning and conducting manned space flight missions; and for conducting medical, engineering, and scientific experiments. There are approximately 3,500 engineers and other staff employed at the Johnson Space Center plus another 7,500 contract personnel. NASA has a total of 22,000 employees nationwide.

ENGINEERING TRAINING PROGRAM

On-the-job training is supplemented with formal classroom instruction as needed to help new engineers become familiar with NASA operating systems and procedures.

QUALIFICATIONS

Engineering positions with NASA require a bachelor's, master's, or doctoral degree in engineering. Administrative positions require a bachelor's or a master's degree in public administration or political science. Work experience combined with college study is preferred.

RECRUITMENT AND PLACEMENT

Recruitment is nationwide. You will work in Clear Lake, near Houston.

SALARY AND BENEFITS

With a master's degree in public administration or political science, the starting salary is in the low twenties. Benefits include health plans, life insurance, liberal retirement, and cash awards as high as $25,000 for money-saving suggestions.

CONTACT

Personnel Department, NASA Lyndon B. Johnson Space Center, Houston, TX 77058.

NATIONAL PARK SERVICE

PARK RANGERS

THE COMPANY

Are you looking for a job that lets you work out of doors? Park rangers manage national parks, historic sites, and recreational areas—over 31 million acres in the United States, Puerto Rico, and the Virgin Islands. They plan and carry out conservation efforts, enforce the law when necessary, and perform rescue work. The National Park Service is a bureau of the Department of the Interior and employs more than 8,000 people.

RANGER TRAINING PROGRAM

You will spend your first year carrying out assignments that include on-the-job training. The training includes courses at the Horace M. Albright Training Center at Grand Canyon, Arizona.

QUALIFICATIONS

You should have a degree in natural science or archaeology.

RECRUITMENT AND PLACEMENT

You may be assigned almost anywhere in the United States—in an urban, suburban, or rural area. Over half of the placements are east of the Mississippi.

SALARY AND BENEFITS

Benefits include health and life insurance, annual and sick leave, and a retirement plan. Check with the national office for the latest beginning civil service salaries.

CONTACT

National Park Service, Interior Building, Room 2328, 18th and C Streets, Washington, DC 20240.

NATIONAL SECURITY AGENCY

COMPUTER SCIENCE • ELECTRICAL AND COMPUTER ENGINEERING • FOREIGN LANGUAGES • MATHEMATICS

THE COMPANY

The National Security Agency collects, analyzes, and assesses foreign signals, safeguards our government's critical communications, and establishes standards for computer security for use throughout the federal government. Using the most sophisticated technologies, often before they become available commercially, NSA employees play a vital part in the functioning of American government. Computers simplify the job of NSA linguists, making extensive dictionaries and glossaries from around the world instantly available. The Agency's computer facility is one of the largest in the world—big enough to be measured in acres. If you pass the security check, you'll be in a position that is both stable and challenging.

ALL TRAINING PROGRAMS

You will receive a combination of formal and on-the-job training with guidance from supervisors, training coordinators, career development panel members, and personnel representatives. The Agency's own National Cryptologic School offers a wide array of courses, covering management and technical skills. You might be sent to any of 12 nearby universities and colleges for advanced study with financial support from NSA.

QUALIFICATIONS

Your degree might be in business, computer science, engineering, languages (Asian, Middle Eastern, or Slavic), or mathematics. You and members of your immediate family must be U.S. citizens.

RECRUITMENT AND PLACEMENT

A thorough background check is part of the hiring process, so allow at least four months for this before graduation or before leaving another job. Experienced persons may contact the Agency directly. The NSA is firmly committed to recruiting members of minority groups, women, veterans, and the handicapped. You will work in Fort Meade, Maryland, between Baltimore and Washington.

SALARY AND BENEFITS

The NSA pays salaries that are competitive with private industry, based on your qualifications. Benefits include: generous holidays and vacations, recreation programs, and a choice of several health and life insurance plans. You will be eligible for tuition reimbursement for advanced study.

CONTACT

National Security Agency, Attention M322, Fort George G. Meade, MD 20755-6000.

NATIONAL SEMICONDUCTOR CORPORATION

COMPUTER SCIENCE • ENGINEERING • MARKETING • RESEARCH AND DEVELOPMENT • SALES • TECHNICAL SERVICES

THE COMPANY

One of the world's largest semiconductor manufacturers, National has grown at a compounded annual rate of nearly 35 percent for eighteen years. In 1986 sales were over $1.4 billion, largely from products featuring proprietary technology. The company now offers customer specific products and anticipates that this will develop into a multibillion-dollar market. National Advanced Systems is a subsidiary that maintains the largest installed base of IBM plug compatible mainframe computers in the world. Datachecker/DTS, a point-of-sale systems subsidiary, offers equipment ranging from low-cost electronic cash registers to the most sophisticated supermarket scanning system available. In 1985 the company spent $3 million on training at the Santa Clara, California, location alone. National has a new 14-acre recreational park for its employees—about 13,000 in the United States, and another 17,000 abroad—where annual business meetings are held. It ranks number 227 in the Fortune 500 largest U.S. industrial corporations.

ALL TRAINING PROGRAMS

National's training centers provide intensive training along with skills learned on the job and closed-circuit TV classes. This is a fairly technical program that will take you through all manufacturing processes of integrated circuit chips before you are assigned to a full position. Management information programmers follow a six-month formal training program. Engineers and technical graduates receive about twelve months of on-the-job training.

QUALIFICATIONS

You should have a bachelor's degree in chemistry, engineering, computer science, information systems, materials science, mathematics, polymer science, or software engineering.

RECRUITMENT AND PLACEMENT

National Semiconductor recruits on many college campuses. You might work in Tucson; Santa Clara or Mountain View, California; Danbury, Connecticut; Maynard, Massachusetts; Portland, Oregon; Arlington, Texas; or West Jordan, Utah.

SALARY AND BENEFITS

Starting salaries for engineers are in the mid- to upper twenties. The College Placement Council Salary Survey for September 1986–June 1987 indicates starting salaries for electrical and electronic machines and equipment companies to be $1,861 a month for those with a B.A. degree in nontechnical curricula and $2,419 with a B.A. degree in technical curricula. M.B.A. starting salaries were $2,784 for a nontechnical undergraduate degree and $2,818 for a technical undergraduate degree. Check with the company for more specific salary information. Your benefits package will consist of insurance and medical benefits, tuition reimbursement, pension and profit-sharing plans, and relocation assistance.

CONTACT

Camille Saviano, Manager, College Relations, 2900 Semiconductor Drive, Santa Clara, CA 95051.

NATIONAL STEEL CORPORATION

ACCOUNTING • ADMINISTRATION • COMPUTER SCIENCE • ENGINEERING • FINANCE • MANAGEMENT • MARKETING • PRODUCTION • OPERATIONS • RESEARCH AND DEVELOPMENT • SALES • TECHNICAL SERVICES

THE COMPANY

The new National Steel is the result of a joint venture between Nippon Kokan, KK, the world's fifth largest steelmaker, and National Intergroup, Inc., formerly the sole parent of National Steel. National is a customer-oriented corporation producing a full range of flat-rolled carbon steels for use in automobiles, construction, and other end-markets. National points with pride to its modern operations—a result, it says, of not being saddled with nineteenth-century equipment as are many of its older competitors. It was the first domestic company with the most modern steelmaking technology: continuous cast. This new collaboration with Nippon Kokan should give National added strength in the steel industry. It has about 12,000 U.S. employees.

MANAGEMENT TRAINING PROGRAM

National has a two-part training program that will give you a comprehensive overview of both the technical and administrative aspects of the company. For business and business-related graduates, the twenty-four-month initiation period includes both formal and informal training. On-the-job training introduces you to a functional area, such as finance/accounting, operations/production, industrial relations, sales/marketing, purchasing, production control, management services, or traffic and transportation.

QUALIFICATIONS

Managerial positions at National Steel are available to college graduates with or without advanced degrees who have specialized in business administration or a business-related field such as accounting, industrial management, computer science, or planning. Engineering positions require a master's degree or doctorate in one of the following disciplines: architectural, ceramic, chemical, industrial, mechanical, or metallurgical engineering. Those engineering positions requiring only a master's degree are in the fields of industrial, mechanical, and metallurgical engineering. Sales positions for which no degree is required are available. As a prospective candidate, you must be a U.S. citizen or hold a permanent-residence visa.

RECRUITMENT AND PLACEMENT

National recruits mostly in the East, Midwest, South, and Southwest. As a new employee you may start work at National's headquarters in Pennsylvania or at one of its facilities in Illinois, Indiana, Kentucky, Michigan, Missouri, or Texas.

SALARY AND BENEFITS

With a bachelor's degree, starting salaries are in the mid-twenties, with a master's, in the high twenties. National Steel's benefits include medical, surgical, hospitalization, and life insurance. The company also offers a stock-purchase plan, a tuition aid program, and a retirement plan.

CONTACT

L. R. Zizzo, Manager, Employment and Development, National Steel Corporation—Steel Group, 20 Stanwix Street, Pittsburgh, PA 15222.

NATIONAL SUPPLY COMPANY

ACCOUNTING · ENGINEERING · FINANCE · INDUSTRIAL RELATIONS · MANAGEMENT · OPERATIONS · PRODUCTION

THE COMPANY

National Supply Company is the world's largest manufacturer and distributor of oilfield machinery and equipment, and it is growing. The company is a division of a larger, diversified company, Armco, which ranks among the Fortune 500 companies based on sales. In about 125 locations in the United States and overseas, national plants, service centers, machinery centers, and supply stores form a network to serve oilfields. There are 21 separate businesses within National Supply Company, offering the potential to move around in a large network.

ALL TRAINING PROGRAMS

The company likes to tell recruits that they may sink their heels into deep carpet the first day on the job, but don't count on it. You'll be just as likely to start with one of its companies, National Cementers, as a helper, then advance to driving a truck. Maybe you'll start by stocking shelves before you ever see a customer. National wants you to have a feel for field conditions, but it won't ignore more formal training. Standard training methods supplement, rather than replace, on-the-job development. Formal training will give you what you need to round out what you learn on the job. It may be a course in effective writing or public speaking, training in supervisory and management skills to prepare you for additional responsibility, or postgraduate courses at nearby colleges.

QUALIFICATIONS

National hires in a variety of degree specialties and levels, such as industrial engineering, accounting, metallurgy, business administration, public administration, marketing, and finance.

RECRUITMENT AND PLACEMENT

National sends recruiters to campuses around the country, or you may apply directly through headquarters. The company has a network of 125 locations in the United States and abroad. Your first assignment might be in Houston, Los Angeles, Dallas, or New Orleans, or at a location that is "not necessarily close to a good restaurant." These locales may be in California, Louisiana, Pennsylvania, Texas, or Canada.

SALARY AND BENEFITS

The College Placement Council Salary Survey for September 1986–June 1987 indicates starting salaries for petroleum and allied product companies to be $1,972 a month for those with a B.A. degree in nontechnical curricula and $2,497 with a B.A. degree in technical curricula. M.B.A. starting salaries were $2,629 for a nontechnical undergraduate degree and $2,970 for a technical undergraduate degree. Check with the company for more specific salary information. Benefits include bonus plans, paid vacations, stock and savings plans, pension plan, education reimbursement, major medical, dental and vision care, life insurance, and Blue Cross-Blue Shield.

CONTACT

Personnel Department, National Supply Company, 1455 West Loop South, Houston, TX 77027.

NAVAL SEA SYSTEMS COMMAND

ENGINEERING · PRODUCTION · RESEARCH AND DEVELOPMENT

THE COMPANY

The Naval Sea Systems Command began in 1842 as the Bureau of Construction and Repair. Since that time its purpose has remained constant—to provide the U.S. Navy with ships and weapons. The command has a budget of over $10 billion and is the single largest component in the Department of Defense. The Naval Sea Systems Command also seeks to foster the development of private industry essential to its mission, including shipbuilders and weapons manufacturers. The command maintains 8 shipyards on both the East and West coasts and over 40 weapons stations throughout the country.

ENGINEERING TRAINING PROGRAM

Training provides well-rounded engineering personnel to staff future management and upper-level positions. The program lasts twenty-four months. Trainees are assigned to field activities for six months to gain on-the-job experience. Two to four weeks of this initial period are spent at sea. Trainees then continue with rotational assignments, field activity assignments, and guided on-the-job training. You will also make field trips, attend formal courses, participate in professional meetings, and receive individual counseling. You will work closely with senior engineers and supervisors.

QUALIFICATIONS

You should have a bachelor's or a master's degree in engineering in any of the following areas: chemical, civil, electrical, electronics, fire protection, materials, mechanical, metallurgical, ocean, and welding.

RECRUITMENT AND PLACEMENT

Headquarters for the Naval Seas Systems Command is Washington, D.C. You may work in any of its shipyards or weapons stations.

SALARY AND BENEFITS

With a bachelor's degree you will start in the $18,000 to $23,000 range; and with a master's, at $27,000. Benefits include sick days and vacation time, paid holidays, life and health insurance, and a retirement plan. Additionally, you will be eligible for tuition reimbursement or for advanced study at universities while your salary continues.

CONTACT

Michele Grimm, Consolidated Civilian Personnel Office-CC, Jefferson Davis Highway, CM#2, Room 515, Washington, DC 20376.

NAVAL UNDERSEA WARFARE ENGINEERING STATION

COMPUTER SCIENCE • ENGINEERING • RESEARCH AND DEVELOPMENT

THE COMPANY

The Naval Undersea Warfare Engineering Station (NUWES) conducts research, development, testing, and evaluation for the U.S. Navy's projects in undersea surveillance, ocean technology, and advanced undersea weapons systems. The center is currently working on the Trident submarine defensive weapons system and is rapidly expanding its computer capacities. A fleet of over 20 vessels is assigned to NUWES to support testing operations in the Pacific. NUWES has about 3,250 civil service employees and another 300 military employees. Headquarters are in Keyport, Washington.

ENGINEERING TRAINING PROGRAMS

The Advanced Technology Training Center will acquaint you with robotics, fiber optics, microprocessor, and general-purpose computer laboratories. NUWES has agreements with several colleges and universities to provide both undergraduate- and graduate-level courses relevant to employees. You may pursue a master's degree through video programs offered by Purdue University, the University of Iowa, and the University of Massachusetts. Self-taught and correspondence courses will also be available to you.

QUALIFICATIONS

NUWES looks for graduates with degrees in computer, electrical, electronics, and mechanical engineering. You will need a minimum G.P.A. of 2.3 and should be familiar with computer systems.

RECRUITMENT AND PLACEMENT

You should apply directly to the Keyport, Washington, offices. You might be assigned to California, Hawaii, or Washington to begin your career.

SALARY AND BENEFITS

With a bachelor's degree, your salary will be about $23,000; about $27,000 with a master's. Benefits include medical and dental plans, flextime options, life insurance, tuition reimbursement, and career counseling.

CONTACT

Mary Russell, Personnel Staffing Specialist, Naval Undersea Warfare Engineering Station, Keyport, WA 98345-0580.

NCR CORPORATION

ENGINEERING • FINANCE • INFORMATION SYSTEMS • PERSONNEL • SALES AND MARKETING •

THE COMPANY

When you go through a supermarket checkout counter or withdraw money from an automatic bank teller, chances are good that an NCR machine handles the transaction. A large, dynamic computer company, NCR has employees in more than 120 countries with revenues of $4.8 billion. Its products are wide-ranging, including everything from ink typewriter ribbons to computer modems and mainframe processors. Data processing centers across the United States provide on-line data processing for special projects and complete information processing for customers who do not have their own in-house systems. Listed among *Fortune*'s most admired corporations, NCR ranks number 75 in the Fortune 500 largest U.S. industrial corporations. Individual achievements are recognized and rewarded with promotion from within. NCR's organizational structure provides you with access to high levels of management from the start of your career.

ALL TRAINING PROGRAMS

You will receive several months of on-the-job training and orientation as you begin your career. As you continue, you will regularly go to formal seminars and courses at headquarters in Dayton and at other worldwide educational centers. Structured self-instruction materials come from the company's independent Learning Center. The NCR Computer Science Institute and NCR Management College provide curricula on sales education, sales support education, product and systems education, and technical, professional, and management development and training programs comprising scores of courses, seminars, and workshops using both traditional and nontraditional formats and media.

QUALIFICATIONS

Your college G.P.A. should be at least 3.0. You should have a bachelor's degree in electrical, mechanical, industrial, or software engineering; business; or liberal arts (for technical writing). Applications from people with one or more years of experience are also welcome.

RECRUITMENT AND PLACEMENT

NCR recruits on many college campuses. Starting locations may be anywhere in the United States.

SALARY AND BENEFITS

Starting technical salaries are in the $23,000 to $27,000 range. Benefits include a matching gifts program, stock purchase, health betterment programs, employee assistance counseling, medical expense coverage, HMO alternatives (in some areas), optional dental coverage, disability income, disability vocational rehabilitation, group life and accidental death insurance. You may also be eligible to participate in voluntary life insurance, automobile insurance, homeowner's insurance, and IRAs through payroll deductions.

CONTACT

Corporate College Relations, NCR Corporation, World Headquarters, Dayton, OH 45479.

NEIMAN-MARCUS

RETAILING

THE COMPANY

Image is everything with this Texas-based specialty retail store. Nurtured by its owners to be THE store catering to the ultrawealthy with high-quality and imaginative merchandise, Neiman-Marcus is legendary for its marketing techniques. For the annual Fortnight celebration, the Dallas store takes on the atmosphere of a foreign country for two weeks in October, generating extensive community involvement—and sales. Merchandise is carefully selected to complement the theme, which is carried through with museum exhibitions, special orchestra performances, and dramatic events. The Neiman-Marcus Christmas Book is the best-publicized Christmas catalog in the world, with outrageous "His and Her" gifts such as camels, airplanes, and mummy cases—and many millions of dollars of sales as a result of its more mundane offerings. Since Neiman-Marcus merged with Carter Hawley Hale Stores in 1968, it has expanded from four Texas stores to a nationwide chain with locations in all the chichi destinations—Beverly Hills, Bal Harbour, and Newport Beach, as well as Chicago; Washington, D.C.; and White Plains, New York. Parent company Carter Hawley Hale is the country's fourth largest department store retailer.

EXECUTIVE DEVELOPMENT TRAINING PROGRAM

In this ten-week program you will start with a week of classroom instruction that covers company policies and procedures, benefits, career paths, systems, and point-of-sale terminal training. After the first week you will begin a series of on-the-job assignments of three weeks each that cover important operating and merchandising departments. This training experience could include sales, buying office, mail order, operations, and finance assignments. During the same period there are two afternoon class sessions per week, for a total of twenty sessions, on subjects ranging from interviewing skills to gross margin. Along with classroom work and on-the-job assignments, each trainee completes an independent research project with another class member. You will take a final examination at the end of the ten-week period. If you pass, you will be interviewed for the first permanent assignment as assistant buyer. Training will continue throughout your career with Neiman-Marcus.

QUALIFICATIONS

Your degree might be in several areas—business or liberal arts perhaps—but equally important will be your excellent academic record and leadership abilities. N-M wants executives who like people, are self-starting, analytical, energetic, flexible but decisive. Youth is not a barrier with this company.

RECRUITMENT AND PLACEMENT

The company recruits nationwide. Training is in Dallas, but you could be assigned to stores in California, Florida, Georgia, Illinois, Missouri, Nevada, New York, or Washington, D.C.

SALARY AND BENEFITS

The College Placement Council Salary Survey for September 1986–June 1987 indicates starting salaries for merchandising (retail and wholesale) and service companies to be $1,594 a month for those with a B.A. degree in nontechnical curricula and $2,141 with a B.A. degree in technical curricula. M.B.A. starting salaries were $2,572 for a nontechnical undergraduate degree and $2,735 for an M.B.A. with technical undergraduate degree. Check with the company for more specific salary and benefits information.

CONTACT

Director, Executive Recruiting, Neiman-Marcus, Main and Ervay, Dallas, TX 75201.

NEW ENGLAND ELECTRIC SYSTEM

ACCOUNTING • COMPUTER SCIENCE • ENGINEERING • FINANCE • MANAGEMENT

THE COMPANY

New England Electric is a progressive investor-owned electric utility serving one million customers in central New England. NEES has pioneered in load management and conservation, long-range planning, coal conversion, fuel management, and rate design. It employs about 5,000 people in engineering, finance and accounting, environmental affairs, energy conservation, fuel supply, and customer service.

ALL TRAINING PROGRAMS

The NEES Career Development Program for engineers is a combination of on-the-job and formal training that lasts twenty-four months. The accounting/finance, and load management and conservation areas are developing similar programs. After a general orientation to company philosophy and policies, you can expect to be rotated to different positions. You will also participate in regular feedback sessions. In 1987, NEES implemented a state-of-the-art Supervisory and Management Development Program for all management-level employees. Current employees and new managers will be trained through 1990. Thereafter all new managers will receive this comprehensive training.

QUALIFICATIONS

NEES is interested in graduates with bachelor's and master's degrees in electrical and mechanical engineering. Applications are also encouraged from graduates with a four-year degree in business or liberal arts, and from technical graduates with one to two years of related experience.

RECRUITMENT AND PLACEMENT

Send a résumé to the company's personnel representative. Placement will be in Massachusetts or Rhode Island. Summer and co-op applicants are encouraged to apply.

SALARY AND BENEFITS

The College Placement Council Salary Survey for September 1986–June 1987 indicates starting salaries for public utilities to be $1,905 a month for those with a B.A. degree in nontechnical curricula and $2,355 with a B.A. degree in technical curricula. M.B.A. starting salaries were $2,403 for a nontechnical undergraduate degree and $2,667 for a technical undergraduate degree. Check with the company for more specific salary information. NEES has excellent fringe benefits, including a tax-deferred, company-matched savings plan and reimbursement of educational expenses.

CONTACT

Suzanne Relyea, Manager of Employment, New England Electric Service, 25 Research Drive, Westborough, MA 01582.

NEW ENGLAND TELEPHONE

ACCOUNTING • COMPUTER SCIENCE • ENGINEERING • FINANCE • MANAGEMENT • MARKETING

THE COMPANY

New England Telephone is a telecommunications company that provides service to Maine, Massachusetts, New Hampshire, Rhode Island, and Vermont. It is headquartered in Boston and employs 40,000 people. New England Telephone is part of NYNEX, one of seven companies that emerged from AT&T's divestiture in 1984, and one of the largest corporations in America.

ALL TRAINING PROGRAMS

NYNEX's centralized training organization has a budget of $45 million and a faculty of 700. The company offers more than 800 different courses. The New England Telephone Learning Center in Marlboro, Massachusetts, offers classroom instruction in virtually every facet of company operations, from computer systems to labor relations, from telemarketing to effective writing. When you join the company you'll probably receive some training at Marlboro, and you may return for supplementary classes several times during your first year on the job. The Learning Center features multimedia classrooms, a resource center, and a closed-circuit television system that enables students to view instructional programs in the comfort of motel-style living quarters.

ACCOUNTING PROGRAM

This department provides an opportunity for accountants to combine their specific training with supervision responsibility. For the nonaccountant, it is an opportunity to gain some knowledge in the area while using already acquired skills in writing and supervision. As a management trainee, you'll be assigned to a methods development, administrative, or supervisory position in any one of the company's areas—such as billing, payroll, or settlement.

QUALIFICATIONS

You should have a degree in accounting or business with a class ranking in the top 50 percent.

ENGINEERING PROGRAM

These departments offer graduates with engineering backgrounds the rare opportunity to combine their technical skills with managerial responsibilities today—not in eight or ten years. Through a two-year Management Training Program, you will develop specifications for and supervise the installation of new plant, switching and transmission systems. Engineers see that buildings are designed to handle new and existing communications equipment, and they make economic studies of alternative plans to determine maximum long-term advantages.

QUALIFICATIONS

You will need a bachelor's or master's degree in engineering and a ranking in the top half of your class.

FINANCE PROGRAM

As a management trainee, you will immediately become involved in research, including economic forecasting and analysis, econometric modeling, cost estimating and pricing for products and services.

QUALIFICATIONS

You should have a bachelor's or master's degree in business or finance.

INFORMATION SYSTEMS ORGANIZATION PROGRAM

Entry-level programmers are trained in data processing theory, structural programming systems analysis, top-down development using different programming languages and JCL training, time-sharing utilization, and an introduction to random-access theory. Advancement within the department can be technical and/or managerial.

QUALIFICATIONS

In addition to a class ranking in the top 50 percent, you will need a bachelor's or master's degree in computer science or information systems.

MANAGEMENT PROGRAM

The Corporate Development Program uses formal training during the first twelve months you are on the job; it runs concurrently with on-the-job training that lasts as long as twenty-four months. You'll be assigned a supervisor to work with you during your first year and to help devise a plan of study. Feedback sessions occur every three months to review your progress and plans for growth. Additionally, the company will grant leaves of absence for graduate study and will reimburse you for your tuition and fees.

QUALIFICATIONS

The company hires from a variety of backgrounds for management, including business, liberal arts, computer science, and marketing.

MARKETING PROGRAM

As an entry-level employee, you'll receive classroom training in marketing and sales in a technical environment. Then, as an associate account executive, you'll move out into the field, where you'll offer sales and service on high-technology information processing.

QUALIFICATIONS

You will meet the company's qualifications if you have a bachelor's or master's degree in accounting, business, computer science, math, physics, liberal arts, marketing, or engineering, and are in the top 50 percent of your class.

ALL PROGRAMS

RECRUITMENT AND PLACEMENT

Representatives of New England Telephone visit many campuses in the Northeast looking for qualified graduates and conducting interviews. The company seeks administrators; civil, electrical, industrial, and mechanical engineers; mathematicians; and computer science personnel. Initial placement can be in Maine, Massachusetts, New Hampshire, Rhode Island, or Vermont.

SALARY AND BENEFITS

The College Placement Council Salary Survey for September 1986–June 1987 indicates starting salaries for public utilities to be $1,905 a month for those with a B.A. degree in nontechnical curricula and $2,355 with a B.A. degree in technical curricula. M.B.A. starting salaries were $2,403 for a nontechnical undergraduate degree and $2,667 for a technical undergraduate degree. Check with the company for more specific salary information. Benefits include medical, dental, and vision insurance; a supplemental medical expense plan; life insurance; 100 percent tuition reimbursement for outside courses; savings plan; stock options; pension; vacations and holidays; and approved moving expenses.

CONTACT

Howard O'Hara, Manager—Employment, New England Telephone, Lincoln Plaza, 103 South Street, Boston, MA 02111

NEW YORK LIFE INSURANCE COMPANY

ACCOUNTING • ACTUARIAL SCIENCE • ADMINISTRATION • COMPUTER SCIENCE • FINANCE • HUMAN RESOURCES • INFORMATION SYSTEMS • MARKETING • RESEARCH AND DEVELOPMENT • SALES

THE COMPANY

New York Life provides a wide variety of life and health insurance, annuities, and pension plans for individuals and groups. Founded in 1845, the company now has more than 18,000 employees and $29 billion-plus in assets. New York Life is the fifth largest life insurance company in the United States, according to the Fortune 50 largest commercial bank ranking, and it is listed among *Fortune*'s most admired corporations.

ALL TRAINING PROGRAMS

You will receive on-the-job training and a series of job rotations to prepare you for your new career.

ACTUARIAL TRAINEE PROGRAM

Training prepares you to deal with technical and practical insurance problems. The company puts you to work learning a wide variety of job duties. Working under an experienced supervisor, you will receive training in the development of new forms of insurance protection, determining proper premium rates and dividends, and calculating the amount of reserves needed to assure payment of future claims. The company provides support to assist you in preparing and passing the Society of Actuaries series of exams. Many of the trainees have passed the first two examinations while in college.

QUALIFICATIONS

An undergraduate or graduate degree in math or a closely related field is required. To become an actuary, superior mathematical ability and the motivation to prepare and pass the series of examinations given by the Society of Actuaries are required.

COMPUTER PROGRAM

New York Life has been an industry leader in the use of electronic data processing equipment. The program combines on-the-job experience with additional instruction as needed. It assists you in learning the principles of life insurance, fundamentals of office methods and procedures, and the operation and programming of large-scale computers. Ongoing professional development is important at New York Life. You are encouraged to continue your learning and to participate in professional associations.

QUALIFICATIONS

New York Life is looking for college graduates with a talent for solving problems in a logical and creative manner. Although not required, mathematics and data processing courses are assets.

GROUP INSURANCE PROGRAM

Training will prepare you to provide low-cost insurance to groups. There are a number of trainee assignments available in the Group Life Insurance Department. You might work as a claims examiner, correspondent, contract analyst, mathematics analyst, or underwriter. Your on-the-job experience may be supplemented with additional instruction to prepare you for certain duties.

QUALIFICATIONS

A specific college degree or academic background is not required. Some of the positions are heavily analytical, and others involve statistical work. Good writing and verbal communication skills are necessary.

ALL PROGRAMS

RECRUITMENT

The company recruits nationally. You will work in the home office in New York City.

SALARY AND BENEFITS

The College Placement Council Salary Survey for September 1986–June 1987 indicates starting salaries for banking, finance, and insurance companies to be $1,889 a month for those with a B.A. degree in nontechnical curricula and $2,135 with a B.A. degree in technical curricula. M.B.A. starting salaries were $2,884 for a nontechnical undergraduate degree and $3,320 for a technical undergraduate degree. Check with the company for more specific salary information. Your benefits package will include life insurance, health and dental insurance, flextime options, pension and profit-sharing plans, and tuition reimbursement.

CONTACT

Angela Coleman, Manager, Advanced and Technical Employment, New York Life Insurance Company, P.O. Box 106, Madison Square Station, New York, NY 10010.

NEW YORK TELEPHONE

COMPUTER SCIENCE • MANAGEMENT • SALES

THE COMPANY

New York Telephone is a major telephone and telecommunications utility. In addition to its mid-Manhattan headquarters, New York Telephone has regional operations centers in New York City, Garden City, Buffalo, Syracuse, Albany, and White Plains. Over 61,000 employees provide communications to more than 6.5 million customers throughout New York State and the Greenwich and Byram areas of Connecticut. In 1984,

New York Telephone joined with New England Telephone as partners in NYNEX, one of seven regional holding companies formed from the 22 Bell System operating companies which were divested by AT&T. As part of NYNEX, with assets of more than $21 billion, New York Telephone offers opportunities which can expand beyond its own corporate structure. New York Telephone is the second largest private employer in New York State. Listed among *Fortune*'s most admired corporations, it is ranked number 3 in the Fortune 50 largest utility companies.

MANAGEMENT TRAINING PROGRAM

The company's Management Career Development Program is an intensive plan that increases your responsibility over an average of two years. You'll be on a fast track designed to challenge your initiative and talent. From your first day in the program, you'll be required to set objectives; make decisions about people and productivity; meet goals, design and implement projects to be measured on quality and cost; initiate new procedures and work in unfamiliar areas. In the process, you'll learn about the business and supervision. You'll be evaluated periodically.

QUALIFICATIONS

To qualify for MCDP, you must have at least a four-year college degree; show scholastic excellence with a ranking in the top third of your class or a B+ average; and demonstrate leadership in extracurricular activities and/or previous business experience. In addition, you must satisfy the company's testing and assessment standards.

RECRUITMENT AND PLACEMENT

Representatives of New York Telephone actively recruit at campuses in the Northeast. All assignments are in New York.

SALARY AND BENEFITS

The College Placement Council Salary Survey for September 1986–June 1987 indicates starting salaries for public utilities to be $1,905 a month for those with a B.A. degree in nontechnical curricula and $2,355 with a B.A. degree in technical curricula. M.B.A. starting salaries were $2,403 for a nontechnical undergraduate degree and $2,667 for a technical undergraduate degree. Check with the company for more specific salary information.

CONTACT

Jon C. Abeles, Staff Director, Management Employment, New York Telephone, 1095 Avenue of the Americas, New York, NY 10036.

NIAGARA MOHAWK POWER CORPORATION

ENGINEERING

THE COMPANY

Niagara Mohawk Power provides electricity and gas to a 24,000-square-mile area of New York. It employs over 10,000 people and maintains headquarters in Syracuse, New York. The company is ranked number 29 in the Fortune 50 largest utility companies.

ENGINEERING TRAINING PROGRAM

Training consists of a combination of formal classroom instruction and supervised on-the-job experience.

QUALIFICATIONS

You should have a bachelor's or a master's degree in chemical engineering, chemistry, civil engineering, computer science, electrical engineering, mechanical engineering, or nuclear engineering. A minimum G.P.A. of 2.0 is required. If you have a technical degree and one to ten years of work experience, you will have an advantage.

RECRUITMENT AND PLACEMENT

The company recruits in the Northeast, the mid-Atlantic states, the Southeast, and the Southwest. Your starting location will be in New York.

SALARY AND BENEFITS

If you have a bachelor's degree, your starting salary will be $23,500. The company will reimburse 75 percent of your tuition and fees for job-related graduate study.

CONTACT

Manager, Employee Relations—Nuclear, Niagara Mohawk Power Corp., 301 Plainfield Road, Syracuse, NY 13212.

NL INDUSTRIES

BUSINESS ADMINISTRATION • COMPUTER SCIENCE • ENGINEERING • GEOLOGY • MINING • SCIENCE

THE COMPANY

NL Industries, formed in 1891, is a leading worldwide manufacturer and supplier of petroleum services and equipment, pigments and specialty chemicals, and fabricated metal products. NL is one of the world's leading producers of drilling fluids, equipment and services for oil and gas well drilling, die casting, and titanium pigments. The industries it serves are a cross section of the economy: aerospace, automotive, appliance, chemical processing, construction, coatings, cosmetics, furniture, natural gas, paper, petroleum, plastic, railroad, and rubber industries. NL industries has 100 plants and mines worldwide. Annual sales top $1 billion. NL ranks number 252 in the Fortune 500 largest U.S. industrial corporations.

ALL TRAINING PROGRAMS

Training is primarily on the job, lasts from six to twelve months, and covers a wide variety of positions. Job rotations are set up about every three months. A multimillion-dollar Career Development Center in Houston offers living accommodations, classrooms, laboratories, an on-site drilling rig, several test wells, and drilling simulation equipment. Both employees and customers may receive training in technical areas, in management development, and in marketing and sales. Programs are performance-oriented and conducted in individualized, self-paced modules. Extensive use is made of specially developed media programs.

QUALIFICATIONS

NL Industries recruits candidates with bachelor's and master's degrees in engineering, chemistry, computer science, geology, materials science, mining, polymer science, and business.

RECRUITMENT AND PLACEMENT

Depending on the division that hires you, placement is possible in any of the fifty states.

SALARY AND BENEFITS

Starting salaries average $24,000 to $32,000. Your benefits package will include comprehensive health and dental care, accident insurance, business travel and life insurance, a pension plan, savings plan, educational assistance program, and an employee stockownership plan.

CONTACT

Manager, College Relations, NL Industries, 19130 Oil Center Boulevard, Houston, TX 77073.

NORFOLK SOUTHERN CORPORATION

ENGINEERING • INFORMATION SYSTEMS • MANAGEMENT • MARKETING • PRODUCTION • OPERATIONS • RESEARCH AND DEVELOPMENT

THE COMPANY

Norfolk Southern Corporation owns and operates the Southern Railway System, headquartered in Atlanta, Georgia, and the Norfolk & Western Railway Company, headquartered in Roanoke, Virginia. Both railroads provide freight service. Norfolk & Western is the oldest of the major railways in the United States. Founded in 1838, its original eight-mile track connected Petersburg and City Point in Virginia. During the first half of the twentieth century the Norfolk & Western Railway made most of its money by shipping coal from West Virginia coalfields to the steel industries of Ohio and Pennsylvania. Today it is listed among *Fortune*'s most admired corporations and has annual sales exceeding $4 billion. It ranks tenth in the Fortune 50 largest transportation companies.

ALL TRAINING PROGRAMS

Training prepares new employees for management positions and for careers in marketing and management information systems. The program takes six to twelve months and offers both classroom and on-the-job experience.

QUALIFICATIONS

You will need a degree in business (B.S. or M.B.A.), mathematics, computer science, marketing, transportation, economics, or engineering—electrical, civil, mechanical, or industrial. The company prefers those in the top third of their class and with a minimum G.P.A. of 2.5. The company is also interested in technical graduates with related work experience.

RECRUITMENT AND PLACEMENT

The company recruits in the East, the Midwest, and the South, hiring about 100 trainees a year. Starting locations are in Alabama, Georgia, North Carolina, South Carolina, Tennessee, and Virginia.

SALARY AND BENEFITS

Starting salaries range from $25,000 to $28,000 for a bachelor's degree and from $27,000 to $30,000 with a master's. Your benefits will include health plans, pension and stock-purchase plans, life insurance, relocation assistance, tuition reimbursement, and deferred compensation and savings plans.

CONTACT

Manager, Employment, Norfolk Southern Corporation, 125 Spring Street, Atlanta, GA 30303.

NORTHERN ILLINOIS GAS COMPANY

ACCOUNTING · ENGINEERING · INFORMATION SYSTEMS · MARKETING · SALES

THE COMPANY

Northern Illinois Gas (NI-Gas) is a public utility engaged principally in the purchase, storage, distribution, and sale of natural gas. Formed from predecessor firms in 1954, NI-Gas has a service territory of about 17,000 square miles in the northern third of Illinois excluding Chicago. The company provides gas energy to an estimated population of 5 million people living in 544 communities and maintains about 24,000 miles of gas pipeline.

ALL TRAINING PROGRAMS

Training for engineers lasts twelve to eighteen months and includes project experience in pipelines, underground storage, station design engineering, and gas system planning. Accountants receive extensive on-the-job training in the preparation of monthly financial statements, government regulations, and the company's sophisticated computerized accounting system. Supervised on-the-job instruction is combined with classroom training.

QUALIFICATIONS

The company is recruiting accountants, auditors (with two to three years of experience), information systems personnel (with two years of experience and knowledge of COBOL), and engineers—chemical, civil, industrial, and mechanical. The company expects you to have good communication skills. Occasional openings also occur in finance, marketing/sales, and public relations.

RECRUITMENT AND PLACEMENT

The company recruits in the Midwest. Corporate headquarters are in Naperville, Illinois, about thirty-five miles from downtown Chicago.

SALARY AND BENEFITS

The College Placement Council Salary Survey for September 1986–June 1987 indicates starting salaries for public utilities to be $1,905 a month for those with a B.A. degree in nontechnical curricula and $2,355 with a B.A. degree in technical curricula. M.B.A. starting salaries were $2,403 for a nontechnical undergraduate degree and $2,667 for a technical undergraduate degree. Check with the company for more specific salary information. Employee benefits include life, medical, and hospitalization insurance; a retirement plan; a stock-purchase plan; a savings investment plan; and an educational assistance program.

CONTACT

Susan C. Virgilio, Senior Recruiting and Training Administrator, Northern Illinois Gas Company, P.O. Box 190, Aurora, IL 60507.

NORTHROP CORPORATION

BUSINESS ADMINISTRATION • ENGINEERING • INFORMATION SYSTEMS • PRODUCTION • RESEARCH AND DEVELOPMENT

THE COMPANY

Northrop Corporation is a high-technology company involved in military aircraft, commercial airframe structures, navigation, and electronics. Northrop's specialty is making aircraft parts for other companies, but it also makes its own aircraft, the F-5 Freedom Fighter jet, which *Forbes* called the "Pinto of the fighter market." The F-5 Freedom Fighter has become the favorite of countries all over the world. The company was founded in 1939 by John K. Northrop, the designer responsible for the Black Widow night fighter of World War I and the Lockheed Vega, which was used by Amelia Earhart in her solo flight across the Atlantic in 1932. Today, Northrop employs 41,500 people in seven principal divisions, a research and technology center, production centers, and offices worldwide. With more than $5 billion in annual sales, Northrop is listed among *Fortune*'s most admired corporations and ranks number 64 in the Fortune 500 largest U.S. industrial corporations.

ALL TRAINING PROGRAMS

Business graduates are trained in an eighteen-month rotation program. You'll spend a few months in finance, materials, contracts, and pricing. All engineering graduates have extensive on-the-job training for six to twelve months under senior-level engineers. Manufacturing engineers spend twelve to twenty-four months in formal training.

QUALIFICATIONS

Northrop hires college graduates primarily in the engineering and engineering-related disciplines, computer science, business, finance, accounting, and physics. Related student work experience will enhance your possibility of being hired.

RECRUITMENT AND PLACEMENT

Northrop recruits extensively across the country through college and university placement offices. Major division offices are in or around Los Angeles, outside Chicago, in Norwood, Massachusetts, and in Kansas City, Missouri.

SALARY AND BENEFITS

The College Placement Council Salary Survey for September 1986–June 1987 indicates starting salaries for aerospace companies to be $1,943 a month for those with a B.A. degree in nontechnical curricula and $2,399 with a B.A. degree in technical curricula. M.B.A. starting salaries were $2,330 for a nontechnical undergraduate degree and $2,475 for a technical undergraduate degree. Check with the company for more specific salary information. You will be eligible for medical and dental coverage, life insurance, and disability protection. Northrop also provides a retirement plan and a savings program, as well as career development programs, tuition reimbursement, a credit union, and a recreation club. Benefits vary according to work location, so check with the specific division or center.

CONTACT

Dr. James McNeely, Manager of Corporate College Relations, Northrop Corporation, 1840 Century Park East, Los Angeles, CA 90067.

NORTHWESTERN MUTUAL LIFE INSURANCE COMPANY

LIFE INSURANCE SALES

THE COMPANY

Known as "The Quiet Company," Northwestern also has a reputation in its home city of Milwaukee as the company that gives its employees a free lunch. The city's largest employer spends about $3 million a year to provide this benefit in a four-star cafeteria but considers the expense well worth the cost since its employees rank as the most productive in the insurance industry. Northwestern introduced the concept of flextime and spent two years retraining employees in a program to revamp job descriptions and minimize boredom for clerical workers.

With more than $20 billion in assets in 1986, Northwestern is the seventy-second largest business in the United States in assets. It has $120.6 billion worth of insurance in force. As a mutual company, Northwestern is owned by its clients. It invests their money soundly but aggressively and returns it in higher dividends. Listed among *Fortune*'s most admired corporations, Northwestern is the tenth largest life insurance company. Agents attend an annual convention in Milwaukee each summer that recharges them for another year of selling. Most Northwestern agents do quite well financially. More than a fourth of the company's 5,134 full-time agents were members of the Million Dollar Round Table for 1985, indicating that their sales totaled a million dollars or more.

SALES TRAINING PROGRAM

You will participate in a five-year training program that emphasizes on-the-job education, with close supervision and training by the local agency and home office. Courses will include: essentials of life underwriting; the sales cycle; client building; advanced personal planning; business insurance planning; and an advanced underwriting seminar. Almost half of Northwestern's agents hold the Chartered Life Underwriter designation. You'll take part in a Personal Progress Program to spot your weaknesses and strengths and will receive counseling as necessary. A student intern program allows college students to try out insurance selling before they graduate.

QUALIFICATIONS

Backgrounds considered helpful are accounting, economics, finance, general business, graduate business, insurance, law, liberal arts, marketing, and management. Northwestern finds that those who enter directly from school and military service do better than those with other occupational backgrounds. You should place a high value on personal independence and be "a confident type who aggressively seeks out what you want in life."

RECRUITMENT AND PLACEMENT

Northwestern recruits on college campuses, or you may contact the nearest sales office for an application. The company has 112 general agencies in major cities and 293 district agencies coast to coast.

SALARIES AND BENEFITS

Your salary is open-ended but you will receive a training allowance for incentive income during the first three years of your career as you build a client base. A recent study of 1,500 agents showed that the average earnings were $30,742, with the average income of NML agents increasing 40 percent from 1982 to 1986. The top 700 agents averaged $126,663 annually (before expenses), and the top 25 averaged $496,074. You receive additional commissions each time a policy is renewed for a nine-year period, and "persistency fees" after that may well make up as much as 40 to 50 percent of your salary when you are established. Benefits include group life and multimedical insurance and a retirement plan.

CONTACT

Northwestern Mutual Life Insurance Company, 720 East Wisconsin Avenue, Milwaukee, WI 53202.

O

☆ ☆ ☆ ☆ ☆

OCCIDENTAL CHEMICAL CORPORATION

SALES/MARKETING

THE COMPANY

Operating as the chemical division of Occidental Petroleum Corporation, Occidental Chemical Corporation (OxyChem) is a diversified manufacturer supplying raw materials, intermediate and finished chemical products, technology, and engineering worldwide. OxyChem concentrates its growth on three core businesses: agricultural products, plastics, and industrial and specialty chemicals. Major recent developments include three key acquisitions: Diamond Shamrock Chemicals Company, Tenneco Polymers, Inc., and the dicalcium phosphate business of American Cyanamid. As a result, OxyChem is now the largest merchant marketer of chlor/alkali and polyvinyl chloride (PVC) resin in the United States. The company is also the world's leading producer of potassium hydroxide, the number one U.S. manufacturer of chrome chemicals, and the number two producer of silicates. OxyChem operates more than 50 manufacturing facilities internationally with more than 12,000 people. Annual sales stood at about $2.75 billion in 1987, making OxyChem the tenth largest chemical company in the United States. The company is looking for young people with an aggressive, competitive outlook blended with a sensitivity and concern for the interests of its customers. OxyChem is interested in what makes you tick as a person: your imagination, your drive, your curiosity.

SALES/MARKETING TRAINING PROGRAM

In the six-month Chemical Sales Training Program, you accompany experienced people on customer calls; visit production and research sites; learn about transportation, purchasing, legal, and customer service departments; and are exposed to current marketing techniques. You will be expected to acquire a working knowledge of the company's products by listening to presentations and reading product literature.

QUALIFICATIONS

OxyChem requires a college degree, preferably technical, a minimum overall G.P.A. of 2.5, participation in extracurricular activities that shows leadership skills, an ability to relate to people, self-motivation, an outgoing personality, an optimistic outlook, and integrity.

RECRUITMENT AND PLACEMENT

The company recruits at several campuses in the fall and spring, and throughout the year at regional sales offices in Edison, New Jersey; Marlton, New Jersey; Atlanta, Georgia; Naperville, Illinois; San Mateo, California; Houston, Texas; and Moreland Hills, Ohio. Sales training is conducted at the headquarters in Dallas with field sales territories throughout the United States.

SALARY AND BENEFITS

The College Placement Council Salary Survey for September 1986–June 1987 indicates starting salaries for chemical, drug, and allied products companies to be $1,964 a month for those with a B.A. degree in nontechnical curricula and $2,457 with a B.A. degree in technical curricula. M.B.A. starting salaries were $2,886 for a nontechnical undergraduate degree and $2,794 for a technical undergraduate degree. Check with the company for more specific salary information. Benefits include tuition reimbursement; major medical, dental, life, and long-term disability insurance; savings and retirement plans; and a relocation plan.

CONTACT

James S. Zolnier, Manager, Sales Training and Recruiting, Occidental Chemical Corporation, 351 Phelps Court, Irving, TX 75015.

OHIO EDISON COMPANY

ENGINEERING • INFORMATION SYSTEMS • MARKETING • PRODUCTION • SALES

THE COMPANY

Ohio Edison is an electric service company based in Akron, Ohio. The company employs about 6,700 people. It has assets exceeding $7 billion and is ranked number 28 in the Fortune 50 largest utilities.

ALL TRAINING PROGRAMS

The program lasts from one to three months and consists of supervised on-the-job experience and classroom instruction. You will be offered seminars and short courses during your career to help keep your skills current.

QUALIFICATIONS

You should have a G.P.A. of at least 2.7. The company is looking for graduates with degrees in computer science, electrical engineering, information systems, mathematics, and mechanical engineering and statistics. Applications are also encouraged from business graduates. Ohio Edison prefers trainees who have some student work experience.

RECRUITMENT AND PLACEMENT

The company hires about 50 trainees a year. Starting locations are in Ohio and Pennsylvania.

SALARY AND BENEFITS

The College Placement Council Salary Survey for September 1986–June 1987 indicates starting salaries for public utilities to be $1,905 a month for those with a B.A. degree in nontechnical curricula and $2,355 with a B.A. degree in technical curricula. M.B.A. starting salaries were $2,403 for a nontechnical undergraduate degree and $2,667 for a technical undergraduate degree. Check with the company for more specific salary information. Ohio Edison offers life insurance, flextime options, relocation assistance, tuition reimbursement, and health plans.

CONTACT

Diane L. Erickson, Employment Coordinator, Ohio Edison Company, 76 South Main Street, Akron, OH 44308.

OHIO POWER COMPANY

ENGINEERING • MANAGEMENT

THE COMPANY

Ohio Power, a subsidiary of American Electric Power Company, is an electric service company. Based in Canton, Ohio, it employs nearly 4,500 people.

ALL TRAINING PROGRAMS

Your training will include both supervised on-the-job experience and classroom instruction.

QUALIFICATIONS

For the engineering program, you should have a degree in chemistry, civil engineering, electrical engineering, engineering science, environmental engineering, environmental science, or mechanical engineering. For the management program, the company is looking for graduates with degrees in business.

RECRUITMENT AND PLACEMENT

Starting locations are in Ohio and West Virginia.

SALARY AND BENEFITS

The College Placement Council Salary Survey for September 1986–June 1987 indicates starting salaries for public utilities to be $1,905 a month for those with a B.A. degree in nontechnical curricula and $2,355 with a B.A. degree in technical curricula. M.B.A. starting salaries were $2,403 for a nontechnical undergraduate degree and $2,667 for a technical undergraduate degree. Check with the company for more specific salary information. The company will reimburse up to 75 percent of job-related continued education.

CONTACT

Gregory G. Pauley, Personnel Services Manager, Ohio Power Company, P.O. Box 400, 301 Cleveland Avenue S.W., Canton, OH 44701.

OLIN CORPORATION

ENGINEERING • SALES/MARKETING

THE COMPANY

Olin Corporation is a diversified company with a concentration on chemicals, metals, and applied physics. Drawing on its expertise in these fields, the company is placing special emphasis on expansion in three high-growth markets: aerospace/defense, electronic materials and services, and water quality management. Headquartered in Stamford, Connecticut, Olin employs 16,000 people worldwide and has annual sales over $1.5 billion. It ranks number 204 in the Fortune 500 largest U.S. industrial corporations.

ENGINEERING AND SALES/MARKETING TRAINING PROGRAMS

The company provides both formal and on-the-job training for new employees in sales and marketing, production, and engineering. The training lasts from one to two and a half years, depending on the group to which you belong. You will receive a general orientation of company philosophy and policies and regular feedback/coaching sessions. Self-study will involve the use of manuals, computer programs, and videotapes. You will be recognized for achievement if you excel in training.

QUALIFICATIONS

Olin seeks qualified men and women for positions in engineering, marketing and sales, finance, accounting, computer science, and data processing. Engineering specialties include aerospace, environmental, chemical, mechanical, industrial, electrical, and metallurgical. You will need a bachelor's or a master's degree in one of these subjects. Your chances of being hired will improve with a high G.P.A., one or more years of related work experience, strong interpersonal skills, versatility, and ambition.

RECRUITMENT AND PLACEMENT

The company recruits from colleges and universities and also accepts applications for employment at all its domestic facilities. New employees are assigned to plants in major metropolitan areas of the Northeastern, Southern, and Midwestern United States.

SALARY AND BENEFITS

The College Placement Council Salary Survey for September 1986–June 1987 indicates starting salaries for chemical, drug, and allied products companies to be $1,964 a month for those with a B.A. degree in nontechnical curricula and $2,457 with a B.A. degree in technical curricula. M.B.A. starting salaries were $2,886 for a nontechnical undergraduate degree and $2,794 for a technical undergraduate degree. Check with the company for more specific salary information.

Olin also provides benefits that include paid vacations and holidays, comprehensive short-term and long-term disability protection, group life insurance, dental care assistance, and a pension plan. Olin provides its employees with generous tuition assistance and a long-term savings 401K plan.

CONTACT

Corporate Manager, Staffing, Olin Corporation, 120 Long Ridge Road, Stamford, CT 06904.

OPPENHEIM, APPEL, DIXON & COMPANY

ACCOUNTING • MANAGEMENT • TAX CONSULTING

THE COMPANY

Oppenheim, Appel, Dixon & Company has been a certified public accounting firm since 1953. But its history goes back to 1919, when Michael Appel had his own accounting practice. Currently the firm offers a full range of auditing and accounting services, tax counseling, and management advisory services. The firm has a growing network of offices in key cities in the United States as well as 60 offices internationally.

ALL TRAINING PROGRAMS

You will be required to take forty hours of continuing education annually, either company-designed programs or educational programs offered by professional societies and organizations. During the first three months you will receive an office orientation, basic auditing and tax training, information on current developments in the auditing field, and specialized industry programs.

QUALIFICATIONS

The company is recruiting accounting graduates, law graduates with undergraduate accounting degrees, and M.B.A. graduates in accounting and taxation.

RECRUITMENT AND PLACEMENT

The company recruits and places new employees nationwide.

SALARY AND BENEFITS

The College Placement Council Salary Survey for September 1986–June 1987 indicates starting salaries for public accounting firms to be $1,834 a month for those with a B.A. degree in nontechnical curricula and $2,155 with a B.A. degree in technical curricula. M.B.A. starting salaries were $2,335 for a nontechnical undergraduate degree, and $2,436 for an M.B.A. with technical undergraduate degree. Check with the company for more specific salary information. Benefits include hospital and medical insurance, disability and group life insurance, tuition reimbursement, and reimbursement of dues and subscriptions for professional societies and publications.

CONTACT

Personnel Partner, Oppenheim, Appel, Dixon & Company, One New York Plaza, New York, NY 10004.

OWENS-CORNING FIBERGLAS CORPORATION

ADMINISTRATION • COMPUTER SCIENCE • ENGINEERING • FINANCE • RESEARCH • SALES

THE COMPANY

Owens-Corning Fiberglas Corporation is the world's leading manufacturer of glass fiber products, which it sells under the trademark Fiberglas. A diversified company, Owens-Corning also has manufacturing operations with related materials and operational units for distribution and wholesaling of company products, as well as installation services, fabrication operations, and construction. The company was founded in 1938 as a joint venture of Owens-Illinois and Corning Glass Works to manufacture and commercially market glass fiber products. Owens-Corning operated as a subsidiary of the two parent companies until it became a public corporation in 1952. Today Owens-Corning's yearly sales are in excess of $3 billion. It has more than 22,000 employees, operates over 70 manufacturing plants in the United States, and has sales offices in 85 cities. Subsidiary and affiliate operations are located in 15 countries. Corporate headquarters are in Toledo, Ohio. Listed among *Fortune*'s most admired corporations, it ranks number 107 in the Fortune 500 largest U.S. industrial corporations.

ALL TRAINING PROGRAMS

If you have less than a year's experience in your field, you will participate in a general development program emphasizing on-the-job training. Expect to receive detailed appraisals and feedback from managers. Monthly progress reports also provide you with self-evaluation. All new employees attend a one-week general orientation school at corporate headquarters, designed to familiarize them with corporate functions and Owens-Corning's philosophy. The program includes presentations by and discussions with top managers from all functional areas of the company. During your initial years with the company, training programs are geared to the development of technical knowledge and skill in your particular area of expertise. You may—at company expense—participate in seminars, workshops, or conferences. As your career develops, training begins to center on acquiring general business knowledge and management skills. As you move into supervisory positions, company training in problem solving and decision making, professional management, field management, and supervisory development are included. You will receive annual performance appraisals to assess whether you are meeting mutually established standards of performance. The company also offers a career self-development program to help you achieve your goals and enhance your job satisfaction.

QUALIFICATIONS

Owens-Corning hires from all educational backgrounds, from bachelor's to doctoral degrees, and is looking for both recent graduates and those with job experience.

RECRUITMENT AND PLACEMENT

The company recruits nationwide. Examples of assignments are: systems analyst, corporate or divisional staff, Toledo, Ohio; researcher, Technical Center, Granville, Ohio; accountant, any of the major manufacturing facilities, Technical Center, Granville, Ohio, or the corporate staff in Toledo; customer service representative, any of 14 service centers or 55 supply centers nationwide. It is common for trainees to be relocated during their initial years of employment.

SALARY AND BENEFITS

Starting salaries for those with a bachelor's degree range from $21,000 to $28,000. Check with the company for starting salaries with a master's or a doctorate. Benefits include group health insurance, salary continuation, long-term disability, life insurance, paid vacations, a savings and deferral investment plan, educational refund plan, retirement, and relocation assistance.

CONTACT

Corporate Employment Department, Owens-Corning Fiberglas Corporation, Fiberglas Tower, Toledo, OH 43659.

Advice from a University Career-Placement Center
Dr. Howard Figler, University of Texas

Dr. Howard Figler, Director of University of Texas Liberal Arts Placement Center, previously spent four years at Dickinson College in Carlisle, Pennsylvania, a liberal arts school, where he was director of the Counseling and Career Placement Center.

☆ ☆ ☆ ☆ ☆

Are companies interested in the liberal arts grad, and if they are, what does the trainee get out of the program?

There have been at least two major studies demonstrating that liberal arts majors advance higher and faster once they have a few years with the company—the AT & T study and the Chase Manhattan study. Today there's much more overall consciousness that liberal arts majors often become leaders. Corporations like their broad analytical skills, and they like their communication skills. This group is able to see the big picture and think broadly, and they're going to communicate it very well, in person and in writing.

From the perspective of the trainee, you learn what it's like to work in a large organization and whether or not you want to be part of a big one, and that's important in decision making for the future. So that would be a good reason to get into a training program, even if you didn't want to stay.

You also get a certain amount of speaking and writing skills. A lot of skills training goes on in those programs that you won't get in a small business. Management skills, organizational skills—they'll teach you anything that they think can be taught. Large organizations have got the money to do it and they're committed to training their future managers as much as they possibly can. A tremendous amount of training goes on at the entry level.

In contrast to some of the training that a student receives in college, training programs emphasize practical application of skills.

Yes, it's all applied training, covering many of the things the liberal arts undergrad may not have gotten in school. Certainly they take good people and make them better, or they may take an unfinished person and make him or her into a smoother product for the business world.

I once, a long time ago, worked in a large corporation, Prudential Insurance, and we did some research and found that people who stayed at least five years tended to stay a long, long time. So the message to the young person is: up to a certain point, if you stay long enough you'd better be prepared to stay forever because there's something about the large organization that can kind of suck you in. My advice to most people is not to stay that long because you've got to try some other things. Now the company may not like that, because the company wants to keep you forever, but you've got to look at it from your own perspective.

In particular today, I think the chance to sample the large organization is important because so many job opportunities are in small organizations. You want to be able to compare large versus small.

Have you seen any changes in training programs during the last ten years?

Maybe fifteen or more years ago, training programs were much more commonplace; everybody got into one, they were in vogue. Companies have become more selective about doing them. They realize that they're very expensive. But recently I would guess they're more technical. There are more mathematical models floating around. There are more financial skills people need to know about. Every new graduate needs to have some exposure to technical skills, because it's a more technical world.

How should a student compare different programs before selecting one?

Every company has its own culture—they're not all like IBM. Aside from the obvious things like the reputation of the company, I would look for those that rotate employees to different departments. If a company doesn't do that, to me that would be a negative, because I think it's important to have direct exposure to several departments. You have a better chance to decide where it is you think you can make the best contribution.

If they stick you in one department and force you to specialize from day one, I think that's a real mistake from a developmental perspective. That would be the main thing I would have students look for.

Get a feeling for the kind of people and how they see their lives, what they're trying to get out of their lives, and why they work there. See if you fit. And no matter how successful the company is, if you don't fit with those people you don't need to be there.

P

☆ ☆ ☆ ☆ ☆

PACIFIC GAS AND ELECTRIC COMPANY

COMPUTER SCIENCE · ENGINEERING · MARKETING · PRODUCTION · RESEARCH AND DEVELOPMENT · SALES

THE COMPANY

Pacific Gas and Electric is the fifth largest investor-owned utility in the country. The utility serves more than 10 million people in northern and central California and is one of the most progressive utilities in the nation. It has a goal of supplying 60 percent of new energy demands through alternative sources of energy, such as biomass, geothermal, wind, solar, and cogeneration, while continuing to use its traditional hydro and fossil fuel plants. With more than $21 billion in assets, Pacific Gas and Electric is listed among *Fortune*'s most admired corporations. The company employs more than 27,000 people in its operations in all major cities in northern and central California. This utility is doing leading-edge work and wants people to have the freedom to express their creativity yet still work cooperatively in a corporate environment.

ALL TRAINING PROGRAMS

Pacific Gas and Electric has an on-the-job plus classroom training program for 50 percent of its work force—the mix varies by department. You can expect to be rotated through different areas of your field as part of the on-the-job training. All formal training takes place in the Bay Area.

QUALIFICATIONS

Pacific Gas and Electric is looking for engineers, computer scientists, and business and economics professionals. Relevant degrees in those areas are necessary, and they're also looking for such intangibles as innovative spirit coupled with ability to be a team player. PG&E prefers graduates who rank in the top 25 percent of their class. The company actively recruits minorities and women.

RECRUITMENT AND PLACEMENT

It's likely you will be placed somewhere in northern or central California. Recruitment is ongoing.

SALARY AND BENEFITS

With a bachelor's degree your starting salary will range from $20,000 to $28,000, increasing to $30,000 with a master's. Benefits will add as much as 40 percent to your total compensation. You will receive life insurance, medical, hospital, dental insurance, pension, stock-purchase and profit-sharing plans, flextime options, and relocation assistance.

CONTACT

Supervisor of College Relations, Pacific Gas and Electric Company, 77 Beale Street, Room F1000, San Francisco, CA 94106.

PAINEWEBBER INCORPORATED

CORPORATE MANAGEMENT • MANAGEMENT INFORMATION SYSTEMS

THE COMPANY

New York-based PaineWebber offers brokerage and investment banking services to clients in the United States and abroad. It underwrites public offerings of securities, advises corporations on mergers and acquisitions, and trades securities for the firm's own profit. The company has helped bring such corporate giants as GTE and McDonald's to market. Founded in 1879, it went public in 1972. PaineWebber has 3,800 brokers in more than 285 offices worldwide.

CORPORATE INTERN TRAINING PROGRAM

In this fast-paced, two-year program you'll receive broad exposure to the many aspects of PaineWebber's business. During the first four months you will be given orientation to the company and the securities industry, followed by a branch office assignment with registration to become a broker. You will also attend a sales training program at the National Training Center. In the second phase you will be given core assignments in PaineWebber Asset Management, Capital Markets, and the Consumer Markets Group. Your training will conclude with eight months of work experience in three of the following: administrative division, branch administration, staff to senior management, advertising and public relations, finance and accounting, operations and systems, and legal and compliance. In addition, you will participate in a series of "Meeting the Management" luncheons to expose you to senior management. Special programs covering time management, effective presentations, conducting a meeting, product training, visits to exchanges, visits to branch offices, career guidance and counseling, and personal improvement modules will round out your training.

QUALIFICATIONS

You should have a bachelor's degree in business or liberal arts, and a G.P.A. of 3.0 or higher, with a solid record of extracurricular achievements. Related work experience or an internship in sales or the financial services industry is desirable.

RECRUITMENT AND PLACEMENT

The company invites résumés, or you may be able to arrange an interview on campus. You will begin your career in New York City.

SALARY AND BENEFITS

The College Placement Council Salary Survey for September 1986–June 1987 indicates starting salaries for banking, finance, and insurance firms to be $1,889 a month for those with a B.A. degree in nontechnical curricula and $2,135 with a B.A. degree in technical curricula. Check with the company for more specific salary information. You will be eligible for a comprehensive benefits plan that includes tuition assistance for M.B.A. study.

SYSTEMS INTERN TRAINING PROGRAM

In this eighteen-month program you will be given a broad exposure to the securities industry through intensive, on-location assignments in PaineWebber business units. You will begin with an orientation to the company and industry, followed by assignment to a branch office. You will become familiar with retail brokerage activities and operations and register to become a securities broker. In the next phase you will be assigned to one or more of the following areas: capital markets, consumer markets, finance and administration, administration, or operations. Finally, you will receive technical training for your initial systems assignment, covering programming languages, operating systems, data communications, database, systems analysis and design, and project management. You could be assigned to computer operations, communications, quality assurance, and one or more projects in systems development. In addition, you will meet members of senior management in a series of meetings and participate in classes on time management, effective presentations, technology updates, interpersonal skills, management training, participation in future recruiting, and stock exchange visits.

QUALIFICATIONS

You must have a bachelor's degree and a high level of academic and extracurricular achievement. Familiarity with computer systems, gained through either an academic environment or related work experience, is desirable. Familiarity with the financial services industry is a plus.

RECRUITMENT AND PLACEMENT

Applications are invited at the New York offices. You will train in New York City.

SALARY AND BENEFITS

The College Placement Council Salary Survey for September 1986–June 1987 indicates starting salaries for banking, finance, and insurance firms to be $1,889 a month for those with a B.A. degree in nontechnical curricula and $2,135 with a B.A. degree in technical curricula. Check with the company for more specific salary and benefits information.

CONTACT

For Corporate Intern Program: Training Center, PaineWebber, 120 Broadway, New York, NY 10271; for Systems Intern Program: Deborah A. Schiavo, Manager, Systems Intern Program, PaineWebber Incorporated, 25 Broad Street, New York, NY 10004.

PALAIS ROYALE
MANAGEMENT

THE COMPANY

Founded in 1921 with a store in downtown Houston, Palais Royale is a clothing chain with an average annual growth rate of 15 percent for the last several years. Sales volume for fiscal 1986 exceeded $130 million. Palais Royale stores' size, floor plans, and strategic locations contribute to sales of $299 per square foot of selling area, double the national average for comparable stores of $144 per square foot. Over 95 percent of the company's recruits who have moved up to management came from Texas colleges and universities.

MANAGEMENT TRAINING

As you prepare for a career as management trainee or assistant area manager, you will spend several months in a Palais Royale store. There, with guidance, you will improve your management skills as you handle day-to-day situations. You will also attend seminars and workshops conducted by senior managers who run the various divisions in the company. They will introduce you to sales supervision/customer service, merchandise presentation, loss prevention, credit, time management, and communication skills.

QUALIFICATIONS

Palais Royale looks for college graduates from a variety of backgrounds with proven leadership ability.

RECRUITMENT AND PLACEMENT

The company recruits on campuses throughout Texas. Placement will be in Houston, Corpus Christi, Beaumont, or Orange, Texas.

SALARIES AND BENEFITS

The College Placement Council Salary Survey for September 1986–June 1987 indicates starting salaries for merchandising (retail and wholesale) and service companies to be $1,594 a month for those with a B.A. degree in nontechnical curricula and $2,141 with a B.A. degree in technical curricula. M.B.A. starting salaries were $2,572 for a nontechnical undergraduate degree and $2,735 for an M.B.A. with technical undergraduate degree. Check with the company for more specific salary information. Your benefits package will include a choice of two medical plans, dental plan, life insurance, 25 percent discount on all merchandise, credit union, two weeks' paid holiday, seven paid holidays, retirement plan, and tuition refund.

CONTACT

Palais Royale, Director of Human Resource Development, 10201 South Main, Houston, TX 77025.

PANNELL KERR FORSTER

ACCOUNTING

THE COMPANY

One of the 15 largest accounting firms in the United States, PKF is a full-service firm whose clients range from multinational corporations to small, hometown operations. PKF specializes in health care, travel, hotels, resorts, real estate, construction, and other industries.

ACCOUNTING TRAINING PROGRAM

An "in-charge" professional is assigned to all entry-level personnel for guidance and assistance. Assignments to projects and responsibilities will increase as skills are developed. Both local office and regional in-house training seminars are available throughout the year.

QUALIFICATIONS

An M.B.A. or a degree in accounting is recommended.

RECRUITMENT AND PLACEMENT

Look for PKF's recruiter on your college or university campus, or contact a local office. Placement may be in any one of 25 states.

SALARY AND BENEFITS

The College Placement Council Salary Survey for September 1986–June 1987 indicates starting salaries for public accounting firms to be $1,834 a month for those with a B.A. degree in nontechnical curricula and $2,155 with a B.A. degree in technical curricula. M.B.A. starting salaries were $2,335 for a nontechnical undergraduate degree, and $2,436 for an M.B.A. with technical undergraduate degree. Check with the company for more specific salary information. Benefits include health insurance, life insurance, sick leave, and a good vacation policy.

CONTACT

Contact one of the 38 local offices, or write Pannell Kerr Forster, 420 Lexington Avenue, New York, NY 10170.

PARKER HANNIFIN CORPORATION

ACCOUNTING • ADMINISTRATION • COMPUTER SCIENCE • ENGINEERING • FINANCE • MARKETING • PRODUCTION • RESEARCH AND DEVELOPMENT • SALES

THE COMPANY

Parker Hannifin produces hydraulic systems and components, flight control systems, and industrial seals. The company makes and markets a complete line of components necessary for connecting, activating, and controlling fluid power systems. Its work force is growing, with about 18,000 employees in the United States and another 7,000 abroad. Listed among *Fortune*'s most admired corporations, Parker Hannifin has annual sales of more than $1.7 billion. It ranks number 201 in the Fortune 500 largest U.S. industrial corporations.

ALL TRAINING PROGRAMS

Engineers get on-the-job training for one year. Your supervisor will see that you are introduced to the company's policies and procedures. Sales trainees go through a six-month program that relies heavily on classroom instruction to present the company's products and selling techniques.

QUALIFICATIONS

Parker Hannifin seeks computer science trainees and engineers. It requires an industrial degree for industrial sales and manufacturing; a mechanical degree for industrial sales, manufacturing, product design, and development; and a mechanical engineering technology degree for industrial sales and manufacturing.

RECRUITMENT AND PLACEMENT

Starting locations are in Alabama, California, Illinois, Kansas, Kentucky, Maine, Michigan, Minnesota, New Jersey, New York, North Carolina, Ohio, Utah, Wisconsin, and Ontario, Canada.

SALARY AND BENEFITS

Average annual starting salary with a bachelor's degree ranges from the low to mid-twenties. Benefits will include life insurance, medical, hospital, dental, pension, stock-purchase, deferred compensation, and savings plans. Parker Hannifin also reimburses up to 100 percent of tuition expenses for advanced study.

CONTACT

W. C. Van Horn, Jr., Manager, Employee Relations, Parker Hannifin Corporation, 17325 Euclid Avenue, Cleveland, OH 44112.

PAYLESS CASHWAYS, INC.

MANAGEMENT

THE COMPANY

Payless building materials centers cater to the growing "do it yourself" market. Its stores, operating under the names Payless Cashways and Furrow Building Materials, supply everything for building, remodeling, repairing, or improving a home. Payless sales are growing fast, from $26 million in 1970 to more than $400 million by the early 1980s to more than $1.5 billion in 1986. The company has about 12,500 U.S. employees and ranks number 49 in the Fortune 50 largest retailers. If you are interested in retail store management, you may have a great opportunity with this expanding company.

MANAGEMENT TRAINING PROGRAM

The Payless Store Manager Program has several phases. You start by working in various store departments, including the lumberyard and warehouse, and by attending training seminars led by experienced managers to learn about Payless' marketing concepts and merchandising procedures. The second phase of your training will help you learn how Payless implements the concepts and procedures learned in the earlier part of your training. You will be working with store managers as you learn about their day-to-day problems as well as their long-range plans.

QUALIFICATIONS

Payless prefers that you have a college degree but will consider you if you have only good related experience.

RECRUITMENT AND PLACEMENT

Payless hires about 150 college graduates a year. On-the-job training takes place in all Payless stores in the following states: California, Colorado, Illinois, Indiana, Iowa, Kansas, Missouri, Nebraska, Ohio, Oklahoma, and Texas.

SALARY AND BENEFITS

With a bachelor's degree you can expect to start at about $18,000; increasing to around $20,000 with a master's; and as much as $25,000 with one to five years' experience. Benefits will include tuition reimbursement, life insurance, medical, hospital, dental, pension, profit-sharing, and stock-purchase plans, and relocation assistance.

CONTACT

Manager of Employment, Payless Cashways, Inc., 2301 Main Street, Kansas City, MO 64111.

JCPENNEY COMPANY

INVENTORY MANAGEMENT · STORE MANAGEMENT · MERCHANDISE BUYING · SYSTEMS

THE COMPANY

In the competitive world of retailing, JCPenney is the third largest retailer by sales volume in the United States. With 170,000 employees now, the company has not forgotten its roots as the little "Golden Rule" dry goods store opened by James Cash Penney in Kemmerer, Wyoming, in 1902. A family atmosphere still prevails throughout the system of 1,600 department stores, stretching across all 50 states plus Puerto Rico. All employees are called "associates." Most stores carry extensive lines of men's, women's, and children's apparel, cosmetics, furniture, housewares, home entertainment electronics, jewelry, and home furnishings; they provide custom decorating and styling salon services as well. Similar merchandise is sold through JCPenney's catalog division, the second largest such operation in the nation. The company also owns the Thrift Drug store chain and the Sarma chain of general merchandise stores in Belgium. In addition, JCPenney Financial Services markets health, life, and casualty insurance and various consumer financial services. Annual sales top $14 billion. The company does not discourage the hiring of additional family members and often has more than one generation working in the same store. Associates tend to stay with JCPenney throughout their entire careers, content with the company's ethical approach to business and its friendly attitudes. Listed among *Fortune*'s most admired corporations, JCPenney is fifth among the Fortune 50 largest retailing companies.

ALL TRAINING PROGRAMS

With the exception of a few positions, expect to do most of your training in a JCPenney store. Large stores may have as many as 100 training programs, with all sales people attending at least one class a year. Training centers also exist in Buena Park, California; Schaumburg, Illinois; Atlanta; and Dallas.

STORE MANAGEMENT PROGRAM

During the first twenty-six weeks of your training you will learn all aspects of merchandising. The most advanced technologies available in retailing today will be at your disposal, including computerized point-of-sale inventory systems that make each cash register a source of data on sales trends. After successful completion of the initial period of instruction, usually in a large or medium-sized store, you will begin managing all aspects of your own department. You may be helping to supervise as much as a half million dollars of annual volume. After nine to twelve months, if you've demonstrated ability, you'll be promoted to merchandising manager.

QUALIFICATIONS

No specific degree is necessary, although study of business administration or retailing would be useful. You must be comfortable with numbers and technology as well as people.

PLACEMENT

You could work anywhere in the United States.

ASSISTANT BUYER PROGRAM

You will work under the supervision of an experienced buyer, getting involved not only in buying decisions but also in reviewing research, evaluating markets, and recommending courses of action. The company buys from over 10,000 suppliers worldwide. You will guide the development, design, distribution, and promotion of products made to specifications for the company—85 percent of the millions of items sold by Penney's. The company has a merchandise testing lab, quality control department, and marketing research and planning department to assist you. Video conferencing via satellite-linked earth stations is used regularly to give merchandise presentations to field offices across the country. You will be given several line assignments to expose you to different aspects of buying for JCPenney.

QUALIFICATIONS

Although you will not need a specific degree to be hired for this position, you should definitely be adept at analysis, communication, leadership, and decision making. The work is demanding; you must often manage many different activities at once.

PLACEMENT

You will usually begin as a buyer at corporate headquarters in New York City.

CATALOG INVENTORY CONTROL TRAINING

A six-week training program will teach you the basics of inventory control. Then you'll be assigned to a specific category of catalog merchandise and given day-to-day responsibility for tracking and ordering it. You will work with buyers, suppliers, and a host of JCPenney departments that will help you forecast sales and analyze trends. Once the eighteen-month training program is successfully completed, you will be considered for promotion to CIC specialist. CIC specialists plan and control the inventory position of about $15 million worth of merchandise, deciding how many of an item to order, in what styles and colors, and to which of the distribution centers they will be sent.

QUALIFICATIONS

In addition to a college degree, you'll need a talent for detail work and considerable mathematical aptitude. Interpersonal skills and ability to work as a team player will be extremely important.

PLACEMENT

You will begin training at New York headquarters.

SYSTEMS ANALYST PROGRAM

You will start with a short training program to acquaint you with JCPenney standards and operating procedures. You will then be assigned to a project team in business applications, telecommunications, or systems software, depending on your area of interest. Early on you'll be expected to handle some fairly complex tasks. JCPenney has one of the largest private telecommunications networks in the world.

QUALIFICATIONS

JCPenney is looking for computer science or management/computer information systems majors. Those who want to work in business applications must have a good knowledge of COBOL.

PLACEMENT

Systems offices are located in Atlanta; Dallas and Plano, Texas; Milwaukee; New York; and Westerville, Ohio. These offices are supported by six corporate data centers spread throughout the United States.

ALL PROGRAMS

RECRUITMENT

JCPenney recruits nationwide.

SALARY AND BENEFITS

The College Placement Council Salary Survey for September 1986–June 1987 indicates starting salaries for merchandising (retail and wholesale) and service companies to be $1,594 a month for those with a B.A. degree in nontechnical curricula and $2,141 with a B.A. degree in technical curricula. M.B.A. starting salaries were $2,572 for a nontechnical undergraduate degree, and $2,735 for an M.B.A. with technical undergraduate degree. Check with the company for more specific salary information. Starting salaries are surveyed periodically to ensure equality. Your benefits package will include comprehensive medical and dental coverage, life insurance, income protection plans, savings and profit-sharing plans, retirement and pension, and discounts on merchandise.

CONTACT

Personnel Recruitment, JCPenney Company, 1301 Avenue of the Americas, New York, NY 10019.

PENNSYLVANIA POWER & LIGHT COMPANY

COMPUTER SCIENCE • ENGINEERING • MANAGEMENT

THE COMPANY

PP&L serves 1 million customers in central and eastern Pennsylvania over a 10,000-square-mile area. One of the top 20 investor-owned utilities in the country (by assets), PP&L designs its own process control computer systems. Assets exceed $7 billion. PP&L is number 31 in the Fortune 50 largest utilities. With general offices in Allentown, the company has almost 8,500 employees. PP&L has two nuclear generating units.

MANAGEMENT TRAINING PROGRAM

Much of your training will be on the job, with formal seminars available in several departments to improve your management skills. Classes may be either in-house or outside the company. A $10 million nuclear training center with an advanced control room simulator will provide hands-on experience.

QUALIFICATIONS

PP&L is looking for graduates with computer science, physical science, and engineering degrees. Familiarity with computers and programming will be helpful, as will be work experience. You should be able to show extracurricular and leadership activities as part of your college history.

RECRUITMENT AND PLACEMENT

The company recruits in Pennsylvania and also accepts applications from experienced personnel. You will work in Pennsylvania.

SALARY AND BENEFITS

With a bachelor's degree, your starting salary will be in the $20,000 to $28,000 range. Benefits include flextime; life and medical insurance; and pension, stock-purchase, and incentive savings plans.

CONTACT

Human Resources and Development Department, Placement Section, Pennsylvania Power & Light Company, 2 North Ninth Street, Allentown, PA 18101.

PEPSICO, INC.

EMPLOYEE RELATIONS • FINANCE • MANUFACTURING • SALES

THE COMPANY

In the 1890s pharmacists used to experiment with mixing soft drinks to sell at their drugstore soda fountains. In New Bern, North Carolina, pharmacist Caleb Bradham hit on a formula that is still a favorite today. He called it Pepsi-Cola and founded a company to produce it in 1896. Through a system of franchises he licensed independent businessmen to bottle Pepsi throughout the country. The company merged with Frito-Lay, Inc., in 1965 and has expanded into other markets with acquisitions such as Wilson Sporting Goods Company, Pizza Hut and Taco Bell, North American Van Lines, and LeeWay Motor Freight. A worldwide organization with headquarters in Purchase, New York, PepsiCo, Inc., has annual revenues of more than $9 billion. Listed among *Fortune*'s most admired corporations, it ranks number 34 in the Fortune 500 largest U.S. industrial corporations. You will enter the company through the Bottling Group rather than headquarters.

ALL TRAINING PROGRAMS

Orientation and training at Pepsi-Cola Bottling Group is based upon two basic principles: on-the-job training from your first day at work; and flexible modular training to enable you to use each job experience as a career builder. To accomplish this, PBG has developed the C.R.E.W. program—College Recruit Experience for Work. Your introduction to Pepsi-Cola Company, PBG, and the functions within PBG, is made up of ten modules. This is followed by in-depth functional training in your area of specialization. In the general orientation you will study videotapes, printed materials, and self-quizzes. By the time you have completed the C.R.E.W. program, you will have spent several months learning about your functional area. Also you will have spent time in the other functional areas, learning their roles and the links to yours. Your supervisor and employee relations manager will work with you during the training period.

EMPLOYEE RELATIONS PROGRAM

You will participate in such activities as grievance procedures; human resource planning; wage and salary administration; recruiting; and assisting operating managers in all aspects of the business involving personnel. You will take on substantial responsibility very quickly. You will act as a human resource adviser to line management in your territory.

FINANCE PROGRAM

You will be trained to assume the position of accountant. So that you will fully understand the company's operations, you will be given detailed exposure to the sales and manufacturing functions. Trainees receive varied responsibilities during period closings, and the post-closing analysis of the results. You will also be involved in special projects, such as tracking shipments of supplies, determining the life expectancies of returnable containers, reviewing procedures, and recommending changes and/or improvements in financial processes. Warehouse audits and other general project work will round out your training.

MANUFACTURING PROGRAM

You will be trained to assume the responsibilities of a production or warehouse supervisor. In addition to the general orientation that all trainees receive, you will be given projects in the areas of quality control, preventive maintenance, planning and scheduling, and warehousing. You will have specific responsibilities and objectives, and will follow up to ensure timely compliance with recommendations. You will gain experience in supervision, and will work on production lines to gain a working knowledge of the bottling line and canning equipment. Assignments may include supervising shift production and warehousing operations.

SALES PROGRAM

You will be trained to become a route manager. Your on-the-job training with each department and function will begin with plant tours conducted by the production manager to acquaint you with manufacturing; night loading observations with the loading supervisor to demonstrate proper truck loading, efficient use of load sheets and warehouse issues; and working closely with a route manager. The route manager will explain space management, new account calls, market checks, route salesperson communication and motivation, accounts receivable, equipment rental, and profit and loss statements. You will also assist on projects with the regional sales manager.

ALL PROGRAMS

QUALIFICATIONS

You should have a strong academic record to back up your graduate or undergraduate degree. Pepsi looks for self-confident leaders who have the abilities to communicate and to solve problems.

PLACEMENT

Locations exist throughout the United States.

RECRUITMENT

The company recruits on college campuses across the country.

SALARY AND BENEFITS

The College Placement Council Salary Survey for September 1986–June 1987 indicates starting salaries for food and beverage processing companies to be $1,834 a month for those with a B.A. degree in nontechnical curricula and $2,301 with a B.A. degree in technical curricula. M.B.A. starting salaries were $3,043 for a nontechnical undergraduate degree and $3,098 for a technical undergraduate degree. Check with the company for more specific salary information. Merit reviews are generally conducted once a year. New hires can expect more frequent merit reviews. Employees are offered options in benefits including comprehensive medical coverage, dental insurance, vision and hearing care, life insurance, tuition reimbursement, and paid holidays.

CONTACT

Manager, Campus Recruiting, Pepsi-Cola Company, Anderson Hill Road, Purchase, NY 10577.

PFIZER, INC.

COMPUTER SCIENCE • ENGINEERING • FINANCE • MARKETING • PERSONNEL • PRODUCTION • RESEARCH AND DEVELOPMENT • SALES

THE COMPANY

Pfizer's $4 billion-plus business encompasses the research, manufacture, and sale of health-care, chemical, agricultural, material science, and consumer products. Included in Pfizer's products are Coty's line of fragrances and cosmetics, lime and limestone products, dental and orthopedic devices, antibiotics, Visine eye drops, and veterinary medicines. Pfizer employs approximately 42,000 men and women worldwide, three fifths of whom work outside the United States. World headquarters are in New York City. Listed among *Fortune*'s most admired corporations, it ranks number 84 in the Fortune 500 largest U.S. industrial corporations.

FINANCE TRAINING PROGRAM

Your training will be informal and on the job. Although formal evaluations are conducted on an annual basis, continuous guidance and feedback are given so that you will always know where you stand. There are no preconceived ideas about how quickly one should move, and Pfizer is not rigidly structured. You might work in corporate internal audit, corporate accounting, or as a business or financial analyst.

QUALIFICATIONS

Pfizer wants M.B.A.s with rigorous academic training, as well as those with practical experience following their undergraduate work.

MARKETING TRAINING PROGRAM

Starting as a pharmaceuticals marketing associate, you will spend approximately six months as part of a product management team. Then another six months will be spent in the field as a pharmaceuticals sales representative. After that introductory year you'll become an assistant product manager, which then leads to product manager. You will use a variety of marketing methods, including traditional selling approaches such as personal calls and distribution of educational literature. In addition, you may be involved in placing advertising in medical journals, direct mail, videotape and audio cassette presentations, closed-circuit television, symposia for physicians and medical personnel, exhibitions at medical conferences, and other promotional techniques.

QUALIFICATIONS

You don't need a technical background, but you should be a business generalist with an M.B.A.

SALES TRAINING PROGRAM

Your training begins as soon as you join Pfizer. Basic orientation to the company is followed by several weeks of classes at New York headquarters. Training in pharmaceutical sales includes: basic course work in human anatomy, physiology, and pharmacology; characteristics of pharmaceuticals offered by Pfizer and other companies; and basic techniques in making presentations. Upon successful completion of the program you will begin your career as a pharmaceutical sales representative, working closely with a district manager to develop your selling skills. If you go into consumer products sales, you will begin training by working with your district manager as you refine your selling skills.

QUALIFICATIONS

A life-science or business degree is helpful, but you may be accepted with any of a variety of degrees. You should be a self-starter, entrepreneurial, creative, and competitive.

ALL PROGRAMS

RECRUITMENT AND PLACEMENT

Pfizer has intensified its efforts in the United States to promote greater employment and advancement opportunities for minorities and women. The work force is broken down as follows: 40 percent United States; 25 percent Europe; 15 percent Asia; 13 percent Canada/Latin America; and 7 percent Africa/Middle East. The company maintains research and production facilities at 123 locations in 43 countries. Pfizer's central research laboratories are in Groton, Connecticut.

SALARY AND BENEFITS

The College Placement Council Salary Survey for September 1986–June 1987 indicates starting salaries for chemical, drug, and allied product companies to be $1,964 a month for those with a B.A. degree in nontechnical curricula and $2,457 with a B.A. degree in technical curricula. M.B.A. starting salaries were $2,886 for a nontechnical undergraduate degree and $2,794 for a technical undergraduate degree. Check with the company for more specific salary information. Sales representatives receive a base salary and bonus, a company car, and complete expense accounting. Contact the company for details on salaries for other entry-level positions. Benefits for all employees include total health-care coverage and a dental program for you and your family, life insurance, retirement annuity and stockownership plans, savings and investment programs, educational assistance, and paid holidays and vacations. For qualified employees, Pfizer also offers military leave and training allowance, and assistance with adoption fees.

CONTACT

For sales, contact the nearest Regional Personnel Manager: Pfizer, Inc., 2400 West Central Road, Hoffman Estates, IL 60196; 16700 Red Hill Avenue, Irvine, CA 92714; Pfizer, Inc., 230 Brighton Road, Clifton, NJ 07012; 4360 Northeast Expressway, Doraville, GA 30340; or Pfizer, Inc., P.O. Box 222249, Dallas, TX 75222. For research and development: Manager, Employment, Central Research, Pfizer, Inc., Eastern Point Road, Groton, CT 06340. For all other jobs: Manager, Employment, Pfizer, Inc., 235 East 42nd Street, New York, NY 10017.

PHILLIPS PETROLEUM COMPANY

ACCOUNTING • CHEMISTRY • ENGINEERING • FINANCE • HUMAN RESOURCES • INFORMATION SYSTEMS • LAW • MANAGEMENT • PHYSICS • REAL ESTATE/INSURANCE • RESEARCH/DEVELOPMENT

THE COMPANY

A major international corporation with more than $12 billion in assets, Phillips has come a long way since it was founded in 1917. The company has leases or production in 35 states and 15 foreign nations, and supplies products and services to customers in 79 countries. More than half of Phillips' worldwide crude oil production and two thirds of its gas production come from the United States, as does nearly all of its production of natural gas liquids. About one fourth of the company's oil and gas production is in the Greater Ekofisk Development in the Norwegian North Sea. Proved reserves of oil and gas are almost evenly divided between the United States and abroad. Phillips is involved in every phase of the petroleum business —exploration and production, transportation, refining, and marketing. In addition, the company is broadly diversified in the petrochemical business. It is also dedicated to research and has earned a reputation as an industry leader. Phillips has more active U.S. patents than any other oil company (5000). It employs 23,000 people and has headquarters in Bartlesville, Oklahoma. Among *Fortune*'s most admired corporations, it ranks number 31 in the Fortune 500 largest U.S. industrial corporations.

ALL TRAINING PROGRAMS

Phillips' programs are structured, enjoyable, and highly flexible. The company has broad-based training programs tailored to meet the specific needs of each of the operating groups and staffs. All training within the company is characterized by structured discussions between employee and supervisor, with a focus on skills assessment, individual training and development, and the employee's career interests. In addition, employee development committees have been established in the areas of engineering, accounting, data processing, employee relations, and materials management. These committees meet regularly to discuss the progress of employees and to consider candidates for placement or development rotations within their functional areas. This procedure gives employees career development opportunities throughout the company.

INFORMATION SERVICES PROGRAM

The corporate Data Processing Employee Development Committee governs policies and practices affecting data processing professionals. It provides entry-level training and orientation and continuing development of experienced personnel. The Data Processing Human Resource Management Program features structured discussions between employee and supervisor, with a focus on skills assessment, individual training and development plans, and employee career interests. Data Processing Technical Training includes more than 900 courses offered in house, including classes taught by software and computer companies, computer-based training, and video/multimedia. In-house instructional technologists assist content experts in evaluating, developing, and teaching courses. The Data Processing Entry-Level Training Program is designed for new college graduates with little data processing experience. It familiarizes new employees with Phillips methodologies, standards, policies, and essential data processing skills. The program lasts three to four months and includes both classroom and on-the-job learning experiences.

QUALIFICATIONS

You will need a degree in computer science or information systems. Phillips prefers graduates who rank in the top 10 to 15 percent of their class.

MANAGEMENT DEVELOPMENT PROGRAM

Technical Professional Ladder programs provide additional opportunities, status, and compensation to outstanding technical professionals who for various reasons do not move into managerial or administrative positions. These programs enable technical professionals to advance to grades equivalent to upper–middle management without having to assume managerial responsibilities. Candidates for TPL are chosen on the basis of nature and scope of work, authority of position, amount of work direction needed, authority of knowledge, creativity and creative accomplishments, communication and persuasion abilities, and knowledge required to solve problems. First-Level Supervisory programs provide new and experienced first-level supervisors with the comprehensive knowledge and skills needed for their managerial responsibilities. Programs include training in basic supervision and management. Middle Management Development Resources programs develop middle managers both as individuals and as organization members. A wide variety of courses are offered both inside and outside the company. The Phillips Advanced Management Program is an intensive three-week learning experience especially designed for Phillips managers. Based on the latest business and management theory, it develops the manager's understanding of the impact of economic, political, social, cultural, and technological changes on management decisions and the organization. Candidates must be nominated by their group or staff and approved by the company's Employee Development Committee. The Professional Development Program develops leadership and managerial skills. Courses include business/technical report writing, oral presentations, financial analysis, effective negotiating, performance counseling for first-level programs, UCLA engineering and management programs, University of Michigan programs, and TELOS leadership and team management programs.

QUALIFICATIONS

The company is looking for recent graduates with bachelor's or master's degrees as well as applicants with related technical experience. Phillips' professional employment needs are primarily in the areas of engineering, accounting, geoscience, computer science, chemistry, technical sales, tax, and business.

RESEARCH AND DEVELOPMENT PROGRAM

R&D training and development are divided into four phases:

- *apprentice* or entry-level training for new college graduates or employees entering new job categories.
- *independent* contributor phase, when employees have demonstrated mastery of basic skills for a job function and are ready to initiate and be responsible for much or all of their functional area.
- *mentor* to supervise and direct the work of other apprentice and individual contributor employees.
- *sponsor* phase (typically senior management) to shape the direction of the organization's growth.

The New Employee Orientation Program smooths new employees' transition to R&D. You will attend six three-hour orientation sessions once a week for six weeks, with coaching continuing for six to eighteen months. Technical training seminars are presented in house for employees with less than five years' experience. They cover a broad range of areas from coal liquefaction to corrosion fundamentals; machinery vibration analysis; process synthetics; and petroleum refining, technology, and economics.

QUALIFICATIONS

Phillips is looking primarily for candidates with advanced degrees in chemistry, geology, geophysics, physics, mathematics, molecular biology/biochemistry, chemical, petroleum, mechanical, and electrical engineering. You will have the best chance of being hired if you rank in the top 10 to 15 percent of your graduating class.

ALL PROGRAMS

RECRUITMENT AND PLACEMENT

Phillips has a formal, centralized recruitment program, which is coordinated by the company's human resources staff. Although recruitment is heaviest in the fall, some spring recruiting is done. Starting locations include Alaska, California, Colorado, Kansas, Louisiana, Michigan, Montana, New Mexico, Oklahoma, Texas, Utah, and Wyoming.

SALARY AND BENEFITS

The College Placement Council Salary Survey for September 1986–June 1987 indicates starting salaries for petroleum and allied product companies to be $1,972 a month for those with a B.A. degree in nontechnical curricula and $2,497 with a B.A. degree in technical curricula. M.B.A. starting salaries were $2,629 for a nontechnical undergraduate degree and $2,970 for a technical undergraduate degree. Check with the company for more specific salary information. Benefits include business travel accident insurance, life insurance, accidental death insurance, medical and dental assistance coverage, short-term and long-term disability coverage, an employee stockownership plan, and a noncontributory retirement plan. Employees also may invest up to 15 percent of their salary in the thrift plan, with the company matching up to 5 percent, dollar for dollar. In addition, employees benefit from vacation and holiday pay, tuition reimbursement, and dependent scholarship programs. Phillips also has an employee suggestion program which offers up to $50,000 for money-saving ideas.

CONTACT

Director, Recruitment/Educational Relations, Phillips Petroleum Company, 5 D4 Phillips Building, Bartlesville, OK 74004.

PHOENIX MUTUAL

ACTUARIAL SCIENCE

THE COMPANY

This 135-year-old New England company has branch offices throughout the country. Ranked 25th among the more than 2,800 life insurance companies in the United States, Phoenix is a financial services institution with an interest in 20 subsidiaries. These subsidiaries offer investment products and services, special insurance concepts, and property-casualty insurance.

ACTUARIAL SCIENCE TRAINING PROGRAM

You will be given a series of rotating job assignments to build a strong foundation for your career as an actuary. Your projects will give you high visibility to top management to offer the best shot at promotion and recognition as you develop work skills. Company-paid study time is available, along with basic company study time of 100 to 150 hours per exam period. Students with two to five exams are eligible to attend a two-week seminar at Georgia State University once each calendar year. You may also attend company-paid courses at the University of Hartford.

QUALIFICATIONS

You should be ranked in the top 20 percent of your class. A major in math or actuarial science is desirable but not required. You should have passed at least one Society of Actuaries exam, but may receive credit for SOA Part 1 on the basis of the Graduate Record Exam advanced math score. If you have otherwise outstanding credentials, such as strong communication skills, this one exam requirement may be waived.

RECRUITMENT AND PLACEMENT

The company recruits nationally. You will start at corporate headquarters in Hartford, Connecticut, or at Group Operations in Enfield, Connecticut.

SALARY AND BENEFITS

You will be hired to start at $24,000 and up, with benefits that include a liberal, noncontributory pension plan; group life and dental insurance; long-term disability insurance; health insurance or your choice of a health maintenance organization; flexible working hours; tuition assistance; a matching gifts program; employee assistance program; one-half fee payment for specified health facilities; and subsidized commuter bus and car pool transportation.

CONTACT

Trentton K. Mack, Associate Manager Employment, Phoenix Mutual, One American Row, Hartford, CT 06115.

THE PILLSBURY COMPANY

ENGINEERING · GRAIN MERCHANDISING · INFORMATION SYSTEMS · MARKETING · OPERATIONS · PRODUCTION · RESEARCH AND DEVELOPMENT · RESTAURANT MANAGEMENT · SALES

THE COMPANY

Established in 1869 on the banks of the Mississippi River, Pillsbury is one of the country's oldest firms. The company started in Minnesota as a flour miller, and is now an international marketing corporation with annual sales of more than $5 billion. It is active in three major segments of the food business: consumer products, restaurants, and agri-products. Among Pillsbury's products are American Beauty pastas, Totino's frozen pizzas, and Green Giant frozen and canned foods. Subsidiaries include familiar restaurant names such as Burger King, Steak & Ale, Bennigan's, Häagen-Dazs, and J. J. Muggs. Extending its food reach even further, Pillsbury's agri-products business includes flour and rice milling, bakery mixes, and grain and feed ingredient merchandising. Pillsbury exports over 200 different products to more than 55 countries. Its manufacturing and marketing organizations operate in 13 foreign countries throughout Europe, Central and South America, and the Far East, with either a controlling or minority interest in 18 separate businesses. Listed among *Fortune*'s most admired corporations, Pillsbury ranks number 61 in the Fortune 500 largest U.S. industrial corporations.

ALL TRAINING PROGRAMS

Your training will be primarily on the job, with experienced supervisors to guide your development.

GRAIN MERCHANDISING PROGRAM

You'll begin at a merchandising office, gathering information on Pillsbury's business and capabilities. Under the guidance of experienced grain merchandisers, you'll learn how to make accurate assessments of the market, allowing for such variables as shipping costs, storage, and processing requirements. Through experience, you'll come to know how to purchase grain and to manage the sequence of events that delivers the commodity to the customer at the correct time and at a competitive price.

QUALIFICATIONS

You should have a business or finance background. Pillsbury is looking for candidates who are self-disciplined and highly motivated. You should be ready to make significant profit-related decisions early in your career.

PLACEMENT

Pillsbury headquarters are in Minneapolis, and there are outlets throughout the country. The company emphasizes the hiring and development of local national employees for overseas positions but also operates an International Group that draws from experienced U.S. employees.

MARKETING PROGRAM

Pillsbury emphasizes that it tries to tailor its development program to you, rather than forcing you to conform to a rigidly structured environment. You will probably find yourself with very important projects in a matter of months after you start. You'll begin as a marketing assistant, working on a major product or a product group and reporting to a marketing manager. You'll be carrying out the details of an already established marketing strategy. If your performance matches your potential, you'll move to associate marketing manager, then to marketing manager.

QUALIFICATIONS

You should have an M.B.A. and an excellent academic record.

PLACEMENT

Pillsbury headquarters are in Minneapolis, but there are outlets located throughout the country.

PRODUCT SUPERVISION PROGRAM

If you are ready to manage right away you'll begin with an on-the-job orientation to your plant's various production departments. This orientation normally lasts less than six months. Then you'll be assigned to the production line as a unit manager. Your prime responsibility will be to supervise 10 to 25 employees engaged in manufacturing, packaging, or shipping food products. You may move to other plant locations to speed your development as a well-rounded manager.

QUALIFICATIONS

You should have an engineering or management degree. Successful candidates have maturity, self-confidence, and excellent interpersonal skills.

PLACEMENT

You could work anywhere in the country.

RESTAURANT MANAGEMENT PROGRAM

Your on-the-job training for Burger King begins in one of the restaurants, followed by additional training at one of the 11 regional training centers. When you are promoted to restaurant manager, you'll be trained in advanced management skills at the regional training center in your area and at Burger King University in Miami.

QUALIFICATIONS

Your specific degree is not important, but you should have a track record of leadership in academics, extracurricular activities, work, or military service.

PLACEMENT

Burger King is based in Miami, and the S&A Restaurant Corporation is headquartered in Dallas.

SALES PROGRAM

You'll begin as a sales merchandiser, calling on retail stores to introduce products, improve product presentations, and generally increase the volume of Pillsbury products through outlets. After you become familiar with product lines and pricing policies, you'll start on-the-job sales training, making calls under the guidance of your district manager. Formal seminars in selling skills will complement your job experience.

QUALIFICATIONS

More important than your degree is a combination of personal qualities including self-discipline, drive, organization, resiliency, and interpersonal skills. You should also be willing to travel and to relocate.

PLACEMENT

You could work anywhere in the United States.

ALL PROGRAMS

RECRUITMENT

Pillsbury actively recruits on college campuses, but those who cannot meet with a company representative or who have extensive experience in their field may send résumés directly to the company.

SALARY AND BENEFITS

The College Placement Council Salary Survey for September 1986–June 1987 indicates starting salaries for food and beverage processing companies to be $1,834 a month for those with a B.A. degree in nontechnical curricula and $2,301 with a B.A. degree in technical curricula. M.B.A. starting salaries were $3,043 for a nontechnical undergraduate degree and $3,098 for a technical undergraduate degree. Check with the company for more specific salary information. Benefits include medical, dental, and life insurance, a retirement plan, tuition reimbursement, savings plan, vacations, holidays, and disability income protection.

CONTACT

College Relations Coordinator, Corporate Staff Personnel, The Pillsbury Company, Pillsbury Center, 200 South Sixth Street, Minneapolis, MN 55402.

PITNEY BOWES, INC.

ADMINISTRATION • ENGINEERING • INFORMATION SYSTEMS AND PROCESSING • MANAGEMENT • SALES

THE COMPANY

"Communication" and "commitment" are the key words at Pitney Bowes. A few years ago, when it became obvious that this office equipment production company needed to update its equipment from electromechanical to electronic, it didn't take the easy way out. Rather than build new factories in the Sun Belt and hire new people, Pitney Bowes set up a training center at its headquarters in Stamford, Connecticut, to teach employees familiar with springs and gears how to solder chips on computer boards. Not a single production worker was laid off. Since 1947, Pitney Bowes has held an annual jobholder meeting for which employees prepare detailed questions that run the gamut from personal complaints to queries about the company's marketing strategy. The president or other high officials chair the meetings, and they stand up there and take it. Another example of the company's involvement with its employees is its Council of Personnel Relations, consisting of an equal number of managers and employees elected by their peers, which meets with management to solve problems. This company of over

27,000 people demonstrates concern and commitment to its employees. Pitney Bowes has annual sales of more than $2 billion and is listed among *Fortune*'s most admired corporations. It ranks number 178 in the Fortune 500 largest U.S. industrial corporations.

ALL TRAINING PROGRAMS

Pitney Bowes offers formal training programs for systems analysis and sales. Management development seminars are conducted by the company's training department. On-the-job training is given to engineers, while a combination of hands-on and formal training lasting eighteen months is given to systems analysts.

QUALIFICATIONS

Bachelor's and master's degrees in computer science, electrical engineering, electronics engineering, information systems, manufacturing information, physics, and software engineering are needed. Applications are also encouraged from technical graduates with one to ten years of related work experience. Graduates with degrees in business are also welcome.

RECRUITMENT AND PLACEMENT

You may be placed at one of the 100 sales offices located in every major city in the United States. However, the main work force is in Stamford, with facilities in Melbourne, Florida; Johnson City, Kansas; and Dayton, Ohio.

SALARY AND BENEFITS

With a bachelor's degree you'll start in the mid- to upper twenties. Salaries for master's degrees are competitive. A consulting firm has ranked the benefits package between second and third in a group of top firms that includes Kodak, GE, IBM, and Xerox. Comprehensive medical, dental, and group life plans, profit sharing, stock purchase, and 100 percent tuition reimbursement are supplemented by a health maintenance plan and an alcohol abuse program. The company has high morale and low turnover.

CONTACT

Michael Xirinachs, Recruiter, Pitney Bowes, Inc., Walter H. Wheeler, Jr., Drive, Stamford, CT 06926.

POLAROID CORPORATION

CHEMISTRY • ENGINEERING • INFORMATION SYSTEMS • OPTICS • PHYSICS • PRODUCTION • RESEARCH AND DEVELOPMENT • TECHNICAL SERVICES

THE COMPANY

In 1928 an eighteen-year-old undergraduate at Harvard, Edwin Land, discovered a method for polarizing light. This process is still used to make sunglasses. Land founded Polaroid in 1937 and introduced the first instant camera in 1948. Today, Polaroid ranks first in instant photography and second in camera and film sales. But the camera and film market is becoming saturated, and Polaroid has begun investing in a future in electronics. Specifically, it is investigating electronic imaging, a process that takes bits of information from a computer and converts them into a picture. This process is used to show the results of ultrasonic tests on unborn fetuses. Polaroid is looking for other marketable applications. The company was an early leader in equal employment opportunity programs and began subsidized child care in 1971. It has about 10,000 employees in the United States and almost 4,000 abroad. Annual sales top $1.6 billion, making it number 211 in the Fortune 500 largest U.S. industrial corporations. Polaroid is also listed among *Fortune*'s most admired corporations.

ALL TRAINING PROGRAMS

On-the-job training lasts from three to six months and gives you an orientation to the company's operating procedures and its expectations about job performance. An experienced supervisor will help you gain the necessary skills and knowledge to get off to a good start in your new position.

QUALIFICATIONS

The company is hiring college graduates and experienced personnel from the following fields: chemistry, business (M.B.A. with a technical undergraduate degree), biochemistry, mathematics, polymer chemistry, pulp and paper technology, and engineering—chemical, electrical manufacturing, mechanical, electronics, and industrial/management. The company prefers applicants in the top third of their class and with a minimum G.P.A. of 3.0.

RECRUITMENT AND PLACEMENT

Starting locations are within a hundred-mile radius of Boston.

SALARY AND BENEFITS

The College Placement Council Salary Survey for September 1986–June 1987 indicates starting salaries for electrical and electronic machines and equipment companies to be $1,861 a month for those with a B.A. degree in nontechnical curricula and $2,419 with a B.A. degree in technical curricula. M.B.A. starting salaries were $2,784 for a nontechnical undergraduate degree and $2,818 for a technical undergraduate degree. Check with the company for more specific salary information. Polaroid benefits include life insurance, medical, dental, and pension plans, profit sharing, and relocation assistance. Part-time study may be reimbursed up to 100 percent.

CONTACT

John D. Litster, College Relations Manager, Polaroid Corporation, 750 Main Street, Cambridge, MA 02139.

PORT AUTHORITY OF NEW YORK AND NEW JERSEY

ENGINEERING • MANAGEMENT

THE COMPANY

Very little could be more critical to maintaining business as usual in the New York and New Jersey region than the successful operation of the Port Authority of New York and New Jersey. This bistate agency operates airports, rail transit, tunnels, bridges, marine terminals, and industrial parks. No responsibility could be more challenging or important, not only to the millions of residents in that region but also to the hundreds of millions of dollars' worth of business that depends on the successful operation of these facilities. The Port Authority of New York and New Jersey will be involved in a multibillion-dollar building and rehabilitation program for the next decade. Some 300,000 New York and New Jersey residents work at permanent jobs related directly and indirectly to Port Authority operations and to transport operators and commercial tenants at its facilities.

ENGINEERING TRAINING PROGRAM

You will receive on-the-job training by working in Port Authority headquarters at the World Trade Center in New York City and at construction sites. The Engineering Department essentially serves as an in-house engineering/architectural and construction management firm. You will be exposed to a broad range of engineering and architectural design, construction supervision and administration, materials inspection, and traffic engineering.

QUALIFICATIONS

You will need a B.S. or M.S. in architectural, electrical, civil, mechanical, or transportation engineering.

MANAGEMENT TRAINING PROGRAM

The one-year program consists of four rotational assignments to operating positions and special projects. Management development seminars are held throughout the year, and you will be exposed to top-level management and key projects. You will work closely with the Management Training Program coordinator and other members of your training group. You will be encouraged to provide critiques, suggestions, and ideas.

QUALIFICATIONS

A master's degree with an emphasis on public administration or business administration, management, or a related area will qualify you for the management training program.

ALL PROGRAMS

RECRUITMENT AND PLACEMENT

Recruitment for both programs begins in February and trainees start summer/fall of that year. Upon completion of the programs individuals are placed based on their technical skills and the needs of the organization. All positions are in the New Jersey-New York metropolitan area.

SALARY AND BENEFITS

The College Placement Council Salary Survey for September 1986–June 1987 indicates starting salaries for public utilities (including transportation) to be $1,905 a month for those with a B.A. degree in nontechnical curricula and $2,355 with a B.A. degree in technical curricula. M.B.A. starting salaries were $2,403 for a nontechnical undergraduate degree and $2,667 for a technical undergraduate degree. Check with the company for more specific salary information. The Port Authority is committed to promotion from within the organization and offers a comprehensive benefits package.

CONTACT

For the Engineering Training Program, send your résumé to Catherine James, Coordinator, College Relations, Port Authority of NY&NJ, One World Trade Center 61N, New York, NY 10048; for management: Yvette Malave Diaz, Coordinator, Management Training Program, Port Authority of NY & NJ, One World Trade Center 61N, New York, NY 10048.

PPG INDUSTRIES, INC.

ACCOUNTING • DISTRIBUTION • EMPLOYEE RELATIONS • ENVIRONMENTAL AFFAIRS • FINANCE • MANUFACTURING • MARKETING • RESEARCH AND DEVELOPMENT • SALES • STRATEGIC PLANNING/BUSINESS DEVELOPMENT

THE COMPANY

PPG Industries is one of America's largest and most diversified manufacturers with annual sales of more than $4 billion. It operates 43 manufacturing plants in the United States and employs approximately 37,000 people. The company has four operating units: the Chemicals Group; the Coatings & Resins Division, the Fiber Glass Division, and the Glass Group. The Glass Group, which produces glass for the transportation and construction industries, is the nation's leading flat glass producer. The Chemicals Group is a major producer of chlorine, caustic soda, potash, herbicides, silica pigments, and fuel additives and is a leader in many of its markets. The Coatings & Resins Division, the country's second-largest coatings maker, produces industrial coatings for automobiles, appliances, and architectural applications, and polyols used in rigid foam insulation, among other things. The Fiber Glass Division produces glass fiber for decorative applications. Founded in 1883 as the Pittsburgh Plate Glass company, PPG was the nation's first successful plate glass producer. Listed among *Fortune*'s most admired corporations, it ranks number 78 in the Fortune 500 largest U.S. industrial corporations.

ALL TRAINING PROGRAMS

PPG's training programs vary in length, but all are relatively informal, pragmatic, and distinctly job-oriented. PPG's operating units and corporate staff departments have training programs, each fashioned to prepare the individual to perform effectively a particular production, sales, research, or administrative function. In this phase of development, you will cover techniques, procedures, processes, policies, organizational relationships, technologies, and the many other elements of business and manufacturing operations that contribute to effective management and professional growth. An ongoing management development program incorporates annual reviews, offering you a chance to make plans for future projects and job assignments. Your participation in in-house seminars, professional activities, seminars conducted by professional societies and trade associations, and other developmental activities will be tailored to your needs. The Controller Training Program, PPG's only formal training program, prepares new employees for financial management positions in plant accounting or electronic data processing departments. The one-year program focuses on basic PPG business and financial policy.

QUALIFICATIONS

PPG's needs are diverse and the company hires from many degree specialties at levels ranging from bachelor's to advanced degrees.

RECRUITMENT AND PLACEMENT

PPG is headquartered in Pittsburgh and has large plants in Lake Charles, Louisiana; Barberton, Ohio; Beaumont, Texas; and Natrium, West Virginia. Small plants exist at other sites. Research and development centers are in Barberton, Ohio; Corpus Christi, Texas; and Chicago. Sales offices are in Boston; Charlotte, North Carolina; Chicago; Cincinnati; Cleveland; Houston; Los Angeles; Minneapolis; Philadelphia; Pittsburgh; Portland, Oregon; St. Louis; San Francisco; and West Orange, New Jersey (near New York City).

SALARY AND BENEFITS

The College Placement Council Salary Survey for September 1986–June 1987 indicates starting salaries for glass, paper, packaging, and allied products companies to be $1,865 a month for those with a B.A. degree in nontechnical curricula and $2,401 with a B.A. degree in technical curricula. M.B.A. starting salaries were $2,945 for a nontechnical undergraduate degree and $2,775 for a technical undergraduate degree. Check with the company for more specific salary information. Benefits include life, dental, and medical insurance, salary continuance during illness or disability, educational assistance, savings and retirement plans.

CONTACT

Personnel Director, PPG Industries, Inc., One Gateway Center, Pittsburgh, PA 15222

PRATT & WHITNEY AIRCRAFT GROUP

ENGINEERING • INFORMATION SYSTEMS • PRODUCTION • PROGRAMMING • OPERATIONS • RESEARCH AND DEVELOPMENT

THE COMPANY

Pratt & Whitney has a history nearly as long as aviation's. Fred Rentschler founded the company in 1925, then joined with William Boeing and Chance Vought, two other aviation pioneers, to form United Aircraft & Transport Corporation in 1928. Their idea was to gather all the industries necessary to build airplanes and operate airlines under one corporate umbrella. They formed what later became United Airlines, and also picked up Sikorsky Aircraft to get the skills of Igor Sikorsky, the inventor of the helicopter.

The company was undone in 1934, however, when Congress, fearing monopolization of the airline industry, forced airplane builders out of the airline business. Boeing and United were split off into separate businesses, and Pratt & Whitney continued to develop airplane engines. During World War II the company supplied half the total power for U.S. planes. After the war it moved into jet engines and then into space and missile work.

The 1960s brought increasing competition and problems with some Pratt & Whitney engines, and falling profits stimulated management into bringing in Harry Gray to find a way out of trouble. Gray brought controversy with him to United Technologies (the parent company of Pratt & Whitney). He quickly diversified, believing that the company needed to be weaned from excessive dependence upon military contracts. United

Technologies bought Otis Elevator Company and Carrier Air Conditioning, both now number one in their fields, and today aircraft technology has a reduced though still hefty rolc in the company as a whole.

In 1979, Gray surprised the industry by installing General Alexander Haig, Richard Nixon's former NATO commander and White House chief of staff, as president and chief operating officer. The company currently has more than 40,000 employees in the United States, and fewer than 500 employees overseas.

ALL TRAINING PROGRAMS

Experimental and manufacturing engineers get a nine-month, on-the-job training program. For performance engineers, a nine-month, formal training program supplements on-the-job experience with classroom instruction. Nearby universities offer degree programs developed jointly with Pratt & Whitney. Computer programmers will attend a three-month formal program.

QUALIFICATIONS

Opportunities are available for mechanical and analytical designers, experimental engineers, and metallurgical materials engineers to design and develop advanced turbine engines. Candidates must have mechanical engineering degrees and experience in the phase of design and manufacture in which they will work. Computer science and business majors are also welcome. Pratt & Whitney looks for an overall G.P.A. of 2.5 or higher, and ranking in the top half of your class. Doctoral candidates in aerospace engineering, mechanical engineering, and metallurgical engineering are also encouraged to apply.

RECRUITMENT AND PLACEMENT

The company recruits nationwide, hiring more than 450 trainees a year. You will start at corporate headquarters in Connecticut, in Georgia, or at the huge West Palm Beach, Florida, Aerospace Division.

SALARIES AND BENEFITS

The College Placement Council Salary Survey for September 1986–June 1987 indicates starting salaries for aerospace companies to be $1,943 a month for those with a B.A. degree in nontechnical curricula and $2,399 with a B.A. degree in technical curricula. M.B.A. starting salaries were $2,330 for a nontechnical undergraduate degree and $2,475 for a technical undergraduate degree. Check with the company for more specific salary information. Fully paid benefits include life, medical, hospital, dental, pension, and stock-purchase plans. You may also participate in fitness programs and a savings plan, and receive career development counseling, relocation assistance, and tuition reimbursement.

CONTACT

Max Fentress, Manager College Relations and Recruitment, United Technologies, Pratt & Whitney, 400 Main Street, East Hartford, CT 06108.

PRICE WATERHOUSE

ACCOUNTING/AUDITING •
MANAGEMENT CONSULTING • TAX

THE COMPANY

The Wall Street Journal says Price Waterhouse is "generally regarded as the 'blue chip' among the nation's largest accounting firms," an opinon echoed by numerous other business observers. Price Waterhouse says its clientele speaks for itself. PW handles more Fortune 500 companies than any other public accounting firm; more of the Forbes 100 U.S. multinational companies; and more companies in the Dow Jones averages than any other firm—and almost half of the industrials on the Dow Jones list. Its network of firms includes almost 400 offices, with over 28,000 professionals in 98 countries and territories. Integrity is also important to Price Waterhouse, the first firm to develop a program of action to combat the credibility and liability concerns facing the accounting field. PW proposed that audit responsibilities include searching for management fraud and reporting on an organization's financial condition as well as its financial position. A PW Technology Assessment Center in Palo Alto operates as a multidisciplinary think tank for research to better anticipate and respond to business needs. The company has seen a 30 percent expansion in number of offices from 1982 to 1986 and a 90 percent jump in revenues. Expect to advance very quickly and to receive varied experience with this leader.

ALL TRAINING PROGRAMS

Your accounting career will begin with a combination of formal continuing education (CE) courses and on-the-job training with performance reports and counseling sessions. CE courses are developed and taught by experienced PW people who are formally trained as instructors, as well as by outside consultants and outstanding faculty of leading executive development programs. The program combines sophisticated learning techniques, small group discussions, problem solving, and hands-on professional activities. Your advanced training will be both educational and enjoyable, with learning facilities in practice offices, resort area training centers, college campuses, conference centers, and hotels around the country. Participating in CE gives you the opportunity to meet hundreds of PW people from U.S. and overseas firm offices, broadening your knowledge at the same time. You will begin serving clients soon after you complete your entry-level course. Ongoing training with each client engagement is an important part of your development. You will be given access to all the latest professional publications and periodicals. Evaluations will follow each major assignment so that you know where you stand, with major reviews twice a year.

QUALIFICATIONS

You should be in the top of your class with an accounting, finance, or business background. Leadership skills, prior work experience, and how you present yourself will be keys to a successful interview.

RECRUITMENT AND PLACEMENT

You may interview with a Price Waterhouse recruiter on your college campus, or contact the office where you would like to work. The company has about 100 U.S. offices.

SALARIES AND BENEFITS

Price Waterhouse maintains its leadership position by paying top salaries. The College Placement Council Salary Survey for September 1986–June 1987 indicates starting salaries for public accounting firms to be $1,834 a month for those with a B.A. degree in nontechnical curricula and $2,155 with a B.A. degree in technical curricula. M.B.A. starting salaries were $2,335 for a nontechnical undergraduate degree and $2,436 for an M.B.A. with technical undergraduate degree. Check with the company for more specific salary information. If you join the firm after college, your starting salary could double in as few as five years. Benefits include medical, dental, group life, accidental death, business travel accident, and long-term disability insurance plans. A 401K savings plan will include a company contribution.

CONTACT

Director—National Recruiting, Price Waterhouse, 1251 Avenue of the Americas, New York, NY 10020.

PROCTER & GAMBLE

MANAGEMENT • SALES

THE COMPANY

Fortune has estimated that 95 out of 100 U.S. homes use P&G products, "a penetration unequaled by any other manufacturer of anything." Familiar brands include Tide laundry detergent, Crest toothpaste, Pampers disposable diapers, Duncan Hines cake mixes, Ivory soap, Head & Shoulders shampoo, Folger's coffee, Crisco shortening, and Cascade dishwashing detergent. The consumer product base also includes soft drinks, orange juice, and pharmaceuticals. Sales exceeding $15 billion consistently place P&G among the top 25 U.S. industrial corporations, and the company is also consistently named one of the best-managed American business organizations. In 1986, P&G ranked number 18 in the Fortune 500 largest U.S. industrial corporations. You'll work hard and be well rewarded for success with this leader. The company's policy is to promote only from within and on the basis of merit, so P&G places great emphasis on individual development.

MANAGEMENT TRAINING PROGRAM

You will be trained on the job to work in customer services or distribution services. After several weeks of personalized training with many levels of personnel plus learning the fundamentals of the company's computer programs, you will be assigned definite supervisory responsibility. New employees must take hold quickly. As a supervisor, you must train and manage a clerical staff and be able to handle personnel administration. Advice and counsel from more experienced personnel will always be available, but you must exercise initiative and make your own decisions.

QUALIFICATIONS

You might have a background in business administration, but P&G frequently hires those with liberal arts and other educational backgrounds. Most important is a demonstrated ability to achieve. Recruiters look for analytical skills, ability to work under pressure, versatility, imagination, and strong communication skills. You should be personable and have participated in extracurricular activities while in school. Leadership ability, demonstrated by holding office of some kind either in or out of school, is essential.

RECRUITMENT AND PLACEMENT

Procter & Gamble visits campuses large and small. You will be asked to take an aptitude test. Headquarters are in Cincinnati, with regional offices in Augusta, Chicago, Dallas, Sacramento, and Trenton, New Jersey.

SALES MANAGEMENT PROGRAM

Your sales management training will be tailored to your needs. You will work in a small group with a management ratio of 1 to 5. Your on-the-job training begins with a two-day orientation in your district. You become acquainted with the company, your brands, your section, and your accounts. At this time you receive your company car, equipment, and supplies. Following orientation, you make sales calls on your accounts with your unit manager or another qualified trainer, observing techniques and performance. You learn the basics of selling as your trainer thoroughly explains each step of the sales call, demonstrates it, lets you try it, and then critiques the sales call with you. In your early months you will attend a five-day new representatives training course in Cincinnati. You'll have an opportunity to tour the company's laboratories and production facilities. An organized reading program is available for self-development to supplement your on-the-job training. This basic approach will continue through your career as you advance to higher levels. There is no set time you will be at each level. A sales representative is responsible for over $4 million worth of sales annually. Travel will be minimal, with little or no overnight travel.

QUALIFICATIONS

A degree is important to Procter & Gamble, but leadership ability and resourcefulness count for more. The company wants to know what you achieved in school and how you achieved it.

RECRUITMENT AND PLACEMENT

P&G recruiters travel extensively. Expect to take an aptitude test. Your sales territory could be anywhere in the United States.

ALL PROGRAMS

SALARIES AND BENEFITS

Starting salaries (base plus generous bonuses) could easily be in the $22,000 range, likely to almost double when you step up to unit manager. P&G offers excellent benefits, including medical and dental insurance, stock options, and profit sharing.

CONTACT

Manager, Corporate Recruiting Coordination, Procter & Gamble Co., P.O. Box 599, Cincinnati, OH 45202.

THE PRUDENTIAL INSURANCE COMPANY OF AMERICA

ACTUARIAL SCIENCE • AUDITING • FINANCE • MARKETING • PENSIONS ADMINISTRATION • PROGRAMMING • SALES • SYSTEMS SUPPORT

THE COMPANY

Prudential's famous slogan is "Get a piece of the rock." The company was founded in 1873 by John Fairfield Dryen, a Yale dropout, who sold industrial insurance to working-class families under the name Widows and Orphans Friendly Society. He changed the name in 1875, and in 1876 he sold 7,000 policies, starting the company on the path to greatness. With a $60 billion portfolio in bonds, stocks, mortgages, real estate, and other investments, Prudential is one of the world's largest institutional investors and one of the largest managers of pension assets in the country. The world's fifth largest corporation and the biggest American corporation in the Fortune 50 largest insurance companies, it is also recognized as a leader in financial services. Bache Group, Inc., the parent company of the Bache brokerage firm, was bought by Prudential to expand its financial services. PruCapital is a subsidiary that Prudential established to engage in a wide range of leasing.

Prudential is headquartered in Newark, New Jersey, and employs over 60,000 people in the United States and Canada. It has more than $103 billion in assets, and is listed among *Fortune*'s most admired corporations.

ALL TRAINING PROGRAMS

You will participate in varied training: on the job, in the classroom, and in rotational assignments.

LIFE INSURANCE PROGRAM

Several departments offer supervised on-the-job training supplemented often with classroom instruction. If you work as an underwriter, your on-the-job training will cover the risk pricing, risk acceptance, and administration of group life and health insurance programs. In Group Pension Department training, you will be exposed to actuarial activities, contracts, systems, and the Administrative and Customer Service divisions. In the Individual Insurance Operations Department, the program covers processing new policy applications, risk evaluation, premium collection, changes in coverage, and the investigation, approval, and disbursement of claims. In the Auditing Section, training provides a number of rotational assignments. You will provide auditing services for individual and group insurance transactions, sales office operations, and real estate investment properties. If you start with the field sales force, the office manager will provide training in the company's various programs, information about the local market, and sales techniques.

QUALIFICATIONS

You should have an undergraduate or graduate degree in business, math, or liberal arts. Prudential is looking for people with strong communication skills, leadership abilities, and a good academic record.

PLACEMENT

Depending on your position, you may work in the home office in Newark, in one of nine regional offices, or at any of Prudential's 1,500 sales offices.

PRUCAPITAL PROGRAM

You may start out with the investment staff, marketing staff support, or portfolio management. You will be assigned to a team of experienced investment experts who will provide you with a thorough orientation to the company's products and customers. A broad exposure to the financial marketplace comes from working with all types of companies. As a member of the investment staff you will be quickly involved in seeking new investment opportunities through direct contact with potential customers and investment bankers. You will be given instruction on evaluating the customer's credit status and determining the appropriate structure for the financing. Upon approval of the financing, the terms of the financing agreement are negotiated. As a member of the marketing staff you will learn strategic planning and new product development methods. As you pursue your career path, you may choose to accept increased responsibilities with PruCapital, which may include managing and training other professionals, or you may transfer to other Prudential subsidiaries.

QUALIFICATIONS

To qualify for PruCapital's program you will need an M.B.A.

PLACEMENT

You might work in the corporate office in Cambridge, Massachusetts, or at one of 11 regional offices.

ALL PROGRAMS

RECRUITMENT

Prudential recruits nationwide.

SALARY AND BENEFITS

The College Placement Council Salary Survey for September 1986–June 1987 indicates starting salaries for banking, finance, and insurance companies to be $1,889 a month for those with a B.A. degree in nontechnical curricula and $2,135 with a B.A. degree in technical curricula. M.B.A. starting salaries were $2,884 for a nontechnical undergraduate degree and $3,320 for a technical undergraduate degree. Check with the company for more specific salary information. Prudential is considered to have an excellent health benefits package including group life, health, and dental insurance, an investment plan, a retirement plan, and tuition reimbursement. Check with the company for information about starting salaries.

CONTACT

For insurance operations: Charles Robbins, Associate Employment Manager, The Prudential, 56 North Livingston Avenue, Roseland, NJ 07068; for PruCapital: Executive Vice-President, PruCapital, Inc., 840 Memorial Drive, Cambridge, MA 02138.

PUBLIC SERVICE ELECTRIC AND GAS COMPANY

COMPUTER SCIENCE • ENGINEERING • MARKETING • OPERATIONS • PRODUCTION • SALES

THE COMPANY

PSE and G is an investor-owned company headquartered in Newark. Founded in 1903, it is currently the nation's third largest combined electric and gas utility. It ranks seventeenth in the Fortune 50 largest utilities, and has more than $10 billion in assets. PSE and G serves nearly 6 million people, almost three quarters of New Jersey's population, and its area of operation encompasses most of the state's largest municipalities. The company maintains a continuous construction program to meet energy needs and is heavily involved in nuclear-produced power with three nuclear power plants producing about a third of its total generating capacity. Public Service Electric and Gas Company built the first synthetic natural gas plant in the United States, installed the first fuel cells ever to supply power for an electric system, and is promoting research into solar energy. The company is also making major commitments to the support of advanced nuclear reactors and coal gasification.

ALL TRAINING PROGRAMS

PSE and G is proud of its nuclear training program and facilities. Its Nuclear Training Center houses classrooms, shops, laboratories, and simulator reactors. Classroom and on-the-job training is given to all Nuclear Department employees. Management-level employees undergo an eight-week orientation. During the first half you will concentrate on management techniques and interacting with supervisors. During the second four weeks you will receive on-the-job training in the department to which you are assigned.

QUALIFICATIONS

A variety of engineering positions are open in the Nuclear Department. The positions range from entry-level to middle management in the areas of training, quality assurance, plan engineering, systems engineering, all phases of plant operations, site maintenance, construction support, radiation protection, nuclear fuels, safety review, and licensing and regulation. In addition, positions are available in the Cost and Scheduling and Management Systems departments. Candidates for these spots should possess bachelor's degrees in the appropriate engineering disciplines. Requirements for the methods and administration positions include degrees in accounting, budgeting, management information, and computer science. Positions also exist in electrical and mechanical engineering and in computer science.

RECRUITMENT AND PLACEMENT

Electrical and mechanical engineers can expect assignment at power plants or distribution facilities. Nuclear Department employees work at the three nuclear power stations run by the company.

SALARY AND BENEFITS

Entry-level bachelor's degree positions start at $25,000 to $27,800. Benefits include four levels of health-care coverage, life insurance, a pension plan, disability benefits, thrift and tax-deferred savings plans, stock-purchase plans, a tuition-aid plan, paid vacations, and an internal Career Opportunity System to help employees up the career ladder.

CONTACT

Manager, Employment and Placement, Public Service Electric and Gas Company, P.O. Box 570, Newark, NJ 07101.

Q

☆ ☆ ☆ ☆ ☆

QUAKER

BRAND MANAGEMENT · SALES

THE COMPANY

With new corporate offices in Chicago and frequent additions of new subsidiaries, Quaker is approaching the 1990s with vigor and strength. Established in 1891 by several independent, regional millers who banded together to form the world's largest oatmeal company, today Quaker is considered one of the preeminent marketers of grocery products. The company consists of three operating segments: U.S. Grocery Products, International Grocery Products, and Fisher-Price (acquired in 1969). In addition to oatmeal, you'll find pork and beans, frozen waffles/pancakes, all types of dog and cat food, ready-to-eat cereals, pancake mix, and pancake syrup among Quaker's current product line. Recent product additions include Gatorade Thirst Quencher (from the acquisition of Stokely-Van Camp), Ghiradelli chocolates, Rice-A-Roni, and Gravy Train. Quaker has sales of over $3.5 billion and, in addition to Fisher-Price, operates subsidiary companies in Europe, Latin America, Canada, and the Pacific. There are more than 29,500 employees worldwide. It ranks number 104 in the Fortune 500 largest U.S. industrial corporations.

BRAND MANAGEMENT TRAINING PROGRAM

You'll enter brand management as a marketing assistant. In this job you will directly affect the brand's performance by gathering and analyzing the information needed for marketing plans, profit objectives and advertising, packaging and promotion plans. You'll forecast sales and profits and develop new products and product extensions. You will be part of a marketing team, which acts as a support group as you develop and execute your plans. You can expect to stay at this level for anywhere from one to one and a half years before moving to assistant brand manager.

QUALIFICATIONS

Quaker is looking for graduates with marketing, business, and related degrees who can demonstrate leadership, creativity, analytical ability, communication skills, and self-motivation. You may also join Quaker with related work experience, such as grocery store management.

PLACEMENT

You will work in Chicago.

SALES TRAINING PROGRAM

As an account representative you will join approximately 725 ambitious, self-motivated members of Quaker's sales team. You will begin your career with a thirteen-week training program. It begins with an intensive, one-week session conducted by your zone sales training manager. During this week you are given all the information you will need to make successful store presentations. Administrative details, company philosophy, and organization structure are covered in the course, as are demonstrations of effective presentation techniques and instruction in the use of sales aids, trade deals, and couponing. In the first few weeks of your sales assignment you will be accompanied and assisted by either the zone sales training manager or the district manager. After you are making calls on your own, part of your job will be to achieve product prominence and availability for consumers by making sales presentations to retail grocery store managers in your territory.

QUALIFICATIONS

Quaker is looking for graduates with marketing, business, and related degrees who can demonstrate leadership, creativity, analytical ability, communication skills, and self-motivation. You may also join Quaker with related work experience, such as grocery store management.

PLACEMENT

Sales representatives will be assigned to a zone in one of the four Quaker regions: Central (Chicago, Columbus, Detroit); Eastern (Baltimore, Boston, New York); Southern (Atlanta, Dallas, Jacksonville); or Western (Kansas City, Los Angeles, San Francisco). Sales representatives live in the trade area boundaries of the zone office to which they report and work out of their homes.

ALL PROGRAMS

RECRUITMENT

Quaker visits college campuses around the country and also welcomes applications sent directly to the company.

SALARY AND BENEFITS

The College Placement Council Salary Survey for September 1986–June 1987 indicates starting salaries for food and beverage processing companies to be $1,834 a month for those with a B.A. degree in nontechnical curricula and $2,301 with a B.A. degree in technical curricula. M.B.A. starting salaries were $3,043 for a nontechnical undergraduate degree and $3,098 for a technical undergraduate degree. Check with the company for more specific salary information. Sales representatives receive a base salary, supplemented by a sales incentive bonus program after six months. A company car is provided, and all necessary business expenses are paid by Quaker. Employees participate in a benefits program that includes a health incentive plan which gives each employee an individual medical expense account. Other benefits include stock and profit-sharing plans, dental insurance, and full tuition reimbursement for outside education and training activities directly related to job responsibilities.

CONTACT

Manager—Human Resources, U.S. Grocery Products Sales, The Quaker Oats Company, Chicago, IL 60654.

QUOTRON SYSTEMS, INC.

DESIGN • ELECTRONICS ENGINEERING • FINANCE • MARKETING • NETWORK SYSTEMS • SOFTWARE DEVELOPMENT

THE COMPANY

Quotron Systems, Inc., has been delivering electronic information to the financial industry since the late fifties. It developed the first electronic stock quotation system and continues to supply on-line, real-time information to clients such as banks, savings and loan associations, and insurance companies, as well as individual investors, corporations, and various exchanges. Citibank acquired Quotron in 1986. Its services go to approximately 72,000 terminals at more than 6,400 customer locations worldwide. With headquarters in Los Angeles, it has about 1,700 employees.

ALL TRAINING PROGRAMS

You will enter a formal training program to introduce you to Quotron's operations and procedures if you are an engineer, technician, programmer, or customer engineer. All other employees receive on-the-job training.

QUALIFICATIONS

Quotron hires at all degree levels from the following specialties: computer engineering, computer science, electronics engineering, engineering technology, information systems, manufacturing engineering, mathematics and applied mathematics, mechanical engineering, software engineering, and systems engineering. In addition to a familiarity with computer systems and software, the company prefers that you have related work experience and above-average communication skills.

RECRUITMENT AND PLACEMENT

The company hires about 30 trainees a year. You will work in California.

SALARY AND BENEFITS

The College Placement Council Salary Survey for September 1986–June 1987 indicates starting salaries for research and/or consulting organizations to be $2,116 a month for those with a B.A. degree in nontechnical curricula and $2,266 with a B.A. degree in technical curricula. M.B.A. starting salaries were $2,512 for a nontechnical undergraduate degree and $2,822 for a technical undergraduate degree. Check with the company for more specific salary information. Quotron's benefits include medical and dental plans, life insurance, a pension plan, flextime options, a fitness program, and incentive savings plan.

CONTACT

Peter Wagner, Technical Recruiter, Quotron Systems Inc., P.O. Box 92759, World Way Postal Center, Los Angeles, CA 90009.

R

☆ ☆ ☆ ☆ ☆

RADIAN CORPORATION

COMPUTER SCIENCE • ENGINEERING • RESEARCH AND DEVELOPMENT • TECHNICAL/PROFESSIONAL SERVICES

THE COMPANY

Radian Corporation is a contract research firm that provides a wide variety of professional and technical services focusing on environmental and energy problems. It began in 1969, with the government as the major client. Now it serves many large oil and chemical companies, manufacturing firms, and utilities. It is a subsidiary of Hartford Steam Boiler Inspection and Insurance Company. Corporate headquarters in Austin, Texas, occupy 200,000 square feet in a 15-acre campuslike complex. The site contains offices, laboratories, a computer center, and a manufacturing facility. The company has four divisions: Chemistry, Resources and Instrumentation, Advanced Systems, and Materials. It has about 1,000 employees.

ENGINEERING TRAINING PROGRAM

After joining the company as a new engineer, you will be assigned to a work project without spending time in a formal training program. The company believes that you will learn best from work projects under experienced supervision. You will work in teams, which will enable you to learn from other technical disciplines. Engineering performance reviews are held twice a year, when you and your supervisor will discuss your performance and progress and review your training and career goals.

QUALIFICATIONS

Radian hires graduates with all types of engineering degrees, including aerospace, chemical, civil, electrical, electronics, industrial, mechanical, and metallurgical engineering. A few computer science, physical science, and biological science majors are also hired each year. Doctoral candidates are encouraged to apply.

RECRUITMENT AND PLACEMENT

The company recruits nationwide. Generally you are placed in your specified area of interest. The location might be in headquarters in Austin or a regional branch office in Sacramento; Washington, D.C.; Durham, North Carolina; or Houston.

SALARY AND BENEFITS

The College Placement Council Salary Survey for September 1986–June 1987 indicates starting salaries for research and/or consulting organizations to be $2,116 a month for those with a B.A. degree in nontechnical curricula and $2,266 with a B.A. degree in technical curricula. M.B.A. starting salaries were $2,512 for a nontechnical undergraduate degree and $2,822 for a technical undergraduate degree. Check with the company for more specific salary information. Benefits include life, health, dental, and disability insurance; tuition assistance; a credit union; stock-purchase plan; and a retirement program.

CONTACT

James L. Grey, Manager, Employee Relations, Radian Corporation, P.O. Box 9948, Austin, TX 78766.

RALSTON PURINA COMPANY, GROCERY PRODUCTS DIVISION

ACCOUNTING • ANIMAL NUTRITION • CHEMISTRY • COMPUTER SCIENCE • ENGINEERING • FINANCE • FOOD SCIENCE • FOOD TECHNOLOGY • MARKETING • PRODUCT MANAGEMENT • SALES

THE COMPANY

In 1893, William H. Danforth decided that he would enter a business that would always be needed, during good times and bad. He chose to go into the feed business in St. Louis. Since then his company has grown into the world's largest producer of commercial animal feeds. Cereals are also manufactured under many well-known labels, and Ralston is the leader of the private-label cereal business, products sold as store brands.

Ralston Purina has diversified into other types of food, such as tuna, cookies, and crackers. Almost 800 Jack-in-the-Box fast-food restaurants as well as 85 full-service restaurants are owned and managed by Purina. The conglomerate also owns resorts and a hockey team. In addition, it is a major soy protein research firm.

In 1986 the company bought Union Carbide Corporation's battery products business (excluding India), adding 18,000 employees to the 47,000 who already work for Ralston Purina.

There are five major divisions within Ralston Purina. The largest, Grocery Products, accounts for one third of the company's sales and over half of its products. Thirty-five consumer products are marketed by this division. The other four divisions are Agricultural Products, Restaurants, Diversified Businesses, and International.

The Grocery Products Division has 14 production plants across the country. Profit centers and management are organized around types of pet and human food.

With $5.5 billion in annual sales, Ralston Purina ranks number 65 in the Fortune 500 largest U.S. industrial corporations. It is listed among *Fortune*'s most admired corporations.

PRODUCT MANAGEMENT TRAINING PROGRAM

The initial training lasts three months and is designed to incorporate any past experiences and specific needs. Meeting and working with staff come first. You will begin by implementing a marketing plan, with your team's attention focused on profit objectives and long-term growth goals. You will work closely with the Market Research Department, sales staff, and financial reporting personnel. The goal is to become an assistant product manager who handles more complex decisions with greater financial responsibility. Training can lead to a position as product manager.

QUALIFICATIONS

The Grocery Products Division looks for educated candidates who demonstrate good communication skills, an ability to motivate and persuade, entrepreneurial spirit, and a single-minded commitment that can be applied to the product.

RECRUITMENT AND PLACEMENT

The company responds only to applicants who fit its current needs. You will be placed as a marketing assistant and be part of a marketing team.

SALARY AND BENEFITS

Ask the company for specifics on its salaries and benefits package.

CONTACT

Grocery Products Personnel Department, Ralston Purina Company, Checkerboard Square, St. Louis, MO 63164.

RAYTHEON COMPANY

COMPUTER SCIENCE • ENGINEERING • PHYSICS

THE COMPANY

Founded in 1922, Raytheon designs and manufactures electronic systems for commercial and government customers. It manufactures radars, sonars, minicomputers, telecommunications and communications systems, computers and displays, missile guidance systems, microwave and solid-state semiconductor devices, heavy construction equipment, and acoustic and high-tech materials. Raytheon is also involved in educational publishing. Its subsidiary, Raytheon Service Company, one of the largest technical service organizations in the United States, produces sophisticated defense systems. Raytheon developed the first successful guided missile, the first laser signal bounced off the moon, and microwave cooking. It employs over 70,000 people worldwide. With more than $7 billion in annual sales, Raytheon is listed among *Fortune*'s most admired corporations. It ranks number 48 in the Fortune 500 largest U.S. industrial corporations.

ENGINEERING TRAINING PROGRAM

Training provides beginning engineers with the information and skills they need to begin work in research or in advanced development and design. Most beginning training is on the job. Advanced in-house training programs are offered. The company sponsors selected employees for full-time study for advanced degrees, including microwave engineering.

QUALIFICATIONS

The company is looking for graduates in computer science, physics, and engineering—electrical, electronics, industrial, manufacturing, materials, materials science, metallurgical, and mechanical.

RECRUITMENT AND PLACEMENT

The company recruits nationwide. Company facilities are located in California, Connecticut, New Jersey, Rhode Island, Tennessee, and Massachusetts.

SALARY AND BENEFITS

The College Placement Council Salary Survey for September 1986–June 1987 indicates starting salaries for electrical and electronic machines and equipment companies to be $1,861 a month for those with a B.A. degree in nontechnical curricula and $2,419 with a B.A. degree in technical curricula. M.B.A. starting salaries were $2,784 for a nontechnical undergraduate degree and $2,818 for a technical undergraduate degree. Check with the company for more specific salary information. Benefits include dental and medical insurance, a disability program, group life insurance, tuition reimbursement, and a pension plan.

CONTACT

Manager, College Relations, Raytheon Company, 141 Spring Street, Lexington, MA 02173.

RCA CORPORATION

ENGINEERING • RESEARCH AND DEVELOPMENT

THE COMPANY

Incorporated in 1919 as Radio Corporation of America, RCA acquired all property and assets of Marconi Wireless Telegraph Company, which then owned substantially all commercial radio communication facilities in the United States. It is now a wholly owned subsidiary of the General Electric Company. RCA pioneered in the development of radio, black-and-white and color television, videocassette recorders and cameras, and videodisc technology. RCA researches, manufactures, distributes, sells, leases, and services all of these products plus audio records and recorded tapes, solid state and electro-optic devices, commercial communications satellites, microwave systems, TV and broadcast equipment and systems, and space and military electronic equipment. Net sales have almost doubled in the past ten years. RCA employs more than 85,000 employees and owns or leases 26 plants in the United States and 18 in other countries. The National Broadcasting Company and Hertz Corporation (rental cars and trucks) are two of its subsidiaries.

ENGINEERING TRAINING PROGRAM

The Engineering Rotational Program gives you work experience on a variety of projects so you can choose the area of work best suited to your talents and interests. You will participate in four five-week engineering assignments as a member of a design team headed by experienced engineers. (If you have a master's degree, you will be given three eight-week assignments.) You may be assigned to one of these areas: government and commercial systems (aerospace and communications systems, and broadcast systems and products), solid state electronics, or consumer electronics (TV, radio, and stereo).

QUALIFICATIONS

You will need a bachelor's or master's degree in electrical, electronics, or mechanical engineering. RCA prefers candidates who place in the top quarter of their class with a G.P.A. of 3.0 or higher. Related student work experience and familiarity with computers will be in your favor.

RECRUITMENT AND PLACEMENT

Initial assignments may be in any of a number of divisions in different locations. Most of the company's facilities are in Indiana, Massachusetts, New Jersey, New York, and Pennsylvania.

SALARY AND BENEFITS

With a bachelor's degree, you will start at $23,000 to $31,000; with a master's, at $28,000 to $35,000; and with a doctorate, at $29,000 to $40,000. Benefits include life, accident, dental, and health insurance; a tuition reimbursement program; savings and pension plans; and relocation assistance.

CONTACT

RCA College Relations, RCA Corporation, Two Independence Way, P.O. Box 2023, Princeton, NJ 08540.

REVCO
MANAGEMENT

THE COMPANY

Revco is the nation's largest pharmacy chain, with more than 1,700 stores over more than half the nation. In 1947 the original store was a conventional drugstore in Detroit. By 1961 the chain had 20 discount drugstores—specializing in low prices for prescription drugs—in the Detroit area and Cleveland. Revco is now opening about two stores a week and also has moved into manufacturing through the purchase of four small drug companies (makers of vitamins, food supplements, cough syrups, liquid antibiotics, and medical shampoos). It ranks number 30 in the Fortune 50 largest retailing companies and has annual sales of $2.7 billion.

MANAGEMENT TRAINING PROGRAM

Pharmacists receive training and on-the-job experience in business skills and management training to become assistant store managers. Revco's continuing education program offers correspondence courses to all professional staff. Lectures in select cities keep you abreast of the latest trends in pharmacy and store sales.

QUALIFICATIONS

The company recruits pharmacists who are interested in store management positions.

RECRUITMENT AND PLACEMENT

Recruitment and placement are primarily in the Northeast, East, South, Southwest, and Midwest.

SALARY AND BENEFITS

The College Placement Council Salary Survey for September 1986–June 1987 indicates starting salaries for merchandising (retail and wholesale) and service companies to be $1,594 a month for those with a B.A. degree in nontechnical curricula and $2,141 with a B.A. degree in technical curricula. M.B.A. starting salaries were $2,572 for a nontechnical undergraduate degree, and $2,735 for an M.B.A. with technical undergraduate degree. Check with the company for more specific salary information. Benefits include health and dental insurance, disability protection, life insurance, a pension plan, profit-sharing and savings plans, and a favorable discount policy providing additional savings on most products in the store.

CONTACT

Senior Vice-President—Store Operations, Revco, 1925 Enterprise Parkway, Twinsburg, OH 44087.

REYNOLDS METALS COMPANY

COMPUTER SCIENCE • ENGINEERING • SALES/MARKETING

THE COMPANY

One of the most popular metals in use today is aluminum, and Reynolds is one of the leading aluminum companies. Founded in 1919, Reynolds Metals has become one of the world's largest producers of primary, recycled, and fabricated aluminum products. A wide range of products include flexible packing, containers, extrusions, sheet, plate, cable, plastic films, and household foil (Reynolds Wrap). Approximately 26,000 employees make up the Reynolds Team in over 50 manufacturing facilities scattered throughout the United States. Listed among *Fortune*'s most admired corporations, Reynolds has annual sales in excess of $3 billion. It ranks number 109 in the Fortune 500 largest U.S. industrial corporations.

ALL TRAINING PROGRAMS

Most entry-level trainee positions at Reynolds consist primarily of comprehensive on-the-job experience under the direction and guidance of a seasoned supervisor. This is supplemented by a once-a-year performance review coupled with various company-sponsored programs in a classroom setting. Courses cover such subjects as management skills and sales/marketing techniques.

QUALIFICATIONS

Reynolds seeks primarily college graduates with degrees in engineering and computer/information systems. Other disciplines include accounting, business, and chemistry.

RECRUITMENT AND PLACEMENT

Reynolds recruits nationwide. Your placement will depend on your area of interest, personal qualifications, academic background, and the company's requirements.

SALARY AND BENEFITS

The College Placement Council Salary Survey for September 1986–June 1987 indicates starting salaries for metals and metal products companies to be $1,782 a month for those with a B.A. degree in nontechnical curricula and $2,353 with a B.A. degree in technical curricula. M.B.A. starting salaries were $2,346 for a nontechnical undergraduate degree and $2,700 for a technical undergraduate degree. Check with the company for more specific salary information. Reynolds' employees enjoy an outstanding benefits package including company-paid medical, dental, and vision care, life insurance, savings plan, and tuition assistance for continuing education.

CONTACT

Thomas J. Nash, Director, Employment and Placement, Reynolds Metals Company, 6601 West Broad Street, Richmond, VA 23230.

RJR NABISCO

ENGINEERING • FINANCE • MARKETING RESEARCH ANALYSIS • PROGRAM ANALYSIS • SALES • SYSTEMS ENGINEERING

THE COMPANY

Formerly R. J. Reynolds Industries, RJR Nabisco assumed its new name in 1986 to reflect its growing diversity. The company produces and markets a wide variety of consumer products worldwide, including foods and beverages, domestic and international tobacco, spirits, wines, imported beer, and packaging products. With more than 200 brands in 39 major product categories, the company had sales exceeding $20 billion in 1986. It is the parent company of Nabisco Brands, Inc.; R. J. Reynolds Tobacco Company; R. J. Reynolds Tobacco International, Inc.; Heublein, Inc.; and RJR Archer, Inc. RJR Nabisco has more than 250 manufacturing plants around the world and sells products in more than 160 countries and territories. Its corporate headquarters are in Winston-Salem, North Carolina. Over half of its 130,000 employees work outside the United States. Listed among *Fortune*'s most admired corporations, it has more than $17 billion in assets. RJR Nabisco ranks number 14 in the Fortune 500 largest U.S. industrial corporations.

FINANCIAL TRAINING PROGRAM

You will participate in four six-month assignments in different financial functions as well as different companies within RJR Nabisco. You will be exposed to financial analysis, general accounting, cost accounting, budgeting, information systems, internal audit, credit analysis, capital budgeting, tax, and treasury. Training is conducted in group sessions and seminars.

QUALIFICATIONS

You should be a recent or prospective M.B.A. with a finance major.

RECRUITMENT AND PLACEMENT

The company recruits nationwide. You will train in Winston-Salem.

SALARY AND BENEFITS

The College Placement Council Salary Survey for September 1986–June 1987 indicates starting salaries for food and beverage processing companies to be $1,834 a month for those with a B.A. degree in nontechnical curricula and $2,301 with a B.A. degree in technical curricula. M.B.A. starting salaries were $3,043 for a nontechnical undergraduate degree and $3,098 for a technical undergraduate degree. Check with the company for more specific salary information. After six months of employment your benefits package will include group life insurance for you and your family, funeral leave with pay, medical and dental coverage, a retirement plan, savings and investment plan, stock-bonus and stock-purchase plan, credit union, paid vacations, and tuition reimbursement.

CONTACT

Personnel Recruiter, RJR Nabisco, Inc., Corporate Headquarters, Winston-Salem, NC 27102.

ROCKWELL INTERNATIONAL

ENGINEERING • INFORMATION SYSTEMS/PROCESSING • MANUFACTURING • RESEARCH AND DEVELOPMENT

THE COMPANY

Rockwell International is the nation's largest independent supplier of domestic microwave communication systems. The company straddles the aerospace, electronics, and automotive industries as well. Rockwell is a prime contractor to the federal government for the NASA Space Shuttle, the Navy's NAVSTAR GPS navigation satellite program, and the Air Force's B-1B long-range combat aircraft. Products manufactured by Rockwell range from defense systems to avionics to printing presses. The company has 110,000 employees in the United States and another 10,000 outside the country. Listed among *Fortune*'s most admired corporations, Rockwell has annual sales of more than $12 billion and ranks number 24 in the Fortune 500 largest U.S. industrial corporations.

ALL TRAINING PROGRAMS

If you join the company as a manufacturing supervisor trainee, you will go through an intensive twelve- to twenty-four-month program. For most engineering positions the training is supervised on-the-job experience combined with classroom instruction.

QUALIFICATIONS

Rockwell looks primarily for college graduates with degrees in engineering and computer science. Individuals trained in other academic fields have some opportunities but are not in as great demand. For computer science graduates, some positions require software language course work in FORTRAN, BASIC, ATLAS, ADA, and Pascal. Microcomputer course work and experience are helpful.

RECRUITMENT AND PLACEMENT

The company recruits nationally, hiring about 1,100 trainees a year. Depending on which division you work for, you could be placed in El Segundo, Anaheim, Canoga Park, or Newport Beach, California; Pittsburgh; Troy, Michigan; Richardson, Texas; Cedar Rapids, Iowa; Tulsa; or Duluth, Georgia.

SALARY AND BENEFITS

The College Placement Council Salary Survey for September 1986–June 1987 indicates starting salaries for aerospace companies to be $1,943 a month for those with a B.A. degree in nontechnical curricula and $2,399 with a B.A. degree in technical curricula. M.B.A. starting salaries were $2,330 for a nontechnical undergraduate degree and $2,475 for a technical undergraduate degree. Check with the company for more specific salary information. Your benefits package will include tuition reimbursement, membership in a recreational facility, group health insurance, long-term disability insurance, dental coverage, retirement and savings plans, and credit union membership.

CONTACT

Personnel Manager, Rockwell International: for aerospace businesses, Mail Code B15-006, 2230 East Imperial Highway, El Segundo, CA 90245; for automotive businesses, Mail Code 292-AU-1, 2135 West Maple Road, Troy, MI 48084; for commercial electronics businesses, Mail Station 407-321, P.O. Box 10462, Dallas, TX 75207; for defense electronics businesses, Mail Code AD-IS, 3370 Miraloma Avenue, P.O. Box 4921, Anaheim, CA 92803; for general industries businesses, Mail Code 706-IG-1, 400 North Lexington Avenue, Pittsburgh, PA 15208; for shuttle launch operations, Jane Beech, Personnel, Rockwell International, Shuttle Launch Operations Division, P.O. Box 21105, Kennedy Space Center, FL 32815; for missile systems, Manager, Employment Administration, Rockwell International, Missile Systems Division, 1800 Satellite Boulevard, Duluth, GA 30136.

ROLM CORPORATION

ENGINEERING • INFORMATION SYSTEMS • MARKETING • RESEARCH AND DEVELOPMENT • SALES

THE COMPANY

ROLM was founded in 1969 by four Rice University engineers who set up shop in an abandoned prune-drying shed in Santa Clara, California. In October 1984, ROLM was acquired by IBM for $1.25 billion—not bad for ROLM, which had posted a growth rate of 60 percent or better each year it was in operation. ROLM started with the idea of the founders (who combined the initial letters of their last names to form the company name) that there should be a good minicomputer for sale to the Defense Department. ROLM made the computer, sold it at a substantial savings over the bid of the nearest competitor, and was launched on the path to success. The company later introduced a computer-driven telephone system that has been eating up the market. ROLM had the golden touch, but Kenneth Oshman, cofounder and chief executive of ROLM, had continually bemoaned the scarcity of suitable venture capital. ROLM and IBM worked together in 1983, IBM to provide capital and ROLM to share its research and planning with IBM. After months of internal staff tensions between the two companies, Oshman agreed to a merger with IBM as a way to settle the disputes. ROLM has 10,000 employees in the United States and another 500 outside the country.

ALL TRAINING PROGRAMS

ROLM has a very comprehensive and intense training program. All positions involve some on-the-job training heavily supplemented with company courses, outside seminars, tutorials, and specific engineering training programs. This company has no set career paths; you make your own, and you will be evaluated carefully as you are circulated through various training assignments.

QUALIFICATIONS

ROLM is looking for design, production, and field service engineers. In addition, applications are desired from graduates with business degrees.

RECRUITMENT AND PLACEMENT

Design and production engineers will likely start in either Texas or California, and field service engineers are needed throughout the United States and Canada.

SALARY AND BENEFITS

The College Placement Council Salary Survey for September 1986–June 1987 indicates starting salaries for electrical and electronic machines and equipment companies to be $1,861 a month for those with a B.A. degree in nontechnical curricula and $2,419 with a B.A. degree in technical curricula. M.B.A. starting salaries were $2,784 for a nontechnical undergraduate degree and $2,818 for a technical undergraduate degree. Check with the company for more specific salary information. One of ROLM's founding goals is that the company be a great place to work. Your liberal benefits package will include medical and dental plans, life and accident insurance, short- and long-term disability, holiday and sick pay, profit sharing, stock-purchase plans, and one very unusual program—a requirement that each employee who works six full years with the company take a twelve-week paid leave. Management believes this freshens you and prevents burnout.

CONTACT

Personnel Manager, ROLM Corporation, 4900 Old Ironsides Drive, Santa Clara, CA 95050.

ROYAL INSURANCE

ACTUARIAL SCIENCE • AUDITING • CLAIMS REPRESENTATION • COMPUTER PROGRAMMING • DATA PROCESSING • ENGINEERING REPRESENTATION • MARKETING • UNDERWRITING

THE COMPANY

Royal Insurance, established in 1845, is an insurance firm specializing in property, casualty, life, and marine coverages. It sells policies through more than 4,000 independent agents and brokers in all 50 states with a network of more than 100 offices and 5,500 employees nationwide. Royal Insurance is part of the International Royal Insurance Group, headquartered in London, offering insurance in more than 80 countries. Its policies are written in 16 languages. The parent company has a staff of 22,000.

ALL TRAINING PROGRAMS

The training program includes one month of formal training and five months of on-the-job training. The company has a complete program of audiovisual training courses.

QUALIFICATIONS

Either master's or bachelor's degree holders may find a job with Royal Insurance.

RECRUITMENT AND PLACEMENT

Data processing graduates are currently in high demand. If you majored in engineering (general, environmental, industrial/management, or mechanical), engineering science, or engineering technology, then Royal Insurance may be the firm for you. Royal also looks for actuaries and auditors. You may also be placed as a claims representative, marketing representative, or underwriter. Royal Insurance has agencies in every state. Starting locations are in California, Georgia, Illinois, Kansas, Massachusetts, Michigan, New Jersey, New York, Pennsylvania, Tennessee, Texas, and Virginia.

SALARY AND BENEFITS

The College Placement Council Salary Survey for September 1986–June 1987 indicates starting salaries for banking, finance, and insurance companies to be $1,889 a month for those with a B.A. degree in nontechnical curricula and $2,135 with a B.A. degree in technical curricula. M.B.A. starting salaries were $2,884 for a nontechnical undergraduate degree and $3,320 for a technical undergraduate degree. Check with the company for more specific salary information. You will receive a full range of benefits, including health-care plans, hospitalization, disability, retirement, life insurance, and savings and profit-sharing plans.

CONTACT

Robert A. Moeller, Employment Manager, Royal Insurance, Suite 140, 8731 Red Oak Boulevard, Charlotte, NC 28210.

Advice from a University Career-Placement Center
Dr. Glenn Payne, University of Southern California

Dr. Glenn Payne is the Director of M.B.A. Career Services in the Graduate School of Business at the University of Southern California.

☆ ☆ ☆ ☆ ☆

When finishing an M.B.A. and beginning to interview companies, what is the advantage of going with a company that does have a strong entry-level program?

The M.B.A. can get graduates a job, anywhere in the company probably. But it might not lead them to the promotions that they would like. If they don't go through one of the training programs, they probably won't get into top management. The programs are intended as an entry route into the main line of money making in a company. They're trying to get you into line jobs. Very few of the programs are for staff jobs. Most are for line money-making people in that business. As a result, if you go through that training program and go out on the line, then you have a lot of credibility in that role. And so I think that letting yourself go through the training program is very important in terms of being indoctrinated into the company. The larger companies really want somebody to be the next president in twenty years. And they're expecting that person to come through that training program. Now, there are training programs and there are fast-track training programs.

How would you distinguish between those?

My classic case in point would be Chevron. I can think of four or five different training programs at Chevron. But there's one that I ran across for M.B.A.s that is a fast-track program. They only take real quality M.B.A.s from prestigious institutions. There are some training programs that are really set up to find the next comptrollers or presidents or whatever.

What's the trend for hiring M.B.A.s, and how has it changed in the last five to ten years?

They're still a valuable commodity. Some companies want M.B.A.s more than other companies. In the banking world, they'll go out of their way to interview M.B.A.s but they don't depend on them. They depend on B.A.s for their training programs. It's not necessary to have an M.B.A., it certainly does help, but it's not a necessity. Whereas I think, to succeed in the world of investment banking, it's a necessity. And to become the treasurer/comptroller for a company, it is definitely an asset. People can do without it, but with the number of M.B.A.s on the market, I think they have a great advantage.

What kind of suggestions or tips would you give to someone who is comparing training programs?

I would look at what usually happens to people when they get out of them. Do they step into a line management division? And what happens to them two or three years out? Try to determine if a company is really depending on the program to bring forth their line managers.

I think M.B.A.s balk at the time taken for these programs. I know that in banking the programs last anywhere from six to eighteen months. Usually M.B.A.s don't want to put time into them, but they actually need to be indoctrinated into the company and to supplement their academic experience. But at the same time they need to evaluate how much they're being taught. For example, in Chicago, at Continental Bank their program is six months long, and at First Chicago it takes a full year or more. But the difference is that at First Chicago they are teaching you how to be an investment banker too. They've got their merchant banking and investment banking mixed in with the regular banking. Then I'd look at the quality of the people who run the place; I'd prefer a former line person or a line person assigned to manage the training program.

And what's your rationale for that?

Because they know what the company is trying to achieve. They have a line perspective and an operations perspective. So one of the questions that a student needs to ask is about faculty, who are they and what kind of experience they have.

Check into placement after the program. A lot of the M.B.A.s are concerned about where they will live when they get through a training program. If you go to work with Chase and go to their training program in New York, can you come back to L.A.? Some companies will make a commitment to you on placement after the program and some won't.

They should also ask about how much they would travel in the training program. I know at GTE and Texas Instruments—and I think TRW too—trainees are in one place for six months and then move to another for six months, and then six months in another, and then you get to decide which place you want to stay for the next three years. But for a year and a half they're going to move around within the company.

A person might also review the overall economics in a particular industry and the position of a company in an area of the business. My case in point is First Interstate Bank in California. They decided to get out of the merchant banking business and they laid off two students from U.C.L.A. and two students from U.S.C. who were in their training program. Now, the training program for commercial banking stayed put, and the real estate program stayed put, but the area that they got out of was shut down. So check out the viability of that particular part of the business when you're considering a training program.

S

☆ ☆ ☆ ☆ ☆

SAFEWAY STORES, INC.

ACCOUNTING · ADMINISTRATION · ADVERTISING · AUDITING · BUYING/ PROCUREMENT · DATA PROCESSING · EMPLOYEE RELATIONS · MERCHANDISING · PUBLIC RELATIONS · RETAIL MANAGEMENT

THE COMPANY

Safeway is the world's largest supermarket chain and one of the three largest retailers in the world, with sales exceeding $20 billion annually. It ranks 3 in the Fortune 50 largest retailing companies. It also manufactures and processes products bearing its own brand names in about 100 plants. Safeway traces its beginnings to S. M. Skaggs, a Baptist minister, who opened a grocery store in American Falls, Idaho, in 1915. Skaggs built sales volume by taking only a small profit on the merchandise sold. In 1926, Skaggs merged with the Southern California chain of Safeway stores. Even today, margins are so slim that a net profit of one penny on the dollar is considered good. Quality circles involve front-line employees in problem solving. Safeway has more than 2,500 store managers.

STORE MANAGEMENT TRAINING PROGRAM

This accelerated training program can prepare you for store management in a year or less. You will begin with a six- to nine-month stint in department training, rotating through departments in a retail store. Evaluation conducted by a department trainer follows each experience. You will supplement this with a self-study program on retailing. If you do well, you will be promoted to assistant manager. The pace of training speeds up, with a comprehensive review of technical information, an analysis of the assistant manager's own store, self-paced study in management skills, and seminars in management, industrial relations, and division staff functions.

QUALIFICATIONS

Safeway is hiring graduates in the fields of mathematics/statistics, business administration, marketing, accounting and finance, and liberal arts with background in food retailing.

RECRUITMENT AND PLACEMENT

Recruitment and placement are nationwide.

SALARY AND BENEFITS

The College Placement Council Salary Survey for September 1986–June 1987 indicates starting salaries for merchandising (retail and wholesale) and service companies to be $1,594 a month for those with a B.A. degree in nontechnical curricula and $2,141 with a B.A. degree in technical curricula. M.B.A. starting salaries were $2,572 for a nontechnical undergraduate degree and $2,735 for an M.B.A. with technical undergraduate degree. Check with the company for more specific salary information. Benefits consist of life, health, dental, accident, and disability insurance; profit sharing; bonus payments; an employees' association; a credit union; a retirement plan; and tuition reimbursement.

CONTACT

Personnel Director, Safeway Stores, Inc., 201 Fourth Street, Oakland, CA 94660.

SALOMON BROTHERS

FINANCE • RESEARCH • SALES • TECHNOLOGY RESOURCE MANAGEMENT • TRADING

THE COMPANY

Salomon Brothers is a major international investment banking and market-making concern. It provides a broad range of underwriting, financial advisory, and research services to governments, corporations, and institutional investors around the world. Services to corporations and real estate clients offer expertise in restructurings, securitization of assets, mergers and acquisitions, and domestic and international debt and equity financing. Headquartered in New York, Salomon Brothers operates affiliated offices in London, Tokyo, Zurich, and Frankfurt, and domestic offices in Atlanta, Boston, Chicago, Dallas, Los Angeles, and San Francisco. Listed among *Fortune*'s most admired corporations, Salomon has assets of more than $78 billion. It ranks number 3 in the Fortune 50 largest diversified financial companies.

SALES AND TRADING TRAINING PROGRAM

You will spend two weeks preparing for the Registered Representative exam and three months in a classroom training program. You will study corporate finance; municipal finance; the fixed income areas of money markets, governments, futures, mortgages, corporate bonds, preferreds, municipal bonds; and the international markets; as well as the equity market. You will study basic concepts about these markets as well as the fundamentals of relative value analysis. The classroom phase is followed by rotational assignments on all sales and trading desks, preparing you to work with corporations and institutional portfolio managers.

QUALIFICATIONS

You will need a record of distinguished academic achievement, superior leadership ability, outstanding entrepreneurial capability, and excellent communication skills. Knowledge of the investment banking industry, a broad range of interests, and a clear commitment to achieve great success are necessary. An academic background in economics, finance, or other quantitative discipline is very important.

RECRUITMENT AND PLACEMENT

Hiring is highly competitive with recruiting done nationally. You could work at any of the company's offices during your career.

SALARY AND BENEFITS

The College Placement Council Salary Survey for September 1986–June 1987 indicates starting salaries for banking, finance, and insurance firms to be $1,889 a month for those with a B.A. degree in nontechnical curricula and $2,135 with a B.A. degree in technical curricula. M.B.A. starting salaries were $2,884 for a nontechnical undergraduate degree and $3,320 for an M.B.A. with technical undergraduate degree. Check with the company for more specific salary information. You will be eligible for bonuses based on your contributions.

CONTACT

Personnel Recruitment, Salomon Brothers, Inc., One New York Plaza, New York, NY 10004.

SAMI/BURKE INC.

CLIENT SERVICE • MARKETING RESEARCH

THE COMPANY

The merger of Selling-Areas Marketing, Inc. (SAMI), and Burke Marketing Services, Inc., combined some of the richest databases in the market research industry. A wholly owned subsidiary of Time, Inc., SAMI/Burke, Inc., is composed of specialized service divisions covering all segments of the marketing research industry. The company is headquartered in Cincinnati, Ohio, with offices in more than 35 U.S. cities. It has conducted over 60,000 individual research projects encompassing almost every kind of business.

The company began about fifty years ago as a field and tabulation service. With more than 3,000 employees, it is the world's largest marketing research company and the nation's most diversified custom research company. Its services include client management, project management, report processing, simulated test marketing and forecasting, and management information systems.

Long respected for its work in the consumer packaged goods arena, SAMI/Burke is experiencing unprecedented research opportunities in industry, telecommunications, data processing, finance, and health care. The company offers an array of complementary services and extensive databases such as planning, collection, and analysis of survey research data; predictive market modeling; testing of advertising effectiveness; store scanner-based test marketing; product movement data; and educational seminars.

ALL TRAINING PROGRAMS

Training is primarily on the job. An individual begins as an associate research analyst or associate project director and gains exposure to all facets of a research study from study design through analysis and modeling. Once experience has been gained, the individual can choose to pursue an analytical, production, or client service track depending on interest and potential.

QUALIFICATIONS

SAMI/Burke recruits candidates with both undergraduate and graduate degrees in marketing, marketing research, quantitative analysis, data processing, and experimental psychology. Ideal candidates have some experience in marketing or behavioral research.

RECRUITMENT AND PLACEMENT

The company recruits nationally. Primary locations are the company headquarters in Cincinnati, Chicago, Westport, Connecticut, New York City, and the San Francisco Bay area. You could also work in Atlanta, Dallas, Detroit, Louisville, Philadelphia, or Los Angeles.

SALARIES AND BENEFITS

The College Placement Council Salary Survey for September 1986–June 1987 indicates starting salaries for research and/or consulting organizations to be $2,116 a month for those with a B.A. degree in nontechnical curricula and $2,266 with a B.A. degree in technical curricula. M.B.A. starting salaries were $2,512 for a nontechnical undergraduate degree and $2,822 for a technical undergraduate degree. Check with the company for more specific salary information. Benefits include health and dental coverage, life insurance, accident insurance, disability income, profit sharing, retirement benefits, a deferred savings plan, and liberal vacations and holidays.

CONTACT

Manager, Professional Development, SAMI/Burke, Inc., 800 Broadway, Cincinnati, OH 45202.

SANDERS ASSOCIATES, INC.

ENGINEERING • OPERATIONS • PRODUCTION • RESEARCH AND DEVELOPMENT

THE COMPANY

Ever wonder who makes all those devices that can tell you if someone has bugged your phone? Sanders Associates makes such gadgets; it is a consulting, engineering, and professional services firm that refers to this activity as "electronic countermeasures." The firm also deals in advanced graphic terminals and systems, printed circuits, microwave products, and consulting services and product manufacture for defense. Sanders employs 9,000 people in the United States and another 2,000 outside the country.

ALL TRAINING PROGRAMS

Training gets you ready to work with state-of-the-art electronics and computer systems. The program consists of twenty-four months of on-the-job and classroom instruction.

QUALIFICATIONS

Sanders is looking for engineering and computer personnel. If you have a background in computer, electrical, electronics, industrial/management, manufacturing, mechanical, ocean, or software engineering, this may be the company for you. Doctoral-level applicants are also encouraged in those fields, as are people with a degree in business. Work-related experience will strengthen your résumé. The company wants applicants in the top half of their class.

RECRUITMENT AND PLACEMENT

Your starting location will be in Nashua, New Hampshire, at company headquarters. International assignments are available to U.S. citizens with one to five years' experience.

SALARY AND BENEFITS

The College Placement Council Salary Survey for September 1986–June 1987 indicates starting salaries for electrical and electronic machines and equipment companies to be $1,861 a month for those with a B.A. degree in nontechnical curricula and $2,419 with a B.A. degree in technical curricula. M.B.A. starting salaries were $2,784 for a nontechnical undergraduate degree and $2,818 for a technical undergraduate degree. Check with the company for more specific salary information. Your benefits package will consist of medical, hospital, and dental plans; life insurance; pension and stock-purchase plans; relocation assistance; and an incentive savings plan.

CONTACT

David Hallee, Coordinator, College Relations, Sanders Associates, Inc., 95 Canal Street, Nashua, NH 03061.

SANTA FE RAILWAY COMPANY

MANAGEMENT • SALES

THE COMPANY

Santa Fe, founded in 1860, certainly got off to a slow start. No track was laid for the first eight years of the company's existence. In 1872 the railroad finally reached Dodge City, and though it made good money from shipping cattle to the East, it was constantly plagued by troublemaking and marauding cowboys. Finally, twenty-two years after it was founded, the company earned its name by reaching Santa Fe, New Mexico. Today the railroad stretches for more than 12,000 miles, from Chicago to California and from Texas to Nebraska. The company is also a major producer of heavy crude oil. Ranked number 7 in the Fortune 50 largest transportation companies, it is listed among *Fortune*'s most admired corporations. Santa Fe's annual revenues exceed $5 billion.

ALL TRAINING PROGRAMS

Your training in the Sales and Service Section will give you effective sales techniques and an understanding of tariffs, freight schedules, and other transportation services. The company also sponsors a cooperative education program leading to a master's degree in management at Massachusetts Institute of Technology or at Harvard University's School of Business Administration.

QUALIFICATIONS

You should have a bachelor's or a master's degree in business administration, economics, marketing, accounting, finance, or labor relations.

RECRUITMENT AND PLACEMENT

Santa Fe recruits primarily in the Midwest, though representatives also visit campuses in the South and West. You can expect to be placed anywhere within the large railroad service area.

SALARY AND BENEFITS

The College Placement Council Salary Survey for September 1986–June 1987 indicates starting salaries for public utilities (including transportation) to be $1,905 a month for those with a B.A. degree in nontechnical curricula and $2,355 with a B.A. degree in technical curricula. M.B.A. starting salaries were $2,403 for a nontechnical undergraduate degree and $2,667 for a technical undergraduate degree. Check with the company for more specific salary information. Benefits include medical and life insurance, an educational assistance plan, a stock-purchase plan, and a retirement program.

CONTACT

Manager of Personnel Development, Santa Fe Railway Company, 80 East Jackson Boulevard, Chicago, IL 60604.

SAV-ON DRUGS, INC.
MANAGEMENT

THE COMPANY

Sav-On started in 1945 in San Bernadino, California, as a single store, a pioneer self-service drugstore. It is now one of the largest-volume chain drug retailers in the United States. The company describes each of its stores as "25,000 square feet of retailing enthusiasm." It has a growth rate goal of 10 percent a year—8 to 15 new stores are added to the chain each year.

MANAGEMENT TRAINING PROGRAM

The goal of the training program is to give you the experience and skills necessary to ultimately become a store manager. As a management trainee, you will receive firsthand experience in every aspect of the store operation. You will learn the latest merchandising and management techniques.

QUALIFICATIONS

The single most important qualification for positions with Sav-On is a willingness to work long hours on the job. The normal workday lasts nine to ten hours, and it is expected that every other week you will be willing to stay until the store closes at night. Weekend work and extra hours because of seasonal or emergency needs also are required.

RECRUITMENT AND PLACEMENT

Sav-On Stores are in California, Nevada, and Texas.

SALARY AND BENEFITS

The College Placement Council Salary Survey for September 1986–June 1987 indicates starting salaries for merchandising (retail and wholesale) and service companies to be $1,594 a month for those with a B.A. degree in nontechnical curricula and $2,141 with a B.A. degree in technical curricula. Check with the company for more specific salary information. You will be provided with (at no extra cost) a host of benefits that include employee discounts; health, dental, and vision care; life insurance; paid vacations and holidays; profit sharing; and retirement benefits.

CONTACT

Director of Corporate Training, Sav-On Drugs, Inc., 150 South Anaheim Boulevard, Anaheim, CA 92805.

SCHLUMBERGER WELL SERVICES

COMPUTER SCIENCE • ENGINEERING • GEOPHYSICS • PHYSICS

THE COMPANY

Schlumberger (pronounced "Schloomber zshay") is Johnny-on-the-spot whenever an oilman wants to know what he's likely to find at the bottom of his wells. The company, which also has an overseas division, sends out a field crew in an electronics-packed van, drops a probe down the well, and deciphers the electrical readings to tell the oilman what's there. The company goes way back. Conrad Schlumberger and his brother Marcel came out of the Alsace region of France in the 1800s. They moved to Paris and experimented with minerals to determine whether they could be identified by their degree of resistance to electricity. By the end of World War I they had a device to sell, and a company was born. Company headquarters moved to Houston in the early 1950s, and Schlumberger was soon probing wells all over the world. Declines in the oil market have led the firm to focus more attention on its electronics divisions with the goal of expanding into international markets. The company manufactures its own testing equipment at plants in Houston and France. World headquarters are now in New York, with North American operations directed from Houston.

ALL TRAINING PROGRAMS

Engineers get training that allows them to function effectively in the many remote and rugged areas where drilling occurs. Domestically based employees get a combination of on-the-job and classroom instruction for six months. Overseas personnel train with the same approach for twelve months.

QUALIFICATIONS

Schlumberger is looking for computer science and engineering personnel for its research and development operations; it needs engineers (electrical, mechanical, and petroleum), geophysicists, and physicists for its operating offices. You should have appropriate degrees for those areas. Previous work experience will help a lot.

RECRUITMENT AND PLACEMENT

Schlumberger has 85 operating offices in 24 states for field engineers. Research and development facilities are in Houston, Ridgefield, Connecticut, France, and England. Overseas operations are active in 70 countries around the world, with the heaviest concentration of locations in the North Sea, West Africa, the Middle East, South America, and the Far East.

SALARY AND BENEFITS

U.S. starting salaries at the bachelor's level are in the $25,000 area. Overseas bachelor's or master's salaries average over $31,500. Benefits are industry-average.

CONTACT

For U.S. operations: C. R. Gadomski, Director of College Relations, Schlumberger Well Services, 5000 Gulf Freeway, Houston, TX 77001; for overseas operations: L. A. Walker, Recruiting Coordinator, Schlumberger Overseas, 3100 Timmons Lane, Houston, TX 77027.

SCOTT PAPER COMPANY

SALES

THE COMPANY

When preparing for a sales career with Scott, bring your combat boots, for you will be entering the "Great Toilet Paper War"! After Scott's fifty years as the number one toilet paper and paper towel seller in the nation, Procter & Gamble has beaten Scott in sales of both products. Accustomed to being number one, Scott is geared up for the battle to regain its top ranking. The company has also taken major steps to revitalize its entire structure, shaking up top management by basing pay partly on their contribution to profits. *Fortune* reports that insiders say "managers who don't produce either get religion or get shown the door, something that never happened before." In addition to toilet paper and towels, annual sales of $3.8 billion come from babies' premoistened tissues, paper napkins, wax paper, and polyurethane foam for carpet cushioning and soundproofing. The company also sells liquid soaps, lumber, and book publishing papers. The Scott family includes approximately 20,600 employees in consolidated operations and more than 19,700 in affiliated companies. Listed among *Fortune*'s most admired corporations, Scott ranks number 115 in the Fortune 500 largest U.S. industrial corporations.

SALES TRAINING PROGRAM

The twelve-week sales orientation program helps you develop professional selling skills, learn the market, and become familiar with Scott's products. You will work directly under a supervisor who will help you learn to manage your market. During the twelve-week program you will also learn more about Scott's marketing strategy and your role within the company.

QUALIFICATIONS

You should have a bachelor's degree in liberal arts or business administration, and a strong desire to progress into sales management.

RECRUITMENT AND PLACEMENT

Scott recruits on many college campuses each year. Training takes place in the sales territory.

SALARY AND BENEFITS

Scott's salaries include bonuses and other incentives. The College Placement Council Salary Survey for September 1986–June 1987 indicates starting salaries for glass, paper, packaging, and allied products companies to be $1,865 a month for those with a B.A. degree in nontechnical curricula and $2,401 with a B.A. degree in technical curricula. M.B.A. starting salaries were $2,945 for a nontechnical undergraduate degree and $2,775 for a technical undergraduate degree. Check with the company for more specific salary information. Its excellent benefits package includes a car (for sales jobs), an expense account, liberal vacations, and a tuition refund plan.

CONTACT

Director of Employment, Scott Paper Company, Scott Plaza 1, Philadelphia, PA 19113.

SEARS, ROEBUCK AND COMPANY

CONTROLLERSHIP • CREDIT SALES • RETAIL MANAGEMENT

THE COMPANY

Sears is the largest retailer in the United States. It started in 1886 as a mail-order catalog business. The Sears catalog has the most widespread distribution of any publication in the United States except the Bible. Company philosophy remains "Satisfaction guaranteed, or your money back." In 1911 it was the first retailer to accept credit. The 110-story Sears Tower in Chicago, one of the world's tallest buildings, houses corporate headquarters and 12,000 employees. Merchandise includes over 90,000 items handled by more than 400,000 employees in over 3,800 locations. Sears pioneered phone shopping, night hours, self-service, and computerized distribution systems. One of every three families has a Sears credit card. With the acquisition of Dean Witter Reynolds, Sears added stockbrokerage services to its financial centers, which bring investment, insurance, and real estate people together in a department store setting. Sears is one of 10 foreign companies listed on the Tokyo Stock Exchange. With more than $44 billion in annual sales, it ranks number one in the Fortune 50 largest U.S. retailing companies.

ALL TRAINING PROGRAMS

You will participate in a course of training that combines on-the-job experience, formal classes, outside study, and job rotation.

CONTROLLERSHIP PROGRAM

The Controllership Program consists of planned job rotation tailored to your particular needs. The type of assignment and length of training depend on your background and skills. You will alternate between each operating department and the controller's office. First you will learn operating procedures; then you will see what the controller's accounting department does with the information, testing for completeness, accuracy, and integrity. After a year you will have been exposed to the entire unit operation. Later you will function as a traveling auditor to the smallest units, accompanied by an expert auditor for the first several trips. It will be your job to evaluate the total operation of the retail stores, catalog centers, and other units in your region. A resourceful individual will find unlimited opportunities for advancement.

QUALIFICATIONS

You will need a degree in accounting, economics, finance, or business administration. You should be willing to work long hours and relocate as necessary.

PLACEMENT

Controller staff positions are available at catalog, territorial, group, and national headquarters offices as well as foreign offices in Canada, Latin America, and Europe.

CREDIT SALES MANAGEMENT PROGRAM

For credit sales, the initial executive training consists of a formal program lasting six to twelve months, depending on the region of the country in which you start. You learn much of the credit business through study and job rotation within credit and collection central offices, a retail store credit department, or the Accounting and Processing Center. You will participate in staff meetings and management seminars to develop skills in human relations and management techniques. Through regular progress discussions you will develop an understanding of credit functions at regional, territorial, and corporate levels. Your first assignment will include preparing work schedules, interviewing new applicants, credit counseling, dealing with unhappy employees, and handling customer complaints.

QUALIFICATIONS

You will need a degree in computer science as well as strong people skills. You should be willing to relocate as needed.

PLACEMENT

Credit sales involve several organization levels working in retail or catalog selling units, credit and collection central offices, accounting and processing centers, and in regional, territorial, and corporate credit offices. Your assignments could take you anywhere in the United States.

RETAIL MANAGEMENT PROGRAM

In retail, programs depend on store location, your background, and the needs of the company at that time. In some areas there are special training stores with training personnel. In others, trainees are assigned to a retail store, with the local manager providing the training. The program lasts eight to twelve months. It consists of on-the-job assignments, informal discussions, films, and outside reading. You will be rotated to several areas of the store, such as basic sales training, installation, auditing, receiving and shipment, personnel, catalog sales, merchandise control, credit sales, operations, customer service, display, and the automotive center. After training, as a division manager your job will be constantly to improve the appearance and operation of your division through local advertising, displays, and effective ordering.

QUALIFICATIONS

Sears is interested in people who have earned a college degree. Important personal qualities include intelligence, curiosity, flexibility, and the ability to work effectively with other people. Willingness to work long hours and relocate are part of the commitment. The retailing business is hectic and may require some of your nights and weekends, perhaps even a move to another city or state.

PLACEMENT

You could work anywhere in the United States.

ALL PROGRAMS

RECRUITMENT

Recruitment is at some 100 schools in all regions, generally in the spring. You must schedule an interview through your college placement officer. Those without college degrees make up only a small percentage of those hired. You may express your career direction preference. Major job paths to management include retail, credit sales, and controllership.

SALARY AND BENEFITS

The College Placement Council Salary Survey for September 1986–June 1987 indicates starting salaries for merchandising (retail and wholesale) and service companies to be $1,594 a month for those with a B.A. degree in nontechnical curricula and $2,141 with a B.A. degree in technical curricula. M.B.A. starting salaries were $2,572 for a nontechnical undergraduate degree and $2,735 for an M.B.A. with technical undergraduate degree. Check with the company for more specific salary information. In four years your salary will have doubled and will continue to grow with the growth rate of the company. At the present rate, in ten years of employment your salary will be four times your starting salary. Company benefits include an additional income program. The company offers life, health, and disability insurance; travel/accident insurance; illness benefits; employee relocation benefits; merchandise discounts; and a pension program, including a profit-sharing plan.

CONTACT

Manager, Executive Resource Planning and Development, Sears, Roebuck, and Company, Sears Tower, Chicago, IL 60684.

SENTRY INSURANCE COMPANY

ACCOUNTING • ACTUARIAL SCIENCE • ADMINISTRATION • COMPUTER SCIENCE • ENGINEERING • FINANCE • INFORMATION SYSTEMS

THE COMPANY

Sentry provides property, casualty, life, and health insurance but is expanding into noninsurance areas such as manufacturing, financial services, building products, communications, and aviation. It employs 8,000 people worldwide and is headquartered in Stevens Point, Wisconsin.

ALL TRAINING PROGRAMS

As a new computer scientist with the company, you will go through training that offers supervised on-the-job experience and classroom instruction. Actuarial technicians receive training on the job provided by a senior supervisor.

QUALIFICATIONS

You are encouraged to apply if you have a degree in business or liberal arts. The company is also looking for more specific majors: actuarial science, computer science, fire protection engineering, information science, information systems, mathematics, engineering, and software engineering.

RECRUITMENT AND PLACEMENT

Sentry recruits throughout the nation; initial placement will usually be in Arizona, Georgia, Massachusetts, or Wisconsin.

SALARY AND BENEFITS

The College Placement Council Salary Survey for September 1986–June 1987 indicates starting salaries for banking, finance, and insurance companies to be $1,889 a month for those with a B.A. degree in nontechnical curricula and $2,135 with a B.A. degree in technical curricula. M.B.A. starting salaries were $2,884 for a nontechnical undergraduate degree and $3,320 for a technical undergraduate degree. Check with the company for more specific salary information. Sentry will give you release time or leaves of absence to pursue job-related graduate study and will reimburse all tuition and fees.

CONTACT

Bob McGowan, Recruiting and Employment Manager, Sentry Insurance Company, 1800 North Point Drive, Stevens Point, WI 54481.

SHEARSON LEHMAN BROTHERS, INC.

FINANCIAL CONSULTING

THE COMPANY

Shearson Lehman began in 1960 as Cater, Berlind, Potoma & Weill. By 1981 the company had acquired 18 financial firms to become the second largest brokerage house (in terms of capital) in the country. In that year it was acquired by American Express for $950 million. More than 5,200 financial consultants offer a wide variety of products and services in 360 offices around the world. Shearson encourages its financial consultants to act like entrepreneurs. The corporation provides a wide variety of product offerings and corporate training support—the individual provides the initiative and energy. The company's Financial Consultant Training Program is thorough and challenging.

FINANCIAL CONSULTANT TRAINING PROGRAM

Shearson has three regional training centers (New York, Chicago, and Los Angeles) that provide training in conjunction with the branch offices. The Financial Consultant Program lasts sixteen months and offers intensive classroom instruction, supervised on-the-job experience, and self-study. After a short introduction to company background and philosophy you spend the first three months in your branch office studying for the basic brokerage, commodities, or insurance exams. All materials are provided, and a staff person is available to answer questions and provide assistance. During the next phase of the program you spend six weeks at one of the regional training centers learning about the company's products and services as well as developing your sales skills. Company speakers with brokerage experience present information about stocks, bonds, commodities, tax shelters, real estate investments, insurance, and other services and products. Classes contain no more than 36 trainees and there is one trainer for every six trainees. You'll get to review your presentations on videotape. The next four months are spent in your branch office learning prospecting and client development skills. Then you'll return to the regional training center for a week of advanced sales training. The training staff will review your client book and suggest strategies to increase your business. Presentations by company speakers and practice sessions make for a busy week. During the next seven months the branch manager will provide on-the-job assistance to help you get your feet on the ground and build your client base. The program ends with a one-week session at the regional training center, but the training staff stays in touch and continues to be available.

QUALIFICATIONS

Shearson looks for self-starters with a desire to succeed in the financial world. You must be eager to learn, enjoy working with people, possess the ability to present yourself and the company's products with confidence, and put in the hours required to be a success. The company interviews candidates from a variety of academic backgrounds and prefers that you have work experience. Persons making career changes are encouraged to inquire about openings.

RECRUITMENT AND PLACEMENT

Shearson recruits and hires through its branch offices around the country. It has a rigorous selection process; recruiters spend about thirteen to fourteen hours with each candidate. Only one out of eighty applicants is hired.

SALARY AND BENEFITS

Your compensation during the training program will be a combination of salary, bonus, and limited commissions. When you finish the program you are entirely on commission. Performance incentives, deferred compensation, and retirement programs are part of a full employee benefits package.

CONTACT

Since you are hired by a branch office, the best approach is to contact the branch in the city where you wish to work. Or you may contact: Staffing Director, Shearson Lehman Brothers, Inc., American Express Tower, World Financial Center, New York, NY 10285.

SHELL OIL COMPANY

ADMINISTRATION • COMPUTER SCIENCE • EMPLOYEE RELATIONS • ENGINEERING • FINANCE • LAND • LAW • MARKETING • PURCHASING • SALES • SCIENCE • SUPPLY • TAX ORGANIZATION • TRANSPORTATION

THE COMPANY

Shell Oil Company, which began operations in 1912, is an oil, gas, and chemical company operating primarily in the United States. It employs more than 30,000 people in many locations, carrying on a tradition of achievement that has made it one of the nation's most successful oil and gas explorers and developers; a leader in offshore production and enhanced oil recovery technology; and an achiever of a number of industry firsts and milestones—many through its own research. Listed among *Fortune*'s most admired corporations, it ranks number 15 in the Fortune 500 largest U.S. industrial corporations.

ALL TRAINING PROGRAMS

Shell encourages your development by providing an intellectually stimulating environment and by helping you obtain a high level of professional qualification through various training programs. Training is considered an important aspect of each employee's development and is provided through various formal methods as well as on-the-job assignments. Training opportunities begin early. These include a variety of in-house technical-professional programs as well as personal-managerial seminars and workshops. Development options are provided through company-sponsored tuition assistance for graduate college and university programs related to your continued professional growth. You will be expected to keep abreast of trends and developments in appropriate areas of science, engineering, business, and management. Continuing education and participation in professional societies are supported with this goal in mind.

QUALIFICATIONS

Major disciplines of interest to Shell are accounting, business administration, finance, law, engineering (electrical, chemical, civil, geological, mechanical, petroleum), and science (chemistry, computer science, geophysics, geology, mathematics, physics, and statistics). Geologists and geophysicists must have master's or Ph.D. degrees.

RECRUITMENT AND PLACEMENT

Shell recruits at approximately 80 campuses across the United States. Corporate headquarters are in Houston. Major exploration and production offices are in Houston, New Orleans, and Bakersfield, California. Manufacturing complexes combining both refining and chemical manufacturing are in Deer Park, Texas; Martinez, California; Norco, Louisiana; Wilmington, California; and Wood River, Illinois. Refineries are in Odessa, Texas, and Anacortes, Washington; and there are other chemical manufacturing plants in Geismar and Taft, Louisiana; Woodbury, New Jersey; and Belpre, Ohio. Sales offices are located in 22 cities across the United States.

SALARY AND BENEFITS

The College Placement Council Salary Survey for September 1986–June 1987 indicates starting salaries for petroleum and allied products (including natural gas) companies to be $1,972 a month for those with a B.A. degree in nontechnical curricula and $2,497 with a B.A. degree in technical curricula. M.B.A. starting salaries were $2,629 for a nontechnical undergraduate degree and $2,970 for a technical undergraduate degree. Check with the company for more specific salary information. At Shell salary advancement is based on the individual's performance, contribution, and level of responsibility. Benefits include comprehensive medical and dental assistance plans; health cost reduction plan; disability benefits; life insurance; vacation and holidays; and company savings and retirement programs.

CONTACT

C. E. Bishop, Manager Recruitment, Shell Oil Company, P.O. Box 2463, Houston, TX 77252.

SIGNETICS CORPORATION

ENGINEERING • INFORMATION SYSTEMS • MANUFACTURING • MARKETING • RESEARCH AND DEVELOPMENT • SALES

THE COMPANY

Signetics Corporation is a major manufacturer of semiconductors and integrated circuits, both analog and digital. The company, established in 1961, has a worldwide employment force of more than 10,000. It is a subsidiary of U.S. Philips Corporation of New York.

ALL TRAINING PROGRAMS

Signetics has a combination program of on-the-job and formal training. Tuition reimbursement is available for job-related courses.

QUALIFICATIONS

The company prefers graduates with a G.P.A. of 3.5 or higher who are already familiar with computers. Depending on the assignment, a bachelor's, master's, or Ph.D. degree is required. Technical graduates with one to ten years of related work experience are also encouraged to apply.

At the bachelor's or master's level, people with the following areas of study are recruited for research and development: engineering (chemical, computer, electrical, and materials science) and chemistry. If you have majored in engineering (chemical, computer, electrical, electronics, manufacturing, materials science, mechanical, or metallurgical), chemistry, engineering technology, or physics, you may be assigned to a production job.

You are eligible for a technical services job if you majored in engineering (chemical, computer, electrical, electronics, or mechanical), physics, computer science, chemistry, engineering technology, or software engineering. If you majored in computer science, you may be assigned to an information systems job. Some electrical engineers go into marketing and sales.

Opportunities for those with a Ph.D. degree are for recruits who have specialties in one of the following areas: chemistry (analytical, general, or physical), engineering (materials science, chemical, computer, or electrical), computer science, general physics, and solid-state physics. Other opportunities exist for graduates with either a business-related B.S. or an M.B.A.

RECRUITMENT AND PLACEMENT

Signetics recruits nationwide, hiring about 70 trainees a year. Starting locations are in California, New Mexico, and Utah.

SALARY AND BENEFITS

With a bachelor's degree, you can expect to start at about $28,000; at $33,000 with a master's; and at $44,000 with a doctorate. Contact the company directly for details of benefits.

CONTACT

Mark Thomas, Staffing Recruiter, Signetics Corporation, P.O. Box 3409, MS-07, Sunnyvale, CA 94088-3409.

SNAP-ON TOOLS CORPORATION

COMPUTER SCIENCE • ENGINEERING • PRODUCTION • RESEARCH AND DEVELOPMENT

THE COMPANY

If you've ever spent any time around a mechanic's shop, you've probably seen the Snap-On Tools truck arrive. With their vans full of tools, Snap-On salespeople crisscross America, keeping mechanics supplied with proper tools. The company's more than 5,000 employees manufacture a range of hand tools and electronic diagnostic equipment. With more than $670 million in annual sales, it ranks number 391 in the Fortune 500 largest U.S. industrial corporations.

ALL TRAINING PROGRAMS

Snap-On Tools is looking for people who can make machinery and people who can set up the computer and paper trails necessary to move the products. Engineers participate in a six-month program of supervised on-the-job training. The program for computer programmers and systems analysts combines hands-on experience and classroom instruction.

QUALIFICATIONS

The company is looking for computer science majors to fill openings for programmers and analysts. It is also seeking architectural, electrical, mechanical, and metallurgical engineers as well as business and liberal arts majors. Work-related experience is a plus. You should have a G.P.A. of at least 2.5.

RECRUITMENT AND PLACEMENT

Your starting location is in Kenosha, Wisconsin, at company headquarters.

SALARY AND BENEFITS

Starting salaries with a bachelor's degree range from $26,000 to $28,000, and from $30,000 to $32,000 with a master's. Your benefits package will include relocation assistance; medical, hospital, and dental plans; career counseling; and a pension plan.

CONTACT

Diane Kastelic, Personnel Representative, Snap-On Tools Corporation, 2801 80th Street, Kenosha, WI 53140.

SOCIAL SECURITY ADMINISTRATION

COMPUTER EQUIPMENT ANALYSIS • COMPUTER PROGRAMMING • COMPUTER SCIENCE • COMMUNICATIONS • INDUSTRIAL ENGINEERING • OPERATIONS RESEARCH ANALYSIS

THE COMPANY

The Social Security Administration provides sustained income benefits to Americans through a computer system that links a network of 1,300 offices across the United States. Nine out of every ten Americans are earning Social Security benefits and one out of six receives a monthly benefits check. One of the world's largest computer systems, the heart of its operation is in the new, state-of-the-art National Computer Center in Baltimore, Maryland (next to SSA headquarters). Of the SSA's 80,000 employees, nearly a quarter work at headquarters with about 3,000 in computer-related jobs, handling everything from processing new number applications to computing benefits for 36 million Americans. The SSA has a commitment to maintaining a technically advanced system to keep pace with increasing demands.

ALL TRAINING PROGRAMS

You will receive a formal introduction to the SSA's program with comprehensive, on-the-job training. The type of orientation varies with the position. As an entry-level data programmer, for example, you will participate in a four-stage course with at least fourteen classes over a twenty-four-month period. College students may join the SSA during their final years of college through the ACCESS/Cooperative Education Program. You will be trained for a job that will be yours upon graduation. Students alternate two or more six-month periods of full-time work with two or more periods of academic study until they receive their bachelor's degree. A Graduate Cooperative Education Program operates similarly.

QUALIFICATIONS

The SSA is primarily looking for graduates with degrees in mathematics and computer science. To be eligible for the ACCESS program, you must be in your junior year at a college with which the agency has a cooperative education agreement, maintain a G.P.A. of at least 2.5, have completed at least sixty semester hours, and be a U.S. citizen.

RECRUITMENT AND PLACEMENT

The SSA recruits on campuses around the country but also welcomes inquiries at headquarters. Most entry-level positions will be in the Baltimore facility.

SALARY AND BENEFITS

Entry-level systems professionals start at the GS-7 level ($18,358), and may be eligible for up to three annual promotions. Cash or honor awards for outstanding performance can boost an employee's salary as much as $2,500. The SSA offers flextime schedules, paid holidays, sick days and vacation leave, health and life insurance, and military leave with pay for reserve training.

CONTACT

Social Security Administration, Recruitment and Placement Branch, Room G-120 West Building (High Rise), 6401 Security Boulevard, Baltimore, MD 21235.

SOUTHERN CALIFORNIA GAS COMPANY

ENGINEERING • GEOLOGY • GEOPHYSICS • INFORMATION SYSTEMS • MANAGEMENT • METALLURGY

THE COMPANY

Southern California Gas Company, a subsidiary of Pacific Lighting Corporation, is the nation's leading natural gas distribution utility. With approximately 10,000 employees, the company serves more than 13 million customers in Southern and Central California. Its revenues are over $1.3 billion. Since 1867, when it was established, Southern California Gas Company has aggressively searched for energy supplies to meet the growing demands of its state. During the 1800s the company went as far as Australia to obtain coal to produce gas for Southern California. After World War II the company brought natural gas from West Texas and Oklahoma. In 1969, Southern California Gas once again began a worldwide energy search for gas supply acquisition opportunities. Currently the company is exploring synthetic fuels such as methane, oil shale, and biomass; the potential of solar-assisted gas energy; and hydrogen as a fuel for the twenty-first century.

MANAGEMENT TRAINING PROGRAM

The Management and Professional Program is designed to select and develop managers and technical leaders. As a new employee, you will work with experienced energy and business specialists. Most training is on the job, with individual projects to analyze, plan, implement, manage, and complete successfully. Field work is an important part of many work assignments.

QUALIFICATIONS

Southern California is looking for graduates in the following fields: chemical, civil, electrical, and mechanical engineering; chemistry; mathematics; industrial engineering; petroleum engineering and geology/geophysics; computer science; mathematics; and business.

RECRUITMENT AND PLACEMENT

The company hires about 120 trainees a year, most of whom work in the Los Angeles metropolitan area. If you're interested in finding out more about the company, you may want to take advantage of its summer employment and cooperative education programs. Summer intern positions in engineering and information systems are available to college students who have completed at least two years of study. The cooperative education program is available to engineering students to work as energy consultants all over Southern California.

SALARY AND BENEFITS

The College Placement Council Salary Survey for September 1986–June 1987 indicates starting salaries for public utilities to be $1,905 a month for those with a B.A. degree in nontechnical curricula and $2,355 with a B.A. degree in technical curricula. M.B.A. starting salaries were $2,403 for a nontechnical undergraduate degree and $2,667 for a technical undergraduate degree. Check with the company for more specific salary information. Benefits include medical coverage, a dental plan, life insurance, disability protection, stock purchase, relocation assistance, and retirement benefits. The company reimburses tuition for college courses and provides a full range of in-house management development programs. Employees also have the opportunity to attend national, regional, and local professional seminars.

CONTACT

Ms. W. Guerra, Professional Staffing Coordinator, Southern California Gas Company, P.O. Box 3249, Terminal Annex, Los Angeles, CA 90051.

SOUTHLAND CORPORATION
STORE MANAGEMENT

THE COMPANY

Who could have foreseen that Uncle Johnny Green's ice dock in Dallas, Texas, would become 7-Eleven, the largest chain of convenience stores in the world? It all began during World War I, when a Consumer's Ice Company summer hand named Joe C. Thompson came up with the bright idea of selling ice-cold watermelons. It was a roaring success, and when Consumer's and four other ice companies joined together in 1927 to start Southland, Thompson became a director. Not long after, an ice dock manager, Uncle Johnny Green, was keeping his ice dock open sixteen hours a day, seven days a week. When he complied with customer wishes to add bread, milk, and eggs to his offerings, the modern convenience store was born. Thompson became president in 1931 and began to build the chain. The original name, Tote'm Stores, was changed to 7-Eleven in 1946. Southland has continued to expand—keeping most stores open twenty-four hours, creating gas and dairy divisions, adding auto parts stores, and opening modern mom-and-pop stores around the world. Its more than 50,000 employees serve more than 7 million customers daily. Can you imagine how much bread, milk, and eggs its almost 7,500 stores now sell every day? The company's dairy operation ranks as one of the country's largest processors of dairy products. Southland Corporation, now run by Thompson's three sons, has grown to a Fortune 500 corporation with annual sales above $11 billion. It ranks number eight in the Fortune 50 largest retailing companies and is listed among *Fortune*'s most admired corporations.

STORE MANAGER TRAINING PROGRAM

You start with 7-Eleven by learning the basics. Manager candidates must complete the New Employee Training Program for store clerks and work as a store clerk before promotion to store manager. The length of this period depends upon your experience, aptitude, and the availability of an opening.

You begin training by participating in the New Employee Training Program under the guidance of a training manager and in a planned, assigned store experience under the guidance of your store manager. All routine store clerical duties and skills, such as customer service, cash register, money orders, handling checks, stocking, money handling, and security, are learned during this period. The objective is for you to be able to operate the store without supervision during a shift. Your next step is Assistant Store Manager Training. This is an on-the-job plan with the store manager acting as a coach. The program includes reading assignments in the system manual for store managers and planned learning experience in the store. Skills that are important for managing the store plant, such as daily paperwork, planning employee schedules, store inspection, equipment inspection, ordering, and stock maintenance, will be your new areas of learning. The time for completing the assistant store manager phase is usually a minimum of thirty days but may take longer.

The Store Manager Training Program is a combination of on-the-job experience and classroom instruction. Before you are promoted to store manager you will spend two weeks learning to plan and analyze the store operation. This entry-level training includes on-the-job work with analysis of the daily store reports, work-load scheduling, controlling expenses, verifying store reports, reviewing audits, processing time sheets, maintaining vendor relations, and getting employees started. At the time of your promotion to store manager you will participate in a three- or four-day classroom program that covers management skills such as meeting Equal Employment Opportunity requirements, employee interviewing and selection, and handling performance problems. After you have been a store manager for approximately three to six months you will attend the advanced classroom program devoted to in-depth training in management skills with role-playing practice.

If you are ambitious and make a good showing as a store manager, the next move up the career ladder is to store supervisor with responsibility for six to twelve stores. The Supervisor Training Program includes self-study, job rotation, classroom instruction, and training at corporate headquarters in Dallas.

QUALIFICATIONS

Southland prefers applicants for its store management training to have college and/or related work experience, and previous retail supervisory experience is a definite plus. If you don't have the experience, you can begin as a clerk and after learning the store operations become eligible for store manager training. If you do have experience, the company will tailor the training program to fit your needs.

RECRUITMENT AND PLACEMENT

There are 7-Eleven stores scattered across the country and each division recruits and trains staff for its geographical area. Southland is recruiting more minorities and women. Your first assignment will be in the area where you apply and are trained.

SALARY AND BENEFITS

The minimum entry-level base salary for the Management Trainee Program is about $21,000. Management supervisors start at $22,500 or more. You can take advantage of medical, life, and dental plans, and participate in the company's profit-sharing program. You will also be eligible for tuition reimbursement and a savings and profit-sharing plan.

CONTACT

The 7-Eleven district or division office in your area or Manager, Professional Staffing, Southland Corporation, 2828 North Haskell Avenue, P.O. Box 719, Dallas, TX 75221.

SPERRY CORPORATION

ENGINEERING · MANAGEMENT · MARKETING · RESEARCH AND DEVELOPMENT · SALES · SOFTWARE DEVELOPMENT · SYSTEMS DESIGN · TESTING

THE COMPANY

Sperry, through its various divisions and operating units, manufactures electronic computer systems for commercial and government applications worldwide. The company researches, designs, develops, manufactures, and services all types of computer systems.

Sperry Computer Systems produces minicomputers and mainframes. A major component of this operation is the Defense Systems Division (DSD), a leading developer, manufacturer, and marketer of digital computer systems and components for defense uses. Another division, Flight Systems, makes aerospace flight control systems and other related electronic and space products. Sperry New Holland manufactures farm machinery and industrial equipment.

ALL TRAINING PROGRAMS

If you are going into a programming or engineering job, you will be given both on-the-job and formal training for six months. Tuition and fees are reimbursed up to 100 percent for job-related graduate study.

QUALIFICATIONS

A bachelor's, master's, or Ph.D. degree is required. A minimum G.P.A. of 2.5 is preferred. Engineers should have at least an M.S. If you are a technical graduate with one or more years of related experience, Sperry is also interested in you.

Sperry Computer systems seeks majors in computer science, engineering (computer, electrical, electronics, industrial/management, mechanical, or software), or mathematics. At the Ph.D. level, Sperry looks for those specializing in computational methods, computer engineering, computer architecture, information science, programming systems, software engineering, electronics engineering, electrophysics, solid-state physics, systems design, and systems science. In addition, M.B.A.s with a technical B.S. or a B.S. in business are sought by the Computer Systems Division. Some marketing and sales personnel are also recruited. Sperry Flight Systems seeks engineers (electrical, electronics, mechanical, software development) with M.S. degrees. Sperry New Holland recruits accountants, copywriters, and engineers (agricultural, industrial, and mechanical—preferably with a farm background), market research analysts, and sales personnel.

Computer Systems assignments include R&D for those majoring in engineering (computer, electrical, electronics, or software), computer science, or mathematics. Information Systems assignments go to majors in engineering (computer or software), computer science, or mathematics. Production jobs go to those who majored in engineering (industrial/management, software, or mechanical) or mathematics. Those who majored in computer science or software engineering may be assigned to marketing and sales. Software engineers may also be assigned to technical services or administration/finance.

RECRUITMENT AND PLACEMENT

Sperry recruits nationwide. Starting locations for Computer Systems are in California, Iowa, Minnesota, Pennsylvania, Tennessee, and Utah. Flight Systems has operations in Phoenix and Albuquerque. New Holland is in New England and Pennsylvania.

SALARY AND BENEFITS

The average annual starting salary with a bachelor's degree is $27,000 to $29,500; with a master's, $29,300 to $32,000. The benefits package provides you with life insurance, medical, hospital, and dental plans, flextime options (at some divisions), savings plans, pension program, and relocation assistance.

CONTACT

Headquarters Staffing Services Manager, Sperry Computer Systems, P.O. Box 500, Blue Bell, PA 19424; or Employment Manager, Sperry Flight Systems, 2111 North 19th Avenue, Phoenix, AZ 85036; or Office Employment Supervisor, Sperry New Holland, Franklin Street, New Holland, PA 17557.

STATE FARM INSURANCE COMPANIES

ACCOUNTING • ADMINISTRATION • DATA PROCESSING • INSURANCE SALES • INVESTMENT ANALYSIS • LAW

THE COMPANY

More than 40 million policyholders count on State Farm's auto, life, home, and health insurance across the United States and Canada. Almost 33,000 employees and more than 17,000 agents and agency managers represent the "Good Neighbor" policies of State Farm. Headquartered in Bloomington, Illinois, State Farm is the world's largest auto insurer and has been the leader in the industry since 1942. The company's operations are decentralized with 53 percent of employees in regional offices and 47 percent in field offices. Assets total more than $7 billion. State Farm ranks number 18 in the Fortune 50 largest life insurance companies.

ALL TRAINING PROGRAMS

You will be assigned to a sponsor who is responsible for seeing that your training program is an effective learning experience. You will meet regularly with this sponsor to review questions and discuss progress. You will advance through the program as fast as you and your trainer feel comfortable. Hands-on assignments will be available as you go through formal training.

QUALIFICATIONS

Your background might be any of the following: liberal arts, business, legal, data processing, or accounting.

PLACEMENT

State Farm locations are found throughout the United States in cities large and small.

FIRE COMPANY PROGRAM

You will begin with a general orientation to the region and company. Following orientation, you will get a walk-through of the total Fire operation from records to underwriting to rating to policy issue. Then a period of general training begins. Time will be allocated for insurance education and management skills training. General training will be completed in about six months and then you will be assigned to a functional area for special training in data processing, agency, or field work. At this point you will begin to assume direct responsibilities and to apply the principles and procedures you have learned. The complete training period generally lasts about fifty-two weeks.

QUALIFICATIONS

Your degree could be in liberal arts, business, law, data processing, or accounting.

PLACEMENT

You might be placed anywhere in the country.

ALL PROGRAMS

RECRUITMENT

State Farm sends representatives to campuses around the country to give information interviews.

SALARIES AND BENEFITS

Salaries are based on a merit system, adjusted for increases in cost of living. Each time the Consumer Price Index changes to the next whole index point, you will receive a corresponding salary adjustment. Private salary surveys in and out of the insurance industry ensure competitive salaries. State Farm offers the following benefits: paid holidays and vacation, a personal time policy, insurance, retirement, relocation program, sick leave, tuition reimbursement, medical services, and an incentive and thrift plan.

CONTACT

Personnel, State Farm Home Offices, One State Farm Plaza, Bloomington, IL 61701.

STEELCASE

ACCOUNTING • COMPUTER SCIENCE • DATA PROCESSING • ENGINEERING • MARKETING • PRODUCTION • RESEARCH AND DEVELOPMENT • SALES

THE COMPANY

Steelcase is the world's leading designer and manufacturer of office furniture, systems furniture, office lighting, and computer-assisted programs for those who plan, provide, and manage effective and efficient office environments. The company employs 15,000 people worldwide and is double the size of its nearest competitor in dollar volume and market share. Its sales representatives benefit from the company's premier position with exceptionally high commission checks.

ALL TRAINING PROGRAMS

The Professional Accelerated Career Entry Program for sales trainees begins at corporate headquarters in Grand Rapids, Michigan, and is followed by transfer to a field sales office. Other training programs also combine on-the-job and classroom instruction. Feedback and coaching sessions as well as job rotation will be part of your training.

QUALIFICATIONS

The company is looking for college graduates (and technical graduates with related work experience) in marketing, computer science, information systems, and engineering—architectural, electrical, manufacturing, mechanical, and safety. The company prefers a class rank in the top 25 percent, with a minimum G.P.A. of 3.0.

RECRUITMENT AND PLACEMENT

The company recruits nationwide. Regional sales offices are located throughout the United States. Manufacturing facilities are in California, Michigan, and North Carolina.

SALARY AND BENEFITS

With a bachelor's degree you can expect to start at $24,000; with a business-related master's and a nontechnical B.S., at $26,000 to $27,000. One to five years' experience will add another thousand or two to your salary. Benefits include a tuition reimbursement plan and a flexible or "cafeteria style" benefits package.

CONTACT

College Relations Recruiter, Steelcase, P.O. Box 1967, Grand Rapids, MI 49501.

STONE & WEBSTER ENGINEERING CORPORATION

ACCOUNTING • COMPUTER SCIENCE • ENGINEERING • GEOLOGY • PHYSICS

THE COMPANY

Stone & Webster provides engineering, design, construction, and management consulting services to power-generating utilities and the petrochemical and petroleum industries. The company traces its origins to a partnership formed in 1889 by Charles A. Stone and Edwin S. Webster to practice the new profession of electrical engineering. By the 1940s it had become involved in the nuclear age. It participated in the first nuclear project in 1942, built much of the Oak Ridge nuclear facilities, and in 1956 engineered the nation's first commercial-scale nuclear power plant. It is well known for its expertise in designing, engineering, and constructing coal- and oil-fired power-generating plants, as well as hydroelectric facilities. The company is also an acknowledged leader in the technology used in ethylene production, petroleum refining, and other hydrocarbon-related processes. Stone & Webster plans to continue to develop alternative energy technologies —solar energy collection, tidal power, geothermal energy, advanced coal technology—and to construct more efficient fossil-fuel and hydroelectric plants.

CAREER DEVELOPMENT TRAINING PROGRAM

The Career Development Training Program offers you a variety of assignments in different work settings so you may choose the career direction most promising for you: design, engineering, cost/scheduling, or procurement. On-the-job training involves a series of assignments, rotating through different groups in a specific division or among different divisions. You are exposed to all of Stone & Webster's capabilities, from conceptual engineering to field operations.

QUALIFICATIONS

Stone & Webster is looking for college graduates with the following engineering specialties: chemical, civil, electrical, environmental, geotechnical, industrial, mechanical, nuclear, and structural. It is also recruiting in construction management, computer science, accounting, geology, and physics. The company prefers graduates who rank in the top 40 percent of their class with a minimum G.P.A. of 2.5.

RECRUITMENT AND PLACEMENT

Starting locations for jobs are in Colorado, Massachusetts, New Jersey, New York, and Texas. Summer employment opportunities and cooperative education programs are available for engineering and computer science college students.

SALARY AND BENEFITS

The College Placement Council Salary Survey for September 1986–June 1987 indicates starting salaries for research and/or consulting organizations to be $2,116 a month for those with a B.A. degree in nontechnical curricula and $2,266 with a B.A. degree in technical curricula. M.B.A. starting salaries were $2,512 for a nontechnical undergraduate degree and $2,822 for a technical undergraduate degree. Check with the company for more specific salary information. The benefits package includes comprehensive medical and dental insurance, disability income, a pension plan, insurance, travel and accident insurance, employee investment and stockownership plans, and tuition assistance.

CONTACT

John Hamlet, Senior Employment Manager, Stone & Webster Engineering Corporation, P.O. Box 2325, Boston, MA 02107.

ST. PAUL COMPANIES

ACCOUNTING/INTERNAL AUDITING • ACTUARIAL SCIENCE • CLAIMS ADJUSTING • MARKETING AND BOND FIELD SUPERVISION • PROGRAMMING • RISK MANAGEMENT REPRESENTATION

THE COMPANY

When you work as an insurance underwriter for the St. Paul Companies, you are part psychologist and part detective. The underwriter makes the final decisions on whether the company will accept or reject a risk offered for insurance. Since 1853, the St. Paul Companies have provided a wide range of insurance services, including coverage for property, liability, life, health, consumer finance, mutual funds, and title insurance. The St. Paul has consistently ranked among the top 20 in assets among over 2,000 U.S. property liability insurance companies. It is the largest medical malpractice insurer, the fifth largest provider of ocean marine insurance, and the seventh largest provider of inland marine insurance. The company has assets of more than $7 billion and annual revenues topping $3 billion. It ranks number 25 in the Fortune 50 largest diversified financial companies.

ALL TRAINING PROGRAMS

Your career with the St. Paul will begin with a short orientation, followed by a short course at the home office. After this you will begin a six- to twelve-month course of intensive on-the-job, self-study, and classroom training under the direction of experienced managers and professional training staff. In some programs you will receive bonuses for exams passed. Upon graduation you will be relocated and promoted. If you are a computer specialist you will have available over 100 different courses a month to enhance your skills.

QUALIFICATIONS

In addition to a degree in liberal arts or social science, you will need strong analytical skills, creativity, a keen sense of judgment, and excellent people skills. Actuarial trainees should have degrees in math or statistics, and have maintained a G.P.A. of 3.2 or better. Course work in communications, insurance, or business will be a plus for actuaries. Trainees for the information systems division may or may not have computer science or management information systems degrees.

RECRUITMENT AND PLACEMENT

St. Paul recruiters visit colleges and universities throughout the United States. You could be sent to work in any of the 150 branch offices in the United States and Canada or at the headquarters in St. Paul.

SALARY AND BENEFITS

The College Placement Council Salary Survey for September 1986–June 1987 indicates starting salaries for banking, finance, and insurance firms to be $1,889 a month for those with a B.A. degree in nontechnical curricula and $2,135 with a B.A. degree in technical curricula. M.B.A. starting salaries were $2,884 for a nontechnical undergraduate degree and $3,320 for an M.B.A. with technical undergraduate degree. Check with the company for more specific salary information. Benefits include life and health insurance, tuition reimbursement, a career planning program, profit sharing, a personal investment program, and a retirement plan.

CONTACT

Supervisor, College Recruiting, St. Paul Companies, 385 Washington Street, St. Paul, MN 55102.

STRAWBRIDGE & CLOTHIER

MANAGEMENT

THE COMPANY

Strawbridge & Clothier is a leading Philadelphia high-fashion department store with an annual sales volume of approximately $300 million and 12,000 employees in 3 states. A separate division, the Clover Corporation, appeals to mass-merchandise customers. In addition to store managers, Strawbridge & Clothier has a limited number of openings in finance, publicity, personnel, and store operations.

MANAGEMENT TRAINING PROGRAM

The goal is to prepare selected candidates for branch divisional manager, branch store manager, divisional merchandise manager, or executive positions. At Strawbridge & Clothier you go through a nine-month Executive Development Program, which supplements your on-the-job experience. Classroom sessions and specialized seminars develop a solid understanding of retail math, inventory control, merchandising reports, fibers and fabrics, customer service, advertising, human relations and communications. Department managers have overall responsibility for the operation of merchandise departments. As a department manager, you would be in charge of planning, buying, sales promotion, administration, inventory, expense control, and selling the most merchandise for the best profit. You might use computers to develop buying strategy, shop the market to discover and promote fast-moving items, and decipher and solve shipping problems. Managers may also develop radio, TV, and newspaper promotion for fashion lines.

QUALIFICATIONS

Strawbridge & Clothier offers opportunities to graduates of liberal arts, retailing, and business or business-related majors. You should rank in the top half of your class with a minimum G.P.A. of 3.0.

RECRUITMENT AND PLACEMENT

Recruitment for this company is in the mid-Atlantic states and New England. The store has one center-city store and 11 suburban branch stores in Greater Philadelphia.

SALARY AND BENEFITS

With a bachelor's degree you can expect to start in the $18,500 to $19,000 range. Benefits include company-paid Blue Cross, Blue Shield, and major medical insurance; group life, disability, and travel accident insurance; a savings plan; employee discounts; and a retirement plan.

CONTACT

Charlotte Waterbury, Executive Recruitment, Strawbridge & Clothier, 801 Market Street, Philadelphia, PA 19105.

SUN COMPANY, INC.

ACCOUNTING • BUSINESS ADMINISTRATION • CHEMICAL ENGINEERING • CHEMISTRY • CIVIL ENGINEERING • EXPLORATION AND PRODUCTION DRAFTING • ELECTRICAL ENGINEERING • ENGINEERING DRAFTING DESIGN • FINANCE • GEOLOGY • GEOPHYSICS • INDUSTRIAL ENGINEERING • INFORMATION SYSTEMS • LAW • MECHANICAL ENGINEERING • METALLURGY • PETROLEUM ENGINEERING • PETROLEUM LAND MANAGEMENT • PETROLEUM TECHNOLOGY • PHYSICS • RESEARCH AND DEVELOPMENT LABORATORIES • SALES • SECRETARIAL • TRANSPORTATION

THE COMPANY

Sun Company, Inc., is an energy resources company with petroleum operations and financial interests in other energy resources (primarily in the United States and Canada). Sun explores for and produces crude oil and natural gas, refines crude oil and its derivatives, markets a full range of refined petroleum products, and trades crude oil and refined petroleum products. Sun mines coal in the United States and produces synthetic crude oil in western Canada. It is also engaged in nonenergy activities. Incorporated in Pennsylvania in 1971 as Sun Company, Inc., the company maintains its principal executive offices in Radnor, Pennsylvania, a Philadelphia suburb. The company employs approximately 20,000 people and ranks number 33 in the Fortune 500 largest U.S. industrial corporations.

ALL TRAINING PROGRAMS

Sun emphasizes on-the-job training with supervision and, in some areas, job rotation to acquaint employees with the company's procedures and philosophy. This early training is supplemented by courses for management trainees held at Sunbrook, Sun's corporate management education facility in Radnor. Sunbrook's curriculum includes courses on management and supervision, counseling, career planning, written business communications, computer applications, and stress management. Each course involves three to five days of intensive training by experienced Sun managers or outside experts. Most of the management training courses require preclass preparation and homework assignments.

ACCOUNTING PROGRAM

QUALIFICATIONS

You will need one or more of the following degrees: B.S., M.S., or M.B.A. The program leads to positions as associate auditor in general accounting, exploration and production accounting, or tax accounting. Associate auditors receive immediate field assignments of one to three weeks with travel required about 40 percent of the time. With an M.B.A. you may move into corporate accounting. You will have broad opportunity to move laterally and upward within the company.

PLACEMENT

You will be placed in Dallas, Philadelphia, or Radnor.

BUSINESS ADMINISTRATION PROGRAM

QUALIFICATIONS

Business school graduates with B.S., B.A., M.S. and/or M.B.A. degrees may start in the Sun corporate organization or in a major subsidiary such as Sun Exploration and Production, or Sun Refining and Marketing. Training in computer programming and analysis is especially useful. Your degrees may take you immediately into programming/analysis or sales.

PLACEMENT

Positions will be in Dallas, Philadelphia, or Radnor.

CHEMICAL ENGINEERING PROGRAM

QUALIFICATIONS

You will need one or more of the following degrees: a B.S. (for field production engineering or sales); M.S. and Ph.D. (for chemical development engineering); B.S. and M.S. (environmental control, gas plant design and processing, materials and field services engineering, plant project engineering, process design and evaluation, process development, process engineering, product research and development, project engineering and reservoir engineering); or an M.S. (planning and economics, process control).

PLACEMENT

Jobs are in the following locations: Marcus Hook and Philadelphia, Pennsylvania, and throughout the Southwest.

CHEMISTRY PROGRAM

QUALIFICATIONS

Sun wants chemists with the following degrees: an M.S. and Ph.D. in physics and physical chemistry (an applied physics position); Ph.D. in organic, inorganic, or physical chemistry (exploratory research); a B.S. and M.S. in combination (product research and development); or B.S. (refinery chemical laboratory, sales).

PLACEMENT

Depending on your specialty, you may be assigned to Marcus Hook, Pennsylvania, any of the refineries, or sales territories in the East and Midwest.

CIVIL ENGINEERING PROGRAM

QUALIFICATIONS

Sun needs many kinds of engineers, including civil. You will need a B.S. (for cost engineering, marketing engineering, or pipeline engineering), or B.S. and M.S. (plant maintenance engineering, plant project engineering).

PLACEMENT

Assignments will be to: Philadelphia; Wayne, Pennsylvania; Tulsa, Oklahoma; Longview, Texas; or any of the refineries.

EXPLORATION AND PRODUCTION DRAFTING PROGRAM

QUALIFICATIONS

Sun hires two-year college graduates. You will need a good math background. Skills in contouring and updating oil well information on geological structural and isopach maps are highly desirable.

PLACEMENT

You will work in Dallas.

ELECTRICAL ENGINEERING PROGRAM

QUALIFICATIONS

With a B.S. you may be recruited for one of the following areas: pipeline engineering, plant project engineering, Sun exploration and production electric engineering, or technical sales. A B.S. and M.S. will prepare you for careers in applied physics, materials and field services engineering, project engineering, and telecommunications.

PLACEMENT

Sun will place you in Marcus Hook or Philadelphia, Pennsylvania; Dallas; the Southwest; or any of the refineries.

ENGINEERING DRAFTING DESIGN PROGRAM

QUALIFICATIONS

You can join Sun in this department with an associate degree from an accredited engineering school or recognized technical training institute. Continued education toward a Bachelor of Science degree in engineering, usually accomplished by attending evening college classes, is recommended.

PLACEMENT

You will work in Philadelphia.

FINANCE PROGRAM

QUALIFICATIONS

Sun expects you to have an M.B.A. and high levels of achievement in graduate study for an economics and planning position. Aptitude and interest in computer utilization are helpful. An M.B.A. can also be your entree to financing. A B.S., M.S., and M.B.A. combination of degrees can lead you to Sun's treasury department.

PLACEMENT

Finance positions are in Philadelphia and Radnor.

GEOLOGY PROGRAM

QUALIFICATIONS

You should have a B.S. and M.S. for a job in exploration and development, or an M.S. and Ph.D. for production research.

PLACEMENT

You will be sent to a field location in the Southwest or the lab in Richardson, Texas.

GEOPHYSICS PROGRAM

QUALIFICATIONS

A combination B.S. and M.S. will prepare you for jobs in either exploration or seismic processing (developing computer programs for digital computers).

PLACEMENT

Jobs are located throughout the Southwest.

INDUSTRIAL ENGINEERING PROGRAM

QUALIFICATIONS

You should have a B.S. for cost engineering, plant project engineering, or technical sales. With a B.S.

and M.S., you will be eligible for industrial engineering.

PLACEMENT

Jobs are located in Philadelphia and Marcus Hook, Pennsylvania, all refineries, and sales territories in the East and Midwest.

INFORMATION SYSTEMS PROGRAM

QUALIFICATIONS

If you have both a B.S. and an M.S. in this field (computer science, engineering, applied mathematics, statistics or quantitative technique), jobs are available in scientific programming/analysis, programming/analysis, systems consultant/analysis, and telecommunications.

PLACEMENT

You may be sent to Philadelphia, Dallas, or Radnor.

LAW PROGRAM

QUALIFICATIONS

Sun wants lawyers with J.D., L.L.B., and L.L.M. for the Exploration and Production Department, Tax Department, and Refining and Marketing Division.

PLACEMENT

Assignments will be to the major offices in Dallas, Philadelphia, and Radnor.

MECHANICAL ENGINEERING PROGRAM

QUALIFICATIONS

With a B.S., you can go into exploration and production drilling engineering, cost engineering, field production, or pipeline engineering. If you have both a B.S. and M.S., Sun may place you in the applied physics laboratory, industrial engineering, materials and field services, plant maintenance, plant project engineering, or product research and development.

PLACEMENT

Jobs will be in Philadelphia, Marcus Hook, or Wayne, Pennsylvania; Tulsa, Oklahoma; Longview, Texas; or any of the refineries.

METALLURGY PROGRAM

QUALIFICATIONS

A B.S. will prepare you for technical sales or refinery materials engineering, while a B.S. and M.S. will make you eligible for materials engineering.

PLACEMENT

Assignments will be to any of the refineries, to headquarters in Marcus Hook, Pennsylvania, or to sales territories in the East and Midwest.

PETROLEUM ENGINEERING PROGRAM

QUALIFICATIONS

With a B.S., Sun might place you in field production engineering, drilling engineering, or production service. Sun wants engineers with M.S. degrees for production recovery research, and B.S. and M.S. degrees for reservoir engineering.

PLACEMENT

Assignments may be to field locations in the Southwest (expect considerable travel during your first year) or to Richardson, Texas.

PETROLEUM LAND MANAGEMENT PROGRAM

QUALIFICATIONS

Sun hires graduates with B.B.A./P.L.M. degrees.

PLACEMENT

Assignments will be in the field throughout the Southwest.

PETROLEUM TECHNOLOGY PROGRAM

QUALIFICATIONS

Sun hires graduates with associate degrees.

PLACEMENT

You will be assigned to a field position in the Southwest.

PHYSICS PROGRAM

QUALIFICATIONS

Whether you choose to work in the field or the laboratory, you will need both M.S. and Ph.D. degrees.

PLACEMENT

You may work in the Southwest or Richardson, Texas.

RESEARCH AND DEVELOPMENT LABORATORIES PROGRAM

QUALIFICATIONS

If you have an associate degree in chemistry or chemical engineering, Sun may start you in research and development.

PLACEMENT

You will work in Marcus Hook, Pennsylvania.

SALES PROGRAM

QUALIFICATIONS

Sun wants sales employees who have B.S., B.A. (liberal arts, marketing, and business administration), B.S. engineering (ChE, CE, Ee, IE, ME, Petro.E, and Metal E) or physical sciences (chemistry, biology, physics, or geology) degrees. Self-reliance and initiative are key personal characteristics for sales representatives.

PLACEMENT

You will be assigned a territory in the East or Midwest.

SECRETARIAL PROGRAM

QUALIFICATIONS

If you have an associate degree in secretarial or administrative secretarial techniques, Sun has many positions throughout the company for you.

PLACEMENT

You may work in any of the company's locations.

ALL PROGRAMS

RECRUITMENT

Sun visits college campuses throughout the country, or you may contact the employment office of the Sun Company that is of interest to you.

SALARY AND BENEFITS

The College Placement Council Salary Survey for September 1986–June 1987 indicates starting salaries for petroleum and allied products (including natural gas) companies to be $1,972 a month for those with a B.A. degree in nontechnical curricula and $2,497 with a B.A. degree in technical curricula. M.B.A. starting salaries were $2,629 for a nontechnical undergraduate degree and $2,970 for a technical undergraduate degree. Check with the company for more specific salary information. Benefits vary slightly from one division to another but may include paid holidays, paid vacations, assistance with medical, dental, and hospital costs, life insurance and disability programs, a savings plan, payment of some college costs, and retirement income.

CONTACT

Sun Company, Inc., 100 Matsonford Road, Radnor, PA 19087; Sun Exploration and Production Company, Campbell Centre II, P.O. Box 2880, Dallas, TX 75221; and Sun Refining and Marketing Company, 10 Penn Center, 1801 Market Street, Philadelphia, PA 19103.

The Corporate Perspective on Training Programs
Pat Cataldo, Digital Equipment Corporation

Pat Cataldo is the Vice-President of Educational Services at Digital Equipment Corporation. He started to work for the company in 1974, was their first international training manager, and held the positions of U.S. training manager and corporate sales manager before taking his present position.

☆ ☆ ☆ ☆ ☆

Describe the approach to training and development at Digital.

At Digital we have a unique organization called Educational Services that's responsible for training both Digital customers and Digital employees. This enables us to take the innovative and creative activities that we plan for our employees and use them for our customers as well.

Do you have any numbers that indicate the amount of financial commitment that Digital makes to training and development?

Our commitment is very large. Every Monday morning we start over 5,400 students in 110 different training locations all over the world. We teach in 17 different languages and offer more than 523 different courses for employees and customers. We have 185 different lecture courses. Then we have a seminar catalog which includes another 55 technical seminars. Last year we delivered over 10 million hours of education to over 251,000 students.

Of those 251,000 students, how many were employees?

About 50 percent. I think it's imperative to make this kind of commitment because of the business we're in. The technology is changing so fast, and obviously DEC has been out on the edge of that as long as we've been in business.

There seems to be willingness for the company to make a serious investment in training.

I think there is, not only at DEC, but for many companies. One of the things we're seeing is more corporate directors and corporate vice-presidents in training today than there were five years ago. I think the rate of change is forcing many major companies to find that they have to integrate training more closely with the strategic mission of the company. Training has become a very critical part of Digital's overall strategy.

I understand you have plans for a state-of-the-art corporate training center. Can you tell me about it?

Yes. We have received approval by the executive committee of the company and the board of directors to proceed with a corporate education center which will allow us to demonstrate the latest technology and also training methodology. It will be in Boylston, Massachusetts, on a 449-acre site. It will be a complete learning facility and will have housing for our employees, classrooms, labs, an auditorium, complete recreational facilities. If all things go well, we think we will be there the latter part of 1990.

Where do you recruit new employees?

There are four sources. One is the college and university. Another one is our direct competitors, other computer companies. Another is noncompeting companies—someone could have banking experience or retail food experience, or come out of the financial sector. And the fourth category is from inside the company. I continue to remind our managers to watch the percentage flow that we're getting from those various categories.

What was it five years ago as compared to now?

Let me talk about three years ago. Three years ago a much larger percentage came from the college campus. The marketplace for talent was highly competitive, and we were off trying to recruit people with prior experience, and so was everyone else. While we got our share, we were growing faster than the industry so we had to hire more from the campuses. As the market has shifted and a number of companies have not been as fortunate as we have, there's been a tremendous population out there for us to draw from—people with computer-related experience. In fact that has also caused us to refine our training programs. Three years ago we had more comprehensive training programs because new employees were less skilled coming in. We have now accelerated a number of courses because of the senior-level people we are now able to attract. That's especially true in the sales area.

How would training be different for someone with five to seven years' experience in engineering as opposed to an engineer who's just graduating and coming off campus?

In sales we have an accelerated program that will move a senior person through the training in three months. People who come either directly from college or with some minimal level of experience—a couple of semesters in computer science and maybe a year in selling—would be in a six-month, intensive program with formal classroom training as well as formal training in the field.

We also offer a tremendous amount of computer-assisted self-study materials and instruction. We've got a lot of interactive video materials and we use a lot of video. We use our private satellite broadcast system called Digital Video Network to do special programs. That all fits into a comprehensive offering that we tailor for either classes or individuals. It's really up to that person and his or her supervisor to put together a professional development plan. While we make a lot available, we rely a tremendous amount on the individual.

T

☆ ☆ ☆ ☆ ☆

TACO BELL

INFORMATION SYSTEMS • MANAGEMENT

THE COMPANY

Glen Bell was certain that there was more to fast foods than hamburgers and hot dog stands. In 1962 he opened the first Taco Bell, a fast-service Mexican food restaurant. Today there are over 2,200 Taco Bell restaurants in 48 states, Canada, Guam, Australia, Panama, Venezuela, and the Philippines. Over 800 restaurants are company-owned; the rest are franchised. Taco Bell plans to add another 700 restaurants in the next three years. It is part of the Pepsico family, an $8 billion international corporation. Pepsico's Food Service Division—Pizza Hut and Taco Bell—has shown dramatic growth in the past few years, with profits increasing over 20 percent annually. Taco Bell has about 30,000 employees in the United States.

MANAGEMENT TRAINING

As a management trainee, you will first be trained to manage a Taco Bell restaurant, a self-contained business with sales of almost $500,000 annually. Initial training is on the job, coupled with a five-week basic training program. Your comprehensive training will include all operational procedures, accounting and financial responsibilities, personnel and employee relations, local store marketing, ordering, inventory, product specs, and equipment. From management trainee, you move to first assistant manager, then restaurant manager. Strong performance in restaurant management will allow you to move rapidly into multiunit management as a district operations manager supervising eight restaurants. The company conducts a series of developmental seminars and follow-up training to prepare you for increased responsibility. The first of a network of training centers has opened near headquarters in Irvine, California.

QUALIFICATIONS

Taco Bell offers career opportunities for college graduates in many areas of liberal arts and social sciences as well as business. With its continued growth, you'll have an unusually good opportunity to move into management rapidly. You should rank in the top quarter of your class with a minimum G.P.A. of 2.5.

RECRUITMENT AND PLACEMENT

The company recruits all across the country. You could work in any of its local restaurants.

SALARY AND BENEFITS

The College Placement Council Salary Survey for September 1986–June 1987 indicates starting salaries for merchandising (retail and wholesale) and service companies to be $1,594 a month for those with a B.A. degree in nontechnical curricula and $2,141 with a B.A. degree in technical curricula. M.B.A. starting salaries were $2,572 for a nontechnical undergraduate degree and $2,735 for an M.B.A. with technical undergraduate degree. Check with the company for more specific salary information. Your benefits will include life insurance, medical, dental, and vision plans; pension and stock-purchase plans; relocation assistance; a fitness program; and incentive savings plan.

CONTACT

Kathy Kjar, Senior Recruiter, Taco Bell Corporation, 16808 Armstrong Avenue, Irvine, CA 92714.

TANDY CORPORATION

MANAGEMENT • SALES • SERVICE

THE COMPANY

"Up from the ashes" is one way to describe Radio Shack's revitalization by Charles Tandy of the Tandy Corporation. Once a bankrupt chain of electronics stores in New England, Radio Shack is now part of the world's largest electronics retailer with retail sales over $3 billion a year. Tandy traces its roots to a family leather business begun in 1919, while the company's flagship operation, Radio Shack, was founded in Boston in 1921. Your neighborhood Radio Shack is one of over 6,900 Tandy stores and dealers in the United States. One of every three households in the United States buys at least one item at a Radio Shack each year. Tandy places great emphasis on its service and support network, providing service for all of its products through neighborhood stores, and fielding more than 100,000 calls a month from customers. Radio Shack computer centers were the first in the industry to offer classroom training for customers. The company has given free computer literacy training to more than 400,000 of the nation's teachers. It ranks number 29 in the Fortune 50 largest retailing companies. An amazing 75 percent of its employees own stock in the company. Promotion from within, an open-door policy, and a down-home image contribute to the friendly, entrepreneurial atmosphere of the Fort Worth-based company.

ALL TRAINING PROGRAMS

As a service technician you will train at headquarters, participating in an in-shop apprenticeship. Field training "blitzes" coincide with the introduction of new products. All salespeople are considered potential managers, so if you begin in a retail position you will learn as you earn, on the job. You will be taught all aspects of running the store, from ringing up sales to creating merchandise displays and balancing the books. You will attend three weeks of classroom product training before you step foot on the sales floor. Weekly follow-up training keeps you abreast of new products and changes to existing products. Training is conducted at a "hub" center near your assigned store.

QUALIFICATIONS

College degrees are not required for sales people or technicians although exposure to computers and marketing is obviously a plus in interviewing. Tandy values enthusiastic people who are willing to work hard.

RECRUITMENT AND PLACEMENT

You can contact the company directly for information about available positions. The 6,900 stores and 212 service centers are located throughout the country. Distribution centers are located in Garden Grove and Woodland, California; Boston; Columbus; Charleston; and Fort Worth. Manufacturing employees work in Fort Worth as do headquarters personnel. Tandy also has employees in Korea, Taiwan, Canada, and France.

SALARIES AND BENEFITS

Salespeople are paid either an hourly rate or sales commission, but almost all employees are elible for bonuses that can boost salaries substantially. The average salary for a Radio Shack store manager is about $50,000. Benefits include a stock-purchase program; deferred salary and investment program; tuition refund plan; college scholarship plan for employees and dependents; and group medical/life, dental, and personal accident insurance plans.

CONTACT

Recruiting, Tandy Corporation, 500 One Tandy Center, Fort Worth, TX 76102.

TEKTRONIX, INC.

ENGINEERING • INFORMATION SYSTEMS AND PROCESSING • MARKETING • OPERATIONS • PRODUCTION • RESEARCH AND DEVELOPMENT • SALES • TECHNICAL SERVICES

THE COMPANY

Tektronix makes more than 700 electronic test and measurement instruments and computer graphics terminals. It is the largest producer of CRT oscilloscopes. Tektronix has created an in-house venture capital unit to maintain ties with employees who want to run their own companies and manufacture products that don't fit neatly into the company's plans. By 1984 two such companies had been formed: Planar Systems, which produces a flat panel display for computers; and Anthro Corporation, which makes furniture for engineering work stations. Tek is Oregon's largest private employer. It is aggressively egalitarian, relaxed, and informal. There are few companywide policies and procedures. A nine-member panel of employees provides information, investigates matters of concern, and prepares monthly educational sessions. The company's philosophy is: "Everybody here is an employee. We just have different jobs." With $1.3 billion annual sales, Tektronix ranks number 242 in the Fortune 500 largest U.S. industrial corporations.

ALL TRAINING PROGRAMS

The company uses supervised on-the-job experience as the primary means of training new employees. You will work with an experienced supervisor who will show you the ropes and introduce you to company operations and the specific needs of your job. The company also offers degree programs developed in cooperation with nearby colleges and universities, as well as workshops and short courses.

QUALIFICATIONS

The company is looking for college graduates (and technical graduates with one to ten years of experience) in the following fields: ceramic engineering, chemical engineering, chemistry, computer engineering, computer science, electrical engineering, electronics engineering, industrial/management engineering, information science, materials science, mechanical engineering, metallurgy, physics, and systems engineering.

RECRUITMENT AND PLACEMENT

Almost all U.S. employees work in the Portland, Oregon, area.

SALARY AND BENEFITS

The College Placement Council Salary Survey for September 1986–June 1987 indicates starting salaries for electrical and electronic machines and equipment companies to be $1,861 a month for those with a B.A. degree in nontechnical curricula and $2,419 with a B.A. degree in technical curricula. M.B.A. starting salaries were $2,784 for a nontechnical undergraduate degree and $2,818 for a technical undergraduate degree. Check with the company for more specific salary information. Benefits are excellent, including a liberal profit-sharing plan and a stock-purchase plan that enables employees to buy Tek stock at a 20 percent discount. Tuition and fees are reimbursed up to 100 percent.

CONTACT

College Relations Manager, Tektronix, Inc., P.O. Box 500, Beaverton, OR 97077.

TENNECO, INC.

ACCOUNTING AND FINANCE • ADMINISTRATION • ENGINEERING • INFORMATION SYSTEMS • PRODUCTION • RESEARCH AND DEVELOPMENT

THE COMPANY

Tenneco operates in a broad range of industries but strives to keep each division small to facilitate efficient and friendly communication. You will not get lost at Tenneco. Its businesses include energy development and petrochemicals, agricultural products, insurance, automotive equipment, and numerous manufactured products. The Tenneco work force is made up of more than 75,000 employees in the United States, and another 30,000 abroad. Listed among *Fortune*'s most admired corporations, Tenneco has annual sales totaling more than $14 billion and ranks number 21 in the Fortune 500 largest U.S. industrial corporations. See also entry on subsidiary Tennessee Gas Transmission Company.

ALL TRAINING PROGRAMS

You will be given responsibility from your first day and be exposed to the knowledge of experienced professionals as you learn on the job.

QUALIFICATIONS

You should have a bachelor's or master's degree in any of the following: actuarial science; chemical engineering; chemistry; computer science; electrical engineering; electronics engineering; environmental science; geology; geophysics; manufacturing engineering; marine engineering/naval architecture; materials science; mechanical engineering; metallurgy; mining; nuclear engineering; petroleum engineering; plastics engineering/polymer science; pulp and paper technology; structural engineering; or systems engineering.

RECRUITMENT AND PLACEMENT

Tenneco recruiters visit campuses around the country. Your starting location might be in California, Colorado, Georgia, Illinois, Louisiana, Michigan, New Jersey, Oklahoma, Pennsylvania, Texas, Virginia, Wisconsin, or Wyoming.

SALARIES AND BENEFITS

The College Placement Council Salary Survey for September 1986–June 1987 indicates starting salaries for petroleum and allied products (including natural gas) companies to be $1,972 a month for those with a B.A. degree in nontechnical curricula and $2,497 with a B.A. degree in technical curricula. M.B.A. starting salaries were $2,629 for a nontechnical undergraduate degree and $2,970 for a technical undergraduate degree. Check with the company for more specific salary information. Benefits include medical and life insurance, hospitalization, dental, pension, and stock-purchase plans, as well as a career development program.

CONTACT

Director, Staffing and Placement, Tenneco, Inc., P.O. Box 2511, Suite T-1035B, Houston, TX 77001.

TENNESSEE GAS TRANSMISSION COMPANY

ACCOUNTING AND FINANCE • ADMINISTRATION • FINANCIAL SERVICES • GOVERNMENTAL AFFAIRS • INFORMATION SERVICES • LAW • LONG-RANGE PLANNING • MARKETING • OPERATIONS • SUPPLY

THE COMPANY

Tennessee Gas Transmission was established during World War II to meet the pressing need for fuel in Appalachian factories. In less than a year the company laid pipeline from Texas to West Virginia across 67 rivers and hundreds of roads, setting a pipeline construction record of more than seven miles per day. Now a major subsidiary of Tenneco, Tennessee Gas Transmission is one of the largest natural gas pipeline networks in the world, stretching far beyond Tennessee. TGT's three interstate pipeline companies—Tennessee Gas Pipeline, Midwestern Gas Transmission, and East Tennessee Natural Gas Pipeline—now combine over 16,000 miles of pipeline serving 25 states. Opportunity exists within the company because many of its 3,100 employees have been with TGT for more than thirty years and will soon be retiring. A progressive employer, TGT gives workers access to the Tenneco Employee Center's health and fitness center in Houston; a private employee club northwest of the city; discounts on tickets to concerts and sporting events; and company van pools to ease commuting. The company also has one of the nation's best and most active employee volunteer organizations.

ALL TRAINING PROGRAMS

The Tenneco conference and training facility in Houston includes a video training room. A wide range of training courses will enhance your technical, interpersonal, and industry skills. You will receive a performance appraisal at least once a year to guide your career direction.

ADMINISTRATION PROGRAM

In this field, you might work in employee relations, training and development, employee communications, safety, or graphic arts. You will enter a department and work under the supervision of experienced personnel who will be responsible for your training. You will be given assignments to develop your abilities such as designing, developing, and implementing new training programs for others. In safety you might be assigned to conduct accident prevention programs or perform safety inspections at each field location. You will be given responsibility from the beginning of your career.

QUALIFICATIONS

You should have an excellent academic record and strong oral and written communication skills. Both recent graduates and experienced professionals are considered for employment. Applicants for employee relations or training and development should have a bachelor's or master's degree, preferably in human resources; safety applicants—a bachelor's degree in safety or health; employee communications candidates—a degree in English, communications, or journalism; and graphic arts applicants—a bachelor's degree in art.

PLACEMENT

You will work in Houston.

ENGINEER PROGRAM

You will begin in the field, the heart of operations, for the first year of training. Under the guidance of seasoned engineers and field managers, you'll be exposed to all areas of operations and field engineering, including corrosion, measurement, compressor, and electronics. After this in-depth portion of the development program, you'll spend six months at corporate headquarters in Houston. You'll work in technical staff departments such as measurement, research, planning, and electronic services. Upon completion of the program, you'll be given a choice about the direction of your career.

QUALIFICATIONS

You should be a recent graduate with bachelor's degree in civil, mechanical, electrical, industrial, or metallurgical engineering. You will need strong oral and written communication skills, and excellent academic credentials.

PLACEMENT

Your first assignment could be in Winchester, Kentucky; Lafayette or Houma, Louisiana; Agawam, Massachusetts; Hamburg, New York; Middleton, Tennessee; or Houston.

FINANCIAL SERVICES DEVELOPMENT PROGRAM

You will work in a variety of departments to learn about the natural gas industry, the operations of Tennessee Gas Transmission, and the role of financial services in the company. You will begin in accounting, rotating through departments such as accounts payable, gas revenue, financial reports, internal audit, then budget, treasury, and possibly systems development. These nine- to thirty-six-month assignments will be supplemented by management development courses that complement your academic training. Progression depends entirely on your ability, performance, and motivation. For each new assignment you will be asked to name five choices, and whenever possible the assignment will come from one of those choices. After completing the program you can decide in which area you want to concentrate your efforts. TGT will reimburse you for the cost of your first CPA exam taken while at the company, and pay membership dues in select local and national professional societies.

QUALIFICATIONS

You should be aggressive, capable, and achievement-oriented. TGT looks for graduates with bachelor's degrees in accounting with a minimum of twenty-seven semester hours in accounting and a G.P.A. of 3.0 or higher. You might also have one to three years of accounting experience.

PLACEMENT

You will begin your career in Houston.

ALL PROGRAMS

QUALIFICATIONS

TGT also hires graduates with degrees in political science for governmental affairs; recent law school graduates and experienced attorneys; M.B.A.s with undergraduate degrees in engineering, mathematics, business, or economics for long-range planning; computer science, math, business administration, engineering, or economics graduates for information service; and graduates with bachelor's degrees in engineering, business, or math for supply.

RECRUITMENT

The company visits campuses around the country.

SALARY AND BENEFITS

Check with the company for specific salary information. TGT salaries are reviewed annually. Benefits make up an additional thirty-three cents for every dollar of your salary. The package will include medical, life, and dental insurance; a long-term disability plan; retirement, thrift, and stock-ownership plans; tuition reimbursement; paid holidays and vacations.

CONTACT

Tennessee Gas Transmission, Employment Office, P.O. Box 2511, Houston, TX 77001. You may call collect to (713) 757-4193.

TEXACO, INC.

ACCOUNTING • CHEMISTRY • COMPUTER SCIENCE • ECONOMICS • ENGINEERING • EMPLOYEE RELATIONS • GEOLOGY • GEOPHYSICS • LAW • MARINE ENGINEERING • MARKETING • NAVAL ARCHITECTURE • PUBLIC RELATIONS • RESEARCH

THE COMPANY

Texaco is one of the largest industrial corporations in the nation and a worldwide leader in petroleum and petrochemicals. The company markets petroleum products in countries and territories around the world. It explores for new oil and gas resources on a global scale and is engaged in producing operations on six continents. Texaco fully or partly owns refineries in dozens of nations. An extensive fleet includes a large number of supertankers and a sophisticated seismic exploration ship, *Percheron*. Company assets top $34 billion and employees worldwide number about 67,000. Executive offices are in White Plains, New York. Listed among *Fortune*'s most admired corporations, it ranks number 8 in the Fortune 500 largest U.S. industrial corporations.

ALL TRAINING PROGRAMS

When you begin work at Texaco you will be expected to set goals for yourself and to review progress toward these goals with a supervisor periodically. During this review you and your supervisor will develop a training and development plan to assist you in improving your skills, knowledge, and experience. Texaco offers courses in leadership skills, management development, advanced management development, labor relations, financial management, and human resource management. You will also be eligible for ongoing technical training within your department or division.

QUALIFICATIONS

Texaco wants high-performance individuals trained in a broad spectrum of disciplines. You might have an undergraduate or advanced degree in any of the following areas: almost any engineering discipline, geology, geophysics, physics, mathematics, business administration, law, analytical or organic chemistry, applied mathematics, computer science, data processing, liberal arts, employee relations, communications, public relations, or economics.

RECRUITMENT AND PLACEMENT

Texaco recruits actively on college and university campuses, but you may also write directly to the college recruiting manager. Depending on your job function, you could be placed almost anywhere in the United States. For example, the marketing department has its headquarters in Houston and operating centers in Chicago; Cherry Hill, New Jersey; Los Angeles; and Bellaire, Texas.

SALARY AND BENEFITS

The College Placement Council Salary Survey for September 1986–June 1987 indicates starting salaries for petroleum and allied product companies to be $1,972 a month for those with a B.A. degree in nontechnical curricula and $2,497 with a B.A. degree in technical curricula. M.B.A. starting salaries were $2,629 for a nontechnical undergraduate degree and $2,970 for a technical undergraduate degree. Check with the company for more specific salary information. Texaco offers a comprehensive benefits program. You will receive medical and dental insurance, liberal vacations and holidays, tuition aid, sickness and disability benefits, leaves of absence, relocation assistance, pension plan, savings and stockownership plan, and life and accidental death insurance. In addition, the company offers credit unions, counseling and health services, organized commuting programs, and athletic activities.

CONTACT

Manager—College Recruiting, Texaco, Inc., P.O. Box 52332, Houston, TX 77052.

TEXAS INSTRUMENTS

ACCOUNTING • ADMINISTRATION • APPLIED OPTICS • APPLIED PHYSICS • CERAMICS • ENGINEERING • COGNITIVE PSYCHOLOGY • COMPUTER SCIENCE • GEOLOGY • GEOPHYSICS • INFORMATION SYSTEMS • LINGUISTICS • METALLURGY • PHYSICS •

THE COMPANY

Texas Instruments is a Fortune 500 company that takes pride in being the world's largest semiconductor supplier. It is the leader, or a major competitor, in more than 20 broad fields of science and engineering. Founded in 1930, TI has more than 50 plants in 18 countries on 6 continents. Its products include semiconductor components and materials, microcomputers and microprocessors, calculators, electronic learning aids, home computers, metallurgical materials, and a fleet of geophysical exploration ships linked by satellite. In 1985, TI's expenditures for research and development were $402 million, with an additional $367 million from customers, primarily the U.S. Government. You'll be on the cutting edge of new technology with this company and have the option of working in a wide variety of locations. The company fosters an entrepreneurial environment with its many small business units called Product-Customer Centers. Each of these 90-plus units has its own product lines or services and sets its own goals. With headquarters in Dallas, TI has about 78,000 employees worldwide and is the third largest nonunion company in the United States. Annual sales exceed $4.9 billion and the company is listed among *Fortune*'s most admired corporations. TI ranks number 72 in the Fortune 500 largest U.S. industrial corporations.

ALL TRAINING PROGRAMS

You will be encouraged to contribute from your first day on the job. TI emphasizes on-the-job training, offering job rotations after a couple of years to broaden your experience. You will have access to top managers from the beginning.

CONTROL MANAGEMENT PROGRAM

In this one-year program you will be encouraged to study TI before you select the area of accounting, control, or finance where you want to work. TI's manager of control development will supervise your work as you complete three to four major assignments. You will work in either an analytical or staff position, with top people at group, division, and corporate levels. You will contribute while you become familiar with the company's business systems and methods of operation. At the end of the program you will choose a permanent analytical or managerial position from openings at that time. You can apply yourself at any level—group, division, corporate, or multinational. Interdisciplinary training is a priority.

QUALIFICATIONS

TI selects M.B.A.s and B.B.A. accounting majors who have records of both academic and extracurricular achievement. You should have a G.P.A. of 3.0 or higher. Computer familiarity will be a plus.

PLACEMENT

Your assignments could be in California, Colorado, Kentucky, Massachusetts, Tennessee, Texas, or at any of the international locations.

EDP/ENGINEERING DEVELOPMENT PROGRAM

If you are accepted into this program, you will attend a local university half time and work half time. When you graduate you become part of the College Recruiting Program and have interviews with the appropriate managers.

QUALIFICATIONS

This program is for employees who want to acquire a bachelor's degree in computer science or engineering. Selection is based on years of service, a 3.0 G.P.A. in any completed academic work, and successful completion of two calculus courses.

PLACEMENT

Employees throughout the TI system are eligible. You continue to work in your local plant.

MANUFACTURING TRAINEE PROGRAM

TI is commited to continued professional development. It has an employee education center in each of its plants. The Manufacturing Rotation Program lasts eighteen months and provides on-the-job experience through three six-month assignments in manufacturing, purchasing, material planning, industrial engineering, or warehouse supervision. A wide variety of technical courses are available in the company's training catalog to supplement your on-the-job experience. After you complete the training, you will be offered three job options.

QUALIFICATIONS

TI needs college graduates with computer science, industrial engineering, or M.B.A. degrees. It is especially looking for persons with a specialty in artificial intelligence.

PLACEMENT

You may work in any of TI's facilities around the country.

ALL PROGRAMS

QUALIFICATIONS

You might have a degree in any of the following specialties: accounting, computer science, engineering (ceramic, computer, electrical, industrial, manufacturing, mechanical, metallurgical, plastics), engineering mechanics, engineering technology, information systems, management information systems, math, or solid state physics.

RECRUITMENT AND PLACEMENT

TI recruits nationwide and has starting locations in California, Colorado, Kentucky, Massachusetts, Tennessee, and Texas. International locations range from Australia to Egypt, Venezuela to China.

SALARY AND BENEFITS

The College Placement Council Salary Survey for September 1986–June 1987 indicates starting salaries for electrical and electronic machines and equipment companies to be $1,861 a month for those with a B.A. degree in nontechnical curricula and $2,419 with a B.A. degree in technical curricula. M.B.A. starting salaries were $2,784 for a nontechnical undergraduate degree and $2,818 for a technical undergraduate degree. Check with the company for more specific salary information. Your benefits package will include relocation assistance, health plans, stock-purchase and deferred compensation plans, fitness programs, and a pension plan.

CONTACT

Corporate Staffing, Texas Instruments, P.O. Box 655474, MS 67, Dallas, TX 75265; or Manager of Control Development, Texas Instruments, P.O. Box 225474, MS 410, Dallas, TX 75265.

3M (MINNESOTA MINING AND MANUFACTURING COMPANY)

ACCOUNTING • ADMINISTRATION • ENGINEERING • FINANCE • INFORMATION SYSTEMS • HUMAN RESOURCES • JOURNALISM • MARKETING • PACKAGING ENGINEERING • PRODUCTION • RESEARCH AND DEVELOPMENT SALES • STATISTICS • TECHNICAL SERVICES

THE COMPANY

Close to half of the world's population benefits in some way from 3M products each day, according to company estimates. Among the 3M products that see daily use are television programs recorded and broadcast on Scotch brand videotape, Scotch-lite reflective road signs, literature printed on 3M lithographic plates, 3M health-care and safety products, 3M sandpaper, and 3M adhesives and Scotch brand tapes. 3M began in 1902 as a mining business and discovered masking tape in 1925. In the 1950s, 3M produced the first office copier, the ThermoFax. The company now has 45 major product lines, more than 40 product divisions, and more than 50 international companies. Production occurs in 91 plants, largely in small towns in the United States, and 97 more in 38 foreign countries.

3M encourages an entrepreneurial spirit among its employees, and welcomes ideas that can be spun off into self-sustaining units. Researchers spend up to 15 percent of their time "bootlegging" or working on whatever interests them. Many of 3M's profitable products (Post-It notes is a recent example) have come from projects that went awry but sparked creative applications in other ways. Management operates by the philosophy that "if you put fences around people, you get sheep." 3M wants to see 25 percent of its sales generated each year by products or services that didn't exist five years ago.

Headquarters are in St. Paul, Minnesota. Listed among *Fortune*'s most admired corporations, 3M ranks number 39 in the Fortune 500 largest U.S. industrial corporations.

ALL TRAINING PROGRAMS

Except for sales and engineering, 3M trains most employees on the job. Sales employees will attend formal seminars in St. Paul and be coached by internal consulting services. Outside experts will be brought in from time to time to keep you current. Sales training programs last for about six months and include product and market knowledge, territory management, and selling skills training. Engineers attend a six-week training program, manufacturing engineers a four- to eleven-week program.

QUALIFICATIONS

3M hires college graduates with degrees in accounting, biochemistry, chemistry, marketing, pharmacology, physics, mathematics, advertising, journalism, communications, all engineering disciplines, and master's in market research, management information systems, and marketing. In sales, a proven record can sometimes offset the lack of a degree (previous sales experience, 3M product knowledge, or experience with industries serviced by 3M).

RECRUITMENT AND PLACEMENT

3M recruits nationwide. Starting locations are in Alabama, California, Iowa, Minnesota, and Wisconsin. Travel requirements for sales and marketing personnel range from 20 to 70 percent, and periodic relocations should be expected.

SALARY AND BENEFITS

With a bachelor's degree, salaries are $27,000 to $30,000; with a master's, $29,000 to $32,000; and with a doctorate degree, $32,000 to $40,000. Benefits include relocation services, flextime, stock-purchase plans, life, medical, and dental insurance, and tuition reimbursement.

CONTACT

Staffing and Employee-Resources/3M, 224-1W 3M Center, St. Paul, MN 55144.

THE TIMKEN COMPANY

ENGINEERING • INFORMATION SYSTEMS • MANAGEMENT • PRODUCTION • RESEARCH AND DEVELOPMENT • TECHNICAL SERVICES

THE COMPANY

The Timken Company, established in 1899, produces tapered roller bearings, alloy steel, and percussion rock bits. Tapered roller bearings are designed to counteract friction on axles and shafts in machines and vehicles of every description. Timken makes its own alloy steel for the bearings and also sells it to other manufacturers. Latrobe Steel Company, a wholly owned subsidiary, produces tool steels, vacuum-melted alloys in various solid shapes, and other custom-made steel products. The company's percussion rock bits are used in the construction, mining, quarrying, and drilling industries. The company employs more than 17,000 people worldwide, and in addition to its facilities in the United States has manufacturing operations in Canada, Great Britain, France, Australia, South Africa, and Brazil. With more than $1 billion in annual sales, Timken ranks number 290 in the Fortune 500 largest U.S. industrial corporations.

ALL TRAINING PROGRAMS

Timken maintains its own Timken Management Institute for management training. It's mostly on-the-job training for positions other than management and sales, and for those spots it's a combination of on-the-job and formal training for eighteen months.

QUALIFICATIONS

The company recruits college graduates with degrees in law, business administration, industrial management, marketing, economics, finance, accounting, computer science, mathematics, physics/chemistry, mechanical engineering, electrical/electronics engineering, industrial engineering, general engineering, industrial technology, and mechanical/electrical technology. In most of these areas, entry-level opportunities exist for people with degrees but little or no work experience. Advanced degrees are also considered.

RECRUITMENT AND PLACEMENT

Timken is headquartered in Canton, Ohio, and you'll probably start there. Other U.S. plants are elsewhere in Ohio, as well as in Colorado, North Carolina, and South Carolina. Latrobe Steel plants are in Pennsylvania and Ohio. The company recruits aggressively, and entry-level access is possible in almost all its divisions.

SALARY AND BENEFITS

The College Placement Council Salary Survey for September 1986–June 1987 indicates starting salaries for metals and metal products companies to be $1,782 a month for those with a B.A. degree in nontechnical curricula and $2,353 with a B.A. degree in technical curricula. M.B.A. starting salaries were $2,346 for a nontechnical undergraduate degree and $2,700 for a technical undergraduate degree. Check with the company for more specific salary information. Benefits include a comprehensive program of insurance and retirement benefits, a savings plan, and a liberal vacation policy. You will also be eligible for up to 100 percent reimbursement for advanced degree study.

CONTACT

Todd P. Miller, Manager, College Relations, The Timken Company, 1835 Dueber Avenue, S.W., Canton, OH 44706.

THE TORRINGTON COMPANY

MANUFACTURING ENGINEERING • MARKETING • PRODUCT AND APPLICATIONS ENGINEERING • SALES

THE COMPANY

Torrington designs, manufactures, and sells just about every basic type of antifriction bearing. It also produces universal joints and precision metal components and assemblies. Founded in 1866, it currently employs 12,000 people and is a subsidiary of Ingersoll-Rand. Torrington recently merged with one of its major competitors, Fafnir, a seventy-five-year-old company. Torrington is now America's largest bearing company.

ALL TRAINING PROGRAMS

You will spend one to two years in Torrington's training program, learning about the company's operations and your new position. Training takes the form of on-the-job experience as well as formal classes.

MANUFACTURING ENGINEERING PROGRAM

Mechanical engineers begin the program immediately. It is twelve months long with an optional six months added at the end for training in supervision. The program consists of on-the-job training on major projects. Formal instruction is provided in oral and written communication, project management, human relations, finance, sales and marketing, product design, production control, research, metallurgy CAD/CAM, quality control, participative management, and productivity improvement. The six-month supervisory segment consists of an assignment as a first-line supervisor in the employee's home plant.

PRODUCT AND APPLICATIONS ENGINEERING PROGRAM

This one-year program emphasizes on-the-job training in bearing design, computerized design and application analysis, bearing selection, metallurgy, lubrication, housing and shaft recommendations, manufacturing processes, and communication skills. You will also receive a general orientation to the company's philosophy and policies.

SALES/MARKETING TRAINING PROGRAM

It is twenty-four months long and consists of on-the-job training in pertinent departments and divisions in the organization. You will receive formal instruction in sales skills, negotiation, time management, human relations, oral and written communication, listening, and certain technical areas such as metallurgy, product design and applications, and manufacturing techniques.

ALL PROGRAMS

QUALIFICATIONS

Torrington takes roughly the top 10 percent of all applicants. You should have a bachelor's or a master's degree in engineering, including mechanical, electrical, electronics, and metallurgy.

PLACEMENT

You can expect to work in Connecticut, Georgia, North Carolina, or South Carolina.

SALARY AND BENEFITS

The College Placement Council Salary Survey for September 1986–June 1987 indicates starting salaries for automotive and mechanical equipment companies to be $1,907 a month for those with a B.A. degree in nontechnical curricula and $2,333 with a B.A. degree in technical curricula. M.B.A. starting salaries were $2,697 for a nontechnical undergraduate degree and $2,986 for a technical undergraduate degree. Check with the company for more specific salary information. The benefits program includes reimbursement of the total amount of tuition and fees for job-related graduate study.

CONTACT

Kenneth M. Keane, Manager, Professional Recruiting, The Torrington Company, 59 Field Street, Torrington, CT 06790.

TOUCHE ROSS & COMPANY

ACCOUNTING · AUDITING · MANAGEMENT CONSULTING · TAX CONSULTING

THE COMPANY

Touche Ross is a Big Eight public accounting firm with offices throughout the country and the world. The company employs more than 20,000 in more than 470 offices in 90 countries and offers a full spectrum of financial services, including auditing, planning, tax services, management consulting, actuarial services, and small-business financial consulting. If you want a lot of responsibility quickly and the chance to travel, you may like Touche Ross.

ACCOUNTING TRAINING PROGRAM

Accountants' on-the-job training starts right away. You will be given assignments of increasing responsibility as you show you can handle them. When you define an area you want to specialize in, you can ask for more assignments in that area and so increase your experience. During the first year you will begin to perform on the job, learn TRAP (the Touche Ross Audit Process), and hone your basic accounting skills. In the second year you will practice development techniques (such as showing a client the advantages of adding services), and develop your communication skills. In your third year you will have the opportunity to build your management skills (including supervising staff members, evaluating performance, and recognizing new business opportunities). When you are ready to study for your CPA exam, you will be provided with a self-study guide for all sections of the exam.

QUALIFICATIONS

You should have a degree in accounting or an M.B.A.

RECRUITMENT AND PLACEMENT

Touche Ross recruits on many college campuses. You may be assigned to work at any one of its many offices (85 in the United States).

SALARY AND BENEFITS

The College Placement Council Salary Survey for September 1986–June 1987 indicates starting salaries for public accounting firms to be $1,834 a month for those with a B.A. degree in nontechnical curricula and $2,155 with a B.A. degree in technical curricula. M.B.A. starting salaries were $2,335 for a nontechnical undergraduate degree and $2,436 for an M.B.A. with technical undergraduate degree. Check with the company for more specific salary information. Overtime is paid on a straight-time basis. You can convert overtime to vacation time with the leisure bank option. Touche Ross also has a good vacation policy and comprehensive medical insurance.

CONTACT

Todd Rossel, Supervisor, University Relations and Recruitment, Touche Ross & Co., 1633 Broadway, New York, NY 10019.

TOYS "R" US
STORE MANAGEMENT

THE COMPANY

Founded in 1948 as a single juvenile furniture store in downtown Washington, D.C., by young entrepreneur Charles Lazarus, Toys "R" Us has grown to become the world's largest specialty toy retailer. The USA division currently operates 273 stores in 31 states, with annual sales in excess of $2 billion. In addition, the company has an international division with units on three continents, with locations ranging from Hong Kong to Montreal, and Singapore to the United Kingdom. Kids "R" Us, a children's clothing division featuring name-brand merchandise at discount prices, operates 23 stores in 9 states. The firm expects to add approximately 30 to 40 new toy stores per year domestically, and roughly 20 new clothing stores annually.

STORE MANAGEMENT TRAINING PROGRAM

Each division trains its own personnel with programs combining classroom instruction and practical on-the-job training. Sessions on your division's merchandising principles will be interspersed with seminars on effective management skills.

QUALIFICATIONS

You should thrive in a fast-paced environment where constant change is the rule. If you are a results-oriented person with analytical skills and the ability to make fast decisions, you will catch the recruiter's attention. A degree in retail management, business administration, or marketing is also important.

RECRUITMENT AND PLACEMENT

Toys "R" Us and Kids "R" Us recruit nationally and welcome résumés from college graduates. Contact the company for specific locations of stores.

SALARY AND BENEFITS

The College Placement Council Salary Survey for September 1986–June 1987 indicates starting salaries for merchandising (retail and wholesale) and service companies to be $1,594 a month for those with a B.A. degree in nontechnical curricula and $2,141 with a B.A. degree in technical curricula. M.B.A. starting salaries were $2,572 for a nontechnical undergraduate degree and $2,735 for an M.B.A. with technical undergraduate degree. Check with the company for more specific salary information. Benefits include stock-option, profit-sharing, and savings plans; free life insurance; low-cost dental and health insurance; salary continuance in times of illness; long-term disability; and paid vacations and holidays.

CONTACT

Toys "R" Us, Recruitment and Placement, 395 West Passaic Street, Rochelle Park, NJ 07662; or Kids "R" Us, Recruitment and Placement, S61 Paramus Road, Paramus, NJ 07662.

THE TRAVELERS COMPANIES
DATA PROCESSING • FINANCIAL MANAGEMENT

THE COMPANY

Travelers writes every form of life, health, accident, group casualty, and property insurance. The company also invests in a variety of businesses and institutions. Travelers claims a number of firsts in the insurance industry. It wrote the first personal accident policy in America, the first automobile policy, and the first policy to insure astronauts during space travel. The company employs 30,000 people in the United States and Canada and has assets of more than $27 billion. Listed among *Fortune*'s most admired corporations, it is ranked number 8 in the Fortune 50 largest life insurance companies.

DATA PROCESSING TRAINING PROGRAM

Travelers' Accelerated Entry Program (Accent) develops computer science graduates for key positions in the data processing department. In your first four to five years of employment you'll be assigned rotating positions in the company's most challenging areas, including systems network architecture, operating systems support, and data administration. At the end of this training period candidates should be ready to assume management responsibilities.

QUALIFICATIONS

You should have a degree in computer science or a related discipline with exposure to software and hardware. Coding experience in BASIC, Assembler, COBOL, or APL is advantageous. Programming experience through summer employment or a cooperative education program is desirable. Personal qualities should include the abilities to work independently, handle pressure, and adapt quickly, communication skills, and willingness to take risks and make difficult judgments.

FINANCIAL MANAGEMENT TRAINING PROGRAM

Travelers offers a fast-paced three-year program with both practical and academic components. You'll learn the basics of financial theory, accounting practice, and the principles of management and acquire an understanding of the financial services industry. A corporate officer will act as your adviser and mentor. Your practical work experience will come from a series of rotational assignments, each lasting for approximately nine months. During the three-year period you will participate in at least four assignments, working in such areas as auditing; financial planning, measurements, and analysis; data processing, financial systems, and support; accounting; tax compliance/planning; and investments. Assignments can be either within corporate finance or one of Travelers' four business groups. In addition, you will attend classes and management seminars and engage in self-study courses. The in-house classes are approximately thirteen weeks long, with three classes offered each year. Over three years you will take classes in accounting and taxation; financial statement analysis; techniques of modeling and decision making; actuarial principles and methods; budgeting and cost accounting; strategic and tactical planning; information and resource management; and performance and people management. Classes are taught by Travelers professionals as well as professors from major Northeastern universities and partners of the Big Eight accounting firms.

After successfully completing your classwork you will be ready to tackle the program's practicum. Here you are presented with a complex business problem. Drawing upon the knowledge and techniques you've acquired through the Financial Management Development Program, you will probe the problem, consider the many alternatives, and ultimately propose a solution. Next you'll be asked to make an oral presentation and defend your solution before management. The practicum is one of the toughest challenges you will face. In addition to classwork, program participants are encouraged to engage in self-study courses and to attend financial management seminars.

QUALIFICATIONS

You should have a bachelor's or M.B.A. degree, preferably with a major in accounting, finance, or a related discipline, and evidence of academic achievement. Previous business experience is an asset. You should also have superior analytical, communication, interpersonal, and leadership abilities. You should be an autonomous thinker and a dynamic "doer"—an independent worker, yet a team player.

ALL TRAINING PROGRAMS

RECRUITMENT AND PLACEMENT

Company headquarters are in Hartford, Connecticut, and offices are located throughout the United States and Canada.

SALARY AND BENEFITS

The College Placement Council Salary Survey for September 1986–June 1987 indicates starting salaries for banking, finance, and insurance firms to be $1,889 a month for those with a B.A. degree in nontechnical curricula and $2,135 with a B.A. degree in technical curricula. M.B.A. starting salaries were $2,884 for a nontechnical undergraduate degree, and $3,320 for an M.B.A. with technical undergraduate degree. Check with the company for more specific salary information. Benefits include life, health, and disability insurance, tuition assistance, a savings plan with company contributions totaling 50 percent of the first 5 percent of your salary, subsidies for commuting costs, a company-subsidized restaurant, special rates for trips, and a retirement program.

CONTACT

Personnel Director, The Travelers Companies, One Tower Square, Hartford, CT 06183-7060.

TRW, INC.

MANAGEMENT

THE COMPANY

TRW is a $6 billion, diversified, multinational company which provides high-technology products and services to the space, defense, automotive, electronics, energy, and information systems markets. The firm began in 1901 with $2,500 and five men as the Cleveland Cap Screw Company. Throughout its eighty-five-year history, the company has had remarkable growth. Listed among *Fortune*'s most admired corporations, it ranks number 58 in the Fortune 500 largest U.S. industrial corporations.

MANAGEMENT TRAINING PROGRAM

On-the-job learning is the primary training method, which takes place at the various company sites for all technical and entry-level business jobs. TRW also offers a two-year Management Associates Program which rotates individuals through many parts of TRW's organization and prepares them for further advancement in management in their area. Regular feedback and coaching sessions are part of TRW's program.

QUALIFICATIONS

For the Management Associates Program you should have a graduate technical or business degree and approximately two years of prior work experience.

RECRUITMENT AND PLACEMENT

TRW does extensive nationwide campus recruiting during the fall and spring. With about 300 locations in 25 countries, the company has opportunities for placement in different geographic areas. Send a complete résumé with cover letter to one of the addresses below only if you are unable to interview on campus.

SALARY AND BENEFITS

The College Placement Council Salary Survey for September 1986–June 1987 indicates starting salaries for electrical and electronic machines and equipment companies to be $1,861 a month for those with a B.A. degree in nontechnical curricula and $2,419 with a B.A. degree in technical curricula. M.B.A. starting salaries were $2,784 for a nontechnical undergraduate degree and $2,818 for a technical undergraduate degree. Check with the company for more specific salary information. Your compensation is keyed to your overall contribution and performance rather than length of service. Benefit plans vary from location to location, but the company emphasizes that its plans reflect TRW's commitment to keep you producing and give you incentive for continued growth and development.

CONTACT

Manager, College Relations & Associates Program, TRW, 1900 Richmond Road, Cleveland, OH 44124; Company Staff, Manager, Human Relations, TRW Executive Offices, 1900 Richmond Road, Cleveland, OH 44124; Automotive Worldwide, Director, Human Resources, TRW Automotive Worldwide Sector, 1900 Richmond Road, Cleveland, OH 44124; Electronics and Defense Sector, Manager, College Relations, TRW Electronics and Defense Sector, One Space Park,

Building 81, Redondo Beach, CA 90278; Information Systems Group, Manager, Human Relations, TRW Information Systems Group, 200 Oceangate, Suite 1200, Long Beach, CA 90802.

U

☆ ☆ ☆ ☆ ☆

UGI CORPORATION

ACCOUNTING • ADMINISTRATION • FINANCE • MANAGEMENT • MARKETING • PRODUCTION • SALES

THE COMPANY

UGI, headquartered in Valley Forge, Pennsylvania, is a diversified energy company with gas and electric utilities in Pennsylvania. Through a wholly owned subsidiary, AMERIGAS, it manufactures and distributes compressed and liquefied gases. It is also involved in natural gas and oil exploration and development in the Southwest. The company employs 3,800 people in the United States.

MANAGEMENT TRAINING PROGRAM

You will participate in an eighteen-month on-the-job training program. Outside workshops and courses will be available as your career progresses. The company encourages advanced degree study with tuition reimbursement of up to 75 percent.

QUALIFICATIONS

UGI is looking for people with business administration degrees; engineers with chemical, mechanical, and petroleum specialties; and salespeople to market industrial gases. Applicants with prior work experience have a head start.

RECRUITMENT AND PLACEMENT

The company recruits mainly in the East, Midwest, and Southwest. Starting locations are in Pennsylvania or Texas.

SALARY AND BENEFITS

The College Placement Council Salary Survey for September 1986–June 1987 indicates starting salaries for petroleum and allied products (including natural gas) companies to be $1,972 a month for those with a B.A. degree in nontechnical curricula and $2,497 with a B.A. degree in technical curricula. M.B.A. starting salaries were $2,629 for a nontechnical undergraduate degree and $2,970 for a technical undergraduate degree. Check with the company for more specific salary information. Your benefits package will consist of life insurance; medical, hospital, and dental plans; pension and stock-purchase plans; and career counseling.

CONTACT

Thomas Hadderman, Manager, Compensation and Recruiting, UGI Corporation, P.O. Box 858, Valley Forge, PA 19482.

UNION OIL COMPANY OF CALIFORNIA

ACCOUNTING • ENGINEERING • FINANCE • INFORMATION SYSTEMS • MARKETING • PRODUCTION AND OPERATIONS • RESEARCH AND DEVELOPMENT • SALES

THE COMPANY

Union Oil is a classic example of a fully integrated company. It is engaged in every aspect of the oil and mining business—research, exploration, mining, production, refining, marketing, chemical production, and minerals processing. It employs 20,000 people throughout the world and is a subsidiary of UNOCAL Corporation of Los Angeles. Union Oil is actively involved in the development of alternative energy sources, such as geothermal resources and oil shale.

ALL TRAINING PROGRAMS

The company will provide you with an extensive training program that can last from eighteen to twenty-four months. Engineers and earth scientists receive on-the-job training; sales and marketing personnel receive a combination of on-the-job and formal training.

QUALIFICATIONS

You should have a bachelor's or a master's degree and at least a 2.8 G.P.A. Related student work experience will be a plus. Union Oil is looking for you if you have a degree in engineering, computer science, or the physical and biological sciences. Your chances are also good if you have a degree in business.

RECRUITMENT AND PLACEMENT

You may work in Alaska, California, Colorado, Illinois, Louisiana, Mississippi, New Mexico, Oklahoma, Texas, or Wyoming. International placement is available after five years.

SALARY AND BENEFITS

The College Placement Council Salary Survey for September 1986–June 1987 indicates starting salaries for petroleum and allied products (including natural gas) companies to be $1,972 a month for those with a B.A. degree in nontechnical curricula and $2,497 with a B.A. degree in technical curricula. M.B.A. starting salaries were $2,629 for a nontechnical undergraduate degree and $2,970 for a technical undergraduate degree. Check with the company for more specific salary information. Benefits include pension and profit-sharing plans; medical, hospital, and dental plans; and a stock-purchase plan.

CONTACT

Russel Groesbeck, Manager, Recruitment and College Relations, Union Oil Co. of California, P.O. Box 7600, Los Angeles, CA 90051.

UPJOHN COMPANY

SALES REPRESENTATIVE

THE COMPANY

The Upjohn Company was founded in 1886, following the invention of a "friable" pill that could be crushed under the thumb—and dissolved after swallowing. Since then it has grown to become one of the world's largest health-product producers with specialties in pharmaceuticals, chemicals, and agriculture. The company is a world leader in the discovery and development of antibiotics, steroids, and prostaglandins. The Agriculture Division includes the Asgrow Seed Company, one of the world's largest producers of vegetable and agronomic seed products. The newest addition to the division is Cobb, Incorporated, a worldwide business that provides breeding stock for broiler chickens. A HealthCare Service Division with more than 250 offices in the United States provides paramedical personnel ranging from homemakers to registered nurses. They deliver health care in homes and in hospitals. Corporate and all division headquarters are located in Kalamazoo, Michigan, along with the company's major research and development complex and its largest pharmaceutical production facility. As a sales representative, you will enjoy knowing that your work with doctors, pharmacies, hospitals, and other health-care professionals helps to keep them informed about the latest advances in medicine. Upjohn ranks number 162 in the Fortune 500 largest U.S. industrial corporations and has annual sales of more than $2 billion.

SALES TRAINING PROGRAM

Upjohn likes to say that your training as a pharmaceutical sales representative begins with your college education and ends when you retire. You will begin with an orientation of several weeks under the direct supervision of the area sales manager concerning initial disease and product information, mechanics of the job, and operations of the sales area office. As training progresses you will learn more about Upjohn's products, policies, and operating procedures and will be involved in a supplemental study of the life sciences. Considerable attention is devoted to the development of professional communication skills through the use of videotape replay and other up-to-date teaching techniques. This portion of the development program lasts for four weeks and is under the leadership of the Professional Training and Development unit in Kalamazoo. Field training begins under the supervision of a district manager, but then you will be on your own. Training and development conferences will be held every four months to keep you current about health-care technology. After about eighteen months in the field and at periodic intervals thereafter, you will return to Kalamazoo for a one-week seminar. You will manage your territory as if you were in business for yourself.

QUALIFICATIONS

While your degree might be in business or a science field, Upjohn is most concerned that you be strongly self-motivated and organized. You must enjoy learning and working independently.

RECRUITMENT AND PLACEMENT

Upjohn recruiters visit campuses around the country, or you may contact the sales area office nearest you. Sales offices are located throughout the world. Most territories are limited in size and will not involve extensive travel.

SALARY AND BENEFITS

The College Placement Council Salary Survey for September 1986–June 1987 indicates starting salaries for chemicals, drugs, and allied products companies to be $1,964 a month for those with a B.A. degree in nontechnical curricula and $2,457 with a B.A. degree in technical curricula. M.B.A. starting salaries were $2,886 for a nontechnical undergraduate degree and $2,794 for a technical undergraduate degree. Check with the company for more specific salary information. In addition to your salary, Upjohn pays a cost-of-living allowance to reflect changes in the economy. Benefits include all types of insurance, retirement and savings plans, and liberal vacations and holidays.

CONTACT

Marketing Personnel Affairs, 9241-88-1, The Upjohn Company, Kalamazoo, MI 49001.

USG CORPORATION

ARCHITECTURE • ENGINEERING • FINANCE AND ACCOUNTING • INFORMATION SYSTEMS • SALES AND MARKETING

THE COMPANY

USG (formerly United States Gypsum Company) changed its name in 1985 to reflect its broadening scope of products for the construction industry. Products include gypsum, wood fiber, acoustical and mineral fiber, metals, adhesives, plastics, refractories, residential steel door systems, shower tub enclosures, chemicals, and carpeting. Listed among *Fortune*'s most admired corporations, USG ranks number 136 in the Fortune 500 largest U.S. industrial corporations. The company employs 22,000 people and has sales over $2.6 billion. With USG's system of subsidiaries that operate like businesses within a business, you will be encouraged to operate as an "intrapreneur." Each is run as an independent unit, providing the benefits of a big company and the feel of a small one.

ALL TRAINING PROGRAMS

In your training you will be exposed to extensive and varied programs that include audiovisual instruction on thc uses and applications of major products in the USG line; internal seminars on a variety of business subjects from letter writing to first-level supervision to stress management; regular management updates on the state of the company; a video news magazine produced four times a year with information on company products and policies; and several print publications, published regularly. A management development program, conducted in conjunction with Northwestern University's J. L. Kellogg Graduate School of Management, introduces selected high-potential employees to both broad business practices and strategies and specifics of the USG business environment.

QUALIFICATIONS

USG hires applicants from a broad range of academic backgrounds, emphasizing both written and oral communication skills, ambition, and personal integrity.

ENGINEERING PROGRAM

Your first project in manufacturing engineering will give you hands-on experience involving capital equipment, mobile equipment, worker safety, or plant protection. You will work under the guidance of a plant engineering or production superintendent, planning and coordinating the project to ensure a safe working environment, quality work, cost control, and timely completion. At some point you will work as relief foreman to prepare you for greater responsibility.

QUALIFICATIONS

USG requires a bachelor's degree or higher in virtually any engineering specialty, an excellent academic record, proven potential for leadership, superior communication and interpersonal skills, and the flexibility to relocate.

PLACEMENT

You could be sent to any one of 100 plants around the country. Engineers also work in staff positions at corporate and subsidiary headquarters, in science and technology, and in sales and marketing. Expect to be transferred as your career advances.

INFORMATION SYSTEMS PROGRAM

You will begin as a programmer trainee, learning skills to design and develop computer programs. A project leader will lead you through courses and on-the-job training in concepts and fundamentals of data processing and programming, programming languages, job control language, systems software, utilities, programming aids, installation support systems, and the test data generator. Test exercises and production programs ranging from simple to complex will be part of your training. At the second level of training, you will begin designing and developing computer programs.

QUALIFICATIONS

You should have a degree in computer science, information systems, business administration, accounting, finance, or management, a mind that can keep pace with the new technology, and the communication skills to deal with management in nontechnical terms.

PLACEMENT

USG maintains data centers in its Chicago corporate offices, in the Graham J. Morgan Research Center in Libertyville, Illinois, in St. Louis, Missouri, and at various locations of the Masonite Corporation.

SALES AND MARKETING PROGRAM

As a sales representative your training will use self-directed audiovisual programs to teach the product line attributes and sound selling skills. Hands-on experience in plant settings and ongoing help from your manager complement formal training. Regular sales meetings cover additional helpful topics. In your territory, assigned at the start, you'll divide your time between promotion of new business, customer service, and constructive communications with management and customers.

QUALIFICATIONS

You should have a bachelor's degree in an area of study that develops clear thinking and solid communication skills, a strong record of extracurricular activity in leadership roles at the college level, top-notch problem-solving abilities, a natural affinity for people, a taste for independent activity and the self-discipline to handle it, a talent for managing time, a mind for facts and figures, and the ability to think on your feet.

PLACEMENT

USG has sales offices in every major market throughout the United States.

ALL PROGRAMS

RECRUITMENT

USG representatives visit college and university campuses around the country. The company also invites résumés from experienced professionals.

SALARY AND BENEFITS

The College Placement Council Salary Survey for September 1986–June 1987 indicates starting salaries for building materials manufacturers and construction companies to be $1,782 a month for those with a B.A. degree in nontechnical curricula and $2,156 with a B.A. degree in technical curricula. M.B.A. starting salaries were $1,666 for a nontechnical undergraduate degree and $2,677 for a technical undergraduate degree. Salaries are based on performance rather than seniority. Check with the company for more specific salary information. Benefits include group insurance; retirement, investment, and stockownership plans; paid holidays and vacations; and a matching gift plan to universities and certain civic/cultural institutions.

CONTACT

USG Corporation, Corporate Employment Office, 101 South Wacker Drive, Chicago, IL 60606-4385.

V

☆ ☆ ☆ ☆ ☆

VANITY FAIR MILLS, INC.

ENGINEERING • MANAGEMENT • MANUFACTURING

THE COMPANY

Vanity Fair, a subsidiary of VF Corporation, is a producer of lingerie, foundation garments, robes, and loungewear. The company employs 7,000 people in the United States.

MANAGEMENT TRAINING PROGRAM

The one-month program of classroom instruction prepares management trainees for their first assignment. Other employees receive on-the-job training.

QUALIFICATIONS

Vanity Fair is looking for industrial and manufacturing engineers and also for graduates with degrees in business. If you have previous work experience, you will be more seriously considered. A minimum G.P.A. of 2.5 is required.

RECRUITMENT AND PLACEMENT

You will work at a plant location in Alabama or Florida. The company recruits all year.

SALARY AND BENEFITS

The College Placement Council Salary Survey for September 1986–June 1987 indicates starting salaries for glass, paper, packaging, and allied products companies to be $1,865 a month for those with a B.A. degree in nontechnical curricula and $2,401 with a B.A. degree in technical curricula. M.B.A. starting salaries were $2,945 for a nontechnical undergraduate degree and $2,775 for a technical undergraduate degree. Check with the company for more specific salary information. Your benefits will include life insurance, medical and hospital plans, and a pension plan. You may be granted time for job-related graduate study.

CONTACT

Manager, Employment and Benefits, Vanity Fair Mills, Inc., Alabama Avenue, Monroeville, AL 36460.

VARIAN

ACCOUNTING • COMPUTER SCIENCE • ENGINEERING • FINANCE • MARKETING • SALES

THE COMPANY

Varian is an international Fortune 500 high-technology company and a Silicon Valley pioneer. Founded in 1948, this Palo Alto firm concentrates on areas of essential need—medicine, communications, defense, science, and industry. It is a leader in linear accelerator technology for medical and industrial applications, one of its earliest innovations. The company is divided into four diversified product groups: the Electron Device Group, Instrument Group, Semiconductor Equipment Group, and Medical and Industrial Products Group. Among its products are microwave and power tubes, nuclear magnetic resonance spectrometers, and ion implanters. Varian employs more than 13,000 people nationwide. It ranks number 325 in the Fortune 500 largest U.S. industrial corporations and has annual sales of more than $900 million.

ALL TRAINING PROGRAMS

To get you started, Varian will assign you to projects that offer measurable results. Support from senior engineers, scientists, and management will guide your first efforts. Varian advocates an informal mentor system to help you learn your new job. Seminars, lectures, and workshops will round out your on-the-job training.

QUALIFICATIONS

Varian hires electrical, industrial, mechanical, and manufacturing engineers; computer scientists (including scientific programming and MIS applications); and business and M.B.A. graduates in accounting, finance, marketing, and sales.

RECRUITMENT AND PLACEMENT

Varian recruits around the country. You will likely be assigned to one of three locations: the Greater Boston Area; Salt Lake City; or San Francisco Bay Area.

SALARY AND BENEFITS

The College Placement Council Salary Survey for September 1986–June 1987 indicates starting salaries for electrical and electronic machines and equipment companies to be $1,861 a month for those with a B.A. degree in nontechnical curricula and $2,419 with a B.A. degree in technical curricula. M.B.A. starting salaries were $2,784 for a nontechnical undergraduate degree and $2,818 for a technical undergraduate degree. Check with the company for more specific salary information. Benefits include life insurance, dental, medical, retirement, stock-purchase, and savings plans; and annual cash profit sharing.

CONTACT

Rob Lawrence, Corporate College Relations Manager, Varian, 611 Hansen Way, Palo Alto, CA 94303.

VF CORPORATION—WRANGLER DIVISION

DATA PROCESSING • ENGINEERING • MANAGEMENT

THE COMPANY

Blue Bell, Inc., merged with VF Corporation in November 1986 to form the world's largest manufacturer of wearing apparel. VF produces Wrangler and Rustler tops and bottoms for men, women, and children. Wrangler and Rustler jeans are among the four largest-selling brands in the United States. Wrangler is headquartered in Greensboro, North Carolina, and has 8,000 employees worldwide.

ALL TRAINING PROGRAMS

You will enter a six-month training program for positions in engineering, manufacturing management, and management information systems. Training takes place at your starting location with emphasis on direct participation in on-the-job activities, supplemented by classroom activities.

QUALIFICATIONS

You will need a minimum of a four-year degree in engineering, business, or computer-related disciplines. Candidates should be aggressive, willing to accept responsibility, and self-motivated.

RECRUITMENT AND PLACEMENT

Wrangler's recruiting program focuses on a select number of schools in the Southern United States, but the company welcomes applicants from campuses not visited. Wrangler hires for entry-level assignments year round.

SALARY AND BENEFITS

Starting salaries for holders of bachelor's degrees are in the $20,000 to $24,000 range. Benefits include insurance and retirement plans and are competitive within the apparel industry.

CONTACT

Sam Tucker, Management Recruiting, Wrangler, P.O. Box 21488, Greensboro, NC 27420.

VISTA CHEMICAL COMPANY

ANALYSIS · CHEMICAL SALES ENGINEERING · CUSTOMER SERVICE REPRESENTATION · RESEARCH AND DEVELOPMENT CHEMISTRY · TECHNICAL SALES REPRESENTATION

THE COMPANY

After Conoco and Du Pont merged in 1981 it became apparent that the large-volume commodity businesses of Conoco Chemicals were not a perfect fit with those of Du Pont, whose interests were in high technology and specialty chemicals. In late 1982 a group of Conoco Chemicals executives and private investors began efforts to buy the company's assets, and a year and a half later completed negotiations to establish Vista Chemical Company. Today the Houston-based company is a privately held corporation with approximately 1,500 employees worldwide. It has international sales offices in Brussels, Tokyo, and Houston with interests in two affiliates in Japan and one in Argentina. Nearly all of the current management team was part of the Conoco staff. Vista is the largest of the three U.S. producers of detergent alkylate, and also utilizes a few feedstocks to produce large-volume commodities such as ethylene, vinyl chloride monomer, linear alkylbenzene, and polyvinyl chloride.

ALL TRAINING PROGRAMS

You will receive on-the-job training for most positions, with supervision and formal evaluations to help you make the best start at Vista Chemicals.

QUALIFICATIONS

You should have a technical undergraduate degree in chemistry (organic, physical, inorganic, analytical, polymer, or surface) or chemical engineering, or an M.B.A. with a technical undergraduate degree.

PLACEMENT

Vista has plant locations in Hammond, Indiana; Lake Charles and Westlake, Louisiana; Baltimore, Maryland; Aberdeen, Mississippi; Ponca City and Oklahoma City, Oklahoma. Sales offices exist in Houston; Santa Ana, California; Saddle Brook, New Jersey; and Oak Brook, Illinois.

CUSTOMER SERVICE REPRESENTATIVE TRAINING

You will spend about two years in this entry-level position and be assigned a mentor for guidance during the first year. Your supervisor will orient you to company procedures and help you evaluate your goals within the company. One week of product and technical training is held twice a year at the Ponca City plant. You will also attend up to three weeks of technical training classes. Beforehand, you will receive the detailed course outline, advance work to be completed, and other instructions. As part of your business knowledge development, you will participate in a series of two- to three-day presentations, held over a month's time, by managers in areas such as law, manufacturing, treasury, and marketing communications. You will also be sent to the Lake Charles complex to observe operations there. In-house and external workshops on personal computers and effective writing are a few of the additional opportunities you may have during your training period.

QUALIFICATIONS

You should have a degree in chemistry, chemical engineering, chem-business, or related fields. Vista stresses the importance of hiring people with initiative, creativity, and a high degree of motivation.

PLACEMENT

You will work in the Houston offices.

ALL TRAINING PROGRAMS

RECRUITMENT

Vista recruiters visit campuses throughout the country. Experienced candidates are encouraged to contact the company with a letter of interest and résumé.

SALARIES AND BENEFITS

The College Placement Council Salary Survey for September 1986–June 1987 indicates starting salaries for chemicals, drugs, and allied products companies to be $1,964 a month for those with a B.A. degree in nontechnical curricula and $2,457 with a B.A. degree in technical curricula. M.B.A. starting salaries were $2,886 for a nontechnical undergraduate degree and $2,794 for a technical undergraduate degree. Check with the company for more specific salary information. You will be offered a comprehensive benefits plan. Technical sales representatives receive a company car and credit cards for travel expenses.

CONTACT

College Relations, Vista Chemical Company, 1590 North Barker's Landing Road, Houston, TX 77079.

The Corporate Perspective on Training Programs
Baxter Graham, Chubb Insurance

Baxter Graham is Vice-President of Corporate Education and Training at Chubb Insurance Companies. Previous to this new assignment he worked for a number of years in the Marine Underwriting Division.

☆ ☆ ☆ ☆ ☆

I understand you're on a special assignment.

Yes. My mission is to review and evaluate our training programs for new hires to determine if Chubb is doing an adequate job and to develop new programs.

How many new hires do you have each year?

About three hundred.

Why were you asked to take on this new assignment?

They wanted somebody who had worked on the line—someone who had actually come through one of the operating departments. They wanted the perspective of a line manager to make sure our training goals fit our business goals. There's a bridge there between training and our business plans. I think that's sometimes overlooked, but we try to make it a priority.

How is entry-level training organized at Chubb?

We have eleven different schools that each focus on a particular line of the business. Eight of these schools deal with specialty underwriting. Underwriting is the essence of our business. We have a school that trains new people for our claims area. And there's a school that trains people coming into our operations area and loss control.

What are minimum and maximum lengths of those programs?

In the specialty programs, the minimum is about a week and the maximum has been six weeks.

How are the programs structured?

We used to have a job rotation program. But what we do now is to provide an initial four-week orientation program. We have forty-seven branch offices, and we recruit and hire for a branch in the local area. Then we will send all trainees to a new introductory property casualty insurance program at the home office. This will cover for four weeks everything from A to Z—what we do, the various lines that we write, how we are organized, and our place in the industry, as well as the fundamentals of insurance. Trainees will then enter their specialty school (underwriting, claims, etc.); these schools are being redesigned with the help of professional educators. All of our courses have really been redesigned and fine-tuned in the methodology and sequence of topics. The specialty programs will vary from one week to six weeks. Once the trainees have successfully completed both segments, they go back to their branches and go through a formal on-the-job training program of approximately three to six months. We try to get them out of that status and into real jobs as quickly as possible. And we try to continue to mix the job with structured training. That's where we get a little more into job rotation, because they move through the operating departments, spending anywhere from a week to three weeks in each area.

What is it you're trying to instill in that initial four-week course at the home office?

Basic insurance building blocks, including: (a) a broader understanding of Chubb's overall operations; (b) coverage offered by the various underwriting departments; and (c) each department's strategies and differences.

What happens as a trainee finishes on-the-job training?

It's important to talk about what happens after a person has been here about one and a half to two years. We are designing and will have in place probably by the fall of 1988 what we will refer to as the Chubb Business School. It's on the drawing board. It's received senior management approval. It looks like it will be approximately two weeks long and will be for employees at that year-and-a-half to two-year level of experience. We're looking at one of two approaches. One approach is to design a program that would be very particular to Chubb. A second approach would be to design an in-house "business school"—more generic in nature and designed with the assistance of one of the more reputable business schools. The best way to describe it is a mini-business course, professionally taught by senior managers and outside faculty, covering such topics as the insurance industry, financial management, marketing, basic management principles, and how we do business as a company. Some of those things are generic, but others will be specific to Chubb.

What will happen after this new business school?

We will not stop at the two-year mark. After that, training is more specific in terms of technical training, managerial training, marketing training, those kinds of things. Trainees begin to have more of a role in deciding what kinds of things they need to do their job and to get ready for the next job.

What do you hope to achieve with this new approach?

I hope it does a couple of things. First of all, it will continue to emphasize the specialty training which is part of the secret of how we do business. Through the four-week program at the home office, everybody will get a more basic understanding of the industry so that they see a larger picture than ever before. With an offering of the basic fundamentals of an insurance operation, and more specific, professionally designed specialty schools, plus a "rounding out" of a mini-M.B.A. program at two years, we have as close to five years' experience as we can achieve in two years. This may create significant advancement opportunities within the operation.

☆ ☆ ☆ ☆ ☆

WACHOVIA BANK & TRUST COMPANY, N.A.

AUDIT · CONTROL · MANAGEMENT · MORTGAGE · OPERATIONS · RETAIL BANKING · SALES FINANCE · SYSTEMS DEVELOPMENT · TRUST

THE COMPANY

Wachovia Bank & Trust, headquartered in Winston-Salem, North Carolina, offers banking and financial services throughout the state and has offices in New York City; Chicago; Tampa; Zurich, Switzerland; and the Cayman Islands. Established in 1879, it employs 6,500 people in the United States. Wachovia operates 213 offices in 89 North Carolina cities and towns.

ALL TRAINING PROGRAMS

The goal of training is to prepare new employees to provide competitive banking and financial services to individuals and institutions. In Wachovia's seven-month training program you will receive both supervised work experience and classroom instruction.

QUALIFICATIONS

Candidates with degrees in business, computer science, information science, and operations research are welcome.

RECRUITMENT AND PLACEMENT

Wachovia recruits mainly in the mid-Atlantic States, the eastern part of the Midwest, and the Southeast. It hires nearly 150 trainees a year. Your starting location is likely to be at company headquarters in Winston-Salem.

SALARY AND BENEFITS

The College Placement Council Salary Survey for September 1986–June 1987 indicates starting salaries for banking, finance, and insurance firms to be $1,889 a month for those with a B.A. degree in nontechnical curricula and $2,135 with a B.A. degree in technical curricula. M.B.A. starting salaries were $2,884 for a nontechnical undergraduate degree and $3,320 for an M.B.A. with technical undergraduate degree. Check with the company for more specific salary information. Your benefits package will include life insurance; medical and hospitalization plans; day-care facilities; career counseling; relocation assistance; pension and profit-sharing plans; and stock-purchase and incentive savings plans.

CONTACT

Jacob Dove, Recruiting and Employment Officer, Wachovia Bank & Trust Company, N.A., P.O. Box 3099, Winston-Salem, NC 27102.

WALGREEN, INC.

ACCOUNTING · FINANCE · INFORMATION SYSTEMS · MANAGEMENT · PHARMACOLOGY · RESEARCH AND DEVELOPMENT

THE COMPANY

Charles Walgreen opened a Chicago retail store in 1901. Eight years later he opened a second store. Walgreen has been growing ever since. He served the first chocolate malted milk with ice cream at the nation's first drugstore soda fountain. His son, Charles Walgreen, Jr., took over the company in 1939, converting the chain stores into a self-service operation. His grandson, Charles Walgreen III, now presides over 650 stores that sell more pharmaceuticals than any other in the country, 300 restaurants, 3 manufacturing plants, and 3 photo-processing studios that turn out more than 80 million color prints a year. Walgreen has 36,000 employees in the United States. With $3.6 billion in annual sales, it is listed among *Fortune*'s most admired corporations and ranks number 27 in the Fortune 50 largest retailing companies.

ALL TRAINING PROGRAMS

As a new employee you will receive both classroom and on-the-job training that can last as long as eighteen months. You will also be able to participate in seminars and workshops to develop management techniques and skills. Evaluations are carried out periodically to keep you up to date on your progress and to maintain company standards.

QUALIFICATIONS

Walgreen is looking for you if you are competent in the areas of data processing, marketing, pharmacology, or finance.

RECRUITMENT AND PLACEMENT

The company recruits primarily at Midwestern colleges and universities, hiring more than 450 trainees a year. It also recruits through advertisements, employment agencies, and interviews. There are 45 district offices in the United States, but you will most likely begin your career in Illinois.

SALARY AND BENEFITS

With a bachelor's degree you can expect your starting salary to be in the $20,000 to $30,000 range. Benefits include medical, life, and hospital insurance; profit sharing; tuition reimbursement; and pension plans.

CONTACT

Ms. Pat Schultz, Consultant, Walgreen, Inc., 200 Wilmot Road, Walgreen, Inc., Room 200, Deerfield, IL 60015.

WALLACE COMPUTER SERVICES, INC.

ACCOUNTING · ENGINEERING · MARKETING · PLANT SUPERVISION · SALES

THE COMPANY

As the world's supply of computers increases, so does the demand for computer supplies. Wallace is a leading producer and distributor of computer supplies, manufacturing computer ribbons, carbon paper, disk packs, and pressure-sensitive labels. It also operates a large direct mail distribution division for peripheral supplies and a software house. A publicly held corporation since 1971, Wallace owns 9 business forms plants and creates everything from catalogs to airline tickets —well over 6,000 different products. This is one of the fastest-growing companies in its field. A solid training program and strong company spirit contribute to Wallace's record for the highest output per employee ratio in the industry.

ALL TRAINING PROGRAMS

You will receive a combination of on-the-job training with supervision and scheduled instruction so that you can put your theoretical education to work.

QUALIFICATIONS

Wallace looks for candidates with strong academic records and a variety of degrees. Exposure to computers would be a plus.

PLACEMENT

You might be sent to any of the following locations: Chicago, Hillside, St. Charles, Wheeling, or Clinton, Illinois; Luray, Virginia; Gastonia or Durham, North Carolina; Marlin, Houston, or Brenham, Texas; Metter or Atlanta, Georgia; Osage, Iowa; San Luis Obispo, Lodi, or Hayward, California; Manchester, Vermont; or Twinsburg, Ohio.

SALES TRAINING PROGRAM

Your training will begin with a thorough self-study program to develop product knowledge, selling skills, and an understanding of territory management procedures. You and your district manager will work together through exercises and role playing to meet your specific needs. At the same time, you will be testing these skills in your territory. After in-district training you will be invited to attend two-week-long basic sales training programs at Wallace's training facility in suburban Chicago. Working in teams with other sales reps, you will refine your skills, study more technical product information, learn how to "systems-sell," and develop a broader understanding of the industry, Wallace, the market, and your role as sales representative. Role playing and simulation exercises will help you investigate and analyze customer needs, design solutions to customers' problems, and make formal professional presentations to sell those solutions. An advanced sales training course and special seminars will be available later in your career.

QUALIFICATIONS

In addition to an undergraduate degree and some knowledge of computers, Wallace looks for candidates with success in sales. Expect to spend at least two years developing your customer base.

PLACEMENT

Wallace has sales offices in over 75 principal cities throughout the country.

ALL TRAINING PROGRAMS

RECRUITMENT

Wallace sends representatives to university and college campuses around the country.

SALARY AND BENEFITS

The College Placement Council Salary Survey for September 1986–June 1987 indicates starting salaries for glass, paper, packaging and allied products companies to be $1,865 a month for those with a B.A. degree in nontechnical curricula and $2,401 with a B.A. degree in technical curricula. M.B.A. starting salaries were $2,945 for a nontechnical undergraduate degree and $2,775 for a technical undergraduate degree. Check with the company for more specific salary information. Your benefits plan will total more than 40 percent of salary. Benefits include profit-sharing plans, supplemental life and accident insurance, hospitalization, dental plan, stock-purchase plan, vacations and paid holidays, tuition reimbursement, and long-term disability.

CONTACT

Vice-President of Human Resources, Wallace Computer Services, Inc., 4600 West Roosevelt Road, Hillside, IL 60162.

WAL-MART

RETAIL MANAGEMENT

THE COMPANY

Founded in 1962 by Sam Walton, this discount retailing firm concentrates on small-town America. Until recently Wal-Mart targeted only towns with populations under 50,000, but in 1987 Wal-Mart had one-stop-shopping outlets in 22 states and was entering big-city markets with several innovative new divisions such as Sam's Wholesale

Clubs, Dot's Discount Drugs, and Helen's Arts and Crafts stores. The firm opened two Hypermart USA grocery stores near Dallas in 1987. Second only to K mart in number of discount stores, Wal-mart expands at the rate of 180–200 new stores a year and shows no signs of slowing down. Wal-Mart's annual sales exceed $12 billion and it is ranked number 7 in the Fortune 50 largest retail corporations.

Wal-Mart takes pride in employee participation and strong company spirit. All employees are called "associates." The company has established a management curriculum for associates at the Walton Institute of Retailing at the University of Arkansas.

RETAIL MANAGEMENT TRAINING PROGRAM

Phase I trainees follow a sixteen-week on-the-job training program covering all aspects of store operations and merchandising. The store manager will give you written exercises and evaluations. In Phase II you will assume responsibility for various areas of the store until you demonstrate readiness for promotion to assistant manager. Both videos and manuals guide you as assistant manager, and you will participate in new-store setups. Management seminars and meetings provide ongoing education.

QUALIFICATIONS

Consider this program if you are willing to relocate and have at least one of the following: a four-year college degree, prior retail management experience, or a recommendation from within the company.

RECRUITMENT AND PLACEMENT

Wal-Mart recruits on college campuses and accepts applications at headquarters. The company is presently placing over 300 trainees annually. Wal-Mart plans to open at least 100 new stores a year through 1990, with locations in Alabama, Arkansas, Colorado, Florida, Georgia, Illinois, Indiana, Iowa, Kansas, Kentucky, Louisiana, Minnesota, Mississippi, Missouri, Nebraska, New Mexico, North Carolina, Oklahoma, South Carolina, Tennessee, Texas, Virginia, and Wisconsin.

SALARIES AND BENEFITS

Average first-year salary is $17,160 plus bonus. Second-year salary is about $18,500 plus bonus. You will participate in profit-sharing and stock-purchase programs that have been especially lucrative on account of Wal-Mart's tremendous growth and profitability. Benefits include health care for employees and their families, term life insurance, business travel accident insurance, long-term disability insurance, paid vacations, discount on purchases, and an assistant manager's bonus program.

CONTACT

Van Johnston, Director of Personnel, Wal-Mart Stores, Inc., P.O. Box 116, Bentonville, AR 72712.

WANG LABORATORIES, INC.

ENGINEERING • INFORMATION SYSTEMS AND PROCESSING • MARKETING • PRODUCTION • RESEARCH AND DEVELOPMENT • SALES

THE COMPANY

Founded in 1951, Wang Laboratories is now widely acknowledged as a world leader in office automation systems. It will be no easy task for Wang to maintain its position; it is in the middle of a highly competitive industry marked by constant technological advances. Wang therefore has a strong commitment to research and development, spending over $100 million on it a year. In 1980, Wang identified six technologies of the automated office as priority areas: data processing, word processing, image processing, audio processing, networking, and human factors. As a result of this focused strategy, Wang became the first office automation company to address verbal communication in the office by means of digital voice exchange, a voice-message storing and routing system. Wang may be the first company given permission to build a computer manufacturing facility in China, if negotiations are successful. The company has 32,000 employees in offices and plants throughout the world. It is listed among

Fortune's most admired corporations. It rings up $2.6 billion in annual sales and ranks number 169 in the Fortune 500 largest U.S. industrial corporations.

ALL TRAINING PROGRAMS

You will receive comprehensive training and educational programs as well as on-the-job training. Research and development facilities are in the Boston area, where there are a number of educational institutions that will meet the needs of technical personnel (Wang will reimburse employees for all tuition payments).

QUALIFICATIONS

You should have at least a 3.5 G.P.A. and a ranking in the top quarter of your class. For its entry-level positions, the company will expect you to have a degree in computer science, electrical engineering, computer engineering, or mechanical engineering.

RECRUITMENT AND PLACEMENT

Your starting location will be at company headquarters in Lowell, Massachusetts.

SALARY AND BENEFITS

Starting salaries range from $20,000 to $30,000. Wang's benefits include profit sharing; stock plans; company-paid dental, medical, and life insurance; child day-care and infant day-care programs; and an employee country club.

CONTACT

Manager of College Relations, Mail Stop 1402A, Wang Laboratories, Inc., One Industrial Avenue, Lowell, MA 01851.

WENDY'S INTERNATIONAL
MANAGEMENT

THE COMPANY

Wendy's has chalked up an impressive growth record since its beginning in 1969. By focusing on the older market, providing a quality product, and using aggressive marketing, Wendy's became the nation's third largest hamburger chain. Its advertising slogan "Where's the beef?" became famous presidential campaign fodder in 1984. To increase its family business, Wendy's has added less expensive menu items. With a network of 3,727 stores across the country, Wendy's is adding new stores, remodeling existing stores, and has added a full breakfast menu in some locations. It has restaurants in 17 foreign countries, and 36,000 U.S. employees. About a third of Wendy's stores are company-owned and -operated; the others are franchises.

MANAGEMENT TRAINING PROGRAM

The program prepares you for the position of assistant manager. Your first day on the job, a Wendy's trainer will give you an orientation to the company and get you started in the Management Development Program. The first phase of the program lasts four to seven weeks, depending on your previous experience and your learning rate. During this time you will study the company manual, work in a store under an experienced manager, and attend classroom sessions where audiovisual programs and lectures provide practical operational and management information. The manual is broken into learning modules. Each week you set a goal of how many modules you will cover. The second phase lasts two to six weeks. During this time you will study another manual and learn the ins and outs of running a shift. When you complete this phase you become an assistant manager. The third phase deals with food ordering and scheduling and may take up to three months. Your next career move is up to co-manager and then store manager.

QUALIFICATIONS

If you have a degree, that's a plus but not the most important thing for Wendy's. It is looking for people who are interested in a career in restaurant management, not afraid of long hours, and are willing to apply themselves to learn Wendy's systems.

RECRUITMENT AND PLACEMENT

Wendy's recruits nationally. You will work in the area where you are recruited and interviewed.

SALARY AND BENEFITS

The College Placement Council Salary Survey for September 1986–June 1987 indicates starting salaries for merchandising (retail and wholesale) and service companies to be $1,594 a month for those with a B.A. degree in nontechnical curricula and $2,141 with a B.A. degree in technical curricula. M.B.A. starting salaries were $2,572 for a nontechnical undergraduate degree and $2,735 for an M.B.A. with technical undergraduate degree. Check with the company for more specific salary information. Wendy's offers quarterly performance and salary reviews, so you have an opportunity to move up fast, adding about $10,000 to your salary by the time you advance to store manager. Benefits include two to three weeks of vacation as well as paid health and life insurance, a pension plan, profit sharing, and stockownership plan.

CONTACT

Your local Wendy's franchise or company store or Personnel Director, Wendy's International, 4208 West Dublin Granville Road, P.O. Box 256, Dublin, OH 43017.

WESTINGHOUSE ELECTRIC CORPORATION

ELECTRONICS • ENGINEERING • HEALTH PHYSICS • INFORMATION SYSTEMS AND PROCESSING • MARKETING • RESEARCH AND DEVELOPMENT • SALES • TECHNICAL SERVICES

THE COMPANY

This huge company is the second largest light bulb manufacturer and the leading manufacturer of nuclear power plants. About 10 percent of its business is supplying the U. S. Government with radar and missile-launching systems. Westinghouse also owns the world's largest 7-Up bottling plant and several radio and television stations. The company began in 1886 and enjoyed tremendous success until recently. In the past decade, however, the company has had many problems, such as building a nuclear power plant on the site of an active volcano. Currently Westinghouse is increasing its defense work and has expanded into robotics. It has 110,000 employees in the United States and another 20,000 outside the country. The company's annual sales exceed $10 billion, and it is listed among *Fortune*'s most admired corporations. It ranks number 28 in the Fortune 500 largest U.S. industrial corporations.

ALL TRAINING PROGRAMS

After a three-day orientation program in Pittsburgh, you will be assigned to a new location every month. You can have as many rotations as you like before deciding on a position. Once you decide, your training continues on the job as you develop your professional skills.

QUALIFICATIONS

Westinghouse is looking for college graduates in engineering, physics, computer science, business, accounting, mathematics, and law. The company prefers graduates who rank in the top third of their class and are familiar with computer systems.

RECRUITMENT AND PLACEMENT

Westinghouse recruits at many college campuses, hiring more than 550 trainees a year. You may be placed in any part of the eastern United States, although your preference will be considered. In the Graduate Placement Program, you will be rotated to a new location every month until you decide where you want to work.

SALARY AND BENEFITS

Westinghouse falls into several industry classifications, including aerospace; electrical and electronic machines and equipment; petroleum and allied products; and transportation. The College Placement Council Salary Survey for September 1986–June 1987 indicates starting salaries for aerospace companies to be $1,943 a month for those with a B.A. degree in nontechnical curricula and $2,399 with a B.A. degree in technical curricula. M.B.A. starting salaries were $2,330 for a nontechnical undergraduate degree and $2,475 for a technical undergraduate degree.

In electrical and electronic machines and equipment companies, the CPC Survey reports the average starting salary to be $1,861 a month for those with a B.A. degree in nontechnical curricula and $2,419 with a B.A. degree in technical curricula. M.B.A. starting salaries were $2,784 for a nontechnical undergraduate degree and $2,818 for a technical undergraduate degree.

In petroleum and allied products (including natural gas) companies, the CPC Survey reports the average starting salary to be $1,972 a month for those with a B.A. degree in nontechnical curricula and $2,497 with a B.A. degree in technical curricula. M.B.A. starting salaries were $2,629 for a nontechnical undergraduate degree and $2,970 for a technical undergraduate degree.

In public utilities, the CPC Survey reports the average starting salary to be $1,905 a month for those with a B.A. degree in nontechnical curricula and $2,355 with a B.A. degree in technical curricula. M.B.A. starting salaries were $2,403 for a nontechnical undergraduate degree and $2,667 for a technical undergraduate degree.

Check with the company for more specific salary information. Your benefits will include medical, life, hospital, vision, and dental insurance; a pension plan; career counseling; fitness program; relocation assistance; and stock-purchase plan.

CONTACT

D. A. Kearney, Manager of Recruiting and Placement, Westinghouse Electric Corp., 1 Gateway Center, Westinghouse Building, Room 706, Pittsburgh, PA 15222.

WEYERHAEUSER COMPANY

ACCOUNTING · BUSINESS ADMINISTRATION · ENGINEERING · SCIENCE · SALES · TECHNOLOGY

THE COMPANY

Weyerhaeuser rates high in all types of polls: for financial soundness, for community and environmental responsibility, and as a good place to work. One of the largest and most diverse forest products companies in the world, Weyerhaeuser was the first company to begin renewing what appeared to be an inexhaustible resource, when it planted the first tree farm in 1941. Except for the U.S. Park Service, Weyerhaeuser has more foresters in its employ than anyone else. Its 6 million acres of productive commercial forest are concentrated in the Northwest and South.

A major user of its own trees, the company is also one of the country's largest builders of single- and multifamily homes. To make sure that people have access to credit to buy them, Weyerhaeuser is the United States' second largest mortgage banker. Developing commercial real estate is another of its major enterprises. In addition, Weyerhaeuser is the largest producer of private-label disposable diapers; manufactures other personal care products; grows and distributes outdoor ornamental plants; markets garden supplies and chemicals; raises salmon; and grows and sells hydroponic vegetables.

The company's three main divisions are: Weyerhaeuser Paper Company, Weyerhaeuser Forest Products Company, and Weyerhaeuser Real Estate and Diversified Businesses. It has about 40,000 employees worldwide with more than $5 billion in annual sales. Listed among *Fortune*'s most admired corporations, it ranks number 62 in the Fortune 500 largest U.S. industrial corporations.

ALL TRAINING PROGRAMS

You will receive both formal and on-the-job training at Weyerhaeuser. This company is on the leading edge in its industry. Your training will prepare you to work in a structured environment and familiarize you with Weyerhaeuser innovative systems and working teams. Engineers receive one year to eighteen months of formal training. Other positions have six-month training periods. Your supervisor will provide orientation to the company's policies and procedures as you begin your new job. Career counseling is available to help you plan your future with the company.

QUALIFICATIONS

Weyerhaeuser hires from a wide variety of degree specialties, including accounting, business administration, computer science, engineering (chemical, electrical, forest, industrial, mechanical, and structural), forest management, horticulture, human resources, marketing, production management, pulp and paper technology, and wood technology. Your class rank should be in the top 30 percent with a G.P.A. of 3.0.

RECRUITMENT AND PLACEMENT

Weyerhaeuser fills many permanent positions from its summer intern program, so consider entering one of these during your junior year. Locations are in Alabama, Arizona, Arkansas, California, Colorado, District of Columbia, Florida, Georgia, Hawaii, Illinois, Indiana, Kansas, Kentucky, Louisiana, Maine, Maryland, Massachusetts, Michigan, Mississippi, Missouri, New Jersey, New York, North Carolina, Ohio, Oklahoma, Oregon, Pennsylvania, South Carolina, Tennessee, Texas, Washington, Wisconsin, and British Columbia. The company also operates in 16 foreign countries.

SALARY AND BENEFITS

With a bachelor's degree you can expect to start at about $20,000; in the low twenties with an advanced science or humanities degree; around $28,000 with a business-related master's and nontechnical B.S. (increasing another $800 with one to five years' experience); and around $30,000 with a business-related master's degree and a technical B.S. (up to $32,400 with work experience). Benefits include life insurance, medical, hospital, dental, pension, and stock-purchase plans, fitness programs, flextime, and relocation assistance.

CONTACT

College Relations and Recruiting Office, Weyerhaeuser, Box C, Tacoma, WA 98477.

X

☆ ☆ ☆ ☆ ☆

XEROX CORPORATION

FINANCE · INFORMATION SYSTEMS · MANUFACTURING · PERSONNEL · RESEARCH AND DEVELOPMENT · SALES

THE COMPANY

With annual sales of more than $9 billion, Xerox is one of the giants of the office information industry, a multinational enterprise of 100,000 people. A leading supplier of all kinds of office equipment and a leading developer of technologies to automate offices, Xerox markets everything from typewriters to word processors, copiers to electronic printers. There are Xerox organizations that market office supplies, operate business equipment stores, provide copying and duplicating services, and offer computer services. Xerox expects its people to be involved in their communities and even offers paid absences of up to a year for those who want to pursue community service. Listed among *Fortune*'s most admired corporations, it ranks number 32 in the Fortune 500 largest U.S. industrial corporations.

ALL TRAINING PROGRAMS

Training takes place mainly on the job. Xerox also has a series of formal training programs to enhance individual skills, develop potential managers, and provide ongoing executive development. The Xerox International Center for Training and Management Development near Leesburg, Virginia, can accommodate nearly 1,000 employees. In addition, the Xerox Reprographic Engineering Division provides a one-year rotational assignment program for interested entry-level employees.

SALES PROGRAM

You will receive several weeks of intensive in-district training before being assigned to a sales team and a geographical territory. During this first selling phase you will receive self-paced training on new products and will be closely coached by your manager. After several months of successful selling you will receive formal training at the Leesburg training center.

QUALIFICATIONS

For sales, you may have a bachelor's degree in any subject. You should have a broad educational background with some exposure to computers. In some sales areas you should also have greater exposure to computers or a degree in computer science, mathematics, information systems, or other technical disciplines. Academic achievement is considered important, because it shows a pursuit of excellence. Your interests and activities are also factors, and previous experience in sales or retailing is a definite plus. You should be energetic, confident, motivated, and ambitious. Salespeople should also be independent, mature, self-motivated, tenacious, and well organized.

RECRUITMENT AND PLACEMENT

Xerox recruits extensively on college and university campuses, and also welcomes résumés for review at headquarters. Placement may be anywhere in the United States.

SALARY AND BENEFITS

The College Placement Council Salary Survey for September 1986–June 1987 indicates starting salaries for computer and business machine companies to be $1,880 a month for those with a B.A. degree in nontechnical curricula and $2,389 with a B.A. degree in technical curricula. M.B.A. starting salaries were $2,633 for a nontechnical undergraduate degree and $2,781 for a technical undergraduate degree. Check with the company for more specific salary information. Benefits include profit sharing, tuition reimbursement, medical insurance, and a dental health plan.

CONTACT

College Relations Manager, Xerox Corporation, Xerox Square 020, Dept. B, Rochester, NY 14644.

Y

☆ ☆ ☆ ☆ ☆

ARTHUR YOUNG

AUDITING • MANAGEMENT CONSULTING • TAX CONSULTING

THE COMPANY

Arthur Young is an international public accounting, tax, and professional services firm with offices in over 85 cities in the United States and more than 370 cities in 65 countries abroad. It was founded in 1894 in Chicago. Most of the company's dramatic growth has occurred in the past thirty years with the addition of tax and management advisory services. Its management services department ranks among the ten largest management consulting organizations in the world. Arthur Young is continuing to develop sophisticated approaches—computerizing the audit process and designing new approaches to managing information technology.

ALL TRAINING PROGRAMS

During your first few years you'll attend a series of core courses to develop your auditing, tax, or management consulting skills. In each office a director of education is responsible for organizing and conducting meetings and seminars based on the needs of that staff. You'll have the opportunity to work with and be counseled by a number of different people during your first years with the company. Your professional development will be carefully monitored, and you'll know exactly where you stand. Video programs and written materials are prepared by the firm's National Education Group in Reston, Virginia; several have been adopted by the American Institute of CPAs. In addition, you will receive financial assistance for taking job-related academic courses.

QUALIFICATIONS

You will need a college degree, preferably with an emphasis on accounting, tax, or management consulting, although there are some opportunities for students with other majors. Equally important as academic performance are self-reliance; an orderly, inquiring mind; ability to communicate; and personal integrity. You can find out what it's like to work for Arthur Young by interning in a local Arthur Young office while you're in college.

RECRUITMENT AND PLACEMENT

Arthur Young recruits across the country. You would work in any of its U.S. offices in more than 85 cities.

SALARY AND BENEFITS

The College Placement Council Salary Survey for September 1986–June 1987 indicates starting salaries for public accounting firms to be $1,834 a month for those with a B.A. degree in nontechnical curricula and $2,155 with a B.A. degree in technical curricula. M.B.A. starting salaries were $2,335 for a nontechnical undergraduate degree and $2,436 for a technical undergraduate degree. Check with the company for more specific salary information. Partners (after ten to twelve years) share directly in the profits of the firm. A full employee benefits program includes group life insurance, a pension plan, and a comprehensive medical insurance plan. The company supports your involvement in national and local professional associations and will pay any expenses you incur in such activities.

CONTACT

Request the list "Worldwide Offices of Arthur Young and Associates" from the national office, and contact the college recruitment coordinator at the Arthur Young office that interests you. Or write: John P. Pendergast, Director of Personnel Development, Arthur Young, 277 Park Avenue, New York, NY 10172.

Z

☆ ☆ ☆ ☆ ☆

ZENITH

ENGINEERING/PRODUCT DEVELOPMENT · FINANCE · HUMAN RESOURCES · INFORMATION SYSTEMS · MANUFACTURING · PURCHASING · SALES/MARKETING

THE COMPANY

In the competitive world of state-of-the-art consumer electronics, Zenith has long been a leader. Started in Chicago as an amateur radio station in 1918, the Zenith Radio Corporation was born five years later to make and sell radio equipment. The company pioneered television and FM radio in the late thirties. With sales of almost $2 billion, Zenith competes aggressively with Far East firms and continues to focus on the products that have been its mainstay—radio and television. Company headquarters are in Glenview, Illinois, a Chicago suburb. It ranks number 191 in the Fortune 500 largest U.S. industrial corporations.

HUMAN RESOURCES TRAINING PROGRAM

Zenith will train you to enter this rapidly growing field through a rotation of job assignments. You will work in employment, labor relations, and wage and salary administration. In these assignments you will become familiar with recruitment, interviewing, equal employment opportunity compliance, union contract administration, grievance handling, employee counseling, job description writing, job evaluation, and wage and salary survey techniques. You will also be involved in the training and development of new employees.

QUALIFICATIONS

You should have a degree in business administration or a related discipline. Zenith will be favorably impressed if you demonstrate strong interpersonal skills and ability to assume responsibility.

MANUFACTURING PROGRAM

Three avenues are open to you in this division. In Manufacturing Methods and Equipment, you will assist management in long-range planning. In Manufacturing Equipment Design, your team will be designing and implementing new electromechanical systems to ensure quality control. The Manufacturing Engineering Group is generally responsible for efficient production processes. You will be assigned to a group where you will work as part of the team on specific projects to develop your understanding of Zenith operations.

QUALIFICATIONS

Zenith looks for candidates with degrees in electrical, mechanical, and industrial engineering, as well as M.B.A.s with undergraduate engineering degrees.

PURCHASING TRAINING PROGRAM

In your initial assignment you will coordinate material shipments from suppliers to Zenith plants. Your duties will range from checking and expediting orders to meeting delivery schedules. You will be expected to maintain strict Zenith material standards. If any material or shipment discrepancies arise, you will be called on to implement viable, timely solutions. This first phase of your materials management future at Zenith will give you an in-depth, working knowledge of the company's vital order and shipment operations. After gaining sufficient experience in this area, you may move into a buying position for materials and services.

QUALIFICATIONS

You should have a degree in business administration or related disciplines, and demonstrate fluent communication skills and analytical strength.

ALL PROGRAMS

RECRUITMENT AND PLACEMENT

Zenith recruiters visit college campuses around the country. You may also send a cover letter and résumé directly to the company. You could be placed in California, Illinois, Indiana, Kansas, Michigan, New Jersey, or Pennsylvania. Zenith also has plants in Mexico, Canada, and Taiwan.

SALARY AND BENEFITS

The College Placement Council Salary Survey for September 1986–June 1987 indicates starting salaries for electrical and electronic machinery and equipment companies to be $1,861 a month for those with a B.A. degree in nontechnical curricula and $2,385 with a B.A. degree in technical curricula. M.B.A. starting salaries were $2,784 for a nontechnical undergraduate degree and $2,818 for a technical undergraduate degree. Check with the company for more specific salary information. Benefits will include life, disability, and medical care programs, educational assistance, profit sharing, retirement, employee savings plan, and paid vacations.

CONTACT

Zenith, College Relations Department, 1000 Milwaukee Avenue, Glenview, IL 60025.

Recommended Reading

Allen, Jeffrey. *How to Turn an Interview into a Job.* New York: Simon & Schuster, 1983.

Bolles, Richard N. *The Three Boxes of Life and How to Get Out of Them: An Introduction to Life/Work Planning.* Berkeley: Ten Speed Press, 1978.

———. *What Color Is Your Parachute? A Practical Manual for Job-Hunters & Career-Changers.* Berkeley: Ten Speed Press, 1987.

Clawson, James G., and David D. Ward. *An MBA's Guide to Self-Assessment & Career Development.* Englewood Cliffs, N.J.: Prentice-Hall, 1986.

Cohen, Steve, and Paulo de Oliveira. *Getting to the Right Job: A Guide for College Graduates.* New York: Workman Publishing, 1987.

Collard, Betsy. *The High-Tech Career Book: Finding Your Place in Today's Job Market.* Los Altos, Calif.: William Kaufmann, 1986.

Figler, Howard. *The Complete Job-Search Handbook: All the Skills You Need to Get Any Job and Have a Good Time Doing It.* New York: Holt, Rinehart and Winston, 1979.

Gardenswartz, Lee, and Anita Rome. *What It Takes: Good News from 100 of America's Top Professional and Business Women.* New York: Doubleday, 1987.

German, Donald R., and Joan W. German. *How to Find a Job When Jobs Are Hard to Find.* New York: AMACOM, 1983.

Hardesty, Sarah, and Nehama Jacobs. *Success and Betrayal: The Crisis of Women in Corporate America.* New York: Simon & Schuster, 1986.

Jackson, Tom. *The Perfect Résumé.* Garden City, N.Y.: Anchor Books/Doubleday, 1981.

Josefowitz, Natasha. *Paths to Power: A Woman's Guide from First Job to Top Executive.* Reading, Mass.: Addison-Wesley, 1980.

Kline, Linda, and Lloyd L. Feinstein. *Career Changing: The Worry-Free Guide.* Boston: Little, Brown, 1982.

Lathrop, Richard. *Who's Hiring Who.* Berkeley: Ten Speed Press, 1977.

Lewis, Diane, and Joe Carroll. *The Insider's Guide to Finding the Right Job.* Nashville, Tenn.: Thomas Nelson Publishers, 1987.

Lico, Laurie E. *Resumes for Successful Women.* New York: Pocket Books, 1985.

Lombardo, Joseph, and Amy Lombardo. *The Job Belt: The Fifty Best Places in America for High-Quality Employment—Today and in the Future.* New York: Penguin Books, 1986.

Medley, H. Anthony. *Sweaty Palms: The Neglected Art of Being Interviewed.* Berkeley: Ten Speed Press, 1984.

Merman, Stephen K., and John E. McLaughlin. *Out-Interviewing the Interviewer: A Job Winner's Script for Success.* Englewood Cliffs, N.J.: Prentice-Hall, 1986.

Mitchell, Joyce Slayton. *College to Career: The Guide to Job Opportunities.* New York: College Entrance Examination Board, 1986.

Munschauer, John L. *Jobs for English Majors and Other Smart People.* Rev. ed. Princeton, N.J.: Peterson's Guides, 1986.

Petros, Ross, and Kathryn Petros. *Inside Track: How to Get into and Succeed in America's Prestige Companies.* New York: Vintage Books, 1986.

Pollack, Sandy. *Alternative Careers for Teachers.* Boston: Harvard Common Press, 1984.

Potter, Beverly A. *The Way of the Ronin: A Guide to Career Strategy.* New York: AMACOM, 1984.

Rogers, Edward J. *Getting Hired: Everything You Need to Know About Résumés, Interviews, and Job-Hunting Strategies.* Englewood Cliffs, N.J.: Prentice-Hall, 1982.

Salzman, Marian L., and Nancy Marx Better. *Wanted: Liberal Arts Graduates: The Career Guide to Companies That Hire Smart People.* New York: Anchor Press, 1987.

Schuman, Nancy, and William Lewis. *Revising*

Your Résumé. New York: John Wiley & Sons, 1986.

Stechert, Kathryn. *On Your Own Terms: A Woman's Guide to Working with Men.* New York: Vintage Books, 1986.

Wegmann, Robert, and Robert Chapman. *The Right Place at the Right Time: Finding the Right Job in the New Economy.* Berkeley: Ten Speed Press, 1987.

Weinstein, Bob. *How to Get a Job in Hard Times.* New York: Cornerstone, 1984.

———. *How to Switch Careers.* New York: Simon & Schuster, 1985.

Indexes

TRAINING PROGRAM INDEX

INDUSTRY INDEX

GEOGRAPHIC INDEX

Most companies indicate which states are likely for starting positions. Companies that have offices all over the United States are listed under the heading "Nationwide assignments." There are also index headings for the following regions of the United States: East, South, Northeast, Midwest, West, Southeast, Southwest. Job possibilities in other countries are indicated under the headings "Canada" and "International assignments."